DRAMA
for Students

Advisors

Jayne M. Burton is a teacher of English, a member of the Delta Kappa Gamma International Society for Key Women Educators, and currently a master's degree candidate in the Interdisciplinary Study of Curriculum and Instruction and English at Angelo State University.

Mary Beth Maggio teaches seventh grade language arts in Schaumburg, Illinois.

Tom Shilts is the youth librarian at the Okemos branch of Capital Area District Library in Okemos, Michigan. He holds an MSLS degree from Clarion University of Pennsylvania and an MA in U.S. History from the University of North Dakota.

Amy Spade Silverman hastaught at independent schools in California, Texas, Michigan, and New York. She holdsa bachelor of arts degree from the University of Michigan and a master of fine arts degree from the University of Houston. She is a member of the National Council of Teachers of English and Teachers and Writers. She is an exam reader for Advanced Placement Literature and Composition.She is also a poet, published in *North American Review*, *Nimrod*, and *Michigan Quarterly Review*, among others.

Mary Turner holds a BS in Secondary Education from East Texas State University and a Master of Education from Western Kentucky University. She teaches English 7 and AP English 12 literature and composition at SBEC in Southaven, Mississippi.

Brian Woerner teaches English at Troy High School in Troy, Ohio. He is also a Program Associate of the Ohio Writing Project at Miami University.

DRAMA
for Students

**Presenting Analysis, Context, and Criticism
on Commonly Studied Dramas**

VOLUME 30

Sara Constantakis, Project Editor

Foreword by Carole L. Hamilton

Detroit • New York • San Francisco • New Haven, Conn • Waterville, Maine • London

GALE
CENGAGE Learning·

Drama for Students, Volume 30

Project Editor: Sara Constantakis

Rights Acquisition and Management:
Robyn Young

Composition: Evi Abou-El-Seoud

Manufacturing: Rhonda Dover

Imaging: John Watkins

Product Design: Pamela A. E. Galbreath,
Jennifer Wahi

Digital Content Production: Allie Semperger

Product Manager: Meggin Condino

© 2013 Gale, Cengage Learning

For product information and technology assistance, contact us at
Gale Customer Support, 1-800-877-4253.
For permission to use material from this text or product,
submit all requests online at **www.cengage.com/permissions.**
Further permissions questions can be emailed to
permissionrequest@cengage.com

Gale
27500 Drake Rd.
Farmington Hills, MI, 48331-3535

ISBN-13: 978-0-7876-9640-5
ISBN-10: 0-7876-9640-4

ISSN 1094-9232

This title is also available as an e-book.
ISBN-13: 978-1-4144-4942-5
ISBN-10: 1-4144-4942-9
Contact your Gale, a part of Cengage Learning sales representative for ordering information.

Printed in Mexico
1 2 3 4 5 6 7 17 16 15 14 13

Table of Contents

The Study of Drama

We study drama in order to learn what meaning others have made of life, to comprehend what it takes to produce a work of art, and to glean some understanding of ourselves. Drama produces in a separate, aesthetic world, a moment of being for the audience to experience, while maintaining the detachment of a reflective observer.

Drama is a representational art, a visible and audible narrative presenting virtual, fictional characters within a virtual, fictional universe. Dramatic realizations may pretend to approximate reality or else stubbornly defy, distort, and deform reality into an artistic statement. From this separate universe that is obviously not "real life" we expect a valid reflection upon reality, yet drama never is mistaken for reality—the methods of theater are integral to its form and meaning. Theater is art, and art's appeal lies in its ability both to approximate life and to depart from it. For in intruding its distorted version of life into our consciousness, art gives us a new perspective and appreciation of life and reality. Although all aesthetic experiences perform this service, theater does it most effectively by creating a separate, cohesive universe that freely acknowledges its status as an art form.

And what is the purpose of the aesthetic universe of drama? The potential answers to such a question are nearly as many and varied as there are plays written, performed, and enjoyed. Dramatic texts can be problems posed, answers asserted, or moments portrayed. Dramas (tragedies as well as comedies) may serve strictly "to ease the anguish of a torturing hour" (as stated in William Shakespeare's *A Midsummer Night's Dream*)—to divert and entertain—or aspire to move the viewer to action with social issues. Whether to entertain or to instruct, affirm or influence, pacify or shock, dramatic art wraps us in the spell of its imaginary world for the length of the work and then dispenses us back to the real world, entertained, purged, as Aristotle said, of pity and fear, and edified—or at least weary enough to sleep peacefully.

It is commonly thought that theater, being an art of performance, must be experienced—seen—in order to be appreciated fully. However, to view a production of a dramatic text is to be limited to a single interpretation of that text—all other interpretations are for the moment closed off, inaccessible. In the process of producing a play, the director, stage designer, and performers interpret and transform the script into a work of art that always departs in some measure from the author's original conception. Novelist and critic Umberto Eco, in his *The Role of the Reader: Explorations in the Semiotics of Texts* (Indiana University Press, 1979), explained, "In short, we can say that every performance offers us a complete and satisfying version of the work, but at the same time makes it incomplete for us, because it cannot simultaneously give all the other artistic solutions which the work may admit."

Thus Laurence Olivier's coldly formal and neurotic film presentation of Shakespeare's *Hamlet* (in which he played the title character as well as directed) shows marked differences from subsequent adaptations. While Olivier's Hamlet is clearly entangled in a Freudian relationship with his mother Gertrude, he would be incapable of shushing her with the impassioned kiss that Mel Gibson's mercurial Hamlet (in director Franco Zeffirelli's 1990 film) does. Although each of performances rings true to Shakespeare's text, each is also a mutually exclusive work of art. Also important to consider are the time periods in which each of these films was produced: Olivier made his film in 1948, a time in which overt references to sexuality (especially incest) were frowned upon. Gibson and Zeffirelli made their film in a culture more relaxed and comfortable with these issues. Just as actors and directors can influence the presentation of drama, so too can the time period of the production affect what the audience will see.

A play script is an open text from which an infinity of specific realizations may be derived. Dramatic scripts that are more open to interpretive creativity (such as those of Ntozake Shange and Tomson Highway) actually require the creative improvisation of the production troupe in order to complete the text. Even the most prescriptive scripts (those of Neil Simon, Lillian Hellman, and Robert Bolt, for example), can never fully control the actualization of live performance, and circumstantial events, including the attitude and receptivity of the audience, make every performance a unique event. Thus, while it is important to view a production of a dramatic piece, if one wants to understand a drama fully it is equally important to read the original dramatic text.

The reader of a dramatic text or script is not limited by either the specific interpretation of a given production or by the unstoppable action of a moving spectacle. The reader of a dramatic text may discover the nuances of the play's language, structure, and events at their own pace. Yet studied alone, the author's blueprint for artistic production does not tell the whole story of a play's life and significance. One also needs to assess the play's critical reviews to discover how it resonated to cultural themes at the time of its debut and how the shifting tides of cultural interest have revised its interpretation and impact on audiences. And to do this, one needs to know a little about the culture of the times which produced the play as well as the author who penned it.

Drama for Students supplies this material in a useful compendium for the student of dramatic theater. Covering a range of dramatic works that span from 442 BCE to the 1990s, this book focuses on significant theatrical works whose themes and form transcend the uncertainty of dramatic fads. These are plays that have proven to be both memorable and teachable. *Drama for Students* seeks to enhance appreciation of these dramatic texts by providing scholarly materials written with the secondary and college/university student in mind. It provides for each play a concise summary of the plot and characters as well as a detailed explanation of its themes. In addition, background material on the historical context of the play, its critical reception, and the author's life help the student to understand the work's position in the chronicle of dramatic history. For each play entry a new work of scholarly criticism is also included, as well as segments of other significant critical works for handy reference. A thorough bibliography provides a starting point for further research.

This series offers comprehensive educational resources for students of drama. *Drama for Students* is a vital book for dramatic interpretation and a valuable addition to any reference library.

Sources

Eco, Umberto, The Role of the Reader: Explorations in the Semiotics of Texts, Indiana University Press, 1979.

Carole L. Hamilton
Author and Instructor of English at Cary
Academy, Cary, North Carolina

Introduction

Purpose of the Book

The purpose of *Drama for Students* (*DfS*) is to provide readers with a guide to understanding, enjoying, and studying dramas by giving them easy access to information about the work. Part of Gale's "For Students" literature line, *DfS* is specifically designed to meet the curricular needs of high school and undergraduate college students and their teachers, as well as the interests of general readers and researchers considering specific plays. While each volume contains entries on "classic" dramas frequently studied in classrooms, there are also entries containing hard-to-find information on contemporary plays, including works by multicultural, international, and women playwrights. Entries profiling film versions of plays not only diversify the study of drama but support alternate learning styles, media literacy, and film studies curricula as well.

The information covered in each entry includes an introduction to the play and the work's author; a plot summary, to help readers unravel and understand the events in a drama; descriptions of important characters, including explanation of a given character's role in the drama as well as discussion about that character's relationship to other characters in the play; analysis of important themes in the drama; and an explanation of important literary techniques and movements as they are demonstrated in the play.

In addition to this material, which helps the readers analyze the play itself, students are also provided with important information on the literary and historical background informing each work. This includes a historical context essay, a box comparing the time or place the drama was written to modern Western culture, a critical essay, and excerpts from critical essays on the play. A unique feature of *DfS* is a specially commissioned critical essay on each drama, targeted toward the student reader.

The "literature to film" entries on plays vary slightly in form, providing background on film technique and comparison to the original, literary version of the work. These entries open with an introduction to the film, which leads directly into the plot summary. The summary highlights plot changes from the play, key cinematic moments, and/or examples of key film techniques. As in standard entries, there are character profiles (noting omissions or additions, and identifying the actors), analysis of themes and how they are illustrated in the film, and an explanation of the cinematic style and structure of the film. A cultural context section notes any time period or setting differences from that of the original work, as well as cultural differences between the time in which the original work was written and the time in which the film adaptation was made. A film entry concludes with a critical overview and critical essays on the film.

To further help today's student in studying and enjoying each play or film, information on audiobooks and other media adaptations is provided (if available), as well as suggestions for works of fiction, nonfiction, or film on similar themes and topics. Classroom aids include ideas for research papers and lists of critical and reference sources that provide additional material on each drama. Film entries also highlight signature film techniques demonstrated, as well as suggesting media literacy activities and prompts to use during or after viewing a film.

Selection Criteria

The titles for each volume of *DfS* are selected by surveying numerous sources on notable literary works and analyzing course curricula for various schools, school districts, and states. Some of the sources surveyed include: high school and undergraduate literature anthologies and textbooks; lists of award-winners, and recommended titles, including the Young Adult Library Services Association (YALSA) list of best books for young adults. Films are selected both for the literary importance of the original work and the merits of the adaptation (including official awards and widespread public recognition).

Input solicited from our expert advisory board—consisting of educators and librarians—guides us to maintain a mix of "classic" and contemporary literary works, a mix of challenging and engaging works (including genre titles that are commonly studied) appropriate for different age levels, and a mix of international, multicultural and women authors. These advisors also consult on each volume's entry list, advising on which titles are most studied, most appropriate, and meet the broadest interests across secondary (grades 7–12) curricula and undergraduate literature studies.

How Each Entry Is Organized

Each entry, or chapter, in *DfS* focuses on one play. Each entry heading lists the full name of the play, the author's name, and the date of the play's publication. The following elements are contained in each entry:

Introduction: a brief overview of the drama which provides information about its first appearance, its literary standing, any controversies surrounding the work, and major conflicts or themes within the work. Film entries identify the original play and provide understanding of the film's reception and reputation, along with that of the director.

Author Biography: in play entries, this section includes basic facts about the author's life, and focuses on events and times in the author's life that inspired the drama in question.

Plot Summary: a description of the major events in the play. Subheads demarcate the play's various acts or scenes. Plot summaries of films are used to uncover plot differences from the original play, and to note the use of certain film angles or techniques.

Characters: an alphabetical listing of major characters in the play. Each character name is followed by a brief to an extensive description of the character's role in the play, as well as discussion of the character's actions, relationships, and possible motivation. In film entries, omissions or changes to the cast of characters of the film adaptation are mentioned here, and the actors' names—and any awards they may have received—are also included.

Characters are listed alphabetically by last name. If a character is unnamed—for instance, the Stage Manager in *Our Town*—the character is listed as "The Stage Manager" and alphabetized as "Stage Manager." If a character's first name is the only one given, the name will appear alphabetically by the first name. Variant names are also included for each character. Thus, the nickname "Babe" would head the listing for a character in *Crimes of the Heart*, but below that listing would be her less-mentioned married name "Rebecca Botrelle."

Themes: a thorough overview of how the major topics, themes, and issues are addressed within the play. Each theme discussed appears in a separate subhead. While the key themes often remain the same or similar when a play is adapted into a film, film entries demonstrate how the themes are conveyed cinematically, along with any changes in the portrayal of the themes.

Style: this section addresses important style elements of the drama, such as setting, point of view, and narration; important literary devices used, such as imagery, foreshadowing, symbolism; and, if applicable, genres to which the work might have belonged, such as Gothicism or Romanticism. Literary terms are explained within the entry, but can also be found in the Glossary. Film entries cover how the director conveyed the meaning, message, and mood of the work using film in comparison to the author's use of language, literary device, etc., in the original work.

Historical Context: in play entries, this section outlines the social, political, and cultural climate in which the author lived and the play was created. This section may include descriptions of related historical events, pertinent aspects of daily life in the culture, and the artistic and literary sensibilities of the time in which the work was written. If the play is a historical work, information regarding the time in which the play is set is also included. Each section is broken down with helpful subheads. Film entries contain a similar Cultural Context section, because the film adaptation might explore an entirely different time period or culture than the original work, and may also be influenced by the traditions and views of a time period much different than that of the original author.

Critical Overview: this section provides background on the critical reputation of the play or film, including bannings or any other public controversies surrounding the work. For older plays, this section includes a history of how the drama or film was first received and how perceptions of it may have changed over the years; for more recent plays, direct quotes from early reviews may also be included.

Criticism: an essay commissioned by *DfS* which specifically deals with the play or film and is written specifically for the student audience, as well as excerpts from previously published criticism on the work (if available).

Sources: an alphabetical list of critical material used in compiling the entry, with full bibliographical information.

Further Reading: an alphabetical list of other critical sources which may prove useful for the student. It includes full bibliographical information and a brief annotation.

Suggested Search Terms: a list of search terms and phrases to jumpstart students' further information seeking. Terms include not just titles and author names but also terms and topics related to the historical and literary context of the works.In addition, each entry contains the following highlighted sections, set apart from the main text as sidebars:

Media Adaptations: if available, a list of audiobooks and important film and television adaptations of the play, including source information. The list may also include such variations on the work as musical adaptations and other stage interpretations.

Topics for Further Study: a list of potential study questions or research topics dealing with the play. This section includes questions related to other disciplines the student may be studying, such as American history, world history, science, math, government, business, geography, economics, psychology, etc.

Compare and Contrast: an "at-a-glance" comparison of the cultural and historical differences between the author's time and culture and late twentieth century or early twenty-first century Western culture. This box includes pertinent parallels between the major scientific, political, and cultural movements of the time or place the drama was written, the time or place the play was set (if a historical work), and modern Western culture. Works written after 1990 may not have this box.

What Do I Read Next?: a list of works that might give a reader points of entry into a classic work (e.g., YA or multicultural titles) and/ or complement the featured play or serve as a contrast to it. This includes works by the same author and others, works from various genres, YA works, and works from various cultures and eras.

The film entries provide sidebars more targeted to the study of film, including:

Film Technique: a listing and explanation of four to six key techniques used in the film, including shot styles, use of transitions, lighting, sound or music, etc.

Read, Watch, Write: media literacy prompts and/or suggestions for viewing log prompts.

What Do I See Next?: a list of films based on the same or similar works or of films similar in directing style, technique, etc.

Other Features

DfS includes "The Study of Drama," a foreword by Carole Hamilton, an educator and author who specializes in dramatic works. This essay examines the basis for drama in societies and what drives people to study such work. The essay also discusses how *DfS* can help teachers show students how to enrich their own reading/viewing experiences.

A Cumulative Author/Title Index lists the authors and titles covered in each volume of the *DfS* series.

A Cumulative Nationality/Ethnicity Index breaks down the authors and titles covered in each volume of the *DfS* series by nationality and ethnicity.

A Subject/Theme Index, specific to each volume, provides easy reference for users who may be studying a particular subject or theme rather than a single work. Significant subjects from events to broad themes are included.

Each entry may include illustrations, including photo of the author, stills from stage productions, and stills from film adaptations, if available.

Citing Drama for Students

When writing papers, students who quote directly from any volume of *DfS* may use the following general forms. These examples are based on MLA style; teachers may request that students adhere to a different style, so the following examples may be adapted as needed.

When citing text from *DfS* that is not attributed to a particular author (i.e., the Themes, Style, Historical Context sections, etc.), the following format should be used in the bibliography section:

"*Candida*." *Drama for Students*. Ed. Sara Constantakis. Vol. 30. Detroit: Gale, Cengage Learning, 2013. 1–27. Print.

When quoting the specially commissioned essay from *DfS* (usually the first piece under the "Criticism" subhead), the following format should be used:

O'Neal, Michael J. Critical Essay on *Candida*. *Drama for Students*. Ed. Sara Constantakis. Vol. 30. Detroit: Gale, Cengage Learning, 2013. 12–15. Print.

When quoting a journal or newspaper essay that is reprinted in a volume of *DfS*, the following form may be used:

Lazenby, Walter. "Love and 'Vitality' in *Candida*." *Modern Drama* 20.1 (1977): 1–19. Rpt. in *Drama for Students*. Ed. Sara Constantakis. Vol. 30. Detroit: Gale, Cengage Learning, 2013. 18–22. Print.

When quoting material reprinted from a book that appears in a volume of *DfS*, the following form may be used:

Phelps, William Lyon. "George Bernard Shaw." *Essays on Modern Dramatists*. New York: Macmillan, 1921. 67–98. Rpt. in *Drama for Students*. Ed. Sara Constantakis. Vol. 30. Detroit: Gale, Cengage Learning, 2013. 26. Print.

We Welcome Your Suggestions

The editorial staff of *Drama for Students* welcomes your comments and ideas. Readers who wish to suggest dramas to appear in future volumes, or who have other suggestions, are cordially invited to contact the editor. You may contact the editor via e-mail at: **ForStudentsEditors@cengage.com.** Or write to the editor at:

Editor, *Drama for Students*
Gale
27500 Drake Road
Farmington Hills, MI 48331-3535

Literary Chronology

1564: William Shakespeare is born in Stratford-Upon-Avon, England. The exact date is unknown but thought to be late April. The date of his birth is often celebrated as April 26, which is the date of his baptism.

1600: *Much Ado About Nothing* is published in the first quarto edition.

1616: William Shakespeare dies on April 23 of causes unknown in Stratford-Upon-Avon, England.

1856: George Bernard Shaw is born on July 26 in Dublin, Ireland.

1886: Zoë Akins is born on October 30, in Humansville, Missouri.

1891: Zora Neale Hurston is born on January 7 in Nostasulga, Alabama.

1898: George Bernard Shaw's *Candida* is published.

1901: John Van Druten is born on June 1 in London, England.

1925: George Bernard Shaw is awarded the Pulitzer Prize for Literature.

1931: Zora Neale Hurston's *Poker!* is first produced.

1935: Zoë Akins's *The Old Maid* is first produced.

1935: Zoë Akins's *The Old Maid* is awarded the Pulitzer Prize for Drama.

1936: Alfred Uhry is born on December 3 in Atlanta, Georgia.

1938: Caryl Churchill is born on September 3 in London, England.

1944: David Feldshuh is born in New York City, New York.

1944: John Van Druten's *I Remember Mama* is first produced.

1945: August Wilson is born on April 27 in Pittsburgh, Pennsylvania.

1950: George Bernard Shaw dies of complications from an injury on November 2 at Ayot St. Lawrence, England.

1955: José Rivera is born on March 24 in San Juan, Puerto Rico.

1957: John Van Druten dies on December 19 in Indio, California.

1958: Zoë Akins dies of cancer on October 29 in Los Angeles, California.

1960: Zora Neale Hurston dies of hypertensive heart disease on January 28 in Fort Pierce, Florida.

1960: Naomi Wallace is born on August 17 in Prospect, Kentucky.

1961: Lisa Kron is born on May 20 in Ann Arbor, Michigan.

1987: August Wilson is awarded a Tony Award and the Pulitzer Prize for *Fences*.

1987: Alfred Uhry's *Driving Miss Daisy* is written.

1988: Alfred Uhry wins the Pulitzer Prize for *Driving Miss Daisy*.

1989: The film version of *Driving Miss Daisy* is released.

1989: David Feldshuh's *Miss Evers' Boys* is first produced.

1990: August Wilson is awarded the Pultizer Prize for *The Piano Lesson*.

1993: The film version of *Much Ado About Nothing* is released.

1993: Jose Rivera's *Tape* is published.

1995: Naomi Wallace's *One Flea Spare* is first produced.

2000: Caryl Churchill's *Far Away* is published.

2005: August Wilson's *Radio Golf* is first produced.

2005: August Wilson dies of liver cancer on October 2 in Seattle, Washington.

2006: Lisa Kron's *Well* is published.

Acknowledgements

The editors wish to thank the copyright holders of the excerpted criticism included in this volume and the permissions managers of many book and magazine publishing companies for assisting us in securing reproduction rights. We are also grateful to the staffs of the Detroit Public Library, the Library of Congress, the University of Detroit Mercy Library, Wayne State University Purdy/Kresge Library Complex, and the University of Michigan Libraries for making their resources available to us. Following is a list of the copyright holders who have granted us permission to reproduce material in this volume of PfS. Every effort has been made to trace copyright, but if omissions have been made, please let us know.

COPYRIGHTED EXCERPTS IN *DfS*, VOLUME 30, WERE REPRODUCED FROM THE FOLLOWING PERIODICALS:

American Drama, v. 10, no. 2, Summer 2001. Copyright © 2001 by *American Drama*. Reproduced by permission of the publisher.—*American Scholar*, v. 75, no. 1, Winter 2006. Copyright © 2006 by *The American Scholar*. Reproduced by permission of the publisher.—*American Theatre*, v. 19, no. 2, February 2002, for "The City That Embraced Naomi Wallace: In Atlanta, a Dozen Theatres Plumb the Depths of One Writer's Work" by Walter Bilderback. Copyright © 2002 by *American Theatre*. Reproduced by permission of the author.—*Back Stage East*, v. 47, no. 14, 6 April 2006.

Copyright © v. 11, no. 16, 15 April 2004; v. 13, no. 16, 20 April 2006. Copyright © 2002, 2004, 2006 by VNU Business Media, Inc. Reproduced by permission of the publisher.—*College Literature*, v. 1, no. 3, Fall 1974; v. 36, no. 2, Spring 2009. Copyright © 1974, 2009 by *College Literature*. Reproduced by permission of the publisher.—*Commonweal*, v. 118, no. 22, 20 December 1991; v. 120, no. 12, 18 June 1993. Copyright © 1991, 1993 by *Commonweal*. Reproduced by permission of the publisher.—*Language in India*, v. 12, no. 3, March 2012. Copyright © 2012 by *Language in India*. Reproduced by permission of the publisher.—*Modern Drama*, v. 20, no. 1, March 1977. Copyright © 1977 by *Modern Drama*. Reproduced by permission of the publisher.—*Nation*, v. 229, no. 2, 14 July 1979; v. 264, no. 19, 19 May 1997. Copyright © 1979, 1997 by *The Nation*. Reproduced by permission of the publisher.—*New Republic*, v. 197, no. 13, 28 September 1987; v. 202, no. 3914, 22 January 1990. Copyright © 1987, 1990 by *The New Republic*. Reproduced by permission of the publisher.—*New York Amsterdam News*, v. 93, no. 9, 28 February 2002; v. 100, no. 13, 26 March 2009. Copyright © 2002, 2009 by *New York Amsterdam News*. Reproduced by permission of the publisher.—*New Yorker*, v. 78, no. 41, 6 January 2003. Copyright © 2003 by Conde Nast. Reproduced by permission of the publisher.—*Newsweek*, v. 152, no. 25, 22 December 2008.

Contributors

Bryan Aubrey: Aubrey holds a PhD in English. Entry on *Miss Evers' Boys*. Original essay on *Miss Evers' Boys*.

Kristy Blackmon: Blackmon is a writer, editor, and critic from Dallas, Texas. Entry on *Tape*. Original essay on *Tape*.

Rita M. Brown: Brown is an English professor. Entry on *Poker!*. Original essay on *Poker!*.

Catherine Dominic: Dominic is a novelist and a freelance writer and editor. Entry on *Well*. Original essay on *Well*.

Kristen Sarlin Greenberg: Greenberg is a freelance writer and editor with a background in literature and philosophy. Entry on *Far Away*. Original essay on *Far Away*.

Sheri Karmiol: Karmiol holds a PhD in literature and is a university lecturer in interdisciplinary studies. Entries on *Driving Miss Daisy* and *Much Ado About Nothing*. Original essays on *Driving Miss Daisy* and *Much Ado About Nothing*.

Amy Lynn Miller: Miller is a graduate of the University of Cincinnati and now resides in New Orleans, Louisiana. Entry on *Radio Golf*. Original essay on *Radio Golf*.

Michael J. O'Neal: O'Neal holds a doctorate in English. Entries on *Candida* and *One Flea Spare*.Original essays on *Candida* and *One Flea Spare*.

April Dawn Paris: Paris is a freelance writer with an extensive background writing literary and education materials. Entry on *The Old Maid*. Original essay on *The Old Maid*.

Bradley A. Skeen: Skeen is a classicist. Entry on *Far Away*. Original essay on *Far Away*.

Candida

GEORGE BERNARD SHAW
1898

Candida is a three-act domestic comedy written by Irish playwright George Bernard Shaw in 1894. The play was first produced onstage in 1897 and published in 1898. The title character (whose name is pronounced CAN-did-uh) is an attractive, vivacious woman who is put in the position of having to choose between two men: her husband, James Morell, a popular, energetic Christian socialist clergyman; and Eugene Marchbanks, a romantic eighteen-year-old poet who has become infatuated with her. Although the play depicts a conventional love triangle, it has survived on the stage because of its witty and provocative exploration of love, marriage, fidelity, and the role and position of women.

Candida is an early play in the Shaw canon. Prior to the mid-1890s, Shaw wrote plays that he characterized as "unpleasant" because they would have forced the audience to face difficult truths. He followed these with a group of four plays he regarded as more "pleasant" and amusing. One of these was *Candida*, which was published in a collection called *Plays Pleasant* along with *Arms and the Man*, *The Man of Destiny*, and *You Never Can Tell*. (This collection was one volume in a two-volume collection titled *Plays Pleasant and Unpleasant*.) These "plays pleasant" are lighter and more comic in tone yet continue to embody thought-provoking views.

Candida is available in *Plays by George Bernard Shaw* (Signet, 1960).

George Bernard Shaw (*The Library of Congress*)

AUTHOR BIOGRAPHY

Shaw was born on July 26, 1856, in Dublin, Ireland, to a lower-middle-class Scots-Protestant family. His father, George, worked as a corn merchant and drank heavily. His mother, Bessie, was a professional singer who fell in love with a musician who went variously by George Lee, George John Lee, George Vandeleur Lee, and Vandeleur Lee. When Shaw was fifteen years old, his mother abandoned him and his father and, with Shaw's sisters in tow, followed Lee to London. Shaw always went by the name Bernard Shaw, rejecting "George" because it was the name of his father and of his mother's lover.

Shaw's education was irregular, for he was never able to adapt himself to any kind of educational system. In 1876, he left Dublin for London, where he lived off of his mother and sister while he pursued a career in writing and journalism, especially art, music, and theater criticism. During these early years in London, he wrote five novels, but all were rejected by publishers. He also began to adopt progressive causes, including vegetarianism and socialism, and became a member of the Fabian Society, a socialist group. He overcame both a stammer and a fear of public speaking on soapboxes at Speaker's Corner in London's Hyde Park, adopting an aggressive, energetic style while delivering speeches about social and political issues.

Shaw wrote his first play, *Widower's Houses*, in 1891. Over the next decade, he wrote nearly a dozen plays, but he had trouble getting them produced. On July 30, 1897, the Independent Theatre Company at Her Majesty's Theatre in Aberdeen, Scotland, gave one performance of *Candida*, which was published the following year in *Plays Pleasant*. In 1898, Shaw married Charlotte Payne-Townsend, a woman of some wealth and a fellow Fabian; their marriage endured until her death in 1943.

At the turn of the century, Shaw's reputation as a playwright began to grow. *Candida* was produced in London and on the Continent, and in the years before World War I, he wrote some of his greatest plays, including *Caesar and Cleopatra* (1898), *Man and Superman* (1903), *Major Barbara* (1907), *The Doctor's Dilemma* (1911), and *Pygmalion* (1914), his comic masterpiece and the play on which the modern Broadway musical *My Fair Lady* is based. The war years (1914–1918) were difficult ones for Shaw. He believed that the war's carnage marked the end of capitalism and empire, and his anti-war newspaper articles made him a target of criticism and accusations of treason. During the war, he wrote only one major play, *Heartbreak House* (1919).

After the war, Shaw resumed his career as Britain's leading playwright. In 1925, he won the Nobel Prize for *Saint Joan* (1924) and donated the cash award to pay for the publication of an English version of the plays of Swedish playwright August Strindberg. In 1928, Shaw published a political tract titled "The Intelligent Woman's Guide to Socialism and Capitalism."

In the decades that followed, Shaw continued to write, but his plays from these years are regarded as minor. In 1950, at the age of ninety-four, Shaw was injured when he fell from a ladder at his home. A few days later, on November 2, he died of complications from his injury at Ayot St. Lawrence in Hertfordshire, England, where he had lived since 1906.

MEDIA ADAPTATIONS

- An audio CD of a radio production of *Candida* was released by the Canadian Broadcasting Corporation in 2003. Running time is about one and a half hours.

- In 2007, the British Broadcasting Company produced a radio adaptation of the play on Radio 7.

- *Candida* is available as an audio CD released by Audio Book Contractors, in 2011. Running time is about two hours and twenty minutes.

- The soundtrack for a musical version of *Candida* titled *A Minister's Wife* was released by PS Classics in 2011.

PLOT SUMMARY

Act 1

Act 1 opens with a description of the setting of the play: the northeast suburbs of London, specifically the parsonage of St. Dominic's Church, where the Reverend James Morell works and lives with his wife, Candida. Morell is seated with his secretary, Miss Proserpine Garnett ("Prossy"), trying to arrange his upcoming speaking engagements. Candida has been away with their two children, but she is expected back later that morning. His curate, the Reverend Alexander ("Lexy") Mill enters and says to Morell's dismay, that his father-in-law, Mr. Burgess, is on his way to pay a call. After Morell leaves the room, Prossy and Lexy discuss Morell's affection for his wife, making it clear that Prossy has feelings for him. She is also critical of Lexy's tendency to try to imitate Morell.

Burgess enters unannounced. Morell returns, and the two men quarrel about the wages that Burgess pays to his workers and about a disagreement the two men had three years previously over a contract to manufacture clothing in Burgess's mill. Burgess indicates that he has raised the wages he pays his workers, but Morell is disappointed when he learns that Burgess has done so only because the local government authorities would not have done business with him otherwise.

Just as the two men patch up their quarrel, Candida enters, having arrived back in London early. She was accompanied on her trip by Eugene Marchbanks, a young poet and the aristocratic son of an earl. Marchbanks enters and is introduced to Burgess, who then leaves. Candida goes to look into the state of the housekeeping, leaving Marchbanks with her husband. In the discussion that follows, Marchbanks confesses that he is in love with Candida and accuses Morell of complacency in his marriage. The confrontation escalates into a quarrel that almost turns physical, and Morell orders Marchbanks to leave. Just as Marchbanks is leaving, Candida returns to the room and invites him to stay.

Act 2

Act 2 begins a few hours later. Marchbanks has a discussion with Prossy about the nature of romantic love and people's need for it. Candida, who has been busy with household chores, announces that her favorite scrub brush has been ruined. Marchbanks is worried about the state of Candida's hands and groans to think that the woman he adores should be saddled with basic domestic chores. Candida responds by laughing and asking him whether he would be willing to replace the scrub brush with one made of ivory and inlaid with mother-of-pearl. Marchbanks makes a poetic response, saying that he would like to replace it with a small boat that could carry them away, far from the petty concerns of the world, to a place where the floors would be washed by the rain.

Morell harshly interrupts Marchbanks's poetic effusions. Candida responds by saying to her husband that he is spoiling the poetry. A few minutes later, Candida and Morell are alone. She asks him what is troubling him and tries to cheer him up by talking about Marchbanks and his need to be loved. She says that she would be willing to teach Marchbanks about love if she did not already love her husband. Candida assumes that the reason her husband remains disturbed is that he believes that social codes and the traditional Christian virtue of fidelity have played no part in her decision. Lexy arrives with Burgess and persuades Morell to honor a commitment he had made to give a lecture. Morell leaves to give the lecture, insisting that

Marchbanks and Candida remain behind. Marchbanks realizes that Morell's motivation is to assert his superiority over the poet.

Act 3

Later that evening, past ten o'clock, Candida and Marchbanks wait by the fire for Morell to return home from his lecture. For the past two hours, Marchbanks has been reading poetry to her, but she appears to be bored with his efforts. Finally, Morell returns, elated at the success of his lecture. At this point, he and the poet decide that Candida has to choose between the two of them. Candida responds by calmly asking each man what he will "bid" for her. Morell says that he will offer her his position and ability, as well as his strength and honesty. Marchbanks can offer only the needs of his own heart. Candida appears to be trying to decide between the two when Morell cries out her name. She responds by saying that she will give herself to the weaker of the two men. Marchbanks understands that she means her husband.

The three characters then sit by the fireside and discuss the situation. Candida explains that her husband needs her more than Marchbanks does. Marchbanks thanks Morell for filling the heart of the woman that he loves and departs. The curtain falls on Morell and Candida sharing an embrace.

CHARACTERS

Mr. Burgess

Burgess, Candida's sixty-year-old father, is the owner of a mill that produces clothing. Shaw writes that he has been "made coarse and sordid" by his involvement in business matters. Burgess is also described as soft and lazy now that he has achieved financial success. He is a "vulgar, ignorant, guzzling man" who does not treat his employees well. Burgess always has his eye out for his own advantage. Early on, he states: "When I pay a man, an' 'is livin' depen's on me, I keep him in his place."

Proserpine "Prossy" Garnett

Shaw describes Prossy as "a brisk little woman" who is "sensitive and affectionate." She is about thirty years old and unmarried. She is "rather pert and quick of speech"; perhaps she is more direct in her manner than is considered polite.

Although she denies it, she is secretly in love with Morell and jealous of his attentions to Candida.

Eugene Marchbanks

Shaw describes Marchbanks as a shy, sensitive young man who is "slight, effeminate, with a delicate childish voice." Marchbanks is a poet, and he is tormented by his infatuation with Candida. He is the only character who changes significantly, coming to admire Morell for filling a place in Candida's heart.

Reverend Alexander "Lexy" Mill

Lexy is Morell's young curate and assistant. His intentions are good, and he is enthusiastic. He idolizes Morell and tries, with limited success, to be like him.

Candida Morell

Candida, age thirty-three, is Morell's wife and the mother of their two young children. Shaw describes her as "well built, well nourished." Candida is charming and does not hesitate to use her charm to "manage people . . . without the smallest scruple." Candida loves her husband, but she finds Eugene Marchbanks's naïveté and poetic nature appealing. At the end, given a choice between her husband and Marchbanks, she chooses her husband, believing that he needs her more.

Reverend James Mavor Morell

Morell is the husband of the title character. He is an energetic and sympathetic clergyman. Shaw describes him as a "vigorous, genial, popular man of forty, robust and goodlooking." Morell is somewhat complacent and vain and perhaps takes his wife for granted. When Marchbanks tells Morell that he loves his wife, Morell grows angry and orders the poet out of his house. Later, convinced that Candida will be faithful to him, he leaves his wife and Marchbanks together. In the end, he "bids" for his wife by offering her his strength, honesty, ability, and position.

THEMES

Socialism

An important contemporary theme that Shaw incorporated into *Candida* is socialism, particularly Christian socialism, a movement that grew out of perceptions that the presumed abuses of capitalism were inconsistent with the lofty ideals

TOPICS FOR FURTHER STUDY

- Locate a copy of *Fabianism and the Empire: A Manifesto by the Fabian Society* (published by Nabu Press in 2011, or available on the Internet Archive website at http://archive.org/details/fabianismempirem00shawuoft). Shaw, one of the first members of the Fabian Society of British Socialists, had a hand in the production of this document. After examining the text, write an essay in which you comment on how Shaw's socialist views might have influenced him in the writing of *Candida*.

- *Candida* is sometimes reprinted together with *Pygmalion*, a play that tells the story of a young Cockney girl, Eliza Doolittle, who is transformed into a lady by a snooty professor of linguistics, Henry Higgins. Read *Pygmalion*, then prepare an oral report in which you trace any similarities (or differences) you find in the two plays.

- Investigate the issue of the position of British women in the late nineteenth century. At a political level, what were their concerns? How did they express those concerns? What groups advocated for improvements in the position of women at the time? What involvement did Shaw have with these groups? To what extent is Candida a "modern" woman? Make a chart that lists the key elements of your findings and share your chart with your class.

- Using the Internet, conduct research on what was called "muscular Christianity" in England at the time when Shaw lived and wrote. What ideas did the phenomenon represent? Who were some of the major figures in the movement? Present your findings to your class in a brief oral report.

- Imagine that you are part of a love triangle, one in which the two people of the same gender have very different personalities, but each is vying for the affection of the third person in the triangle. Write a brief one-act play in which you dramatize some aspect of the relationships. Recruit a couple of your classmates and perform your play for the other students in the class.

- A recent young-adult novel, one turned into a highly successful feature film, is *The Hunger Games* (Scholastic Press, 2008) by Suzanne Collins. This book, like *Candida*, features a love triangle. Read the book, then prepare a PowerPoint presentation for your class exploring how each work is a reflection of the culture that produced it (remembering that *The Hunger Games* is a futuristic fantasy novel).

- Read Tanuja Desei Hidier's *Born Confused* (Scholastic Press, 2003), a young-adult novel about an Indian American girl living in New Jersey, her blonde, blue-eyed friend, and the love triangle that emerges with an Indian boy, Karsh Kapoor. Now, imagine that Candida from Shaw's play is a good friend to the girl—a teacher or neighbor, or perhaps an aunt. Write a letter in the voice of Candida advising the heroine of *Born Confused* as to what to do.

of Christianity. That the Reverend James Morell is a socialist is made clear in the narrative description of him at the beginning of act 1, where his bookcase reveals socialist works, including, for example, *Progress and Poverty*, a widely read book by Henry George published in 1879 under the full title *Progress and Poverty: An Inquiry into the Cause of Industrial Depressions and of Increase of Want with Increase of Wealth: The Remedy*. Morell opens a copy of *The Church Reformer*, and the reader is told that he is a member of the Guild of St. Matthew and the Christian Social Union, organizations committed to socialist ideals. Morell's socialism is apparent in his discussion—which turns into an argument—with his father-in-law, Burgess, in act 1, where Burgess is depicted as a selfish, oafish, exploitative mill owner who pays the workers subsistence wages, at best.

Women's Rights

In act 1 Lexy refers to the "Woman Question," and Shaw capitalizes the words to suggest that this issue was one of particular importance and discussion at the time. The Woman Question had to do with the changing roles of women and raised such questions as whether women should be allowed to pursue higher education, take part in politics, seek employment in the business world, and vote. Also important was the question of a woman's role in the household relative to her husband and children. Shaw was a proponent of women's freedom. He supported extension of the right to vote to women and maintained that women could provide the compassion and other attributes that he saw as missing from government as it was currently constituted. Thus, he would have been a supporter of a group such as the Women's Liberal Federation, an organization formed in 1886–87 and that Lexy refers to in act 1 when he quotes a statement Morell made to the organization in a speech: "Ah, if you women only had the same clue to Man's strength that you have to his weakness . . . there would be no Woman Question."

Candida examines the Woman Question from a unique angle. On the one hand, Candida is supposed to be a powerful woman. She has always supported her husband, who owes much of his success to her. She is beautiful, engaging, and intelligent. She is a good mother to her children, having come all the way back to London to get flannel because the children were ill. (At the time, it was believed that flannel was an effective health measure that could keep warmth in and illness out.) She has little interest, however, in Morell's socialism; when he returns home triumphant about an address he has delivered, her only response is to ask about the amount of money collected. By the same token, she has little interest in Marchbanks's poetry. When he recites poetry to her, she dozes off. Her goal is to provide Marchbanks with motherly care simply because he seems to need it, and, at the end of the play, when she chooses her husband over Marchbanks, it is because he needs her more (although earlier it is made apparent that she loves him as well). Ultimately, then, the play is satirical, for Candida clings to the conventional role of wife and mother, implicitly

granting her husband permission to maintain his complacency and self-sufficiency. As she notes in her lengthy monologue near the end of the play:

> When there is money to give, he [Morell] gives it: when there is money to refuse, I refuse it. I build a castle of comfort and indulgence and love for him, and stand sentinel always to keep little vulgar cares out. I make him master here, though he does not know it.

Working Class

Shaw was vitally interested in the plight of the industrial working class in late-nineteenth-century England. From the middle of the century, workers could make more money in the factories than they could on farms. Accordingly, many moved from the countryside to work and live in the cities and larger towns. The conditions they faced were usually brutal. Men, women, and children worked long hours for little pay. An employee who was injured and could not work would in most cases simply be let go. As the number of workers in the factory towns increased, wages declined so that by the 1890s, weavers such as those Burgess employs earned only ten to sixteen shillings a week; children working in jobs such as this earned perhaps three to four shillings a week—this at a time when a loaf of bread cost about one shilling.

People such as Morell and organizations such as the Fabian Society recognized the effects of the factory system and fought to regulate it. This conflict is depicted in *Candida* in act 1, where Morell and his father-in-law, Burgess, quarrel. Morell is speaking for Shaw when he responds to Burgess's claim that in submitting a low bid on a contract three years ago, he was acting in the interests of taxpayers:

> Yes, the lowest, because you paid worse wages than any other employer—starvation wages— aye, worse than starvation wages—to the women who made the clothing. Your wages would have driven them to the streets to keep body and soul together.

Shaw's depiction of Burgess is hardly flattering to him; in commenting on his need to raise wages to appease the local government, Burgess says:

> Why else should I do it? What does it lead to but drink and huppishness in workin' men? . . . you never think of the 'arm you do, puttin' money into the pockets of workin' men that they don't know 'ow to spend, and takin' it from people that might be makin' a good huse on it.

Eugene Marchbanks, a young poet, tries to woe Candida. (© Victorian Traditions / Shutterstock.com)

Romantic Love

Candida presents a sharp contrast between romantic, poetic love, represented by Eugene Marchbanks, and a steadier, more conventional and domestic kind of love, represented by James Morell and Candida. Although Marchbanks is present as a sincere character, it is clear that Shaw is satirizing the kind of love Marchbanks represents. At the beginning of act 2, for example, he has an awkward conversation with Prossy about romantic love. The stage directions emphasize Marchbanks's melancholy, mournfulness, and dejection. He is said to collapse into a chair as he discourses on love. He presents a "tragic mask" to Prossy.

Later, when Candida announces that her favorite scrub brush has been ruined, a scene of high comedy follows. Marchbanks, dismayed that the woman he adores should be burdened with domestic chores, cries out, then says "horror, horror, horror." He bows his head on his hands. Burgess is present, and he says: "What! Got the 'orrors, Mr. Morchbanks! Oh, that's

bad, at your age. You must leave it off grajally." Candida dismisses the problem as "only poetic horror."

Marchbanks's romantic love is also satirized in act 3 as he sits with Candida reading poetry to her. She wants him to stop, saying, "Come and sit down on the hearth-rug, and talk moonshine as you usually do. I want to be amused." This kind of remark indicates to the audience that Candida regards Marchbanks, his poetry, and his romance with tolerant bemusement and that she has no intention of being unfaithful to her husband.

STYLE

Dialogue

Obviously, the keystone of a work of drama is its dialogue, although actors supplement dialogue with facial expressions, mannerisms, dress, action, and other visual elements. Shaw is well known for his witty, incisive dialogue, dialogue that is often comic (as in *Candida*) but that conveys serious underlying perspectives on the themes he wants to develop. A reader could find a scene of sharp, incisive dialogue almost by opening a copy of the play at random.

In act 2, Candida punctures some of her husband's pretensions in an exchange about his popularity as a preacher: "James, dear, you preach so splendidly that it's as good as a play for them. Why do you think the women are so enthusiastic?" Morell is "shocked" and can only exclaim "Candida!" His wife continues, teasing him but making it very clear that she truly believes many of the women in the congregation "have Prossy's complaint." When Morell asks her what she means, she explains that Prossy is

> in love with you, James: that's the reason. They're all in love with you. And you are in love with preaching because you do it so beautifully. And you think it's all enthusiasm for the kingdom of Heaven on earth; and so do they. You dear silly!

An exchange such as this accomplishes multiple purposes. It suggests Candida's tolerance and affection for her husband, along with her refusal to take him too seriously. She mentions that part of Prossy's job is to "peel potatoes and abase herself in all manner of ways for six shillings a week less than she used to get in a city office." This remark grounds the issue in the domestic sphere and undermines the seriousness of Morell's ideology, especially considering that Prossy works for lower wages than she could otherwise earn, a bone of contention between Morell and his father-in-law. The discussion touches on the idea that personal relationships and emotions do more to determine people's happiness than theories and beliefs. The dialogue also subtly comments on the position of women, both in the world of business and in the domestic sphere.

Problem Play

Candida is a specific kind of play referred to by many theater scholars as a "problem play." The problem play is a subgenre of drama that emerged in the nineteenth century to examine controversial social issues in a realistic way, expose social ills, and provoke thought and discussion. Shaw was a socialist, and he was committed to the emancipation of women. He supported the right of women to vote, and in his plays he tried to depict strong, independent women—women such as Candida, who is courageous, stable, confident, guided by common sense, and able to impose her will on the men around her.

At the same time, Candida is depicted as maternal; indeed, in the initial description of her in act 1, the reader is told that she is endowed with "the double charm of youth and motherhood." Later, Shaw states: "A wisehearted observer, looking at her, would at once guess that whoever had placed the Virgin of the Assumption over her hearth did so because he fancied some spiritual resemblance between them." (The "Virgin of the Assumption" should read *The Assumption of the Virgin*, the name of a famous sixteenth-century painting by Titian that depicts Mary, the Virgin Mother of Christ, being assumed, or taken up, into heaven.) Thus, Shaw sets up a highly conventional dramatic situation, a love triangle, but it turns out that it is the woman, not one of the men, who is morally strong enough to make the critical decision, settle the dispute, and come down on the side of conventional, stable, pragmatic marriage.

Narration

Typically, a printed play does not provide extensive stage directions or commentary. Shakespeare's plays, for example, have virtually nothing in the way of stage directions, and many of the very brief stage directions they do have are provided by editors. One exception to this common practice is American playwright Eugene O'Neill, who provides extensive stage directions, descriptions of settings and characters, and the like. Another noteworthy exception is Shaw, whose plays in some ways read almost like novels consisting of narration interspersed with dialogue. Thus, for example, act 1 opens with an extensive description of the setting that surrounds the parsonage where Morell and Candida live, a narrative description little different from that which might be found in a novel. The action of the play takes place entirely indoors, so in one sense the description of the neighborhood is irrelevant, but this description gives the reader a firmer sense of the social and economic environment that surrounds the characters and the action of the play.

Shaw also provides extensive descriptions of his characters, thus giving stage producers and directors guidance on the characters' appearance, dress, and mannerisms. He often seems to leave scant room for actors to interpret their parts, for he provides running commentary on how characters react to the statements of others. Thus, for example, as Morell and Marchbanks quarrel in act 1, Shaw writes: "Morell, angered, turns suddenly on him. He flies to the door in involuntary dread."

Additionally, Shaw freely comments on the motivations of characters, interpreting those motivations in ways that the character himself could not. In act 1, for example, as Morell and Burgess try to smooth things over after their quarrel, Morell makes a remark that Shaw then comments on and interprets:

> The effect of this observation on Burgess is to remove the keystone of his moral arch. He becomes bodily weak, and, with his eyes fixed on Morell in a helpless stare, puts out his hand apprehensively to balance himself.

The effect of this type of narration is to enable Shaw to write not just what amount to scripts for stage actors but fully realized works of literature that can be enjoyed both in performance and on the printed page.

HISTORICAL CONTEXT

Christian Socialism

The Reverend James Morell describes himself as a Christian socialist. Christian socialism was a movement that emerged in Britain in the

COMPARE
&
CONTRAST

- **1890s:** The Fabian Society, founded in 1884, advocates the gradual reform of the social and economic order through legislation and education rather than Marxist revolution.

  Today: The Fabian Society in Britain, as well as in other countries, continues to advocate evolutionary socialism. British Fabians are affiliated with the nation's Labour Party.

- **1890s:** The Christian Social Union has been in existence since 1889.

  Today: The Christian Social Union merged with the Industrial Christian Fellowship in 1919, but the Fellowship continues to pro-

mote social progress, business ethics, and similar goals in Great Britain.

- **1890s:** British socialists win a victory in 1894 when legislation levying death duties (that is, inheritance taxes) is passed, leading to the breakup of large estates over the next century, especially after the deaths of estate owners who fought in World War I.

  Today: The issue of death duties, both in Britain and the United States, continues to arouse heated debate, although relatively few estate owners in both countries are affected by the tax.

---

mid-nineteenth century with the goal of applying the teachings of Christianity to modern industrial life. Christian socialists believed that wealthy capitalists were too often guilty of exploiting workers who, in England's industrial cities, led squalid, precarious lives working brutally long hours for low wages and no job security. Within this movement, activists called for social programs that would ameliorate conditions for workers and reform wealthy business owners by exposing the potential evils of capitalism and individualism. As the century went on, "Christian socialism" was a term used more generally to refer to any movement or social philosophy that tried to combine the ethical convictions of Christianity with the basic aims of socialism.

The roots of Christian Socialism lay with the utopian socialism advocated by French philosopher Henri de Saint-Simon in the early nineteenth century. Saint-Simon was a proponent of a new kind of Christianity that would concern itself primarily with the condition of the poor, and his followers, called Saint-Simonians, believed that social development could be achieved only through a spirit of association and cooperation rather than competition. They believed that under the influence of Christianity,

association and connectedness would replace individualism and competitive antagonism as the dominant social and economic pattern. The Saint-Simonians believed, for example, that inheritances should be abolished. Doing so would free up capital for the use of society as a whole and remove it from the hands of selfish capitalists and the idle rich. Steps such as this, they believed, would help alleviate poverty.

The term "Christian socialism," however, was first used by a trio of prominent figures. One was Frederick Denison Maurice, an English theologian and Church of England minister known for his social work. In 1848, he helped create Queen's College, which provided for the education of governesses. He promoted and helped found the Working Men's College in 1854, and in 1874, he joined forces with Frances Martin to establish the Working Women's College. Another early leader in the movement in England was the novelist Charles Kingsley, who wrote articles for *The Christian Socialist: A Journal of Association* and whose novels highlighted the plight of the working poor. A third major figure was John Malcolm Ludlow, the author of *Progress of the Working Class: 1832–1867* (1867).

These men founded the Christian socialist movement after the collapse of the Chartist movement in 1848. This was a movement based on the People's Charter of 1838, which called for a variety of political reforms, including universal suffrage (for men). Its failure was seen as a repudiation of the legitimate claims of the nation's workers. The stated goal of the new Christian socialists was to establish a Kingdom of Christ (a phrase used in *Candida*) with authority over industry and trade. Their belief was that socialism was the true Christian revolutionary force of the century.

Although his name is largely forgotten today, Ludlow was a driving force in the movement. He looked to France, where various cooperative workers' societies were being formed. He and others helped finance a number of small cooperative societies in England where workers would share in an enterprise's profits. Although the specific movement that Ludlow and his colleagues formed would dissolve, the spirit of the movement lived on, and a host of Christian socialist organizations were formed in England in the last decades of the century. Morell, for example, is a member of the Christian Social Union, an organization founded in 1889. This was the "mainstream" organization whose membership was made up largely of members of the orthodox Church of England. An alternative organization, whose members were largely nonconforming Christians, was the Christian Socialist League, which lasted only from 1894 to 1898. The Christian Socialist Society, which lasted from 1886 to 1892, was the most ecumenical of such societies, with membership open to all.

Morell is also a member of the Guild of St. Matthew, an organization founded in 1877 by the radical Anglo-Catholic curate Stewart Headlam, one of Shaw's lifelong friends, at St. Matthew's Church in Bethnal Green, a district in the East End (London's working-class district). In act 1 of the play, the audience learns that Morell has been invited to speak at various radical, anarchist, communist, and progressive groups, including the Women's Liberal Federation. These and other organizations continued to advocate social reform through education and legislation rather than the kind of convulsive revolution advocated by the followers of Karl Marx.

Muscular Christianity

Another important influence on society in the late nineteenth century was "muscular Christianity," a term whose meaning has historically

The Reverend James Mavor Morell is married to Candida. *(© Lisa S. | Shutterstock.com)*

been somewhat fluid. One connotation of the term has to do with the concept that a healthy body helps produce a healthy mind—that is, the belief that a true Christian should remain physically fit. This view was the impetus behind the formation of such organizations as the Young Men's Christian Association (YMCA) and the Young Women's Christian Association (YWCA), both of which promoted sport.

The term, however, was also used to refer to a perspective on and an attitude toward Christianity: a forthright, manly, plainspoken, candid assertion of Christianity and Christian values, one that rejected asceticism (spiritual discipline through self-denial) and restraint. The term probably originated in an 1857 review of Kingsley's novel of that year, *Two Years Ago*. The phrase was also used in reference to *Tom Brown's School Days*, an 1857 novel written by Kingsley's friend, Thomas Hughes. The press took up the term and started calling the two writers muscular Christians and applying the term "muscular

Christianity" to adventure novels that embody noble principles defended by manly Christian heroes.

CRITICAL OVERVIEW

Shaw was a theater critic. What did he think of *Candida*? According to Allan Chappelow, in *Shaw the Villager and Human Being: A Biographical Symposium*, *Candida* was Shaw's favorite play, a prototype of the new drama that he wanted to write in opposition to the conventional drama that he believed was a plague on the English stage.

Early commentary on *Candida* focused on the play in performance. In an unsigned review in the *Aberdeen Journal* in 1897, the theater critic responded to a production of *Candida* in a lukewarm fashion, writing:

> There are not a few smart sayings throughout the play, but on the whole it lacks robustness. A little more of the butterman [i.e., Burgess] and a trifle less of the poet would be a decided improvement.

Oliver Elton, reviewing a performance of the play for the *Manchester Guardian*, was troubled by its ending:

> The whole passage...strikes us as sentiment wrapped up in ingenuities, and it is some strain on belief that even Morell should welcome his reward with such rapture when receiving it as the corollary of his weakness from his direst critic, who has upset his whole theory of himself.

In the years that followed, however, enthusiasm for the play grew. In her book *Bernard Shaw*, Pat M. Carr notes that after a performance of the play at the Neues Theater in Berlin, Germany, in 1904, "the German critics were enchanted and called the play a 'masterpiece,' a 'brilliant success,' that had 'dazzling fantasy, unique dialogue, bold humor and deep emotion.'" Carr also states that by 1905, "*Candida* was recognized as one of the great European dramas, and the French critic Henri Odier called it 'one of the most beautiful and finished contributions to the contemporary drama.'"

Later critics comment less on particular performances and more on the text. In "The Case against *Candida*," an essay included in his book *The Art and Mind of Shaw: Essays in Criticism*, A. M. Gibbs quotes Oliver Elton in commenting on what he regards as inconsistent characterization in the play. Gibbs then notes:

> The problems surrounding the characterization of Morell are closely related to confusions in Shaw's conception...of the character of Candida. Shaw clearly intended Candida to be seen as an extremely powerful character.... But Shaw obviously had difficulty in finding satisfactory ways of representing this power in dramatic terms.

Gibbs concludes: "Having decided to show her as being entirely without interest in either Christian Socialism or poetry, he fell back on unctuous maternalism as her most positive form of communication."

In "The Virgin Mother," Margery M. Morgan examines a related issue. After noting that "in some ways *Candida* is a bad play, with excruciatingly written passages," Morgan takes a somewhat more positive view of the maternalism of the play: "Instead of playing up the titillating possibilities of the adultery motif, Shaw has chosen to develop the thesis-character of the play in an analysis of the actual role of woman in contemporary English society." Morgan then concludes: "instead of woman as the immature plaything of man, Shaw emphasizes her maternal aspect, her influence over men and their dependence on her strength."

Tracy C. Davis, in an essay titled "Shaw's Interstices of Empire: Decolonizing at Home and Abroad," examines the broad ideological underpinnings of the play, both in the context of gender issues and in Shaw's critique of British colonialism. Her thesis is that the domestic drama played out in the Morell household is an oblique commentary on ruler and ruled, on colonizer and colonized, on master and subject. Thus, *Candida*

> provides the paradigmatic example of Shaw's ability to relate the microeconomy and power of a household to the macroeconomic concerns of global capitalism, its product (colonialism), and the complicity of colonialism in gender ideology and racism.

As an example, Davis comments on the relationship between Prossy and Morell, stating that it represents "a matter of one gender's willingness to extend unlimited credit (in the form of fidelity and nurturing) and the other gender's willingness to exploit this credit fulsomely for its own glory or profit." Eldon C. Hill, in *George Bernard Shaw*, buttresses this point when he notes that "it is not surprising that, at the end of the play, [Candida] has settled back into her cozy domestic situation—and has failed to exhibit the attributes of the New Woman."

CRITICISM

Michael J. O'Neal

O'Neal holds a PhD in English. In the following essay, he examines Shaw's development of theme through paradox in Candida.

"Paradox" refers to a self-contradictory statement or to a set of incompatible ideas whose very incompatibility exposes a truth or sparks an insight. Shaw was a master of the paradox. He is the source, for example, of the statement (usually quoted by older people) that youth is wasted on the young; the actual quote is "What a pity that youth must be wasted on the young." Shaw's admirers will use the term "Shavian" to describe this kind of statement; "Shavian" is the adjective form of the name Shaw (like "Shakespearean") that has come to connote Shaw's wit, sophistication, intellectual rigor, moral complexity, sparkling language, and theatrical bravura. A considerable part of Shaw's appeal for theatergoers and readers is his ability to hold in suspension two apparently contradictory beliefs—that is, to explore the paradoxical nature of the human condition and to greet all accepted wisdom, all conventional viewpoints, with piercing skepticism.

The opening scene of *Candida* provides a simple example. Shaw himself was firmly committed to socialist ideals. He was an early member of the Fabian Society, which promoted those ideals. He cooperated with the society in the production of *Fabianism and the Empire: A Manifesto by the Fabian Society*. He backed numerous progressive causes. However, the play's opening scene, which establishes the Reverend James Morell's socialist credentials, has a distinctly tongue-in-cheek, comic tone. As Prossy tries to arrange her employer's numerous speaking engagements, the audience is flooded with the names of organizations, from the Hoxton Freedom Group (which Prossy characterizes as a group of communist anarchists) to the English Land Restoration League to the Social-Democratic Federation—culminating in a demand from the Fabian Society, to which Morell responds: "Bother the Fabian Society!" The paradox, of course, is that Shaw can back the

views of organizations such as these yet at the same time recognize that their proliferation, along with their incessant demands on the time of someone like Morell, can lead to a comic ridiculousness, as though everyone surrounding Morell is tied up with radical causes with which Morell himself seems almost to be growing impatient: "Just like Anarchists not to know that they can't have a parson on Sunday!" Shaw's own socialism gets the gimlet eye.

In act 3, Shaw gives Candida a line that, taken by itself, could almost be said to contain the essence of the play. Candida chastises her husband for his attitude toward Marchbanks and toward the relationship between the poet and his wife. She says to him: "Put your trust in my love for you, James, for if that went, I should care very little for your sermons—mere phrases that you cheat yourself and others with every day." Moments later, she is more severe: "James—you understand nothing." Morell, of course, is shocked by her words. She responds with a line that represents the pith of the play: "Oh, you're only shocked! Is that all? How conventional all you unconventional people are." She then goes on to explain:

> This comes of James teaching me to think for myself, and never to hold back out of fear of what other people may think of me. It works beautifully as long as I think the same things as he does.

This exchange could be seen as the core of the play: James, a socialist, much like Shaw himself, believes that he teaches the habit of independent thought to others, including his wife.

WHAT DO I READ NEXT?

- *How He Lied to Her Husband*, a one-act comedy Shaw wrote in 1905, involves three characters: Aurora Bompas, who manages to pass herself off as young and beautiful; her husband, Teddy Bompas; and Henry Apjohn, who bears comparison with Marchbanks for his impetuosity and for having written romantic poems to Aurora. The play is available online at Pennsylvania State University's Electronic Classics Series at http://www2.hn.psu.edu/faculty/jmanis/gbshaw/Lied.pdf.

- *Saint Joan* (1924) is based on the life and trial of St. Joan of Arc, the fifteenth-century folk heroine who led French forces to victories in the Hundred Years' War but who was tried and executed by the English for heresy when she was just nineteen years old. The play, which led to Shaw receiving the Nobel Prize for Literature, is available in numerous editions.

- Oscar Wilde, an Irish author born just two years before Shaw, is the author of "The Soul of Man under Socialism," an 1891 essay that defended his views as an anarchist. The essay is available online at the Project Gutenberg website at http://www.gutenberg.org/ebooks/1017.

- Perhaps Wilde's best-known play is *The Importance of Being Earnest* (1895), but almost equally popular is *Lady Windermere's Fan*, a comedy about marriage published in 1893.

- Roy Hattersley's *The Edwardians* (2005) examines the era in which Shaw came of age, launched his career as a playwright, and achieved fame. Although the Edwardian era technically encompasses the period of King Edward VII's reign (1901–1910), most social and cultural historians extend the boundaries back to the 1880s and forward to the years after World War I.

- Shaw was an avid proponent of English spelling reform. His 1906 letter to the editor of the *New York Times* outlining his views can be found at "G. B. Shaw Would Save English by Phonetics" at the *New York Times* archive website at http://query.nytimes.com/mem/archive-free/pdf?res=F10816F9395512738DDDAC0A94D1405B868CF1D3.

- Just as Shaw tried to raise his audiences' awareness about social issues through his plays, so too did African American playwright August Wilson, whose "Pittsburgh Cycle" of ten plays about the African American experience earned him two Pulitzer Prizes. The plays were written between 1985 and 2007, and each of the ten plays is set in one of the ten decades of the twentieth century.

- Shaw was a great admirer of Norwegian playwright Henrik Ibsen, one of early modern theater's major proponents of psychological realism. Among Ibsen's most famous plays is *A Doll's House*. Premiering in 1879, the controversial play, which was sharply critical of traditional marriage norms, helped inspire *Candida*, which Shaw wrote partly in response to Ibsen's play.

- Lensey Namioka's young-adult novel *An Ocean Apart, A World Away* (2002) presents a modern take on the issue of women and their roles in society.

Socialism by its very nature questions the established order, and the Christian socialism of the nineteenth century called for an evolutionary process of change that would in time overthrow received wisdom. However, Morell's brand of Christian socialism can itself, paradoxically, become received wisdom among a certain set. It can become conventional. This is what prompts

Marchbanks was a poet. (© *Gayvoronskaya_Yana | Shutterstock.com*)

the line, "How conventional all you unconventional people are." Further, Candida has little interest in her husband's socialism, and she seems also to have little interest in his Christianity ("mere phrases" used to "cheat" people). Again, paradoxically, the play suggests that Morell owes much of his professional success to the support he has received from his wife.

If Candida does not adhere to her husband's brand of Christian socialism, to what does she adhere? Again, the play presents a fundamental paradox. In the play's final scene, Candida declares her purpose of remaining with her husband—paradoxically, the stronger man by most measures, the muscular Christian, whom she sees as weaker in comparison with Marchbanks. Note the contradiction. Morell is self-confident. He is in demand in the world at large. He cuts a wide swath. Others, like Lexy, want to imitate him. The ladies, like Prossy, develop crushes on him. In contrast, Marchbanks is weak and young. He is physically timid. He shies away from Morell in physical fear. He spouts poetic "moonshine," as Candida calls it. When he reclines with his head on her lap, one can

imagine the audience rolling its collective eyes in amusement, yet in a highly paradoxical reversal, it turns out that Marchbanks, at least for Candida, is the stronger man of the two. The audience, too, recognizes that while Morell (and to a certain extent, Candida) is a static character, Marchbanks is capable of growth and insight. Accordingly, he has less need of her than Morell does.

The final paradox has to do with the play's attitude toward marriage. The love triangle consists of a conventional husband and wife. Candida is presented as a strong, independent woman, yet she exerts her strength within the boundaries of a highly traditional marriage. Her attitude toward her husband is not romantic. In fact, it is almost cynical. At the same time, there is no selfishness in her nature. These characteristics enable her to be clear sighted about her husband. She recognizes him for who he is, and she accepts him as he is. Unlike Prossy, or even Lexy, she does not idolize him. In this way she suggests that for Shaw, marriage was not a trap, or slavery; nor was marriage an institution based on sentimental ecstasy. Marriage was a social institution, one rooted in fact. It was an alliance, one that enabled the couple to confront the world, raise children, and create a space for themselves in the portion of the world that they inhabit. In a traditional marriage, the wife regarded the husband as her knight, her protector. She saw him as paradoxically strong, a warrior in the world, and weak, like a child who requires her guidance and her willingness to bandage his bruises. Thus, the resolution of *Candida* expresses the paradox that Morell, a stalwart, "muscular" man of the world, is too small to get by on his own. He needs the support of a woman who can think for herself. To the extent that he chafes at that need, he is one of the conventional unconventional people whom Candida chides.

In the end, Shaw presents his readers with three conflicting sets of ideals. None is adequate. All, however, have appeal. One set of ideals are those of Christian socialism and muscular Christianity, as represented by Morell. A second set are those of romantic love and sentimentality, as represented by Marchbanks. The third set of ideals revolve around motherhood and domesticity; indeed, Shaw himself referred to *Candida* as "the Mother Play" (quoted by William Storm in *Irony and the Modern Theatre*).

Candida herself is a paradox, for in one sense she is the kind of woman whom Shaw, outside the theater, might have despised, at least on an intellectual level, for her matronly domesticity is at odds with Shaw's political beliefs in women's emancipation. As she is depicted, however, she is irresistible, a kind of combination of the Virgin Mary (see the description of the painting *The Assumption of the Virgin* over her mantel) and of the New Woman of nineteenth-century British progressivism.

In a larger sense, the play is never resolved. Shaw wants to depict that "New Woman" in the context of the "Woman Question," yet he recognizes that within the home, passions, prejudices, tradition, and a host of other factors render the politics of the streets and debating societies irrelevant. Perhaps that is the most fundamental paradox of all. Shaw wanted to write a "problem play"; he wanted theater to be the theater of ideas, yet with a creation such as Candida, ideas play second fiddle to tradition. In the end, the status quo endures. Nothing has changed in the lives of the Morells.

Source: Michael J. O'Neal, Critical Essay on *Candida*, in *Drama for Students*, Gale, Cengage Learning, 2013.

> **MOREOVER, THE WORD 'CANDIDA' ALSO MEANS 'FUNGUS' AND SHAW HAS CLEVERLY TITLED HIS PLAY WITH THE SAME NAME SO AS TO INFORM HIS READERS THAT HE DISCUSSES IN THIS PLAY HOW MARRIAGE AND ECONOMIC SYSTEMS, LIKE FUNGUS, DECAY THE SOCIETY AND RESTRICT THE LIFE FORCE."**

A. Kayalvizhi

In the following essay, Kayalvizhi focuses on how Shaw attacks the institution of marriage and the economic system of the society in the play.

This article focuses on how George Bernard Shaw attacks the most popular institution marriage and the economic system of the society in his domestic play *Candida*. He conveys in this play that marriage is only a sexual contract between a man and a woman. Moreover, woman's economic dependence on man makes her a slave in the house, and it is also a hindrance to the free movement of Life Force, believes Shaw.

OUTLINE STORY

Candida, a pretty woman of thirty three, is married to James Mavor Morell, a popular man of forty and a first rate Christian Socialist clergyman, and they are the parents of two children. Outwardly, Morell and Candida seem to be a happy couple, living harmoniously without any kind of dissatisfaction between them. However, the intervention of Eugene Marchbanks, an eighteen year old poet, turns things into a different shape. He ascertains that Morell does not deserve Candida, for he is just a religious windbag, and treats her as a slave. And he realises that his poetic soul has a natural resemblance with the soul of Candida. He shows his love to her, and she responds to him impulsively.

Suddenly Marchbanks, who turns out to be daring, tells Morell that he is no match for Candida, and he himself would be the suitable person to be her husband. First Morell does not take this seriously; but then he starts worrying, because of the assertion of Marchbanks. Morell, at last, lets Candida choose between them.

Candida finds herself for auction and asks the rivals to announce their bids. Morell offers his strength for her defence, his honesty for her surety, his ability and industry for her livelihood, and his authority and position for her dignity. Marchbanks offers his weakness, his desolation, and his heart's need. Though Candida is impressed by Marchbanks's bid, she declares her decision to remain with the weaker of the two rivals, i.e., Morell. Her choice shocks Marchbanks, yet he leaves the household of Candida without any complaint, but with a secret in his mind.

HEROISM OF MARCHBANKS

Shaw's depiction of his hero Marchbanks is completely different from the hero concepts of other playwrights. He is an eighteen year old youth who is shy and physically weak, but mentally he is very strong. The portrayal of Marchbanks by Shaw is observed by Innes: "Hypersensitive, fearful, physically puny, Marchbanks is a typical Shavian contrast to the conventional hero. Yet he represents both the idealist and an ideal."

Marchbanks has the intellectual competence to judge others correctly, and it is he who finds the incompatible combination of the couple Morell and Candida, whereas they seem to be an ideal couple for others. Shaw introduces Morell as a respectable, popular, first rate clergyman of forty, and having the unaffected voice with perfect articulation of a practiced orator. In spite of the fact that he is highly regarded by the people, Marchbanks sees him as a religious windbag. He opines about Morell to the typist Proserpine, "I can see nothing in him but words, pious resolutions, what people call goodness." He degrades the oration of Morell as that which merely excites people and rouses their fervour but makes no change in their conducts. He even compares Morell to King David, who danced before people to make them enthusiastic and was despised by his wife for that.

UNINTENTIONAL TREATING OF WIFE AS A SLAVE—MARCHBANKS' WORLD VIEW

Morell is, of course, an ideal husband and is very much devoted to his wife, but he treats his wife like a slave unintentionally. Marchbanks finds out that there is no real love between Morell and Candida though he adores his wife. According to Marchbanks, the conventional, pig-headed Morell cannot match up with the idealistic, noble Candida. His view is that if a man really loves his ladylove, he would wish to keep her happy and free from toiling, albeit to be idle and useless. So he wants to rescue her from the chores, and asks Morell to give up his wife. He condemns Morell, "your wife's beautiful fingers are dabbling in paraffin oil while you sit here comfortably preaching about it: everlasting preaching! preaching! words! words! words!" But what he, Marchbanks, can provide her is that, he says poetically:

> a tiny shallop to sail away in, far from the world, where the marble floors are washed by the rain and dried by the sun; where the south wind dusts the beautiful green and purple carpets. Or a chariot! To carry us into the sky, where the lamps are stars, and dont need to be filled with paraffin oil every day.

A HIGHER GOAL?

Marchbanks may seem to be a wicked man for intruding into the affairs of a perfect couple and flirting with the wife of another man. But it is not true, for he does not seek sensual pleasure from her. His desire is only to see to it that Candida lives happily and this quality of his character can be perceived from his suggestion to Morell:

> Oh, Morell, let us both give her up. Why should she have to choose between a wretched little nervous disease like me, and a pig-headed parson like you? Let us go on a pilgrimage, you to the east and I to the west, in search of a worthy lover for her: some beautiful archangel with purple wings—.

Thus, in Marchbanks are seen this honesty and exquisiteness of the soul. The frail Marchbanks, who trembles in fear when Morell tries to attack him, is strong in his conception, and brave enough to fight against the notions of a clergyman.

CANDIDA'S LOVE FOR MARCHBANKS

Shaw describes Candida as a woman with the double charm of youth and motherhood who frankly and instinctively handles people by appealing to their affection. As evaluated by Marchbanks, Candida is a woman with a great soul, craving for reality, truth, and freedom. She ties her husband with her abundance of love, but does not have a high estimation of him. Her opinion about Morell is similar to that of Marchbanks. For her, his preaching is not worth mentioning, that the big crowd listening to him do not follow his words but they take it as an entertainment for them. His sermons are, she says, "mere phrases that you cheat yourself and others with every day."

But the poet Marchbanks appeals to her soul very much that he is an extraordinary, quick-witted, and cleverer than Morell. She finds him well-suited to her own temperament. She expresses her love to him without any hesitation. She is bold enough to tell Morell about her increasing love for Marchbanks. Goodness and purity, which Morell expects from her, are little care for her, since she says, "I would give them both to poor Eugene as willingly as I would give my shawl to a beggar dying of cold, if there were nothing else to restrain me." Candida's fascination with Marchbanks is not to be taken as sexual magnetism. It is well-explained by Holroyd:

> But the affinity between them is that of mother and son, and the weapon that guards them from Hell is the taboo of incest. It is because the Virgin Mother outlaws sex that she is Shaw's ideal. Candida reduces all men to children by emotional castration. (317)

CANDIDA'S OUTLOOK OF MEN

Morell recognises that Candida holds Marchbanks in high regards, and not him. Candida's outlook on both men is thoroughly expressed in her speech, for she tells Morell, "He is always right. He understands you; he understands me; he understands Prossy; and you, darling, you understand nothing." Her words, which hurt Morell, clearly show her esteem and affection for Marchbanks.

PREFERENCE OF CANDIDA

Morell, unable to stand his intolerable jealousy and the insistence of Marchbanks to give up Candida, asks her to choose her mate between them. In a situation of selecting a man, she finds herself as a thing being auctioned, and therefore asks the bids of the rivals. Morell says, "I have nothing to offer you but my strength for your defence, my honesty for your surety, and ability and industry for your livelihood, and my authority and position for your dignity. That is all it becomes a man to offer to a woman." And Marchbanks's bid is, "My weakness. My desolation. My heart's need" which is admired by Candida.

After a while, surprisingly she announces that she wants to give herself to the weaker of two; by this she means that she wants to remain

with her husband. She justifies her decision to Marchbanks that he can do without her, but Morell needs her very much, as his mother, sister, wife and mother to his children. Bentley comments on Shaw's converse view on the topic of weaker sex: "instead of the little woman reaching up toward the arms of the strong man, we have the strong woman reaching down to pick up her child."

Marchbanks does not feel depressed for being rejected by Candida. He proves to be a gentleman unlike the jealous Morell, and he departs her without any hostility. His response towards Candida and Morell is purely benevolent, not malevolent. He tells Morell, "I no longer desire happiness: life is nobler than that. Parson James: I give you my happiness with both hands: I love you because you have filled the heart of the woman I loved. Goodbye." Holroyd observes his attitude:

> It is Eugene Marchbanks who experiences the metamorphosis from sensuality to spirituality and artistic dedication. Looking upon the suffocating commonplaces of the Morell household, he concludes that domesticity, security, and love are inferior ends compared with the sublime and lonely renunciation of the artist. (316)

Candida thinks that her decision must have shown him about the character of women. So she enquires him: "How old are you, Eugene?" and the philosophical reply of Marchbanks is, "As old as the world now. This morning I was eighteen" which implies that he becomes matured enough to understand the nature of the women.

PURPOSE OF SHAW

The intention of Shaw to make Candida take this decision is that, in spite of being an idealist, she cannot overcome the traditional economic morality of the society. Though a romantic, she is not influenced by illusions. Life Force, the power of Nature, utilizes woman, its willing agent, as equipment for the fulfilment of evolutionary process. It concerns only for betterment of the race, and individual's happiness is not considered. Candida, in order to bring up her children well, needs economical help from man. Her insight enables her to assess the two men, and she perceives that it is her husband who can provide a more secured home and sustenance for her and her children.

The poets are intellectuals and help the Life Force in the enhancement of the human race, but they may fail to be successful breadwinners.

Hence she renounces her happiness so as to obey the order of Life Force. She is prepared to continue her life at Morell's home where she is a mistress as well as a slave. She tells Marchbanks, "I build a castle of comfort and indulgence and love for him, and stand sentinel always to keep little vulgar cares out. I make him master here, though he does not know it, and could not tell you a moment ago how it came to be so" (Shaw).

FOCUS ON BIOLOGICAL NEED

Nature intends women to propagate children and sustain the human race. If so, her sexual relationship with man is not the result of higher love but of her physical hunger. Therefore, man and woman live together for biological need, and fulfil their duty demanded by Nature, even though there is no true love and mutual understanding. Therefore the preference of Candida for Morell is not the outcome of real love. Bentley puts it, "The axis about which Candida revolves is that of strength and weakness, not love and hate" (71). Shaw exposes effectively the hollowness of marriage in the present society through this play. According to him, any marriage will be proved to be failure if it is checked up inherently. The people want to maintain their relationship by suppressing their mental distress with the wrap of happiness and peace.

IMPACT OF ECONOMIC DEPENDENCE

Furthermore, Shaw discloses how the economic dependence of woman impedes the free movement of Life Force. Life Force, whose sole duty is to produce better intellectual human race, urges the woman on choosing a competent mate for its purpose. In this case, Candida finds Marchbanks superior to Morell in fulfilling the requirement of Life Force. Had Candida been economically independent, she would have chosen Marchbanks. Therefore her economic slavery obstructs her from picking the right person for mating.

IMPLICATIONS OF "CANDIDA"

Shaw has his own intention for naming his heroine "Candida." The different implications of the word "candida" such as white, bright, and light vividly describe the personality of his heroine. The purity of her soul is represented by "white." She is "bright" and clever in making better decisions. And she is a light in the sense that she illuminates her surroundings with her charisma. Moreover, the word "candida" also means "fungus" and Shaw has cleverly titled his

> " SHE WILL STILL TRIM THE LAMPS, PEEL THE NASTY LITTLE SPANISH ONIONS, AND KEEP THE 'CASTLE' IN GOOD RUNNING ORDER, BUT MORELL WILL KNOW THAT SHE DOES IT FOR LOVE, NOT SIMPLY BECAUSE SHE IS HIS WIFE."

play with the same name so as to inform his readers that he discusses in this play how marriage and economic systems, like fungus, decay the society and restrict the Life Force.

CONCLUSION

The actual reason behind the decision of Candida and the influence of the social conventions on it may be the secret in the poet Marchbanks's heart. Thus, the worthlessness of morality of society and its ideal of happiness are drawn attention to in this play. Shaw's aim to attack the purport of marital love and domestic happiness is well achieved. And how the customs of the society become the setbacks of the progress of the human race is excellently depicted.

Source: A. Kayalvizhi, "The Treatment of Marriage in George Bernard Shaw's *Candida*," in *Language in India*, Vol. 12, No. 3, March 2012, pp. 190–97.

Walter Lazenby

In the following excerpt, Lazenby examines aspects of irony, imagery, and plot through the visualization of the character of Candida.

Most critics of Shaw's *Candida* have approached the play "as if it were a geometry problem whose basic axioms can be located in *The Quintessence* and other Shaviana." They have assumed that Shaw was here merely illustrating his three types (Philistine, Idealist, Realist) and that the play demands a simplistic stock response: automatic scorn for Idealists and Philistines, automatic approval for Realists—that is, after one has identified the characters who represent the types. Unfortunately, they have not been able to agree on whether Morell is Idealist or Philistine; whether Marchbanks is Idealist or Realist; and, curiously, whether Candida herself is a Realist or a Philistine!

One who surveys critical opinions on the play will not find much detailed, cogent analysis of what actually happens in it. True, there has been considerable general discussion of how the play's action affects Marchbanks and Morell, resulting in agreement that both come to be enlightened. But several specific questions remain to be explored: what and how does Eugene learn about love, and what is Morell's state of mind at the end? More important, critics have neglected Candida's reactions to the play's events; in fact Eric Bentley's emphatic assertion that she is merely a link between the two men and alone remains "unchanged at the end" seems to have put an end to consideration of her as a character capable of growth. What does happen in her story?

By attending to patterns in the plot, to hitherto neglected imagery (particularly visual aspects of the staging), and to the effects of dramatic irony, I hope to refine perceptions about the play and to answer these questions. I propose to show that each major character becomes more "vital" (in Shaw's sense) in proportion as he learns more about the reality of love and that this pattern of vitalization, subsuming developments related to all three major characters, earns for each a measure of approval, of dramatic sympathy, which mere recognition of him as a "type" would rule out. The result may be a reappraisal of the overall effect of the play.

CANDIDA'S EMANCIPATION

At various times in the play Candida exhibits different aspects of her multi-faceted character; and it is extremely difficult, as is evident from faulty and contradictory critical statements about her, to frame valid generalizations about her character. Shaw's own overstated generalizations (applicable to only one aspect or another of her character) have tended to obfuscate rather than to clarify: he called her "the Virgin Mother and nobody else," said that she possessed "unerring wisdom on the domestic plane," and averred that she was a thoroughly immoral woman. Similarly Beatrice Webb's characterization of her as a "sentimental prostitute" focuses on only one scene in the play. In her earliest appearances she seems the efficient managing woman, in firm control of the household (though not always of the situation developing there); later she takes on the role of concerned wife and helpmeet to Morell, and nurse or mother to Marchbanks. In Act Three she combines sacred and profane love,

and appears as a "heavenly" mother posing temporarily as a siren. Finally, her role culminates in a scene where she extends her motherliness not to her own biological children (in fact they never appear on the stage) but to her husband as well as her young guest.

In studying a character who exhibits such multiplicity it might be easy to mistake gradual revelation of these facets of character for actual change; yet I shall maintain that she does indeed change. Though Candida begins by playing the role of subservient wife deferring to her husband's authority, she gives evidence of being an independent thinker in Act Two and finally takes courage, in the auction scene, to emancipate herself completely from her pretense—in fact from the abstractions that can render a marriage lifeless. And the change results from her new perception of self, husband, and marriage—a perception brought about by her involvement with and love for Marchbanks.

Throughout Act One and well into Act Two, she manages and maneuvers her menfolk in efficient, business-like fashion, her relationship to each submerged in her role as manageress-automaton. Her initial words in the play are a command to her husband: "Say yes, James." Subsequently she orders him to go out to pay the cabman, and tells her father not to miss his train and to come back in the afternoon. With more subtlety she exhibits control over Marchbanks by a gently ironic speech: "And youll go to the Freeman Founders to dine with him [her father], wont you?" But as she exits, she issues these instructions to him: "Give me my rug.... Now hang my cloak across my arm.... Now my hat.... Now open the door for me . . ." The force of her commands is seen in his behavior while she is out of the room, when at her bidding he twice declines the expected invitation to lunch. When she re-enters, now wearing "her house-keeping dress," she makes the disheveled poet stand still, takes him by the coat, moves him, buttons his collar, ties his neckerchief, arranges his hair, and tells him to stay to lunch. Then, maintaining the fiction that Morell is master, she makes a show of deference to his authority by asking, "Shall he stay, James, if he promises to be a good boy and help me to lay the table?" And in Act Two, she continues to bustle about, busy with household chores, suggesting at one point that Eugene might take over the job of trimming the lamp. She scolds James for not looking after things properly: her favorite scrubbing brush has been used for blackleading. After Eugene's attack of the "poetic horrors" at the thought, she says that she will *allow* him to give her a new brush, and specifies the kind: "a nice one, with an ivory back with mother-of-pearl." Subsequently she rebuffs Morell for deflating Eugene's poetic flight and then punishes Eugene for taunting Morell by telling him that tomorrow he will have to perform Morell's chore, cleaning the boots. When Candida must return to the kitchen to peel onions, she tells her admiring guest to come and help. Dragging him out by the wrist, she scandalizes her father, who says that she should not handle an earl's nephew like that. Even later, in the prologue to her wifely confrontation with Morell, she sprinkles her conversation with imperatives, as usual: "Come here. . . . Let me look at you. . . . Turn your face to the light. . . . Here . . . youve done enough writing for today. Leave Prossy to finish it. Come and talk to me."

So far, Candida has given little evidence of tenderness or kindliness to dispel the impression that she is behaving automatically, from a habit of bossiness, except in her gentleness to the young poet (even so, she has spoken unfeelingly to him of his "queerness," laughed at his wanting to overpay the cabman, and called him a "great baby"). Now her compassionate nature becomes more evident. On her first occasion to be alone with Morell, she begins the conversation with seeming wifely concern; but before the scene ends, her candor harrows his feelings. In her charge that his preaching does little good, she seems intentionally cruel because she does not know of the doubts that Marchbanks has awakened in his mind during the morning. Turning the conversation to their young guest, of whom she has grown quite fond recently, she admits to being jealous *for* him, because he does not receive the love he ought to, whereas Morell receives more than his share. She inadvertently repeats some of the things that Marchbanks has said, hurting Morell more painfully.

From this point on, the widening discrepancy between Morell's awareness and hers, known to us through dramatic irony, undercuts her seeming wisdom, at the same time increasing sympathy for him. She tells Morell that Marchbanks is ready to fall in love with her, but Morell knows that he has already fallen. Her candid revelation that she pities the love-starved

youngster and cares what he may think of her in later years if she does not teach him about love increases Morell's uneasiness more than she can know. If she did not have some illusions about Morell and their marriage, she could not be surprised at his parsonlike response, that he puts confidence in her goodness and her purity. As it is, she taunts him by saying, "What a nasty uncomfortable thing to say to me! Oh, you are a clergyman, James . . ." and later, "Ah, James, how little you understand me . . ." She unconventionally avers that she would give her purity and goodness to Eugene as readily as she would give her shawl to a beggar dying of cold—if she were not restrained by her love for Morell. Interpreting his apparent shock as arising from rigid conventionality, she taunts him further and gives Eugene, returning, occasion to remonstrate bitterly with her over what he interprets as cruelty to Morell. When Morell thwarts her wish that she and the others should all attend his evening lecture, by insisting that the two potential lovers should stay alone in the house during the others' absence, she loses control of events. Unnerved slightly by Morell's now obviously unconventional move and protesting that she does not understand, she cannot know just how "heroic" his behavior is at this point. Momentarily, at least, she is not the all-wise managing figure she has been; she is subject to Morell's incomprehensible wishes and puzzled.

At the beginning of Act Three, Candida's feeling for Marchbanks moves her to appear in a new role or aspect. Though she momentarily becomes the seductress (without, however, seeming overly aggressive), she is at the same time being true to her "divine" instinct to mother the men around her. Her behavior arouses suspense regarding the question whether a good woman will "lose" her character or reputation—a staple of interest in many plays of the period by Oscar Wilde, Henry Arthur Jones, and Arthur Wing Pinero. But her unconventional outlook revealed in her earlier conversation with Morell does not allow her to worry about such a question. As the curtain rises, she *looks* significantly different: now instead of bustling about, she is sitting almost paralyzed, staring at the poker in her hand. Mesmerized by it, she seems virtually powerless, not even in control of herself. Her immobility might suggest the stillness of the spider waiting for its prey, an image that Shaw applied to other women characters, if we had no inkling of her kindly intentions. Presumably still considering her companion's need for love, she is either pondering how she can teach him about love short of allowing herself to be seduced or debating whether to give herself to him. But her exact thoughts must remain ambiguous if the later auction scene is to be effective.

The only clue to her thoughts, aside from what dramatic irony provides, is the poker itself, to which Shaw calls a great deal of attention by allowing it to engage the attention of both characters. Largely ignored until Charles A. Berst commented on it rather extensively in 1973, this symbol has one meaning in relation to Candida's state of mind and, as we shall see, another in relation to Eugene's; but both meanings share sexual connotations. Berst sees two alternatives: the poker represents either Candida's "subconscious desire for the virility of the absent Morell" or "her even more subliminal desire for physical satisfaction from the vital boy-poet." Yet in context with her unconventional talk in Act Two, her fascination with it may signify her awareness that she is about to stir the boy's passion. Could it not also denote her awareness of the unconventionality of her behavior (disregarding her "duty" to her husband) and—if she is the wise woman we like to think—of the potential psychological harm she might do to the sensitive, young, uninitiated male? If the young man had finical reticence or puritanical notions, he might become frightened or disgusted, and she might be transformed in his eyes into a castrating female or ogress or bitch. She has earlier called him, by implication, a "poetic" man (which may mean "naive") who imagines "all women are angels" (though of course Marchbanks does not, for instance, consider Prossy so). In either case, she is metaphorically playing with fire.

Evidently, she decides to proceed toward a staged seduction. To please Eugene, she lays the poker aside and invites him to establish physical intimacy with her by sitting on the hearthrug near her feet to "talk moonshine." Her discarding the poker makes her seem more passive; but in effect, she is maneuvering him into the position of a suppliant approaching a deity or a lover extolling his mistress. She is also now playing the role in which he has cast her. When he begs to be allowed to say "wicked" things, she denies him the pleasure but encourages him to say whatever he sincerely feels. By demonstrating her affection in this rather daring way, she frees him from the need to pose as a love-starved unfortunate. She succeeds

in eliciting from him an incantatory prayer to his "goddess" and then pointedly—suggestively—asks him if he wants anything more than to be able to pray. His reply, that he has come into heaven "where want is unknown," relieves her of the necessity to seek further clarification of his wants. Perhaps it also indicates that she has satisfied his surprisingly meager need.

Her behavior upon Morell's return shows her reversion from siren to housewife (she goes out to dismiss a servant) to motherly type: on re-entering, she vows her determination to protect her "boy" (Morell) and foreshadows her choice in the auction. After the interlude with the other characters returning from their champagne supper, she treats *both* Morell and Marchbanks as little boys having an argument—an argument which she as "mother" must settle, but momentarily revives the pretense that her husband is master when she defers to his wish that the poet remain in the room. Her discovery that Marchbanks has declared his love for her that morning finally explains to her the deep perturbation underlying Morell's uncharacteristic behavior during the afternoon. Now learning that they are seriously proposing that she should choose between them, she realizes how far things have got out of hand; it would not be inappropriate for her to laugh hysterically. In another situation not of her own making, their wills are being imposed on her.

Her behavior beyond this point restores her own authority and gives her greater independence than ever before. By quick cleverness she throws off the roles both men have cast her in, but she also acts in such a way as to bring each man to a new realization of self. Told that the men await her decision, she says, "Oh! I am to choose am I? I suppose it is quite settled that I must belong to one or the other," dramatizing her awareness that she is, or can be, her own possession. Regaining control of the situation by offering to be her own auctioneer and pretending that she is indeed up for auction, she proceeds: "And pray, my lords and masters, what have you to offer for my choice?" echoing her ironic pretense earlier that Morell was "master" in their home and expressing her scorn of them for treating her like chattel and misunderstanding her love. By suggesting the bidding, she gains time to decide how to reply, but also incidentally offers each bidder a chance to clarify his own self-appraisal, with happy consequences, as it turns out.

Candida does not take the bids at their apparent rhetorical value, wisely aware that both bidders misunderstand their own worth. She must be aware of the deep irony in Morell's posing as her strong defender while exhibiting apparent weakness (he breaks into tears, falters when he tries to speak, and almost suffocatedly cries out her name) and a similar irony in Eugene's stoically enduring the ordeal while pleading weakness. But paradoxically, weakness is the winning card in this game. Her riddling choice of the "weaker" grows from her perception of the ironies. Of course she is not literally choosing between the two men; it was not her idea to make (or pretend to make) such a choice. She is only expressing her deep affection for Morell, the warm affection without which marriage would be intolerable, according to Shaw. Now, more than ever, she can be sure of Morell's sincere love for her, on the evidence of his near breakdown. But going through the form of the auction fortuitously gives her the chance to reveal the truth to Morell, freeing him from his illusions of strength and self-sufficiency, and at the same time to disappoint Eugene gently, flattering his ego and completing his process of growing up. All her early responses to Eugene's blandishments have been discouragingly down-to-earth, tending to dampen the poetic spirit in which they were uttered (true, on one occasion she scolded Morell for spoiling the effect of one of Eugene's speeches). They suggest, along with her inattentiveness to Eugene's poetry and her missing the point of his allusions to medieval chivalric codes, that she would be ill-cast in the role of the goddess whom Eugene wants to worship perpetually.

More important from her point of view, the auction gives her a chance to escape from the conventionality of her wifely role, of which she has only recently become aware. At the beginning of the play she has come back from her visit in the country "with her mind and ideas thoroughly aired out" by Eugene. She has become convinced that he is "always right," and his comments have led her to a new perception of her status in the marriage. If she is not willing to become Eugene's goddess, neither is she now the subservient or slavish wife willing to pretend forever that she needs her husband's proffered abstractions: his "strength...honesty...ability and industry...authority and position..." During the play she has come to realize that Morell views her as his *dutiful* helpmeet, bound to him by such abstractions as the notions of purity and goodness. When she emphatically states that she Gives Herself to the weaker, she stresses her freedom from abstractions and her ability to exercise her will in making a free gift of her love. She does not have to run away with a poet to achieve her freedom.

In thus redefining her role in the marriage, she redefines herself. Breaking out of the mold of Womanly Womanliness which Morell has seemed to want, she becomes an independent woman who freely gives her love. Thus she emancipates herself, according to Shaw's prescription: "... unless Woman repudiates her womanliness, her duty to her husband, to her children, to society, to the law, and to everyone but herself, she cannot emancipate herself." By her completely free "choice" of Morell, she abolishes the compulsory character of her marriage to him, affirming that she is bound by only the silken cords of love.

In the adult, friendly discussion which follows, she explains, by her long account of Morell's upbringing and her recapitulation of Eugene's difficulties with his family, how she has been used as a means to the ends of building up Morell's ego and image, and of serving as a substitute for Eugene's old nurse. (To be so used, said Shaw, is to be denied one's right to live.) Gone is the pretense that Morell is the tower of strength, for it is she who builds "a castle of comfort and indulgence and love for him." Gone also is any hint of condescension to Eugene; she has "mothered" him in the best sense, helping him to become a man. Her account serves as edification and enlightenment for both men, but it also satisfies her own desire for recognition of her efforts. Her revelation to Eugene of the nature of her love for Morell is partly reciprocation for Eugene's helping her to see her marriage in a new light, partly realization that she did not need to seduce him to teach him about love.

Thus the denouement is especially happy for Candida. Though her nature has not changed, her outlook has; and through her timely action she has altered her status. She will still trim the lamps, peel the nasty little Spanish onions, and keep the "castle" in good running order, but Morell will know that she does it for love, not simply because she is his wife. She has become completely vital herself and has brought vitality to their marriage....

Source: Walter Lazenby, "Love and 'Vitality' in *Candida*," in *Modern Drama*, Vol. 20, No. 1, March 1977, pp. 1–19.

Charles A. Berst

In the following excerpt, Berst argues that complex emotions and characterization are more important than ideas in Shaw's work.

A year before Shaw wrote *Candida* the prominent critic William Archer reviewed his first play, *Widowers' Houses*, in the London *World*. Archer was most condescending: "It is a pity that Mr Shaw should labour under a delusion as to the true bent of his talent, and... should perhaps be tempted to devote further time and energy to a form of production for which he has no special ability and some constitutional disabilities... it does not appear that Mr Shaw has any more specific talent for the drama than he has for painting or sculpture." Such critical condescension was to be cast upon Shaw for many years, hindering popular acceptance of his plays for a decade and enduring even to the American production of *Saint Joan* in 1923. By 1923, however, the critics were more wary, qualified, and humble. By that time Shaw had become so great a force in the theater that few could afford to be supercilious, and most were content to generally acknowledge his greatness while jabbing at him here and there, faulting individual characters or scenes, or deploring his looseness and verbosity.

Time and Shaw's genius have buried most of his least perceptive detractors. However, many of their echoes persist, a few of which possess the power, and concomitant danger, of half-truths. Half-truths have the virtue of frequently provoking new insight, but they have the vice of also being half-false, with their portion of truth rendering their falsehood unusually tenacious. Such is the case with the recurring assertions that Shaw is overly intellectual as a dramatist, his plays are plays of ideas, his characters are mere Shavian mouthpieces, his structures are loose, and his dialogue expands for its own sake where it might well be trimmed or excised. These noises from the past

impinge upon the present, and since Shaw wrote so much (his corpus of plays and playlets numbers over fifty) evidence can always be ferreted out in support of one or another of them. What they neglect most frequently is a balanced appraisal of the special aspects of Shaw's talent, those aspects which either grandly incorporate such seeming flaws, transmuting them into considerable art, or which contradict them almost entirely as irrelevant to his major plays. *Candida* is an important work to consider in this context, since it is an early play and refutes many of the facile critical generalizations so often repeated about Shavian drama. If Shaw had firm control of his medium at such an early stage, his later development as a playwright may be seen to derive from sound and even impressive dramatic sensibilities.

In *Candida* emotions and characterization are far more important than ideas, the characters are complex individuals greatly removed from Shaw, the structure is extremely tight, and the dialogue is masterfully concentrated to reveal the most about the dramatic situation in the least possible time. The objection to Shaw as a man and playwright too exclusively intellectual and deficient in the profounder depths of the emotions has some merit. A part of his appeal indeed results from the cerebral sparkle of his wit, and he seldom descends into the lachrymose regions of Dickens or the heart-wringing pathos of Tennessee Williams. Yet clearly the central element of *Candida* has less to do with Morell's socialism or Marchbanks' poetic idealism than with their love relationship to Candida, a love which in each case is profoundly felt and serves as a fulcrum for the play's action. Although Marchbanks sounds distinctly Shavian at the end of Act I as he challenges Morell—"I'm not afraid of a clergyman's ideas. I'll fight your ideas."—it is clear that he is motivated less by intellect than by his infatuation with Candida. And Morell's response to this challenge is less that of an insulted preacher than an indignant, hurt, and threatened husband. Candida, in her turn, is less concerned with the ideas of either Marchbanks or Morell than with her role as a mother to both and a wife to one. Her world is primarily that of her marriage and secondarily one of tender care toward an idealistic adolescent. Ideas are involved in the characters' varying concepts of love and marriage, but they are informed in a most basic way by layers of deepfelt emotions.

And before either emotions or ideas come complex factors of personality and personal disposition. Contrary to those critics who for so long insisted that Shaw provided himself only with so many mouthpieces, the three principal characters of *Candida* are richly individualistic. Only if we fully perceive their individualism can we clearly appreciate the dynamics of their interaction and the subtle reaches of the play. Even more than most great playwrights, Shaw rejected stereotypes, being highly sensitive to the fact that they dehumanize the individual and reflect a melodramatic consciousness which is false to the vital wellsprings of life. Stereotyping is the refuge of the unimaginative, thoughtless, insensitive man who regards human affairs as well as fiction in terms of black-or-white distinctions. Shaw's eye, in contrast, explores the ubiquitous gray shades of life where good and evil, right and wrong, justice and injustice may be all mixed, inverted, or perverted. So the critic who too easily pigeonholes Candida, Morell, or Marchbanks is likely to be in error, reflecting his own tendency to stereotype, misrepresenting Shaw's ambiguous art. The essence of *Candida* lies outside easy categories, engaging fully the contradictions which exist in each individual, and, even more, the multifold perspectives which result from the complexities of one character confronting the complexities of another.

Candida herself is the most outstanding case in point. As a vibrant actress such as Katharine Cornell would play her (and the part demands such a vibrant actress) Candida will emerge as forceful, charming, practical, dignified, intelligent; she will be a projection of the person whom Shaw describes in his introductory description of her—an ideal of femininity and motherhood—and may well live up to his praise in a letter to the actress Ellen Terry: "Candida, between you and me, is the Virgin Mother and nobody else." But there is an underside to her character which makes her even more intriguing. Shaw hints at it in his description of her ability to "*manage*" people, as one who makes "*the most of her sexual attractions for trivially selfish ends.*" The play itself qualifies her further. If we are observant, we can see a strong strain of vanity moving Candida as she not only glories in being the center of attention but manipulates the men to acknowledge her primacy. Her humor is self-serving and her world view is ultimately mundanely cramped and domestic. Her very virtues have an obverse side: her charm and forcefulness serve to reduce men to children (there is a sub-strain of emasculation); her practical nature instinctively values household matters

more than the socialism or idealism of the men; and her intelligence contrives to abet her vanity, promote the emasculation, and rationalize the supreme importance of her domestic role. In short, behind the beauty and charm is a feminist conceit; behind the Virgin Mother is a variety of witch. And as the latter emerge in large part through the attractiveness of the former, her portrait is charged with life and fascination.

More obviously Marchbanks is also a bundle of contraries. As he is introduced to Burgess he is painfully shy and inept, a youth so hypersensitive and shrinking that he seems scarcely past puberty. In his adoration of Candida he reveals all the blindness and exuberance of adolescent romanticism, the impulse of youth reaching out tentatively toward the mystery of an attractive older woman whose appeal rests somewhere between that of platonic ideal and mother's womb. Regarding Morell, on the other hand, he is boldly, brilliantly aggressive, a skilled rhetorician, ruthless iconoclast, and daring rival in love. Marchbanks' character, so full of contraries, has the full vitality of its extremes. The contraries, far from rendering him inconsistent, provide him with the urgent tremor of their interaction, giving his portrait the depth of each quality and the variety of all. Keen insight regarding Morell, blindness regarding Candida, aggressiveness in iconoclasm, and shyness in society go hand in hand to compassionately depict the sensitivities of a poetic youth newly engaging the complexities of life.

Morell is perhaps the easiest role to misrepresent, especially if we take him at the valuation of the other two major characters. In Act I Marchbanks effectively exposes Morell's complacent ministerial assumptions, his touch of pomposity, his inflated rhetoric. In Act II Candida charmingly but at the same time ruthlessly and cruelly reduces him further—he is an ineffectual sermonizer to Sunday Christians, a romantic idol of numerous Prossys, a stolidly convention-ridden husband. But such observations are only half true, and the actor who plays up Morell's pomposity and thick-headedness will be missing the full reverberations and strength of his character which result from contrary qualities. As weaknesses lie beneath Candida's strengths, strengths lie beneath Morell's weaknesses. He reveals how it is possible to be a windbag but also sincere beneath inflated rhetoric; to be a complacent minister but also a sensitive, kindly man; to be vain and conventional but also humble, serious, hard-working, socially-conscious, and compassionate. As Shaw carefully notes in his introductory description of him, Morell is "*a first rate clergyman.*" The admiration afforded him by Lexy and Prossy, and his kind treatment of them, cannot be dismissed too lightly; but even more telling are the hard-headed respect he has won from Burgess as a practical social reformer, his constant generosity of spirit, and his genuine sensitivity to the attacks of Marchbanks and Candida. Such qualities interpenetrate the dignified, self-satisfied portrait, giving it reverberant humanity and rendering Morell in many ways the most admirable character in the play.

Lexy, Proserpine, and Burgess are distinct characterizations in their own right, though they function primarily to reflect on the major characters. They reveal Shaw's skill at sharply etching a convincing personality with a few brief strokes in the process of utilizing it for a larger purpose. His minor characters are seldom dull dramatically even when dullness is a part of their nature. Lexy, the least memorable, augments Morell by his sycophancy and feeble attempt to be a carbon copy, personifying a clerical shallowness which Morell so naturally transcends. Prissy Prossy, seemingly so minor, grows the more one examines her. She not only serves generally as an example of "Prossy's complaint" in her adoration of Morell, but functions personally and dramatically as a vital antagonist to the men's adoration of Candida, to Burgess' superciliousness toward the working classes, and to Marchbanks' blindness regarding the attractiveness of Morell.

Burgess, though more heavily drawn, effectively personalizes the very human duplicity of a "good" businessman. Coarse, vulgar, ignorant, and with an avaricious talent for exploiting the labor of others, he esteems himself as a sensible, personally admirable exponent of the free-enterprise system. He is necessary to the play not only as he acknowledges and emphasizes Morell's social importance (Morell is "hinfluential," having shamed the Board of Guardians into refusing Burgess' sweat-shop product), but also as he gives us a clue about Candida's temperament. When Candida denigrates Morell's social influence in Act II she appears to be less knowledgeable and generous than her father in Act I; and via Burgess it is clear that Candida's marriage, while being a step downward economically for her, was a step upward socially: she candidly

(hence "Candida") embraced a gentleman (and a higher morality, hence "Morell"), shaking off her bourgeois ("Burgess") boots. Thus despite her assertion in Act III of Morell's total debt to her, Candida owes him much more than she deigns to recognize. And further, in her insensitivity to the true poetic depths of Marchbanks we may perceive her bourgeois origins. In sum, the Burgess part of Candida offers a penetrating rationale for the assertive bourgeois woman behind the genteel madonna.

If one appreciates the full complexity of these characters, both major and minor, one can hardly fall into the error of tagging any of them as Shavian mouthpieces or as dramatized ideas. Certainly there *are* ideas aplenty here, but they rise naturally out of the stirring interaction of deeply founded, various characterizations rather than from an overriding thesis. The real action of the play derives from the major characters asserting different attitudes toward life, different value systems, attitudes and systems rising out of their most basic psychological promptings and estimates of reality. To Morell, reality is based in his happy, conventional marriage to an attractive woman and in his Christian Socialism which seeks to bring a bit of heaven to earth for all to share. To Marchbanks, reality resides in a poetic aspiration for beauty and love and truth above the grimy mundanities of the world. To Candida, reality is her own role in her domestic sphere of home, husband, and family, ultimately as mother to all, indispensable to the spoiled husband and the aspiring poet, both of whom she manages so well.

Shaw himself may in part be seen (if one wishes to dig him out) in Morell's socialist work ethic, in Marchbanks' iconoclasm, and in Candida's feminist assertiveness, but so is any great artist to some degree in all his characters, and in the case of these three there are at least as many qualities he would deplore as support. Morell's complacency and conventionality, Marchbanks' adolescent artistic escapism, and Candida's bourgeois domestic values make each of them strongly non-Shavian in a fundamental way. The basic problem, the essence of the conflict and drama, is that these three do not deeply understand one another because of their divergent views of reality. Hence the repeated refrain of "I don't understand" and its debased complement in Burgess' referring to others as "mad." All three are in a dramatic context where their understanding of themselves and the others is explored and tested. Notably, Morell and Marchbanks each grows in understanding by the end of the play, while Candida remains self-righteously, self-consciously, self-adoringly static. . . .

Source: Charles A. Berst, "The Craft of *Candida*," in *College Literature*, Vol. 1, No. 3, Fall 1974, pp. 157–73.

William Lyon Phelps

In the following essay, Phelps comments that Shaw's works whet the appetite for more because they ask more than they answer.

Shaw's pages bristle with ideas; and every living idea is a challenge. This is why his plays are so much more interesting than most plays. They answer no questions, but they ask many. For some in the audience the end of his play is the beginning of mental activity. Instead of giving us food, he gives us an appetite.

Bernard Shaw in one respect is the exact opposite of Shakespeare, and in this particular his dramas are the opposite of true drama. Shakespeare has presented every aspect of human life, and we do not know whether he was a Christian or an atheist, an aristocrat or a democrat, an optimist or a pessimist. His plays reach the goal of objective art—there is no alloy of the author in any of the characters, as there is in *The Ring and the Book*. Now Shaw is wholly subjective: even if he had not written the brilliant *Prefaces*, every play and every person represent the author. That he did write the *Prefaces* is a proof of his aim; so far from concealing himself, he uses every means to reveal himself.

He is a great Teacher; and if you ask me, What does he teach? I confess I do not know. The main business of the teacher is not to impart information, to transfer facts from his skull to the skulls of the pupils with as little friction as possible. The business of the Teacher is to raise a thirst.

Although Bernard Shaw is an original writer, if there ever were one, he has learned much and been greatly influenced by his predecessors. That he has been profoundly affected by Schopenhauer, Nietzsche, and Ibsen would be perfectly clear even if he had not denied it; his debt to Samuel Butler he takes pleasure in acknowledging.

Although Rousseau and Shaw are about as different as two men could be, Rousseau's weapon being Sentiment and Shaw's Reason, still the latter shares the fate of all modern artists, thinkers, and writers in being influenced by Jean-Jacques, who was not only the greatest Force but the greatest Source in modern times.

Nothing could indicate more clearly that the mass of men are swayed by emotion rather than by thought, than the absolutely universal influence of that eighteenth-century Frenchman. I had not supposed that it would be possible to point out any specific indebtedness, however, until I happened to see in the *Athenaeum* some years ago, the suggestion that Shaw took the hint for *Pygmalion* from Rousseau.

Shaw's plays are cleanly, antiseptic, stimulating; his laughter clears the air. But plays that substitute the laughter of reason for the warm glow of romance lack something that is generally believed to be essential; instead of having an emotional interest, they have the keen play of dialectic. It is the same with his characters; even his greatest single character, *Candida*, has no charm; there is in all his plays only one figure that has any charm, and that is the Lion. The beast is irresistible; everybody in the audience wants to stroke him.

Source: William Lyon Phelps, "George Bernard Shaw," in *Essays on Modern Dramatists*, Macmillan, 1921, pp. 67–98.

SOURCES

Banerjee, Jacqueline, "Frederick Denison Maurice (1805–1872)," in *Victorian Web*, February 2007, http://www.victorianweb.org/religion/maurice/bio.html (accessed July 17, 2012).

Carr, Pat M., *Bernard Shaw*, Frederick Ungar, 1976, p. 88.

"The Case for Death Duties," in *Economist*, October 25, 2007, http://www.economist.com/node/10024733 (accessed July 17, 2012).

Chappelow, Allan, *Shaw the Villager and Human Being: A Biographical Symposium*, Macmillan, 1962, p. 201.

Davis, Tracy C., "Shaw's Interstices of Empire: Decolonizing at Home and Abroad," in *The Cambridge Companion to George Bernard Shaw*, edited by Christopher Innes, Cambridge University Press, 1998, p. 219.

Elton, Oliver, Review of *Candida*, in *George Bernard Shaw: The Critical Heritage*, edited by T. F. Evans, Routledge, 1976, pp. 72–73; originally published in *Manchester Guardian*, March 15, 1898, p. 8.

Everett, Glenn, "Chartism or the Chartist Movement," in *Victorian Web*, 1987, http://www.victorianweb.org/history/hist3.html (accessed July 17, 2012).

"George Bernard Shaw: Biography," Nobel Prize website, http://www.nobelprize.org/nobel_prizes/literature/laureates/1925/shaw-bio.html (accessed July 17, 2012).

Gibbs, A. M., "The Case against *Candida*," in *The Art and Mind of Shaw: Essays in Criticism*, St. Martin's Press, 1983, p. 82.

Hewett, Caspar, "The Scientific Revolution and Enlightenment: Henri de Saint-Simon: The Great Synthesist," Great Debate website, http://www.thegreatdebate.org.uk/Saint-Simon.html (accessed July 17, 2012).

Hill, Eldon C., *George Bernard Shaw*, Twayne, 1978, p. 54.

"History of St. Matthew's," St. Matthew's-Bethnal Green website, 2005, http://www.st-matthews.co.uk/history.html (accessed July 17, 2012).

Industrial Christian Fellowship website, http://www.icf-online.org/ (accessed July 17, 2012).

Michaels, Steven, "A Teacher's Resource Guide," McCarter Theatre Education Department website, http://www.mccarter.org/Education/candida/index.html#contents (accessed July 16, 2012).

Morgan, Margery M., "The Virgin Mother," in *George Bernard Shaw: Modern Critical Views*, edited by Harold Bloom, Chelsea House, 1987, pp. 121, 123; originally published in *The Shavian Playground: An Exploration of the Art of George Bernard Shaw*, Methuen, 1972.

Phillips, Paul T., *A Kingdom on Earth: Anglo-American Social Christianity, 1880–1940*, Pennsylvania State University Press, 1996, p. xiii.

Putney, Clifford, "Muscular Christianity," Infed website, http://www.infed.org/christianeducation/muscular_christianity.htm (accessed July 17, 2012); originally published in *Men and Masculinities: A Social, Cultural, and Historical Encyclopedia*, ABC-CLIO, 2003.

Review of *Candida*, in *George Bernard Shaw: The Critical Heritage*, edited by T. F. Evans, Routledge, 1976, p. 69; originally published in *Aberdeen Journal*, July 31, 1897, p. 4.

"Shaw, George Bernard," in *Merriam Webster's Encyclopedia of Literature*, Merriam Webster, 1995, pp. 1020–21.

Storm, William, *Irony and the Modern Theatre*, Cambridge University Press, 2011, p. 83.

Uffelman, Larry K., "Charles Kingsley: A Biography," in *Victorian Web*, August 2002, http://www.victorianweb.org/authors/kingsley/ckbio.html (accessed July 17, 2012).

"Women's Liberation Federation," Liberal Democrat History Group website, January 4, 2010, http://www.liberalhistory.org.uk/item_single.php?item_id=50&item=history (accessed July 18, 2012).

FURTHER READING

Bevir, Mark, *The Making of British Socialism*, Princeton University Press, 2011.

This book chronicles the history of British socialism from its origins in the late nineteenth century. It examines debates about such topics as revolution, capitalism, gender relations, and utopian communities, and it includes discussion of prominent literary figures, including William Morris, Oscar Wilde, and Shaw.

Davis, Tracy C., *George Bernard Shaw and the Socialist Theatre*, Praeger, 1994.

This volume examines Shaw's work in theater along with his economic theories, his critiques of colonialism, and his views on women's issues. Throughout, the book traces the connections between Shaw's politics and the socialist theater.

Holroyd, Michael, *Bernard Shaw: The One-Volume Definitive Edition*, Norton, 2005.

This biography condenses Holroyd's standard multivolume biography of the author. It includes information about both the public and the private Shaw. The book emphasizes that although Shaw's plays dealt with issues of public interest, they were also intensely personal.

Laurence, Dan H., ed., *Bernard Shaw: Theatrics: Selected Correspondence of Bernard Shaw*, University of Toronto Press, 1995.

This volume gathers one hundred of Shaw's most illuminating and interesting letters. In them, Shaw discusses a range of issues having to do with the world of theater and theatrical performance, including censorship, theater politics, intrusive journalists, and radio and television performances.

Laurence, Dan H., and James Rambeau, eds., *Agitations: Letters to the Press, 1875–1950*, Frederick Ungar, 1985.

Readers interested in Shaw's political views and aggressive, opinionated writing for newspapers will find this collection useful. The selections demonstrate his thoughts on a range of issues, including opera, the abolition of Christmas, and the atomic bomb. Some of the pieces were part of debates he carried on with such luminaries as G. K. Chesterton, Arthur Conan Doyle, and H. G. Wells.

SUGGESTED SEARCH TERMS

British socialism

Early twentieth century AND British theater

Fabian Society

George Bernard Shaw

George Bernard Shaw AND Candida

George Bernard Shaw AND domestic comedy

Guild of St. Matthew

Henrik Ibsen

Industrial Christian Fellowship

Oscar Wilde

Plays Pleasant and Unpleasant

Woman Question

Driving Miss Daisy

1989

Driving Miss Daisy is a 1989 film that spans twenty-five years in the life of Daisy Werthan, who is seventy-two years old when the film begins. The film documents her relationships with her black chauffeur and with her son and his wife. *Driving Miss Daisy* is based on the play of the same name by Alfred Uhry, who also wrote the screenplay for the film. Morgan Freeman stars as the black chauffeur, Hoke. He is the one original stage actor who made the move from play to film. Jessica Tandy stars as Daisy, and Dan Aykroyd plays Daisy's son, Boolie. In the play there are only three characters—Daisy, Hoke, and Boolie. In the play, most of the action takes place offstage and is recounted by the three actors who converse onstage. There is no car prop, and all driving is portrayed via two stools placed on the stage. The film *Driving Miss Daisy*, to the contrary, actually brings to life the world in which Daisy and Hoke live.

The themes in *Driving Miss Daisy* focus on racism and segregation, discrimination, aging, friendship, and trust. The time frame, which spans the years between 1948 and 1973, includes the pivotal years in the civil rights movement. The social, political, and cultural changes that occurred during that time period are depicted in the film. The setting for the play and film is Atlanta, Georgia. Filming took place in Atlanta and in Decatur, Georgia.

FILM TECHNIQUE

• Beresford uses close-up camera shots in several scenes as a way to depict what people are thinking but not actually saying. The dialogue often provides one idea, while the actor's face tells a different story or a story in more depth. The looks in Hoke's eyes, as well as those in Daisy's eyes or on Boolie's face at key points, are important strengths of the film and of the actors' performances. Initially Daisy looks at Hoke with irritation at having this man in her home. She is also resentful at having to rely on him to drive her. She conveys these emotions on her face and without speech, emotions that the close-up camera shots convey. In one early scene she walks down the street while Hoke drives along beside her. Daisy's smile to her watching neighbors is tightly pleasant, but quickly turns to irritation when she glances at Hoke, whom Daisy thinks is embarrassing her.

• The close-up camera shot is also used when Boolie tries to convince his mother that she cannot drive any longer. She is so resistant that she begins to sing so that she will not have to listen to her son. In this and other scenes where Daisy refuses to listen to Boolie, the camera lingers on Boolie's face, which reveals resignation as he recognizes that she will not listen to him.

• In the scene when the state police approach Hoke and Daisy and ask to see the car registration and license, there is much tension as the officers look at Hoke. When the officers leave, the camera lingers on Hoke's face after he gets back into the car. There is relief and a certain amount of fear still etched there, which the close-up camera shot

shows very clearly. For a black man, being questioned by police in the 1950s South was indeed an occasion to elicit fear, but while the police were questioning them, Hoke never allowed his face to give away his fear. Hoke has no dialogue here, but his face says a lot about the close call and how much danger he was potentially facing. The camera also catches Daisy letting her breath out as the police walk away. She has also understood the danger that Hoke faced.

• During the course of *Driving Miss Daisy*, twenty-five years pass in Daisy's and Hoke's lives. The director uses subtle reminders in several scenes to depict the passage of time; instead of flashing numbers on the screen, Beresford approaches the passage of time in nuanced ways and with very little duplication. For people familiar with automobile design, the varying selection of cars helps to indicate that time has passed, since many are recognizable by year and design. In some cases the date is inscribed on an item that figures prominently in a camera shot, such as on a record label or on an award presented to Boolie. In other cases the passage of time is revealed though changing weather seasons and even through the date on a greeting card. Beresford also has the camera linger on the cars' license plates, which show the year. Another way to mark the passage of time is with changes in hair color, thinning hair, and the addition of age spots and wrinkles. The aging of the actors in *Driving Miss Daisy* is very subtle and, even with camera close-ups, done so well that it is not obvious to viewers.

Directed by Bruce Beresford, *Driving Miss Daisy* was nominated for nine Academy Awards and received four, for Best Picture, Best Actress for Tandy, Best Makeup, and Best Adapted Screenplay for Uhry's script. Freeman was also

nominated as Best Actor, as was Aykroyd as Best Supporting Actor. Bruno Rubeo and Crispian Sallis were nominated for Best Art Direction, and Mark Warner received a nomination for Best Film Editing. The remaining nomination, for Best

© *Pictorial Press Ltd | Alamy*

Costume Design, went to Elizabeth McBride. *Driving Miss Daisy* also won three Golden Globe Awards, for Best Picture, Best Actor for Morgan Freeman, and Best Actress for Jessica Tandy. The screenplay won the Writers Guild of America Award for Best Adapted Screenplay.

The theatrical play, *Driving Miss Daisy*, was first performed at Playwrights Horizons Theatre in 1987. This is a very small, seventy-four-seat nonprofit theater in New York City. *Driving Miss Daisy* proved to be very popular with audiences, and after its initial five-week run was extended and then was later moved to a larger theater. The play won Uhry the Pulitzer Prize for Drama in 1988.

PLOT SUMMARY

Driving Miss Daisy opens in 1948 with Daisy Werthan preparing to leave her home. Idella, the cook and housekeeper, works in the kitchen and watches out a window as Daisy starts her car. She backs her car into a neighbor's yard and very nearly into a ravine. Soon, everyone gathers around to watch the car being removed by a tow truck. The event is certainly of interest to the neighbors, who enjoy refreshments on their front porches. Daisy complains that it was the car's fault it backed into the neighbor's yard, but Boolie warns her that the insurance company will cancel her insurance.

As Boolie predicted, Daisy can no longer drive. A series of small scenes reveal that Daisy hates being trapped at home, but she refuses to call Boolie to pick her up. When Boolie offers to have someone pick her up, she tells him no.

At Boolie's factory, work is delayed when an elevator will not work. Hoke walks in and suggests a way to fix the elevator. Hoke is at Boolie's factory to interview for the position of chauffeur for Daisy. Hoke is a local black man who was most recently the chauffeur for a judge, until the judge died. Hoke needs a job and is confident that he can work with Daisy, but Boolie warns Hoke that his mother does not want a driver and will be difficult. The initial part of this scene, with the broken elevator, is not in the play, but Hoke's quiet demeanor in suggesting how the elevator can be repaired reveals his wisdom. The addition of the scene helps to add depth to Hoke's character.

Boolie has told Daisy that she can no longer drive and he is hiring a driver to take her wherever she needs to go. Daisy hates the idea of losing her freedom, and she tells Boolie no, but he is insistent. When Hoke and Boolie arrive, Daisy refuses to even come downstairs to meet Hoke. Hoke and Idella get along just fine, but Daisy tells Hoke not to waste Idella's time with talk. Hoke tries to do chores around the house to keep busy and feel useful, but Daisy chastises him at every step. When Daisy needs to go to the market, she will not allow Hoke to drive her. As she walks to the store, he drives along beside her. Because the neighbors are watching this spectacle, a very embarrassed Daisy is finally forced to get into her own car and allow Hoke to drive her. Even when she does agree to allow him to drive her, Daisy insists on giving Hoke orders about how to drive the car, how fast to drive, and which direction to take. He politely disagrees with her directions and takes the shortest route to the store. Once they arrive, Hoke calls Boolie to tell him that Daisy finally allowed Hoke to drive her. It took six days.

While Daisy is at her synagogue, Hoke waits outside talking to the other drivers. Daisy is concerned when her friends see that she now has a driver. It turns out that Daisy does not want a driver because she fears her friends will think she either has become very wealthy, and is putting on airs by having a chauffeur, or is too old to drive. Daisy thinks that acknowledging her wealth is vulgar, and she has no desire to be thought old. Hoke tells her that he needs a job, and she needs a chauffeur, so they should quit arguing about things.

One morning Daisy calls Boolie and asks him to come right over. When Boolie arrives, Daisy tells her son that Hoke has stolen a can of salmon. She is in fact accusatory of all black people, who are all thieves, according to Daisy. When Idella and Hoke arrive, Boolie and Daisy are waiting. Before they speak with him, Hoke apologizes for eating a can of salmon the day before and explains that he stopped on his way to work that morning to buy a replacement can.

In 1951 Hoke drives Daisy to the cemetery, where she asks him to place a plant at a friend's grave. That is when she discovers he cannot read. Daisy is a retired schoolteacher, and when she learns that Hoke is illiterate, she teaches him to read.

It is 1953, and Boolie and his wife, Florine, are celebrating Christmas, which makes Florine feel less Jewish and more in tune with their Christian friends and neighbors. Florine is rude to their black cook and treats servants like they are inferior. Daisy and Hoke talk comfortably as they drive toward Boolie's house, where they find that Boolie's home is extensively decorated for Christmas. When they arrive, Daisy gives Hoke a gift, a book to help him improve his writing. In the next scene, Boolie takes Hoke with him when he goes to buy a new Cadillac for his mother. Hoke, in turn, buys Daisy's old Hudson, which he has been driving for the past five years.

When Hoke drives Daisy to her brother's birthday party, they must leave Georgia to drive to Mobile, Alabama. Daisy keeps the map with her in the back seat and gives Hoke directions about where to turn. Hoke tells Daisy that he has always lived in Georgia and this is his first time crossing the state line. As they spend more time together, Daisy begins to like Hoke,

and she grows to respect his goodness and humanity. She also begins to understand what a restricted life he has led, having never left the state before. She tells Hoke how she first traveled to Mobile in 1888, when she was twelve years old. Two Alabama state policemen approach Daisy and Hoke when they stop for lunch. The policeman call Hoke "boy" and ask to see his license and car registration, which Hoke shows to them. As the car drives off, one of the policemen says, "An old nigger and an old Jew woman taking off down the road together. Now that is one sorry sight."

Daisy, who is holding the map, tells Hoke to turn at the wrong place on the road, and they must drive back a short distance. Having to turn around will make them a bit late for their arrival in Mobile. When Hoke needs to stop and use the bathroom, Daisy tells him to wait until they arrive. Hoke explains that he could not use the bathroom in the gas station because "colored" are not permitted to use white bathrooms. Hoke insists on stopping the car and explains to Daisy that he must stop and that he is a man and not a child or animal. She is frightened while waiting alone in the car, but Hoke quickly returns, and soon enough they arrive in Mobile, and Daisy celebrates her brother's ninetieth birthday.

It is 1961, and Hoke goes to visit Boolie to tell him that one of Boolie's cousins has been trying to hire him. Boolie offers Hoke more money, with a raise to seventy-five dollars a week. One afternoon, while Daisy and her friends play mah-jongg, Hoke and Idella watch television in the kitchen. Idella, who has become quite elderly in appearance, suddenly collapses and dies. Boolie and Florine accompany Daisy and Hoke to Idella's funeral. Daisy decides that she does not want to hire another housekeeper and will take care of the house herself. Hoke gives Daisy advice on cooking, and the two of them cook together. They also tend the vegetable garden together and clearly have become good companions. When the power is out due to a snowstorm, Hoke is thoughtful and brings Daisy fresh hot coffee.

In 1966, Boolie is chosen Atlanta businessman of the year. In the next scene, Daisy and Hoke drive to her synagogue. When the traffic is forced to stop, they learn that Daisy's synagogue has been bombed, but Daisy cannot believe anyone would bomb a synagogue. Hoke's response is that there are always people who hate and do hateful things, and he tells Daisy about a lynching that he saw when he was a child. Daisy does not realize that the attack on the synagogue is similar to the lynching of blacks; each act is an act of hatred. This bombing is an event that occurred in real life, but it actually occurred in 1958 and not in 1966, as the film suggests.

Daisy decides to attend a Jewish dinner honoring Dr. Martin Luther King Jr. She asks Boolie to attend with her, but he declines and suggests that she ask Hoke. Boolie cannot go because attending would make him seem too Jewish and too much in favor of equal rights for black people; to attend a dinner for King would be a bad business decision. Hoke would like to attend but is too proud to ask, and it never occurs to Daisy that Hoke would want to hear Dr. King speak. When Daisy finally does ask Hoke, he declines. Daisy finally understands that she has insulted Hoke in the way that she invited him. The film includes excerpts from King's speech about the need for equal rights and for silent people to take action and speak up. Hoke listens to the speech on the car radio. The truth of her actions finally occurs to Daisy, who sits inside next to the empty chair that should have gone to Hoke.

By 1971, it has become clear that Daisy can no longer live alone. Hoke arrives one morning to find Daisy confused and looking for papers she graded for school. She has forgotten the year and that she is no longer a teacher and has not been for decades. Hoke tries to calm her, and she tells him he is her best friend. She takes his hand, and he continues to try and calm her. The house is sold in 1973, and Daisy is now ninety-seven years old and very frail. Hoke no longer drives, but his granddaughter drives him to see the house one last time before the new owners move in. After Hoke and Boolie walk through the house, they go to visit Daisy, who now lives in a retirement home. Daisy has difficulty feeding herself, and Hoke begins to feed her. Boolie has continued to pay Hoke's salary, even though he no longer drives Daisy. The film ends with a snippet of film showing the car driving away in the distance.

CHARACTERS

Beulah
Sylvia Kaler plays Beulah. This character does not actually appear in the theatrical play *Driving Miss Daisy*. In the film, Beulah is a minor

character who plays mah-jongg with Daisy and is part of her circle of women friends.

Hoke Colburn
Morgan Freeman plays Hoke, who at the beginning of the film is a sixty-year-old black man who has had a difficult time finding a job. Jobs for black men are hard to find, and jobs for older black men are nearly impossible, according to a comment that Hoke makes to Boolie when he is interviewed for the job as Daisy's chauffeur. Hoke needs the job badly, but his tolerance of Daisy's prejudice and his resistance to her best efforts to control his driving are not all based on his needing a job. Hoke's nature is to be patient and kind. He is also pragmatic and adaptable to any situation. His kindness to Daisy eventually wins over her lifetime prejudice against black people, and by the end of the film, Hoke and Daisy have become comfortable companions, although their relationship is never one based on equality.

Hoke has a manner that both is subservient but also demands that Daisy acknowledge his humanity at the same time. He agrees to do what she asks but all the while does as he knows is correct. When Daisy refuses to allow him to take a break to use the bathroom, Hoke reminds her that he is not an animal; he is a human being with the needs of any human being. Although Hoke is uneducated and has been illiterate throughout his life, until Daisy teaches him to read, he does understand human nature. He also understands that there is no moral difference between racism and anti-Semitism; hatred is hatred, no matter how it is described. Regardless of how he is treated, Hoke responds with dignity but is always an advocate for human rights.

Idella
Esther Rolle plays the part of Idella, who in the original play is spoken about but never appears onstage. In the film, Idella is seen mostly in the kitchen preparing food and occasionally in conversation with Hoke. She has been the family cook and cleaning lady for more than thirty years, since Boolie was a teenager. She resists change, as does her mistress, Miss Daisy. Although Boolie has purchased a new vacuum cleaner for her, Idella refuses to use it because she has always cleaned the carpets in the same way for her entire adult life. When Idella dies,

Daisy, Hoke, Boolie, and Florine all attend Idella's funeral.

Miriam

Muriel Moore plays Miriam, one of Daisy's friends. This character never appears onstage in theatrical productions of *Driving Miss Daisy*. In the film, Miriam is a minor character who plays mah-jongg with Daisy and is part of her circle of women friends.

Boolie Werthan

Dan Aykroyd plays the role of Daisy's son, Boolie. He is forty years old when the film begins. Boolie is a successful businessman who has risen to prominence in Atlanta, based on his management of the company that his father originally founded. Boolie is concerned for his mother's well-being. He takes care of her financially and makes sure that her health is maintained. He is sometimes careless about hurting her feelings, though. Boolie understands that there is prejudice against Jews in the community, and so he distances himself from his Jewish roots, celebrating Christmas and staying away from events that would identify him as Jewish. Boolie is concerned that his business would suffer if he were to be too closely identified as being Jewish. In most of his scenes, Boolie listens to his mother's complaints with minimal irritation and is politely resigned to her many demands.

Daisy Werthan

Jessica Tandy plays Daisy, a seventy-two-year-old widow when the film begins. Daisy is a retired schoolteacher who is used to being independent. After she has an accident driving, her son hires a driver, but Daisy is stubborn and likes to do things her own way. She is not appreciative of her new chauffeur and regards the need to be driven as an infringement of her freedom to do what she wants when she wants. Although she is initially distrusting of Hoke, as the film progresses, so does Daisy's regard for Hoke. She converses easily with him and shares her feelings freely. She teaches Hoke to read and write and begins to treat him in a more companionable way.

At the beginning of the film, Daisy has some deep-seated prejudices against black men and women, but through the twenty-five years covered in the film she grows and changes, and one of the things that changes is her prejudice against blacks. Daisy becomes an advocate for civil

rights for black people and an advocate for the end to Jim Crow laws and discrimination against blacks. Because of her growing relationship with Hoke, Daisy begins to see black people as individuals and not simply as a group of people to be distrusted.

Daisy has an authoritative manner that has served her well throughout her life. She is accustomed to giving orders and having her own way, but she learns to be more tolerant and patient because of Hoke's patient responses to her demands. At the end of the film, Daisy is ninety-seven years old. She is frail and suffers from some form of dementia. She must move into a nursing home, but her relationship with Hoke is not forgotten.

Florine Werthan

Florine is never seen in the theatrical version of *Driving Miss Daisy*; Patti LuPone plays this role in the film. Her scenes are few, but she is largely presented as gaudy and tasteless, with over-the-top Christmas decorations that allow the home she and Boolie share to be seen a fair distance away in the darkened sky. With a careless shrug of her shoulders, Florine sometimes appears to resent the demands that Daisy makes on Boolie. Florine is also rude and disagreeable to her servants, and so Boolie frequently has to hire new servants for the house.

THEMES

Friendship

Driving Miss Daisy has much to say about the nature of friendship, including how it is defined and how it evolves. When Hoke first begins working for Daisy as a chauffeur, a friendship between Hoke and Daisy seems unlikely. Yet over the course of many years a kind of friendship does develop and is represented in several ways in the film. To achieve a companionable relationship, Hoke and Daisy must first achieve parity. Parity begins in the scene at the cemetery when Daisy learns that Hoke cannot read. As her chauffeur, Hoke performs a service for Daisy, even though he is paid for it. Hoke drives her, and he makes driving Daisy tolerable by maintaining his dignity and being respectful and kind. His job requires that he be deferential toward her, but he goes beyond just being polite. Because he is so good to her, Daisy feels

READ, WATCH, WRITE

- Uhry made very few changes to the dialogue in transforming the play of *Driving Miss Daisy* into a film. He added just enough new dialogue to add depth to the characters' personalities. Read the play *Driving Miss Daisy*, and compare the characters of Daisy, Hoke, and Boolie in the play to the same characters in the film. Write down several scenes that are expanded on in the film, and choose three to discuss in greater depth, including one scene for each of the three major characters. Then present an oral report on your findings, showing clips from the film if you choose.

- *Driving Miss Daisy* was nominated for an Academy Award for Best Costume Design. Research clothing styles in 1948, 1953, 1960, 1966, and 1973. Create a PowerPoint presentation showing the evolution of clothing styles and comparing those styles to the clothing worn in the film. Include some analysis about what the different clothing styles reveal about southern society and how people live.

- In *Driving Miss Daisy*, viewers see only a small part of Boolie's life. Obviously he has a very full and interesting life as a husband and businessman, but the film shows him largely as Daisy's son. Write a short story in which you extrapolate an episode from *Driving Miss Daisy* from Boolie's point of view, focusing on his personal and business life.

- Uhry based the characters and events in *Driving Miss Daisy* on his own family, the way they behaved, and their experiences living in Atlanta in a mix of Jewish and black society. Research Jewish life in Georgia, and write a research paper that explores the his-

tory of Jews in Georgia and their contributions to Georgian life.

- *Driving Miss Daisy* was a play before it was a film. To understand how a play is changed when it is filmed, it is helpful to understand the kinds of film techniques that Beresford used in creating this film. Working in small groups with two or three classmates, create a glossary of film and camera terms. Some terms to consider include *point of view*, *montage*, *dissolve*, *high angle*, *wide tracking shot*, *pan shot*, *close-up shot*, and *short*, *medium*, or *long shot*. In your glossary, define each term and then provide an example of how it is used in Beresford's film. In addition to creating a written film glossary, you and your group partners should prepare a video of examples that illustrate your glossary terms. Download the film clips that you have selected into a computer presentation, which you can then show to your classmates.

- The young-adult novel *Black and White* (2006), by Paul Volponi, is about the friendship between two teenage boys, one white and one black. After reading this novel, write an essay in which you discuss the dynamics between the two lead characters in both the novel and the film *Driving Miss Daisy*. Both this novel and the film reflect different ages and periods of time. Note the things that have changed and the things that remain the same with respect to trying to make an interracial friendship work.

- Research the major changes in civil rights legislation that occurred between 1948 and 1973, and create a PowerPoint presentation that describes those changes and in which you link scenes from *Driving Miss Daisy* that reflect the changes in legislation.

---

obligated to Hoke. After she learns that Hoke cannot read, she teaches him to read. She then gives him a gift for Christmas even though she

tells him she does not give Christmas gifts. It is evidently very important to Daisy that there is a level of reciprocity in their relationship. She is happier after she is able to give him something of herself, and this notion of reciprocity is an important element of friendship. The ability to give of themselves and to achieve parity within the relationship helps to define Hoke and Daisy's growing relationship.

After Idella dies, Daisy begins cooking her own meals. The scene in the kitchen where Hoke tells Daisy that the pieces of chicken cannot touch one another makes clear that their relationship has changed significantly. Their verbal exchanges have become very casual, and their manner is easy. In some ways they are like an old married couple cooking together. The difference is that she eats by herself in the dining room, while he eats alone in the kitchen. Daisy's sphere of society at that time would not allow a black man and a white woman to share the same table.

In still another scene, Daisy is snowed in, and there is no power. Hoke drives to her home on icy roads to bring Daisy fresh, hot coffee. When he leaves the room, she tells him to sit with her, and he replies that he will get wood to build a fire. Daisy and Hoke have now achieved such a level of companionship that they can easily sit together in the same room, but it is only near the end of the film that Daisy verbalizes what she thinks is true about the nature of their relationship. She considers Hoke to be a friend, and she tells him, "You're my best friend." Other than her son, Boolie, and his wife, Hoke has been the one constant in Daisy's life for nearly twenty-five years. *Driving Miss Daisy* shows the evolution of their relationship from employer-employee to that of companionable friends.

Outsiders

Both Hoke and Daisy are outsiders in their community. Racism keeps Hoke an outsider, but anti-Semitism also makes Jews outsiders. Jewish settlers may have resided in Georgia for more than 250 years, but as non-Christians they were always outsiders in the community. When the Jewish temple to which Daisy belongs is bombed, Daisy is in disbelief. Initially she thinks Hoke must be wrong. Daisy leads such an insular life that she fails to recognize that she is from a certain perspective no different from Hoke. Hoke tries to commiserate with her and explain that he, too, knows how discrimination and violence feel, but Daisy cannot recognize that she and Hoke share a common position as outsiders in the community.

The Jewish position as outsiders within the community comes up again when Boolie tells Daisy that he cannot attend the dinner to honor Dr. Martin Luther King Jr. Boolie has achieved solid respectability as a businessman in Atlanta. His factory has grown and become a sizable industry, and he feels he has done so in spite of being Jewish. Boolie and Florine bury their Jewishness in Christmas decorations and music. To attend a dinner honoring Dr. King would remind everyone that Boolie is Jewish. He tells his mother that he might lose business and his standing in the community if he appears to support the Jewish position that favors equal rights for blacks. This conversation with Daisy is a reminder for the audience that Jews do not really fit into Atlanta life.

At the King dinner, Daisy sits alone, with an empty chair next to her. Boolie cannot sit there, and she has insulted Hoke by assuming that all blacks know all other blacks and that since he must already know Dr. King, Hoke would not want to attend. As a result, Hoke will not occupy that empty chair. At that moment, Daisy finally understands that she is an outsider just as Hoke is.

Unlike Daisy, Hoke has always known that he is an outsider in Atlanta. For a man of Hoke's age who is also illiterate, there are only limited employment opportunities available. He is too old to do heavy work, and that leaves only domestic service suitable for an older illiterate black man. He wants the job as Daisy's driver because he needs to work, which is exactly what he tells Daisy. When they drive to Mobile for her brother's birthday, Hoke cannot use the men's bathroom at the gas station, which is for whites only. As a result, Hoke must stop the car later to wander away from the highway to relieve himself. Daisy leads such a sheltered existence that Hoke must remind her of the limitations put upon black men, who cannot use many public bathrooms.

The scene with the state police officers was added just for the film. The contempt with which the policemen remark on the old Jewish woman and the black man together as the car drives off is designed to remind the audience that Daisy and Hoke are at heart the same—outsiders in the American South.

© *AF Archive | Alamy*

STYLE

Costumes

The costumes featured in *Driving Miss Daisy* are used to reveal status and also the passage of time. Daisy is always dressed up, even when just at home. Her hair is always coifed, and her dress is neatly pressed and always belted. In summer she carries a white handbag, wears white shoes, and either wears or carries white gloves. She also wears a summer hat. In winter, Daisy wears a fur piece over her wool coat. Her shoes are dark, as are her handbag and her gloves. She wears a hat with a veil. The graying of Daisy and Hoke's hair is another facet of the costuming of the actors. As they are aged through makeup over twenty-five years, their hair becomes grayer and eventually white.

Hoke typically wears a shirt, tie, and suit, with suspenders. As time passes, Daisy's clothing remains very formal, while Hoke's style of dress does not change much. However, the clothes of the people who move in and out of Daisy's and Hoke's lives change to reflect changing styles. The costumes that Florine wears are certainly worth mentioning. Her clothing is always gaudy, tasteless, and too much of everything. In one scene, Florine wears a bright green and orange sweater and 1950s poodle skirt. It is obvious that Florine spends a lot of money on clothing, but her clothes reveal her personality, which lacks refinement.

Musical Score

The musical score for *Driving Miss Daisy* was composed by Hans Zimmer. Because of a very small budget, there was no orchestra or even live instruments to record the film score. Instead, Zimmer used an electronic synthesizer to create the music. The music for *Driving Miss Daisy* is often a light melody, but occasionally it becomes more dramatic, as when Daisy calls Boolie to come to her home one winter morning to tell him that Hoke stole a can of salmon. In this case the music becomes very dramatic, as if Daisy's holding up the empty can of salmon is the revelation of a major crime. The music for this film also has undertones of jazz and the blues. The musical score for *Driving Miss Daisy* was nominated for a Grammy Award in 1990.

Setting

The southern setting of *Driving Miss Daisy* almost functions as a character, since the location is especially revealing of the plot and the actions of the main characters. For instance, in the play, the family business is a printing company, but in turning the drama into film, Uhry changed Boolie's business into cotton, which is a highly recognizable southern crop. Throughout the film there are multiple camera shots of gracious older homes, with shutters and brick facades, sitting along wide, tree-lined streets. There is lovely woodwork along the frames of doors and windows and going up the stairs. The furniture is gracious, and the rooms are large, with wallpapered walls and elaborate chandeliers hanging from the ceilings. The windows are hung with drapery, and the walls reveal casually hung family photos, designed to reveal the family's long history in the home. The actual Atlanta home that was used was selected because it had never been remodeled and genuinely looked like a 1940s–1950s era home in Atlanta. On film, Daisy's home is gracious and welcoming but not overdecorated. Her home reflects her personality, which is traditional and tasteful.

The yards in Daisy's neighborhood are filled with flowers and flowering shrubs and green grass. Cars pull around back and do not park in front of the homes; the back is where the garage is set so that it is not visible from the street. In addition, the food referenced in *Driving Miss Daisy* is traditionally southern. Idella shells peas, and after Idella's death, Daisy and Hoke cook okra and fried chicken together. Daisy also shops at the Piggly Wiggly, a grocery store with locations that are still very familiar to people living in the southern states. When Daisy's neighbors gather to watch Daisy's car being towed from her neighbor's yard, the neighbors are served iced tea by their black maids. Daisy wears a hat and gloves when she leaves her home. All of these evoke both a period and a place—southern living in the mid twentieth century.

CULTURAL CONTEXT

Georgia's Jewish Community and Anti-Semitism

In writing and filming *Driving Miss Daisy*, Uhry and Beresford worked hard to re-create the cultural and social community in which Daisy lived.

For instance, Boolie tries to fit into the Atlanta business community by not reminding anyone that he is Jewish. He and Florine celebrate Christmas and decorate their home so thoroughly for the holiday that their home would rival that of any Christian home in their neighborhood. When Daisy offers Boolie a ticket to attend a dinner honoring Dr. King, Boolie declines because he fears that his presence in support of Dr. King would hurt his business. Although Jews had lived in Georgia for 250 years and in Atlanta for more than a hundred years, they were still outsiders in the community.

The Jewish community in Atlanta, Georgia, was first established in 1844, but there had been Jews in Georgia since just after the colony was founded early in the eighteenth century. Some of these earliest Jews were German Jews, while others were Spanish or Portuguese. These two groupings had different religious, cultural, and dietary customs, and so even as early settlers, some Jews were outsiders within their own community. Eventually most of the German Jews moved to South Carolina, but the Jews who remained in Georgia still found themselves to be outsiders within their community.

As non-Christians, Jews were accustomed to being considered outsiders. In Europe they had not been permitted to own land and were often restricted to working only certain kinds of jobs. In Georgia, many of these restrictions were lifted, but a history of hundreds of years of oppression meant that Jews understood what it meant to be different. As such, they were especially sympathetic to the plight of African Americans in Georgia, who were victimized by Jim Crow laws that kept blacks and whites separate and blacks subservient to whites. Their support of blacks also meant that Jews were identified as opponents of racism. This further set them apart in white society.

There are two notable historical examples of violence directed toward the Jews of Atlanta. The first was the trial of Leo Frank in 1913. Frank had been accused of murdering a young girl and was found guilty at trial. In 1915 a vigilante group broke into the jail and drove Frank outside Atlanta, where they lynched him. This vigilante group was eventually transformed into the Georgia Ku Klux Klan. Scholars today think that Frank was innocent and that anti-Semitism fueled his conviction.

© *AF Archive | Alamy*

The 1958 attack on the Jewish synagogue represents the kind of prejudice that was part of cultural life in Atlanta in the middle of the twentieth century. Because Jewish leaders, especially the rabbi at the Atlanta temple, spoke publicly about supporting the civil rights movement, Jews in Atlanta became targets for neo-Nazi groups and other racists who did not want equality for black citizens. Although the temple bombing occurred on a Sunday and thus did not result in any deaths, this was because the bomber was so ignorant of Jewish custom that he or she did not know that Jews worship on Saturday morning and not on Sunday morning, as is common for many Christians. It is worth noting that the five white defendants who were tried for the bombing were acquitted after using an anti-Semitism defense. The temple bombing was a reminder for Atlanta's Jews that even if they seemed to be a part of Atlanta's white society, their Jewishness set them apart.

Black and White Interaction

During the course of the twenty-five years covered in *Driving Miss Daisy* there were many changes in the laws governing the separation of blacks and whites in southern society. There were also many changes in how African Americans were perceived in the southern United States during this period of time. The relationship between Hoke and Daisy reflects the many changes in southern life. In 1948, there were still many rules of etiquette that governed how people of different races should interact. One of the most important rules in the first half of the film is that friendship between a black man and a white woman cannot exist. Although Daisy and Hoke are not romantically linked, white fear of white-black romance still permeated southern society. It was illegal for blacks and whites to marry one another throughout the South until 1967, when antimiscegenation laws forbidding interracial marriage were declared illegal by the U.S. Supreme Court, although antimiscegenation laws still existed in two southern states until 1998 (South Carolina) and 2000 (Alabama).

By 1948, many African Americans had begun to protest Jim Crow laws, which were first enacted late in the nineteenth century as a way to segregate black people from their white southern neighbors. These laws were designed to separate blacks from whites on public transportation, in public restaurants and theaters, at drinking fountains, and in city parks. Sharecropping practices prevented black farmers from owning their own land. Separate school systems kept black children from receiving an education equal to that received by white children. These laws kept blacks and whites apart and made it much more difficult for interracial friendships to evolve. As a result, blacks and whites often knew very little about one another. Daisy reveals prejudice when she concludes that Hoke is a thief because she thinks that all black men are thieves. Hoke, in turn, thinks that Boolie and Daisy are money-pinching Jews because he thinks that all Jews hoard money. In the film, both whites and blacks have preconceived ideas about the other group because they have not had opportunities to know one another as individuals.

CRITICAL OVERVIEW

Driving Miss Daisy was generally well received by film critics upon its release in 1987. In his review for the *Chicago Sun Times*, Roger Ebert labels *Driving Miss Daisy* "a film of great love and patience." Ebert is especially complimentary of the film's efforts to delve into the characters and explore their lives and feelings, "as few films take the time to do." Ebert suggests that *Driving Miss Daisy* is a film that effectively focuses on body language and movement and not on dialogue to develop the story being related. The use of body language and facial expression is especially helpful in revealing Hoke's humanity, according to Ebert, who says that "Freeman's performance is a revelation," one that shows Hoke to be wise but not "obsequious" or "ingratiating." His humanity is revealed via Freeman's small gestures and expressions, which result in "a three-dimensional" character who is "completely convincing." Ebert also celebrates Tandy's fine performance, saying that her Daisy "is one of the most complete portraits of the stages of old age" that he has ever seen in film. Ebert finishes his review by complimenting Beresford, who as director created a film that allows the audience to peer into the hearts of the characters depicted on screen.

In his review for *Time* magazine, film critic Richard Schickel is just as enamored of *Driving*

Miss Daisy as is Ebert. What Schickel notes is the film's ability to take on larger issues of importance, such as the change in racial attitudes during the twenty-five years that the film covers, and to do so without "broad sentimentality or the slightest pomposity." What emerges on-screen is, according to Schickel, a "marvelously understated movie." After noting the acting abilities of the two leads, Schickel states that "one cannot speak too highly of the subtlety that two great actors, Freeman and Tandy, bring to their roles." As does Ebert, Schickel also notes the strength of the changes of expression that Beresford uses in place of dialogue. *Driving Miss Daisy* is a film, states Schickel, that "aspires more to complex observation of human behavior than to simple moralism about it." This critic hoped that audiences would respond to *Driving Miss Daisy* with the accolades it was seen to deserve.

After first complaining that *Driving Miss Daisy* is a play that focuses on the lives of two Jewish characters (Daisy and Boolie) but does not contain a Jewish actor in either role, film critic Desson Howe of the *Washington Post* finally admits that this adaptation of Uhry's hit play is done with "intelligent restraint." Howe also gives much of the credit for the film's success to Freeman's depiction of Hoke, whose character Freeman transforms "and plays like a rascal within the Negro limitations," as he so often does in playing "whatever black parts Hollywood has thrown his way." Howe also acknowledges the strengths of Aykroyd's "adroit" and Tandy's "assured and lovely" performances, but he reserves his deepest compliments for Freeman, whose acting in both the stage production and the film served to "make this ride more than worth the trip."

CRITICISM

Sheri Karmiol

Karmiol holds a PhD in literature and is a university lecturer in interdisciplinary studies. In the following essay, she discusses the complex interplay of race, religion, and economics that forms the basis of the relationship between Daisy and Hoke in the film version of Driving Miss Daisy.

Although *Driving Miss Daisy* was nominated for eight Academy Awards and won four, received three Golden Globe Awards, was awarded several smaller critics' awards, was

WHAT DO I READ NEXT?

- *The Rosa Parks Story* is a 2002 television film starring Angela Bassett. The film dramatizes the life of Parks, who in 1955 became a modern African American hero after she refused to give up her seat on a bus in Montgomery, Alabama, to a white man. Her refusal to obey this segregation law helped to fuel the civil rights movement. The film has been released on DVD.

- *To Kill a Mockingbird,* the classic 1962 film based on Harper Lee's novel and starring Gregory Peck, focuses on prejudice and racism in Alabama. In 2012, a fiftieth-anniversary edition of the film was released on DVD.

- The 2005 DVD *Martin Luther King, Jr.: I Have a Dream* includes King's memorable speech of August 28, 1963, as well as footage from King's 1963 March on Washington for Jobs and Freedom protest. The DVD also presents news film from several early 1960s civil rights protests, with narration by Peter Jennings. Although reading the speech is always important, the single largest benefit of this film is hearing King's stirring voice delivering his words.

- *Nothing but a Man* (1963) was one of the earliest independent films, with a mostly black cast, created for an integrated audience. The film focuses on a black man who insists to his white bosses that he must be treated with dignity and respect. The film is not focused on civil rights for the black community but rather is a plea for personal rights.

- *A Raisin in the Sun* (1961) is another drama that has been transformed into film. Like *Driving Miss Daisy, A Raisin in the Sun* features a black man employed as a chauffeur. Unlike Hoke's quiet acceptance of his position, Walter Lee fights against having to work a job he thinks is demeaning. The film version of *A Raisin in the Sun,* adapted from Lorraine Hansberry's drama, stars Sidney Poitier and Ruby Dee.

- *Australian Rules* is a 2002 young-adult film about interracial friendship between an Australian teenager and an Aboriginal teenager. The film is based on a young-adult novel, *Deadly, Unna?,* by Phillip Gwynne. This coming-of-age film was directed by Paul Goldman from a screenplay by Gwynne and himself.

loved by audiences, and was celebrated by many film critics, it was also the subject of much critical panning by those who thought that the depiction of Hoke, a black male chauffeur, was too close to stereotypes of the black servant obediently bowing down to the white master. Critics have argued that Daisy holds all the power in the relationship, but a closer look at *Driving Miss Daisy* reveals that Daisy and Hoke's relationship through twenty-five years spent together is simply that of employer and employee, not of servant and master or of best friends. While Hoke is obviously a black outsider in white Atlanta, he is not the only outsider in the film. Even though Daisy is a wealthy white

widow, as a Jewish woman, she is also an outsider in the closed white Christian society that existed in 1950s Atlanta. The two characters' racial and religious differences add nuanced common ground as well as limitations to what might otherwise be an evolving relationship between two older people. A study of *Driving Miss Daisy* shows how the relationship that Daisy and Hoke create together in the film reflects a complex, multidimensional merging of race, religion, and economics.

In his essay "White Wash," David Denby argues that *Driving Miss Daisy* is a hit because it offers a soothing friendship between a black man

> A STUDY OF *DRIVING MISS DAISY* SHOWS HOW THE RELATIONSHIP THAT DAISY AND HOKE CREATE TOGETHER IN THE FILM REFLECTS A COMPLEX, MULTIDIMENSIONAL MERGING OF RACE, RELIGION, AND ECONOMICS."

and a white woman that endures for twenty-five years and that ignores the turmoil occurring in the world outside the theater doors. Denby suggests that the predominantly white audience for *Driving Miss Daisy* finds in this film an acceptable reassurance of "the public fantasy that everything is just swell in this country." In contrast to the reality of the many political, economic, and racial problems facing the United States during this period in history, the film presents a dream in which "two elderly people can work out their problems of respect and affection." This is a film, according to Denby, that exists in a dream world. What bothers Denby and several other critics is that Daisy, who is white, has all the power in the relationship. Although the end of the film presents Hoke feeding Daisy, who seems dependent on him, Denby writes that Hoke achieves only "*personal* power, in the sense of dignity and authority." Hoke is not revealed to have achieved any sort of social or political power. Denby is bothered that Hoke appears confident and mature, but other than the one incident in which he stands up for himself to stop the car to relieve himself, Hoke "never really challenges Miss Daisy." Of course that is not totally true. Hoke is insistent on doing his job and living his own life to the best of his abilities, whether that means taking the best route to the grocery store and ignoring Daisy's instructions, or refusing to eat what she tells him to eat.

Denby also makes clear that his problem with *Driving Miss Daisy* is not that the movie depicts the reality of 1950s Atlanta or that Hoke is hired to be an employee and thus is required to take orders from Daisy. Denby has a problem not with the film itself but with the audience, because *Driving Miss Daisy* fills a need for the audience, who wants to find this relationship comforting and not confrontational. Denby points out that

people have "long known that blacks and whites are equal," but in championing this film, "the country is mooning over a movie in which a black servant is content with his lot," while his "white mistress learns to trust the goodness of his soul." That people celebrate this friendship is abhorrent to Denby, not because the movie is not well made or because the actors are not doing fine work, but because the movie does not demand that the audience question the state of race relations. What Denby ignores is that Hoke is no patsy. He may be an uneducated black man over age sixty, but he is very capable of negotiating a raise from Boolie. It is true that Hoke is sometimes forced to compromise, but even his level of compromise has limits, as when he refuses to sit with Daisy at the dinner honoring Dr. King. Hoke would rather listen to the speech on the car radio than sit at a table with Daisy, whose assumptions about black men—they probably all know one another, and she knew he would not want to attend anyway—reveal that she is guilty of prejudice herself. This is one case when Hoke demands that Daisy respect him, and he forces her to accept him and to face her own racism. He is, of course, employed as a servant, but jobs for illiterate senior citizens are not plentiful at any time in history.

Denby is not alone in raising concerns about the depiction of blackness in *Driving Miss Daisy*. In their article "*Driving Miss Daisy*," Hélène Vann and Jane Caputi attack the stereotypes they see present in the film. After noting that Hoke approaches Boolie to ask about the position as Daisy's driver, Vann and Caputi claim that having Hoke ask Boolie for the job "is a standard convention in White films about Blacks as servants, serving to deftly sidestep any recognition of White exploitation since Blacks themselves beg for the menial jobs." Vann and Caputi reduce Hoke to the one-dimensional stereotype of a "good natured, unflappable, subservient, and folksy" black man, who is both "a White dream" and an "'Uncle Tom' who unfailingly knows his place." It is worth noting that Vann and Caputi also think that Daisy is a stereotypical feisty old lady who is little more than "a caricature and an insult" to elderly women everywhere.

The views of Denby, Vann, and Caputi are not isolated. In her book *Two Covenants: Representations of Southern Jewishness*, Eliza R. L. McGraw summarizes the views of several writers who, like Denby, Vann, and Caputi, complain that *Driving Miss Daisy* makes Hoke an obedient near slave, whom Daisy orders about with all the imperialism of her position as his employer. As a rebuttal to this view, McGraw claims that the complexity of Hoke's blackness and of Daisy's Jewishness moves *Driving Miss Daisy* above such simple divisions of black and white, while Hoke and Daisy's twenty-five-year relationship is too complex a relationship to define so simply. For instance, Daisy is initially uncomfortable with the idea of a driver, but Hoke's color is not the initial problem. Daisy is later suspicious of Hoke, who as a black man uncovers in Daisy a lifetime of prejudices against blacks that she had never acknowledged in the past. But Hoke eventually wins Daisy's trust, and as McGraw suggests, "as they age, the two forge a strong and complicated bond that challenges some socially proscribed mores, but leaves others intact." The fact that Daisy and Hoke's relationship cannot be defined as one-dimensional is one of the reasons why McGraw can so carefully dismiss complaints about a supposed servant-master relationship that is designed to make audiences feel better.

Nor can Daisy be reduced to a label like "white master" or "feisty old woman." If Hoke is necessarily depicted within a narrow framework as a black servant/driver, Daisy is similarly isolated within her own narrow social milieu. She is shown in her home, in her car, at her synagogue, at the Jewish cemetery, in the homes of her family members, and at a Jewish dinner honoring Dr. King. Daisy's world is a narrowly defined one of southern Jewishness. Daisy rejects the white Christian world of her son and daughter-in-law and makes clear that she finds Florine's willingness to submerge her Jewishness in favor of appearing to be a white Christian completely unacceptable. In fact, Daisy's embrace of her southern Jewishness makes her an outsider in Atlanta's white world.

McGraw also notes the class structure at work in the southern community of Atlanta and reminds viewers that Daisy is as much an outsider as Hoke is. Although Daisy seems unaware of the requirements of her social class as a wealthy widow, Hoke knows how women of wealth are to behave, and he reminds her that rich Jewish women have no business riding the trolley. Daisy has a driver because women of her financial means employ drivers. What Daisy objects to is not having a driver; it is the definition of herself as a rich Jewish woman. McGraw points out that "'Jewish' remains the unspoken modifier for Daisy, but her fear of being imagined as rich demonstrates an associated fear of being thought stereotypically Jewish, amassing fortunes in the nefarious way" that is the stereotype too often applied to Jews. McGraw reminds readers that Daisy would have been a grown woman when Leo Frank, a victim of anti-Semitism, was convicted and then lynched for a crime for which he was later exonerated. Daisy understands that Jews are outsiders, and she wants nothing associated with her life that will remind people of the term "rich Jews."

Daisy's and Hoke's status as outsiders is reinforced in the scene where the two Alabama police officers ask to see the registration for Daisy's car. Although he is an elderly man, Hoke is addressed as "boy" and immediately put in his place as a subservient black male. When the policeman asks Daisy what kind of name Werthan is, her response that the name originates in Germany just reinforces the policeman's notion that Daisy is an outsider. As Hoke and Daisy drive away, one of the policemen says, "An old nigger and an old Jew woman taking off down the road together. Now that is one sorry sight." In the policeman's eyes, there is no difference between Hoke and Daisy. Neither one of them is a privileged white southerner. This point is reinforced when Daisy's temple is bombed and Daisy is reminded that to be Jewish is to be an outsider in their community. She rejects Hoke's reminder that he has also experienced hatred and thus understands her fear and grief. In Daisy's narrowly defined world, Hoke is her employee and she is his employer, and their experiences cannot be similar nor shared. For Daisy, though, the bombing of the temple is a frightening reminder of the precarious position that Jews hold in the community.

McGraw is correct when she argues that the relationship between Hoke and Daisy cannot be reduced to simple terms. McGraw writes that Daisy's "story, framed within her relationship with Hoke, is more than either a depiction of an unlikely friendship or white southern condescension toward African Americans." Over a span of many years of shared experiences, Daisy begins to regard Hoke as a friend, but there is no suggestion that she regards him as an equal. Nor is there any evidence that Hoke

© *Moviestore Collection Ltd / Alamy*

regards Daisy as a close or best friend. He never forgets that she is his employer. As the film comes to a close, Daisy tells Hoke, "You're my best friend." After initially refuting her words, Hoke utters, "Yassum." He does not say that she is his best friend. Throughout the film Hoke shows Daisy much kindness that goes beyond driving her on errands and to synagogue. He has worked around the house, planted a vegetable garden that both of them tend, helped her cook meals, and even driven through an ice storm to bring Daisy fresh hot coffee at a time when the power was out. Hoke is clearly a good, kind, and considerate man. He is also paid to help Daisy, and while there can be no doubt that Hoke exceeds his duties in caring for his employer, he is still paid well to do so. Even in the final scene of the film, when Hoke helps to feed Daisy, he has already admitted that Boolie has continued to pay his salary even though he no longer drives Daisy. Obviously feeding Daisy is not a part of his duties, and there can be no doubt that this good man, who throughout the film has revealed himself to be a caring

individual, is acting out of genuine affection for his onetime employer. However, he is still paid as if he remained an employee.

There is simply no evidence in *Driving Miss Daisy* that Hoke regards Daisy as his best friend. Their relationship is not that simple. Audiences are never provided with enough knowledge about Hoke's life to make that assumption. Critics are correct that the film ends with a scene that is designed to make the audience feel good about the relationship between these two elderly individuals. But they are individuals, and their relationship would have ended no differently if Hoke had been a white chauffeur. To reduce *Driving Miss Daisy* to a film that is only about the relationship between a white woman and a black man does a disservice to the film. *Driving Miss Daisy* is about two individuals, who after twenty-five years of shared experiences and educating one another have found that they have far more in common than they ever expected.

Source: Sheri Karmiol, Critical Essay on *Driving Miss Daisy*, in *Drama for Students*, Gale, Cengage Learning, 2013.

Stanley Kauffmann

In the following review, Kauffmann notes the fine acting of Jessica Tandy and Morgan Freeman.

Jessica Tandy and Morgan Freeman are first-rate in *Driving Miss Daisy* (Warner Bros.). It would be surprising if they weren't. Two such exceptional actors could not miss the opportunities in Alfred Uhry's screenplay, which, like his play on which it's based, was constructed as a sure thing. This is not to say that any other two actors would have been as good as Tandy and Freeman, only that any two good actors could climb aboard this tidy little vehicle and ride off to huzzahs and talk of Academy Awards. That's what Uhry's piece exists *for*.

Tandy plays an aging, well-to-do Atlanta widow, Jewish, who is getting too old to drive. Freeman is the somewhat younger—though not young—black man engaged by Tandy's married son, Dan Aykroyd, to be his mother's chauffeur. Tandy, proud and independent, resents the arrival of Freeman, patient and wise, who understands both her resentment and her tacit need of his help. The whole film then lies plain before us. Her resentment is going to fade, and through the years they are going to become friends.

I've read somewhere that Uhry drew his play from his family's history, so I don't suppose that he set out consciously to provide another item in the genre that includes *The Zulu and the Zayda* and *A Majority of One*—a genre in which a Jewish person and a very different kind of person, initially distant, grow close and prove that all the peoples of the world could get on together if only we'd get in there and try. But *Daisy* ends up just one more of that soppy breed.

As in any pop genre when well executed, *Daisy* has its melty moments. ("Extraordinary how potent cheap music is," says the heroine of Coward's *Private Lives*.) But the whole piece exists to stroke the audience reassuringly. The old woman asserts often that she has no prejudice, though she has no black friends. Freeman's granddaughter, at the end of the years traveled through, is a high school biology teacher, though Aykroyd is insufficiently concerned even to know of this. *Daisy* tells us that if we just keep on as we're going, allowing carefully stratified friendships to blossom here and there, everything is going to be OK. If Stanley Kramer were still active in film production, he would have rushed to buy the screen rights of Uhry's play.

In the theater the piece had only three characters: all the others were suggested. Suggested, too, were the settings and the successive cars that Miss Daisy acquires through the years and that her chauffeur drives. This Thornton Wilder approach lent the play a veneer of imagination. The screenplay is of course "opened up," with the other characters present, with the places and the cars real. Thus the veneer is stripped away, and the piece is all the more clearly revealed as a cozy tearjerker. This is emphasized by Peter James's cinematography, which lays on a golden haze that might give Hallmark itself some pause.

But Tandy and Freeman are fine. Primarily they are tasteful. They understood what plums they had been handed, and instead of cutting loose, they worked with truth and care. Freeman gives an extended, but not inflated, version of his theater performance in this role, with all the dignity allowed a man in his circumscribed position, with humor and sagacity, and with as valid a depiction of advancing age, free of actor's hokum, as I can remember. To see this film right after seeing Freeman's ex-slave Union soldier in *Glory* is to be reassured about the survival of imaginative acting in our beleaguered film and theater worlds.

Tandy has a sense of proportion. All of Miss Daisy's attributes—defensive pride, restrained

gratitude, tempered dislike of her daughter-in-law, loyalty to her standards—are made part of a woman, not facets of a virtuoso performance. Toward the end Miss Daisy has an attack of senile dementia that is especially moving because Tandy has given us such a lustrous portrait of the disciplined woman who is now wandering. This scene, like all of what she does here, reminds us that we are enjoying the fruit of a long, lovely career. (Tandy was Cordelia to John Gielgud's Lear in the 1940 production directed by Harley Granville Barker. This, by the way, was 13 years after her debut!)

Tandy and Freeman do what prime actors have very often done: they make the piece they are in seem better than it is.

Source: Stanley Kauffmann, "Cars and Other Vehicles," in *New Republic*, Vol. 202, No. 3914, January 22, 1990, pp. 26–28.

Robert Brustein

In the following review, Brustein considers the film "an experience of considerable power and sensitivity."

Alfred Uhry's *Driving Miss Daisy*, which might sound...unappealing in bare outline, proved to be an experience of considerable power and sensitivity.

It was also exquisitely acted and directed, one of those rare moments in theater when every aspect of production seems to be controlled by a single unifying imagination. *Driving Miss Daisy* plays for about 90 minutes without intermission, further documenting my only formula for popularity on the stage these days—that critics and audiences will embrace most warmly those productions that last an intermissionless hour and a half....

Driving Miss Daisy has both appealing brevity and considerable quality. It is a first play by Uhry, who has hitherto been associated with musicals (he wrote book and lyrics for *The Robber Bridegroom*). If his talent holds against the inevitable pressures, we have another gifted playwright in our midst. Uhry comes from a German-Jewish family in Atlanta. His play is apparently autobiographical, a series of vignettes about the relationship between an aging Southern Jewish matriarch (presumably his grandmother) and her only slightly less venerable black chauffeur.... The play concerns the evolving intimacy between these two aged people, the gentle, bemused black man and the cranky Southern

Jewess who resists his services—a kind of *I'm Not Rappaport* without the jokes. The old alliance between Jews and blacks is somewhat strained these days. It was already strained in the South during the period of the play, 1948 to 1973. Although "Miss Daisy" (as Hoke calls her, using the common form of subordinate Negro address) persists in believing that she feels no bigotry toward blacks, she is deeply opposed to Hoke's presence in her house, and not just because he reminds her of her helplessness. Daisy embodies all the racial prejudices of her class toward the "other" that Hoke represents.

Including an assumption about thieving black people. Daisy complains to her son that she is missing a can of salmon, having found the empty can under the coffee grounds. Hardly a generous spirit, she assumes that Hoke has stolen this 33-cent item and wants him dismissed. Hoke enters, offering her another can of salmon, to admit he helped himself because the pork chops she gave him were "stiff." . . .

They disagree about everything and Hoke spends his days moping in the kitchen, a talkative man deprived of conversation. Only when they drive to visit her husband's grave does some intimacy spring up between them. Unable to make out the writing on the gravestone, Hoke arouses Daisy's tutorial instincts by admitting he's illiterate. Before long she is teaching him to read phonetically, and later gives him a handwriting copy book as a gift.

Daisy denies this is a Christmas present. She disapproves deeply of Jews who observe that holiday, chief among them her daughter-in-law, Floreen, whose idea of heaven on earth, she says, is "socializing with Episcopalians." Floreen is an invisible character, deftly characterized by the playwright with simple strokes through Daisy's attitude toward her. Floreen puts reindeer in her trees, a Christmas wreath in every window. ("If I had [her] nose," snorts Daisy, "I wouldn't go around saying Merry Christmas to anyone.") Despite her nose, Floreen ends up as a Republican National Committee-woman, the type of woman who goes to New York to see *My Fair Lady* rather than attend the funeral of Daisy's brother in Mobile.

The trip to Mobile inspires tender and nostalgic memories in Daisy, who recalls tasting salt water on her face at her brother's wedding. As for Hoke, he admits to having never left Georgia before, and "Alabama ain't lookin' like much so far." Yet even this intimate journey inspires arguments. Hoke has to pass water; Daisy wants him to wait until they reach a Standard Oil gas station. But colored people aren't allowed to use white rest rooms and Hoke, shouting he will not be treated like a dog, stops the car and disappears into a bush. Her small piping "Hoke?" signifies a belated realization of just how much she needs him.

Going to the synagogue one morning, both of them see a big mess in the road. The temple has been bombed. By whom? "Always the same ones," says Hoke. Daisy is convinced the hoodlums meant to bomb the conservative synagogue, but as Hoke observes, "A Jew is a Jew—just as in the dark we're all the same nigger." This shared suffering moves Hoke to speak of a time when the father of his friend was lynched, his hands tied behind his back and flies all over his body. "Why did you tell me that story?" asks Daisy. "Stop talking to me."

By the time she's nearing 90, and extremely feeble, Daisy has developed enough social conscience to help organize a United Jewish Appeal banquet honoring Martin Luther King Jr. Now it is her son, a successful banker with business to conduct with a racist clientele, who is hesitant about public demonstration of Jewish-black friendship. But Daisy persists. "Isn't it wonderful the way things are changing?" she says to Hoke, who grumbles, "Things ain't changed that much." Daisy has waited until the very day of the King memorial to invite him to join her at the banquet—and with quiet pride he refuses.

Growing senile in her 90s, confused and rambling, convinced she's teaching school again, Daisy realizes, with a start, that Hoke, the black man, is her best friend. And when her son and Hoke come to visit her in the nursing home, it is Hoke she wishes to talk to. "How old are you?" he asks. "I'm doing the best I can." "Me too," he responds, ". . . that's all there is to it." In the final action of the play, a sweet, delicate moment, he feeds her two pieces of pie.

This odd love story, though it never underestimates the difficulty of intimacy between the races, could easily grow mawkish. It is a tribute to Uhry's discreet understatement that the sentiment does not grow into corn—or into *The Corn Is Green*. . . .

Driving Miss Daisy is all of a piece, combining elements of sense and sensibility, not to mention generous portions of pride and prejudice. It is the work of decent people, working against odds to show how humans still manage to reach out to each other in a divided world....

Source: Robert Brustein, "Energy for Old Age," in *New Republic*, Vol. 197, No. 13, September 28, 1987, pp. 28–30.

SOURCES

Branch, Beverly, "Southern Society in *Driving Miss Daisy*," in *Motion Pictures and Society: Proceedings of the Eighth Annual Kent State University International Film Conference, April 17–18, 1990*, Vol. 8, edited by Douglas Radcliff-Umstead, Kent State University Press, 1990, pp. 74–78.

Cooksey, Elizabeth B., "Judaism and Jews in Georgia," in *New Georgia Encyclopedia*, 2009, http://www.georgiaencyclopedia.org/nge/Article.jsp?id = h-3169 (accessed August 26, 2012).

Denby, David, "White Wash," in *New York Magazine*, Vol. 23, No. 15, April 16, 1990, pp. 68, 70.

Driving Miss Daisy, DVD, Warner Brothers, 1989.

Ebert, Roger, Review of *Driving Miss Daisy*, in *Chicago Sun-Times*, January 12, 1990, http://rogerebert.suntimes.com/apps/pbcs.dll/article?AID = /19900112/REVIEWS/1120301/1023 (accessed August 15, 2012).

Howe, Desson, Review of *Driving Miss Daisy*, in *Washington Post*, January 12, 1990, http://www.washingtonpost.com/wp-srv/style/longterm/movies/videos/drivingmissdaisypghowe_a0b249.htm (accessed August 15, 2012).

McGraw, Eliza R. L., "Southern Jewishness on Screen: *Driving Miss Daisy* and Southern Jewish Documentary," in *Two Covenants: Representations of Southern Jewishness*, Louisiana State University Press, 2005, pp. 113–40.

Schickel, Richard, Review of *Driving Miss Daisy*, in *Time*, Vol. 134, December 18, 1989, p. 91.

Uhry, Alfred, *Driving Miss Daisy*, Theatre Communications Group, 1986.

Vann, Helene, and Jane Caputi, "*Driving Miss Daisy*," in *Journal of Popular Film & Television*, Vol. 18, No. 2, Summer 1990, pp. 80–82.

Wormser, Richard, Introduction to *The Rise and Fall of Jim Crow*, St. Martin's Griffin, 2004, pp. xi–xii.

FURTHER READING

Aronson, Marc, *Race: A History beyond Black and White*, Ginee Seo Books/Atheneum Books for Young Readers, 2007.

    This young-adult book is a history of racial and ethnic prejudice that traces such prejudice back to the Sumerians. This volume compels readers to ask serious questions about how societies define race and what color or ethnicity means to people. The author discusses religious and ethnic prejudice, as well.

Greene, Melissa Fay, *The Temple Bombing*, Da Capo Press, 2006.

    Greene recounts the history of 1950s civil rights legislation, the support for these changes provided by the Jewish community that joined with the black community in demanding equality for all people, and the response from those citizens who did not wish to see change. These events resulted in the 1958 bombing of the temple of the Hebrew Benevolent Congregation, a Reform Jewish congregation in Atlanta that was established in 1867. Greene provides an easy-to-read narrative that all ages can understand.

Harmon, David Andrew, *Beneath the Image of the Civil Rights Movement and Race Relations: Atlanta, Georgia, 1946–1981*, Garland, 1996.

    This book focuses closely on events in Atlanta between 1946 and 1981. Harmon argues that the perception of Atlanta as a southern city that was progressive in efforts to be socially, racially, and economically advanced was in contrast with the realities of the period, when the inhabitants of the city still struggled with segregation and racial and economic inequality.

Packard, Jerrold M., *American Nightmare: The History of Jim Crow*, St. Martin's Press, 2002.

    The author traces the origination of slavery as a legal institution and of Jim Crow laws, which were common in both the southern and northern United States. Packard provides many details about the history of segregation, how it functioned, and the court cases that brought an end to Jim Crow.

Ritterhouse, Jennifer, *Growing Up Jim Crow: The Racial Socialization of Black and White Southern Children, 1890–1940*, University of North Carolina Press, 2006.

    The author explores how children learned the unwritten and carefully socialized rules of segregation. This book looks for answers about how parents taught their children about segregation and how the differences between public and private behaviors were defined during this period of American history.

Rose, Michael, *Atlanta Then & Now*, Thunder Bay Press, 2001.

    This book is a photographic history of Atlanta, pairing older photographs with new ones to show how the city has grown and changed. The photographs are designed to demonstrate Atlanta's southern charm and the beauty of the city.

Sniderman, Paul M., and Thomas Piazza, *Black Pride and Black Prejudice*, Princeton University Press, 2002.

    The authors provide an often-provocative look at race relations in the United States. The focus is on how African Americans view themselves and how they perceive they are viewed by other groups. Some of the topics covered include black pride and black intolerance and racism.

Westridge Young Writers Workshop, *Kids Explore America's African American Heritage*, 2nd ed., John Muir Publications, 1996.

    This book is designed for younger middle-schoolers. The authors explore African American culture through literature, music, crafts, food, and the history of civil rights.

SUGGESTED SEARCH TERMS

Driving Miss Daisy AND Alfred Uhry

Alfred Uhry AND drama

Driving Miss Daisy AND Jessica Tandy

Driving Miss Daisy AND Morgan Freeman

Driving Miss Daisy AND Bruce Beresford

Driving Miss Daisy AND racism

anti-Semitism AND Atlanta

temple bombing AND Atlanta

civil rights AND Georgia

Far Away

CARYL CHURCHILL

2000

Caryl Churchill is generally regarded as among the greatest of living playwrights. Her body of work represents a hard-line socialist critique of British society. *Far Away* uses the apocalyptic roots of Marxism and presents political ideas in what can nearly be described as a religious allegory. Churchill draws heavily on the European tradition of leftist theater, and *Far Away* is heavily influenced by the surrealists' "theater of cruelty" and the epic theater of Bertolt Brecht. Churchill feels she can no longer directly convey her political analysis and so turns to a style thick with symbols, creating a dramatic world in which the power of language itself fails.

AUTHOR BIOGRAPHY

Churchill was born in London, England, on September 3, 1938. Her family moved to Montreal, in Canada, ten years later, but she returned to England to attend Oxford University beginning in 1957. Churchill says that while she wrote enthusiastically since childhood, at Oxford she began to specialize in drama and had her plays (such as *Downstairs* and *Having a Wonderful Time*, neither of which has been published) performed by college drama societies. In 1960, she published an article in *The Twentieth Century* praising the work of the Royal Court Theatre, which had been founded in 1956 to produce

Caryl Churchill (© Scott Wintrow / Getty Images Entertainment / Getty Images)

avant garde (experimental) theater. She would go on to develop a close relationship with the Royal Court, which has been responsible for the premieres of most of her plays, including *Far Away* (2000). In 1961, Churchill was introduced by a mutual friend to the prominent literary agent Peggy Ramsay, who worked to establish Churchill's career. After graduation, Churchill married the barrister (a type of attorney) David Harter, with whom she had three children. She began to write brief radio plays, beginning with *The Ants* (also unpublished), which premiered on the British Broadcasting Corporation (BBC) radio in 1962. Throughout the 1960s, Churchill continued to write more radio plays that were generally directed on the air by John Tydeman. She also worked on stage dramas, but she did not have her breakthrough on the stage until 1972, when the Royal Court Theatre put on her *Owners*. By 1974, she was the resident writer at the Royal Court, where Tydeman has became a leading director.

Churchill is unusually reclusive for a modern author and does not give interviews with the press or speak out in the usual academic and critical venues to explain her work. The main theme of Churchill's plays is social justice. Her husband too has gradually given up a more standard law practice and works as an advocate for the poor and oppressed. Among her best regarded plays, *Top Girls* (1982) addresses the compromises and choices that the new roles offered by feminism place on women, and *Serious Money* (1987) deals with the problem of greed in the financial industry. *Blue Heart* (1997) is about the limitations that language imposes on drama. *Far Away* was staged as a successful production in 2000 at the Royal Court Theatre, directed by Stephen Daldry, and has been revived since then all over the world.

In 2009, Churchill's *Seven Jewish Children*, a ten-minute play criticizing Israeli attitudes toward Palestinians, premiered at the Royal Court, and it has brought her even greater fame. It plays on the irony of a nation that was founded in reaction to the Holocaust oppressing a minority. She encourages it to be produced by letting it be performed without royalties so long as the proceeds are donated to charities for Palestinians. It has been more widely performed than any of her other works. Although she has won a number of awards for her plays (including the Susan Smith Blackburn Prize in 1983 and 1987 and the *Evening Standard* Prize, also in 1987), they are too experimental in nature for her to have been in the running for mainstream awards such as the Tony or the Pulitzer.

PLOT SUMMARY

According to Philip Roberts in his book *About Churchill*, the playwright "increasingly in her work delivers her text to those she trusts to create it in performance." As a practical matter, this seems to mean that there is considerable variance between the published form of her work and the productions in which she is personally involved. What has been left out of the published texts can sometimes be reconstructed from the comments of Roberts and other critics who viewed the original production. In other cases, the difference are tantalizingly vague. For instance, Roberts says that there are four speaking roles in the play, though there are only three in the printed text. The printed text contains virtually no stage directions or descriptions, since Churchill feels those creative decisions should be left to the director, crew, and actors of the play.

Far Away is divided into three acts, indicated simply by boldfaced numbers in the script. The second act is divided into six scenes. As the initial production begins, the curtain is down, showing a painting of the English countryside. When the curtain rises, Harper is singing the hymn "There Is a Happy Land Far, Far Away," which refers to the Christian idea of heaven. This is evidently the inspiration for the play's title.

Act 1

The first scene takes place in the bedroom of Harper, the aunt of Joan, the main character of the play. When the play is performed, Joan has been presented as a small child in this scene, played by a different actress than in the later acts.

Joan is visiting her aunt Harper, who lives in the country. One night at 2:00 a.m., long after her bedtime, the little girl goes into her aunt's room and complains that she cannot sleep. Harper suggests all sorts of reasons this might be, such as sleeping for the first night in a strange bed or missing her pet. But it is none of those. Joan finally admits that she is cold, and Harper, ignoring possible metaphorical meanings of the term, takes her statement at face value; she offers to solve the problem with more blankets. But the issue is not really resolved, and the aunt continues questioning the child. Harper reveals that she had gone outside—not through the front door but through her window onto the roof. Harper is naturally upset to hear this, because there is some risk of falling in that case. But Joan turns the conversation toward how much brighter the stars seem in the country than in the city. As slowly as possible, Joan lets Harper drag out of her what actually happened.

Joan went out through her window because she heard a noise: someone screaming. Hiding in the tree by the house, Joan saw her uncle (Harper's husband, who does not appear as a character in the play) pushing someone into a shed. There were many people inside the shed crying. Joan could hear them because she climbed down from the tree and listened with her ear against the wall. She also noticed a great deal of

blood on the ground. Harper denies this, but Joan says, "I slipped in it." Harper claims it must have come from a dog that had been run over earlier in the day.

Joan does not press the point any further, but she asks why there were children in the shed. The light in the shed was on, and she could see that there were children in there, some of whose faces were covered in blood.

Now Harper acknowledges that there was something secret going on in the shed and tells Joan what is going on. She insists that Joan's uncle is helping the children and adults in the shed to escape. Harper doesn't go into unnecessary detail, as one might not to a child, but the audience is led to believe that these people are under threat from some kind of tyrannical government. If Joan ever reveals the secret she'll be in danger too. Harper suggests that Joan's uncle is doing something along the lines of hiding Jews in Nazi-occupied Europe and smuggling them to safety. Harper now admits that what she had said before (suggesting the injured dog, for example, to explain the blood) was a lie, to keep the secret. She assures Joan: "I'm trusting you with the truth now. You must never talk about it or you'll put your uncle's life in danger and mine and even your own. You won't even say anything to your parents."

But this isn't everything Joan saw. She saw her uncle beating a man and a child. Harper explains that this was a traitor who had infiltrated their rescue operation. The child was the traitor's son. Harper reassures Joan that now she is a hero for helping to keep the secret. In the morning she can do more by helping her aunt to clean up the blood.

Act 2

It is now several years later; the setting is a hat maker's shop. Each scene in act 2 takes place one day after the previous scene.

ACT 2, SCENE 1

Joan, now an adult, is sitting at a work bench with Todd, and they are both making hats. There is a good deal of incidental conversation about the work that they are doing, but again a hint is given that provides background for the audience and moves the plot along. Joan has just finished a university degree in millinery, or hat making. Joan understood that she has been hired by the most prestigious hat workshop, but Todd lets her know that there are many things wrong with the place. Work rules are always being changed to make matters more difficult and reduce their pay. He sounds her out about some kind of joint action to oppose the management.

ACT 2, SCENE 2

Churchill has made a point in the play of writing lines that are much more like real conversation than dramatic dialogue. Action often begins and ends in the middle of conversations without context. But at the beginning of this scene, as Joan and Todd continue to work the next day, that begins to break down. The dialogue is literally incomprehensible:

Joan: Your turn.

Todd: I go for a swim in the river before work.

Joan: Isn't it dangerous?

Todd: Your turn.

Joan: I've got a pilot's license.

The *your turns* could mean they're taking turns using some hat making equipment; only the director could establish that by what he has the actors do on stage. If, on the other hand, the two are playing some kind of game where they reveal something unexpected about themselves in turn, that would actually provide some kind of context for Joan's "I've got a pilot's license," which does not seem to follow logically from Todd's earlier statement. Another possibility is that the conversation is being picked up in the middle, so there is no way to follow it. But the logical breakdown of the dialogue that begins here worsens throughout the play until words have no meaning left.

Todd mentions that he stays up late at night watching the trials on television. So far the audience has no way of understanding what that means. Todd also expresses concerns that the business practices of the workshop's executives are corrupt. He also starts courting Joan.

ACT 2, SCENE 3

This scene revisits the content of the previous one. Joan and Todd grow closer, and Todd complains about the management. The point is to model the repetitions that fill everyday life. It develops that the increasingly ridiculous hats they are making will be worn in a parade.

ACT 2, SCENE 4

Todd tells Joan he is going to confront their boss about improving work conditions. Besides what he considers the rightness of his cause, he is prepared to use blackmail. Todd knows certain details about improprieties in the workshop's finances and a journalist who might be interested. If he loses his job over it, Todd says, the only thing he would miss is Joan.

ACT 2, SCENE 5

The scene shifts to a parade of prisoners on their way to execution. They are wearing the hats that Todd and Joan made, and other hats that are equally ridiculous.

ACT 2, SCENE 6

Joan has won an award for one of the hats she made for the last parade. It will be preserved in the worship museum. In general, however, the hats are burned together with the bodies of the prisoners. Todd and Joan are clearly more concerned about the hats than the people.

Joan is beginning to return Todd's affection. While before she was indifferent to his concerns about their wages and work rules, she now flatters him by saying she feels inspired by his political and economic consciousness. Todd speaks briefly about what happened at the meeting he had the previous day. This was exactly nothing, but he imagines he must be on the verge of improving their situation. Joan volunteers that if Todd is fired, she will quit too.

Act 3

Several years later, Todd is hiding out at Harper's house. Joan is asleep in a bedroom upstairs. Todd and Harper talk about how animals are starting to kill people. They are taking sides with the various nations who are all fighting each other, the cats with the French and the ants with the Moroccans. The dialogue becomes more and more chaotic and meaningless, just random phrases snatched out of thin air. Todd has been fighting in the war, taking a sadistic pleasure in massacring children and animals. Joan comes downstairs and delivers a long final speech about her own perilous journey to reach the house, during which she may or may not have been attacked not just by animals, but by a river.

CHARACTERS

Harper

Harper is Joan's aunt with whom she is, in all probability, spending part of her summer vacation from school as a young child. Joan comes to her aunt because she is overwhelmed, having just seen her uncle brutalize and evidently murder at least some of a group of people he has locked in his garden shed. The girl is unable to say clearly what she has seen, but she wants her aunt to make the experience go away; she is unable to deal with it. The coldness that Joan complains of is emotional numbness. She slowly tells her story, recalling what she did and what she saw one step at a time.

Harper knows exactly what has been going on that night, but she responds to each segment of her niece's story as if it were the end, and that stage was all the girl witnessed. She does this because she desperately wants her niece not to know anything that has happened. At each new detail that Joan reveals, Harper provides an explanation that makes the thing witnessed seem innocent, but which is a lie. When Joan says she saw her uncle on the lawn, Harper tells her he was out for a walk. When Joan reveals that she saw him forcing someone to go into a shed, either a woman or a young man, the audience may well think the uncle was committing some kind of sexual assault, but Harper responds: "Well I have to tell you, when you've been married as long as I have. There are things people get up to, it's natural, it's nothing bad, that's just friends of his your uncle was having a little party with." Whatever Harper means by this, the audience will think the uncle was involved in something that one would not want to discuss with a little girl and suspect that is what Harper was trying to cover up. She is constantly trying to persuade Joan with a false story that seems to explain the facts so far but without giving anything else away. But then Joan says she stepped in a pool of blood. Harper invents a dog run over by a truck, even supplying a made-up name and description of the animal. Finally, when Joan says that she saw her uncle torturing and murdering people, even children, Harper admits that everything she has said before is a lie, but she offers a new explanation that makes her husband out a hero. Supposedly he is helping innocent people escape the forces of oppression, and the people he killed were traitors. She had had to lie to protect Joan from knowing the

dangerous truth. Young as she is, even Joan can see the improbability in this; she quite sensibly asks: "Why did you have me to stay if you've got this secret going on?" Harper has an answer for this too: while they help ferry truckloads of these people to safety periodically, the truck that came that night was unexpected. Joan finally accepts this as the truth.

But the audience may not be so reassured. Since Harper was lying about everything else, explaining everything away to her own advantage, why should this last story be any different? Doesn't it seem probable that the uncle is an agent of the forces of oppression, and he is torturing, terrorizing, and murdering because his purpose is to torture, terrorize, and murder? Other government agents and secret police in the history of the twentieth century also had families to whom they pretended to be virtuous heroes while they were really cowardly murders. People who live under totalitarianism (a system in which the government holds great power over every aspect of citizens' lives) to a surprising degree accept and internalize the propaganda of the state. They learn to explain away the horrors they witness every day by the kind of reasoning and fictions that Harper uses to persuade Joan. Harper is a symbol of the education and acceptance of falsehood that repression depends upon. Churchill's point in bringing this "education" into a home environment is to invite the audience to consider whether they might not have been re-educated in this way without realizing it.

Joan

Joan is the central character of the play, as well as a vehicle for Churchill to deliver her political message to the audience. *Far Away* is the story of Joan's growth and gaining of self-awareness. It is vital therefore to see the three acts of the play as corresponding to the three stages of Joan's life: childhood, physical maturity, and intellectual or spiritual maturity. The basis of Joan's characterization comes from her being portrayed at three different ages. In the first act, she is a small child who still sleeps with a stuffed animal. In the second act, she is a new graduate who is on her first day of the job. In the last act she is a mature adult, not necessarily many years older than in the second act, but with a completely altered perspective. This is clear in productions of the play, where Joan is generally played by two different actresses, a child in the first act and an adult in the other two, although Churchill stays as silent about this in the printed text as she does other details of staging.

One way to read the play is as the process of Joan's education. In the first act, she is taught to ignore or explain away the alarming facts about the world around her, and in the second she has learned her lesson and is oblivious to the atrocities she is witness to and even a participant in. In the third act, she throws off her childhood lessons and begins to be aware. As a result, the world she sees seems threatening and insane. Joan stands in for the audience. Churchill is using a very thin veil of fiction to tell the viewers that their life histories have been the same as Joan's. They were conditioned as children to ignore the forces of oppression and violence that are present in modern Western society, and continue to ignore their own share of the blame. She is calling on her audience to wake up and see the world in the same way that she does.

The Parade
Churchill lists the parade as a collective character in the *dramatis personae* (a list of the characters given at the beginning of the script). The individuals making up the parade appear in only one scene, completely detached from the rest of the action of the play. Whereas the rest of the play takes place either in Harper's bedroom or the hat workshop, the parade must take place in some unspecified prison yard or place of public execution. The scene, without dialogue, is described only in the briefest terms in the text of the play: "A procession of ragged, beaten, chained prisoners, each wearing a hat, on their way to execution. The finished hats are even more enormous and preposterous than in the previous scene." Churchill also specifies the number of actors in the parade in the dramatis personae: "five is too few and twenty better than ten. A hundred?" Her point is for there to be an overwhelming number of people in this parade. In some productions, the parade is acted in deathly silence; in others, there is an emotive musical score.

The parade's members are wearing the hats that were being made by Joan and Todd. This comes as a shocking surprise. During the earlier part of the second act, it would be natural to assume that the hats were to be worn during some sort of happy, festive parade such as that held at Mardi Gras, not a public execution. But the prisoners are made to wear the hats as a strategy to dehumanize and humiliate them, to distract the members of the public who are watching them. Roberts comments in *About Churchill*, "Nothing demonstrates the utter contempt the prisoners are held in [more than] that they are fodder for millinery."

The dialogue between Joan and Todd makes it clear that the execution that will happen after the parade will be watched on national television by a large audience. Furthermore, while discussing Joan's prize-winning hat after the parade, they make it clear that the prisoners are burned along with the hats. The audience is left wondering if the prisoners might be burned alive, although no such brutal details are spelled out.

Todd
In the second act, Todd functions as the love interest for Joan, in what might be called a satire of a love story. His role in the third act, like Harper's in the first act, is simply to provide explanation about a world at war with itself, and that scene does nothing to build his character. In the second act, Todd complains about the working conditions at the hat workshop and engages in vaguely described political maneuverings to try and improve them. He thinks he has succeeded, but he seems too unsophisticated to realize that his employers have given him only meaningless bureaucrat-speak ("these things must be thought about") that means nothing will change. This is usually taken by scholars as Churchill's criticism of the failure of the British trade union movement as an instrument of socialist reform.

THEMES

Apocalypse
The Greek word *apocalypse* means the bringing to light of something that has been hidden away. Often translated as *revelation*, apocalypse is the name given to a genre of literature that emerged in Judaism about the third century BCE and which was later taken up by early Christian writers. The subject matter of an apocalypse is the revelation of secrets about the universe given to the author by an angel or other divine agent. In the earliest apocalypse, the First Book of

TOPICS FOR FURTHER STUDY

- There are many videos posted at various places on the Internet that cut together stock footage in order to create a film trailer. As if you were mounting a production of *Far Away*, edit your own trailer for the play and post it to the Internet. Gather stock and other footage that may itself be unrelated to the play but whose images, edited together, suggest the themes of the play. Examples can be found online: for instance, one that was done for a student exercise (http://www.youtube.com/watch?v = czqFJa VmZxk) and one done for a professional stage production (http://www.youtube.com/ watch?v = sCcgwuE0EJ8).

- Elin Diamond has suggested, without fully developing the idea, that *Far Away* presents a view of the world that is exactly opposite that given in an ancient Greek work, Seneca's *Thyestes* (which Churchill has translated). Read that play and write a paper comparing the two works, particularly paying attention to their views of the role of power in society.

- "Exquisite Corpse" is a game invented by the surrealists to demonstrate the creative power of the human unconscious. It is meant to produce writing that on the surface makes no sense but that is capable of provoking a deeper meaning within the reader. The gradual breakdown of ordinary sense in

the dialogue throughout *Far Away* is deeply indebted to this surrealist view of language. Organize a few rounds of this game among your classmates, splitting them into groups of five or six. To play, the group leader writes out on a sheet of paper a column of the names of the parts of speech in an order that makes a sentence, like so: article_____ noun_____ verb_____ article_____ noun_____. The paper is handed around to each member of the group a who writes down an actual word of the indicated kind on the line, then folds the paper so the next player cannot see what was written before and passes it on, until the sentence is complete. The leader then reads what was written, makes any necessary adjustments for agreements of number or case, and reads out the randomly created sentence. The title of the game is itself a striking phrase created by this kind of random generation that would be unlikely to have been made up on purpose.

- The surrealist tone of *Far Away* would make it ideal for a graphic adaptation. For comparison, Shaun Tan's 2006 *The Arrival* is a graphic novel for young adults that uses surrealist imagery to deal with the theme of immigration. Make your own graphic novel based on an act or scene from *Far Away*.

Enoch, the author is a given a tour of the universe. The Revelation of St. John, at the end of the New Testament, records visions of the future, specifically the end of the world in devastating war and natural disasters.

The point of the genre is to show its readers that the world is fundamentally different than is usually assumed and that a changed way of living is called for as a consequence. This makes the apocalyptic genre very suitable for Churchill's purposes, since in *Far Away* she calls into

question the common assumptions that the modern world is a place of freedom and justice. Churchill uses, as a model, the apocalypse that is described in Revelation. *Far Away* ends in a catastrophic global war in which all the nations of the earth fight against each other. Animals join in, with each species fighting for or against one side or another, and finally nature itself rises up against humanity. This is all described in the third act of *Far Away*, which begins with Todd and Harper discussing which nations and

The factory is the main setting of the play. *(© Lucian Coman / Shutterstock.com)*

animals are to be trusted and describing attacks against people by deer and house cats. The climax of the play comes in Joan's narration of her trip to Harper's house:

> I could hardly walk but I got down to the river. There was a camp of Chilean soldiers upstream but they hadn't seen me and fourteen black and white cows downstream having a drink so I knew I'd have to go straight across. But I didn't know whose side the river was on, it might help me swim or it might drown me.

The theme of warfare between men and animals is drawn directly from the Bible:

> And I looked, and behold a pale horse: and his name that sat on him was Death, and Hell followed with him. And power was given unto them over the fourth part of the earth, to kill with sword, and with hunger, and with death, and with the beasts of the earth (Revelation 8:6, King James Version).

The very last lines of the play tie in with the theme of apocalyptic mythology and much else. When Joan steps into the river, Churchill is recalling a whole raft of mythology, from Jesus's baptism in the river Jordan to the river of

forgetfulness that, in Greek myth, the dead must cross to enter the underworld:

> I knew it was my only way of getting here so at last I put one foot in the river. It was very cold but so far that was all. When you've just stepped in you can't tell what's going to happen. The water laps around your ankles in any case.

This relates to the afterlife, referred to in the play's title as a place far away. In the declaration "you can't tell what's going to happen," Churchill is denying the whole of prophecy that the apocalypse depends on, but even that is no more than a symbol for her denial of literature. The play ends in nonsense because Churchill has a sense that literature, or at least the possibility of communicating genuine meaning through literature, has ended.

Romantic Love

In *Reflections on "The Name of the Rose,"* novelist Umberto Eco offers the opinion that a self-reflective character cannot tell someone he loves that he loves her madly because the words that he might use have been used in romance novels and become ridiculous. But such a character could avoid the debasement of his feelings through cliché by telling his beloved that he loves her madly, just like a character in a romance novel. This is a classic postmodern analysis: one that references its own genre.

Eco is pointing out the absurdity that is part of the postmodern condition, but in *Far Away*, Churchill goes one step further. She constructs a romance in the play between Joan and Todd by dropping hints here and there in their dialogue throughout the second act. Todd starts to court Joan by inviting her out to eat and saying he wishes she would drop by his apartment. He compliments her work with praise that is obviously flattery. Joan gradually begins to return his interest, praising his judgment and seniority, and she defers to his opinions. He says that the only drawback to potentially losing his job would be that he would miss her—but in that case, she responds, she would quit. By the end of the act, when they are bickering who will let the other use some beads that they both want for their work, the audience is in no doubt about their feelings, and indeed in the third act, they are a couple. The whole thing proceeds with far more subtlety than a romance novel, but no one could mistake it for a genuine depiction of love either. Churchill is telling the audience: *romance between the two main characters is the most common device to drive a plot forward; I am showing you the conventional signs of romance, and you will read them.* Churchill does not need to show her audience reality. For her, all literature is clichéd, so a sort of summary of it is all that is required. She is pointing out that the entire idea of the romance plot is absurd.

STYLE

Postmodernism

Modernism was a literary and artistic movement of the late nineteenth and early twentieth centuries. It looked to the new world created by the industrial revolution as one of boundless possibility, advancing toward prosperity and order at a rapid, unstoppable rate. Modernist literature is confident about the future, about science and industry constantly making the world better, creating more wealth, more equality, and more freedom. The optimism of modernity met deep challenges in the crises of the twentieth century. The forces that had seemed to drive civilization forward came to endanger civilization in the two world wars, the failure of capitalism in the Great Depression, the failure of Communism in the

Stalinist purges, the failure of science and industry in the environmental degradation produced by modern society, and the failure of all the systems working together in producing nuclear weapons and the Cold War. The human race and all life on earth seemed on the verge of extinction. The old confidence and faith in progress were shattered.

Postmodern art, especially after World War II, reacted to the collapse, not of civilization, but of confidence in civilization. Painting and sculpture used became more abstract, exploding viewers' perception of the world, and literature moved away from forms like rhyme and meter in poetry and traditional formats of the novel. While late modernist writers like T. S. Eliot (writing between the world wars) felt devastated by the breakdown of modernity, the typical response of a postmodernist writer is to view the broken landscape of the world comically, almost as a playground. Churchill's postmodern outlook is reflected in her view of society and government as inherently oppressive. *Far Away* is, on the one hand, set in modern Britain, but on the other in an oppressive state that can be compared to Stalin's Soviet Union or George Orwell's fictional Oceania in his novel *Nineteen Eighty-Four*. The message is that British society—one of the most liberal in the world—is oppressive and its citizens simply do not realize it. If Churchill were pressed to explain her work, she might say that the violence and tyranny of the parade stand for the human suffering caused by the poverty and social inequality that persists in even the most advanced Western countries, whether in spite of or because of government polices and interventions. The absurdist or comic element of her work is revealed in the ridiculous hats that become the symbol of totalitarianism.

Theater of the Absurd

The theater of the absurd has developed since the 1950s out of the existentialist literature of Albert Camus and is seen in the work of British dramatists such as Samuel Beckett, Harold Pinter, and Tom Stoppard. It is one of the main forms of modernist drama. Its main idea is that human life and art have no meaning, and the attempt to communicate through the drama itself is broken down as the irrational nature of existence is exposed by the play. Absurdism leads to an inability to communicate, ending not in a dramatic climax but in silence. Churchill takes the ideas of the theater of the absurd almost as her script for *Far Away*. Katherine Tozer (who played the adult Joan in the original production) recalls the rehearsal process of *Far Away* in a reminiscence written for Philip Roberts's *About Churchill*:

> I had stopped saying the last line—"The water laps around your ankles in any case"—like it was the last line and we had a major breakthrough. The play just needed to be left hanging there, and the great heavy front cloth [curtain] bashed into the stage with an amplified thud like the building was falling down and the theatre had been broken.

The play builds up to fantastic pitch of absurd rejection of reality and then simply ends, falling silent with no possible resolution.

HISTORICAL CONTEXT

Public Executions

In all Western countries, executions of criminals were public affairs viewed by large crowds until late in the nineteenth century. Think of all the cowboy films that show public hangings in the Old West. Executions in Victorian London were festivities attended by thousands of people, with vendors and entertainers catering to the crowds. Public executions were justified on the grounds that because so few criminals were caught and punished, it was the only way to keep the fear of punishment in the public consciousness.

But the executions as practiced in *Far Away* go far beyond this. It is evident from the work pace kept up by Todd and Joan that they must make the hats for several parades a year, and there are other workshops besides theirs that they compete against for prizes. Todd also mentions at one point that there are other parades in which hats are not used but which are marked by some other similar special features. So Churchill is envisioning a version of British society in which no fewer than several thousand people are publicly executed on nationwide television every year. This level of mayhem can only be part of an apparatus of state terror. The goal is not to control crime but to stifle political dissent. The real-world counterparts that come to mind are the show trials in Soviet Russia in the 1930s, in which thousands of innocent people were convicted and executed on false charges of treason and counter-revolution. The executions themselves in that case were not public, but the trials were filmed and shown as newsreels. The same means of social control today is used by the Islamic Revolutionary government of Iran, albeit on a smaller scale.

As odd as it seems, the use of special costumes like Churchill's hats for criminals being executed also have historical precedent. They are part of a strategy to humiliate the condemned and make them seem different, so that the audience can be convinced to fear and hate them, never identify with them. The audience supports the executioners rather than their victims. In the Roman Empire, condemned criminals were often executed during the public games held in the Coliseum at Rome and in smaller amphitheaters throughout the Empire. During the lunch hour when there was a lull in the schedule of gladiatorial combats and wild beast hunts, the theater floor would be used for executions. Often, to increase the spectacle, they were dressed in costumes depicting mythic characters, and the manner of their execution sometimes re-enacted scenes from mythology (such as the legendary traitor Tarpeia being flung from a cliff). When Christians were executed, they were sometimes humiliated by being forcibly dressed in costumes representing the pagan gods. During the counter-reformation in the sixteenth and seventh and seventeenth, the Spanish Inquisition would organize mass executions of dozens of heretics at a time in a spectacle they called an *auto de fe*, or act of faith, considering that the executions would be an expression of public virtue. In that case, the victims were dressed in elaborate silk gowns with masks and pointed hats.

CRITICAL OVERVIEW

Although *Far Away* has developed a favorable reputation among scholars and has been frequently revived, its initial reception was not completely enthusiastic. Reviewing the original production in 2000 in the *Guardian*, Michael Billington found that "although this 50-minute play about a descent into the dark ages' shocks and surprises, it moves from the real to the surreal in ways I found less than convincing." His dissatisfaction stemmed from the rapid pace of the play's development. The play moves from realism into "cosmic chaos" in a way that is impressive but "too swift to be dramatically convincing." He felt the viewer is forced to believe Churchill's argument rather than be persuaded, commenting: "while I am prepared to accept Churchill's thesis that we are slowly sliding into barbarism, I would prefer the case to be argued rather than presented as a dramatic given."

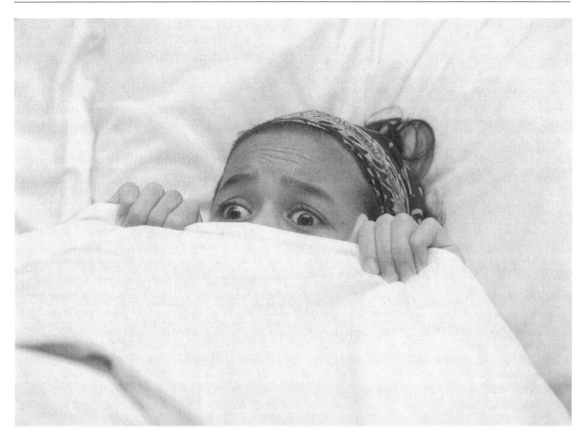

Young Joan can't sleep. (© Juriah Mosin | Shutterstock.com)

Ann Wilson, in her article "Hauntings: Ghosts and the Limits of Realism in *Cloud Nine* and *Fen* by Caryl Churchill," says that Churchill uses a "stunning theatricality . . . to critique social relations." That is, she uses the conventions and expectations of theater to make the audience think about elements of politics, economic life, and other important social issues. Churchill herself, though, seems to give much of the credit to the way the plays are staged by the Royal Court Theatre.

Unusually for a living author, Churchill is the subject of a volume in the Cambridge Companion series. Writing in this series, Dan Rebellato, in "On Churchill's Influences," judges that "*Far Away* . . . has a claim to being the most influential play of the 2000s." In the same volume, Elin Diamond's essay "On Churchill and Terror" considers *Far Away* in connection with the ancient Roman play *Thyestes*, by Seneca, in which power and horror are seen as opposite to ordinary life; in *Far Away*, though, power and horror become part of the characters' everyday lives. Diamond finds, however, that the ending

of *Far Away* nevertheless offers hope to its characters. Any serious analysis of *Far Away* sees it as a socialist allegory criticizing the British government. Siân Adiseshiah, in her 2009 book *Churchill's Socialism: Political Resistance in the Plays of Caryl Churchill*, argues that the general consensus that Churchill is a feminist playwright is at best a partial picture of her work; instead, she finds the origin of Churchill's thought in classic socialism, which Adiseshiah feels is too often shifted into the background in discussions of Churchill. She views *Far Away* as a reaction to the NATO interventions in the former Yugoslavia and Kuwait in the 1990s, which Churchill viewed as thoroughly imperialist.

CRITICISM

Bradley A. Skeen

Skeen is a classicist. In the following essay, he analyzes Churchill's use of her literary influences in Far Away, *especially Bertolt Brecht's epic theater and Sophocles's* Oedipus Tyrannus.

WHAT DO I READ NEXT?

- *The Blind Owl* (1937, translated into English in 1958) is a novel by the Iranian writer Sadegh Hedayat. It uses the imagery and techniques of surrealism in an attempt to break through to a deeper understanding of the meaning of existence.

- *A Kestrel for a Knave* (1973) is a classic young-adult novel by Barry Hines. It tells the story of a working-class boy from the north of England who is alienated from the oppressive environments of his family and school. The only thing that holds any meaning for him is a kestrel (a type of falcon) that he raised from a chick and taught to hunt. He finds new meaning in life through his connection with the natural world. It offers an alternative to the bleak view of humanity at war with nature in *Far Away*.

- *Caryl Churchill: A Casebook*, edited by Phyllis R. Randall and published in 1988, offers an early assessment of Churchill's life and work through a collection of scholarly articles.

- The fourth and most recent volume of Churchill's collected works, *Plays: 4*, was published in 2009. It contains a selection of her recent work, including *Cloud Nine*, *Bliss*, *Hotel*, *This Is a Chair*, *Blue Heart*, *A Number*, *Drunk Enough to Say I Love You?*, and her translation of August Strindberg's *A Dream Play*.

- Elaine Aston's 2010 *Caryl Churchill* offers a biography of Churchill and critical readings and commentaries on the most important of her plays.

- *Theatres of the Left, 1880-1935: Worker's Theatre Movements in Britain and America*, written by Raphael Samuel, Ewan MacColl, and Stuart Congrove and published in 1985, provides a history of the early Marxist drama that forms the historical background for the socialist themes in Churchill's work.

The initial reaction to Churchill's *Far Away* is invariably to call it surreal. After his initial reading of it, Max Stafford-Clark, the artistic director of the Royal Court Theatre, recorded in his diary (quoted by Philip Roberts in *About Churchill*): "The play is compressed and surreal but epic." The term *surreal* is often used informally to mean an image or text that seems irrational. But in the history of art and literature, surrealism was the dominant artistic movement of the 1930s, created by artists such as Salvador Dalí and writers such as André Breton. Surrealism indeed seems irrational at first glance because it depends on the logic of the unconscious mind, rather than the conscious mind. It creates meaning using intuitive connections and symbolic correspondences. As bizarre as *Far Away* may seem, it is not really surreal in this strict sense, but Churchill is indebted to the surrealists, particularly in using techniques and material that would shock the audience members into replacing their conventional conception of reality, which the surrealists regarded as superficial and deceptive, with a truer and more insightful one. This tendency was developed by the playwright Bertolt Brecht, most famous for *The Three-Penny Opera*, into what he called epic theater, and this movement is probably the best generic category for *Far Away*.

In his 1938 essay "The Theatre of Cruelty," the surrealist playwright, actor, and director Antonin Artaud expressed regret that because the world had become so immoral, the artist had to treat his audience with violence and cruelty. He meant that the playwright had to mercilessly strip away the delusions and illusions that everyone cherishes, in order to shatter false reality and expose the truth. He imagines the process to be analogous to the murder and rebirth of the audience's consciousness, or burning down the theater to build it up again. It is a development of one of the basic ideas of surrealism formulated by Dalí (quoted by Hans Richter in *Dada: Art and Anti-Art*): "Surrealism is destructive, but destroys only what it considers to be shackles limiting our vision." Artaud did not make much headway toward putting his bold new idea into practice (he was committed to psychiatric care by 1939), but he has been a profound influence on postmodern drama, and particularly on Churchill.

In the 1950s, the German playwright Bertolt Brecht developed Artaud's idea of the theater of

FAR AWAY IS CHURCHILL'S ANSWER TO THE
RIDDLE OF THE SPHINX FROM CLASSICAL
MYTHOLOGY."

cruelty into *epic theater*. The name reflects in part the effect of grandeur that Brecht hoped to achieve and in part paid homage to the elements of Greek drama that Brecht used. He also called it *Neo-Aristotelian drama*, referencing Aristotle's *Poetics*, the first surviving example of dramatic criticism. Brecht perceived that drama was an inherently artificial form and that attempts to achieve realism on the stage were doomed to tend toward emotional appeals and therefore melodrama. Brecht thought a better approach was to come to terms with the artificiality of theater and to constantly distance the audience from the play by reminding them that they are watching a drama. The main way that he did this was to describe rather than show the action. This has precedent in the messenger speeches of ancient Greek drama. Very often in the plays of Sophocles, Euripides, and other Greek dramatists, the climax of the play occurs off-stage and is described by a messenger who was not otherwise a character in the play but is introduced as an eyewitness to describe what took place. In this way, Brecht kept stagecraft down to a minimum; he used simplified sets, props, and costumes and in general wanted to avoid creating illusion, because he aimed at revealing the truth.

It is easy to see how Churchill in *Far Away* follows many of the conventions established by Brecht. Although she shows the parade of condemned political prisoners, precisely for its surrealistic shock value, she does not, in fact show the executions themselves on-stage. The other main actions of the play occur off-stage and are reported by Joan to Harper, as if Joan were the messenger in a Greek tragedy. These are the events in the garden shed that are the subject of the first act, and the cataclysmic war of nature against humanity and of humanity against itself that is the subject of Joan's final speech at the end of the third act.

Far Away is epic in Brecht's sense not only in its apocalyptic surface appearance but in the basic themes it explores. The first act of the play is in many ways the most interesting, since its plot takes the form of an investigation and thus plays on the popular detective genre, as the second act plays on the romance genre. One cannot help but feel that Churchill has two particular investigations in mind, and that she sets the two against each other to produce her meaning.

The first investigation might seem the furthest afield, but it provides the structure for the first act. *Far Away* is Churchill's answer to the riddle of the sphinx from classical mythology. The sphinx was a monster that the gods had sent to plague the city of Thebes. She sat at the crossroads outside the city and strangled any traveler that could not answer its riddle: What goes on four legs in the morning, two legs at noon, and three legs at sunset? A young traveler, Oedipus, faced her test and gave her the answer: a human being, who crawls as an infant, walks upright as an adult, and uses a cane in old age. Thwarted, the sphinx threw herself over a cliff, freeing Thebes from its curse. Oedipus went into the city and found that its king, Laius, had been killed while he was on a journey to ask the gods what to do about the sphinx. The people of Thebes made Oedipus their king, and he married the dead king's widow, Jocasta. Years later, the gods curse Thebes with a plague, and the oracle sends word that to end it, Oedipus must drive the murderer of Laius out of the city. That is the beginning point of Sophocles's play *Oedipus the King*. The play covers the course of Oedipus's investigation to discover the murderer. At every turn of the play, when Oedipus finds some new clue, he forms a new theory. First he thinks there was a conspiracy of citizens, later he thinks the seer Tiresias was the murderer, then he thinks it was a band of robbers. At each step Oedipus formulates a new explanation of the crime, because he is resisting the true explanation, which finally becomes so obvious that he can no longer deny it. At the same time Laius was killed, Oedipus himself had killed an arrogant man who insulted him on the road. It was none other than Laius. He also discovers, much against his will, that Laius and Jocasta had had a son whom the oracle had ordered them to expose on the mountainside, the same mountainside where he had been found as an infant by a shepherd who had given him to his foster parents. The reason he had left his parent's home was because the oracle had told him that

Young Joan says she saw her uncle loading bloody children into the back of a lorry. *(© Andrey Tirakhov /*
Shutterstock.com)

he was doomed to murder his father and marry his mother. He wanted to get as far away from them as possible to prevent the prophecy coming true, but that had led him to unwittingly kill his true father and marry his true mother. But he had known this secret all along since the oracle told him, and he simply denied it.

The investigation that Joan carries out by asking Harper what her uncle was doing in the shed is exactly parallel. Harper supplies a new theory of events as each new piece of evidence is revealed, but Joan knows all along what she saw: her uncle killing two people before her eyes and torturing others. She accepts Harper's final theory because it is more bearable to believe than the face the truth. Her process is the opposite of that of Oedipus: Joan knows the truth and finds a lie that gives her comfort. The purpose of her investigation is not to discover the truth but to hide it away. During the course of the play, Joan goes through the same three stages of development as in the sphinx's riddle: miseducated child, ignorant adult, and finally wise older person.

Churchill works this astonishing reversal of the investigative process because she believes that this is what everyone does. The world is filled with monstrous truths, in Churchill's view; for example, poverty and the suffering of the poor and downtrodden are created not by impersonal forces but by the actions of individuals and governments that are never held to account for it. Everyone, Churchill is saying, has to go through the same process that Joan does in order to live with this conflict between the way things really are and the way it is bearable to believe they are without acting to change them.

This is where the other half of Churchill's statement comes in. In George Orwell's novel *Nineteen Eighty-Four*, Winston Smith is a political dissident in the fictitious totalitarian state of Oceania (a circumstance recalled in the final lie that Harper tells Joan). He has been arrested and is being interrogated, or "re-educated," by the police officer O'Brien. O'Brien cannot blot out Smith's knowledge of the evil and tyrannical nature of the state—indeed, he has no interest in doing so—but he uses torture to make him accept the government's truth through "double-think." This means simultaneously knowing the truth and earnestly believing the opposite; in this case, knowing that Oceania is a brutal regime that tortures its own citizens and also that it is a benevolent, virtuous state. Churchill makes Joan reach the same point of double-think, not through coercion but because she comes to think that it is in her own interest to do so, so that she can grow up from a child to an adult and retire into old age with a career and a life of relative comfort, so long as she does not object to the tyranny of the state and society she lives in. It is double-think that allows her to play her role in mass executions while thinking she is only making hats. Joan's path to double-think is, if anything, more dangerous than the torture in Orwell's novel because it is voluntary. Churchill believes this is the same double-think that everyone in the real world of her audience has to engage in. It is also the real point of *Nineteen Eighty-Four*. That novel was published in 1948, and Orwell originally wanted to title it *Nineteen Forty-Eight*, making a clear connection to the real world in which the writer and the readers lived. His publishers would not allow it, because it would make the book-buying audience too uncomfortable. In the case of *Far Away*, Churchill's chief aim is to make her audience uncomfortable.

Source: Bradley A. Skeen, Critical Essay on *Far Away*, in *Drama for Students*, Gale, Cengage Learning, 2013.

Jeremy McCarter

In the following review, McCarter notes the disturbing and bizarre reality of the play.

George W. Bush's presidency hasn't been especially accomplished, or ennobling, but it has turned out to be awfully fantastical. Almost by the month, things that once seemed barely imaginable became all too real: an election better suited to a banana republic than a mature democracy, airliners converted to lethal weapons (see also exploding sneakers, powdery letters of death), an American city left to drown. Though countless earnest dramatists made countless earnest attempts to respond to these events (including David Hare, Sam Shepard and, most regrettably, Tim Robbins), nobody has done a better job capturing the uniquely cataclysmic ways that life has gone screwy than the British playwright Caryl Churchill. In early 2001, she wrote *Far Away*. Dark, disjointed and bizarre, it's essentially a nightmare in three scenes. And the

more her play veers from recognizable reality, the more disturbingly exact a record of our time it becomes.

The story, like the decade, begins on a deceptively placid note. A girl named Joan tells her aunt that she can't sleep. Joan has heard shrieks, ventured outside and found people tied up in a shed. Aunt Harper assures her that her uncle is only trying to help the detainees, but the lie doesn't work. "He was hitting a man with a stick. I think the stick was metal," says Joan. "He hit one of the children." Before the brutality has been explained, Churchill skips ahead a few years. Now a young woman, Joan works in a shop designing hats so huge and ornate they'd make a pimp self-conscious. They are worn, we soon learn, by scraggly prisoners who are paraded before fashion judges on their way to execution. In the final scene, Churchill ventures even further into deadpan science fiction, as Joan and Harper discuss the shifting allegiances in a weird war that rages all around them. "The cats have come in on the side of the French," Harper reports. "The Bolivians are working with gravity," says Joan.

When the play reached New York in 2002, the final scene's vision of all-out war offered a twisted but true-to-life reflection of the paranoia we were feeling in those post-9/11 days. Six years later it speaks well of Churchill's prophetic powers that the other scenes now seem just as timely. The nighttime beatings that Joan witnesses (and the sorry excuses her aunt supplies) anticipate waterboarding, "stress positions," rendition. The hellish parade of hat-wearing prisoners now seems a grisly metaphor for the way that soldiers toyed—sometimes fatally—with inmates at Abu Ghraib.

Yet the real resonance of Churchill's play lies deeper than in eerie parallels. The arc of Joan's story reminds us how easy it is to forget the value of human life, how quickly we can become dehumanized ourselves. By the last scene, Joan tosses off the news that on her way to Harper's she's killed "two cats and a child under 5." The fact that we've fought two wars, abrogated a treaty here and there, and squandered the affection of much of the species doesn't necessarily mean that fashion-show executions are nigh. But after all the strange twists of the past eight years, we might wake up to a reality that's weirder still.

Source: Jeremy McCarter, Review of *Far Away*, in *Newsweek*, Vol. 152, No. 25, December 22, 2008, p. 56.

Rebecca Mead

In the following review, Mead discusses the dramatic centerpiece of the drama, the thirty-five hats.

Caryl Churchill's new play, *Far Away*, depicts a surreal dystopia, not too far in the future, in which a totalitarian government performs weekly mass executions to the accompaniment of tinny martial music; a global war has escalated so that not only have the French and the Chinese formed strategic alliances but so have the world's cats, crocodiles, and rivers; and the millinery trade has been taken over by the government, to perverse and sickening ends. The dramatic centerpiece of the play, which is currently showing at New York Theatre Workshop, is a stunning cavalcade of thirty-five hats, among them one in the shape of a black galleon, another with a bright-red wimple and enormous globes over the ears, like something that might be worn by a punk nun. The unfortunate wearers of the hats—they include an athletic-looking man whose hat is bedecked with a big rose, and a wan woman who trails a train of red net bigger than she is—are destined for a rather less pleasant fate than a day out at the Easter Parade, as is revealed by the rest of their outfits, which consist of prison pajamas and manacles around their wrists and ankles.

The hats were created by Catherine Zuber, the show's costume designer. "The structure of the hat is born out of the hat telling you, in a way, what it needs to be," Zuber explained one recent chilly morning, backstage at the theatre. She drew her inspiration from hat history—the galleon hat is based on an eighteenth-century illustration—and from contemporary haute couture. The showstopper hat, a midnight-blue snake of fabric rising in coils above its wearer's head, with a silver star burst on top, is a copy of a Philip Treacy design. (A milliner in Washington named Ted Stumpf was responsible for much of the actual hatmaking.) To assemble the hats, Zuber raided the storerooms of other theatres—one headpiece of antlers decorated with flowers had previously done service in *The Merry Wives of Windsor*—and specialty stores for such necessities as vulture feathers and large quantities of ostrich plumes.

Zuber said that she thought the symbolic role of the hats was to show how creative people can become complacent about the political sufferings of those around them; but she admitted that that was only her own interpretation of Churchill's millinery motif. "The hats needed to have a joy and a level of creativity," she said. "If the hats were badly made, it wouldn't show the tenderness and the beauty, even in this bleakness." The actors who appear in the nightly hat parade have become attached to their assigned headgear, in spite of the dark purposes to which the hats are put. "People get really sad if they don't get the hat they want," Zuber said. Her own favorite is one in the shape of a bouquet of roses, perched aslant on the head, though the hat she'd chosen to wear that day was a more modest production: a burgundy-colored knit skullcap. "I got it at Barneys," she said.

Source: Rebecca Mead, "Hats to Die In," in *New Yorker*, Vol. 78, No. 41, January 6, 2003, p. 32.

SOURCES

Adiseshiah, Siân, *Churchill's Socialism: Political Resistance in the Plays of Caryl Churchill*, Cambridge Scholars Press, 2009, pp. 195–218.

Artaud, Antonin, "The Theatre of Cruelty," in *The Theater and Its Double*, translated by Mary Caroline Richards, Grove Press, 1994, pp. 89–100.

Billington, Michael, "Surreal Shocks from Caryl Churchill," in *Guardian*, December 1, 2000.

Brecht, Bertolt, *Brecht on Theatre: The Development of an Aesthetic*, edited and translated by John Willett, Hill and Wang, 1964, pp. 22–24, 179–205.

Churchill, Caryl, *Far Away*, Nick Hern, 2000.

Diamond, Elin, "On Churchill and Terror," in *The Cambridge Companion to Caryl Churchill*, edited by Elaine Aston and Elin Diamond, Cambridge University Press, 2009, pp. 125–43.

Eco, Umberto, *Reflections on "The Name of the Rose,"* Secker & Warburg, 1985, p. 67.

Esslin, Martin, *Theater of the Absurd*, 3rd ed., Vintage, 2004, pp. 15–28.

Orwell, George, *Nineteen Eighty-Four*, Harcourt Brace, 1949, pp. 246–73.

Rebellato, Dan, "On Churchill's Influences," in *The Cambridge Companion to Caryl Churchill*, edited by Elaine Aston and Elin Diamond, Cambridge University Press, 2009, pp. 163–79.

Richter, Hans, *Dada: Art and Anti-Art*, Thames & Hudson, 1997, p. 194.

Roberts, Philip, *About Churchill: The Playwright and the Work*, Faber and Faber, 2008, pp. xv–xxi, 145–50, 257–61.

Sophocles, "Oedipus the King," in *The Complete Greek Tragedies, Sophocles I*, translated by David Greene, University of Chicago Press, 1954, pp. 9–76.

Wilson, Ann, "Haunting: Ghosts and the Limits of Realism in *Cloud Nine* and *Fen* by Caryl Churchill," in *Drama on Drama: Dimensions of Theatricality on the Contemporary British Stage*, edited by Nicole Boireau, MacMillan, 1997, pp. 152–67.

FURTHER READING

Churchill, Caryl, *Top Girls*, Methuen, 1982.
  Top Girls is a study of the role and failures of feminism in Britain during its first few years under the influential prime minister Margaret Thatcher. It is probably Churchill's most influential play and is generally credited with forming the shape of modern British theater.

Cousin, Geraldine, *Churchill the Playwright*, Heinemann, 1989.
  A volume in the Methuen Theatre Profiles Series, this work provides an introduction to Churchill's life and her early work.

Lynn, Jonathan, and Anthony Jay, *Yes Prime Minister: The Diaries of the Right Hon. James Hacker*, Vol. 2, Guild, 1987.
  Adapted from the BBC television series *Yes Prime Minister*, this volume is a highly realistic (as opposed to surreal) satire of the British political system. The chapter "The Patron of the Arts" deals with the relationship between the government and the arts community; it notes the paradox of the government having to pay through arts grants to support playwrights who do nothing but criticize the government. Although she is not named, Churchill is partly the target of the satire. The book as a whole gives insight into the political realities that Churchill is satirizing in an entirely different manner in *Far Away*.

Orwell, George, *Animal Farm: A Fairy Story*, Secker and Warburg, 1945.
  Orwell criticizes the history of the Russian revolution through allegory. He sets his story on an English farm on which the animals revolt, drive the farmer off his land, and begin to work the farm for themselves. The various historical figures of the revolution, such as Vladimir Lenin, Leon Trotsky, and Joseph Stalin are represented as pigs and other domestic animals.

SUGGESTED SEARCH TERMS

Caryl Churchill

Far Away AND Churchill

theater of the absurd

theater of cruelty

surrealism

allegory

socialism AND theater

Thyestes

I Remember Mama

JOHN VAN DRUTEN
1944

I Remember Mama, a two-act play by John van Druten, was adapted from the book *Mama's Bank Account*, by Kathryn Forbes. It was first produced by Broadway legends Richard Rodgers and Oscar Hammerstein in 1944 and was immediately popular. Perhaps this heartwarming play was comforting to an America under the cloud of World War II. The story highlights the coming of age of a young writer and portrays a Norwegian American family as they struggle with a tight budget and interfering relations. The script of *I Remember Mama* is no longer in print, but inexpensive used copies, for example the acting edition published by Dramatists Play Service, are readily available online.

AUTHOR BIOGRAPHY

Van Druten was born in London on June 1, 1901. His father, Wilhelmus, was Dutch, and his mother, Eve, was an Englishwoman of Dutch descent. Van Druten attended University College School in London from 1911 to 1917. He knew at a very young age that he wanted to be a writer, but his father insisted on a more practical profession. While continuing his efforts as a writer, Van Druten studied law at the University of London and worked at a law firm for five years. Because he enjoyed exploring the academic side of the field better than practicing as

John Van Druten (© Daily Mail | Rex | Alamy)

I Am a Camera was adapted as the popular Broadway show *Cabaret* in 1966 and made into a film of the same name six years later.

In addition to his success in theater, Van Druten worked in film. He wrote screenplay adaptations of his own plays, including *Young Woodley* (film 1930) and *Bell, Book, and Candle* (play 1950, film 1958), and contributed to the stories and screenplays for several original films, including the classic *Gaslight* (1944). Van Druten also directed the film adaptations of some of his own plays as well as, on the Broadway stage, the musical *The King and I* (1951). He also tried his hand at fiction: he turned *Young Woodley* into his first novel and wrote a few others, but it was his work as a playwright that made his reputation.

Near the end of his life, Van Druten became interested in religion and wrote many articles and a book, *The Widening Circle* (1957), examining his beliefs. His dedication to his craft shows in *Playwright at Work* (1953), which is partly a memoir and partly a playwright's how-to manual. Van Druten lived for many years on a ranch in Indio, California, where he died on December 19, 1957.

a solicitor, he lectured in English law from 1923 to 1926 at the University College of Wales.

The same year Van Druten earned his law degree, his first play was produced: *The Return Half* (1923). His second play, *Young Woodley* (1925), was banned in the United Kingdom for several years because of its subject matter. The play tells the story of a young student's romantic interest in a teacher's wife, and English censors disapproved of the implied criticism of the British school system. *Young Woodley* was produced in New York, however, and did well enough to establish Van Druten in his chosen profession.

Throughout the next three decades, Van Druten wrote more than two dozen plays, including *I Remember Mama*, which was first produced in 1944. One of his most successful works, in terms of popularity and critical acclaim, was *The Voice of the Turtle* (1943), which portrays a soldier visiting New York City for the weekend. The play was never banned, but it was controversial because it challenged the strict social rules of the time regarding sex outside of marriage, as did *I Am a Camera* (1951), which is based on Christopher Isherwood's stories about his time living in Berlin.

PLOT SUMMARY

I Remember Mama is set around 1910. The playwright specifies that the central role, Katrin, should be played by an actress able to portray the character both as an adult in her twenties and as a young teenager. He suggests that her hair might be pulled up when she is an adult and then let down for a more youthful look. She might also wear a short dress that would be suitable for a young girl but could be hidden when she is an adult, writing at her desk.

Act 1

Seated at a desk, Katrin begins to read what she has written. She explains how her mother and father came to San Francisco because Mama's sisters had already moved there from Norway. Katrin also mentions her brother, Nels, and her sisters, Christine and Dagmar. Dagmar is the youngest and is regarded by everyone as the baby of the family, whereas, even when envisioning the past, Katrin thinks of herself and her brother and Christine much as they appear at the time she is writing. Katrin always pictures her mother as she appeared when she was about

MEDIA
ADAPTATIONS

- DeWitt Bodeen adapted the screenplay for the 1948 film version of *I Remember Mama* from Van Druten's stage play. The movie was directed by George Stevens and stars Irene Dunne, Barbara Bel Geddes, and Oscar Homolka.
- An audiobook of *Mama's Bank Account*, the novel by Kathryn Forbes that served as the source for Van Druten's play, was produced on CD in 2008 by Recording for the Blind & Dyslexic.

forty years old. The family has a boarder, Mr. Hyde. He is an Englishman and a former actor. He reads to the family in the evenings and impresses Mama with his good manners and polished way of speaking.

The playwright gives specific stage instructions indicating that the lights directed toward Katrin at the front of the stage should be dimmed and those illuminating the main stage should be brought up to reveal the kitchen, which is the heart of the family home. The furniture is described in detail: a table with chairs and a bench, a stove, a dresser where dishes are displayed, and a painted backdrop of the San Francisco hills visible through the windows.

As the action of the play shifts to the main stage, Mama is opening an envelope containing a handful of coins. She asks Papa to call the children, because "Is good they should know about money." Mama tells Papa that he must call especially loudly for Katrin, because she might be in her "study," a small space in the attic that she has set up for writing.

Eight-year-old Dagmar is the first of the children to enter the kitchen. She brings her cat, Elizabeth, with her. Papa points out that the cat appears to have been in a fight, but Dagmar is unconcerned. Christine appears next. She is thirteen and is described as being "cool, aloof, matter-of-fact." Mr. Hyde, the

boarder, enters the room. He wears shabby clothes and speaks in lofty, poetic turns of phrase. He leaves to buy tobacco but promises to return in time to read to the family.

Mama has to call again before Nels and Katrin come, but then the Hanson family gathers around the kitchen table to divide Papa's salary. The process takes on the air of a ritual, with Mama counting out the proper amount of money and the children handing the coins down the table to Papa to wrap in paper. As they pass each handful of coins, they repeat Mama's words: "For the landlord" and "For the grocer," until all of the money has been set aside for their bills. When they are finished, Mama says, "Is good. We do not have to go to the Bank."

As Mama gathers up leftover coins, Nels tentatively asks if he might be able to go to high school. He has gotten a list of possible expenses from a friend, and Christine fetches the "Little Bank" so that Mama can count the money they have in reserve. They do not have enough, but Nels promises to get a job in the local grocer's store after school, Papa offers to give up tobacco, and Christine and Katrin will help by babysitting. Mama decides that these extra efforts will be enough to raise the money.

Dagmar asks questions about the bank, not understanding why no one wants to go there. Christine explains that if they used all the money in the bank account, they would have no emergency fund, and "they'd turn us out like Mrs. Jensen down the street."

Aunt Trina arrives and wishes to speak to Mama alone. She confesses that she wants to get married. Mr. Thorkelson from the funeral parlor has proposed, but Trina is afraid to tell the other sisters, Sigrid and Jenny, because she is afraid that they might laugh at her. Mama promises to talk to Sigrid and Jenny but insists that Mr. Thorkelson must talk to Uncle Chris, whom the sisters consider the head of the family. Jenny and Sigrid arrive, and Trina hides while Mama tells them of the marriage. She makes certain they will not laugh by threatening to tell Trina embarrassing secrets about them.

Mr. Hyde appears, and Jenny asks Mama if he has paid his rent. The aunts ask to see the children before they leave. Dagmar brings her cat, which the aunts seem to disapprove of. Nels points out that the cat is male, so Dagmar renames it "Uncle Elizabeth." The aunts leave, and Mr. Hyde reads to the family. Katrin explains how her imagination was sparked by Mr. Hyde's books.

The scene changes, showing Jenny, Trina, and Sigrid talking. Sigrid explains how Uncle Chris took her son, Arne, to the hospital for surgery to repair a knee injury without her knowledge. She is angry and persuades Jenny and Trina to come with her to confront Uncle Chris.

Uncle Chris visits the Hanson house. Katrin tells him that Dagmar is sick with a bad earache. The doctor appears, having seen Dagmar, and wants to operate on her ear immediately. Mama is concerned about the expense, but Uncle Chris offers to pay, and the doctor says they only need pay what they can afford at the clinic. Uncle Chris angers the doctor by insisting he will watch the operation, but Mama smooths things over.

The children admit to Uncle Chris that he frightens them. He does not understand that his loud voice and gruff manner are intimidating, but he says that he enjoys frightening the aunts. This makes the girls laugh and feel less afraid. The aunts arrive. They are scandalized to see a "woman" in Uncle Chris's car. They know that the woman is not his wife and do not approve of their relationship. Sigrid tries to confront Uncle Chris about Arne, and Trina tries to introduce Mr. Thorkelson, but it is time to take Dagmar to the clinic. The aunts are shocked that Mama would ride in the car with "the woman," but Mama is too practical to be bothered.

At the hospital, Sigrid is upset that she is not allowed to see Arne. Uncle Chris gives his permission to Trina to get married but is outraged when Mr. Thorkelson hints about a dowry for her. It has been several hours since they brought Dagmar in, and the doctor finally emerges to tell them that her surgery went well. Mama is not allowed to see Dagmar and worries that she will be frightened when she wakes up.

Mama lets Nels take her home, but she frets about Dagmar being alone. She has an idea and brings Katrin back to the hospital with her. Katrin waits, composing overly dramatic poetry, while Mama pretends to be a cleaning woman, mopping the floors so that she can get by the nurse at the front desk. Mama is able to see Dagmar and feels relieved.

Uncle Chris visits Arne in the hospital and teaches him to curse as a way to deal with his pain. Uncle Chris is surprised that Mama was able to get in to see Dagmar when he cannot,

but he seems to admire Mama's resourcefulness. He tells her and Katrin that he is going to get drunk when he leaves the hospital. He says that he has no family of his own, even though he is the "head of the family."

Act 2

As with the first act, the second opens with the adult Katrin at her desk. She remembers how busy her mother always was and how surprised Katrin was when she suggested they celebrate Dagmar's recovery with an ice-cream soda. It made Katrin feel "like a grown-up person" to sit alone with her mother for a talk. The scene shifts to the past. Mama orders a soda for Katrin and coffee for herself. Katrin asks Mama when she may have coffee, and Mama explains that she cannot say exactly when it will be: "Comes the day you are grown up. Papa and I will know." Mama talks a little about her life in Norway before coming to America.

The play jumps to the next day, when Dagmar comes home from the hospital. Nels is nursing Uncle Elizabeth, who has been in another fight. Nels tries to prevent Dagmar from seeing the cat, but she pushes past him. Dagmar insists that her mother can heal the cat's injuries. She says, "Mama can do everything." Mama, Papa, and Nels decide they must put the cat to sleep. Papa gives Nels money to get chloroform.

Mr. Hyde appears to say goodbye. He must leave, he explains, because of a letter he received. He gives Mama a check for $110, which pays for his room and board for the four months he has lived with the Hansons. Mama is happy to get the money but sad that there will be no more reading in the evenings. Mr. Hyde also leaves his books behind for the family, which pleases all of them. Later, Aunt Jenny appears with bad news: Mr. Hyde's checks are no good. He has left town without paying local merchants what he owes. Mama insists that "he pay with better things than money."

No one knows how to go about putting the cat to sleep. Mama does not want to hold the cat and watch him die, so they cover the cat snugly with blankets and put in a big sponge soaked in chloroform. The next morning, Dagmar checks on Uncle Elizabeth. Mama is horrified, but Papa feels it would be better to let Dagmar think the cat died from its injuries. They are shocked to find the cat alive—the chloroform drugged him and gave him a sound rest rather than killing him.

Mama wants to tell Dagmar the truth: "Is not *good* to let her grow up believing I can fix *everything*." Papa, however, thinks it is a wonderful thing for a little girl to feel that kind of security.

Katrin is preparing for her part in the school play and getting ready for her graduation. Christine feels Katrin is being selfish by thinking only of her own activities and not paying attention to more important things, like the fact that Papa has been on strike and not working for four weeks. Katrin talks with her friends, Dorothy and Madeline, about the presents they believe they will get upon their graduation. Katrin wants a dresser set that she saw in the drugstore, but Christine tells her that Mama plans to give her a *solje*, a traditional Norwegian brooch made of silver that is a family heirloom.

Katrin is thrilled to receive the dresser set she wanted. She wants to take it to the performance of the school play so that she can show it to her friends, but Christine tells her that Mama had to trade her brooch to the owner of the drugstore to get the lavish gift for Katrin. Papa cannot attend the play because he has to go to a meeting about the strike, but he seems happy when the decision is made to go back to work.

Because she is upset, Katrin is not good in the play. That night she is late getting home, and Mama is worried about her. When Nels and Katrin finally arrive home, he explains that Katrin went to the home of the drugstore owner to convince him to return the brooch. She had to promise him that she would work in his store after school because he had planned to give his wife the brooch as a birthday present. She tries to give it back to Mama, but Mama insists that it was her graduation present and pins it on Katrin's dress. Katrin promises to keep it forever. Through nods and significant looks, Mama and Papa decide that Katrin is ready for her first cup of coffee. Because she now understands the importance of the family heirloom and did so much to get it back, she has proven herself to be grown up.

A telegram arrives telling Mama that Uncle Chris is dying. Mama, Katrin, and the aunts go to his farm to say goodbye. Jenny objects to visiting "that woman," but Mama insists. All of them say goodbye to Uncle Chris and speak with the woman for the first time. Her name is Jessie Brown (they pronounce it "Yessie" in a Norwegian accent), and Uncle Chris asks Mama to make sure to give her a little money once his

farm is sold. Jessie will not inherit anything legally because they are not married.

Uncle Chris dies, and Jenny is indignant that there is no money for his surviving relatives. Mama then reads from a small notebook, listing children's names. He had been lame himself and spent much of his money to pay for doctor visits and surgery for these children, including Arne, his nephew, so that they would not be lame.

The story skips forward in time. Trina is married now, with a young baby named after Uncle Chris. She and Mr. Thorkelson plan a little party to celebrate their anniversary. The scene shifts to the Hanson house. Katrin has been sending out stories to magazines, and she receives another rejection letter. She is discouraged and thinks she will never become a writer.

Papa sees a newspaper interview with Florence Dana Moorhead, "celebrated novelist and short story writer," and Mama decides to go and see the author, hoping to get some advice for Katrin. Mrs. Moorhead tells Mama that she has made it a rule to never read people's unpublished writings, but Mama noticed in the newspaper article that Mrs. Moorhead likes to cook. Mama promises to write out some of her best recipes while Mrs. Moorhead reads one of Katrin's stories.

Successful, Mama returns home and relates what Mrs. Moorhead told her: Katrin has talent but must write what she knows instead of the fanciful, dramatic stories she has been working on so far. Mama suggests that Katrin write about Papa.

Katrin writes a story according to Mrs. Moorhead's advice, and it is accepted for publication. She is paid $500. Everyone is thrilled. Katrin wants Mama to use some of the money to buy a new coat and then take the rest to the bank. Mama admits that the family never had a bank account. She and Papa pretended because "Is not good for little ones to be afraid . . . to not feel secure." Katrin reads the story aloud to her family, and they learn that she wrote the story about Mama.

CHARACTERS

Arne

Arne is Aunt Sigrid's son and the Hanson children's cousin. He hurt his knee a few months before the main action of the play, and Uncle

Chris takes him to the hospital for surgery to have the injury repaired. At the end of the play, Arne is running and playing, giving the family (and the audience) a living, breathing illustration of Uncle Chris's generosity.

Jessie Brown

Throughout most of the play, Jessie Brown is referred to as "the woman" or "that woman" by the aunts. It is not until Uncle Chris is dying that she introduces herself. The aunts do not wish to speak to her because they know she lives with Uncle Chris but is not married to him. Mama is more practical and forgiving of supposed indecorousness than her sisters. She does not hesitate to get into Uncle Chris's car with Jessie when Dagmar needs to go to the hospital, and she promises to make sure Jessie will get some of the money when Uncle Chris's farm is sold after his death.

Uncle Chris

Uncle Chris is the "head of the family." Because he is loud and bossy, he frightens the children—and sometimes even frightens the aunts. Under his gruff exterior, he has a kind heart. After his death, Mama finds his notebook, which lists the names and medical conditions of all the children he has helped. He is lame in one leg, and he has spent a lot of money over the years to get many children the care they need so that they will be able to walk.

Dorothy

Dorothy is one of Katrin's friends from school. Near the end of the play, Dorothy, Madeline, and Katrin are discussing what they expect to receive as graduation gifts. Dorothy's father is the owner of the drugstore where Katrin sees the dresser set she covets.

Christine Hanson

Christine is the middle daughter, and Papa calls her "the stubborn one." She is scolded by Mama for being rude to the aunts and is sometimes unkind to Katrin, such as when she tells how Mama traded her brooch for Katrin's graduation present. She knows that her parents do not want her to tell, but she did not like "the smug way" Katrin was behaving over her gift. She stands by what she believes to be right: although she apologizes to Mama, she still insists, "But I'm not sorry I told." She thought Katrin should know the truth and would not back down.

Dagmar Hanson

Dagmar is the youngest of the Hanson children. She loves animals and has a parade of pets, including Uncle Elizabeth the cat, whose miraculous recovery after an injury makes Dagmar think her mother can fix anything. Dagmar has a serious ear infection that requires surgery, and Mama find a way in to visit her even though hospital rules usually require visitors, even parents, to wait twenty-four hours.

Katrin Hanson

Katrin is a central character of the story. At the start of the play Katrin appears as an adult, and the main action of the story consists of her memories of the time just before she graduated from junior high school. She hopes to be a writer. Papa calls her "the dramatic one," and she has a very active imagination. She is swept up by Mr. Hyde's stories.

As the scenes progress, Katrin matures. She starts out writing melodramatic stories and poems but by the end learns to write more realistic, thoughtful stories inspired by her family. Although she is a bit self-centered at the beginning of the play, Katrin begins to think about the importance of others' feelings, so that Mama and Papa decide she is grown up enough for her first cup of coffee.

Lars Hanson
See Papa

Marta Hanson
See Mama

Nels Hanson

Nels is the oldest Hanson child and the only boy. Papa calls him "the kind one," and he does seem to be a very kind and helpful boy. He is always willing to lend a hand when asked, from trying to nurse the injured cat back to health to carrying his youngest sister when she is ill. He wants to continue his education, but he knows it will be expensive—he asks if it might be possible rather than assuming he can have what he wants, and he is willing to work hard himself at an after-school job to make it happen.

Mr. Hyde

Mr. Hyde is the Hansons' boarder. He is a former actor. With his dramatic way of talking and his English accent, he impresses Mama. He skips town owing four months' rent, but he gave the family many pleasurable evenings by reading aloud while he lived there, and he left his collection of books behind when he left.

Jenny

Aunt Jenny is one of Mama's sisters. She is the most critical and bossy of the sisters. She encourages Sigrid to stand up to Uncle Chris after he took Arne to the hospital without telling her, and she pushes Trina and Mr. Thorkelson to ask Uncle Chris for a dowry. When Jenny learns that Mr. Hyde's rent check is no good, she seems gleeful when she tells Mama. Jenny always disapproves of Uncle Chris's relationship with Jessie Brown and almost refuses to go into the house to say goodbye when he is dying because Jessie is there.

Dr. Johnson

Dr. Johnson takes care of Dagmar when she has her ear infection. Uncle Chris almost makes Dr. Johnson abandon his patient by being bossy and demanding to watch the surgery, but Mama is able to keep Uncle Chris's interference to a mimimum.

Madeline

Like Dorothy, Madeline is one of Katrin's friends from school.

Mama

As is clear from the title of the play, Mama is an important and influential character. She is kind and level-headed, and she seems to be an almost-perfect wife, sister, and mother. Mama is patient with her sisters, even bossy Jenny, but does not hesitate to speak sharply to them to keep them in line. Trina comes to her for help when she wants to marry because she is afraid her other sisters will laugh at her.

As a parent, Mama does everything she can to help her children. She sneaks into the hospital, pretending to be the cleaning woman, because she does not want Dagmar to be alone and wants to see for herself that Dagmar is all right. She goes to see a famous author and bribes her with recipes to get advice about writing when Katrin gets discouraged. When Nels wants to continue his schooling, she juggles the family finances and puts off buying herself a new winter coat so that he can do so. Not forsaking sternness and sensibility, she scolds the children when necessary and brings them into the process of paying the bills, teaching them life lessons they need to learn.

Mama is also fair and kind to people outside the family. When she and Katrin go out for a soda and a coffee, she tips their waiter generously and thanks him graciously. She is the only one among her sisters who is willing to give Jessie Brown a chance and promises Uncle Chris without hesitation that she will help Jessie after he dies.

Florence Dana Moorhead

Florence Dana Moorhead is a famous writer in the play. Papa sees an article about her in the newspaper, and Mama goes to see her, taking some of Katrin's stories. Mrs. Moorhead does not want to read anything unpublished, but Mama tempts her with recipes, and Mrs. Moorhead finally passes on advice for Katrin: to write what she knows.

Papa

Although the play concentrates on Mama's importance in the family, Papa is also a kind and capable parent. He works as a carpenter to support the family and is an affectionate father. When Nels wants to continue in school, Papa immediately offers to give up tobacco to save money. Papa also has patience and a sense of humor when it comes to dealing with Mama's troublesome sisters.

Mama and Papa seem to have a solid marriage. Papa appreciates Mama's strength and kindness and clearly loves and admires her. When Dagmar thinks that Mama miraculously healed her injured cat, Mama wants to tell Dagmar the truth, but Papa thinks it is better to let Dagmar have the security of that feeling. "Is best thing in the world for her to believe," he says, adding, "Besides, I know *exactly* how she feels." The strength of their relationship also shows in the important moment of Katrin's first cup of coffee. They are able to communicate very easily without talking.

Sigrid

Aunt Sigrid is another of Mama's sisters. She follows Jenny's lead, but where Jenny is controlling and bossy, Sigrid tends to complain. Uncle Chris takes Sigrid's son, Arne, for surgery without telling her. She is angry, but at the end of the play, Arne is healthy, and Sigrid is touched by the notebook full of the names of children like her son who are able to walk because of Uncle Chris.

Peter Thorkelson

Mr. Thorkelson is the man who wants to marry Trina. He works at the funeral home, and Sigrid calls him "Little Peter," seeming to refer to his timidity as well as his small stature. When Mr. Thorkelson asks for a dowry for Trina, Uncle Chris is able to talk him out of it, convincing him that he does not want to be the kind of man who would not marry her without a dowry.

Trina

Aunt Trina is one of Mama's sisters. She is meek and shy. She wants to marry Mr. Thorkelson, but she asks Mama to tell the other sisters because she is sure they will laugh at her. At the very end of the play, Trina is happily married with a new baby.

The Woman

See Jessie Brown

THEMES

Female-Male Relations

Throughout *I Remember Mama*, Van Druten provides a subtle portrait of the relations between the sexes. The story takes place around 1910. Therefore, it would be easy to assume that the family behaves according to traditional social rules, and some events do follow a traditional pattern. For example, Papa is the breadwinner of the Hanson family, leaving the house each day to work as a carpenter. Also, everyone refers to Uncle Chris as the "head of the family" because he is the oldest male member, and when Trina wants to get married, her fiancé goes to Uncle Chris to ask for her hand.

However, there are many ways in which this traditional social structure, where the men are in charge, is overturned. Although Mr. Thorkelson does indeed ask Uncle Chris for permission to marry Trina, it is Trina herself who fetches Mr. Thorkelson and drags him to the meeting. Papa does earn most of the money, but Mama takes in a boarder to supplement the family budget. Uncle Chris might be called the head of the family, but he has to resort to secrecy to do what he wants, such as taking Arne to the hospital without telling Sigrid because he knows she will not allow it. Uncle Chris is rarely around, and Mama and the aunts are the ones who are truly in charge of the family.

There are positive aspects to this disruption of old-fashioned social traditions. Instead of showing a domineering father figure who makes all of the family decisions and a weak, obedient mother, the play instead features a more modern family dynamic. Mama is capable and strong, and Papa is kind and loving. Mama and Papa are partners. They make decisions together, such as whether Katrin is ready for her first cup of coffee. They also make sacrifices together, as when Nels wants to continue his schooling; Mama gives up her new coat, and Papa gives up tobacco.

Family Relationships

The title of the play is a large clue to the reader or audience that family relationships will be important throughout the story. Mama is, of course, central to the family. All of the children seem to think, like Dagmar, that "Mama can do everything," and even Papa seems to agree. Because Mama is such a strong and caring person, her entire family feels secure, even though they struggle financially. The strong marriage between Mama and Papa also contributes to this feeling of family security.

There is conflict in the family, of course, especially when one looks at the relationships between the sisters. Katrin and Christine bicker at times, and it is Christine who tells Katrin about Mama trading her brooch for Katrin's graduation present, just because Christine did not like the way Katrin was acting. Christine felt Katrin was showing off. This is typical of rivalry between sisters.

The older generation of sisters has conflict as well. Right at the beginning of the play, Trina tells Mama that she is afraid that Jenny and Sigrid will laugh at her for wanting to get married—not the congratulatory reaction one might reasonably expect from women who ought to want their sister to be happy. Even Mama stoops to using slightly childish tactics to force Sigrid and Jenny to behave as she wants them to: she threatens to tell Trina embarrassing stories about them if they laugh at Trina's engagement to Mr. Thorkelson.

In spite of these relatively minor disagreements, clearly Van Druten wants to stress the significance of family. Uncle Chris says he wants to get drunk because "I haf no family." Because he does not have a wife and children, he is unhappy and wants to forget himself in alcohol.

TOPICS FOR FURTHER STUDY

- It was more common in the 1910s for Scandinavian immigrants to settle in the countryside and work on farms. How would the Hanson family live differently if they had made their home in the Midwest? Would Dagmar enjoy keeping animals as pets if she had to do chores to help take care of livestock? Would Katrin still imagine growing up to be a writer if she attended a one-room rural schoolhouse? Would Mama keep a boarder? Choose a scene from the play and rewrite it with the setting as a remote farm instead of San Francisco. Perform the scene with your classmates.

- Research life of immigrants to the United States in the 1910s to see what things were like for the Hansons living in San Francisco. Find images representative of immigrant life of the time: the places they left behind, their travels to America, and the new city neighborhoods they settled in once they arrived. Create a PowerPoint presentation of these pictures, and provide commentary while sharing it with your class.

- Read *Bread Givers* (1925), by Anzia Yezierska, which relates the story of Sara Smolinsky. Like the Hansons, the Smolinskys are poor immigrants struggling to make their way and find their places in a new country. Think about how the characters of Sara in this novel and Katrin in *I Remember Mama* are similar and how they are different. Write a short story or a play-like scene in which Katrin and Sara meet, or compose an essay in which you imagine what they might think of one another.

- Carefully read the stage directions and author's notes in the script for *I Remember Mama*. Lay out and sketch your own designs for the stage, including sets and props. You may incorporate Van Druten's detailed instructions or ignore them and use your own ideas. Share your designs with your class, explaining why you included the various elements.

The closest thing to a villain in the play is Mr. Hyde, the boarder who abandons the Hansons without paying what he owes them, and when he leaves, even he seems to appreciate the importance of family ties. He thanks Mama for her "most kind hospitality" and specifically asks her to "say good-bye to the children for me." He also leaves his books behind "for the children," indicating that he enjoyed his cozy evenings reading with the family as much as they did.

STYLE

Stage Directions

Some playwrights give next to no stage directions in their scripts, leaving directors and producers to decide how to create the sets and providing very few cues to the actors regarding how the lines ought to be read. Throughout *I Remember Mama*, however, Van Druten includes many descriptions about how the actors should say their lines and how they should move on the stage. For example, in Uncle Chris's death scene, there are multiple directions for the actor, such as "Handing MAMA the empty glass," "With a glance at JENNY," and "Shouting." Van Druten has a clear idea about how he wants the final scene to appear, and he does his best to communicate this vision through his script.

Van Druten is also very particular about how he wishes the stage to be set up. The stage design that he describes is meant to highlight the nature of the story. There are two turntables, revolving platforms, at the front of the stage for when Katrin is her older self, reminiscing, and for shorter scenes that do not take place in the Hanson home. Van Druten also indicates when curtains should be used to hide the main

Katrin is writing an autobiographical novel, which is how the audience hears the story of the Hansons.
(© olly | Shutterstock.com)

set on the stage, helping to make changes of scene clear, such as in switching from the kitchen to the hospital or Uncle Chris's house.

Van Druten writes that the turntables are not essential, but he insists that some method for setting up and removing any props (furniture, for example) needed for these scenes must be devised. The props cannot be left on the secondary stage areas for the entire play because they would obstruct the view of the main stage, and changes must be done quickly so as not to draw the audience's attention. Van Druten wanted to preserve the realism of the story. Van Druten was a playwright who believed in making the action of the play as close to real as possible. He wanted to reduce any distractions for the audience that might detract from their becoming absorbed in the story.

Accents

The characters in *I Remember Mama* speak with various accents, and Van Druten uses the way the

characters speak to indicate something more significant about them. For example, the children, born in San Francisco, have American accents, whereas their Norwegian-born parents have Norwegian accents. This defines the pattern on the simplest level, but the use of accents is a bit more subtle than just that. Van Druten specifically mentions in the script that Papa speaks with less of an accent than Mama: "His English throughout is better than hers, with less accent." This makes sense, considering that he works outside the house and converses with a more diverse group of people, while Mama's responsibilities keep her busy in the family home.

Uncle Chris seems to have the strongest accent of all. He introduces his common-law wife as "Yessie Brown" because in Norwegian the letter *J* is pronounced like an English *Y*. He also says "von" for *one* and "vant" for *want* and usually calls the children by the Norwegian versions of their names. When he is dying, he reverts to speaking Norwegian: "Farvell, Katrinë." It is

COMPARE & CONTRAST

- **1910s:** Immigrants newly come to the United States are likely to live in separate communities with others from their homeland. Because of this social isolation, they might maintain traditions like a bride's family providing a dowry when she marries. On the other hand, there is social pressure on immigrants to conform—to give up the traditions of their country if they want to be accepted into mainstream American society.

  Today: Immigrants are more likely to live in integrated neighborhoods. There is also more acceptance of people retaining their traditions and culture even if they have immigrated to the United States.

- **1910s:** Scandinavians are much more likely to settle in the Midwest on farms or in small towns than in a large city, as with the Han-

sons. This sets Scandinavians apart from most immigrants, who tend to live in cities, where there are more jobs.

  Today: Of the more than 4.5 million people of Norwegian ancestry in the United States, 55 percent live in the Midwest, while 21 percent live on the West Coast, in Washington, Oregon, and California.

- **1910s:** Around the turn of the century, a carpenter might earn between $2 and $3 per day, or between $500 and $900 per year. A check for $110, like Mr. Hyde's, may be worth four months of room and board.

  Today: A skilled carpenter might earn $40,000 per year or more. Inflation has raised the value of a check worth $110 in the 1910s to approximately $2,500 now.

appropriate that Uncle Chris, as the oldest member of the family, would have the strongest links to the old country. He is of the older generation, and his thicker accent stresses his resistance to change.

HISTORICAL CONTEXT

Work and Financial Matters in the Early Twentieth Century

Personal finances in the very early years of the twentieth century were very different from today. Inflation makes today's salaries seem much higher, but buying power may be lower. Even where a profession's basic salary is proportionally comparable now to what it was a hundred years ago, modern workers are much more likely to have other compensations from their jobs that simply did not exist back then.

For example, not all jobs today include a health-insurance package or paid vacation time, but in the 1910s, such benefits were almost unheard of. Today, if a worker is sick, he or she can usually take time off work to recover. With many health-insurance programs, if a person visits the doctor, he or she might have to pay only a relatively affordable co-payment, and the insurance company will pay the rest of the bill. One hundred years ago, most workers would lose their wages for the day if they were ill. Today, the Family and Medical Leave Act requires employers to allow workers to take time off to care for a new baby or a sick family member without losing their jobs. If a person is injured on the job, there are laws in place to ensure that the employer will pay for medical expenses, but no such laws existed at the turn of the twentieth century.

Workers were then just beginning to ask for these kinds of benefits and protections. Labor unions were beginning to form that allowed workers to speak as one, giving them more

Mr. Hanson is eventually forced to return to Norway to look for work. (© Pincasso / Shutterstock.com)

bargaining power than one person alone could have. Sometimes unions would go on strike, refusing to work until management met their demands. There is some discussion of Papa being on strike near the end of *I Remember Mama*, for example. It was a gamble to go on strike, however. At that time, waves of new immigrants were arriving, many of them desperate for work, so it was likely that management could easily find people to take the places of the striking workers.

The ways in which banks, businesses, and individuals handle money have also changed. After the Great Depression, when many financial institutions failed and people lost their savings, the federal government put protections in place to insure the money in banks. Before that, however, banks were not insured. If a bank's investors mismanaged the money and the bank failed, depositors might have lost their money.

In the very early twentieth century, there was no such thing as a credit card. A local storekeeper might have offered credit to a recognized neighborhood customer, but there were no credit cards as known today: a card that can be used almost anywhere to pay for just about anything.

Credit cards have changed the way people live. People can use credit to tide themselves over when things get tight financially. However, there is a decidedly negative aspect to this: it is easier to overspend than when commerce was based mostly on cash.

CRITICAL OVERVIEW

The sheer number of plays produced by Van Druten speaks to his popular and commercial success, and the critical reception of his work was also mostly positive. His first widely reviewed play, *Young Woodley*, is pronounced by Stark Young in *New Republic* to be "a delightful and gentle thing." Otis Chatfield-Taylor, writing in *Outlook*, calls Van Druten's play *After All* "a keenly observant and delicately ironical study."

The subtlety of Van Druten's dialogue is often commended. Richard Dana Skinner's 1932 review of *There's Always Juliet* points out that Van Druten "appreciates the importance of unspoken words, and also the significance of sheer nonsense and banter covering up much deeper emotions." In a review of *The Voice of the Turtle* in *American Mercury*, George Jean Nathan admires how Van Druten writes "skillfully,... without the least chicanery or subterfuge," with "deceptive immaculateness and simplicity." Grenville Vernon, in remarks in *Commonweal* in 1941, praises Van Druten's general talent: "Van Druten is one of the few men now writing for the stage who knows how to write high comedy. His touch is at once delicate and sure: his sense of comedy ... keen and subtle: his dialogue witty, often distinguished."

In a *New York Times* review of the film adaptation of *I Remember Mama*, Bosley Crowther describes how the play's "genial personality" translates well from stage to screen. Crowther appreciates how the format of the presentation, with its movement between Katrin as an adult and flashbacks to her youth, which "was effectively used for the play," also works well for the film.

Critics and audiences alike seem to enjoy Van Druten's work. In the *Saturday Review*, John Mason Brown sums up the general reaction with broad praise, claiming that Van Druten is "a dramatist who cannot write a play without some merits."

CRITICISM

Kristen Sarlin Greenberg

Greenberg is a freelance writer and editor with a background in literature and philosophy. In the following essay, she examines how van Druten uses the story line of the bank account to sustain Mama as a realistic character in I Remember Mama.

Throughout his play *I Remember Mama*, John van Druten provides ample evidence that Mama is a remarkable woman. Although she is only a hardworking wife and mother of a blue-collar family, she seems almost too good to be true. She is a dream parent: patient and loving, teaching her children important life lessons, and acting as a good partner to her husband. However, a character who is too perfect is not realistic, and Van Druten, as a playwright, believed that realism was best for the theater. Therefore he introduced elements into the story that make Mama more human.

WHAT DO I READ NEXT?

- *Mama's Bank Account* (1943) is the autobiographical novel by Kathryn Forbes that was the basis for Van Druten's play *I Remember Mama*. The novel's greater length allows for more of the Hanson family's adventures to be included.

- In *The Brief Wondrous Life of Oscar Wao* (2007), Junot Díaz brings to life a first-generation American who at first seems very different from Katrin Hanson. However, just as Katrin is swept away by Mr. Hyde's evening reading, Oscar is fascinated by the worlds created in science-fiction novels. Both teens try to find their places in the world between their families' traditions and values and contemporary American culture.

- Ole Edvart Rolvaag's 1927 novel *Giants in the Earth* portrays a Norwegian immigrant family working to establish a farm on the Dakota plains in the 1870s. Rolvaag drew from his own experience, as well as that of his wife, when writing the novel.

- American husband and expectant father Eric Dregni moved his family to Norway for a year to learn more about his Scandinavian roots. He writes of his experiences and illuminates many surprising aspects of Norwegian culture in his 2008 memoir *In Cod We Trust: Living the Norwegian Dream*.

- Van Druten's play *I Am a Camera* (1951) is based on Christopher Isherwood's stories written about living in Berlin in 1931. It was an exciting and frightening time, with the Nazis coming to power in Germany in the years leading up to World War II.

- The immigrant experience is a central theme in the short-story collection *Interpreter of Maladies* (1999) by Jhumpa Lahiri. Lahiri's stories illustrate that a person does not leave one culture behind when adapting to a new one.

THE MENTIONS OF THE BANK ACCOUNT
THREADED THROUGHOUT THE PLAY ADD TENSION
TO THE ENTIRE STORY, AND IT IS ALSO WHAT
RESCUES MAMA, AS A CHARACTER, FROM BECOMING
TOO SAINTLY TO BE BELIEVABLE."

The first time the audience sees Mama's merits is when she is put in comparison with her sisters. Sigrid is whiny, Jenny is bossy, and Trina is rather silly. In contrast, Mama is intelligent and even-tempered. When Uncle Chris visits accompanied by "the woman," Sigrid and Jenny are shocked that he would dare bring her with him. They are not married, but she lives with him, in a state of cohabitation that was unsettling to many people at the time. Mama has good reason to ignore such social rules: Dagmar is ill and needs to be taken to the hospital, and Uncle Chris will give them a ride in his car. Sigrid says, "You *can't* go in his automobile.... Because *she's* in it." But Mama makes clear that she thinks Sigrid is being ridiculous: "So it will kill me, or Dagmar, if we sit in the automobile with her? I have see her. She looks nice woman." Mama is too practical to refuse a ride in Uncle Chris's car simply because Jessie Brown is also sitting in it.

Mama very much wants to get Dagmar to the hospital quickly, but it is not only because of this practical concern that she agrees to ride in the car with Jessie and Uncle Chris. Van Druten makes clear that Mama truly does not judge Uncle Chris or Jessie negatively because of their relationship. As Uncle Chris is dying, Mama promises him that Jessie will receive some of the money from the sale of his farm. She also suggests to Jessie that she come to live with them—first as a guest and then later as a boarder, once she is able to find work. Mama will not shun Jessie, as it seems Jenny and Sigrid might do, simply because of her supposedly inappropriate relationship with their uncle. Mama is forgiving of the unofficial couple's faults—if she even sees their not being married as a fault. It seems that Mama considers Jessie a member of the family, and Mama knows that family is important and welcomes Jessie into her home.

Mama's positive qualities are also illustrated in her behavior when Dagmar is in the hospital. Dr. Johnson explains that the hospital has a rule that a patient may have no visitors, even parents, for twenty-four hours after being admitted. Mama protests: "But, Doctor, she is so little. When she wakes she will be frightened." However, the rule is firm, and Mama is not allowed in. Yet because she is concerned for her little girl, Mama finds a way. Pretending to be a cleaning woman, Mama manages to get past the nurse at the front desk and visit Dagmar as she promised. She is a devoted mother and cannot bear the thought that Dagmar will be alone and scared.

Mama's affectionate devotion does not imply that she is overly indulgent. She does not hesitate to correct or scold the children if they do something wrong, such as when Christine tells Katrin about Mama's trading away her brooch. Van Druten includes a stage direction indicating Mama's behavior when she learns what has happened: Mama is "rising with a sternness we have not seen before." Christine makes an excuse, saying she "hated the smug way" Katrin was behaving over her graduation present, but Mama is firm. "Is no excuse," she says; "Is not your business.... Is not for you to judge. And you know I do not want you to tell. I am angry with you, Christine." While not harsh or cruel, Mama makes Christine understand that she disapproves. Mama does everything she can to teach her children right from wrong.

One of the funniest moments in the play is also one of the most poignant: the resurrection of Uncle Elizabeth. Dagmar is heartbroken to come home from the hospital only to find her beloved pet injured in a fight. Nels tries to nurse the cat back to health, and Dagmar is sure that Mama will be able to heal him. "Mama can do everything," she says. Poor Mama is at a loss. She does not think the cat will survive, and everyone but Dagmar feels that it would be cruel to try to keep him alive. They decide to put the poor animal to sleep, but Mama is too softhearted to push a chloroform-soaked cloth over the cat's face and "watch him die." Instead, she soaks a sponge in the chemical and puts it in the bed with Uncle Elizabeth, covering him with a blanket, believing he will pass away gently while he sleeps.

However, instead of euthanizing the cat, the chloroform just gives him a "good sleep." Dagmar is thrilled: "Oh, Mama, I *knew* you'd fix him." It is an amusing moment: the family's horror at Dagmar's cuddling the cat, which they assume to have died, changing to surprised joy when they see his tail twitching and realize that he is alive. It is also an important emotional moment, because it shows a parent's dilemma regarding how much truth to force on a young child. Mama does not want to take the credit for the cat's recovery, not wanting to give Dagmar illusions about what her mother can accomplish, but Papa tells her it might be a very good thing for a little girl to believe that her Mama can fix everything, to make her feel safe and secure.

On the one hand, this event confirms Mama's remarkable qualities; it is as if she can bring a beloved pet back from the dead, even if only by accident. On the other hand, this is also where the audience starts to see that Mama is a real person. For all that the final result was positive, it was only due to a mistake that the cat survived. Mama is not infallible, and in the end she is willing to allow the truth to be sacrificed for her child's peace of mind.

There are several plotlines that reverberate throughout the play. Van Druten uses this stylistic approach to impress important themes upon the audience—the idea of coffee being a privilege for adults, for example. From time to time, Papa gives the kids a sugar cube dunked in coffee, but if the children ask when they can have real coffee, in a cup, Mama answers, "Comes the day you are grown up. Papa and I will know." There are several instances when Dagmar or Katrin asks about drinking coffee, so that by the end of the play, when Papa and Mama give Katrin her first cup, the audience thoroughly understands its significance.

Similarly, there are many times when the issue of the bank account is raised. In the opening scene, when the family is counting out coins to pay the bills, Dagmar asks if the bank is "like a prison" because she does not understand why Mama never wants to go there. Christine explains, "Because if we went to the Bank all the time, there'd be no money left there. And then if we couldn't pay our rent, they'd turn us out like Mrs. Jensen down the street."

The importance of money also comes up when Dagmar is ill. Mama knows that Dagmar's ear infection must be treated, but she is concerned about the cost. She pours out what little money the family has in the "Little Bank," and Mama asks, "Is enough without we go to the

Bank, Doctor?" Because this issue is brought up several times throughout the play, we know that Van Druten wants the audience to pay attention.

The overarching story of the bank account is crucial. The original novel was called *Mama's Bank Account*, after all. The mentions of the bank account threaded throughout the play add tension to the entire story, and it is also what rescues Mama, as a character, from becoming too saintly to be believable. Mama is lying. There is no bank account. If the family spends Papa's salary for the week and their Little Bank is empty, the family will have to give up something in their already modest budget. Mama has been doing her best, but they are poor, without any savings. Mama is not perfect, but she and Papa are doing the best they can. Mama realizes that the children's feeling safe is more important than a lie in this case. And it is this lie, as well as this struggle to make her children feel secure and provide for them, that makes Mama more human, which in turn makes her that much more admirable.

Source: Kristen Sarlin Greenberg, Critical Essay on *I Remember Mama*, in *Drama for Students*, Gale, Cengage Learning, 2013.

Harold Clurman

In the following excerpt, Clurman commends Liv Ullman's portrayal of Mama in the musical version of I Remember Mama.

I Remember Mama, a musical with a score by Richard Rodgers, lyrics by Martin Charnin and Raymond Jessel and book by Thomas Meehan, based on John Van Druten's play of the same name, is a placid show which would hardly be noteworthy were it not for the presence of Liv Ullman. Her warm womanliness and simple truthfulness in the character of Mama represent her best work on the New York stage to date. I could not help thinking as I watched her that she is one of the very few real *women* among present-day actresses. There are hardly more than three or four now on the distaff side of the stature of Ethel Barrymore, Laurette Taylor and Pauline Lord whom—quite apart from sheer acting talent—I could designate "true women." Something seems to have happened.

Source: Harold Clurman, Review of *I Remember Mama*, in *Nation*, Vol. 229, No. 2, July 14, 1979, pp. 59–60.

SOURCES

Brown, John Mason, "Van Druten, John (1901–1957)," in *Modern American Literature*, 5th ed., Vol. 3, St. James Press, 1999, pp. 314–15; originally published in *Saturday Review*, December 15, 1945, p. 15–16.

Chatfield-Taylor, Otis, Review of *After All*, in *Modern American Literature*, 5th ed., Vol. 3, St. James Press, 1999, pp. 313–14; originally published in *Outlook*, December 16, 1931, p. 502.

Crowther, Bosley, "Irene Dunne and Oscar Homolka Head Brilliant Cast in RKO's *I Remember Mama*," in *New York Times*, March 12, 1948, http://movies.nytimes.com/movie/review?res=9C06E3D9173FE23BBC4A52DFB5668383659EDE (accessed September 7, 2012).

Eisenbach, David, "Federal Savings and Loan Insurance Corporation (FSLIC)," in *Encyclopedia of the Great Depression*, edited by Robert S. McElvaine, Macmillan Reference USA, 2004, pp. 354–56.

"Family and Medical Leave Act," U.S. Department of Labor website, http://www.dol.gov/whd/fmla/ (accessed September 13, 2012).

Feinberg, Richard A., and Cindy Evans, "Credit Cards," in *St. James Encyclopedia of Popular Culture*, edited by Sara Pendergast and Tom Pendergast, Vol. 1, St. James Press, 2000, pp. 628–30.

"John van Druten," Classic Theatre Festival website, http://www.classictheatre.ca/john-van-druten (accessed September 7, 2012).

"John William Van Druten," in *Dictionary of American Biography*, Charles Scribner's Sons, 1980.

"John (William) Van Druten," in *International Dictionary of Theatre*, Vol. 2, 1993.

Lebergott, Stanley, "Wage Trends, 1800–1900," National Bureau of Economic Research website, http://www.nber.org/chapters/c2486.pdf (accessed September 13, 2012).

Nathan, George Jean, Review of *The Voice of the Turtle*, in *Modern American Literature*, 5th ed., Vol. 3, St. James Press, 1999, p. 314; originally published in *American Mercury*, April 1944, p. 465.

Nelson, Daniel, "Labor," in *Dictionary of American History*, 3rd ed., edited by Stanley I. Kutler, Vol. 5, Charles Scribner's Sons, 2003, pp. 3–10.

"Norwegian-Americans," in *Norway: The Official Site in the United States*, http://www.norway.org/News_and_events/Norway-in-the-US/Norwegian-American-Organizations/Norwegian_Americans/ (accessed September 13, 2012).

Skinner, Richard Dana, Review of *There's Always Juliet*, in *Modern American Literature*, 5th ed., Vol. 3, St. James Press, 1999, p. 314; originally published in *Commonweal*, March 2, 1932, p. 495.

Van Druten, John, *I Remember Mama*, Dramatists Play Service, 1944.

Vernon, Grenville, "Van Druten, John (1901–1957)," in *Modern American Literature*, 5th ed., Vol. 3, St. James Press, 1999, pp. 314–15; originally published in *Commonweal*, January 10, 1941, p. 303.

Young, Stark, Review of *Young Woodley*, in *Modern American Literature*, 5th ed., Vol. 3, St. James Press, 1999, p. 313; originally published in *New Republic*, December 23, 1925, p. 134.

FURTHER READING

Brockett, Oscar G., and Franklin J. Hildy, *History of the Theatre*, Allyn & Bacon, 2007.
This is the fortieth-anniversary edition of a book often called the bible of theater history because it is such a comprehensive volume, providing expert commentary and hundreds of photos and illustrations.

Brown, Joanne, *Immigration Narratives in Young Adult Literature: Crossing Borders*, Scarecrow Press, 2010.
Brown has done extensive research about immigration and theories of adolescent development and presented her findings in an engrossing analysis of the immigrant experience as reflected in over two dozen young-adult novels.

Ehrenreich, Barbara, *Nickel and Dimed: On (Not) Getting By in America*, Metropolitan Books, 2001.
Like the Hanson family, counting out coins to pay the bills from their "Little Bank," many of today's families struggle financially. In *Nickel and Dimed*, Ehrenreich writes of her financial experiment: she accepted various jobs—sales clerk, waitress, and maid, among others—earning minimum wage and struggling to make ends meet. Her experiences highlight the difficulties of America's working poor.

Van Druten, John, *The Voice of the Turtle*, Dramatists Play Service, 1998.
This inexpensive actor's edition of one of Van Druten's most critically acclaimed plays gives a taste of the playwright's work that is more controversial than the family-oriented *I Remember Mama*.

SUGGESTED SEARCH TERMS

John Van Druten

John Van Druten AND twentieth-century theater

John Van Druten AND realistic theater

I Remember Mama

I Remember Mama AND theater

Norwegian immigration

history of banking

Mama's Bank Account

Miss Evers' Boys

DAVID FELDSHUH
1989

Miss Evers' Boys is a play by American dramatist David Feldshuh. It was first produced by Center Stage in Baltimore, Maryland, on November 17, 1989. Over the next two years it was performed in Los Angeles, California; Atlanta, Georgia; and Minneapolis, Minnesota. It was also nominated for a Pulitzer Prize. The play is based on the Tuskegee syphilis experiment, an infamous episode in twentieth-century American history that took place between 1932 and 1972.

The study was conducted by the U.S. Public Health Service in Tuskegee, Alabama, on 399 poor African American sharecroppers (tenant farmers) in Macon County, Alabama. The men all had syphilis and were told they were being given free government health care, although they were never told what disease they were suffering from. The men in fact received only very limited treatment for syphilis, which was then stopped altogether because the purpose of the study was to document the progress of the disease in African American men when it was untreated. The experiment was intended to continue until the men died. Even when penicillin became available in the 1940s and was known to be an effective treatment for syphilis, it was not made available to the men in the study.

Miss Evers' Boys centers around the memories and reflections of the fictional character Eunice Evers, an African American nurse, as she struggles to deal with her long involvement

in the deception. The victims of the study are personified in the fictional figures of four African American tenant farmers, ranging in age from nineteen to fifty-seven when the play begins. The play documents how mistakes and wrong judgments can be made with good intentions but lead, if uncorrected over the years, to an egregious violation of people's human rights. An edition of the play is currently available, published by Dramatists Play Service in 1995.

AUTHOR BIOGRAPHY

Feldshuh was born in New York City in 1944. He graduated from Dartmouth College with a degree in philosophy and trained as an actor at the London Academy of Music and Dramatic Art. He joined the Guthrie Theater in Minneapolis, where he remained for seven years first as an actor and then as a director. He also completed a doctorate degree in theater at the University of Minnesota. Feldshuh also studied to become a medical doctor and completed a residency in emergency medicine at Hennepin County Medical Center, Minneapolis. He is a board-certified emergency medicine physician at Cayuga Medical Center in Ithaca, New York. He travels to the Dominican Republic each year on a medical mission, helping sugarcane workers.

His first published play was *Fables Here and Then*, which appeared in *Minnesota Showcase Four Plays: Do Not Pass Go, Buchner's Woyzeck, Fables Here and Then, The Cookie Jar*, published in 1975 by the University of Minnesota Press. The play is a collection of comic and tragic stories from around the world. It was produced at the Guthrie Theater.

Feldshuh wrote *Miss Evers' Boys* in 1989. It was a finalist for a Pulitzer Prize in 1992. The play was adapted for television by Walter Bernstein for HBO in 1997 and won five Emmy Awards including Best Picture. Feldshuh also coproduced the documentary film *Susceptible to Kindness*, for which he interviewed people involved in the Tuskegee syphilis study, including some survivors. In 1994, the film won the Cine Golden Eagle, the Intercom Gold Plaque, and the International Health and Medical Film Festival award. He has received a distinguished service award from the National Center for Bioethics at Tuskegee University.

At Cornell University, Feldshuh was professor of theater and artistic director of the Schwartz

MEDIA ADAPTATIONS

- *Miss Evers' Boys* was made into an HBO television film in 1997, starring Alfre Woodard as Evers and Laurence Fishburne as Caleb, directed by Joseph Sargent.

Center for the Performing Arts for nearly twenty-eight years, until his retirement from that position in June 2011. He directed many theater productions, many of them large-scale works. He was also the Menschel Distinguished Teaching Fellow for 2011–12 in the Center for Teaching Excellence at Cornell University.

PLOT SUMMARY

Act 1

PROLOGUE

The prologue takes place in 1972, in the Possom Hollow Schoolhouse in rural Macon County, Alabama. Miss Eunice Evers is giving her testimony to a U.S. Senate committee. While she recites the oath she took when she first became a nurse, four black men who were part of the study enter the schoolhouse and stand in the background.

SCENE 1

It is 1932, and the scene takes place in a schoolhouse in the early evening. Present are four black tenant farmers, Willie Johnson, Caleb Humphries, Hodman Bryan, and Ben Washington. They have been told by Kirk, a white local landowner who owns the land they farm, that they must go to the schoolhouse to see a government doctor. The men are nervous and do not know what to expect. Willie and Caleb recall their school days there. Willie recalls his teacher Miss Jane Teeters and how she instilled ambition into him. Ben, the oldest of the four, never attended school.

Miss Evers arrives by car. As the local nurse, the men already have heard of her. She explains that she has been sent by Dr. Eugene Brodus, a black hospital administrator in Tuskegee. She informs the men that the federal government is offering them free medical treatment if they have "bad blood," a euphemism for syphilis. She also tells them they may have bad blood even if they have no symptoms. The men are skeptical about why the government is offering them free treatment.

Willie tells Evers that the four men form a dance band, and they are going on Saturday to compete in the Macon County Victrola Gillee Competition. They believe they will win, and they invite Evers to come. The scene ends with music and dance as the men play their instruments (drum, washboard, and harmonica), and Evers joins in. The men sign up for the free medical treatment. Evers, looking back from the vantage point of 1972, says that the men won the competition.

SCENE 2

Two months later, at the schoolhouse, Ben, Caleb, and Willie wait in line as Hodman argues with Douglas, the white doctor. Hodman does not understand the questions he is being asked until Evers gets the doctor to speak in words he is able to understand. Douglas then gives a technical explanation to all the men about how syphilis is contracted, although he does not use that term. The men do not understand a word he says until Evers puts it in plain language. In a flash forward to Evers' testimony in 1972, she reveals that all four men tested positive for syphilis. The following week, treatment begins.

SCENE 3

Douglas draws blood from Willie, but the two men do not communicate well. Douglas tells Evers that Willie inherited the disease from his grandfather. Evers tells him to talk to Willie in a more personal way. Douglas reveals to Willie that he likes their kind of music and has even been to the Cotton Club in Harlem. Willie is excited, and the two men discuss a dancer named Ruby Blue, whom Douglas saw perform. Douglas even dances as a demonstration. Willie says he would like to have some life insurance to go along with the medical treatment. Then he would be able to have a decent burial in a real coffin.

SCENE 4

Six months later, the men are massaging each other's backs with mercury, which is part of the treatment. They are in good spirits, as is Evers. Flashing forward to 1972, Evers reveals that the men won lots of music competitions in the first six months of the treatment. Then the government ended the treatment program.

SCENE 5

Dr. Douglas and Dr. Brodus discuss the situation. Evers is also present. Douglas says there is no more money. He suggests they continue the program but turn it into a study of the effects of untreated syphilis. He thinks this will be an important study. When it is publicized, he says, it will motivate the government to provide more money for treatment, not only in Macon County but throughout the country. He also believes the study will show that black people are affected by the disease in the same way that whites are. He mentions that a study already has been done in Oslo, Norway, based on autopsy reports of three hundred whites who died of syphilis.

Brodus is cautious at first, but eventually he is convinced by Douglas's arguments. He accepts that more money will be forthcoming within two years at the maximum. Evers protests that the men need treatment, but Douglas and Brodus insist that the men must believe that nothing has changed, that they are still receiving treatment. He suggests that heat liniment be used as a substitute for mercury rubs. Douglas says he can get fifty dollars worth of life insurance for each man, as an incentive for them to stay in the study.

SCENE 6

The men are about to receive spinal taps as a test for neurological syphilis. In order not to scare the men, the taps are referred to as "back-shots." Evers prepares Caleb. Douglas arrives and performs the procedure, injecting a needle several times into Caleb's back. The procedure is painful. The doctor collects some fluid. Caleb mistrusts the procedure and asks Evers if it is making him healthy. She does not answer him directly.

SCENE 7

In the presence of Evers, Brodus reviews the results of the spinal taps. She tells him she is unhappy about lying to the men and wants to tell them the truth. Brodus replies that they would not understand and would not be around for treatment when the money comes through.

She says she has a job offer in New York City, but he urges her to stay.

SCENE 8

One week later, there is a gillee competition that night. Evers teaches the illiterate Ben how to write his name on the blackboard. She tells him she is leaving soon for New York. Ben says the men cannot manage without her. Evers then drives the men to the competition. They all enjoy themselves in the car. In a flash forward to Evers's 1972 testimony, she reveals that that night she decided not to move to New York.

Act 2

SCENE 1

It is 1946. Willie is practicing his dancing. In her testimony, Evers says the men looked healthy at that time and felt good, although she knew that could be deceptive. Then in 1946, a new and very effective treatment for syphilis became available: penicillin. Evers believed that her patients would be first in line for treatment.

Willie starts getting pains in his leg that affect his ability to dance. Evers tells Brodus that her patients need penicillin. Brodus says it could be risky for those who have had the disease a long time. It might produce an allergic reaction that could kill the patient. He says the government is assessing the level of risk involved. Meanwhile, the other men encourage Willie to overcome his leg pain and keep dancing. They have a competition to win.

SCENE 2

One month later, at a treatment center, Willie and Caleb says they have come for penicillin, but Evers says he cannot have it because he is a government patient. They say they know other men who are receiving penicillin. Evers points out that unlike those men, Willie and Caleb have had "bad blood" for years, and penicillin might be dangerous for them. Willie accepts what she says, but Caleb does not.

SCENE 3

Willie's bad leg is examined by Drs. Brodus and Douglas. They notice that he drags his right foot when walking and conclude that the symptom may be due to syphilis. They still refuse to offer him penicillin, however, even though the risk has been found to be small for those with late-stage syphilis. They think that should Willie die from the treatment, many of the six thousand people in the

county who, unlike Willie, have contagious syphilis and whom the doctors wish to treat with penicillin, would be frightened and refuse treatment that could help them. Evers protests, but Brodus overrules her. Brodus confirms to Willie that he has "bad blood" but says they cannot help him. Evers gives him a hat to wear during the upcoming competition, to bring him luck.

SCENE 4

Hodman is giving Willie a homemade cure made of molasses and sulfur that he has to take as he follows a ritual under moonlight that Hodman prescribes. Caleb is skeptical and says it will not work. He says they should have penicillin and is angry that it is being denied to them. Ben defends Evers.

Douglas and Brodus have a disagreement. Brodus says there is no longer a need for their study because both black and white people are cured of the disease through penicillin, which shows that both races react in the same way. Douglas says that only through showing the devastation caused by the disease will there be enough political will, generated by fear, to eradicate it.

SCENE 5

Three months later, Caleb urges Evers to give Willie penicillin, but Evers says she is not permitted to do so. Caleb says he has found a way of getting penicillin. He says he is going away for good and asks Evers if she will go with him. Evers says she is staying where she is because she is dedicated to the people she serves.

SCENE 6

Four months later, Ben is sick. He is in a wheelchair in the hospital. Evers gets him to sign a document that will permit an autopsy on him and also pay fifty dollars toward burial expenses. He expresses his appreciation to Evers for all that she has done to help him. Evers is emotionally touched by this, and the two hold hands.

SCENE 7

Two months later, Douglas tells Brodus that it is too late to treat the men with penicillin; it will not cure them. Brodus insists it will stop them from getting any worse. He tries to persuade Douglas that the fourteen years of data they have is sufficient, but Douglas insists that the study must be continued to its end point, that is, the death of all the participants. Evers protests, but Douglas insists on issuing orders that no doctor in the area is to treat the men in the study with penicillin.

SCENE 8

Two days later, Evers confronts Hodman, who is having vision problems. She has obtained some penicillin and persuades Hodman to let her inject it into his hip. Within four weeks, Hodman has had a psychotic breakdown and dies after ingesting a poisonous mold mixed with turpentine that he believes is medicine. Evers believes she is partly responsible for his madness and death and feels guilty.

EPILOGUE

It is 1972, and Evers is giving her congressional testimony in the schoolhouse. She says that Willie did receive penicillin when he moved to a different county. Caleb also left Macon County. She adds that 127 patients still remain in the study. Outside, Caleb, now a clergyman, confronts Douglas and hints that he is going to take legal action over what happened to him. Douglas still believes that the study did some good, but Brodus appears to regret his role in the affair.

Caleb convinces Willie that Evers behaved badly toward him, and Willie, who now walks with a limp and with the aid of a cane, confronts her. She insists that she acted as a friend toward him, but he rejects her and exits. Caleb continues to remonstrate with Evers as she tries to defend her actions. She was doing what the doctors told her to do, and nursing was her life. In her closing words, she reveals that she has faced hostility in the county because of the publicity, but she continues to insist that she loved the men who were under her care.

CHARACTERS

Dr. Eugene Brodus

Dr. Eugene Brodus, a forty-year-old African American, is the administrative head of Memorial Hospital in Tuskegee, Alabama. He allows himself to be influenced by Douglas's arguments about continuing the study of untreated syphilis. At first he is cautious, unconvinced, but Douglas talks him into it. Brodus thinks that a study that shows that both blacks and whites are equally affected by the disease will put an end to the notion that syphilis is predominantly a black person's disease. The government will then be prepared to put more money into fighting it.

Hodman Bryan

Hodman Bryan is a thirty-seven-year-old African American tenant farmer. He has had little formal education and may be illiterate. Like the other men in the study, he plays in the band that they call Miss Evers' Boys. Hodman believes in folk remedies for ailments rather than standard medicine. When Caleb's child was sick, Hodman prescribed a remedy, but it did not work, and the child died. When the disease progresses in Hodman, it affects his eyesight and his mind. Evers persuades him to take the penicillin she has gone to great lengths to get for him. It does not seem to help him, however, and he persists in pursuing his own strange remedies. He dies after drinking a combination of turpentine and mold.

Dr. John Douglas

Dr. John Douglas is a thirty-four-year-old white doctor, a field physician with the U.S. Public Health Service. At first he talks to the men in technical language, and he does not know how to get through to Willie, but they get along better after Douglas reveals that he appreciates African American music and has been to the Cotton Club in Harlem. Douglas is a well-intentioned man who genuinely wants to help the men in the study. He is disappointed and frustrated when the money runs out.

However, it is he who then comes up with the idea of conducting a study on untreated syphilis. He believes it will be an important study that will document the progress of the disease in black people and will show if there are any differences in how the disease affects whites. He expects more money to be forthcoming in six months. He maintains his belief in the validity of the study even when it is clear that no more money will be coming.

When penicillin becomes available in 1946, Douglas refuses to allow the men in the study to receive it. He believes that his work will help to eradicate syphilis, and he is quite high-minded and idealistic about it. However, he does not take into consideration the negative effects endured by the men who are guinea pigs in the study.

Eunice Evers

Eunice Evers is a twenty-eight-year-old African American public-health nurse. Her father died when she was five, and she has been a nurse since she was about twenty. When hard times hit in 1930, she lost her job as a nurse and did whatever domestic work she could find. Then in 1932

Dr. Brodus invited her to be a part of the new treatment program.

Evers never marries. Instead, she devotes herself to nursing, and in her own mind, she does the best job she can, even though she does not agree with the decision to withhold medicine from the men, especially penicillin. Although she protests and makes her feelings known to the doctors, she nonetheless follows whatever instructions the doctors issue. She does think of leaving Macon County and has a job lined up as a night supervisor in New York City, but she develops an affection for the men she cares for and decides to stay in Macon County, Alabama.

Evers is genuinely dedicated to her profession, and she takes as good care of the patients in her charge as she can. She even manages to get some penicillin for Hodman. At the end of the play, during her testimony, she says she loved the men, but she also has feelings of guilt, especially in the case of the death of Hodman.

Caleb Humphries

Caleb Humphries is a thirty-seven-year-old African American tenant farmer. He had a wife and child, but they both died. He is angry that he has to work with his hands rather than his brain, and he does not like living in a poor area where no one ever gets ahead. He is also suspicious of the treatment program he is in and wonders whether it is doing him any good. He is wary of white people. No white people came to help him when his wife was sick and gave birth to a sick child. Caleb thinks that the anger he feels about his situation in life is what keeps him going.

Caleb is also a good talker, and when he was a boy he used to entertain his friends by imitating the local clergyman's sermons. In 1946, he manages to get treated with penicillin from somewhere else in the county. He leaves Macon County, as he has long wanted to, and eventually becomes a preacher. He wants Evers to go with him, but she turns him down. In 1972, when the news breaks about what the treatment program was really about, Caleb rebukes Evers for her role in it, although he does make some effort to understand her point of view.

Willie Johnson

Willie Johnson is a nineteen-year-old African American tenant farmer. He has had only two years formal schooling, but he is ambitious. He is the dancer in the men's music group, and he

hopes to use that skill to move north and perform in clubs. According to Dr. Douglas, Willie inherited syphilis from his grandfather, passed on through his mother. By 1946, Willie has pain in his leg, and this affects his dancing skills. Ten years later, he leaves Macon County and moves to Tennessee, where he is able to receive some penicillin. This stabilizes him as far as the progress of the disease is concerned.

At the end of the play, Willie walks with a limp, with the aid of a cane. He is angry with Evers, having found out that she was a party to the fact that he was refused penicillin. He confronts her, saying the medicine could have saved him a lot of pain and enabled him to go on dancing.

Kirk

Kirk is the white man who owns the land where Willie, Caleb, Hodman, and Ben farm. Kirk sends them to the local schoolhouse to see the government doctor.

Ben Washington

Ben Washington is a fifty-seven-year-old African American tenant farmer. He has never had any formal schooling and is illiterate, and he regrets his lack of education. He works hard on the land he farms, for little reward. He says that if he had children he would try to ensure they went to college. In the band, Ben plays the washboard. At the beginning of the play, Ben is nervous about being at the schoolhouse and is apprehensive about dealing with any authority figures, especially whites. In fact, he does not like dealing with white people at all, because in his experience it leads to trouble.

During the course of the play, Evers teaches Ben how to write his name. By 1946, he is showing symptoms of the disease. He is in a wheelchair and has difficulty breathing. He dies at the age of seventy-four. Unlike the other men, who turn against Evers, he dies before the full truth is unveiled. He expresses appreciation to her for the efforts she made on his behalf. He is also proud of the certificate he received from the U.S. government that shows he participated in the study for fourteen years.

THEMES

Ethics

Of the three characters who administer the study, only one, Eunice Evers, shows any conscience about the part she played in it. In contrast, Dr. Douglas,

TOPICS FOR FURTHER STUDY

- In 1991, Cornell University, where David Feldshuh teaches, wrote to all its incoming freshmen urging them to attend a campus performance of the play. The university thought that its racially diverse student body would benefit from seeing such a play. Take a look at a YouTube video that is an advertisement for a Howard University production of the play (http://www.youtube.com/watch?v = 8wkQ6Twq4Qc). Then get together with a group of three or four other students and make your own video in which you discuss the play, read excerpts from it, and explain why you think it is a play that everyone must see.

- Watch the 1997 film version of the play, directed by Joseph Sargent, and write an essay in which you discuss how the film differs from the play. Which version do you prefer, and why?

- When the Tuskegee Syphilis Study was revealed to the public, some people compared it to the experiments done on humans by the Nazis in Germany during the 1930s and 1940s. Was this a fair comparison? Read *Nazi Germany* (2000) by Ted Gottfried, a book for young adults that explains who the Nazis were and what they did. Give a class presentation in which you explain what might prompt such a comparison and explain whether you believe it is valid or not.

- The Tuskegee Syphilis Study unfortunately was not the only time that the U.S. Public Health Service got involved in unethical research. In 2010, it came to light that from 1946 to 1948 the Public Health Service had deliberately exposed 1,300 people in Guatemala to sexually transmitted diseases as part of a research study. With some of your colleagues, research this case, beginning with the website of the Presidential Commission for the Study of Bioethical Issues (http://www.bioethics.gov/). With your colleagues, give a class presentation in which you explain what happened. What measures have been put in place to ensure that such abuses do not occur again? Could they occur again?

---

at the end of the play, insists to Caleb Humphries that the study was not racist but a matter of following "research options that were appropriate at the time." He still believes in the value of the study. Dr. Brodus is not so confident, saying to Douglas "Those men could have been given a choice," but he does not express any personal regret about his involvement in the study.

For Evers, however, it is different. She struggles to reconcile her devotion to nursing and to the men who were in her charge with the fact that she was also part of the deception that was practiced upon them. Dramatically, the stage is set for the examination of her struggle with these ethical questions in the prologue, where she is shown during her 1972 congressional testimony reciting the pledge she took as a nurse. The

pledge includes the words, "To devote myself to the welfare of those patients committed to my care." With that, the play begins.

Evers has misgivings about telling the men they were still being treated when they were not, and she expresses her concern to the doctors, but she has no power in the situation and goes along with the instructions she is given. Later, in her testimony, she asks the senators to remember the time and place where the study was done. It was a very poor area, and the fifty dollars of life insurance offered the men so they could have a decent burial meant a lot. Evers talks about the "messy middle ground," to the senators; she is making the point that the situation was not as black and white as it appears. The men did get some benefit from their participation. Nevertheless, at the time, she felt uncomfortable not telling them the truth. In act 1, scene 7, she says to Brodus, "I just want to tell the men what's going on. The straight truth." However, in the testimony she speaks in act 2, scene 1, she admits that as the years went by and the men still appeared healthy, she became reconciled to the situation.

The availability of penicillin, and the fact that it was denied to the men, raised once more the ethical issues that she had pushed aside. When Evers takes the matter up with Dr. Brodus, he deflects her by warning of possible allergic reactions to penicillin. Eventually Evers argues that the men should at least be given the choice of whether or not to take penicillin. When the government decides that the risk of an allergic reaction is small, Evers expresses her frustration at Dr. Brodus's continued refusal to allow the men to have the medicine. Later, in her testimony, she says that she was "deeply uneasy" about the situation, with "more and more doubts," but she did not speak those doubts out fully to Dr. Brodus. Finally, in act 2, scene 7, she does stand up to both doctors, saying she will not go along with their instructions anymore, and indeed she does manage to obtain some penicillin for Hodman.

Over the years, Evers struggles with a difficult ethical dilemma: whether to follow her own conscience or to follow authority. Gradually the voice of conscience becomes louder in her, although she admits in her congressional testimony in the Epilogue that after 1946, she "tried to stop thinking about it." At the end of the play, she clearly has regrets about what happened but seems to feel that she does not deserve the blame she is receiving from people in her community.

Racism

The injustice of the study is plain to see. The play shows that the men in the study are denied medical treatment that might have helped them. They are lied to, and the lies go on for a period of forty years. Compounding the injustice is the fact that it is racially slanted. All the men in the study are black. Not only that, they are poor and, in the case of Ben and possibly Hodman, illiterate. This suggests that they were chosen because their lives were not considered very valuable and they could just be experimented on without any thought of how it would affect them as individuals.

However, the theme of racism is not treated in an overt way. Dr. Douglas is shown as being a

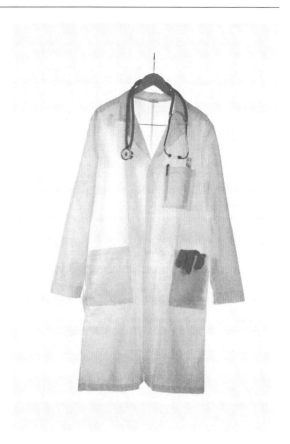

In a forty-year-long study, doctors injected the patients with syphilis without their consent to study its effects. (© mikeledray | Shutterstock.com)

fan of African American music, and he genuinely believes that the study is scientifically valid. The case of Dr. Brodus is even more interesting, because he is African American. He convinces himself that African Americans as a group will in the long run benefit from the study. He identifies strongly with being a research scientist. He tells Willie, "Research means finding new things to help people. That doesn't mean every single person is helped but it means that more people are helped than hurt." In other words, he believes that it is justifiable to allow individuals to suffer so that a greater good may emerge. He genuinely believes he is serving his race, as he explains to Evers at the end of act 2, scene 7. However, most playgoers are likely to reach the conclusion that whatever the protestations to the contrary, the men in the play—Willie, Caleb, Hodman, and Ben—suffer ill treatment in part because they are black and that the arguments put forward in favor of the study draw a convenient veil over some of its darker motivations.

STYLE

Dramatic Irony

Dramatic irony is a type of irony that takes place when a character on stage says something to another character that has a different or more complex meaning for the audience than it does for at least one of the characters. There is an example of dramatic irony in act 2, scene 6. Ben is very sick, but he makes a point of appreciating what Evers has done for him. He says, "You stood by us. You always treated us special. We always knew we'd be cared for, and that you'd be watching out for us." His words affect Evers emotionally, and she begins to cry. Ben tells her she has "nothing to be crying about." The audience is aware, however, of what Evers knows but Ben does not, that Ben's gratitude is based on his lack of information about what really happened. Evers did in a sense do her best, but in other ways she knows, as does the audience, that she has let Ben down, and that is at least part of the reason she cries. The dramatic irony lends poignancy to the scene.

Nonnaturalistic Structure

Because the play takes place in part through the lens of Evers's memory, as she looks back over the previous forty years from the vantage point of 1972, a number of the scenes are nonnaturalistic in the sense that they switch back and forth between different time frames. Evers is often the focal point on stage as she gives her testimony in 1972, which sometimes follows directly from an incident in 1932 (as happens in act 1, scene 4, for example).

Sometimes, as in act 2, scene 1, the structure is reversed, and the scene begins with her testimony and then moves swiftly into several scenes from 1946 in which Evers also takes part. In act 1, scene 1, the scene set in 1932 suddenly jumps to Evers's later testimony and then returns immediately to the former action. Other examples of variations on this structure occur at the end of act 2, scene 3, in which Evers turns and speaks directly to the audience, and especially in act 2, scene 8, in which Evers is present in two different times and scenes that unfold simultaneously: her emotional reaction to Hodman is also her reaction to the senator who is questioning her.

The split perspective conveys well her emotional turmoil. In general, the nonnaturalistic structure has the effect of keeping the entire Tuskegee Study over the course of forty years very much in the minds of the audience. No one is allowed to get temporarily lost in the details and forget the entire tragic process and outcome over this long period of time.

HISTORICAL CONTEXT

The Tuskegee Syphilis Study

The origins of the Tuskegee Syphilis Study lie with a project begun in six southern counties by the Public Health Service (PHS) in 1929. Nearly fourteen hundred black men and women were treated for syphilis. Officials were intrigued by the fact that in the later stages of the disease, some patients seemed to do well even without treatment, while others did not. The PHS then began another, smaller program in which only men who were in the later stages of the disease would participate. When funding for the project ran out, the PHS officials saw an opportunity to study the effects of untreated syphilis. What became known as the Tuskegee Syphilis Study began in Macon County, Alabama, in the area around Tuskegee, in 1932.

The study involved 399 men who had late-stage syphilis and 201 who did not have syphilis but served as controls. The researchers wanted to know more about what happened during the final stages of the disease. The aim was not to treat the disease but to observe it and compile data about it. The men recruited for the study thought they were being treated, although they were never specifically told that they had syphilis. The men agreed to participate in the study largely because of the small benefits they were offered: free physical exams, free car rides to and from the clinics, hot meals on the day of the exam, and a fifty-dollar burial stipend paid to their survivors. By 1969, about one hundred of the men in the study had died.

The study continued until it was exposed by a reporter, Jean Heller of the Associated Press, in July 1972. There was an immediate public outcry about the immoral and highly unethical nature of the study. Particular attention was drawn to the failure to administer penicillin to the men once that drug became an effective treatment for the disease in the mid-1940s. James H. Jones, in his

COMPARE
&
CONTRAST

- **1930s–1940s:** In the 1930s, standard treatment for syphilis, with an arsenic compound called Salvarsan, is of limited effectiveness and can have serious side effects.

- **1970s–1980s:** Penicillin remains an effective treatment for syphilis, and researchers in the field of public health feel able to focus their attention on other sexually transmitted diseases, especially AIDS in the 1980s.

  Today: Treatment for syphilis is with one injection of penicillin, an antibiotic, which will cure the disease if it has been present for less than one year. More than one dose of penicillin is required for those who have had the disease for more than a year.

- **1930s–1940s:** In the early 1930s, 60,000 children in the United States are born with syphilis. Up to 20 percent of patients in mental institutions have the disease. In the United States in 1940, 10.7 out of every 100,000 people die of syphilis. There are 573,593 reported cases in 1940. In 1943, there is a breakthrough when penicillin is shown to be an effective treatment for syphilis, with a rate of cure between 90 and 97 percent.

- **1970s–1980s:** The number of cases of syphilis steadily falls. In 1970, 91,382 cases are reported. In 1980, the figure is 68,832. In the 1970s, 0.2 out of every 100,000 people die of syphilis in the United States, down dramatically from 1940.

  Today: The number of cases of syphilis continues to decline. There are 13,744 cases reported in the United States as a whole in 2010. There are 260 cases of syphilis reported in Alabama in 2010. This ranks Alabama tenth in the nation for such cases, in terms of rates of infection per 100,000 residents.

- **1930s–1940s:** In many states in the rural South, it is not uncommon for African Americans to go all their lives without seeing a doctor, even though diseases such as tuberculosis and syphilis are common. In Macon County, Alabama, the disparity in health care between whites and blacks is marked, because very few black people can afford to pay for a doctor. For health care they rely on traditional home remedies rather than modern methods.

- **1970s–1980s:** The revelations about the Tuskegee study in the early 1970s make many African Americans suspicious of the health care system. When the disease AIDS appears in the early 1980s, within a few years it is more common among black people than whites. Many in the black community believe that the disease is the result of a government conspiracy that targets African Americans for genocide.

  Today: Several studies demonstrate that racial bias exists in the diagnosis and treatment of disease in the United States. The result is that often African Americans receive less effective treatment than whites.

---

book, *Bad Blood: The Tuskegee Syphilis Experiment*, commented:

> Not since the Nuremberg trials of Nazi scientists had the American people been confronted with a medical *cause célèbre* that captured so many headlines and sparked so much discussion. For many it was a shocking revelation of the potential for scientific abuse in their own country.

As a result of the Tuskegee Study, the U.S. government took steps to ensure that such a thing could not happen again. In 1974, the National Research Act created the National Commission for the Protection of Human Subjects of Biomedical and Behavioral Research. The commission made recommendations to the Department of Health, Education, and Welfare

Miss Evers was one of the study's nurses who comforted the patients despite knowing what the outcome would be. *(© Blend Images / Shutterstock.com)*

about the ethical principles governing research on human subjects. In 1974, government regulations were issued that required researchers to obtain informed consent from all persons who took part in Department of Health, Education, and Welfare studies.

In May 1997, at a White House ceremony that was attended by survivors of the study, President Bill Clinton apologized on behalf of the US government for the Tuskegee Study. He described the study as "shameful." Clinton proposed, among other measures, a $200,000 planning grant for a bioethics center at Tuskegee University.

CRITICAL OVERVIEW

A number of theater critics reacted with cautious praise to *Miss Evers' Boys*. Laurie Winer, reviewing

the first-ever production, at Center Stage in Baltimore, Maryland, in the *New York Times*, describes the play as "intelligent if schematic." Winer found some fault with the characterization of Dr. Douglas and Dr. Brodus. "While it's fascinating to follow their increasingly self-deluding logic, the doctors remain only mouthpieces for medical thinking that views humans as subjects rather than patients," Winer writes. She also comments,

> Dr. Feldshuh has simplified matters by making each of the men good hearted and kind, but the director, Irene Lewis, compensates by extracting vibrant performances from the patients, the only characters unburdened by weighty arguments and guilt.

When the play was performed for the first time in New York in 2002, in a production by Melting Pot Theater at the McGinn/Cazale Theater, Bruce Weber reviewed it for the *New York Times*. He writes that because of the "stunning outrage" of the historical event on which the play is based, "the play isn't a subtle piece of drama-turgy." Weber regards the two characters Brodus and Evers, as the most interesting. Brodus is "beguiled by his own sense of self-importance," while Evers "slowly and inexorably loses moral ground" as the years go by. Weber concludes, "The play's main achievement is its refusal to let her off the hook while at the same time illustrating the torment of a good soul." The play has contin-ued to be performed into the 2010s. It was pro-duced at the Grand Theatre, in Salt Lake City, Utah, for example, in February 2012. Blair Howell, for the *Deseret News*, calls it "a harrowing yet deeply rewarding experience."

CRITICISM

Bryan Aubrey

Aubrey holds a PhD in English. In the following essay, he examines the attitudes of the two doctors in Miss Evers' Boys *and the ethical dilemma of Eunice Evers.*

When news of the Tuskegee Syphilis Study first broke in 1972, there was a public outcry against the unethical nature of the study. There was a feeling of dismay that such a thing could happen in the United States. Newspaper editor-ials thundered against it, as did lawmakers. In his book *Bad Blood: The Tuskegee Syphilis Experiment*, James H. Jones quotes Senator John Sparkman of Alabama, who called the study "a disgrace to the American concept of justice and humanity." Senator Edward M. Kennedy, who held hearings on the matter before the Subcommittee on Health of the Com-mittee of Labor and Public Welfare, described the Tuskegee study as "an outrageous and intol-erable situation which this Government never should have been involved in."

By the late 1980s, when David Feldshuh wrote *Miss Evers' Boys*, the passage of time had somewhat moderated the initial sense of outrage. Feldshuh, whose interest in the matter was aroused by Jones's book, approached his dramatization in a more subtle way than might perhaps have been expected. This is not a play with clear-cut villains or heroes, which would have been easy to do but would have resulted in a melodrama far less interesting than the play Feldshuh actually wrote.

It would have been easy, for example, to present Dr. John Douglas as an overt racist,

but what makes the play more intriguing is that he is nothing of the sort. He is well intentioned. He believes in the virtue and scientific validity of the study. His awkwardness in dealing particu-larly with Willie in one of the early scenes (act 1, scene 3) is not due to a racist attitude but simply to his rather stiff personality and his difficulty in talking in layman's terms to the men. He is grate-ful to have Nurse Evers with him to help him communicate. "I've always been a good medi-cine doctor. I've never been a great patient doctor," he confides to Evers.

Douglas is in fact very deliberately shown by the dramatist to lack racial prejudice. That is the purpose of having him tell Willie that he has been to the Cotton Club in Harlem and that he really enjoys the kind of music that is played there. He bandies around some names of musi-cians and dancers with Willie and even dances with him to show what a dancer like Ruby Blue was like. After that, he and Willie seem to enjoy each other's company for a while.

If Douglas is unbending in his insistence in continuing the study as it is, even after penicillin is available, it is not because he is a racist. What his stubbornness shows is that even someone who is well intentioned and dedicated to his profession can be blinded by too great an attach-ment to a theoretical idea. The result is that he loses the ability to see his pet project through the eyes of those who are most immediately affected by it, the men under his care: Willie, Hodman, Caleb, and Ben. Douglas is so attached to his scientific project that he does not realize that in effect he is using human beings as guinea pigs, when he should be doing all he can to cure them.

The reason he is able to do so—which also happens to be the reason given by many people throughout human history who have perpetrated

WHAT DO I READ NEXT?

- *Examining Tuskegee: The Infamous Syphilis Study and Its Legacy* (2009) by Susan M. Reverby has attracted many positive reviews. It is a detailed analysis of the Tuskegee study, including the study of medical records only recently made available. Reverby examines how the study was viewed by all sides in the matter, from participants and their families to the medical authorities, and why it has made such an impact on the American mind since it was first made public in 1972. The book includes a chronology, tables, and charts.

- *The Tuskegee Study* (2002) by civil rights attorney Fred Gray is an account of the Tuskegee Study by the man who represented the survivors of the experiment. He describes the study and the lawsuit that they brought against the Public Health Service and the State of Alabama, as well as the events that led up to the apology by President Clinton on behalf of the U.S. government in 1997.

- *The Normal Heart*, by Larry Kramer, is an outspoken play about AIDS, set in New York City. The play was first produced in 1985, when the disease was new and seemed to affect mostly homosexual men. Facing public indifference, a young activist tries to raise awareness about this devastating disease, which in its early years almost always proved fatal. The play opened on Broadway for the first time in 2011, at the Golden Theatre. It is available in an edition published by the Dramatists Play Service.

- African American dramatist Katori Hall's play *The Mountaintop* (Methuen Drama, 2011) is set at the Lorraine Motel in Memphis, Tennessee, in 1968, the night before

Martin Luther King Jr. was assassinated. The play received stellar reviews when first produced in London in 2009 and won the Best New Play at the 2010 Olivier Awards. It opened on Broadway in September 2011. In the play, King considers his life and destiny, and the future of African Americans, in conversation with a fictional hotel maid.

- *The Tuskegee Experiments: Forty Years of Medical Racism*, by Michael Uschan (Lucent Library of Black History, 2005) is a 112-page book for young-adult readers about the Tuskegee Study. Uschan explains all the details of the study, from its origins to its public disclosure in 1972 and the aftermath of that revelation. The book includes photographs and sidebars for easy reading. It also includes an annotated list of further reading.

- *Fierce and True: Plays for Teen Audiences* (2010) consists of four plays written for and produced at the renowned Children's Theatre Company of Minneapolis. Edited by Peter Brosius and Elissa Adams, the plays are aimed at a twelve- to eighteen-year-old audience and focus on various dilemmas and problems faced by young people. The plays are *Anon(ymous)* by Naomi Iizuka, *The Lost Boys of Sudan* by Lonnie Carter, *Five Fingers of Funk* by Will Power, and *Prom* by Whit MacLaughlin and New Paradise Laboratories.

- Feldsuh's only other published work is *Fables Here and Then*, which appeared in *Minnesota Showcase Four Plays: Do Not Pass Go, Buchner's Woyzeck, Fables Here and Then, The Cookie Jar*. This collection was published in 1975 by the University of Minnesota Press but is now out of print.

---

egregious acts of wrongdoing—is that he thinks he has the greater good in mind. In act 2, scene 3, for example, set in 1946, he fears that Willie might have an adverse reaction to penicillin and

that would scare off the six thousand patients with contagious syphilis in Macon County that he is trying to reach. (Willie and the other men have late-stage syphilis, which is not contagious.)

Douglas, although he does not overtly frame it to himself in this way, is prepared to sacrifice a few in order to benefit the many. Historically, of course, this benefit to the many did not happen. There is no evidence that anyone benefited at all from the denial of penicillin to these men or, in a wider sense, from the Tuskegee Syphilis Study.

Dr. Brodus, the African American doctor and administrator, adopts a similar argument. He is intent on bringing to fruition a study that shows that black people and white people are affected by syphilis in exactly the same way. He also wants to alter the perception in the (white) medical establishment that syphilis is "a colored man's disease." For today's audience, the first statement may sound like odd reasoning: why would anyone think that black and white people are affected differently by this disease? But the fact is that in the nineteenth century and well into the twentieth century, doctors did believe such notions.

In *Bad Blood*, Jones cites a research study published in 1921 based on 1,843 syphilitic patients at a charity clinic. The study reported, according to Jones, that "bone and cardiovascular syphilis were much more common in blacks than whites, while, by contrast, whites suffered higher incidences of neural involvement." Such studies are discounted by modern researchers, who know much more about how the disease progresses. However, Jones comments that studies such as that "no doubt influenced many clinical diagnoses and stood as a powerful reminder of how racial attitudes could influence the medical profession's perceptions."

Dr. Brodus, to his credit, is convinced that such theories—that blacks and whites experience the disease differently—are false, but like Douglas, Brodus is so interested in proving his ideas through the study that he is unable to see that he is contributing to the harm of people he claims he wants to help. He sincerely believes, as he explains with some force to Evers in act 2, scene 7, that he is serving his race by piloting a study that will disprove the bias of the white medical establishment. Like Douglas, he justifies neglecting the few in order to advance the good of the many.

In this way, *Miss Evers' Boys* shows clearly how good intentions, combined with a rigidity of approach, can lead to callous and unethical behavior. Neither Douglas nor Brodus are able take a step back from their entrenched theoretical

positions to see what is in front of their eyes. They show a lack of compassion for the men who are supposedly under their care and whom they are deceiving.

Caught between the misplaced idealism of the doctors and the real suffering of the men in the study is the main character in the play, nurse Eunice Evers; it is not an enviable position for anyone to be in. As Feldshuh, the dramatist, was conceiving the character of Evers, he turned to Jones's book, *Bad Blood*, where he found detailed descriptions of the activities of the real nurse in Macon County who acted as liaison between the Public Health Service doctors and the men in the study. Her name was Eunice Rivers, and the Eunice Evers of the play is very closely based on her.

Nurse Rivers exhibited many of the qualities that the dramatist transferred to his own character. She was devoted to the men in the study. She visited them at their homes to check up on them and visited even more frequently when they were sick. She got to know their families. She went to their funerals. Like Evers in the play, Rivers helped the doctors get the hang of how to communicate with the men, and they respected her and accepted her advice. Like Evers, too, she never gave the men clear explanations of their medical condition. A subject of the study recalled, as quoted by Jones, "The answer she would give me was: 'You just got bad blood and we is trying to help you,'" which is almost exactly the way Evers in the play deals with the men's concerns. Nurse Rivers also went to some lengths to reassure the men (falsely) that they were in fact receiving treatment.

Nurse Rivers, however, does not seem to have ever been troubled by any ethical concerns regarding the study. As Jones writes, "she saw herself as a good nurse, one who always did what the doctors ordered. Not once did she advocate treating the men." It is here that Feldshuh departs from his source, because he needs to inject some drama and conflict into his play. He creates Nurse Evers as a woman who is deeply troubled about the role she is asked to play. Evers swings back and forth between questioning and protesting about what is unfolding and accepting it. As a nurse, not a doctor, she is not in a strong position to argue, but she does her best to advocate for the men, although during many years she accepts the premise of the

Alabama sharecroppers, Miss Evers' boys thought they were getting free health care. (The Library of Congress)

study and does her part to prevent the men from receiving proper treatment.

The dramatic heart of the play shows this good, kind, responsible woman revealing to the congressional committee with sometimes painful honesty how she felt during all those forty years the study was being conducted. She cuts a sad figure by the end of the play as she reveals that she has been shunned by people in her own community for her part in what happened. There is dignity in her final pronouncement, which no one would have reason to doubt: "I loved those men. Those men were susceptible to kindness." Indeed they were, and they received many kindnesses from her, but unfortunately not those that they really needed.

Source: Bryan Aubrey, Critical Essay on "Miss Evers' Boys," in *Drama for Students*, Gale, Cengage Learning, 2013.

New York Amsterdam News

In the following review, a contributor argues that the cast helped bring the atrocious story to life.

This week's Casting Pearls series find us in the Times Square area of New York City for the

Red Fern Theatre Company's (RFTC) powerful off-off Broadway production of *Miss Evers' Boys* by David Feldshuh. Superbly directed by RFTC's founder, Melanie Moyer Williams, the poignant drama opened on March 19 and will run through April 5 at the Shell Theater in the Times Square Arts Building at 300 West 43rd Street at Eighth Avenue.

Boasting a gem of a cast that includes both seasoned and new talent, *Miss Evers' Boys* is in keeping with the Casting Pearls objectives of introducing emerging, well-trained actors who are coloring the various New York City stages, as well as those on the global cinematic screens. In addition, this series serves to acknowledge the legendary and seasoned talent on whose shoulders these newcomers stand. However, before introducing the cast, here's a brief overview of the play.

Miss Evers' Boys, a runner-up for the 1992 Pulitzer Prize in Drama, is the third and final play of the RFTC's 2008–2009 *Season of Secrets*. Based on true events, the story, which is set in Alabama, spans the period between 1932 through 1972, and focuses on the lives of four illiterate African-American sharecroppers, who are used as human guinea pigs by the U.S. federal government to study the effects of untreated syphilis. Known as the Tuskegee Syphilis Study, this non-curative experiment, which was conducted on 399 Black American citizens, became the lengthiest known medical exercise on mankind in medical history.

The atrocious, inhumane story unfolds through the voice of Eunice Evers, a nurse from the community who struggles with her allegiance to the medical ethics of her profession as she witnesses the deteriorating health of the men from her community, who use music to try to maintain their sanity throughout their horrendous ordeal.

In keeping with its continuing mission to "produce socially conscious plays while partnering, with philanthropies whose missions assist those affected by the issues addressed in the play," RFTC has partnered with the Nordoff Robbins Music Therapy Foundation for the production of *Miss Evers' Boys*. The Nordoff-Robbins Center for Music Therapy at New York University offers music therapy services for children and adults "on the autistic spectrum and a wide variety of other disabilities."

Bringing this incredible story to life is an amazing cast, which includes the veteran actor David Pendleton (Ben Washington), whose credits go back to such Broadway classics as Charles Gordone's *No Place to Be Somebody* and Micki Grant's *Don't Bother Me, I Can't Cope,* as well as the LORT productions' of *The King and I* and *Same Time Next Year* opposite Diahann Carroll.

In addition are the solid, seasoned actors Nedra McClyde (Eunice Evers), Alex C. Ferrill (Dr. John Douglas) and Evander Duck (Dr. Eugene Brodus). In addition, the triple threat Jason Donnell Bush (Willie Johnson), a graduate of the American Musical and Dramatic Academy who also studied acting, voice, speech and dance, is a very interesting showman.

This week, the Casting Pearls choices are Garrett Lee Hendricks (Caleb Humphries) and newcomer Marty Austin Lamar (Hodman Bryan). Hendricks, who received his training from the University of the Arts, the British American Drama Association, the William Esper Studio and the Penny Templeton Studio, has appeared on stage at the New Federal Theatre, the Roust Theatre Company and the Castillo Theater. A strong actor with a powerful stage presence, Hendricks' moving performance throughout *Miss*

Evers' Boys is memorable. His powerful spinal tap scene-stealer is the epitome of an actor who knows his craft. Congratulations to Mr. Garrett Lee Hendricks from the Casting Pearls series. Bravo!

Lamar, who is making his off-off-Broadway debut in *Miss Evers' Boys*, received his MFA from the University of Florida (2008). Amongst his special honors is the Irene Ryan ACTF nominee in Acting (2006) and as the musical director for *Sunday in the Park with George* and *Jesus Christ Superstar*. Some of his credits are: *Big River* at the Mill Mountain Theatre, *Lysistrata* in Athens, Greece, *The Trial of William Shakespeare* at the Florida Shakespeare Festival, and the Essential Theatre's productions of *Dreamgirls*, and *Five Guys Named Moe*. Lamar's engaging work in *Miss Evers' Boys* projects the range of his enormous talent for comedy and drama. A Casting Pearls toast to Mr. Marty Austin Lamar. Bravo!

The series would also like to acknowledge the director, Melanie Williams, for casting the wonderful ensemble of *Miss Evers' Boys*, who collectively have also been selected for a Casting Pearls ensemble choice. Bravo!

In addition, the series and the New York Amsterdam News Centennial Anniversary Committee salute the Red Fern Theatre Company in presenting this superb Equity Approved Showcase. We'd also like to acknowledge RFTC and the Nordoff Robbins Center for Music Therapy at New York for their visionary spirit of community partnership, which utilizes theater and music therapy to present this strong sociological message about the brutal impact of human experimentation....

Source: "Casting Pearls: Gem of a Cast Brings *Miss Evers' Boys* to Life," in *New York Amsterdam News,* Vol. 100, No. 13, March 26, 2009, pp. 19–23.

New York Amsterdam News

In the following review, a contributor analyses the approach of the director in illustrating Feldshuh's inspiration.

The Melting Pot Theatre Company (Larry Hirschhorn, artistic director) is proud to present the New York premiere of *Miss Evers' Boys* as the second show of their sixth season at their new home, the McGinn/Cazale Theatre, above the Promenade at 2162 Broadway (at 76th Street).

This powerful play has become a classic in our country's regional theater's but has never been seen in New York before. The Melting Pot, the winner of a Special Drama Desk Award last season for *COBB*, is the company that brought you *Woody Guthrie's American Song* and *The Devil's Music: The Life and Blues of Bessie Smith.*

Written by David Feldshuh, this is a warm, humane, surprisingly humorous and moving play. Inspired by the book *Bad Blood: The Tuskegee Syphilis Experiment*, by James H. Jones, and by a number of primary sources, it is a fictional account of a true government study carried out from 1932–72 of what untreated syphilis would do to the African-American male. It makes a powerful moral statement for our time and has been hailed throughout the country as one of our great American plays.

Director Kent Gash returns to The Melting Pot, having done the much-acclaimed revival of *Home*, and is currently the associates artistic director of the Alliance Theater Company in Atlanta. Last season, he directed Debbie Allen in *Harriet Returns* at the Kennedy Center.

The Melting Pot has put together as cast Broadway veterans: Terry Alexander (*Northeast Local, Streamers*), J. Paul Boehmer (*An Ideal Husband*) Chad L. Coleman (*North Atlantic, Force Continuum* and, recently, O.J. Simpson on TNT's *Monday Night Mayhem*), Helmar Augustus Cooper (*Oh Kay!St. Joan*), Byron Easley (*Fosse, Play On*), Daryl Edwards (*The Colored Museum*) and Adriane Lenox (*Kiss Me, Kate, How to Succeed in Business Without Really Trying, Dinah Was*) as Miss Evers.

Sets are by Emily Beck, lighting by William H. Grant III and costumes by Earl Battle.

Feldshuh has been artistic director at the Center for Theatre Arts at Cornell since 1984. His play *Miss Evers' Boys* has been produced throughout the United States, receiving the New American Play Award nominated for the Pulitzer Prize and winning seven Emmy Awards as an HBO movie. He-co-produced the video *Susceptible to Kindness*, for which he interviewed observers and survivors of the Tuskegee syphilis study. In 1994, the video won three awards: the INE Golden Eagle, the Intercom Gold Plaque and the International health and Medical Film Festival Award.

Feldshuh continues to practice medicine and lectures frequently on the subject of human experimentation and the use of theater in exploring important social issues.

Source: "Melting Pot Premieres *Miss Evers' Boys*," in *New York Amsterdam News*, Vol. 93, No. 9, February 28, 2002, p. 23.

G. Weales

In the following excerpt, Weales points out that despite the focus on individuals, the play's message about a horrible event rings out.

A close-knit group is also at the heart of David Feldshuh's *Miss Evers's Boys*, a play that has been in process since 1986 and has been moving from one regional theater to another since its 1989 debut at Baltimore's Center Stage. I saw it at a recent production at the Philadelphia Theatre Company. Feldshuh, a physician as well as a director and playwright, has used the celebrated/infamous "Tuskegee Study of Untreated Syphilis in the Negro Male" as the starting point for his play. The treatment, which was in fact nontreatment, began in 1932 and continued until 1972 (even after the discovery of penicillin in the 1940s) so that the effects of the disease could be recorded. The play is set in 1932, when both Nurse Evers and her patients believe the men are or are about to be treated for "bad blood," and 1946, when an attempt is made to keep the men from the penicillin which has now become available at anti-venereal clinics. These scenes are intercut with direct statements from Miss Evers's testimony at the 1972 Senate hearing on the project, and an Epilogue in which Miss Evers ("What kind of friend could do what you did?") and the doctors are accused by the crippled Willie.

The group here are four men (representing the 400-odd study participants) who are held together not by their work (farming) but by their band, which they name Miss Evers's Boys, and their desire to dance and play their way out of the hardscrabble world in which they live. The two doctors—the black scientist from Tuskegee and the white one from Washington—might be villains in a doctrinaire play, but here it is never clear how self-deluding they are in their quests for racial equality and scientific knowledge. The moral center of the play is Miss Evers, the dedicated nurse, the friend of the men she looked after, who finally recognized what she was part of but, after the death of a man to whom she belatedly gave penicillin, "just fell in line." Although Feldshuh's focos is on the individuals involved, the play inevitably chronicles a horror story, an American shame perpetrated while we were all being properly outraged at Nazi science.

Source: G. Weales, "Infectious Groupings," in *Commonweal*, Vol. 118, No. 22, December 20, 1991, pp. 750–51.

SOURCES

Aloi, Daniel, "David Feldshuh Reflects on an Era in the Theater," in *Chronicle Online*, May 5, 2011, http://www.news.cornell.edu/stories/May11/FeldshuhProfile.html (accessed August 20, 2012).

"Clinton Apologizes to Tuskegee Experiment Victims," CNN website, May 16, 1997, http://edition.cnn.com/ALLPOLITICS/1997/05/16/tuskegee.apology/ (accessed August 20, 2012).

"David Feldshuh," Cornell University Department of Performing and Media Arts website, http://pma.cornell.edu/people/feldshuh.cfm (accessed August 20, 2012).

Feldshuh, David, *Miss Evers' Boys*, Dramatists Play Service, 1995.

Howell, Blair, "Stage Review: 'Miss Evers' Boys' Harrowing, Rewarding," in *Deseret News*, February 6, 2012, http://www.deseretnews.com/article/print/705398825/Stage-Review-Miss-Evers-Boys-harrowing-rewarding.html (accessed August 20, 2012).

Jones, James H., *Bad Blood: The Tuskegee Syphilis Experiment*, Free Press, 1993, pp. 11, 28, 159, 163, 214.

"Sexually Transmitted Disease—Effective Treatment Developed," Science Encyclopedia website, http://science.jrank.org/pages/6103/Sexually-Transmitted-Diseases-Effective-treatment-developed.html (accessed September 4, 2012).

"Syphilis," Human Diseases and Conditions website, http://www.humanillnesses.com/original/Se-Sy/Syphilis.html (accessed September 4, 2012).

"Syphilis Treatment and Care," Centers for Disease Control and Prevention website, http://www.cdc.gov/std/syphilis/treatment.htm (accessed September 4, 2012).

"Tuskegee Syphilis Study," Encyclopedia of Alabama website, http://www.encyclopediaofalabama.org/face/Article.jsp?id=h-1116 (accessed September 10, 2012).

"2010 Sexually Transmitted Diseases Surveillance," Centers for Disease Control and Prevention website, http://www.cdc.gov/std/stats10/tables/25.htm (accessed September 4, 2012).

Weber, Bruce, "A Tale of a Moral Woman and an Immoral Deception," in *New York Times*, March 16, 2002.

Winer, Laurie, "Patients Sacrificed in the Name of Research," in *New York Times*, December 21, 1989.

FURTHER READING

Brandt, Alan M., *A Social History of Venereal Disease in the United States Since 1880*, Oxford University Press, 1987.

> In addition to examining the various responses of the medical establishment to venereal disease over a period of a century, Brandt examines how American attitudes to venereal disease have been shaped by cultural variables such as sexuality, gender, ethnicity, and class.

Carter, Dan T., *Scottsboro: A Tragedy of the American South*, Louisiana State University Press, 1969.

> Carter examines the notorious case in Alabama in the 1930s, in which nine teenage African American boys were accused of raping two white girls. The book illuminates racism in Alabama in the 1930s and shows how it corrupted the legal profession.

Hoberman, John, *Black & Blue: The Origins and Consequences of Medical Racism*, University of California Press, 2012.

> This is a unique study because it examines racial bias not in the past but in the present, showing how US physicians' views of racial differences affect the way they treat their patients.

Washington, Harriet A., *Medical Apartheid: The Dark History on Medical Experimentation on Black Americans from Colonial Times to the Present*, Anchor, 2008.

> Washington shows that the Tuskegee Study was by no means the only example of medical experimentation on African Americans. In the twentieth century, movements such as eugenics (attempting to use medicine and science to improve the genetic composition of the human population) and social Darwinism were used to provide theoretical justification for such abuses, which were practiced by the government, the military, prisons, and private institutions.

SUGGESTED SEARCH TERMS

Syphilis

Tuskegee Syphilis Study

Venereal disease

Miss Evers' Boys

David Feldshuh

human experimentation

Macon County, Alabama

U.S. Public Health Service

Much Ado About Nothing

1993

Much Ado About Nothing is a 1993 romantic comedy, adapted from the Shakespearean play of the same name. Shakespeare's 1600 comedy is a timeless comedy of gender miscommunication that incorporates two love stories and the machinations of a black-sheep brother. The 1993 film of *Much Ado About Nothing* is based on a screenplay by Kenneth Branagh, who also stars in and directed the film. Emma Thompson, Denzel Washington, Robert Sean Leonard, and Kate Beckinsale also star in the film, which was produced by Stephen Evans, David Parfitt, and Kenneth Branagh. The music was by Patrick Doyle and includes a number of vocal selections as well as instrumental pieces. Filming took place at the fourteenth-century Villa Vignamaggio, Greve in Chianti, Tuscany, Italy.

The very title of this film and the Shakespearean play upon which it is based, *Much Ado About Nothing*, promises a story that is about something, even as the title says it is about nothing. This contradiction fits the game-playing and word play that are the focus of Shakespeare's plot. *Much Ado About Nothing* is about the cruelty of love and the happiness that it brings. It is also about honor and the value placed upon honor. One plot focuses on the unacknowledged attraction between Beatrice and Benedick, who are in love but refuse to admit their love. A parallel love story between Hero and Claudio provides the serious romantic complication of the second plot when dark

FILM TECHNIQUE

- Sideways tracking shots occur when the camera follows the movements of a character as she or he walks or moves along. There is the same continuity to the scene as there would be in real life as the individual actors in a scene move from one location to another. For example, as the soldiers arrive at Leonato's villa, they begin stripping off their clothing and running to the outdoor baths to bathe. The camera follows the men as they undress and then as they jump into the water. Meanwhile, the women all run to their dormitory-style room and begin pulling off their white gowns as they too begin preparing for the meeting with the returning soldiers. The camera shots that follow these actors allow the audience to view the action as if present.

- *Much Ado About Nothing* includes wide lens, long shots, and close-ups in several scenes, including the film's opening sequence. In one of the opening scenes, the camera focuses on Don Pedro and his men, who are off in the distance but are approaching on horseback. This is a long-distance shot, but several members of Leonato's family stand in the foreground with the camera seeming to peek over their shoulders toward the approaching riders. The camera briefly lingers in a close-up shot of each of the approaching riders before the camera lens shows Don Pedro and his men all lined up in a wide-angle shot that fills the screen with the film's title sequence across the front. The camera then shifts to another wide-angle shot of Beatrice, Hero, and the other men and women in Leonato's family group cresting at the top of a small hill above the men. The next shots are a series of close-up individual shots of members of each group, both soldiers and Leonato's family, and even of

the horses. The shifting of camera shots from long to wide lens to close-up is accomplished smoothly and makes the audience feel as if they were present for this exciting reunion. Close-up shots also reveal emotion and work to focus the audience's attention on the Hero-Claudio romance. In the opening of the film, Leonato reads a messenger's letter that explains that the men are returning from war. When Leonato mentions Claudio's name, the camera focuses tightly on Hero's face to show her blushing. This close-up provides the first signal to the audience that Hero is romantically attracted to Claudio.

- Film editing is often invisible to the viewer of a film. If done correctly, the film moves from one scene to the next without any visible break in the action or narration. One of the nicest examples of film editing occurs near the beginning of the film as the camera shifts from Don Pedro and his men approaching on horses to Leonato's family, with Beatrice and Hero in the front, running down a hill to meet them. The scene shifts from wide-angle shots of each group to close-up shots of each of the participants, both on horseback and on foot. The shift in scene is smooth and relates the excitement with which each group greets the other. Another example of effective editing occurs in a scene with Beatrice and Benedick alone in the chapel. Beatrice is on her knees, but the audience glimpses her over Benedick's shoulder. Benedick looks straight at the camera, and the audience sees him finally understand Beatrice's anger. He responds by agreeing to challenge Claudio to a duel. These shots flow seamlessly together without the audience realizing that each has been carefully staged.

© *Moviestore Collection Ltd | Alamy*

forces interfere in their love for one another. As is the case for the Shakespearean play, *Much Ado About Nothing*, the film is predominantly about how romantic games and misunderstandings can impede true love. But unlike some of Shakespeare's other comedies, *Much Ado About Nothing* has a very serious undertone that reveals the social ostracism that results when a young woman's chastity is questioned. The theme of illegitimate offspring and the lack of social position that results are also an important part of the secondary Claudio-Hero plot, which also includes Don Pedro and Don John.

Much Ado About Nothing's costume designer, Phyllis Dalton, was nominated for Best Costume Design by the British Academy Film Awards. The film was also nominated for Best Motion Picture—Musical or Comedy by the Golden Globe Awards. Emma Thompson won a Best Actress Award from the Evening Standard British Film Awards, and Kenneth Branagh won British Producer of the year from

the London Film Critics' Circle. At the Cannes Film Festival, Branagh was nominated for the Palme d'Or, which is awarded to the director of the best feature film entered at Cannes. *Much Ado About Nothing* is readily available on DVD from MGM studios.

PLOT SUMMARY

The film opens with the sound of spoken music, song lyrics that are recited and not sung, and words printed on a black screen. Beatrice speaks the words of the song, and the audience watches as she reads from a book. Shakespeare's play does not begin with this song, but Branagh intends *Much Ado About Nothing* to be an adaptation rather than a filmed play. The introduction of the film lyrics, which are carefully displayed for the audience to read, makes clear that this film will be about love and the battle between men and women to commit to love. Branagh also cuts out much dialogue, nearly 50 percent of Shakespeare's text, in fact. Many of Branagh's cuts describe people, their clothing, or the setting, but he occasionally cuts whole scenes that he finds less important to the film's purpose. In film, the audience can see appearances and clothing, and these descriptions do not need to be stated.

After the initial words on screen, the film opens with men and women lying on the green grass, enjoying a picnic while Beatrice reads to them. The picnickers are Leonato, Beatrice's uncle, his daughter, Hero, and various members of his household, all enjoying a day of sun.

A messenger arrives with the news that the war has ended and Don Pedro and his men have been victorious. The news that Don Pedro and his men will soon be arriving at Leonato's villa brings much excitement, especially to Hero and Beatrice, who are excited to learn that Claudio and Benedick will soon arrive. When the army arrives, Claudio is obviously enamored of Hero, while Benedick and Beatrice begin exchanging their customary witty insults, which are designed to cover their happiness at seeing one another again. Don John sulkily accompanies the men, and although he fought against the army of his brother, Don Pedro, during the rebellion, Don Pedro has forgiven him. However, forgiveness appears not to have resolved Don John's animosity toward his brother. Don John looks ill pleased to be in his present company.

Claudio tells Benedick that he loves Hero, but Benedick is sarcastic, and his reply to Claudio is anti-marriage in words and tone. Claudio also tells Don Pedro that, although he loves Hero, he has no experience wooing a woman. Don Pedro offers to help his young friend. That very evening there will be a masked ball to honor the soldiers and the victorious end to the war. Don Pedro tells Claudio that at the masked ball he, Don Pedro, will speak to Hero on Claudio's behalf. One of Don John's friends, Borachio, hears this plan and tells Don John that they can ruin Claudio and Don Pedro's friendship by convincing Claudio that Don Pedro really wants Hero for himself. Don John is in ill humor and happy to know that he can cause problems.

At the masked ball, Beatrice gives a speech about the problems of men and her intent never to marry. After the ball begins and everyone is

dancing, there is much role playing in costume and much joking. In the midst of this fun, Don Pedro speaks to Hero, who is quite won over by Claudio's expressions of love. Claudio, however, initially believes Don John's story that Don Pedro is speaking to Hero on his own behalf. Claudio laments his poor luck in trusting Don Pedro to woo Hero. Don Pedro tells Claudio of Hero's willingness to accept Claudio and says that Don Pedro only wooed her in Claudio's name. Luckily, Claudio chooses to believe Don Pedro and not his devious brother, Don John. Leonato is happy to have Claudio marry his daughter and immediately begins planning a wedding. Also at the masked ball, Beatrice takes advantage of her mask to tease Benedick. Don Pedro watches the couple and decides that a practical joke might be a way to make Beatrice and Benedick admit their love for one another. Beatrice says that her heart has already been broken once by Benedick and that she has no intention of having it broken again. She is unaware that there is a plan underfoot to change both her and Benedick from verbal enemies to acknowledged lovers.

There now occurs a second singing of the opening song, "Sigh No More, Ladies," a melancholy song about love and untrustworthy men. The next day, Don Pedro, Leonato, and Claudio stage a conversation they intend Benedick to hear. They talk about how much Beatrice loves Benedick and say that she thinks her love for him is quite hopeless. This conversation, which is overheard by Benedick, is accompanied by much slapstick, as Benedick tries to overhear the full conversation and even tries to sneak up on the speakers to hear all the details. When alone again, Benedick is thrilled to think that Beatrice loves him.

Meanwhile, Hero and her maids stage a similar conversation in front of Beatrice, where they talk about Benedick's hopeless love for Beatrice. The camera shows both Benedick and Beatrice dancing with happiness at learning that each one loves the other. Now that each of them knows that the other is in love and that their love is returned, they decide to act on their knowledge of reciprocal love.

There is a brief scene with Dogberry, the constable, and his deputies. Dogberry explains to his deputies how to identify a bad man and how such a man might best be recognized. The scene is full of foolishness, but there is an earnestness in Dogberry's plan to protect Leonato's villa and its inhabitants.

When the plot to end Claudio and Don Pedro's friendship does not work, Don John makes a new plan to convince Claudio that Hero was not honest and chaste. Don John convinces Claudio and Don Pedro to spy upon Hero's window, where he mistakes Margaret for Hero. Borachio has convinced Margaret to disguise herself as Hero and to stand at Hero's window. She thinks the plan is a funny jest and does not realize that there is another part of the plan that involves deceiving Claudio. In the play, it is Borachio who actually creates this plan and convinces Don John to endorse it.

Dogberry and his deputy overhear Borachio boasting about the plot, and they arrest the men, but by then the plot has been a success, and Claudio and Don Pedro have seen Margaret at the window and believe that she is Hero, who has been untrue to Claudio. Dogberry tries to tell Leonato what he thinks he knows, but he muddles the conversation so much that Leonato dismisses him and tells him to go and drink wine. In Shakespeare's play, the window scene is not staged. It is only reported and imagined, but the audience never witnesses it.

The next day is Hero's wedding to Claudio. Claudio waits until the wedding is under way to declare Hero unfaithful and unchaste. Claudio throws Hero to the ground and screams accusations at her in front all the guests who are gathered to witness the wedding. When Leonato asks Don Pedro if he supports Claudio, Don Pedro accuses Hero of infidelity with other men. With both Don Pedro and Don John supporting Claudio's accusations, Leonato is convinced that his daughter has shamed their household. He yells at Hero, accusing her of shameful acts and threatening to kill her. Friar Francis, who has witnessed all these accusations, is not convinced that they are true. He tells everyone that they need to hide Hero until they know what has really happened and who is behind it. The friar insists that everyone be told that Hero has died of grief.

Although the moment following this confrontation and cancelled wedding is painful, Beatrice and Benedick admit they love one another, but Beatrice insists that Benedick must uphold her family's honor and challenge Claudio to a duel. Benedick is reluctant to do this, but his love for Beatrice pushes him to undertake the challenge.

This is followed by a brief scene in which Dogberry appears before the sexton to have Don John's men accused of creating the crime in which Hero was falsely accused and rejected at her wedding to Claudio.

Leonato belatedly comes to his daughter's defense; he and his brother, Antonio, make known their displeasure with Claudio and Don Pedro. Claudio and Don Pedro are told that Hero is dead, but they continue to believe that their honor is at stake and refuse to be reconciled with Leonato and Antonio. Neither Claudio or Don Pedro shows regret at Hero's death, which they see as a just punishment for her lack of chastity. Before a duel can be fought between Benedick and Claudio, Dogberry arrives with his prisoners, and the whole story of the plot to ruin Claudio and Hero's happiness is revealed. The sexton, who is also present, tells everyone that Don John has fled Messina.

Claudio is distraught at this turn of events and asks how he can make amends. Leonato tells Claudio that he must marry Antonio's daughter and hang an epitaph at Hero's tomb. Claudio agrees, and a wedding is quickly promised for the next day. A nighttime ceremony honors Hero, during which Claudio speaks of his love for Hero and cries at her memorial.

The wedding is to take place the next day at dawn. As everyone makes preparations, Benedick recites a sonnet he has written to Beatrice. When Beatrice appears, the two exchange their typical witty remarks, but this time with love rather than sarcasm. As Benedick prepares to ask Beatrice to marry him, they are interrupted by word that it was Don John who perpetrated the crime and that Hero's reputation has been restored. Benedick asks the friar to officiate at his wedding to Beatrice that day.

At the wedding, Hero hides under a veil and Claudio prepares to marry Leonato's niece, a woman he has never seen. When Hero lifts her veil and Claudio sees her face, the couple's happiness at being together is obvious. Hero swears to Claudio that she is still a virgin and the two embrace.

When Beatrice and Benedick are forced to exchange the sonnets they have each written, they agree to be married but still feign reluctance. News comes that Don John has been captured and will soon be back in Messina. The film ends with much celebration and dancing and another singing of "Sigh No More, Ladies," this time with much joy and happiness.

CHARACTERS

Antonio

Antonio is Leonato's brother. Brian Blessed plays this role. Antonio's task is to make sure that the estate is run efficiently. He backs up Leonato in accusing Claudio and Don Pedro of dishonoring Hero.

Beatrice

The role of Beatrice is played by Emma Thompson. Beatrice is intelligent and quick-witted. She is also beautiful and independent and not interested in being controlled by any man, including a husband. Although Beatrice is attracted to Benedick, she has no intention of admitting that attraction. There is a suggestion that Benedick broke Beatrice's heart at some point in the past, and she is very cautious about having it broken again. Beatrice is Leonato's niece and Hero's cousin and closest friend. She has claimed many times that she will never marry, but she enjoys her witty exchanges with Benedick and is obviously attracted to him. Beatrice is not a melancholy person. She is just the opposite—happy and good-natured. One of Leonato's speeches describes her as always laughing.

Beatrice is slightly older than her cousin and friend Hero. The added maturity is what Beatrice uses to mask her feelings. On the outside, she pretends to be uninterested in romance and deals with her attraction to Benedick by being sarcastic. It is only after she is told that he has feelings for her that Beatrice lets down her guard toward him. Branagh deletes text that makes clear that Beatrice has had many admirers in the past but has found none of them suitable for marriage. In Shakespeare's text, Leonato complains that Beatrice mocks all her suitors.

Thompson won a Best Actress Award at the Evening Standard British Film Awards. She was also nominated as Best Female Lead at the Independent Spirit Awards.

Benedick

The role of Benedick is played by Kenneth Branagh, who was married to Thompson at the time the film was made. Benedick is a soldier and serves under Don Pedro's command, but he is also an aristocrat from Padua, in Italy. Benedick is funny and keeps himself entertained through his witty comments, which tend to border on being sarcastic. He is good friends with Don Pedro and Claudio. Benedick hides his attraction to Beatrice by being especially sarcastic and dismissive toward her.

Benedick has been at war, and like his comrades and friends, who have also been away from loved ones for an indeterminate period of time, Benedick is ready to spend time on love instead of war. His lack of interest in Beatrice is only superficial, and when he learns that she is supposedly in love with him, he is willing to take a chance. In Shakespeare's play, Benedick is a ladies' man with a history of involvement with many women, but he always manages to resist their attempts to marry him. Branagh eliminates all text suggesting that Benedick is a philanderer who might well break Beatrice's heart.

Borachio

Gerard Horan plays the role of Borachio, a servant of Don John. Borachio is Margaret's lover, and he convinces her to play a trick on her mistress that he assures her is a harmless jest. After he is arrested and brought before Leonato, Borachio is genuinely sorry for his part in the deception that ruined Hero's reputation. The textual cuts that Branagh made in Shakespeare's play leave the impression that Borachio follows Don John's orders in setting up the false accusations against Hero, but in the play, Borachio has a much larger role, and Don John's role in the plot is diminished. In the play, there is also a suggestion that Borachio was a thief at one time in the past and that his dishonest nature is a part of his personality. Branagh does not provide any suggestion of a back story for Borachio in the film.

Claudio

The role of Claudio, a brave and loyal soldier in Don Pedro's military service, is played by Robert Sean Leonard. Like Benedick and Don Pedro, Claudio is a nobleman. Claudio was attracted to Hero before he went to war and wants to marry her now that the war is over, but he is inexperienced in matters of love and feels at a disadvantage as a potential husband for Hero. Claudio is ready to seize his opportunity, but he lacks sufficient courage to do so himself. Instead, Claudio elicits Don Pedro's help in wooing Hero. Claudio is also appreciative of Hero's wealth as her father's only heir. In Shakespeare's play, Claudio is even more focused on Hero's wealth and on the lack of a male heir to Leonato's estate. Branagh softened Claudio's interest in money and also made him seem much younger and more innocent than in the play.

Even though Claudio loves Hero, he is easily convinced that she has been unfaithful. His repudiation of his bride at their wedding is cruel. Once Hero is revealed to be alive, she guarantees to Claudio that she is still a virgin and inexperienced with men, which is something that matters a great deal to Claudio, who is very focused on honor.

Dogberry

Dogberry is the comedic relief and the clown in this film. Michael Keaton plays this role. Dogberry is the Constable of the Watch. He holds the key to Hero's innocence, but he is so in awe of the noblemen that he can barely speak in their presence. Dogberry is pretentious in his use of language, easily mixing up words and speaking malapropisms that are often unintelligible. He genuinely wants to do the right thing, but he is nearly overwhelmed by his responsibility as Constable of the Watch. Dogberry is the stock character of the clown, a role that is common in both Shakespeare's comedies and his tragedies.

Friar Francis

The role of the friar is played by Jimmy Yuill. Friar Francis is the household chaplain. He is to officiate at Hero's wedding to Claudio but instead helps her family fake Hero's death after Claudio rejects her at the altar. The friar is the voice of common sense and reason after Hero is cruelly rejected. He knows Hero well enough to know that the accusations against her cannot be true.

Hero

Hero is Leonato's only child. The role is played by Kate Beckinsale. Hero is in love with Claudio, who loves her in return. She is very beautiful, but her virtue and chastity are valued more than her beauty. When Hero's chastity is questioned, she loses value as a potential wife. Once Claudio determines that Hero remains pure, she actually feels the need to reaffirm this fact at their reunion. In addition to Hero's innocence and beauty, she participates in the joke played on Beatrice in convincing her that Benedick loves her. Hero's participation in this joke is the only action in both the film and the play that elevates her beyond the stereotype of the falsely accused virgin. It is worth noting that more than 70 percent of Hero's lines in the play were cut by Branagh for the film. The result is that the filmed Hero appears more docile, less outspoken, and more obedient than she does in Shakespeare's text.

Don John

Don John is the illegitimate brother of Don Pedro. Keanu Reeves plays the role of the melancholy, unhappy, and discontented brother, who seeks to disrupt the lives of others so that they might know as much unhappiness as he does. Don John is jealous of the success and admiration that his brother, Don Pedro, receives. Although Don Pedro is generous, even his generosity finds disfavor with Don John, who creates mischief just to see people suffer. The character of Don John is poorly developed in both the Shakespearean play and in Branagh's film. His illegitimacy is suggested as the cause of his melancholy and as a reason for his devious actions, but his character is little more than a stereotype.

Reeves was nominated as Worst Supporting Actor by the Golden Raspberry Award.

Leonato

Governor Leonato is Hero's father and the head of the household at the villa where the action occurs. He is governor of Messina, where the action is set. The role of Leonato is played by Richard Briers. Leonato is a widower, well liked and much respected in the community. He has only one child, his daughter Hero, whom he cherishes. Leonato's niece, Beatrice, who is his ward, also lives in his household. When Hero's honor is impugned at her wedding to Claudio, Leonato also loses honor. Leonato is shamed by his daughter's behavior—or what he takes to be her behavior. His failing as a father is that he immediately believes the slander even though he should know that the accusations are false. Leonato believes Don Pedro and Claudio because they are men of social class and distinction. In this case, the accusers' social class outweighs truth and causes Leonato to reject his only child. What matters more than his daughter's happiness is Leonato's own honor and the honor of the family within the community. His role is of the stereotypical irate shamed father, which does not really fit his character, given both his obvious love for his daughter and the nature of the slander, which is so out of character for her that is scarcely believable.

Margaret

Imelda Staunton plays Margaret, one of Hero's maids and confidantes. Margaret's lover, Borachio, convinces her to play a trick on her mistress, Hero. Margaret thinks the trick is a harmless jest, but she unintentionally makes it appear as if Hero is not chaste. When Leonato learns that Margaret is a party to the evil trick perpetrated by Don John and his men, Leonato very nearly punishes her. Only Borachio's defense of Margaret as having been an unwitting participant saves her from being punished. Margaret is not expected to be chaste, as Hero is, because Margaret is of the servant class for whom chastity is not as important. The role of a servant used to either betray or assist her mistress is a stock character in Shakespeare's comedies. Most of Margaret's spoken lines in the text are cut for the film. Many of her lines in the text are witty and somewhat sarcastic, but in the film, she is more an actor and less a speaker, which leaves her personality underdeveloped on film.

Don Pedro of Aragon

Don Pedro is played by Denzel Washington. He commands a troop of soldiers, who, as the film opens, have just returned from fighting in a war. Don Pedro and his men have done well and are acknowledged to be very brave and honorable men. Don Pedro is strongly focused on the importance of honor and wants all of his men to behave in an honorable manner. Although he is attracted to Beatrice, Don Pedro does the honorable thing and tries to match her with Benedick, whom Don Pedro knows is in love with her. Don Pedro backs up Claudio when it appears that Hero has been unchaste and shows no regret when told that she has died. Instead, Don Pedro appears satisfied that her death is a result of being identified as unchaste. Branagh captures Shakespeare's creation of Don Pedro as an idealized leader who always keeps the well-being of his subjects first in his mind and actions. At the end of the film, Don Pedro is standing alone and is clearly melancholy. He is the only character who seems left out of the celebration.

Ursula

The role of Ursula is played by Phyllida Law, who is Emma Thompson's mother in real life. Ursula is one of two maids in the household who function as Hero's confidantes. Her role is minimal, but she does bring word to Beatrice and Benedick that Hero has been found innocent of all changes and that Don John is guilty of plotting against Hero.

Verges

Verges, played by Ben Elton, is Dogberry's deputy and loyal minion. Verges is proud of his position and helps Dogberry in assigning duties to the watchmen. Much of the time, Verges stands behind or alongside Dogberry and admires his superior's position as constable.

THEMES

Communications

The ability to communicate well is a familiar theme in several of Shakespeare's comedies. Miscommunication and mistaken communication, or in the case of *Much Ado About Nothing*, no communication, are all issues in this film. Beatrice and Benedick unknowingly court one another via their verbal exchanges. They are both witty characters who trade barbed comments as a way to communicate with one another. They love each other, but neither of them is willing to communicate that love until each of them is told that he or she is loved in return. There is safety in knowing that love is returned. Both Beatrice and Benedick use words effectively. Their barbed exchanges form much of the humor in *Much Ado About Nothing*. For instance, Beatrice says to Benedick "How tartly that gentleman looks! I never can see him but I am heart-burned an hour later." Both Beatrice and Benedick enjoy these witty exchanges, which for them form a kind of courtship formula. As a result, communication, even the barbed sarcasm of these two characters, is an effective means to achieve closeness. In contrast, Hero and Claudio leave much unsaid. Claudio asks Don Pedro to speak for him to court Hero. As a modest young woman, Hero can say little and must wait for Claudio to initiate the courtship. The hyperbole of courtship language depends on exaggeration of one another's attributes, but this communication depends on even less reality and truth than the barbed wordplay that engages Beatrice and Benedick's attention. At their wedding, Claudio does not communicate directly with Hero. Instead, he speaks to her father, Leonato, telling him that his daughter only pretends to be pure. Hero is left standing, an outsider at her own wedding, as the two men in her life reject her.

READ, WATCH, WRITE

- The Dogberry character might be compared to Barney Fife, the role played by Don Knotts on the television program *The Andy Griffith Show*. Watch two or three episodes of this television show and study the Barney character. Then prepare an oral presentation in which you compare Barney and Dogberry and their separate approaches to maintaining the law. Include video clips from both *The Andy Griffith Show* and *Much Ado About Nothing* and discuss both the actor's portrayals and their skill in portraying these similar roles.

- The two brothers, Don Pedro and Don John, are similar to two brothers portrayed in Shakespeare's tragedy *King Lear*. Edgar and Edmund are also half-brothers, with one a legitimate heir and the other an illegitimate son who is a social and economic outcast. *Much Ado About Nothing* is a comedy, while *King Lear* is a tragedy. The actions of Don John and Edmund are based on many of the same feelings of being illegitimate and the desire to make someone pay for the bastard brother's suffering. There are a number of film adaptations of *King Lear*. Choose one of the films to watch and then write an essay in which you compare these two sets of brothers. Discuss their actions, their physical portrayal on screen by the actors cast in these roles, and the speeches they make to justify their actions.

- Read Shakespeare's play *Much Ado About Nothing*. After reading the play and watching the film, choose one scene that you think is especially important in revealing something critical about the characters's personalities, actions, and choices. Ask your friends to take on key roles in the scene you choose and have them act out a scene, using modern dress and modern language. Videotape the performance to show your classmates and then discuss what your classmates learned from seeing this scene in modern dress and language.

- *Much Ado About Nothing* includes two different romantic pairings, with two distinctive and different gender-assigned roles. Hero is happy to assume the traditional dependent role in her relationship with Claudio. Beatrice is more independent and rejects that traditional role. Watch the film with a partner and study the actions of these two characters, each of you focusing on one character. Take careful notes describing what you observe and then prepare a debate with your partner debating the virtue of his or her character's choices while you debate the choices that your character makes. Ask your classmates to vote on which character they most identify with.

- Although set in Messina, the behavior of Shakespeare's characters is based on English custom and moral codes. Research marriage rituals and traditions in Renaissance England and write a paper in which you explain how these customs are portrayed in *Much Ado About Nothing*.

- Read the 2012 young-adult novel *In the Bag* by Kate Klise. This is also about miscommunication and witty exchanges between a couple who do not yet realize they should be a couple. Compare this romantic couple to Beatrice and Benedick. What do you notice about their communication style and how they solve differences? In a class presentation, read relevant sections from the novel and compare them to similar scenes from the film. Ask your classmates to tell you what they learned about communication and communication styles.

- Research the re-created Globe Theatre in London, where *Much Ado About Nothing* was performed in the summer of 2011. Create a PowerPoint presentation that includes diagrams of the theater, including the stage area and seating for the audience. Be sure to include information about costuming and staging of plays.

© *Pictorial Press Ltd / Alamy*

As was the case with Claudio's excessive claims of love, his rejection of Hero is filled with hyperbole. Shakespeare also uses communication as slapstick humor. Instead of physical pratfalls, Dogberry is guilty of verbal pratfalls. His vocabulary is quite extensive, but like a student who relies on a thesaurus to choose words, Dogberry's use of language is just a bit off kilter. He chooses words that sound similar to the words he really wants to use, but within the context of his speech, the words do not fit correctly; as a result, his communication is filled with holes and malapropisms and a series of confusing phrases.

Illegitimacy

Much Ado About Nothing contains an important plot arc that explores illegitimacy. Don John is the half-brother of Don Pedro but is also known as "the bastard." Don John cannot inherit legally because he is not a legitimate offspring. This accounts for his melancholy and his plotting against his brother. The war that Don Pedro and his men fought before the film and play began was a rebellion led by Don John. Don John will never have the social status given to his brother. He cannot rise to the same level of aristocracy and wealth as Don Pedro. Although the setting is Messina, the play is about English values. In Renaissance England an illegitimate son could not inherit his father's estate. As a result, the bastard son, Don John, will always be dependent on his legitimate half-brother for support and care and will never have the life of privilege that Don Pedro enjoys.

Truth

The events in *Much Ado About Nothing* move quickly and without a lot of rational thought. There is insufficient time for truth seeking, which leads to a near disaster for Hero and Claudio's romance. When confronted with the seeming evidence of Hero's disloyalty, Claudio never bothers to ask Hero if she was sleeping in her room while Margaret was engaged with her lover. The truth was there all the time, but it is buried under a superficiality that forces the action to keep moving quickly toward the conclusion. Margaret never admits that she was in Hero's room, and no one ever asks why she was in Hero's room. The words of others are not designated as truth. Instead, Claudio and Don Pedro trust what they think they see. Only after the evidence against Don John is irrefutable, does Claudio recognize the truth, but he has required proof of law and the testimony of the arrested conspirators. Neither Hero's words nor those of others are counted as truth until the law pronounces the truth. Truth also underlies the pranks played on Beatrice and Benedick to force them to admit their love for one another. Neither of them can admit the truth since each one fears rejection by the other. More importantly, neither one wants to acknowledge that he or she loves the other. Even in the final scene of the film, they deny that they love one another. By then, the audience does not know if what is being shown on stage and in film is the truth and that they have witnessed the blossoming of true love. However, the reality of true love is completely unimportant at the moment, since the film presents a happy ending.

STYLE

Costuming

The setting for *Much Ado About Nothing* is the Tuscan countryside. The film does not evoke a specific period or date. The women wear loose-fitting white gowns with low necklines and soft, flowing cloth. The top button on Beatrice's gown is left undone, and the gown thus focuses on the character's femininity even though her speech is strong and assertive. The effect is one of sexual innocence since the women are unmarried and virginal, as the white color suggests. The loose-fitting gowns are also sensual and reflect the heat of the Messina countryside and the fecundity that awaits in marriage. The women's hair is undone and worn loose and unkempt, which also reveals an informality and a suggestion of sexuality. Several of the men are either shirtless or have their shirts partially undone, further emphasizing the potential sexuality of the relationships between men and women. The men's uniforms are undone at the top in an informal style that makes clear that they are no longer at battle. While the men carry swords and march with authority, they are not menacing. The heat of the Italian countryside is reflected in the choice of costuming.

Phyllis Dalton, who designed the costumes for *Much Ado About Nothing*, was nominated for Best Costume Design by the British Academy Film Awards.

Music

There are a number of vocal and instrumental numbers in *Much Ado About Nothing*. The music is intended to establish the mood of the film, which is why the song, "Sigh No More, Ladies," which opens the film and appears twice more is so important. The melancholy words of this song warn of men as deceivers and caution women not to sing more love ditties for men. The manner in which this song is sung fits the action of the play. In the first scene, Beatrice sings the song as contemplative, which sets the tone for the film to follow. Later the song appears in a romanticized garden setting, while in the final scene, the song is sung joyously, as if the words of warning no longer matter amid so much festivity.

Another vocal is the song "Pardon, Goddess of the Night," which is a mournful song performed at Hero's memorial service. The tone of this song fits with Claudio's realization that his distrust of Hero and his rejection of her is responsible for her death. This music is reminiscent of a funeral dirge and is accompanied by Claudio's weeping.

The instrumental music is often adapted to fit the changing tone of the film. In the scene after Benedick overhears that Beatrice loves him, he speaks of his happiness. As Benedick speaks, the music builds to a crescendo with the strings of the orchestra matching Benedick's mood. In the next scene, Beatrice overhears a similar story about Benedick's love for her. The music is whimsical and light to match the tenor of the joke being played upon Beatrice. Once the joke is firmly played and both Beatrice and Benedick have been convinced that each is in love with the other, the music is joyous and happy with much reliance upon percussion and cymbals to celebrate their happiness.

Setting

Shakespeare sets *Much Ado About Nothing* in Sicily, but director Branagh chose Tuscany for the film because he thought the landscapes of Tuscany were more lush and more verdant. The area is filled with olive trees and vines that have existed for centuries and aid in creating a romantic and sensual film without evoking a specific period. The wealth of greenery is meant to evoke thoughts of an idyllic paradise. In the film's opening scene, the picnic is staged amid a lush field of grasses and flowers. When the women learn that Don Pedro and his men will arrive soon, the camera follows them dancing across the field in what is easily seen to be an idyllic pasture-like setting. The heat of the location adds to the sensual nature of a play that is focused on love and marriage and the importance of sexual purity even as the landscape suggests unrestrained sexuality.

Stock Characters

Stock characters are not unusual in theater or film or literature. They provide conventional character types that make it easy for the audience to identify key roles. Many of these roles are easy to identify in *Much Ado About Nothing*. The clown (Dogberry) is a common role in Shakespearean theater; the many others include the scheming villain (Don John), the innocent virgin (Hero), the sharp-witted unmarried older woman (Beatrice), the foolish or confused father (Leonato), and the female servant-confidante (Margaret). These characters behave in easily identified ways that quickly help the audience grasp the intricacies of the plot. Knowing who are stock characters in a play or film also helps the audience distinguish between stock behaviors and deviations from the plot. For instance, the friar is a stock character in many Shakespearean plays. Making fun of friars and other church officials is common in British literature, as in Chaucer's *Canterbury Tales* and in Shakespeare's plays such as *Henry V*, where church officials are scheming to protect their wealth. In *Romeo and Juliet*, the friar's actions are one cause of the tragedy, but in *Much Ado About Nothing*, Friar Francis behaves counter to character and acts to save Hero. Knowing how certain stock characters are supposed to function adds to the audience's enjoyment of the play or film.

CULTURAL CONTEXT

Love, Courtship, and Marriage in Elizabethan England

Much Ado About Nothing might be set in Messina, Italy, but regardless of where the play is set, the characters and their actions are always English. That is why it is important to understand how love, courtship, and marriage functioned in Shakespeare's England. Although *Much Ado About Nothing* appears to suggest to the audience that love is an important part of Elizabethan courtship and marriage, nothing could be less true. In Shakespeare's day, marriage was more often a business arrangement that benefited both sets of parents. Marriages were arranged, and the more noble or aristocratic the couple, the less likely it was that love played any role. In many cases, the bride and groom might never have met before the marriage was arranged although the man might have been shown a miniature portrait of the woman to help finalize the deal. For lower-class couples, marriage might also settle an old grudge between neighbors or cement a property exchange, but love was not the critical component that Shakespeare's play or Branagh's film suggests.

While *Much Ado About Nothing* does not make clear Hero's age, she would have been old enough to marry, since marriage was legal anytime after age twelve. However, most women did not marry until much later, often closer to age twenty or older. Couples did not date, and they were not often left alone. The families of both partners would be involved during the courtship stage, and once an agreement to wed was reached, the couple would be required to join

hands in a symbolic promise betrothal. Technically, the couple could call one another husband and wife after this hand-fasting ceremony, but to be legally wed, the couple would next be required to publish the banns of marriage at their church for three Sundays. This constituted a public announcement of their intention to marry. If no one objected to the proposed marriage, the couple could then be married in their church. All of these steps take a good deal of time, and thus, both the initial and the second hastily planned marriages between Hero and Claudio, as well as Benedick's same-day request of the friar to marry Beatrice, could not have happened as they do in the play. At least a month, if not more time, would have to elapse between the initial promise to marry and the actual wedding. Should a woman be pregnant before marriage, a legal swearing that neither couple had entered into a previous contract to marry might cut the waiting time to one week of published banns, thus permitting a more hasty wedding.

Marriage during Shakespeare's time was primarily about creating a legal contract that involved wealth and property. Although a priest or the family friar would likely officiate, the wedding was not first and foremost a religious event. The purpose of marriage was to ensure the familial and financial status of a family line. A marriage contract, then, was a legal document that united a man and a woman of a similar social class that was intended to guarantee the legal status and inheritance of any children that might result from the union. Before marrying, the parents of both the bride and the groom had to agree upon a dowry to be paid to the groom's family. The dowry spelled out a monetary exchange, whether in land, money, or goods. In the film *Much Ado About Nothing*, Claudio is told that Hero is the sole heir to Leonato's estates, but there is no mention of a dowry, which would have been quite common. It was also common to discuss a jointure in case the husband died so that his widow would not be left penniless after his death.

Chastity

A woman's chastity and virtue were much prized by prospective grooms and closely guarded by male relatives during the English Renaissance. A woman was worth more in a marriage contract if she was pure, and indeed, her chastity was often praised as essential to her ability to secure a successful match. During the English Renaissance,

© AF Archive / Alamy

women were made respectable and worthy of marriage if they were also pure. Chastity not only meant a man need not worry that another man had fathered his heirs, it also meant that a woman was able to exercise control over lust. Her ability to remain pure for marriage was seen as a positive character trait. In England, the clergy preached about the importance of chastity in their sermons, and church courts were often willing to excommunicate women who had violated rules of chastity.

Another reason that chastity was so valued is that a chaste wife adds to a man's honor. In short, female chastity equals male honor. The man is in control of his household, which we see in *Much Ado About Nothing*, when Leonato is shamed by Hero's perceived loss of purity. Women are property in marriage and in the family. Fathers who fail to control their daughters are as bad as husbands who fail to control their wives. The man's reputation is at stake. One reason that Don John chooses to target Hero is that Don Pedro has pushed for the match between Claudio and Hero. If Don Pedro is wrong about the purity of the intended bride and she is therefore not a suitable bride, his

honor is diminished. That explains why he does not hesitate to accuse Hero once he thinks they have irrefutable evidence against her. In a stratified society such as the one depicted in *Much Ado About Nothing*, Don Pedro is an aristocrat. Leonato maintains his own honor by rejecting his daughter, who he believes has been promiscuous and has dishonored the family by failing to obey her father and remain chaste.

CRITICAL OVERVIEW

Branagh might have worried that his choice to include American actors in a film of Shakespeare's *Much Ado About Nothing* would be controversial for some critics. He probably also suspected that his cuts to Shakespeare's text might elicit some complaints, which might explain why the film was released in the United States before it was released in England. But in fact, most reviews of *Much Ado About Nothing* were quite positive. This was certainly the case for Vincent Canby's review in the *New York Times*. Canby notes that Branagh's film is accessible to everyone and especially viewers who are not familiar with the Shakespearean play.

Canby labels *Much Ado About Nothing* a film that "uncovers a radiant heart." With regard to Branagh directorial choices, Canby writes that Branagh has "made a movie that is triumphantly romantic, comic and, most surprising of all, emotionally alive." Although Canby wishes for fewer close-ups of Branagh and Thompson, he finds little else to dislike in what he claims is "ravishing entertainment."

In his review for the *Washington Post*, Desson Howe also observes the ease with which Branagh has made Shakespeare accessible to modern audiences. Howe compliments Branagh for having "blown away the forbidding academic dust" of Shakespearean comedy. Thanks to Branagh, suggests Howe, even Shakespeare's language is given "modern life" and made more enjoyable. Branagh's changes to Shakespeare's text are just fine with Howe, who finds these textual alterations made "imaginatively." Although the American actors might not all be perfect in their use of Shakespeare's language, for Howe these few problems fail to distract from the "poetic flame" of the original play.

In Roger Ebert's review of *Much Ado About Nothing* for the *Chicago Sun Times*, Ebert cites the opening scene of the film as a predictor for the kind of movie that audiences will be watching. Branagh opens the film with a scene full of "healthy, joyful young people" singing and dancing amid flowers and verdant hillsides. According to Ebert, these are characters who will be able to survive "the dark double-crosses of Shakespeare's plot." The film's progression through a series of dinners and banquets and dances amid courtships is appealing to Ebert, as is the rapid pace of the film, which the critic thinks moves along at a pace "just this side of a Marx Brothers movie." However, in addition to verdant hills, lively entertainment, or a fast pace, what really works for Ebert are the lead actors, especially Thompson and Branagh, who "aim their insults so lovingly that we realize, sooner than they do, how much they would miss their verbal duets." Ebert ends his review by noting that this production of *Much Ado About Nothing* is especially appealing to the non-Shakespearean scholar in the audience, who can enjoy this film and who will find that Branagh has taken Shakespeare's text and given it "its own reality," which makes it accessible to everyone.

In contrast, the review in *Rolling Stone* by Peter Travers makes clear that Travers is less enamored

> INDEED, IN *MUCH ADO ABOUT NOTHING,* SHAKESPEAREAN COMEDY IS TRANSFORMED INTO FAIRY-TALE ROMANCE WHERE THE REALITIES OF HONOR AND DISHONOR ARE ECLIPSED BY THE IDEALIZED ROMANCE OF A FAIRY-TALE WEDDING. "

of Branagh's vision for *Much Ado About Nothing*. Travers thinks that much of the film "is overripe." After complaining that Branagh "doesn't know when to stop," Travers also complains about the actors, who are, with the exception of Thompson and Washington, too "overripe" as well, with performances that are, as in the case of Branagh, "a ham in thrall to his plummy vocal dexterity." Clearly, Travers is not as enthralled with *Much Ado About Nothing* as are other reviewers who found much to enjoy in this revisioning of Shakespeare's *Much Ado About Nothing*.

CRITICISM

Sheri Karmiol

Karmiol is a university lecturer in interdisciplinary studies. In the following essay, she discusses how chastity, honor, and romantic comedy are presented as an idyllic fairy-tale romance in Branagh's film version of Much Ado About Nothing.

Shakespeare's plays are most often divided into easy-to-define genres of tragedy, comedy, history, and romance. These divisions are often used in classrooms as a quick and easy way to discuss the plays. *Much Ado About Nothing* is always included in the list of comedies. It appears chronologically just after *The Merry Wives of Windsor* and just before *As You Like It*. Scholars have no doubt where *Much Ado About Nothing* belongs. It is a comedy—except in Branagh's hands, where Shakespeare's comedy is transformed into romance. Indeed, in *Much Ado About Nothing*, Shakespearean comedy is transformed into fairy-tale romance where the realities of honor and dishonor are eclipsed by the idealized romance of a fairy-tale wedding.

In the book of the same title that Branagh wrote to accompany the release of *Much Ado*

WHAT DO I READ NEXT?

- The 1973 film *Much Ado About Nothing* is a filmed presentation of the New York Shakespeare Festival and was also shown on CBS. This film stars Sam Waterson (Benedick) and Kathleen Widdoes (Beatrice) and is directed by Nick Havinga and produced by Joseph Papp. It differs from the Branagh *Much Ado About Nothing* in that it is a filmed play. This unrated film is available as a DVD from Kultur Studio (165 minutes).

- Another Shakespearean romantic comedy, *As You Like It*, was filmed in 2006, and stars David Oyelowo (Orlando), Alfred Molina (Touchstone), Kevin Kline (Jaques), Richard Briers (Adam), and Bryce Dallas Howard (Rosalind). *As You Like It* is about mistaken identity, mistaken gender, the pursuit of love, and star-crossed lovers. Branagh directed this film of *As You Like It*, which was released by Medusa Video (127 minutes). This film is rated PG.

- *Twelfth Night* (1996) is another Shakespearean play adapted to film. This comedy is about mistaken identity, mistaken gender, and the games that are played when people are in love. *Twelfth Night* stars Helena Bonham Carter (Olivia), Imogen Stubbs (Viola), Steven Mackintosh (Sebastian), and Toby Stephens (Duke Orsino) and is directed by Trevor Nunn. The DVD was released by Image Entertainment (134 minutes). This film is rated PG.

- In 1989, Branagh directed and stared as *Henry V*. This film adaptation of Shakespeare's history play of the same name focuses on King Henry's decision to invade France and fight a war to regain a portion of France that by inheritance belongs to the English king. *Henry V* also stars Derek Jacobi (Chorus), Brian Blessed (Exeter), Richard Briers (Bardolph), Judi Dench (Mistress Quickly), Paul Scofield (King Charles VI of France), and Emma Thompson (Katherine). The music is by Patrick Doyle. The DVD was released by MGM (137 minutes). This film is rated PG-13.

- Although most of the Shakespearean films that Branagh has chosen to direct are adaptations of the original plays, *Hamlet* is a four-hour rendering of the Shakespearean tragedy with almost every word of the original play spoken on screen. *Hamlet* is about deception, spying, betrayal, revenge, and murder, all set in Denmark after the mysterious death of King Hamlet. Branagh directs and stars (Hamlet) in this film. *Hamlet* also stars Julie Christie (Gertrude), Derek Jacobi (Claudius), Kate Winslet (Ophelia), Michael Maloney (Laertes), Richard Briers (Polonius), Brian Blessed (Ghost of Hamlet's father), Judi Dench (Hecuba), and Robin Williams (Osric). Warner Home Video released the DVD (242 minutes). This film is rated PG-13.

- The 2000 film adaptation of *Love's Labour's Lost*, another Shakespearean comedy, was directed by Branagh, who also stars (as Berowne). *Love's Labour's Lost* is about a man who swears off women, but then meets a woman he cannot resist. Additional actors include Alicia Silverstone (Princess), Emily Mortimer (Katherine), Nathan Lane (Costard), Timothy Spall (Armado), Natasha McElhone (Rosaline), and Richard Briers (Sir Nathaniel). This musical incorporates the music of Cole Porter, Irving Berlin, Jerome Kern, as well as others. The DVD was released by Miramax (93 minutes). This film is rated PG.

- *Shakespeare, the Animated Tales*, were created between 1992 and 1994 by the BBC. The entire set of twelve plays was released on DVD by Ambrose Video (300 minutes). The animated films are not rated.

About Nothing, he writes that the film is deliberately lacking in identifying costumes or setting that might impede the audience's imagination. Branagh did not want the members of the audience to be focused on anything that might distract them from the words and actions that appear on film. Instead, Branagh wanted his audience to see *Much Ado About Nothing* as a romantic fairy tale and as a product of imagination that emerges on film from the countryside where the cast was filming. Branagh notes that the filming took place in Tuscany with "a magical landscape of vines and olives that seems untouched by much of modern life." This setting creates a backdrop to the film that seems more magical than real. This is where Branagh could create "a visual idyll" that would propel the story toward a romantic ideal, which is in keeping with the fairy-tale motif. Even the opening of the film, which first appears as a watercolor painting of a beautiful idyllic villa before dissolving into a lush, verdant hillside picnic, fits the idealized romantic fairy-tale genre.

Of course, there is nothing especially romantic or fairy tale-like about the Claudio that Shakespeare envisioned. In Shakespeare's play, Claudio is pragmatic and focused on Hero's wealth as Leonato's only heir. Claudio may love Hero, but love is not sufficient reason to marry. In his screenplay, Branagh eliminates Claudio's question to Don Pedro, "Hath Leonato any son, my lord?" The only reason to ask this question is to determine Hero's financial worth, and Claudio asks this question before agreeing to have Don Pedro woo her for him. He may be inexperienced with love, but Claudio understands the importance of economics in marriage, as does Don Pedro, who endorses Claudio's suit. Claudio has no problem allowing Don Pedro to do his wooing for him, and Don Pedro's social position and his friendship with Claudio make the latter's suit more attractive to both Hero and her father. In Shakespeare's text, Claudio has no qualms about using Don Pedro's aristocratic lineage to his advantage. However, Branagh makes this wooing of Hero less about money and status by making his Claudio appear especially young and inexperienced. Robert Sean Leonard plays Claudio as youthful and innocent, as if he were barely out of his teens. In her review of both the film and Branagh's own published book about the filming of *Much Ado About Nothing* in the *New York Review of Books*, Anne Barton points out that Leonard's Claudio

is played as "much less sophisticated and knowing than Shakespeare's character." The Claudio depicted in Branagh's film is, according to Barton, "meant to be a very young man, barely past adolescence, who remains...emotionally vulnerable and unsure" of himself. As a result, the audience sees a filmed Claudio who is steeped in innocence and romantic idealism. Instead of Shakespeare's cad, Claudio becomes the romantic fairy-tale prince whose job is to be happily married to the princess at the conclusion of the story.

It is not just the casting of Leonard as Claudio that transforms this character from Shakespeare's vision to Branagh's vision. In her essay "'Silence is the perfectest herald of joy': The Claudio-Hero Plot in Kenneth Branagh's *Much Ado About Nothing*," Sofía Muñoz Valdivieso looks at the textual deletions in Shakespeare's play and the camera shots that Branagh utilizes in the film. Valdivieso argues that, through these changes, Branagh "tries to dissolve the dark strain of cruelty in the Claudio-Hero story so as to subsume it into the bright festivity that shines through the action." Valdivieso notes the many close-ups of Hero's and Claudio's faces, which are designed to show blushing romance to the viewing audience. Shakespeare's play often presents Hero as a strong but opinionated maiden, but since Shakespeare provides no stage directions, Branagh is free to keep her silent and let the camera linger on her adoring face as she gazes at Claudio. Branagh eliminates Claudio's speeches in the fifth act of the play that reveal him to be cold, calculating, and cruel. With textual deletions and camera use, Branagh's film attempts to cast Claudio as a deceived groom who is reconciled with his bride as a result of Dogberry's efforts. It is the comedy of Dogberry that helps to overshadow the less than appetizing darker moments in the film.

It is important to understand how valued chastity was during Shakespeare's time. Chastity ensures that a man's sons and heirs are his own. He is not leaving his titles and estate to another man's offspring. Hero qualifies as a perfect bride for two reasons. She is wealthy, as has been established, and she is a virgin. Claudio expects to marry a chaste bride, but the trick that is played by Don John makes Hero appear to have been unfaithful to Claudio. If Claudio continues with the wedding after learning that Hero has been unfaithful, his honor will be diminished. To Don Pedro, who is Spanish, honor, especially the honor of aristocrats, is how he defines his own life; as a young, impressionable nobleman, Claudio emulates Don Pedro in many things, including this notion of honor's importance. To retain his honor, Claudio must reject Hero, but he chooses to do so very publicly at their wedding. In Shakespeare's text, Claudio says, "If I see anything tonight why I should not marry her, tomorrow, in the congregation where I should wed, there will I shame her." Claudio does not say he will expose Hero or reject her. Instead, he will *shame* her and destroy any possibility that she might be judged honorable. A private rejection would have been kinder, but Claudio has no kindness in him. Branagh cannot eliminate the harshness of the rejection on screen, but he deletes these words and substitutes a camera shot of Claudio with tears in his eyes when he learns that his intended bride has betrayed him. When offered Hero's cousin as a bride, Claudio quickly accepts since this new bride will inherit what Hero would have inherited had she lived.

To make *Much Ado About Nothing* work as romance, Branagh has to do more than make Hero and Claudio look like innocent, love-struck teenagers. He has to defuse the dark plot that attacks Hero's reputation. Revealing the truth about Don John's plot is not the problem. It is necessary to redeem Claudio, who not only insults Hero on their wedding day, calling her a "rotten orange" and "an approved wanton," and even throwing her to the ground. Don Pedro also joins the attack and claims that he stands dishonored because he contrived to "link my dear friend to a common stale." The attack on Hero is done in front of a hundred guests who have gathered for this wedding. In publicly shaming her, Claudio rejects his fairy-tale prince status for that of the villain, but it is always necessary for Branagh to redeem this young hero. To make Claudio seem more sympathetic as he does this, Branagh shows Margaret having sex with Borachio as they appear in the window. This scene is not shown in Shakespeare's play. There, Claudio only learns that Borachio was in Hero's bedroom; the explicit sexuality of the scene is not part of Shakespeare's play, but for Branagh to make Claudio's actions less distasteful, he must appear as the grievously wronged prince. Thus the scene in the window is included and expanded upon in the film.

To create the required romantic ending, Branagh has to find a way to make Claudio more palatable for the audience. In the play Claudio visits Hero's tomb after he learns of her innocence. He reads a scroll that he has presumably written proclaiming her innocence. He then fastens the epitaph to the wall of her monument. Claudio promises to repeat his visit to Hero's tomb each year and then wishes his companions good night and leaves. He is not weeping, nor does he appear especially remorseful. In contrast, in the filmed version, Branagh has the camera focus on a weeping Claudio who appears barely able to control himself as he mourns at Hero's tomb. Claudio's grief make clear that the fault for Hero's death lies with Don John and Borachio, not with Claudio himself. In keeping with the romance genre, Dogberry and his men provide the information that clears Hero's name and allows the fairy-tale wedding at the conclusion. This is achieved via a *deux ex machina* twist in the plot. The sole purpose of the *deux ex machina* is to introduce either a character or an event that solves an insolvable problem. Dogberry plays this role, clearing Hero's name, which allows a wedding and the plot resolution to take place.

The entire notion of romance in *Much Ado About Nothing* is carefully calculated to appear authentic and happenstance. Don Pedro speaks words of love to Hero not for himself but for Claudio, who is apparently in love with Hero but cannot tell her so. He can, however, reject her totally and competently soon enough. He has no problem speaking up at that point. Claudio loves her so little that he rejects her based on evidence that is entirely fabricated; only when she is proved innocent beyond a doubt is he capable of mourning her death—something he did not do previously. To assuage his honor he agrees to marry a woman he has neither met nor seen. The entire romance, denunciation, mourning, and second wedding create a contrived romance that is indeed about nothing, but they are in keeping with the notion of a romantic fairy tale. Branagh takes his audience outside into bright sunlight. With Hero's earlier pain forgotten and Claudio's lines in the final act of Shakespeare's text nearly completely eliminated, the film is able to achieve its romantic ending. As an audience, we enjoy the illusion of romance and a happy ending, but for Hero and Claudio, romance and love might only be an illusion fostered upon them by an audience who wishes to

© *AF Archive | Alamy*

see this couple wed. In Shakespeare's play, tragedy hovers just below the surface. In a different ending, Hero might really have died and her innocence established only after her death. Because *Much Ado About Nothing* is a comedy and not a tragedy, the play requires a different ending. Hero and Claudio wed, but a cynical viewer might wonder if this marriage appears as little more than an arrangement needed to fulfill the required romance of *Much Ado About Nothing*.

Source: Sheri Karmiol, Critical Essay on *Much Ado About Nothing*, in *Drama for Students*, Gale, Cengage Learning, 2013.

Richard Alleva

In the following review, Alleva examines the value of each actor cast in the film adaptation.

Theater critics can break your heart with their eloquence about performances that are no more. When Stark Young tells us that one of Doris Keane's was ". . . all music and security of outline, like a swan on water, and something we long to believe can never cease to exist," we must take his word for it because that performance has ceased and now lives only in Young's prose.

But Emma Thompson's Beatrice is ours forever. This definitive performance is on film.

So you don't have to take my word for it that Thompson begins the movie, *Much Ado About Nothing*, by reading the words of the song, "Sigh no more, ladies," with inflections that not only mock love but mock the mockery of love, that make us share Beatrice's double realization that love makes us fools and that love is inescapable. And don't trust me when I say that all the following is so: In the masquerade ball, Thompson shows us with the tiniest shift of facial expression the exact moment when Beatrice realizes that her disguised tormentor is Benedick, and that the discovery now enables her to torment him.

In her reply to Don Pedro's teasing "you have lost the heart of Signor Benedick," Thompson doesn't rattle out the words ("he lent it me awhile; and I gave him use for it," etc.) in the way most actresses do, like Vassar girls at a 1920s' mixer, but speaks as a woman who has been Benedick's lover already, been trifled with, and doesn't intend to be burned again. This emotional weighting of a passage usually passed off as banter gives the Benedick-Beatrice sparring matches a background that deepens them, embitters them.

And, in the play's most famous scene, when Benedick calls upon Beatrice to set him a task that will prove his love, Thompson's "Kill Claudio!" is limpid rage springing out of her bottomless love for her wronged cousin, Hero. It is as great a piece of acting as I ever hope to see on screen or stage.

And must you credit me when I state that the actress does all of the above without sacrificing any of the lightness, speed, or fun of her role? No! Emma Thompson's Beatrice flourishes in technicolor in a theater near you. Drop this magazine and go.

Those readers who haven't instantly obeyed me will now be punished with a lot of pro and contra concerning the rest of the movie.

Kenneth Branagh's production is handsome, brainy, purposefully bustling, securely paced, well-attuned to Shakespeare's unblinkered view of humanity. Branagh has done what any good director does with any complex play: he has seized upon the reality of the central situation. The igniting action of *Much Ado* is the return of soldiers from war, danger, enforced celibacy, and their entrance into a household full of friendly, nubile women. Branagh makes this fact so alive for us in the first ten minutes that everything else naturally flows out of it.

The setting is Shakespeare's Italianate one but relocated to a sort of streamlined version of the nineteenth century. The cavaliers crest a hill overlooking a Tuscan villa. The music—Patrick Doyle's score is irresistibly Bacchic—drowns out any shouts from the men but we can read the expressions on their faces. They are beautifully lustful. And down in the villa, the news of the army's approach has caused a frenzy. The women strip and bathe and we catch brief glimpses of their nakedness before they throw on their finery. Soon the soldiers, in another part of the estate, are also naked as they plunge into a pond and then suit up in formal attire. Once all the

uniforms of peace, male and female, are on, war breaks out again, the war of love that can be waged now that mortal combat is finished.

The heat of the Italian summer never lets the heat of battle die down. Cicadas drone as young Claudio reveals his love of Hero to Don Pedro, and the sun beats down as they rehearse the tactics necessary to capture the lady. But though the maneuver goes according to plan only a few hours later, Claudio already seems to have forgotten about it and suspects his senior officer of having swiped his girl. Reading the play, one may suspect Shakespeare of nodding or we may give up on Claudio as a dolt; but in all the drowsy, droning, bemusing sunlight with which Branagh fills the screen, everything seems to proceed with logical craziness. Branagh has made *Much Ado* into *A Midsummer Day's Dream*, and the lovers behave as they do because they are dazzled by sunlight, exhilarated and exhausted by heat, blinded by the physical beauty of flowers and flesh, and always at least a little pixilated from being young, alive, and accepted.

For me, this is a convincing view of the play and everything Branagh does with camera, cutting, physical setting, costume, and music realizes his conception. His use of the Tuscan villa is often inventive, always appropriate: when the treacherous Don John and his cronies conspire to destroy love, they are in an underground stone room where the sunlight that so intoxicates sweethearts is sealed off. When Benedick and Beatrice, warm for each other but dismayed by the disaster that has overtaken the younger lovers, declare their hearts, it is in a chapel that is well lit but roofed against the heat.

Yet all is not well with this movie. Shakespeare's plays are supreme in their characterizations, and I am forced to note that not only no other performance in this movie matches Thompson's (that would be too much to expect) but that, of the several male roles, only two are fulfilled, Richard Briers is ripe as Leonato and, as his brother, Brian Blessed, is maturely cherubic. But the rest of the males, the young males who must give this play its fire and commotion (Beatrice giving it heart and wit), are all problematic, and the best of the lot—Branagh himself—is the most problematic of all.

Robert Scan Leonard has the basic substance for Claudio. The fire of first love is in his eyes and he convincingly shows how such unconditional adoration can turn into equally unconditional hate. But his diction wavers and, both in speech and deportment, he brings America too insistently into this utterly European work of art.

Denzel Washington, on the other hand, is well-spoken as Don Pedro and cuts a fine figure. Yet this is a callow performance, more like a warm-up than a finished work. Don Pedro can certainly be played by a young actor but the seniority of rank and pride of command must be communicated. Washington seems detached rather than lordly.

Keanu Reeves is quite bad as Don John. He holds onto one sneering note throughout and never shows us the villain's pleasure in his own malice.

Michael Keaton apparently decided that Dogberry's troubles with the English language are rooted in fundamental problems with the human race, so he plays the constable as a comic psychotic receiving his thoughts from some alien's spaceship in the heavens. Keaton is often fascinating in his weirdness but never funny. And he and director Branagh have severely damaged the movie by allowing Dogberry to maul and gouge not only the villains that the constable captures but his own deputies. And he trots about on an imaginary horse. Dogberry can be convincingly portrayed as quietly mad but not as openly, dangerously crazy, for then why would the sane citizens of Messina accept him as a guardian of civic order?

Like Keaton's Dogberry, Kenneth Branagh's Benedick is a performance wriggling in the grip of a concept. But, unlike Keaton, Branagh finally wriggles free and delivers a human being. Branagh's Benedick is a fellow who has diminished himself by denying his feeling toward Beatrice. When he is tricked into admitting to himself his love, he becomes whole. Good approach, but I found the actor's execution of it too blatant in the play's first half. Trying to establish Benedick's foolishness, Branagh screeches, caws like a crow, does unfunny bits with collapsing chairs. This excess backfires because it keeps us from seeing Benedick's potential, the compassion and true wit that will be released once he becomes a worthy lover. After all, no matter how captious he may be toward Beatrice, Benedick is well regarded by his fellow soldiers and courtiers. After the mutual declaration of love, Branagh is splendid: ardent with his lover, sagacious in aiding the slandered family,

and (how rare this is with most Benedicks!) truly menacing when he challenges Claudio.

A great Shakespeare film? No, it hasn't got a majority of successful performances. But it does have what few Shakespeare films, what few movies of any sort, possess: zest.

And there's always Emma Thompson, wit of the sixteenth century (courtesy of Shakespeare), sensual apparition of nineteenth-century Italy (courtesy of this production), and heroine of the 1990s. Courtesy of herself.

Source: Richard Alleva, Review of *Much Ado About Nothing*, in *Commonweal*, Vol. 120, No. 12, June 18, 1993.

SOURCES

Amussen, Susan Dwyer, *An Ordered Society: Gender and Class in Early Modern England*, Oxford University Press, 1988, pp. 70–76, 104–11, 116–17.

Barton, Anne, "Shakespeare in the Sun," in *New York Review of Books*, May 27, 1993, http://www.nybooks.com/articles/archives/1993/may/27/shakespeare-in-the-sun/?pagination=false (accessed August 14, 2012).

Branagh, Kenneth, *Much Ado About Nothing by William Shakespeare: Screenplay, Introduction, and Notes on the Making of the Movie*, W. W. Norton, 1993.

Brugger, William, "Sins of Omission: Textual Deletions in Branagh's *Much Ado About Nothing*," in *Journal of the Wooden O Symposium*, Vol. 3, 2003, pp. 1–11.

Canby, Vincent, Review of *Much Ado About Nothing*, in *New York Times*, May 7, 1993, http://movies.nytimes.com/movie/review?res=9F0CE7DD133DF934A35756C0A965958260 (accessed July 26, 2012).

Crowl, Samuel, *Shakespeare and Film: A Norton Guide*, W. W. Norton, 2008, pp. 162–65, 191–92.

Ebert, Roger, Review of *Much Ado About Nothing*, in *Chicago Sun-Times*, May 21, 1993, http://rogerebert.suntimes.com/apps/pbcs.dll/article?AID=/19930521/REVIEWS/305210302/1023 (accessed July 26, 2012).

Harmon, William, and Hugh Holman, *A Handbook to Literature*, 11th ed., Pearson Prentice Hall, 2009, pp. 508, 527.

Howe, Desson, Review of *Much Ado About Nothing*, in *Washington Post*, May 21, 1993, http://www.washingtonpost.com/wp-srv/style/longterm/movies/videos/muchadoaboutnothingpg13howe_a0afbc.htm (accessed July 26, 2012).

Marner, Bruce, *Film Production Technique: Creating the Accomplished Image*, 5th edition, Thomson Gale, 2008, pp. 10–12, 28–31.

McDonald, Russ, "Men and Women: Gender, Family, and Society," in *Bedford Companion to Shakespeare*, 2nd ed., Bedford/St. Martins, 2001, pp. 253–72, 292–93.

Much Ado About Nothing, DVD, Samuel Goldwyn, 1993.

Santas, Constantine, *Responding to Film: A Text Guide for Students of Cinema Art*, Rowman & Littlefield, 2002, pp. 57–67.

Shakespeare, William, *Much Ado About Nothing*, in *The Norton Shakespeare, Based on the Oxford Edition: Comedies*, edited by Stephen Greenblatt, W. W. Norton, 1997, pp. 521–84.

Sheppard, Philippa, "'Sigh no more Ladies'—the Song in Much Ado About Nothing: Shakespeare and Branagh Deliver Aural Pleasure," in *Literature/Film Quarterly*, Vol. 33, No. 2, April 2005, pp. 92–100.

Travers, Peter, Review of *Much Ado About Nothing*, in *Rolling Stone*, May 7, 1993, http://www.rollingstone.com/movies/reviews/much-ado-about-nothing-19930507 (accessed July 26, 2012).

Valdivieso, Sofía Muñoz, "'Silence is the perfectest herald of joy': The Claudio-Hero Plot in Kenneth Branagh's *Much Ado About Nothing*," in *Sederi*, Vol. 8, 1997, pp. 191–95.

Vaughn, Virginia Mason, "Daughters of the Game: Troilus and Cressida and the Sexual Discourse of 16th-Century England," in *Women's Studies International Forum*, Vol. 13, No. 3, 1990, pp. 209–20.

FURTHER READING

Bentley, James, *The Most Beautiful Country Towns of Tuscany*, Thames & Hudson, 2001.

This book is a pictorial guide to Tuscany, the setting for the filmed *Much Ado About Nothing*. The photographs in this book reveal the different architectural influences found in Tuscany. The narrative section of the text not only describes the uniqueness of each town, but also includes information about the museums, art, food, and history of each village.

Cressy, David, *Birth, Marriage, and Death: Ritual, Religion, and the Life-cycle in Tudor and Stuart England*, Oxford University Press, 1999.

The author creates a picture of what it was like to live in England during the sixteenth and early seventeenth centuries. Of particular interest is the discussion of social and culture change during Shakespeare's lifetime and the influence of those changes on his work.

Greenblatt, Stephen, *Will in the World: How Shakespeare Became Shakespeare*, W. W. Norton, 2004.

In this biography of Shakespeare, Greenblatt uses historical documents as well as Shakespeare's texts to create a picture of the man and his work within the historical context in which he lived.

Kastan, David Scott, ed., *A Companion to Shakespeare*, Blackwell, 1999.

Kastan has assembled a collection of twenty-eight scholarly essays about Shakespeare's world and his work. Each essay offers a focused examination of one aspect of the playwright's world. Individual essays focus on politics, religion, playwriting, economics of theater life, censorship, and printing.

O'Hara, Diana, *Courtship and Constraint: Rethinking the Making of Marriage in Tudor England*, Manchester University Press, 2000.

This text provides a study of social customs and the economics of courtship in sixteenth-century England. Much of O'Hara's source material is taken from church records, legal documents, and wills.

Pritchard, R. E., ed., *Shakespeare's England: Life in Elizabethan & Jacobean Times*, Sutton, 1999.

Pritchard has collected a large selection of primary documents from Shakespeare's time. These first-hand reports provide a glimpse of what it was like to live in England in the late sixteenth and early seventeenth centuries. Pritchard includes excerpts from letters, diaries, pamphlets, plays, and poetry to reveal what writers had to say about the time in which they lived.

Wells, Stanley, *Shakespeare for All Time*, Oxford University Press, 2003.

This is an illustrated and easy-to-read narrative of Shakespeare's life and legacy. Wells includes a thoroughly researched biography as well as many interesting details about the plays and their reception in the 400 years since Shakespeare wrote them.

SUGGESTED SEARCH TERMS

Much Ado About Nothing AND Shakespeare

Much Ado About Nothing AND Kenneth Branagh

Much Ado About Nothing AND Emma Thompson

Much Ado About Nothing AND Denzel Washington

Much Ado About Nothing AND romantic comedy

Much Ado About Nothing AND feminine chastity

Kenneth Branagh AND Shakespeare

Shakespeare AND comedy

Beatrice AND Benedick AND romantic love

The Old Maid

ZOË AKINS

1935

Zoë Akins's *The Old Maid* is an adaptation of Edith Wharton's novel by the same name. The five-episode melodrama takes place in New York City in the nineteenth century. Set in a time when Victorian sensibilities determined a woman's role and choices in life, the play explores the themes of jealousy, love, class, and sacrifice. Produced in 1935, *The Old Maid* won the Pulitzer Prize for drama and ran for two years. The play was so successful that it was adapted for a film that was released in 1939.

First published in 1935, *The Old Maid* is no longer in print, but an eBook version is available on Questia. This book contains racially charged language in one episode that some readers may find offensive.

AUTHOR BIOGRAPHY

Zoë Akins was born in Humansville, Missouri, on October 30, 1886. Her family moved to St. Louis in 1898 when her father, Thomas Jasper Akins, was made the State Chairman for the Republican Party. She graduated from high school in 1903 and was engaged to Marion Reedy when she was seventeen. Reedy was the editor of the *Mirror*, a weekly publication where Akins submitted her poetry and criticism. Encouraged by Reedy and the poet Sara Teasdale, she published her first collection of poetry in 1912 titled *Interpretations*.

MEDIA ADAPTATIONS

- The film *The Old Maid* is an adaptation of Akins's Pulitzer Prize-winning play. Released in 1939, the movie stars Bette Davis and Miriam Hopkins.

Other poetic influences included Willa Cather and Emily Dickinson.

Akins attended college in New York after her engagement to Reedy ended in 1905. *Papa* was her first play. It was produced in New York City in 1914 but was a not a commercial success. The moderate success of her 1919 play, *Declassee*, however, sealed her reputation as a playwright. Her next popular play was *Daddy's Gone-A-Hunting* in 1921. She moved to Los Angeles in 1928 where she wrote screenplays. She also and adapted some of her plays for film productions. Although she was successful in Hollywood, Akins continued to write plays for the theater. Her next successful Broadway play, *The Greeks Have a Word for It*, ran from 1929 through 1930. In 1932, she married Hugo Rumbold. An artist and set designer, Rumbold died the same year they married.

Akins's greatest success was an adaptation of Edith Wharton's novel *The Old Maid*. Interest in the 1935 production began slowly, but winning the Pulitzer Prize for drama soon spurred ticket sales. The Pulitzer was a surprise because other plays were preferred by critics, according to Alan Kreizenbeck's *Zoe Akins: Broadway Playwright*. Akins continued to write poetry, plays, and screenplays long after the success of *The Old Maid*. She was working on an autobiography when she died in her Los Angeles home of cancer in 1958.

PLOT SUMMARY

The Old Maid is a divided into five episodes. The episodes take place between 1833 and 1854. They follow the lives of Delia Lovell and her cousin Charlotte.

First Episode, 1833

The first episode takes place ten minutes before the wedding of Delia Lovell to James Ralston. Delia and her maid, Nora, are finishing her wedding preparations. Delia assures Nora that she is not nervous about her marriage. Nora, however, is superstitious, and she is concerned because Delia does not have "something borrowed and something blue." Nora is loaning Delia her garter, so she will have something borrowed, when Delia's cousin Charlotte knocks on the door. Charlotte is poor and has been given a dress for the wedding. When Delia asks Charlotte, or Chatty as she calls her, if she has anything blue, Charlotte replies that she does. She has a wedding present from Clem Spender, a blue turquoise necklace. Delia sends Nora away to speak with Charlotte privately.

Clem has been in Italy the past two years attempting to launch an art career. Delia promised to marry him upon his return, but she could not wait. Unfortunately, he returns on Delia's wedding day to James. Delia makes Charlotte promise to take care of Clem at the wedding. Charlotte is dismissive when Delia swears that she loved Clem. Charlotte vows that she would have waited. They both acknowledge that a marriage to a wealthy Ralston will be more comfortable, financially speaking, than marriage to Clem would have been, but Charlotte does not envy Delia because she does not marry for love. She reveals that she will be an old maid because the man she loves does not love her in return. The episode ends with Delia regaining her composure and walking out to the wedding march.

Second Episode, 1839

The second episode takes place at Charlotte's nursery for underprivileged children. It begins with five-year-old Clementina, called Tina, being taunted by the other children because she lives with an African American family. Charlotte comes in and scolds the children, threatening to keep them from her nursery because of their cruel behavior. After being scolded, the children apologize and sing a song for Charlotte as a wedding present.

One of the mothers, Jennie, praises Charlotte for everything she does to help them, pointing out that most women in her class do not care what happens to the children of the less fortunate. She believes that Charlotte will leave the nursery once she is married, but Charlotte tells her that she has no plans to leave the children. She asks Jennie to come work for her when she learns that the young mother has lost her position. Tina is still at the nursery, and Charlotte explains to Jennie that she has supper with them every night because she requires more care than the other children.

Dr. Lanskell arrives at the nursery with Mrs. Mingott, the aunt of Charlotte's fiancé, Joseph Ralston. Joe is James Ralston's brother and Delia's brother-in-law. Mrs. Mingott has come to tell Charlotte that she will give her five hundred dollars of her own once she is married. Charlotte plans on using the money for her nursery, but Mrs. Mingott thinks that Joe will not approve of her keeping the nursery after the wedding.

James, Joe, and Delia come in to see Mrs. Mingott. Mrs. Mingott asks to see Charlotte's children, but only Tina remains. James and Joe are concerned that the children Charlotte works with are diseased. Tina is nervous when Bridget, Charlotte's assistant, brings her out. Mrs. Mingott discovers that Tina is the infamous hundred-dollar baby. She was left on an African American family's porch with a one-hundred-dollar bill pinned to her bib. Tina is drawn to Delia, and Charlotte is anxious to separate them.

Joe stays behind with Charlotte after the others leave. They are both happy about the upcoming wedding. Charlotte tells Joe that her relatives no longer condescend or pity her. Joe admits that he is jealous of Charlotte's affection for Tina and the children in her nursery. He promises that she may give the nursery money, but he will not allow her to work with the children after they are married. He is concerned that she will catch a disease from them. Her health troubles him because she traveled south six years earlier because of an illness. Joe leaves, and the future of their relationship is unclear. Bridget brings Tina in to say goodbye to Charlotte. Charlotte kisses Tina goodnight as she is summoned for the final fitting of her wedding dress.

Third Episode, 1839
This episode occurs in James and Delia's home a few hours after Charlotte and James quarrel. Delia and Mrs. Mingott are chatting in the drawing room. Mrs. Mingott informs Delia that Clem used to speak highly of both her and Charlotte, and she is relieved that Chatty chose Joe over Clem. Clem is now married to someone else and has given up art. According to Mrs. Mingott,

"the spark's gone." Dr. Lanskell enters and asks for some music. He and Mrs. Mingott move to another room where she begins to sing and play the piano.

Delia answers the door and sees Charlotte, who asks to speak with her alone. Charlotte informs Delia that the wedding is off because Joe wants her to give up her children. She confesses that Tina is her daughter and she cannot give her up. Delia is sympathetic, promising to help Charlotte, until she learns that Clem is Tina's father. Charlotte had been in love with Clem since she was a child, but she knew that he only loved Delia. They chose to comfort each other after Delia's wedding, and he never knew that Charlotte was pregnant as a result. Delia promises to help in the way that she thinks best and sends Charlotte upstairs.

Charlotte and Joe love each other, but Delia refuses to allow the marriage to take place. She tells Joe that Charlotte is sick, knowing he will break the engagement. Dr. Lanskell, who has protected Charlotte's secret for six years, knows that Delia lied about Charlotte's illness. After Joe leaves, he tells her that he does not approve of her meddling. Delia informs Lanskell that she plans on raising Tina herself, but Lanskell makes her promise not to take Tina away from Charlotte. Delia argues that Charlotte left Tina in an unsuitable home, but Lanskell reminds her that Tina is living with Charlotte's childhood nurse. Delia reluctantly agrees to the doctor's demands, and she convinces James to pay for a house for Charlotte and Tina. At the end of the episode, Delia tells Charlotte what she has done, and a heartbroken Charlotte leaves her engagement ring with Delia.

Fourth Episode, 1853
The fourth episode takes place fourteen years later at Delia's house. Charlotte sits alone in the drawing room with Dr. Lanskell. Tina; Delia; her daughter, Dee; Dee's husband, John; and John's cousin, Lanning, are singing in another room. Lanskell comments about the happy life that Tina has had since Delia took them in after James's death twelve years ago. Charlotte only replies that Delia has spoiled Tina, particularly since Dee married John the year before. The group emerges as Dr. Lanskell is leaving.

Charlotte chides Tina for being late when they are expected at a party. Lanning and Tina both mock Charlotte's severity, and it is clear that Charlotte does not approve of Lanning. Tina complains about leaving the party early with John and Dee, but Delia demands that Tina do so. The partygoers exit the room to get their coats, and Tina, calling Delia "mamma," asks her to come with them. Tina continues talking about compliments she has been given on her appearance when Charlotte scolds her for her vanity. Tina is cruel to Charlotte, saying: "You think mamma spoils me, but she doesn't! It's just that *she* understands me—while you don't. Mamma knows what it is to be young and have everyone fond of her—while you—" Charlotte exits to the kitchen, and Delia gently reprimands Tina before the group leaves for the party.

Alone, Charlotte and Delia discuss Tina. Charlotte explains that she rehearses what she says to Tina so that she will sound like an old maid instead of a mother. She brings up the subject of Lanning's interest in Tina. Delia cannot help but think of Clem when Charlotte tells her that Lanning is planning a trip to Paris. Charlotte is concerned that Lanning has no interest in marrying Tina because "every careful mother we know has warned her sons against becoming interested." She knows Tina's lack of wealth and family will impede her marriage to anyone. Charlotte insists on waiting up for Tina because she is concerned about her behavior with Lanning. Delia tells her that she should trust her daughter, but Charlotte's reply is "My mother trusted me."

Charlotte wakes up when Tina and Lanning return. Because they missed all the carriages, he has walked her home in the snow. They discuss his trip to Paris as he takes off her wet stockings and warms her feet. Delia walks in while they are kissing. She sends Tina to bed and tells Lanning goodnight. Charlotte, however, is outraged. She demands that Lanning never come to the house again. Tina lashes out at Charlotte, accusing her of hatred and jealousy because she is "hideous and dried up."

After sending Tina to bed, Delia and Charlotte talk. Charlotte believes that it was a mistake to stay where people know about Tina's history. She plans on taking Tina away where no one knows her so that she will have a chance to find a husband and have a family. Delia is not willing to part with Tina, the child of the man she loved. She asks Charlotte for permission to adopt Tina and give her money, which will make her acceptable to Lanning's family. Initially,

Charlotte refuses, but she silently assents before Tina asks her "mamma" to come up and say goodnight.

Fifth Episode, 1854

It is the night before Tina's wedding to Lanning. Mrs. Mingott is at Delia's house with Dr. Lanskell, John, and Dee while Tina tells Delia and anyone else who can hear her how happy she is. Charlotte is busy making arrangements in the background. Charlotte insists that Tina go to bed, and Delia reluctantly backs up the decision. Tina walks Lanning out. Alone with Dr. Lanskell, Delia says that she is sure Charlotte must be happy now because Tina will never suspect the truth.

Tina comes in and tells Delia how grateful she is for everything she has done for her. She does not care who her mother is because she would have chosen Delia. She insists that she loves Delia more than Dee does and that Delia loves her best. Charlotte is on the stairs and hears the conversation. Tina goes on to tell Lanskell that Charlotte gave her all of her grandmother's jewels and the veil she would have worn at her own wedding. Tina has rejected the veil, choosing to wear Delia's, and she comments that she cannot believe anyone would have ever married Charlotte. She ends her babbling by showing Lanskell the turquoise necklace Delia gave her. It is the same necklace Clem Spender sent to Delia on her wedding day.

Tina goes upstairs to wait for her mother. Before leaving, Lanskell asks if Charlotte attributes Tina's happiness to Delia. Delia assumes that Charlotte does know Tina owes her happiness to Delia. She reminds Dr. Lanskell of his reproach for breaking up Joe and Charlotte. He replies that she has paid for her mistake by spending her life with a jealous woman.

Charlotte confronts Delia angrily after Lanskell leaves. Charlotte demands the right to give Tina maternal advice about her wedding night. After a heated exchange about how Delia did everything to turn Tina against her, Charlotte informs her cousin that she will tell Tina the truth and be a mother to her child for at least one night before she loses her forever. Charlotte goes upstairs, leaving Delia alone. Dee comes in and gives Delia some flowers to give to Tina when she goes up talk to her. She also tells Delia that she is pregnant. After Dee leaves, Charlotte comes back downstairs and asks Delia to go up and talk to Tina because she is the mother Tina wants. Delia tries to convince Charlotte to come with her, but she refuses and exits to the garden.

As Charlotte leaves, Tina comes downstairs. Delia tells Tina that they will talk, but she wants her to go see Charlotte before their discussion. For the first time, Delia informs Tina that Charlotte gave up a good marriage to keep Tina with her. Tina feels guilty about her cruelty to Charlotte. She readily agrees to Delia's request that Charlotte be the last person she kisses when leaving for her honeymoon. The play ends with Tina running out to the garden to find Charlotte.

CHARACTERS

Bridget
Bridget helps Charlotte run her nursery. She cooks Tina's meals and takes the child home in the evening.

Chatty
See Charlotte Lovell

Clementina
See Tina

Dee
Dee is the daughter of Delia and James Ralston. She is married to John Halsey. The night before Tina's wedding, she tells Delia that she is going to have a baby.

Delia Halsey
See Dee

John Halsey
John is Dee's husband. He is also Lanning's cousin.

Lanning Halsey
Lanning is John's cousin. He has no money of his own and no business skills, making him very much like Clem. He cares about Tina, but he knows that he cannot marry her because she has no money or family name. After Delia adopts Tina, she becomes an acceptable wife, and the play ends the night before their wedding.

Dr. Lanskell
Dr. Lanskell is the only one besides Charlotte and Delia who knows the truth about Tina. He

sends Charlotte south when she is pregnant, telling everyone that it is for her health. He refuses to allow Delia to physically separate Charlotte from Tina when Delia tells him that she wants to raise Tina herself.

Charlotte Lovell
Charlotte is Delia's cousin. She comes from a respectable family, but she lacks Delia's wealth. As a young woman, she falls in love with Clem Spender. She knows that Clem is in love with Delia, but Charlotte and Clem comfort each other after Delia marries James. Charlotte is sent away to give birth secretly. When she returns to New York City, she leaves Tina with her own childhood nurse.

Charlotte is engaged to Joseph Ralston six years after Delia's wedding. She loves Joe, but they quarrel when he demands that she stop working in her nursery after they marry, which would mean giving up access to Tina. Charlotte is afraid to tell Joe the truth about Tina, and she begs Delia for help. Delia chooses to punish Charlotte for having Clem's baby by breaking up her engagement to Joe. Charlotte allows herself to become dependent on Delia for Tina's sake.

Charlotte takes on the disguise of an old maid to keep Tina from knowing that she is her mother. She allows Delia to adopt Tina so that her daughter will be accepted by society. The night before Tina's wedding, she considers telling her daughter the truth, but she remains silent and allows Delia to continue her role as Tina's mother.

Delia Lovell
Delia is Charlotte's cousin. She comes from wealth and is condescending to Charlotte. She is in love with Clem Spender and promised to marry him when he returned from Paris. Delia does not have the strength to wait for Clem, however, and she chooses to marry James Ralston. Her marriage secures her place in society, and she has everything she wants but the man she loves.

Delia is willing to help Charlotte keep Tina and marry James's brother, Joseph Ralston, until she discovers that Clem is Tina's father. Motivated by jealousy, she convinces Joe that Charlotte is too sick to marry. After James dies, Delia takes in Charlotte and Tina. Delia is indulgent and steals away Tina's affection. She adopts

Tina to make her socially acceptable, breaking Charlotte's heart.

Delia redeems herself at the end of the play by attempting to reconcile Charlotte and Tina. She tells Tina that Charlotte sacrificed her own marriage to keep her. She makes Tina promise to kiss Charlotte last before leaving for her honeymoon.

Mrs. Jennie Meade

Jennie's child is cared for at Charlotte's nursery. She praises Charlotte for doing work that many members of the upper class would refuse. Charlotte offers Jennie a position at the nursery when she learns that she is out of work.

Mrs. Mingott

Mrs. Mingott is the aunt of James and Joseph Ralston. She resides in Paris and returns to New York for family weddings. At first, she intimidates Tina, but she comes to care for Tina as Delia's adopted daughter.

Nora

Nora is Delia's maid at the beginning of the play. She is concerned that Delia does not have something borrowed or blue on her wedding day. She loans Delia her garter for the ceremony.

James Ralston

James is wealthy and comes from an influential family. He marries Delia, and they are important members of society. He is afraid of catching a disease and does not approve of Charlotte working with needy children because he thinks that they are contagious. He insists that Joe give up the idea of marrying Charlotte when Delia tells them that Charlotte is ill. He agrees to provide a house for Charlotte and Tina after the engagement is broken. This arrangement only lasts until his death two years later.

Joseph Ralston

Called Joe by Charlotte and his family, Joseph Ralston is James Ralston's brother. He is engaged to Charlotte and truly loves her. He does, however, share his cousin's idea about the poor carrying diseases, and he does not want Charlotte to work at her nursery after they marry. He agrees to end his engagement to Charlotte after Delia tells him that Charlotte has poor health and is unable to marry anyone.

Clem Spender

Clem never appears in the play. Both Delia and Charlotte love Clem when they are young women, but he only wants to marry Delia. Clem is Tina's father, but Charlotte never tells him.

Tina

Tina is Charlotte and Clem's daughter, but this knowledge is kept from her. Charlotte leaves Tina and a one-hundred-dollar bill with her own childhood nurse, who happens to be African American. This creates a scandal in New York society, and Tina is known as the hundred-dollar baby. When Tina is a young child, Charlotte cares for her in the nursery.

After James dies, Tina lives with Delia and Charlotte in Delia's home. Delia spoils and indulges Tina, making her forget that society will never accept her. Tina loves Delia, but she is cruel to Charlotte, who she believes never understood love. Tina falls in love with Lanning, but he cannot marry her because of her scandalous past and lack of money. She becomes engaged to Lanning after Delia legally adopts her. At the end of the play, she feels guilty about her behavior toward Charlotte.

THEMES

Jealousy

Many of the actions in *The Old Maid* are motivated by jealousy. Charlotte and Delia are jealous of each other, and this jealousy leads to feelings of hatred that damage their relationship. As the wealthier cousin, Delia is condescending to Charlotte. Delia believes that Charlotte should be jealous of her wealth and position. In the first episode, however, Charlotte states: "But, I don't envy you Delia." She would not trade places with Delia because Delia sacrifices love for security. Charlotte's first outburst of jealousy occurs when Tina and Delia first meet. She dislikes how comfortable her child is with Delia and quickly calls Tina away.

Delia, who never expected to envy Charlotte, finds herself jealous of her cousin's dalliance with the man she loved but rejected. She chooses to punish Charlotte after learning that Clem is Tina's father. Jealous that Charlotte has Clem's child and she does not, Delia plots to raise Tina herself. Only Dr. Lanskell is able to

TOPICS FOR FURTHER STUDY

- Read Brenda Woods's young-adult novel *The Red Rose Box* (2003), which tells the story of ten-year-old Leah. She lives in Louisiana under Jim Crow laws and is enamored by the life that her wealthy aunt Olivia has in California. In an essay, explain how you think Tina in *The Old Maid* feels about the family raising her. Also consider what advice Leah might give about being bullied.

- Select a play from *Six Plays by Lillian Hellman*. Hellman was a contemporary of Akins and a competitor for the 1935 Pulitzer Prize for drama. Carefully examine Hellman's themes and style, and write an essay comparing your chosen play with *The Old Maid*. What are the similarities and differences between the two plays? Why do you think that some critics preferred Hellman's subject matter?

- Research the Great Depression, carefully noting how artistic expression changed over the years. Create a web page with a timeline of the Great Depression. Include links to important artistic works at the time. Be sure to include art, literature, and performing arts.

- Read *Interpretation*, a volume of poetry by Akins. Choose a poem that you feel shares a theme you found in *The Old Maid*. Create a visual representation of the poem using handmade drawings or a computer program. Share your work with the class.

- Research one-act plays. Write a one-act play that shares a theme with *The Old Maid*. Perform the play with a small group and record your performance. When you are finished, share the performance with the rest of the class. Classmates will critique how well the themes in your play mirror the themes in *The Old Maid*.

convince Delia not to take Tina away from Charlotte. Delia has both Charlotte and Tina live with her, but she indulges Tina and steals the child's affection away from Charlotte. Tina mistakenly believes that Charlotte is jealous of her, but Charlotte is content with the knowledge that Tina is "really mine." This contentment ends once Delia adopts Tina.

The night before Tina's wedding, Lanskell tells Delia that he understands "no jealous woman was ever easy to live with." He knows that Charlotte has always been jealous of Tina's affection for Delia. Charlotte's anger surfaces shortly after Lanskell leaves, and she asks, "Do you suppose it's been easy all these years to hear her call you *mother*?" The play resolves when both women are able to release their jealousy. Charlotte gives up the desire to act on her emotions and tell Tina that she is her mother. She keeps her secret for Tina's sake. Delia releases her jealousy by telling Tina that Charlotte sacrificed her engagement to keep Tina, hoping to mend their relationship.

Social Class

Class distinctions are evident throughout *The Old Maid*. Set in New York City in the nineteenth century, family and wealth are factors that determine every aspect of life, including whom a person marries. Delia is in a better position than Charlotte. Both women have a good family name, but Delia's immediate family has money and Charlotte's does not. Charlotte is a poor relative who must rely on her extended family for support. Marriage to Joe offers her a chance to escape this dependent role. As she says, "They've all stopped patronizing me now—now that I'm not going to be a poor relation all my life." Delia's actions keep Charlotte trapped and reliant on Delia.

Another example of classism occurs in Charlotte's nursery. Joe and James both fear catching an illness from the children simply because they are from poor families. Mrs. Mingott and other members of the upper class call the children "paupers." James calls Tina "it" and warns Delia not to touch the orphaned child. The distaste for Tina changes after Delia takes her in, but she is not truly part of the upper class.

Although Tina has all that she wants while living with Delia, she is not socially acceptable. Charlotte knows that Tina can never marry well because she has a scandalous past. The mothers

The Old Maid has all the twists and turns of a modern-day soap opera. (© Elzbieta Sekowska / Shutterstock.com)

of young men may like her, but they will not allow their sons to marry her. Only legal adoption into the Ralston family and the promise that she will inherit Delia's money allow her entrance into New York society.

Sacrifice

Sacrifice separates Charlotte from Delia throughout the episodes of *The Old Maid*. Delia is motivated by selfishness, and Charlotte is motivated by sacrifice. In the beginning of the play, Delia is unwilling to wait for the man she loves. She chooses James Ralston because it is a good match, but she is in love with Clem. Charlotte, on the other hand, would rather be an old maid than marry for convenience. She is willing to sacrifice social and financial security for the sake of love.

Charlotte sacrifices her own happiness to keep Tina in her life. She refuses to give up her nursery when she marries Joe. She maintains her resolve despite her love for Joe and the

knowledge that her decision jeopardizes her engagement. After Delia selfishly tells Joe that Charlotte is too ill to marry, Charlotte allows the man she loves to believe the lie for a chance to live with her daughter.

Charlotte sacrifices her child's love and affection in an attempt to conceal the fact that she is illegitimate. Unlike Delia, Charlotte resists the urge to be overly affectionate because she is afraid that Tina will suspect the truth of their relationship. Tina comes to love the indulgent Delia, calling her mother. She is cruel and dismissive to her actual mother who goes out of her way to protect her.

Charlotte is content in knowing that Tina is her daughter, but she sacrifices the only happiness she has left when she gives her consent for Delia to adopt Tina, hoping her child will be able find a suitable husband as a result. The night before Tina's wedding, Charlotte is tempted to tell the truth and take back her daughter. Instead, she stays silent and makes her final sacrifice for her daughter's happiness.

STYLE

Episode

The Old Maid is not written with traditional acts and scenes; rather, it is broken down into five separate episodes. According to William Harmon in *A Handbook to Literature*, each episode is "an incident presented as one continuous action. Though having a unity within itself, the episode in any one composition is usually accompanied by other episodes woven together." Each episode of *The Old Maid* has its own resolution, but the episodes build on each other to the conclusion. For example, Charlotte's confession in the third episode and Delia's decision to sabotage her cousin's relationship with Joe play out as a concise story with a conflict and resolution. The decisions made in this episode, however, affect what happens in the fourth episode, which takes place fourteen years later.

Melodrama

According to Holman, a melodrama typically has a happy ending. In the play, "poetic justice is superficially secured, the characters (either very good or very bad) being rewarded or punished according to their deeds." In *The Old Maid*, Charlotte sacrifices everything for the sake of

COMPARE
&
CONTRAST

- **1830s:** Women have few rights in the 1830s. In most states, married women cannot own property or assets. The Women's Rights Movement addresses property laws along with voting rights.

- **1930s:** Women have the right to vote after the Nineteenth Amendment is ratified in 1920. They also have property rights and opportunities to be independent. Women, however, still face legal discrimination.

  Today: Laws are in place protecting women from discrimination. The Equal Employment Opportunity Act of 1972, for example, prohibits discrimination in the workplace.

- **1830s:** The economy is weakened because of an overextension of debt. The Panic of 1837 occurs when banks are unable to cover debts called in by creditors.

- **1930s:** The stock market crash on October 24, 1929, signals the beginning of the Great Depression. Unemployment remains high

throughout the decade, and the economy is unstable until World War II.

Today: The economy remains a source of concern since the economic crash of 2008. Unemployment remains high, and recovery is slow.

- **1830s:** Women do not have a role outside of the home. Most women are expected to marry and be devoted wives and mothers. It is unusual for a woman to choose work over domestic life.

- **1930s:** More women pursue higher education and careers, and many choose to both work and marry. There are limitations placed on jobs women can do because of discrimination.

Today: Women can pursue any career they choose, and they do not have to decide between work and marriage. Women are employed in the military, run businesses, and hold public office.

---

her daughter, including the love of her child. This directly contrasts with Delia's selfishness as she destroys Charlotte's chance to marry Joe and plots to steal Tina's affection from Charlotte.

Despite all that Charlotte suffers in the play, *The Old Maid* has a happy ending. Tina is able to marry the man she loves, and Delia has a change of heart, helping to reconcile mother and daughter. As Kreizenbeck explains, "Delia's explanation...allows clear closure to the story: ambiguity is lost, replaced by the melodramatic convention of a happy ending."

HISTORICAL CONTEXT

Great Depression
The Old Maid was produced in 1935 during the Great Depression. Beginning with the New York

stock market crash on October 24, 1929, the Great Depression affected nations around the world. Banks began to fail, losing the resources to remain solvent. The unemployment rate began to rise, and many families suffered in extreme poverty. By 1930, over 3.2 million people in the United States were unemployed, and food riots broke out in 1931. In response to the economic collapse under President Herbert Hoover, Franklin Delano Roosevelt was elected president in 1932. The economy of the 1930s was further damaged when large dust storms appeared in the Midwest in 1934. The storms were caused by unsustainable farming practices, and they ruined farmland, creating the Dust Bowl. Some farmers lost everything, and many traveled to California in search of work.

Despite Roosevelt's attempt to create economic recovery with his New Deal, unemployment rose again in 1937. In 1938, Roosevelt requested 3.75 billion dollars to stimulate the economy. The stimulus did little to end unemployment according to *The American Experience*. The Great Depression officially ended with World War II because industry increased with the war effort.

Artistically, audiences during the Great Depression became more interested in stories that they found relatable. Realism became prominent in literature, movies, and plays. Writers such as Akins who dismissed realism were criticized. Kreizenbeck explains this feeling in the critical response to Akins winning the Pulitzer. "None of the critics who took the Pulitzer to task said that *The Old Maid* was a *bad* play: most of them only wanted a selection with more relevance to modern life."

Women in the 1800s

Although *The Old Maid* was produced in the 1930s, it is set in the 1830s. The expectations placed on women, along with their role in society, drives the choices that the characters make. In the early part of the nineteenth century, husbands owned their wives' property. Widows could only inherit their own property if their husbands willed it to them. Many women were financially dependent on their husbands or male relatives.

Reforms, however, began in the 1830s. According to Carole Shammas in the *Journal of Women's History*, "a few state legislatures in the U.S. introduced laws protecting certain types of property a wife brought to a marriage from her husband's creditors." Advocates for women's rights pressed the issue of personal property. Over the next few decades, states created more legislation protecting the property of women. Despite the inequality, marriage provided some women with the best hope of financial security, particularly members of the upper class who had no marketable skills.

In addition to financial dependence, women were expected to follow strict moral standards in nineteenth-century American society. As Lori D. Ginzberg explains in the *Journal of American History*, "Viewed as inherently moral, women were to instruct by example." Any hint of scandal associated with a woman's behavior would have consequences on the rest of her life. If it became known that an unmarried woman kissed a man, her reputation in society would be ruined.

Women who did marry had to follow another set of moral standards. They were

Delia marries a blueblood after getting over her crush on the Italian painter and lives happily ever after. (© Michail Pogosov | Shutterstock.com)

expected to be excellent wives and mothers who rarely left their homes. Wives were placed under the expectations of domestic idealism, having no identity beyond that of wife and mother. This caused some women, particularly women's rights advocates, to resent or delay marriage. Abby Kelley, for example, feared "public opinion . . . would impose on her the wife's traditional role, and . . . push her into the home," according to Françoise Basch's article for *History Workshop*.

CRITICAL OVERVIEW

Akins had greater commercial success than she did critical acclaim. Even many of her positive reviews contain negative comments. For example, Mitchell Kennerley, in his review of her poetry collection *Interpretations*, praises her artistry, but states: "A certain rhythmic monotony may be mentioned." He also calls the book

WHAT DO I READ NEXT?

- Jim Callan's 2005 history book, *America in the 1930s*, presents an overview of the decade. Specifically designed for a young-adult audience, the nonfiction text includes an invaluable glossary and bibliography that are perfect for students who want a better understanding of life during the Great Depression.

- Cara Chow's young-adult novel *Bitter Melon* was published in 2010. The book is about Frances, a Chinese American teenager who faces the pressures placed on her by society and her mother. Like Charlotte, she must choose between what she loves and what is expected.

- *American Cinema of the 1930s: Themes and Variations* (2007), edited by Ina R. Hark, is a collection of essays that examines the greatest films of the decade. Readers will learn what made screenplays marketable as they study Akins's Hollywood.

- Edited by Catherine Parks in 1994, *In the Shadow of Parnassus: Zoe Akins's Essays on American Poetry* is a collection of criticism that reveals Akins's thoughts and feelings about art and poetry.

- *The Era of Franklin D. Roosevelt, 1933–1945: A Brief History with Documents* by Richard D. Polenberg is a nonfiction book published in 2000. This is an excellent resource for anyone interested in understanding Roosevelt's policies and the political climate under the New Deal.

- Published in 1989, *Notable Women in American Theater* is a collection of biographical essays. This nonfiction volume edited by Alice Robinson, Vera Mowry Roberts, and Milly S. Barranger shows the contributions women have made to theater in the United States.

"emotionally feminine." In 1938, Marion Strobel's review in *Poetry* balanced praise and disapproval. She calls Akins's nature poems "unarresting in meter and imagery." She does say, however, "her psychology is at times subtle, always clear, and the presentation admirably restrained."

Criticisms of Akins's plays were equally divided. Early reviews of *The Old Maid* were positive but not glowing. The review in *Time* praises Akins's past success in female characterizations and successfully characterizing them again in *The Old Maid*. She "brought them together with a resounding impact." Many critics, however, were outraged that *The Old Maid* won the Pulitzer because they considered it an out-of-date adaptation. For example, Brooks Atkinson's article in the *New York Times*, as quoted by Kreizenbeck, considers the play, "a system of social manners that have only antiquarian interest now."

As audience interest began to shift toward realism, Akins's critics grew even more dismissive. For example, the 1941 review of *The Happy Days* in *Time* states: "the delicately written play is not at fault if it and adolescent trials nowadays seem somewhat irrelevant." The review of *Mrs. January and Mrs. Ex* in *Time* shows less restraint by saying the play is "pretty much an assault upon the eardrums." Despite later claims of irrelevance, Akins had a long and successful career on Broadway and Hollywood. She adapted her play *The Greeks Had a Word for It* for the film *The Greeks Had a Word for Them* in 1932. The story stood the test of time, and another film version of the play was created in 1953 titled *How to Marry a Millionaire*.

CRITICISM

April Dawn Paris

Paris is a freelance writer with an extensive background writing literary and educational materials. In the following essay, she argues that deception unites Charlotte and Delia in The Old Maid.

Delia and Charlotte are bound together by deception in *The Old Maid*—neither woman is who people perceive her to be. By the end of the play, people believe that Charlotte is a prudish old maid who never knew or understood love. Delia, on the other hand, appears to be independent and selfless. Each woman takes on traits

EACH WOMAN TAKES ON TRAITS OF THE

OTHER. DELIA DOES SO OUT OF JEALOUSY, AND

CHARLOTTE DOES SO TO PROTECT HER DAUGHTER."

of the other. Delia does so out of jealousy, and Charlotte does so to protect her daughter.

In the beginning of *The Old Maid*, Delia's impending wedding will provide her with wealth and strengthen her social standing. Delia should be happy, but she is giving up the only man she ever loved by marrying into the Ralston family. She does not have the strength of spirit to wait for Clem to return from Paris. Additionally, when Charlotte tells her that he has returned, she turns her back on her last chance for happiness. She resolves to "do well" and marry James Ralston. As Alan Kreizenbeck states in *Zoe Akins: Broadway Playwright*, "Delia has everything except what she most desires—a passionate spirit and independent mind, which are the only two things that Charlotte possesses."

Although Charlotte does not have the wealth and social standing of Delia, she is strong and independent. She chooses never to marry if it is not for love, a decision that many women in her position would not make. Charlotte is a poor relation who will depend on the kindness of her extended family if she does not marry for money. As Delia turns her back on the idea of suffering for love, Charlotte embraces the idea of self-sacrifice. She is unsympathetic to Delia's difficult decision. Delia defends her actions saying, "one gets lonely; one wants children, and a home of one's own." Charlotte's reply, "*I could have waited*," implies that she has strength of character that Delia lacks.

Delia goes on to live the life that is expected of her, restrained by the social conventions of her time. Charlotte, however, continues to live life by her own rules. She has a nursery for underprivileged families, an outrageous idea to many people in the upper class, including her fiancé, Joe. As one mother points out, Charlotte's interest in poor children is abnormal. "They wouldn't interest most young ladies in your class—not enough for 'em to give all their

time to a lot of strange brats," Charlotte, however, refuses to bend to convention and sees no reason why she should give up her nursery just because she is getting married.

Everyone else, however, expects Charlotte to stop working with the children. James and Joe are concerned that the children carry disease because they are poor. Charlotte's family refers to the children as waifs and paupers, and James calls Tina "it." They believe it is perfectly reasonable that Charlotte should stop her work and take on the role of a wife as dictated by society. She is expected to emulate Delia, who fulfills her role perfectly as a hostess, household manager, and mother.

Charlotte's hope that Joe will join her in her charitable work is destroyed when he demands that she give it up, not realizing that it would also mean relinquishing her child. Kreizenbeck points out that this creates an internal conflict: "the desire for emotional fulfillment in a marital relationship, a conventional and appropriate feeling, versus the love and responsibility she feels for her daughter...inappropriate by the circumstances of her birth." Again, Charlotte is willing to risk everything for love, but she has to choose between two different loves.

After her disagreement with Joe, Charlotte's only hope to keep both Joe and Tina lies with Delia. Delia, however, resents Charlotte for having the independence and strength that she lacks herself. When she realizes that Tina is Clem's daughter, she chooses to punish her cousin rather than help her. Limited by her role as a wife, the only power Delia has over her own life is through manipulation. More than one person remarks on her ability to convince James to do anything she wants. Delia chooses to use her powers of manipulation to end Charlotte and Joe's engagement, even when Joe says he is willing to allow Charlotte continue her work. Dr. Lanskell does not approve of Delia's manipulation, telling her, "I think it's a sacrilegious thing to lay so much as a finger on another person's destiny." Delia further manipulates Charlotte by threatening to stop helping her and Tina if she refuses to cooperate.

Fourteen years after Delia's interference, she and Charlotte have changed dramatically. Charlotte "is the typical old maid in appearance as well as manner; harsh, and inclined to be tyrannical." Delia, on the other hand, "is still rosy and fair." By outward appearances, Delia appears to be the romantic and passionate cousin, while Charlotte seems to be passionless. Charlotte's behavior is part of a carefully orchestrated role that she plays in order to protect Tina from knowing that they are mother and daughter. She tells Delia, "I always practice what I'm going to say to her, if it's anything important, so I'll sound like an old maid cousin talking; not a mother." The irony here is that the mother of an illegitimate child models the maidenly virtues demanded by society.

Delia's change is due to the death of her husband and the successful manipulation of Tina's affection away from Charlotte. As the widow of a doting husband, Delia has wealth, influence, and independence. Delia is finally free to forge a close relationship with the child of the man she loved. Her apparent act of selflessness in taking in Tina and Charlotte is actually her selfish way of punishing Charlotte and taking away her child. With her own daughter married, Delia indulges Tina who adores her and calls her "mamma." Beneath her exterior, however, Delia is ruled by society rather than passion.

Charlotte and Delia's deception is successful, and no one can see past their exteriors. As Kreizenbeck states: "Tina accepts Charlotte's ruse of being passionless and dependent and believes that by emulating Delia she will avoid those stigmas." Tina is more like Charlotte than she realizes. She feels things passionately. Sadly, much of her passion is rage directed at her mother, whom she sees as an interfering old maid.

Having a passionate and independent spirit means that Charlotte understands Tina much better than Delia does. Charlotte knows that Tina's emotions place her at risk of repeating her mother's past indiscretions. It is Charlotte who notices the way Tina behaves around Lanning and discerns why he keeps coming to visit them with Dee's husband. Delia simply says, "Tina's happy with us. She doesn't need to marry anyone." Tina's flirtation with Lanning, however, mirrors Charlotte's affair with Clem. Like Clem, Lanning has no money, no skills, and no intention of marrying Tina. When Tina and Lanning are caught kissing, Charlotte sees herself with Clem. "I saw *us*—long ago—walking home to a darkened house." Tina, however, is madly in love with Lanning and cannot see that her situation is anything like Charlotte's.

Although Tina and Charlotte are both passionate, Tina's spoiled upbringing by Delia blinds her to truths in life that are all too clear for Charlotte. Charlotte never believed that she would marry Clem, but Tina is certain that she can marry Lanning despite her lack of wealth and family. She is accustomed to having her way, whereas Charlotte was never given what she wanted. This leaves Tina's character weaker than Charlotte's because she is not able to accept the realities of life. Charlotte decides that the only solution is to take Tina away where no one will know about her questionable parentage.

Unwilling to let Charlotte have her daughter, Delia chooses to adopt her. Again, Delia manipulates Charlotte's love by telling her that taking Tina away is selfish. Delia knows that Charlotte's only comfort comes from knowing that she is Tina's true mother. Delia admits to considering adoption earlier, but she uses Charlotte's feelings as an excuse for hesitating. Charlotte, however, knows why Delia never mentioned the idea. "Perhaps you weren't sure how others would take it." Delia's love is still governed by the pressures of society, proving that she lacks Charlotte's passion and independence.

Seen as an act of love by Tina, taking full custody of Clem's daughter is Delia's last punishment for Charlotte. Charlotte accepts Delia's final punishment because, as Kreizenbeck states, "the things that Delia *does* have—position, money, and influence—are the things Charlotte must have to gain a secure future for Tina." Tina never suspects the depth of Charlotte's love. She remains devoted to Delia, the mother of her choice, while Charlotte suffers in silence to protect her lie.

Tina does not understand Charlotte, which damages their relationship. The night before Tina's wedding to Lanning, however, Delia allows her to see a glimpse of Charlotte's true character. In an act of contrition, Delia tells Tina that Charlotte sacrificed her own marriage to keep Tina. As Kreizenbeck points out, she "very nearly tells the truth about [Tina's] birth," but Delia withholds the secret that she and Charlotte have worked together to hide. Mother and daughter are momentarily reconciled, but the deception remains intact at the end of the play.

Source: April Dawn Paris, Critical Essay on *The Old Maid*, in *Drama for Students*, Gale, Cengage Learning, 2013.

Tice L. Miller

In the following review of Alan Kreizenbeck's book on Akins, Miller offers a brief overview of Akins's career as a writer.

Between 1919 and 1944, eighteen of Zoe Akins's plays appeared on Broadway. In total, she wrote or adapted over forty plays in her lifetime, with her adaptation of Edith Wharton's *The Old Maid* winning a Pulitzer Prize for Drama in 1935. At one time she was a force in the New York theatre, and Alan Kreizenbeck's well-written biography provides us with a glimpse into her life and work.

Zoe Akins was born in Humansville, Missouri, in 1886, into a wealthy and influential family. Kreizenbecks explains: "Part of discovering Zoe Akins is to discover what it meant to be the daughter of a politically prominent upper-middleclass Midwestern family that had ancestral ties to traditional Southern gentility and practical connections to the turn-of-the-century Republican Party"(12). She began her literary career as a poet encouraged by the publisher William Marion Reedy (with whom she was engaged) and the poet Sara Teasdale. In many ways Akins and Teasdale were kindred spirits. They wrote about women who wanted their independence and at the same time traditional marriage, home, and family. As the author suggests, they expressed unconventional opinions but with conventional methods (34). Akins also became friends with Emily Dickinson [*sic*] and Willa Cather and looked to them for advice and encouragement. While still Victorian in many ways, they served as mentors, encouraging Akins to tell the truth about the world around her.

Akins's poems seem more Victorian than modern as evidenced in her first book of poetry *Interpretations* in 1912. Yet, in her best work, her images are striking and possess a haunting kind of beauty. At times Akins seems a modernist as evidenced in the following verse from "Mary Magdalen" published in her second book of poetry *The Hills Grow Smaller* in 1937:

> I asked and asked: what should a woman do
> What should a woman be who would not live
> Dumbly from birth to death and leave no sign
> That she had come and gone save newer lives
> Sprung from her own to linger and repeat
> This vanity, futility, disease?

"Mary Magdalen" demonstrates both Akins's strength as a poet and her limitations. Like the poet herself, her women characters rebel against their place in society but in the end bow to societal conventions. This is evidenced when Mary Magdalen, after refusing to give up the self that she has created, in the end accepts Christ's

forgiveness and sacrifices her "baser" self for a "higher" one. This surrender of self to love, according to Kreizenbeck, was the conventional Victorian solution to a woman's place (45). Perhaps more important than her poetry is her volume of literary criticism, *In the Shadow of Parnassus*, that some scholars have compared to T. S. Eliot's criticism.

Akins left St. Louis for New York "around 1905" to study acting. When financial support from home ceased, she turned to writing plays as a means of support. One of the first lessons she learned about writing for the theatre was that her job was to satisfy audience expectations, not challenge them (70). While she might create women characters who asserted their independence, audiences demanded that by the final curtain, they would come to their senses and discover that happiness lies in a heterosexual marital relationship. In this regard her plays resemble those of Rachel Crothers. Clearly the expectations of her audiences had a lasting influence on her writing.

Before Akins's first New York production, she had written at least 15 plays, some seriously considered by producers (75). Her *The Magical City* presented by the Washington Square Players in 1916 was a critical success and established her as a promising newcomer. Her commercial break through next came with *Declassee* in 1919, which ran for 257 performances. Two years later her *Daddy's Gone A-Hunting* ran for 129 performances further enhancing her rising reputation. For the next decade, Akins produced about a play a year on Broadway and several were very successful. Her characters usually were upper class, witty, articulate and focused on sex, love and romance (108). Usually there was the conflict among her woman characters between love and freedom. Kreizenbeck argues that what she learned to write was a "modernized version of American melodrama, but with a literary 'feel' provided by the epigram-filled dialogue that her characters often spoke"(108). Her success as a playwright led to offers to write for the movies. By the end of the 1920s she had abandoned New York for Hollywood where several of her plays were filmed including *Declassee* and *Daddy's Gone A-Hunting*.

The economic depression in the 1930s drove a wedge between audiences wanting standard

Broadway fare of domestic comedies and drama, and those wanting realistic social dramas reflecting the turmoil in the world outside the theatre. Akins disliked the latter, considering it akin to "washing humanity's dirty linen on the public stage"(158). She stated that she aimed her plays for the educated and refined playgoer, not for the "yokels." Her greatest success came in 1935 when her adaptation of Edith Wharton's novella *The Old Maid* became a hit, running two years on Broadway and winning the Pulitzer Prize for Drama in a controversial decision (Lillian Hellman's *The Children's Hour* was favored). Directed by Guthrie McClintic and starring Helen Menken and Judith Anderson, the play drew mixed reviews but appealed to a receptive female audience. The play was filmed in 1939 and became one of the top twenty grossing films in 1939–40 (187). Akins had some success as a screenwriter in the 1930s, mainly for her own plays and for Greta Garbo's *Camille*. But her day was passing as noted by most of the critics. By 1940 her style of drama had been surpassed by that of a new generation of writers led by Eugene O'Neill. The author notes that when she died in 1958, her plays had been absent from Broadway since 1944 (210).

While more details about her film career would have been enlightening, Alan Kreizenbeck's biography of Zoe Akins is well researched and written. The author does not claim greatness for Akins but instead recognizes that she was a woman who competed in a man's world and gained a measure of success. She learned how to craft a play for the Broadway audiences of the 1920s, and continued to supply plays for this audience into the early 1940s. While she was not an innovator, she was a successful Broadway playwright and her best work is worth our attention today.

Source: Tice L. Miller, "Zoë Akins: Broadway Playwright," in *Theatre History Studies*, Vol. 25, 2005, p. 193.

American Women Playwrights, 1900–1950

In the following excerpt, Akins's relationship with Edith Wharton as Akins wrote the play and the circumstances of the early reviews are explained.

. . . Akins was part of a literary circle which included novelists and poets. She enjoyed giving dinners for such people as Elinor Wylie, Carl Van Vechten, Willa Cather, and Edith Wharton. When she dramatized *The Old Maid* (1935), Wharton trusted her so much that she never asked to read the script. Akins made a faithful adaptation of the poignant story, and provided Judith Anderson with one of her finest roles, that of Delia, the wealthy woman who rejects a poor suitor, Clem, but later finds her greatest happiness in her love for his illegitimate child, Tina. She sees the child in Charlotte's school for poor children and is immediately drawn to her. When Charlotte must choose between marrying Delia's brother-in-law and giving up her school, she confesses to Delia that she comforted Clem and bore his child in secret. Jealous of Charlotte and eager to have Clem's child, she breaks off the engagement by saying that Charlotte is too ill to marry. She then takes mother and daughter into her house and adopts Tina so she can make a good marriage.

The development of Charlotte's character from a good, generous, kind woman into a nit-picking, critical old maid is a very interesting aspect and gave Helen Menken a fine role. Tina grows to hate her, unaware that she is her true mother. On the evening before Tina's marriage, Charlotte flies out at Delia, saying that she knows Delia hates her and that she never wanted to help her, but that it was all for Clem Spender and his child:

> I'm not wicked. I wouldn't have done to you what you've done to me. From the beginning, you've deliberately divided me from my daughter! Do you suppose its been easy all these years to hear her call you *mother*? Oh, I know that it was agreed between us that she must never guess! But you needn't have perpetually come between us! If you hadn't, she'd have had to love me! But for all your patience and generosity, you've ended by robbing me of my child. That's why I can talk of hatred here before this altar tonight! And that's why—before she's his tomorrow: tonight, just tonight, she belongs to me! That's why I won't let her call anyone else *mother* tonight!

Charlotte goes to Tina's room to tell her the truth, but realizes it would be useless: Tina's father loved Delia and the child loved Delia and Charlotte has turned into an embittered old maid for nothing.

There was an unfortunate circumstance regarding the first reviews. The opening conflicted with the opening of Robert Sherwood's *The Petrified Forest*. So the reviewers were taken by bus to Baltimore and reviewed a matinee while it was still in out-of-town try-outs. Most critics felt the performances were not particularly good—they obviously improved by the time the play was performing in New York because they were later remembered as outstanding. A typical reaction was expressed by William Boehnel who called it a good play which was neither great nor significant ("Akins Play at Empire"). Almost all the critics praised the denouement, which, according to Arthur Ruhl, left the men moved and the women weeping. He called it "an affecting work, beautifully played" and said "it never creaks and the atmosphere is excellent" (*The Old Maid*). The critic for the *New York Sun* summed up his response in the title "Valentine of Yesteryear." He called the play "a pretty water-color of yesteryear with an aura of wistfulness and sentiment which is affecting, but the play is more tableau than drama." He noted, which most critics did not, that it was unfair to judge the acting at the matinee in Baltimore.

One problem with the play is that the original material is not inherently exciting—Wharton's novel is a low-key, intense picture of the relationship between two women in a society which has no forgiveness for a woman who has an illegitimate child. The critic for the *New York American* called the adaptation neat, straight-forward, restrained, and well-tempered, "which will probably imply to you that it is not a notably exciting one, however. It isn't. Perhaps it couldn't be" (*The Old Maid*). Arthur Pollock said Akins was too faithful to the novel which he called "stiff and old-fashioned" (*The Old Maid*). Some critics praised the work of director Guthrie McClintic and everyone praised the beautiful settings of Stewart Cheney. One of the few really negative reviews (which may have been written by George S. Kaufman) appeared in *Variety*. The reviewer described it as "a bad play which should make money . . . a woman's play from every standpoint. It had charm, lavender and old lace, and the scenery and the costumes were the high point of the show" (*The Old Maid*).

There were almost no rave reviews, but most had some good things to say about the production

and *The Old Maid* pleased audiences. The Pulitzer prize committee awarded it the prize for the year's best play and there was an intense and unpleasant reaction. Clayton Hamilton said on the radio "The Pulitzer prize committee has labored and brought forth a mouse. Miss Zoë Akins herself very likely would be the last to claim that this is an original American play." He concluded that the major elements were all Edith Wharton's. Percy Hammond called it a "first-class second rater" and said the award should have gone to Hellman's *The Children's Hour*. Hellman's director, Herman Shumlin, intemperately said, "I think it's quite the worst selection the committee could possibly have made from all the plays now current on Broadway" (qtd. in Toohey 127). The committee was attacked on all sides and Akins was criticized as well. The newspapers had a field day printing comments from critics and writers. Only George S. Kaufman, who had won a Pulitzer Prize three years earlier, refused to comment, saying, "I'm in a swell place to keep my mouth shut" (qtd. in Toohey 128).

For Akins the award brought a mixture of pain and pleasure, as it had Glaspell. However, Akins did not withdraw from the theatre, but went to Hollywood, her worth increased by the prize, and planned more plays for the future. She was able to salve her wounds with the knowledge that the play ran 305 performances. She also received the annual award from the Theatre Club Incorporated which described the play as the "most outstanding and dramatic production of the season" ("Brief Sketches of Winners of Pulitzer Prizes"). . . .

Source: "Part One: Zoë Akins (1886–1958)," in *American Women Playwrights, 1900–1950*, 1995, pp. 58–78.

SOURCES

Akins, Zoë, *The Old Maid*, D Appleton-Century, 1936.

Basch, Françoise, "Women's Rights and the Wrongs of Marriage in Mid-Nineteenth-Century America," in *History Workshop*, No. 22, Fall 1986, pp. 18–40.

Ginzberg, Lori D., "'Moral Suasion Is Moral Balderdash": Women, Politics, and Social Activism in the 1850s," in *Journal of American History*, Vol. 73, No. 3, December 1986, pp. 601–22.

Greasley, Philip, A., "Zoë Akins," in *The Authors: Dictionary of Midwestern Literature*, Indiana University Press, 2001, pp. 30–31.

Harmon, William, "Episode," in *A Handbook to Literature: Ninth Edition*, Prentice Hall, 2003, p. 188.

———, "Melodrama," in *A Handbook to Literature: Ninth Edition*, Prentice Hall, 2003, p. 305.

Kennerley, Mitchell, Review of *Interpretations: A Book of First Poems*, in *Poetry*, Vol. 1, No. 3, December 1912, p. 97.

Kreizenbeck, Alan, *Zoe Akins: Broadway Playwright*, Praeger Publishers, 2004, pp. 158, 163, 166, 169, 181.

"New Plays in Manhattan: Review of *Mrs. January and Mr. Ex*," in *Time*, Vol. 43, No. 15, April 10, 1944, p. 17.

"New Plays in Manhattan: Review of *The Happy Days*," in *Time*, Vol. 37, No. 21, May 26, 1941, p. 37.

"New Plays in Manhattan: Review of *The Old Maid*," in *Time*, Vol. 25, No. 3, January 21, 1935, p. 25.

Shammas, Carole, "Reassessing the Married Women's Property Acts," in *Journal of Women's History*, Vol. 6, No. 1, Spring 1994, pp. 9–30.

Strobel, Marion, "Four Women," in *Poetry*, Vol. 51, No. 4, January 1938, pp. 223–25.

"Timeline of the Great Depression," PBS website, http://www.pbs.org/wgbh/americanexperience/features/timeline/rails-timeline/ (accessed September 1, 2012).

FURTHER READING

Akins, Zoe, *Papa: An Amorality in Three Acts*, Kessinger Publishing, 2010.

> This volume showcases Akins's early work as a playwright. First published in 1913, the play was not commercially successful, but it is one of her best-loved creations.

Craats, Rennay, *History of the 1930s*, Weigl Publishers, 2001.

> Craats's brief nonfiction book is aimed at young adults. This volume is a concise history that also includes information about the entertainment industry at the time.

Kyvig, David, *Daily Life in the United States, 1920–1940: How Americans Lived through the Roaring Twenties and the Great Depression*, Ivan R. Dee, 2004.

> Kyvig's account examines the evolution of American life and culture. He includes changes in technology and the entertainment industry during the decades when Akins wrote most of her scripts and plays.

Rauchway, Eric, *The Great Depression and New Deal: A Very Short Introduction*, Oxford University Press, 2007.

> Rauchway's examination of the Great Depression is a brief but thorough text. Students will find the analysis of the New Deal programs insightful and the illustrations helpful.

Roth, Benjamin, *The Great Depression: A Diary*, PublicAffairs, 2009.

> This autobiography goes beyond the dates and facts of the Great Depression. Roth's first-hand account of his life during the Great Depression shows what the average middle-class American experienced in a time of economic uncertainty.

Wharton, Edith, *The Old Maid*, Dover Publications, 2012.

> Akins adapted Wharton's story for her play by the same name. The original book shares the hidden thoughts and feelings of the characters. When the novel is compared with the play, it becomes clear where Akins had to provide emotional insight through dialogue and action.

SUGGESTED SEARCH TERMS

Zoë Akins

Zoë Akins AND biography

Zoë Akins AND The Old Maid

American theater AND history

Great Depression AND literature

Zoë Akins AND criticism

1930s AND United States

1830s AND United States

women's rights AND history

women's rights AND United States

One Flea Spare

NAOMI WALLACE
1995

One Flea Spare is a two-act play written by American playwright Naomi Wallace. The play was first produced at London's Bush Theatre in 1995. Its American premier was at the Humana Festival in Louisville, Kentucky, in 1996, and in 1997, it made its New York premier at the New York Shakespeare Festival.

One Flea Spare is set in London in 1665, when the bubonic plague was spreading death throughout the city. The play is in part the result of Wallace's reading of Daniel Defoe's 1722 *A Journal of the Plague Year*, a semi-fictional treatment of the London plague of 1665. The play's title comes from an erotic love poem by John Donne, "The Flea," first published in 1633, which uses the phrase "one flea spare" in the first line of the second stanza (*spare* being used as a verb, not an adjective). *One Flea Spare*, Wallace's most frequently produced play, was awarded the Susan Smith Blackburn Prize, the Fellowship of Southern Writers Drama Award, and the Kesselring Prize, all in 1996. In 1997, the play won an Obie Award (given to Off-Broadway plays) for Best Play. In 2009, the French national theater, the Comédie-Française, permanently included the play in its repertoire, making Wallace the second American playwright to achieve this distinction in the three-hundred-year history of the Comédie-Française; the other was Tennessee Williams.

One Flea Spare contains a few instances of obscene language, and some scenes have sexual

The characters in One Flea Spare *are quarantined together for twenty-eight days.*

(© DeepGreen / Shutterstock.com)

undercurrents that may render them unsuitable for younger readers. *One Flea Spare* is available from Broadway Play Publishing (1997).

AUTHOR BIOGRAPHY

Wallace was born on August 17, 1960, one of six children, five of them girls, and was brought up on a farm in Prospect, Kentucky, just outside of Louisville. Her father, Henry F. Wallace, had been a journalist but turned to farming. During Wallace's childhood, he remained active in the civil rights and anti-Vietnam War movements. Her mother, Sonia de Vries, came from a family that had taken part in the Dutch resistance to the Nazis in World War II. Wallace credits the influence of her parents for her deep commitment to social issues.

Wallace attended progressive schools in Kentucky and then spent a year with her mother

in Amsterdam after her parents divorced. Back in the United States, she attended Hampshire College in Amherst, Massachusetts, where she began to write poetry. She enrolled in the Iowa Writers Workshop at the University of Iowa, receiving a master of fine arts degree in 1985. After she turned her efforts to writing plays, she received a second master's degree from the Theater Arts Department at the University of Iowa in 1993. In the meantime, she married, had three children, and lived for a period of time with her husband in England.

Wallace's first plays to be produced, both in 1993, were *The War Boys* and *In the Fields of Aceldama*. Her first play to receive widespread attention and critical acclaim was *In the Heart of America* (1994), a critique of media coverage of the first Persian Gulf War (1990–91). In 1992, she was reading Daniel Defoe's *A Journal of the Plague Year* when riots broke out in Los Angeles after four police officers were acquitted on charges of police brutality in the beating of Rodney King, a black motorist. *One Flea Spare*, first produced in 1995, was the outcome of the confluence of the riots and Wallace's reading of Defoe.

Other notable plays by Wallace include *Slaughter City*, which premiered at London's Royal Shakespeare Company in 1996, about labor unrest in a meatpacking plant; *Birdy* (1996), a theatrical adaptation of a 1978 novel by William Wharton, and *The Trestle at Pope Lick Creek* (1998), the first of her plays to make its world premier in the United States. She wrote the script for the movie *Lawn Dogs*, which was released in 1997. In 1999, Wallace was the recipient of a "genius" grant from the MacArthur Foundation. More recently, she has written *One Short Sleepe* (2009), *The Hard Weather Boating Party* (2010), and *And I and Silence* (2011).

PLOT SUMMARY

Act 1

SCENE 1

Morse Braithwaite, a twelve-year-old girl wearing a dirty, tattered dress that she has pulled up over her face, is alone onstage, locked in an empty room. She appears to be repeating words that an interrogator might have used. The interrogator is asking her why she is out of her grave. He then asks what happened to the gentleman and his wife, and he asks her about the blood on her sleeve. Morse responds by talking about the fish in the channels, as well as the ships. She alludes to the war with the Dutch, to the heat of the summer, and to "the Visitation."

She then talks about the fever that overtook the city and that caused strange things to happen, such as sparrows falling dead out of the sky, dogs walking in the robes of dying men, and children born with beards. She also alludes to two children who were locked in their own house but who had to remain confined for only three more days. She then says that "we" came in through the basement and across the roofs. They then died.

Bunce, a sailor in his late twenties, comes into the room, which is now transformed into the Snelgraves' room. Morse says that he came in through the cellar, thinking the house was empty. William Snelgrave, a wealthy, elderly man, along with Darcy Snelgrave, his elderly wife, enter the room and catch Bunce in the act of urinating in a vase.

SCENE 2

Morse is hiding in the Snelgraves' room, watching the scene as the Snelgraves pull away from Bunce in fear. The Snelgraves believe he has the infection and try to get him to leave the house. Bunce, however, denies that he is infected. The Snelgraves examine him, looking for marks of the infection, and Snelgrave finally concedes that Bunce appears to be clean. Morse comes forward and says that she is the only daughter of Sir Nevill Braithwaite and his wife, whom the Snelgraves say they know. Sir Nevill has died of the plague, and Morse has entered the Snelgrave house to hide from the infection. Kabe, a watchman and guard, appears at the window, offering to fetch provisions for the Snelgraves. A workman is boarding up the Snelgraves' house, having seen two people (Morse and Bunce) enter the night before; the Snelgraves thus have to quarantine themselves for twenty-eight days. The scene ends with the Snelgraves accepting Morse as a member of their family.

SCENE 3

As Bunce eats an apple, Snelgrave enters the room. He learns that Bunce is a sailor. He then mentions that he works for the Navy Board and that he and a friend, Samuel, control the Royal Dockyards, the nation's largest commercial venture. Snelgrave and Bunce discuss life at sea, including storms and Bunce's travels to various exotic locales. Bunce describes how he avoided the press gangs of the British navy by wounding himself to appear as though he had scurvy.

SCENE 4

Morse, Bunce, Darcy, and Snelgrave are in a room, enduring the tedium of having nothing to do. Morse sings a song that appears to offend Snelgrave. Morse wants to see Darcy's neck, which she thinks is a thing of beauty. Morse then speculates that Darcy's neck will have on it the marks of the hangman or marks left by the fingers of someone who hates her. Morse has fond memories of her mother, but she claims that her father hit the family's servants. She then imagines what death is like, saying that the sound of it is like the tearing of her dress, which she demonstrates. Bunce joins the discussion and reveals that he was a coal miner in Northumberland when he was a child and that he lost a younger brother in the mines. Bunce describes what it was like to try to pick up the crushed body of his brother in his arms.

SCENE 5

Kabe appears on the street, reciting the "Bills," that is, the list of the number of deaths in the local parishes that week; the numbers are in the hundreds for each parish. Morse appears at the window and tells Kabe that Snelgrave thinks ill of him and believes that he wants the Snelgraves to die so that he, Kabe, can loot the house. Morse wants Kabe to obtain for her a certificate of health from the lord mayor, which would allow her to leave the city. Kabe claims that no authorities are around to issue such a certificate, but he says that he can get her one if she allows him certain sexual favors. He then offers to obtain candy ("sugar knots"), an apple, and a tangerine for her. Kabe asks Morse to steal a piece of Darcy's jewelry for him

SCENE 6

Snelgrave has taken Bunce on as a servant. Bunce is cleaning the floor with vinegar as Snelgrave watches. The men discuss death in the context of rich and poor; Snelgrave wonders why the rich are dying of the plague, although he concedes that the fine clothes of the rich do not always signify good morals. Attention turns to Snelgrave's fine shoes; Snelgrave has Bunce put on the shoes, leading to a discussion of history and how the poor will never wear such shoes. Bunce tries to use Snelgrave's cane, but he does not use it properly at first. The scene ends with each man asserting that he is not cruel. Snelgrave exits, locking the door behind him.

SCENE 7

Darcy brings Bunce a clean shirt because the wrappings around his torso, which bandage an old injury he received as a sailor, are falling apart. She also brings new bandages, but Bunce will not let her rewrap the wound or even see it. Darcy and Bunce discuss his career as a seaman, both in the merchant service and in the navy. Darcy gives Bunce a pair of earrings, apparently as payment, although she calls the gesture an act of charity. He returns them to her, worried that Snelgrave would accuse him of stealing them. He and Darcy discuss his relationship with another seaman named Killigrew. Darcy describes the symptoms of the plague. She mentions that she once had a lover. Bunce decides to accept the earrings, which he will hide.

SCENE 8

Morse, her wrists bound, is accused of stealing some of Snelgrave's Spanish gold coins and a brooch. Morse tells Snelgrave that Darcy has given some of his gin to Bunce. Snelgrave is disturbed that his wife has checked Bunce's bandage. He forces her to remove the glove from the hand that touched Bunce. The hand is scarred from burn injuries received many years ago as she tried to save a horse from a stable fire. Darcy describes the fire and the reaction of her horse. As the scene ends, Morse puts her hand in Bunce's hand.

SCENE 9

The scene opens with Kabe on the street preaching. He refers to various unnatural phenomena caused by the plague as evidence of the wrath of God. Snelgrave has sent Kabe to procure quicksilver (mercury) and a walnut shell to contain it; according to a pamphlet, hanging the shell around the neck can ward off the plague. Kabe is able to find only a hazelnut shell. Kabe has also been unable to procure oil and frankincense. He has only a toad to give Snelgrave. Kabe continues to preach, commenting on how the poor will die during the plague and noting that the rich, as well as the king and his courtiers, have fled the city. Snelgrave has offered to make Kabe rich if he lets the Snelgraves escape. Kabe withdraws a small vial of liquid that he calls Solomon Eagle's plague-water, which he sells to Snelgrave. (Solomon Eagle, or Eccles, is a historical person mentioned in Defoe's *A Journal of the Plague Year*.) Kabe says that Morse Braithwaite is dead—that she has been found dead with her family. Snelgrave learns that

Kabe's family were Levellers and Diggers (members of a scorned Protestant agricultural sect). Kabe's father had died by choking on one of Kabe's toads. Kabe explains how to use the toad to ward off disease.

SCENE 10

Snelgrave grows impatient with Morse's babble. Morse questions Darcy about her burns and whether she can feel anything on her skin. Snelgrave wants to confirm Morse's identity by examining her for a scar that Kabe claimed she has on her belly. Snelgrave tries to force Bunce to strip her and examine her, but Darcy stops him. The audience learns that Darcy's severe burns affected much of her body, and the dialogue suggests that Snelgrave has not touched his wife since the fire. Snelgrave accuses her of lying to him and orders Bunce to beat her. The scene ends with Morse wetting herself.

SCENE 11

The scene begins much as scene 1 does, with Morse onstage, alone, apparently responding to the questions of an interrogator. She refers to a girl her age named Lissa. She notices that she has wet herself, and she removes her dress. Darcy, who has entered, takes the dress away. Morse seems to describe her own illness, when she was nursed by Darcy. She then indicates that Lissa's father, Mr. Braithwaite, died, and then her mother died. Lissa, she says, died more slowly.

Act 2
SCENE 1

Bunce and Snelgrave converse about Bunce's experiences at sea. Snelgrave questions Bunce about how he dealt with his sexual urges on a ship crowded with men. Bunce forces Snelgrave's finger into an orange, then drinks the orange's juice from the hole in the rind.

SCENE 2

Snelgrave taunts Bunce, poking him with his stick. Bunce confesses that he thinks about Darcy. When Snelgrave confronts him with his stick, Bunce pushes him back into a chair, where he and Morse tie him up. Kabe appears at the window and tosses Morse an orange. Kabe talks about the terrible scenes that are to be seen at the pits where the dead are thrown. Bunce strips Snelgrave of his shoes, and Morse puts the orange in Snelgrave's mouth.

SCENE 3

As Snelgrave sleeps, Bunce and Darcy converse. Darcy probes Bunce's wound with her finger and confesses that she thinks about him in a sexual way. Bunce tries to elicit feeling from Darcy's scarred skin, and as he talks about the violence of his experiences at sea, he touches her in an intimate way.

SCENE 4

With Snelgrave still tied up, Morse narrates a kind of fairy tale about birds singing. The two discuss the early stages of the plague and how Snelgrave and the Braithwaites treated servants who contracted the disease. Morse burns one of two dolls she has that are made of sticks.

SCENE 5

The scene opens with the characters putting on each other's clothing. Snelgrave rejects Darcy because of her relationship with Bunce. The characters discuss the lack of any kind of marital relationship between Snelgrave and his wife since the fire that scarred her.

SCENE 6

Morse unties Snelgrave, but he is dead, although he has not died of the plague. Morse recites a monologue about herself, a bird, and the death of Lissa.

SCENE 7

Bunce tries to persuade Kabe to allow him to escape, but Kabe refuses.

SCENE 8

Bunce, planning to leave, gathers items in a bundle as Morse watches and inquires into his plans. Darcy appears, and she is feverish. She has the plague, and Bunce tries to treat her sores with hot coals and by piercing them with a knife, causing her great pain. Morse then helps Darcy stab herself to death.

SCENE 9

With the bodies of the Snelgraves in the background, Morse imagines a time after the plague. Kabe appears and covers the faces of the Snelgraves. Morse takes an orange from her pocket, and after Kabe recites a rhyme about the plague, she tosses it into the air. The play ends as she catches it.

CHARACTERS

Morse Braithwaite

Morse is a twelve-year-old girl who suddenly appears in the Snelgraves' house, along with Bunce. She is in effect an urban refugee trying to find shelter from the plague. Throughout, she acts in an enigmatic, mysterious, intuitive fashion. She claims that she is the daughter of one of the Snelgraves' neighbors, Sir Nevill Braithwaite, although the play suggests that she is actually a servant girl in the Braithwaite household. Morse, wise beyond her years, delivers haunting monologues about the fever in the city, vegetables and fruits rotting in their crates, and the old and sick. At one point, she improvises a fairy tale about doomed lovers.

Bunce

Bunce is a sailor, having served both on merchant ships and in the British navy. He has an old unhealed wound on his torso. Like Morse, he is an urban refugee trying to find a place where he can hide from the plague. The Snelgraves take a great deal of interest in Bunce. They make him a kind of servant, and they question him about his experiences in the world outside of London. Throughout the course of the play, Darcy Snelgrave comes to have sexual feelings for him.

Kabe

Kabe, something of a roguish comic character, is the guard who patrols the streets outside of the Snelgraves's house. His role is to enforce the quarantine, making sure that people such as the Snelgraves who are exposed to the plague remain behind closed doors. He tries to gain sexual favors from Morse in exchange for a certificate that would allow her to leave the city. He also reads the "Bills," that is, the lists of the number of dead in each parish of the city. He provides a particularly vivid description of the "pits" where people who have died of the plague are buried.

Darcy Snelgrave

Darcy is William Snelgrave's wife. The two have been married for many years, but they have not been intimate since Darcy was horribly scarred in a stable fire long ago. Eventually, Darcy becomes attracted to Bunce.

William Snelgrave

Snelgrave is a wealthy but haughty and petulant businessman who says that he works for the

TOPICS FOR FURTHER STUDY

- Locate a copy of the film *Lawn Dogs* (1997), for which Wallace wrote the script. Although the movie's setting is very different from that of *One Flea Spare*, you might be able to discern common themes, particularly those having to do with social class. Watch the film, then prepare a report describing what the film and the play have in common. (Note, too, that the protagonist of *Lawn Dogs* is played by the same actress, Mischa Barton, who played Morse in the New York premier of *One Flea Spare*.) Students should be cautioned that this film is rated R for sexuality/nudity, violence, and language

- Read Laurie Halse Anderson's *Fever 1793* (Simon and Schuster, 2002), a young-adult novel about an outbreak of yellow fever in Philadelphia. Prepare a chart for your classmates tracing the similarities and differences between the novel's heroine, sixteen-year-old Mattie Cook, and Morse in *One Flea Spare*.

- One source of inspiration for Wallace in writing *One Flea Spare* was Daniel Defoe's *A Journal of the Plague Year*, first published in 1722. Read Defoe's semi-fictional work, and then prepare a written report that explains specific ways in which you think it inspired Wallace.

- Wallace has stated that one source of inspiration for the play was the rioting that took place in Los Angeles in 1992 after four police officers were acquitted on charges of brutality in the beating of a black motorist, Rodney King. The beating was caught on videotape by a local resident, and the tape was shown repeatedly on news broadcasts. Investigate the incident, and then prepare an oral report in which you comment on how the Rodney King affair may have influenced Wallace in writing *One Flea Spare*.

- Nancy Farmer's *A Girl Named Disaster* (reprinted by Scholastic in 2012) tells the story of eleven-year-old Nhamo, a young African girl who is an orphan and is forced to flee her isolated village when a cholera epidemic strikes and she is condemned as a witch. Imagine a dialogue between Nhamo and Morse from Wallace's play in which they discuss their experiences with epidemic disease. Find a classmate who is willing to help and perform your dialogue for the class.

- Go to the British Library website at http:// www.bl.uk/learning/histcitizen/uk/plague/ gov/localgov.html. There, under "Making of the UK: 1500–1750," is a section titled "Local Government Source," which includes reproductions of orders by the Lord Mayor of London and the city's aldermen for taking precautions during the Great Plague. Make a modern English transcription of the orders, then share them with your class using Flikr or another similar tool. Discuss with your classmates the extent to which *One Flea Spare* reflects these orders.

- Prepare a timeline of the events surrounding the Anglo-Dutch Wars of the seventeenth and eighteenth centuries. Share your timeline with your classmates and comment on why Wallace chose to include details about the Second Anglo-Dutch War in her play.

Navy Board and that he and a friend run the Royal Dockyards, the nation's largest commercial venture. He and his wife, Darcy, have had a marriage in name only for many years after Darcy was burned and scarred in a fire. Snelgrave is intrigued with Bunce and his experiences at sea. He is conscious of his position in the social hierarchy, but ironically he is replaced in Darcy's affections by Bunce. Near the end of the play, he is tied to a chair, where he dies (although not from the plague).

THEMES

Death

Clearly, death is a pervasive theme in a play about the Black Death. In the play's first line, spoken by Morse, an imagined voice asks her what she is doing out of her grave. Morse goes on in the play's first scene to comment on the ships' "hulls plowing the dead up out of the water." Later she says that sparrows fell dead from the sky, that dogs walked in the robes of dying men, and that two children locked in their room died. Later, in act 1, scene 4, Morse says "I already know what it's like. To be dead.... Just lots of nothing to see all around you and nothing to feel, only there's a sound that comes and goes." The sound is that of a tearing dress, which Morse demonstrates with her own dress.

Bunce talks about the loss off his brother in a mining accident and describes the experience of retrieving his crushed and mutilated body. Kabe comes around and announces the "Bills," that is, the number of deaths from the plague in each of London's parishes that week; the numbers for the parishes are all in the hundreds. He also describes the horror of the pits, where the dead are buried, in act 2, scene 2:

> What's terrible at the pits isn't the dead. What's terrible is that there are persons who aren't dead but are infected with the plague and they come freely to the pit, shouting, delirious with fever ... and they throw themselves into the pits, on top of the dead, and expire there.

Kabe goes on:

> Others are still dying. They leap about the pit, roaring, tearing the clothes from their bodies ... cutting open their sores to relieve the pain.... Ay, that's what's terrible. Not death, but life that has nothing left but still won't give itself up.

Social Class

The theme of social class is related to the theme of death, for the disease does not distinguish between rich and poor. The essential structure of the play is that William Snelgrave and his wife, Darcy, are wealthy, whereas Bunce and Morse, who break into their home, are impoverished, bringing the social classes into conflict. Snelgrave raises the issue of social class in act 1, scene 6, when he says to Bunce:

> I heard the crier this morning. The Bills have almost doubled this week. Mostly the Out Parishes of the poor. But it's moving this way. A couple of persons I know personally have died. Decent people. Good Christians on the surface. But there's the key. On the surface. When the poor die, the beggars, it's no riddle.... When the rich die, it's harder to tell why God took them; they're clean, attend the Masses, give alms. But something rotten lurks.... A fine set of clothes does not always attest to a fine set of morals.

The scene continues with a discussion of shoes. Snelgrave suggests that the poor will never wear fine shoes. He slips out of his shoes and urges Bunce to put them on. He then states that the only reason Bunce is wearing fine shoes is that he, Snelgrave, a rich man, allows him to. Snelgrave concludes: "I can't change the fact that you'll never wear fine shoes." In a later scene, the characters put on each other's clothing, further underlining class distinctions. These kinds of class distinction pervade the play. Darcy, for instance, is a woman of means and social standing, yet she is attracted to Bunce, the coarse, lower-class sailor. The play makes clear that people with money have been able to flee the city, while poor people such as Morse and Bunce are left behind.

The plague, however, is the great leveler. As Morse notes in act 1, scene 11, "In the pits their faces looked the same. Dried out by grief." Thus, *One Flea Spare* is Wallace's critique of class distinctions, showing how circumstances can make such distinctions meaningless.

Sensuality

One Flea Spare is in many respects a play about the breakdown of the social order and the erasure of many of the markers that identify people, including social class, economic circumstances, age, and gender. In this vein, the play illustrates the breakdown of norms that generally govern sexual behavior. A simple example is when Kabe tries to extract sexual favors from Morse, who is only twelve years old, in exchange for a way to escape London.

A more complex example involves the trio of Bunce, Darcy, and Snelgrave. The audience discovers that Snelgrave and Darcy have not been intimate for many years. The apparent reason for this is that Darcy was horribly scarred by a fire when she was still a teenage bride, although Snelgrave is characterized as self-righteous and moralistic, suggesting that he might find sexual relations of any kind uncomfortable. Her scars are covered by clothing, and much of her skin seems to have little or no feeling.

As the tension mounts, the play deals with boundaries. (© iconspro | Shutterstock.com)

Under ordinary circumstances, Darcy would not have any type of sexual interest in a character like Bunce, a coarse, tight-lipped sailor, yet in act 2, scene 3, Bunce and Darcy engage in a kind of strange sexually charged conduct. Bunce has an unhealed wound on his torso. Darcy says that she wants to touch it. Bunce then guides her hand under his shirt, allowing her to probe the wound with her finger. Moments later, Darcy confesses: "every night I ravish you in my sleep." Later in the scene, Bunce touches Darcy in an intimate way, all while discussing the violence he experienced as a sailor. This connection suggests that sexuality and violence are somehow bound up with one another.

STYLE

Imagery

A considerable amount of poetic imagery pervades *One Flea Spare*. One set of images has to do with fire and burning. The most prominent example of this is the fire that scarred Darcy

when she was a teenage bride. This fire determined the nature of her relationship with Snelgrave for decades to come. Elsewhere, Morse lights one of her stick dolls on fire. The play also has repeated images of penetration. Darcy, for example, penetrates the wound on Bunce's torso with her finger, and she herself is penetrated by a knife, causing her death in act 2, scene 8. Bunce forces Snelgrave's finger into an orange, and in another scene, Snelgrave pokes Bunce with a stick.

Images of decay and stench are not surprising in a play about the Black Death. For example, in the play's first scene, Morse says:

> In summer. A summer so hot vegetables stewed in their crates. The old and sick melted like snow in the streets. At night the rats came out in twos and threes to drink the sweat from our faces.

Images of injury run throughout the play; Bunce has an unhealed wound on his torso, and Darcy was scarred by fire many years ago.

All of this imagery creates a pervading atmosphere of death, decay, and disease. Against these distasteful images are images that are more pleasant. Morse, for example, tells Darcy:

> My mother said to me that once a tiny piece of star broke off and fell from the sky while she slept in a field of wheat and it pierced her, here . . . and from that piece of star I was born.

The implication is that Morse, elsewhere described in terms suggesting angels, is a bright spot in the bleak landscape of plague-ravaged London.

Symbolism

A number of symbols recur throughout *One Flea Spare*. One symbol has to do with fruit, something that was probably a rarity in London during the plague and whose presence would provide a contrast to the horror of the disease and its effects. Mention is made of an apple and a tangerine, and in act 2, oranges play a prominent role. An orange becomes a sexual symbol in act 2, scene 1, when Snelgrave is questioning Bunce about how he controlled his sexual urges when he was aboard ship, packed together with other men. Bunce is disgusted, and in response to Snelgrave's intrusive questions, he forces Snelgrave's finger through the rind of an orange. He pulls Snelgrave's finger out and then squeezes the orange, drinking the juice that runs out of the hole in the rind.

At the end of the play, Morse has an orange, which she pulls out of her pocket. She tosses it into the air, and the play ends as she catches it, perhaps ending the play on an optimistic, forward-looking note. Meanwhile, Kabe sings the first bit of a nursery rhyme: "'Orange and lemons,' sing the Bells of St. Clements." The rest of the rhyme refers to other parishes in London:

"You owe me five farthings" say the Bells of St. Martin's

"When will you pay me?" say the Bells of Old Bailey

"When I grow rich" say the Bells of Shoreditch

"When will that be?" say the Bells of Stepney

"I do not know" say the Great Bells of Bow

"Here comes a Candle to light you to Bed

Here comes a Chopper to Chop off your Head

Chip chop chip chop—the Last Man's Dead."

The catalogue of parishes recalls the list of parishes when Kabe calls out the "Bill" indicating the number of deaths in each parish.

Clothing and shoes also serve symbolic functions. Morse, for example, has a name that does not identify her as male or female, and her clothing reflects this, for although she wears a dress, underneath she wears what appears to be a boy's set of long johns. In act 1, scene 6, shoes are used as a marker of class distinctions. So, too, is Snelgrave's cane. In act 2, scene 5, one of the few moments of merriment in the play, the characters exchange clothing: Morse takes off Darcy's dress, Snelgrave wears Bunce's clothing, and Bunce puts on Snelgrave's pants. This exchange of clothing suggests the leveling of social class distinctions among the characters.

Rhythm

Normally, rhythm is an element discussed in connection with poetry, although literary prose can often have a distinct "poetic" rhythm. In a play script, the playwright would normally allow the actors, in concert with the director, to establish the pacing and rhythm of the lines. In many places, however, Wallace provides clear guidance about the rhythm with which the lines should be delivered. In the play's opening

scene, for example, Morse is speaking. The script includes the italicized word *Beat* in parentheses in several places, indicating that the actress is to pause for a beat before continuing.

In other places, the syntax is deliberately broken up, such as in act 1, scene 2, when Darcy says (in reference to Bunce having urinated in a vase): "He's relieved himself. In my vase." Normally, such a statement would most likely be written as one sentence. There are other instances where sentences are punctuated in unconventional ways. In act 1, scene 5, Bunce is speaking about his brother, who was killed in a mining accident: "His body. It was like. What? Like water. What was left of him. I couldn't take him up in my arms. He just. Spilled away."

It is difficult to be certain about Wallace's purpose in including these markers of rhythm. One possibility is that she was consciously trying to steer performers away from the tendency to say their lines as if they were giving formal set speeches. Rather, the performers, if they follow Wallace's guidance, will deliver the lines as though they are piecing together their thoughts in a more intimate, true-to-life way, with all of the normal hesitations and uncertainties that find their way into spontaneous speech.

HISTORICAL CONTEXT

The Black Death

By 1665, Europe had long been familiar with the plague, often referred to as the Black Death because one of its symptoms was the clotting of blood under the skin, which then turned black. As early as the sixth century, the Black Death was epidemic in Europe, and other outbreaks of the plague occurred repeatedly during the late medieval period. Some European cities felt fortunate if a decade went by without an outbreak of the plague.

The plague took several forms. The most common one was the bubonic form, which is caused by *Bacillus pestis*. This disease normally afflicts rodents, but it can spread from infected rats to humans through flea bites; the source of the plague was most likely Asia. Infected rats often made their way around the world on ships during the seventeenth century. This form of the plague was called "bubonic" because a primary symptom was bubos, or large, painful swellings in the lymph nodes. The disease spread

COMPARE
&
CONTRAST

- **1665:** The Great Plague erupts in London and other areas of England.

- **1995:** The worldwide incidence of plague in modern times will peak in 1997 at 5,419 cases.

  Today: The plague still occurs today, but the chances of catching it are small, and modern antibiotics are effective if administered soon after symptoms start.

- **1665:** England and Holland are bitter maritime rivals, leading to the outbreak of the Second Anglo-Dutch War in June.

- **1995:** The United Kingdom and the Netherlands are staunch allies as members of the European Union.

Today: The United Kingdom and the Netherlands are trading partners, and their close economic relationship allows companies such as Royal Dutch/Shell and Unilever to be joint British-Dutch enterprises.

- **1665:** London's theaters, which had just reopened after the restoration of Charles II to the throne of England in 1660, are closed because of the plague.

- **1995:** The 1990s witness the emergence of the "in-yer-face" theater movement in Britain, which emphasized plays that were highly provocative and confrontational.

Today: Experimental, innovative, and unconventional plays are routinely produced in Great Britain at numerous small venues.

rapidly, with a relatively short incubation period, and some 90 percent of the people who contracted it died. Another form was pneumonic plague, which was spread by droplets of fluid passing from person to person, usually as a result of coughing. This form of the plague was 100 percent fatal in the seventeenth century, but today can be treated with antibiotics.

The Black Death in England culminated in what came to be called the Great Plague of 1665, the worst outbreak in England since the mid-fourteenth century. During the Great Plague, London lost some 15 percent of its population. The official death toll was 68,596, but it is likely that not all deaths were recorded and that the number was over 100,000. The earliest cases were reported in the spring in a parish called St. Giles-in-the-Fields, located just outside the city's walls. Throughout the spring and unusually hot summer, the death toll steadily increased, peaking at 7,165 during one week in September.

Those who had the means fled the city. King Charles II and his court left in July, taking refuge at Hampton Court and then in Oxford. Parliament was dissolved (although it reassembled in

Oxford in the autumn), and law court cases were moved to Oxford. The Lord Mayor, Sir John Lawrence, and the city's aldermen remained behind to enforce Charles's orders for dealing with the plague. The city was populated at this point largely by the poorest people, some of whom were cared for by Dr. Humphrey Brookes, most likely the "Dr. Brooks" to whom Snelgrave alludes in *One Flea Spare*. Watchmen (like Kabe) were appointed to guard infected houses and enforce quarantines. Searchers looked for bodies and took them to the pits for interment at night. Trade was halted, putting large numbers of people out of work, and Scotland closed its border with England.

By early 1666, the Great Plague had spent its fury. It is thought that the Great Plague of 1665 was the last to strike England because the species of rat that was typically infested with the fleas that carried the plague was largely supplanted by another species of rat that did not become infested with fleas that carried the plague.

Anglo-Dutch Wars
In act 1, scene 1 of *One Flea Spare*, Morse refers to the war with the Dutch, and in later scenes,

An abstract painting of a medieval doctor (© Eugene Ivanov / Shutterstock.com)

Bunce and Snelgrave also allude to the conflict. During the seventeenth and eighteenth centuries, a series of wars between England and Holland erupted; collectively, they are referred to as the Anglo-Dutch Wars. The wars were the product of trading and naval rivalries between the two nations as each fought for supremacy on the oceans, along trade routes, and in potentially lucrative colonies.

The first of these wars was fought in 1652–54. It was precipitated by an English law limiting cargo trade into England, thus harming Dutch commerce. After a series of naval battles, the English blockaded the Dutch coast. The war ended with the Treaty of Westminster, signed on April 15, 1654, but the terms of the treaty were unfavorable to the Dutch, setting the stage for the Second Anglo-Dutch War of 1665–67, the war referred to in the play. The war erupted after King Charles II meddled in affairs of Dutch governance and the English once again tried to thwart Dutch trade. Of particular importance were the English conquest of the island of Curaçao, English seizure of potential colonies in western Africa, and the acquisition of New Amsterdam—that is, New York (renamed after James II, the Duke of York, the king's brother). After a series of naval engagements beginning on June 13, 1665, the war ended with the 1667 Treaty of Breda.

Two additional Anglo-Dutch Wars would later be fought: the Third Anglo-Dutch War (1672–74) and the Fourth Anglo-Dutch War (1780–84).

CRITICAL OVERVIEW

The reactions of critics and reviewers to *One Flea Spare* are decidedly mixed. When the play premiered in England, critics there were largely enthusiastic. Typical of comments in the British press are those of Lyn Gardner, who writes in the *London Guardian* that the play is one in which "issues of class and politics are probed with a fierce, searing tenderness." Gardner adds that the play is "rich and dense" and calls it a "tough and transcendent piece of proper grown-up theatre."

In the United States, critics tend to be less enthusiastic, and in some instances they are sharply dismissive of the play. John Simon, a prominent cultural critic in New York City, calls the play "pretentious and boring but also empty, pointless, and totally preposterous." He also describes it as "sophomoric" and is puzzled that the play garnered awards, including an Obie Award for Best Play. Similarly, Peter Marks, writing in the *Washington Post* (in a review whose title contains the word "dismal"), calls the play "puzzlingly lifeless" and faults the author's "overworked and image-drenched dramatic language." In the same review, he describes the script as "mannered" and laments its "dreary effect."

In *Chicago Theater Beat*, Scotty Zacher is somewhat more positive. He summarizes the play in this way: "sexual bargaining, class warfare, homoeroticism . . . *One Flea Spare* explores these tasty ideas with a steady mix of poetry and prose, absurd comedy and claustrophobic tension." However, Zacher adds that "the experience is more intellectual than visceral" and finds portions of the play "convoluted." Regarding the play's New York City premier, Ben Brantley, writing in the *New York Times*, also seems to be

WHAT DO I READ NEXT?

- Wallace's essay "On Writing as Transgression" is subtitled "Teachers of Young Playwrights Need to Turn Them into Dangerous Citizens." The essay, first published in *American Theater* in January 2008, examines the author's philosophy of play writing and is available online at http://www.play wrightsfoundation.org/images/previous%20 teachers/at_jan08_transgressionFINAL.pdf.

- Wallace's *Slaughter City* (Faber and Faber, 1997) is a play set in a meatpacking plant where workers are subjected to harassment and production schedules that are virtually impossible to meet.

- *The Great Plague* (Scholastic, 2008) by Pamela Oldfield is a young-adult novel that tells the story of Alice, a young girl who has a fairly ordinary life with her father and her aunt until the Great Plague of 1665 changes everything. The story is told through journals, diaries, and letters.

- Mary Hooper's *At the Sign of the Sugared Plum* (Bloomsbury Children's Books, 2003) is a young-adult novel that tells the story of Hannah, a teenager. Hannah accepts an invitation from her older sister, Sarah, who operates a candy shop, to visit her in London in 1665. Hannah arrives in the city, only to be trapped there by the plague.

- *The Decameron* is a collection of one hundred tales written in the mid-fourteenth century by Italian author Giovanni Boccaccio. The stories are linked by a frame story, which is that ten young people flee from Florence, Italy, to the countryside during

an outbreak of the plague. They hide in an abandoned villa, and to pass the time, each of the ten has to tell ten stories over a period of two weeks. The book is available in a 2003 edition published by Penguin Books.

- Jan Hudson's *Sweetgrass* (Puffin, 1999) is an award-winning young-adult novel about a girl who is a member of the Blackfeet tribe in western Canada during the nineteenth century. She and her tribe face famine and the ravages of a smallpox epidemic.

- Steven Johnson's *The Ghost Map: The Story of London's Most Terrifying Epidemic—and How It Changed Science, Cities, and the Modern World* (Riverhead, 2007) is a nonfiction account of a cholera outbreak in London in 1854. The outbreak led to innovations in the provision of clean water, sewage systems, and garbage collection that would change modern cities.

- Michael Bigelow Dixon and Liz Engelman edited *Humana Festival 1996: The Complete Plays* (Smith and Kraus, 1996), a collection that includes *One Flea Spare*. The annual Humana Festival in Louisville, Kentucky, features new plays. This collection includes, among other entrants, Anne Bogart's *Going, Going, Gone*, Jimmy Breslin's *Contract with Jackie*, Tony Kushner's *Reverse Transcription*, Craig Lucas's *What I Meant Was*, John Patrick Shanley's *Kissing Christine*, and Jane Martin's *Jack and Jill*, which won the American Theatre Critics Association citation as outstanding play of 1997.

---

of two minds. On the one hand, he calls the writing "densely lyrical" and praises Wallace for exhibiting "the poet's precision in sustaining and developing metaphors." On the other hand, he describes the play as "self-conscious" and adds that "the work remains stiff, schematic

and surprisingly unaffecting." Brantley also writes: "It's too firmly anchored in its conscientious set of symbols—of unhealing wounds, sexual bartering and penetration, fire, water and decay—for its characters to spring into autonomous life."

At least two American critics are unreservedly positive. Everett Evans opens his review in the *Houston Chronicle* by writing, "A strange and beautiful poetry pervades *One Flea Spare*." He then praises the author for her ability to write "lines and speeches that shine with originality and distinction, passages that project a near-Shakespearean grandeur in their passion for language and for life." John Lahr writes in the *New Yorker* that "*One Flea Spare* is built to provoke, not to distract, and it doesn't surrender its meanings easily. But the play's powerful sexual subtext and its beautiful poetic surface reveal an original theatrical imagination."

CRITICISM

Michael J. O'Neal

O'Neal holds a PhD in English. In the following essay, he examines One Flea Spare *as an example of avant-garde theater.*

During the nineteenth century, the phrase "well-made play" was coined by French playwright Eugène Scribe. In French, the expression is *pièce bien fait.* A well-made play has the characteristics that most mainstream theatergoers expect to see on the stage: a play with a strong, clearly defined narrative line, with exposition, complications, and rising action leading to a climax, a denouement, and falling action. For the past century or more, such plays have often been dismissed by some theater aficionados as conventional, stuffy, and artificial, although such prominent playwrights as George Bernard Shaw and Henrik Ibsen adopted many of the conventions of the well-made play, and these conventions could be considered accepted features of contemporary television shows and mainstream Hollywood movies.

In the twentieth century, many playwrights rejected the conventions of the well-made play and adopted a new set of theatrical conventions that were designed to puzzle, bewilder, provoke, disorient, challenge, and perhaps even anger the theatergoer. The goal was not to allow the audience member to remain a passive spectator but to engage the audience in the construction of the play's meaning, to overturn the audience's ordinary perceptions of the social order, and to redefine the relationship between actor and audience. If earlier drama was regarded as bourgeois, this new type of drama was regarded as being in the

> THEATERGOERS AND READERS CAN READILY SPOT THE DIFFERENCE BETWEEN A CONVENTIONAL, WELL-MADE PLAY WITH TRADITIONAL ROOTS AND A PLAY THAT IS EXPERIMENTAL AND PART OF THE AVANT-GARDE—A PLAY SUCH AS *ONE FLEA SPARE.*"

vanguard, as avant-garde (another French term, literally translated as "advance guard").

"Avant-garde" is a term that refers to any artistic, cultural, and political views that emphasize innovation and nonconformity, along with a rejection of mass culture and mainstream points of view. On the stage, avant-garde plays are often discussed under the term "experimental theater." These terms tend to be used interchangeably, and their precise meaning is debated. Indeed, the terms are resistant to precise definition. Theatergoers and readers can readily spot the difference between a conventional, well-made play with traditional roots and a play that is experimental and part of the avant-garde—a play such as *One Flea Spare.*

The question for many theatergoers is how they are to respond to such a play. In an article in the *New York Times*, theater critic and Columbia University professor Margo Jefferson provides the everyday theatergoer with a "primer" for making sense of avant-garde plays that at first seem simply bewildering. She makes four suggestions: Do not look for a straightforward story line; recognize that theater is now a hybrid form that includes speech, dance, visual design, music, and lighting; see avant-garde theater as occupying a border area, where oppositions and contractions are forced into uneasy alliance; and relinquish your assumptions about how plays are "supposed" to be written. Jefferson then makes this point:

> Remember, the avant-garde is not a designated tribe of rebel outsiders anymore. It is a set of tools and practices; certain styles and attitudes. And pre-eminent among those attitudes is skepticism. For more than a century artists across the board have been questioning fundamental assumptions about art. What makes something art?

Wallace might very well reject a term such as "avant-garde" in describing *One Flea Spare*, for ironically, the avant-garde can quickly evolve into a kind of new mainstream: if everyone is in the advance guard, then no one is. Nevertheless, a reader/audience member is likely at times to be disoriented and even bewildered by the play, which clearly rejects the conventions of the well-made play of the nineteenth century. At every turn, Wallace turns audience expectations upside down.

In the opening scene, for example, the audience is presented with a character wearing a dress, but underneath it she has a pair of boy's pants or long underwear, leaving the audience disoriented as to the character's gender. There is no exposition; the reader does not know who she is. She speaks enigmatically, using words that seem to have been spoken to her by an interrogator. She makes reference to a "Gentleman," but the audience has no idea who the gentleman is nor why Morse has blood on her sleeve. She launches into a monologue about fish burning in the channels, ships plowing the dead up out of the water, fever, dying sparrows, children who are confined but then die. Then Bunce enters the room, and the audience learns that he has urinated in a vase. This is not George Bernard Shaw.

Throughout, the audience is confronted, and challenged, with this kind of enigmatic experience—both action and dialogue that defy rational explication. For example, in act 2, scene 6, Morse narrates a kind of fairy tale, in which she says that "Sir Braithwaite's daughter had a bird. A green and black bird. Whack, whack went her stick on my back when I swept. Then she'd let me hold the bird so I'd stop my crying." The tale goes on to discuss the death of "Lissa," apparently the daughter. This hints that Morse is not Nevill Braithwaite's daughter but rather was a servant in the family, but the audience is never told directly who Lissa is. After Lissa's death, presumably from the plague, Morse put the bird in Lissa's mouth, in much the same way that she puts an orange in Snelgrave's mouth in act 2, scene 3.

These kinds of motifs link the various scenes in the play. That is, scenes are tied together thematically by a wide range of images and references: disease (not just the plague but, for example, the diseased marriage of Snelgrave and Darcy), clothing, birds, fire, oranges, fingers inserted into objects (such as an orange) or people (such as Darcy's finger probing Bunce's wound), knives and sticks (used to penetrate

and pierce, much as Morse says that she was "born from a piece of broken star that pierced my mother's heart"), dirt, blood, urine, vinegar, hot coals, binding (Morse's wrists are bound, Snelgrave is bound in a chair, and Darcy's flesh is bound in clothing designed to hide her scars), and exposure of the body (Morse lifts her dress and "flashes" Snelgrave, Bunce opens his pants, and Darcy reveals her scarred skin). The attentive reader could probably find more such motifs, for the play is thick with them.

The question for the audience is what the poetry, imagery, symbolism, and layers of motifs add up to. For some critics, the answer was very little. These critics regarded the play as self-indulgent, pointless, and overdone. Others saw it as a poetic evocation of a set of views that challenge the accepted social order and the "normal" relationships among people in times of crisis. For at bottom, the play's language makes it a play about the body and about the integrity of a person's body. Clearly, the plague is an assault on that body. It destroys the body, turning it into a thing that has to be thrown into a pit for burial.

The bodies in the play, however, are assaulted by so much more. Darcy's was assaulted by fire. Bunce's brother's body was crushed in a mine. Bunce himself was pierced and left with an unhealed wound that would protect him from seizure by the British navy. Snelgrave's body is tied up, and an orange is forced into his mouth. Bunce is poked with Snelgrave's stick, just as Darcy is pierced by a knife. All of the characters are or have been under assault in some way. All have faced death, and ironically, the wealthier, upper-class characters are the ones who die, while Morse, Bunce, and Kabe survive. All of the characters are forced by circumstances to expose themselves in some way. Thus, the play can be read as an elaborate metaphor for a social infection that has to be cleaned by the revelation of truths. Although the setting is London in 1665, similar themes could be played out in any setting, at any time, where people are thrown together in volatile situations ruled by crisis and unpredictability.

Source: Michael J. O'Neal, Critical Essay on *One Flea Spare*, in *Drama for Students*, Gale, Cengage Learning, 2013.

Paul Birchell

In the following review, Birchall commends the dialogue delivery in this California production.

An artistic rendering of the Black Death (© James
Thew | Shutterstock.com)

17th Century." Director Sam Roberts' briskly
paced and intimate production engrossingly captures the era's squalor and edginess, and the
shut-in environment is depicted with admirable
tension. There's decay all over the place, and the
mood suggests that death is actually the characters' fifth roomie.

The dialogue is sharp and often scathingly
funny, delivered with assured comic timing and
emotional wisdom by the crack ensemble, which
is unusually effective at hinting at the chasm of
class differences that yawns between them. Laurino is enthralling as the tightly wound, but
quickly unraveling William, who locks horns
with Freeman's gruffly earthy Bunce. Also
engaging are Matus' touchingly sad and rather
lost Darcy and Sussman's fiery tempered orphan
girl. Ashley Rice's run-down manor basement
set is unusually evocative, and so are Valerie
Bart's fine-gone-to-shabby costumes.

Source: Paul Birchell, "*One Flea Spare* at the Santa
Monica Playhouse," in *Back Stage West*, Vol. 11, No. 16,
April 15, 2004, p. 13.

Madeleine Shaner

*In the following review, Shaner comments that
"this is an important play that belies the peculiar
theory that nobody writes good plays anymore."*

Death has been termed the final leveler that
makes all persons equal. Naomi Wallace, in her
1995 play written 300 years after the event it
memorializes, substitutes the Great Plague of
1665 as the real leveler, the societal yardstick
that made all men equal in the face of murderous,
rat-borne disease. During the plague, which
flamed in populous cities like London, those
who could afford to fled to the country: doctors,
lawyers, men of the cloth, wealthy merchants.
Those who remained suffered mostly from a nox-
ious sense of entitlement: They were too important, it couldn't happen to them—until it did.

Mr. & Mrs. Snelgrave (Robe Monroe and
Christal Montgomery), quarantined in their
home because their servants have died, have
reached the end of their spousal ropes and
almost the end of their house arrest, when two
strangers sneak into their arid lives seeking asy-
lum until the plague has run its course. Bunce
(Steve Spiro) is a deadbeat sailor with language
and manners to match; Morse (Meghan Lynch)
is a spooky 12-year-old girl who says she is the
daughter of dead neighbors. Noticed by the

Naomi Wallace's 1995 play takes place at the
Armageddon—but it's an Armageddon that happened back in 1665, in a London ravaged by the
Black Plague. Wealthy William Snelgrove
(Michael Laurino) and his wife Darcy (Susan
Matus) are quarantined in their mansion, while
waiting to find out if they're "clean" of the dreaded
disease laying waste to the city. The couple's cozy
environs are invaded by a pair of thieves—unemployed sailor Bunce (Clark Freeman) and orphan
girl Morse (Mariah Sussman)—who are then
bricked up in the house with the owner couple.

The four unlikely housemates are forced to
live together for a month, until the doors are
unlocked, with their only news from the outside
world coming from a sleazy guard (Frank
Smith), who trades tangerines for sexual favors.
In the claustrophobic atmosphere, the four prisoners' engrained class differences all start to fall
away. Darcy becomes smitten with the sexy
Bunce, who himself realizes that William ain't
that much different from him under the belt.

Wallace's play is equal parts historical
drama, social satire, and "Big Brother in the

greedy Kabe (Alan Loayza)—a sometimes guard, sometimes slime-ball procurer—the expanded household's quarantine period is extended for a month. The enforced isolation of the four disparate people creates its own furnace of festering anger and sexual heat. Deprived of the social contract, with inevitable role reversals as the balance of power shifts from the privileged to the despised, decency and dignity and respect for the humanity of the other are speedy casualties in this dismal microcosm.

Monroe has well mastered the repulsiveness of the callous, twisted aristocrat he portrays. Montgomery, at first demure and oppressed, excitingly morphs into the woman she might have been. Spiro makes his disreputable sailor a memorable character, almost noble by comparison with the upper-class, lily-livered boor he is expected to serve. Lynch, though not always audible, projects an otherworldly quality as the pixilated child. Loayza, playing a character removed from the suffocating center of the drama, is a less effective voice for Wallace's fiercely political poetry.

This is shattering subject matter, and the writing is original and brilliant, but Jennifer Ruper directs the spare, madly sensual nightmare as if it were a slow-paced dirge, which diminishes its power to disturb. The urgency of the drama and its visceral potential dissipate as key players are masked by others; characters upstage one another or are littered against the back wall as if the director didn't know what to do with them; too many speeches are delivered facing upstage so clarity is lost, and dubious accents make the dialogue sometimes hard to follow.

Nevertheless, this is an important play that belies the peculiar theory that nobody writes good plays anymore.

Source: Madeleine Shaner, "*One Flea Spare* at the Lillian Theatre," in *Back Stage West*, Vol. 9, No. 29, July 18, 2002, p. 14.

Walter Bilderback

In the following essay, Bilderback relates the reasons that Vincent Murphy, artistic producing director of Atlanta's Theater Emory, chose Wallace's work for his festival.

To call Vincent Murphy, artistic producing director of Atlanta's Theater Emory, a fan of the work of Naomi Wallace is an understatement. Her writing, he says, is "Brecht seen through the lens of Faulkner and Caryl Churchill."

> SHE DOESN'T SHY AWAY FROM GENUINE COMPLEXITIES, AND THE PLAYS RAISE QUESTIONS THAT URGE US TO FIND CONNECTIONS EVERYWHERE— AMONG SUCH PHENOMENA AS HOMOPHOBIA, RACISM, MILITARISM, GENDER ATTITUDES, SEX, THE BODY… AND POETRY."

Murphy illustrates his admiration by describing a scene from Wallace's 1998 drama *The Trestle at Pope Lick Creek*. The couple Gin and Dray, rural factory workers in Depression-era Kentucky, are discussing their situation: Dray has been laid off from his job, and Gin works in a glass factory where a new process has turned the hands of the women workers glow-in-the-dark blue. Their teenage son is in jail on suspicion of murder, and they're having difficulty remembering why, years ago, they fell in love with each other (a love that, as in all of Wallace's plays, is frankly sexual). As they talk, Wallace's text requires that they throw a plate back and forth—and that it shatter at the end of the scene.

"Who does this? Who thinks this way?" Murphy marvels, as he remembers being "blown away" by the scene when the play debuted at the Actors Theatre of Louisville Humana Festival. "This is a voice we don't understand"— which for him is the mark of a potentially great writer.

Never one to let his enthusiasms lie untested, Murphy asked himself—and the entire Atlanta theatre community—a question: "What if a dozen theatres across Atlanta got together to present the works of this not-so-well-known American playwright, Naomi Wallace?" His colleagues were mostly unfamiliar with Wallace's work (none of her plays had ever been produced in Atlanta), but Murphy's case for her literary importance was as convincing as his ardor was contagious: In short order, the theatres of Atlanta had signed on to Murphy's mammoth challenge.

As plans for the autumn-long festival developed, Wallace's stock grew, especially when the Kentucky-born writer was named a MacArthur "genius grant" winner in 1999. Murphy served as yenta for the project, attempting to match Wallace's plays with the strengths and styles of the theatres taking part. In most cases, his suggestions worked out. "I didn't think *One Flea Spare* was the right play for us," commented Hope Minis of the four-year-old Sychronicity Performance Group. "Then I read the play." Synchronicity's Michele Pearce credits Murphy with "a knack for matching companies with plays," which comes from a deep understanding of "who these Atlanta companies are."

The final pieces fell into place when Wallace agreed to allow Theater Emory to workshop *The Inland Sea* (formerly titled Fugitive Cant), a new play commissioned by the Royal Shakespeare Company, this past April as part of its Brave New Works series, and to participate in the festival herself over the course of a week in November; when she would see the various productions and answer questions for the public.

The prospect of having personal access to Wallace electrified the theatres involved and brought the Georgia Shakespeare Festival into the mix—artistic director Richard Garner asked to direct a further developmental reading of *Inland Sea* for the festival, saying he was "smitten with the imagery, the poetry, the mystery, the lustiness, the gutsiness—all the good Naomi stuff."

In the end, three theatres agreed to mount full productions: In addition to *One Flea Spare* at Synchronicity, Murphy would direct *Trestle* at Theatre Emory, and (most ambitiously) Push-Push Theatre would take on three plays in rotating rep—*In the Heart of America, The Girl Who Fell Through a Hole in Her Jumper* (a children's piece co-written with Wallace's partner Bruce MacLeod) and *The Bone Gardens*, an early work that had never received a professional production—all under the direction of PushPush founder Tim Haberger. Other theatres staged readings or site-specific performances of Wallace plays, monologues and poetry.

As preparations continued over the summer; there was a growing sense of excitement at being involved in a common endeavor. Then came Sept. 11.

The day before the terrorist attacks, the Naomi Wallace Festival was an interesting experiment in theatrical community-building for the participants. By the next day, like so much else in the world, it had become something else: a laboratory of questions about what theatre can

and should provide in a time of crisis, an examination of the role of art in the wake of tragedy.

Rehearsals for *One Flea Spare*, set to begin on Sept. 11, were delayed for five days when director Rachel May was unable to fly out of Boston's Logan International Airport. Was this kind of theatrical enterprise even "necessary" (some of the artists involved asked themselves), given the situation? What would the reaction be to a festival of works so charged with a left-wing critique of society? Two of the plays, *In the Heart of America* and *The Retreating World*, dealt with the aftermath of the Gulf War—the former tied American military involvements over the past half-century to male fear of otherness; the latter, a monologue scheduled at Actor's Express, was told from the standpoint of an Iraqi solder reeling from Desert Storm. Would these pieces be seen as unpatriotic? Was it appropriate to present notions critical of the American government's past Mideast policies during the new "war on terrorism"?

At Actor's Express, director Wier Harman and actor Brad Davidorff discussed dropping the production. Davidorff worried that the piece might be "anachronistic in the changed climate." But watching the television coverage of the World Trade Center and the Pentagon, the actor found himself thinking that Americans had a "new vulnerability" that would help them understand the horrors inflicted on the retreating Iraqi army described in *Retreating World*. Harman began to see the show's carefully delineated character, a man opposed to Saddam Hussein yet conscripted into his army, as an antidote to stereotypes of Arabs and Muslims.

"It would have been inappropriate to do it at this time if it had just been agitprop," Harman told interviewer Jennifer Deer in a half-hour special on Atlanta public radio. Instead, he found his "emotional investment" in the project soaring. "At a time when a lot of artists are questioning the value of art, I'm reminded of its clarifying value in a moment like this, when I am lucky enough to be working on a piece that is so meaningful," the director declared.

Other artists shared Harman's response. Events in the plays gained deeper meaning as connections to the larger world presented themselves. Pearce, listening to the first run-though of *One Flea Spare*, a tale of the London plague of 1665, found "the fear of dying striking me in a way it never had before." Stranded in Boston, May found new relevance in a play "about an invisible enemy, and people isolating themselves to keep from getting hurt." Flea actress Kathleen Warns was struck by other parallels: "We're all suspicious of each other and the air we breathe and the water we drink. Are we in danger?"

Wallace herself was strongly affected by the convergence of the festival and the tragedy. "I was feeling like less than nothing, as many are, in the face of all this," she wrote in response to an e-mail confirming the Atlanta theatres' dedication to the festival. "That you and others are doing my work gives my spirit a purpose and a lift."

From the festival's first performance—a testosterone-infused staged reading of Wallace's *War Boys* (like *Bone Gardens*, never professionally produced in the U.S.) at Dad's Garage Theatre Company—it was obvious that something special was happening, and that Murphy's brainstorm had been visionary.

The sense of purpose the artists found radiated off the festival's stages and individual performances. *Flea* and *Trestle*, both excellently directed, featured superb ensembles, made more remarkable because their central characters were played by adolescents (most notably, 15-year-old Rachel Durston in *Flea*) whose work melded seamlessly with that of their experienced cast mates.

The opportunity to take in so much of Wallace's work in a short time seemed to justify Murphy's belief in her importance as an American writer. Taken as a whole, her body of work is far less didactic than it may appear on the page or in individual productions. She doesn't shy away from genuine complexities, and the plays raise questions that urge us to find connections everywhere—among such phenomena as homophobia, racism, militarism, gender attitudes, sex, the body...and poetry. The plays (with the exception of *Trestle*) exhibit a surprising amount of humor and an unexpected sense of the craving for forgiveness, or rather the craving to forgive.

Finally, there is the eroticism of Wallace's writing: In the worlds of her plays, breath or the imagination can be as potent as an embrace. (Indeed, directors and actors would do well to examine skeptically any urge for physical contact not specified in Wallace's stage directions.) She speaks to, and for, the body as eloquently as any American writer since Walt Whitman. And, as director Gayle Austin points out, Wallace's imagination and generosity of spirit allow her to speak for both women and men. Murphy admires the

playwright's "recognition that we're all halves of something, that we're all much more erotic and tender and forgiving than we can allow ourselves to be," due to the impact of society.

At the end of the month of readings and productions, this observer felt an almost crazy sense of optimism, of hope for the future. Murphy praises Wallace for "actually believing things can be different," and I found myself sharing some of that conviction in Atlanta theatres. This was not a bad goal before Sept. 11; it feels all the more important now.

Wallace herself felt similar emotions. In an open e-mail to festival participants, she wrote: "Attending the festival of my plays in Atlanta was the most moving experience I have ever had in theatre, and perhaps may ever have. It wasn't only the sheer volume of work that was done, not the consistently high quality, but a feeling of my work having a dynamic home in Atlanta that is not just for today, but for tomorrow as well. The festival gave my work a wide-open space in which to be considered and challenged and debated. That is what my work longs for."

Source: Walter Bilderback, "The City That Embraced Naomi Wallace: In Atlanta, a Dozen Theatres Plumb the Depths of One Writer's Work," in *American Theatre*, Vol. 19, No. 2, February 2002, pp. 54–58.

Laurie Stone
In the following excerpt, Stone feels that a liveliness is missing in this production of One Flea Spare.

Naomi Wallace's *One Flea Spare* (Public Theater) is lousy with ideas and gorgeous writing, but it never quite quickens so you believe in the characters. John Patrick Shanley's *Psychopathia Sexualis* (Manhattan Theater Club) has hardly any ideas and sometimes sounds like a smart sitcom, but the play—its first, dud scene notwithstanding—is plenty alive. *Peter and Wendy* (New Victory Theater), a version of J.M. Barrie's tale of flying runaways, limbos lower into kiddie theater by presenting the play as a puppet show; but via the avant-garde factory Mabou Mines, the evening lifts off its moorings of innocence and sentimentality, becoming a meditation on exile so plangent the audience sobs. Go figure.

Championed by Tony Kushner and boosted by Vivian Gornick's profile in the *New York Times Magazine*, *Flea* arrived as a challenge to

American audiences. Wallace, a political play-wright, has been well received in Britain but not here, the understanding being that Brits are more open to excavations of class. The case can be made. Brit playwrights Edward Bond, Caryl Churchill, Jim Cartwright and Barrie Keefe extend a tradition, embracing chimney sweeps and Artful Dodgers, fens and colonial high jinks, squatters on the dole, nohopers and soccer head-bashers. Our political playwrights—Kushner, Maria Irene Fornes, Romulus Linney, Mac Well-man—are concerned with class but also identity, be it a hunt for ethnic roots or the chase for minority rights. In their work, politics is a way of seeing, not so much flagged ideas. *Flea* sounds like a Brit play because class is its bold-print focus; sex and sexual politics are present too, but class is its passion, as in eat, . . . and kill the poor.

And Wallace, by setting her play in plague-ridden London, 1665, has conceived a brilliant situation to level the classes, so that a pound of rich flesh is in just as much peril as a pound of poor flesh. A 12-year-old girl and a fugitive sailor steal into the home of a high-born couple quar-antined there. Outside, enforcing the restrictions, is a watchman from the starving classes, the per-fect scavenger whose wits have sharpened him for this ordeal. The contest winds up four against one: a rich old white guy whose privilege can't protect him, besieged by females and underclass men. The old guy is petty, prurient and lacks the imagina-tion to understand his disadvantage. That's what kills him—not seeing the present or future.

There's grittiness in the sensual detail Wal-lace builds: The watchman begs to kiss the foot of the little girl as she flirts with him; the sailor recalls loving a cabin boy; the lady dips her hand into a wound in the sailor's side that won't heal. We see possibilities for Wallace's dreaminess in these riffs, but the sensuality can't slink out of the service to which it's put. The play wants to teach more than let the characters breathe. Still, a livelier production would have helped. Under Ron Daniels's direction the piece seems under water, the actors slogging through, though as the sailor, Bill Camp stirs excitement with his animal sensitivity to hurt and need. Dianne Wiest, encased in a voluminous gown, is wooden, and young Mischa Barton in the difficult role of the child Morse is out of her depth. . . .

Source: Laurie Stone, Review of *One Flea Spare*, in *Nation*, Vol. 264, No. 19, May 19, 1997, p. 34.

SOURCES

Brantley, Ben, "Prisoners in Their Home, Facing the Twin Ravages of Plague and Power," in *New York Times*, March 10, 1997, http://www.nytimes.com/1997/03/10/theater/prisoners-in-their-home-facing-the-twin-ra vages-of-plague-and-power.html?pagewanted = all&src = pm (accessed July 30, 2012).

Chambers, Mortimer, et al., *The Western Experience*, 7th ed., McGraw-Hill, 1999, pp. 355–56.

Cummings, Scott T., "Naomi Wallace," in *Dictionary of Literary Biography*, Vol. 249, *Twentieth-Century Ameri-can Dramatists, Third Series*, edited by Christopher Wheatley, The Gale Group, 2001, pp. 345–52.

Defoe, Daniel, *A Journal of the Plague Year*, edited by Louis Landa and David Roberts, Oxford University Press, 1999, p. 258.

"England and the Netherlands: The Ties between Two Nations: The Anglo-Dutch Wars," Koninklijke Biblio-theek website, http://www.geheugenvannederland.nl/?/en/collecties/nederland_engeland/zeeoorlogen (accessed July 31, 2012).

Evans, Everett, "*One Flea Spare* Is Haunting and Beau-tiful," in *Houston Chronicle*, April 25, 2008, http://www.chron.com/entertainment/article/One-Flea-Spare-is-haunting-and-beautiful-1598696.php (accessed July 30, 2012).

"Fact about Pneumonic Plague," Centers for Disease Control and Prevention website, http://www.bt.cdc.gov/agent/plague/factsheet.asp (accessed November 9, 2012).

"From Rivalry to Mergers: A Brief History of the Anglo-Dutch Business Model," in *Economist*, February 10 2005, http://www.economist.com/node/3651687 (accessed August 7, 2012).

Gardner, Lyn, Review of *One Flea Spare*, in *London Guardian*, April 6, 2011, http://www.guardian.co.uk/stage/2011/apr/06/one-flea-spare-review (accessed August 1, 2012).

"The Great Plague of 1665–6," National Archives (UK) website, http://www.nationalarchives.gov.uk/education/lesson49.htm (accessed July 31, 2012).

"In-Yer-Face Theatre," *Seirz: New Writing for the British Stage* website, http://www.inyerface-theatre.com/what.html (accessed August 3, 2012).

Jefferson, Margo, "The Avant-Garde, Rarely Love at First Sight," in *New York Times*, July 8, 2005, http://www.nytimes.com/2005/07/08/theater/newsandfeatures/08jeff.html?pagewanted = all (accessed August 5, 2012).

Lahr, John, Review of *One Flea Spare*, NC Stage Com-pany website, http://www.ncstage.org/pages/productions/mainstage-season/one-flea-spare.php (accessed August 6, 2012); originally published in the *New Yorker*, May 24, 1997.

Marks, Peter, "Forum Theatre's Dismal *One Flea Spare*," in *Washington Post*, February 23, 2011, http://www.

washingtonpost.com/wp-dyn/content/article/2011/02/22/AR2011022206780.html (accessed July 30, 2012).

"Naomi Wallace: Broadway Play Publishing Inc. Playwright of the Year 1997," Broadway Play Publishing website, http://www.broadwayplaypubl.com/WALLACE.HTM (accessed July 26, 2012).

"Oranges and Lemons," Rotherham Paranormal website, http://www.rotherham-ghosts.com/grimnurseryrhymes.htm#110293399 (accessed August 5, 2012).

"Plague," Human Diseases and Conditions website, http://www.humanillnesses.com/original/Pan-Pre/Plague.html (accessed July 31, 2012).

"Risk of Death from Plague Today and in History," Bandolier website, http://www.medicine.ox.ac.uk/bandolier/booth/risk/plague.html (accessed August 1, 2012).

Simon, John, *John Simon on Theatre: Criticism 1974–2003*, Applause Books, 2005, pp. 664–66.

Wallace, Naomi, *One Flea Spare*, Broadway Play Publishing, 1997.

"Well-Made Play," in *Merriam-Webster's Encyclopedia of Literature*, Merriam-Webster, 1995, pp. 1190–91.

"What Holds the World Together in a Plague," International Centre for Environmental Health website, http://www.iceh.net/?p = 207 (accessed August 1, 2012).

Zacher, Scotty, Review of *One Flea Spare*, in *Chicago Theater Beat*, April 16, 2011, http://chicagotheaterbeat.com/2011/04/16/one-flea-spare-review-eclipse-theatre-chicago/ (accessed July 30, 2012).

It explores how these devastating diseases changed the course of history.

Knopf, Robert, and Julia Listengarten, eds., *Theater of the Avant-Garde, 1950–2000: A Critical Anthology*, Yale University Press, 2011.

> Readers interested in modern avant-garde theater will find this collection fruitful. It includes essays by theatrical practitioners and focuses in part on the dynamic relationship between text and performance.

Moote, A. Lloyd, and Dorothy C. Moote, *The Great Plague: The Story of London's Most Deadly Year*, Johns Hopkins University Press, 2004.

> This volume examines the Great Plague of London in 1665. A. Lloyd Moote is a historian, and Dorothy C. Moote is a microbiologist. Together, they focus on the experiences of nine individuals during the plague, including those of the famous diarist Samuel Pepys.

Underdown, David, *A Freeborn People: Politics and the Nation in Seventeenth-Century England*, Oxford University Press, 1996.

> This volume will appeal to readers interested in the history of England during the seventeenth century. The author explores how the political cultures and beliefs of the higher social classes and the common people intersected during the century.

FURTHER READING

Fisher, James, *Historical Dictionary of Contemporary American Theater: 1930–2010*, Scarecrow Press, 2011.

> Readers interested generally in contemporary theater will find in this volume discussion of the plays, people, movements, and institutions that shaped the American stage from 1930 to 2010. The book includes a chronology, an introductory essay, an extensive bibliography, and more than 1,500 cross-referenced dictionary entries.

Giblin, James Cross, *When Plague Strikes: The Black Death, Smallpox, AIDS*, HarperCollins, 1997.

> This volume, written for young adults, traces the history of three major diseases, including the Black Death—that is, the bubonic plague.

SUGGESTED SEARCH TERMS

Anglo-Dutch wars

avant-garde theater

Black Death

bubonic plague

Daniel Defoe AND Journal of the Plague Year

experimental theater

Great Plague

John Donne AND The Flea

Los Angeles AND riots 1992

Naomi Wallace

Naomi Wallace AND One Flea Spare

Rodney King

Poker!

ZORA NEALE HURSTON

1931

Zora Neale Hurston was a leading figure of the Harlem Renaissance but fell into obscurity after her career was clouded by scandal and changing tastes. Her work as a writer and a folklorist has come back into vogue since the 1990s, and she is recognized as a great American writer. *Poker!*, a political allegory set among the criminal gangs of Harlem, was performed for only a week in 1931 before it fell victim to the economic troubles of the Great Depression. When Hurston's life ended in poverty, the play's single surviving manuscript was almost burned as waste, but it was rescued and restored to the world by the efforts of the Library of Congress where the play was read in 2005. Its first publication soon followed in 2008. *Poker!* draws on a rich tradition of black folklore and verbal artistry, while at the same time reflecting the underside of the Harlem Renaissance.

AUTHOR BIOGRAPHY

Hurston was born on January 7, 1891, in the small town of Notasulga in Alabama. At that time, African Americans faced official and even legal discrimination. Schools and neighborhoods were segregated, and blacks, especially in the South, were generally denied the right to vote. Because of limited economic opportunities, the black community was far poorer than

Zora Neale Hurston (The Library of Congress)

America as a whole. Nevertheless, Hurston was born into relatively favorable circumstances. Her father, John, was a Baptist minister and moved his family to the town of Eatonville, Florida, which had a mostly black population. There he took over a larger congregation and eventually became the mayor of the town.

Hurston's mother died in 1904, and her father remarried. Her new stepmother had her sent off to a boarding school and then cut her off entirely from any family support. Hurston worked for several years as a maid for a white opera singer and then won a scholarship to Morgan Academy (an exclusively black preparatory school in Baltimore). In order to qualify, Hurston had to claim she had been born in 1901, which led to confusion about her biography until recently. She then attended Howard University where she published her first short story, "John Redding Goes to Sea," in 1921 and earned an associate's degree. In 1924, she won a prize for her short story "Drenched in Light" from the national black magazine *Opportunity*.

The awards ceremony for the prize in Harlem was an important turning point in her life. She decided not merely to visit but to move to New York. At the banquet, she met Langston Hughes and other leading intellectuals of the Harlem Renaissance and quickly became integrated into their circle.

Her contacts secured her a scholarship to Barnard College, then the women's college of Columbia University, where she became its first black student. At Barnard, she worked under the anthropologist Franz Boas and completed a bachelor's degree in anthropology. She also worked for two years on a master's degree but never completed it. Under Boas's guidance, Hurston studied the language and folklore of the black community in Harlem. She would spend the next twenty years studying black culture in the American South and the Caribbean, resulting in the publication of studies of folklore, such as *Mules and Men* (1935), as well novels and other literary forms that also reflected her research, such as *Their Eyes Were Watching God* (1937), which is generally considered her masterpiece.

Hurston believed that she had a good understanding of the theater from her years spent as a maid in an opera company dedicated to productions of Gilbert and Sullivan operas. She wrote a number of plays, but she never became an established playwright. Part of her difficulty in this area arose from a conflict over authorship she had with Langston Hughes regarding their play *Mule Bone*. *Poker!* was part of a group of four one-act plays Hurston wrote for the revue *Fast and Furious* in 1931. This was an all-black revue meant to capitalize on interest in the Harlem Renaissance, but it closed in a week. The Great Depression had dried up the white audience for black theater.

Hurston's writing was supported by grants from various Works Projects Authority programs and the Guggenheim Foundation, as well as by the private patronage of Charlotte Osgood Mason, a white heiress who lavished money on the leaders of the Harlem Renaissance. In 1948, Hurston was falsely accused of child molestation, and though she was acquitted in court, her reputation never recovered. Her patronage and grants evaporated, and she was no longer able to publish. She was only able to put into print a handful of small articles in local newspapers in Florida, where she relocated. She fell into poverty and had to work again as a maid, a substitute teacher, and a library clerk.

She continued to write copiously, however, and the Library of Congress has a large collection of her unpublished manuscript material. *Poker!* was never published in her lifetime and was salvaged from the papers left at her death. Hurston suffered a stroke in 1959 and had to move into the Saint Lucie County Welfare Home, where she died the next year on January 28. The janitor there was on the verge of burning Hurston's papers when a security guard suggested they might be sold to help pay off her debts. The play was finally published in 2008.

PLOT SUMMARY

Poker! begins with the *dramatis personae*, or list of characters, and a description of the set. Even these perfunctory sections hint at Hurston's interest in black folk traditions. The characters are all identified by colorful nicknames, a common practice in the black community of the time. The set is described as the "front room of a shotgun house." A shotgun house is a narrow structure, one room wide, with a door in the front room opening directly into the next room and so on until the back door with no hallways. This kind of house was very common in the large free black community in New Orleans in the first half of the nineteenth century. The floor plan seems to have been brought to New Orleans by Haitian immigrants, and it may owe something to architectural styles from Africa. After the civil war, shotgun houses became common throughout the South and, during the Great Migration of Southern blacks to the northern industrial cities that peaked during World War I, in neighborhoods in the North as well.

The play begins in the middle of a card game. Five men are sitting around the table while a sixth, Nunkie, is playing a piano against the wall. Nunkie is newly arrived, and the others invite him to come to the table so the next hand can begin. They verbally spar by exchanging insults with each other over who is the better poker player. Nunkie defers and first goes through an extended line of patter telling a story organized around the thirteen cards in a suit. It is a blues song-like story about a tragic love affair that ends in betrayal and murder, and it works its way around to a reassertion of Nunkie's skill at gambling. The text is organized into rhyming couplets but does not scan as poetry

(that is, there is no regular pattern of stressed and unstressed syllables in the lines):

> The King stands for Sweet Papa Nunkie and he's goin' to wear the crown, So be careful you all ain't broke when the deal goes down!

When Nunkie finally sits down at the table, Tush Hawg, the host of the game, demands a two-dollar fee from him (a working man's salary in 1931 might have been one or two dollars a day). Nunkie pays it but again turns it into an assertion of his status as a superior gambler: "I didn't put it down because I knew you all goin' to be puttin' it right back in my pocket." They are playing draw poker, in which each man is dealt five cards and discards up to three cards to receive the same number of new ones.

As the draw goes around the table, the players continue to try to top each other. Sack Daddy asserts that his hand is bad, but Black Baby suggests that this complaint is deceptive and says he will be on guard against Sack Daddy having a good hand. When the players are not claiming superiority over one another, they link their luck at cards to their success or failure in romantic relationships.

After the drawing is done but before the last round of betting begins, Aunt Dilsey emerges into the front room from deeper within the house, coming in through a set of portieres, or curtains used in place of a door. She tells the players, "You all oughter be ashamed of yourself, gamblin' and carryin' on like this! . . . If you don't stop this card playing', all of you all goin' to die and go to hell." Black Baby insists that the game is innocent. Having delivered her warning, Aunt Dilsey goes back through the curtain.

While Aunt Dilsey was in the room, all of the card players looked at her, and each of the players takes advantage of the distraction to cheat by switching cards from his hand with others he had previously hidden in his clothes against just such a chance. After she leaves, the final round of betting is conducted, which brings the pot to one hundred and fifty dollars. While they are betting, the men cannot keep from taunting each other and even threatening violence. The threats are not serious but are just the kinds of phrases they commonly use in conversation. For instance, when Too-Sweet says the proverbial, "Put your money where your mouth is," Tush Hawg replies, "I'll [put] my fist where yo' mouf is!"

As the cards are revealed the dialogue, becomes more intense and the threats more substantive. The language moves beyond black dialect to the argot (secret language) of the criminal gangs of 1920s Harlem, about which very little is known. Sack Daddy was the last to bet and so reveals his cards first, showing four aces. Tush Hawg immediately reveals that he too has four aces, which is impossible and a sure sign that someone is cheating. Tush Hawg accuses Sack Daddy, "Don't try to carry the Pam-Pam to me 'cause I'll gently chain-gang for you!" This probably means something like: *don't lie to me, I'll have you arrested for cheating*. Sack Daddy responds with yet another threat of violence to defend himself. The meaning of his statement, "Then I'll give my case to Miss Bush and let Mother Green stand my bond!" is probably irrecoverable, but he maintains that he was dealt the aces fairly.

Nunkie now reveals that he has four aces also, insists the other two are lying about not cheating, and threatens murder to defend his claim to the pot. Peckerwood speaks up on behalf of Tush Hawg, threatening to kill Nunkie for insulting him. Black Baby has four aces as well and brandishes his straight razor in a threat to kill anyone else who claims the pot. Too-Sweet and Tush Hawg now both produce pistols. Between the two of them, they kill the other four players and each other, so that in the space of a few seconds of stage business all of the men are left lying dead. Hearing the gunshots, Aunt Dilsey now returns and ends the play with a punch line: "It sure is goin' to be a whole lot tougher in hell now!"

CHARACTERS

Aunt Dilsey

Given the brevity of *Poker!*, more a scene than a full act, there is little room for character development, and so the characters are all recognizable stereotypes. Aunt Dilsey is a middle-aged churchgoing lady, a type as familiar from the literature of the Harlem Renaissance as she must have been in real life. She is presumably the aunt of Tush Hawg, who is hosting the game, but this is never made clear. The term "aunt," however, could be an affectionate colloquialism for a more distant relative or even a family friend. It could also be a general term of respect in view of her maternal qualities, which seems to be the case from the fact that Black Baby also addresses her as Aunt Dilsey. Her condemnation

of the gamblers' sinful lifestyle is a commonplace of black church morality, but Hurston included her final line more as a humorous punch line than as a reflection of her character.

Black Baby

By the time Hurston wrote *Poker!* in 1931, she had already conducted several years' worth of anthropological field work in Florida, collecting folktales from small towns and in the labor camps that grew up around factories and other centers of employment for casual laborers. The results of her research would be published in *Mules and Men* in 1935, where she identifies her informants by their nicknames. Many of the names of the characters in *Poker!* were derived from these nicknames, including Black Baby. Hurston found that issues of status in the black community were constantly negotiated through social interaction, and the use of nicknames, which could be badges of honor or shame, were part of this process. Interestingly, although the characters with these nicknames in *Poker!* are all male, many of the real people they are derived from were women. This gender switching may be Hurston's comment on the exaggerated machismo, which many young black men felt they had to adopt. Black Baby, like all the male characters in the play, is a low-level gangster or hustler in the terminology of 1930s Harlem, as ready to cheat at cards as to commit murder. Although he really fares no worse than any of the others, Hurston puts him in the unfortunate position of bringing a straight razor to a gunfight.

Nunkie

Although it would be hard to say that *Poker!* has a main character, Nunkie has far more lines than any other character because of his verbal display at the beginning of the drama. His character is somewhat more developed than the others because he excels as a verbal artist, which is a source of pride and respect. He, of course, begins the play with his extended patter that in many ways is the most interesting section of the play. He is always ready with clever word play and complex expressions. Even in the extreme circumstances that lead up to the final horrific violence at the end of the play, Nunkie cannot restrain himself from an extravagant pun such as: "Both of you is lyin'! Lyin' like the cross-ties from New York to Key West!" playing on *lie*, to deceive, and *lie*, to lie on the ground like railroad ties.

Peckerwood

Peckerwood is perhaps the least developed character among the poker players. He seems to be subordinate to Tush Hawg because he comes to his defense against the charge of cheating even once it is obvious that they were all cheating. His nickname is the most conventional of any of the characters, denoting inexperience and ineffectiveness. He is also the only one who does not declare his own hand and insist on taking the pot. Hurston does give him a very well-crafted and evocative turn of phrase as his own death threat: "I'm going to bust hell wide open with a man!"

Sack Daddy

Sack Daddy is another name Hurston borrowed from her anthropological field work. In general, the poker players are all highly superstitious. Because of the general powerlessness of blacks in American society and the uncertainties of a life of crime, the hustlers have little control over their lives, so the world seems to them to be controlled by mysterious powers that must be negotiated and appeased in the same way as the people they interact with. Sack Daddy, for instances thinks that fate or luck governs his life and will express itself in the same way in one part of his life as in another. Therefore, he sees his bad luck at poker as a sign that his girl-friend must be cheating on him too: "My gal must be cheatin' on me. I ain't had a pair since John Henry had a hammer!" The remark also shows Hurston's interest in black folklore through the reference to the folk hero John Henry, subject of a popular folk song ("John Henry Had a Hammer").

Too-Sweet

Too-Sweet was another of Hurston's informants from Florida, a woman with whom she became close friends, whose name was borrowed for *Poker!* The character Too-Sweet may be a bit more prone to violence than the other gangsters, because he is the first to draw a gun in the final altercation at the end of the play. This invites investigation into why all of the card players are so prone to violence, which is to say, why they became gangsters in the first place. Too-Sweet and the others live in a community that is oppressed by racial discrimination, a factor that prevents them becoming successful in life through their own efforts. They cannot carve out an identity, particularly a masculine identity,

by participating in the "American dream," working themselves into a position where they could support a stable family through their own hard work and effort.

As a result, they cannot simply discount challenges to their manhood through confidence in their own success in conventional terms. The only thing they have is their ability to defend their *honor* (i.e., their masculine identities) through acts of personal violence. This why their conversation consists almost entirely of insults and responses to insults through threats or humor, which is merely a disguised kind of aggression. Too-Sweet and the other players are constantly negotiating their positions within the group through verbal violence and their ability to back up their words with violence. If they accept dishonor and humiliation, for example, by admitting they are cheating at cards, there is nothing left of their identities, so they lose very little by actually resorting to physical violence and murder, actions that are always just below the surface for them.

This is why they are willing to risk their own lives to win the pot. The money is on the one hand as much as an ordinary worker might see in several months, but the value of the money is trivial compared to what it signifies: the status of each man depends on his ability to claim the pot. Malcolm X became the same kind of petty gangster in his youth in Harlem and describes their psychology in exquisite detail in his autobiography:

> Full-time hustlers never can relax to appraise what they are doing and where they are bound. As is the case in any jungle, the hustler's every waking hour is lived with both the practical and subconscious knowledge that if he ever relaxes, if he ever slows down, the other hungry, restless foxes, ferrets, wolves, and vultures out there with him won't hesitate to make him their prey.

Tush Hawg

Tush Hawg is the host of the poker game because he collects a fee from Nunkie to join the game. Tush Hawg therefore probably lives with Aunt Dilsey, who may well be his aunt. Tush Hawg may also be a leader of higher rank within the criminal hierarchy in which the poker players function, because Peckerwood seems to exhibit some kind of subservience to him. Tush Hawg also initiates the round of murders that end the play.

THEMES

Crime

New York was a magnet for many in the United States as a city of opportunity, and Harlem was specifically appealing because, in comparison with other black communities in the country, it was relatively prosperous. Harlem attracted not only the intellectuals who made the culture of the Harlem Renaissance but every kind of individual, as the civil rights leader Malcolm X recalled in his autobiography, "I had heard a lot about 'the Big Apple,' as it was called by the well-traveled musicians, merchant mariners, salesmen, chauffeurs for white families, and various kinds of hustlers I ran into." Segregation made the black community less likely to divide itself into neighborhoods based on class.

The young Malcolm soon found himself among the thick of the organized crime element in Harlem, encountering them in the bars before working men got off of their jobs: "these were the cream of the older, more mature operators in Harlem. The day's 'numbers' business was done. The night's gambling and other forms of hustling hadn't yet begun." The top levels of crime in Harlem operated a lottery—the *numbers*—that was a vital part of Harlem culture, because, despite the relative prosperity of the neighborhood, blacks still had few means of really advancing themselves because of their segregated and second-class status within American society. Many ordinary citizens of Harlem looked to the numbers as their only hope of gaining any kind of comfortable life, fantastic as that hope might have been in reality.

It is no doubt because of this special status of organized crime in the Harlem community that Aunt Dilsey is willing to tolerate a relative who was a gangster living in her house. A life of crime was not as shocking as it would have been in the more prosperous white community, and segregation limited everyone's options. In addition to the numbers, the gangs also ran drug dealing, other forms of gambling, and every kind of theft and swindling imaginable, what Malcolm calls *hustling*. He goes on to say that by socializing with these criminals, "I was thus schooled well, by experts in such hustles as the numbers, pimping, con games of many kinds, peddling dope, and thievery of all sorts, including armed robbery."

The male characters in *Poker!* are hustlers of the kind described by Malcolm X, not the sophisticated senior gangsters who patronized him but relatively violent and thuggish criminals on the lower rungs of the criminal order. They are all experienced card cheats and are ready at a moment's notice to use deadly violence when they are exposed as cheats. They prefer to kill rather than suffer the humiliation and loss of status that their failure at cheating would bring. In Hurston's Harlem of the 1920s, the criminal element existed but was more marginal than in Malcolm's Harlem of the 1940s following the Great Depression. By 1931, the time of *Poker!*, crime would already have been on the upswing in tandem with poverty in the black community.

Black Culture

Hurston was trained in anthropology at Columbia University and devoted her career to studying black folk culture; even her fictional works are firmly rooted in the black folk tradition. In *Poker!* Hurston is particularly interested in the way language traditions are used to define status—and to vie for status—within the black community. Language display takes on a special importance in black culture because the poverty and powerlessness imposed on the black community by segregation interfered with other kinds of display, such as showing off wealth or displays of political and economic power.

Much of the dialogue in *Poker!* consists of boasting and one or more other characters undercutting another's boast, which is a way of negotiating status within the group. At the very beginning of the play, for instance, Nunkie boasts of his card-playing prowess, and Black Baby immediately responds, "Aw, you can be had," gainsaying the boast and then making his own: "My britches is crying for your money!" Then Nunkie repeats his boast, and so on. This kind of exchange could grow into a ritualized trading of insults, the point of which was to show off one's verbal ability in improvisation known in the black community as *playing the dozens*. This is the subject of two of Hurston's other plays in *Fast and Furious*. It may go back to the call and response pattern of formal, public speech in West African culture.

In *Poker!*, however, Nunkie instead makes another kind of display. Nunkie launches into an extraordinary improvisation that cannot be completely described as poetry or storytelling

TOPICS FOR FURTHER STUDY

- Most of Hurston's literary output was informed by her investigations into black folk culture. This is part of a larger phenomenon that began in the eighteenth century in which traditional stories and songs were collected from many cultures by intellectuals, most famously the Brothers Grimm. These collections are often treated as children's literature (under the category of fairy tales), although they were not especially intended for children in their original cultural contexts. Haitian folklore had been treated the same way, in collections like Diane Wolkstein's 1997 *The Magic Orange Tree*, or Mereille Lauture and Kathleen Minkier's 2010 *Bobo, Chen Odasye A | Bobo the Sneaky Dog*. Hurston, however, always used the same kind of material in literature intended for an adult audience. Read some Haitian folktales, and write your own short story based on the plots, themes, or characters that you find most interesting.

- Hurston was frequently filmed and made many film clips and sound recordings in connection with her anthropological work. Although there has been no systematic collection of them on a dedicated website or formal publication, many are posted on the Internet. Use search engines and look on YouTube to find some of these recordings and videos. Most of the originals of Hurston's films are housed at the Library of Congress, and although this material is not available online, they do provide links to a number of sound recordings she and other Works Progress Administration researchers made in Florida (http://international.loc.gov/ammem/collections/florida/). Survey various Hurston-related video and audio materials and present them to your class within a chronological framework based on your research into her life and career.

- Hurston's novel *Jonah's Gourd Vine* grew out of the same folklore researches that received formal publication in her *Mules and Men*. Write a paper identifying and commenting upon shared folklore themes in the two books.

- Stage a production of *Poker!* with your classmates as actors. Film it, and post it to the Internet.

---

or any other simple genre. He mentally walks through the thirteen cards of a suit, tying each one to a successive element of a story out of a blues song, about a lover's betrayal ending in a horrifying act of vengeance. Obviously Hurston has carefully composed the text as she wrote her play, but it reflects the kind of spontaneous verbal artistry that Hurston encountered in her anthropological field work and, indeed, in the communities where she grew up and lived.

Nunkie positively plays with language, not only building up the whole composition from the card game they are playing, but working in references to popular culture ("Eight means eight hours that she Sheba-ed with your Sheik" playing on the popular the film *The Sheik*, as well as making a *double entendre*), and finally turning the whole discourse around to another prediction of his coming triumph in the card game. The other men cannot answer his virtuoso performance, signaling the boost he has given his own status.

STYLE

Dialect

A form of English has existed for centuries in the black community of the United States that is quite distinct from the standard English taught in schools and generally used in the mass media

The poker game takes place in a shotgun house. *(© Robynrg | Shutterstock.com)*

(such as in news reports) and that is comparable to a large degree with regional accents. The black slaves that were transported from West Africa to the British and French colonies in North America during the seventeenth and eighteenth centuries originally spoke hundreds of different languages. They were quickly forced to learn English pidgin, a simplified form of English that allowed for basic communication between them and the crews of the slave ships. In the early days of the slave trade, this evolved into a creole, a regular growing language with its own rules and vocabulary that slaves spoke among themselves. This survives in the isolated islands off the coast of South Carolina and Georgia in the language known as Gullah.

This process parallels the history of English itself, which began as a simplified pidgin that allowed communication among speakers of various Germanic languages in early medieval England and which today is technically a creole. The language spoken by the majority of American blacks is not directly connected to Gullah but is a form of English very closely related to that of white southerners that owes many of its

particularities to the language spoken in the West Country of England, where much of the white southern population originated. It is distinct from the eastern form of English that predominates in New England or the Oxfordshire dialect that is often used as the standard of British English today.

Although many linguistically naïve observers at first think that black English is a mistaken form of standard English, it is simply a different dialect with its own coherent rules and forms that differ from other forms of English for historical reasons. It is no more or less correct than any other language. However, perceptions are often more important than reality in social relations, and blacks are often forced to use standard English in order to gain advantages in education and employment.

Because language is a social, and even a political issue, it is often a source of contention within the black community itself, as Robert McCrum and his collaborators in *The Story of English* observe,

> It remains controversial even in the Black community. For some, it is an authentic means of

self-expression for Black English speakers throughout America and the world. For others, who prefer the norms of Standard English, Black English represents the disadvantaged past, an obstacle to advancement, something better unlearned, denied or forgotten.

The latter attitude is reflected in the *Autobiography of Malcolm X*, whose author considered speaking in dialect as a show of willing inferiority that blacks had to put on to impress white people with their servility:

> It didn't take me a week to learn that all you had to do was give white people a show and they'd buy anything you offered them....The dining car waiters and Pullman porters knew it too, and they faked their Uncle Tomming to get bigger tips. We were in that world of Negroes who are both servants and psychologists, aware that white people are so obsessed with their own importance that they will pay liberally, even dearly, for the impression of being catered to and entertained.

For him, speaking in dialect was like volunteering to act in a minstrel show, complying with a humiliation that whites demanded. Hurston had an entirely different attitude to language, however. As an anthropologist, she was trained to record faithfully what she observed. She wrote *Poker!* in black dialect because in its time and place, it was almost inconceivable that its characters would have spoken in any other form of language. For her, the use of dialect was merely authentic.

These two opposite approaches to black dialect have alternated in and out of favor with black intellectuals over the last hundred years, and while Hurston's approach was acceptable in the 1920s, it was already being rejected by the 1930s, and her reliance on dialect had already put her out of the mainstream in the black literary community. Prominent novelist Richard Wright makes this clear in his review of Hurston's *Their Eyes Were Watching God* in the *New Masses*, savaging Hurston on the use of black dialect, and in particular on the mind-set that its continued use implied to him: "Miss Hurston *voluntarily* continues in her novel the tradition which was forced upon the Negro in the theatre, that is, the minstrel technique that makes the 'white folks' laugh." Black dialect, however, is neither more nor less forced upon American blacks than standard English.

Word Play

Poker! is filled with clever word play. An example occurs early in the play where the character Nunkie says, "I plays poker, I plays the piano and Gawd knows I plays the Devil." This sentence depends on the parallelism of *play* in all three clauses, yet the meaning of the word in each case is quite different. In the first clause it means to participate in a game, while in the second it means to operate. The third clause is far more evocative. In the simplest reading, it means Nunkie acts like the devil, that is, in a wicked manner. In a sense this could qualify the first two usages, meaning he plays in the ribald and enthusiastic manner characteristic of black music of the period and participates in a game that was generally considered sinful by "respectable" society.

In addition, the sentence has elements of folklore that probably derive from Hurston's anthropological research. In European folklore, the devil is an accomplished musician. The same idea also appears in southern folklore, as reflected in the popular song *The Devil Went Down to Georgia*. This is a reminder that, while black folklore may have African elements, it has also embraced European tradition along with European language. The devil, as a musician, is often presented in a musical contest against a human musician. Particularly by invoking God as a witness, Nunkie suggests that he too is engaged in a contest with the devil, because "play the devil" can just as well mean to play against as to imitate him. This evokes the folktale of the pact with the devil where the hero makes a deal with the devil to enjoy the sinful pleasures of life but still hopes to cheat him and win salvation, a point that is highly relevant to the development of the play. Hurston displays her skill by compressing all of this into a single sentence.

HISTORICAL CONTEXT

The Harlem Renaissance

In the nineteenth century, the interface between black performers and white audiences was the minstrel show. This was a kind of musical and comedy revue in which both black and whites performed, invariably made up in *black face*, a racist caricature of blacks. In the late-nineteenth and early-twentieth centuries, as the entertainment industry grew through many advances and innovations, such as the dance hall, the night club, and radio and records, blacks were able

COMPARE
&
CONTRAST

- **1930s:** All forms of gambling, even private poker games, are illegal throughout the United States, although a lottery run by organized crime known as the numbers is an important part of the economy and culture of Harlem. Gambling is almost universally viewed as a moral failing.

  Today: Casino gambling has been legal in the United States since the 1980s, and state governments run national lotteries to fund public schools. On August 21, 2012, a federal judge ruled that poker was a game of skill, not chance, and so could not be outlawed as gambling, but the ramifications of this decision will take years to play out.

- **1930s:** Racial discrimination and segregation are both commonplace and enforced by law.

  Today: Although racial discrimination and segregation still exist, they are now proscribed by law and are diminishing.

- **1930s:** Plays in the form of revues, a series of short musical and comedy sketches unrelated to each other (a form that descends from the minstrel show), are common on the stage.

  Today: This format exists for the most part on television, on shows like *Saturday Night Live.*

to perform more authentically and developed new forms of entertainment such as ragtime and jazz.

The economic prosperity of the 1920s created the Harlem Renaissance, in which black entertainers such as Josephine Baker and Cab Calloway performed in venues in the segregated black neighborhood of Harlem for largely white audiences. Malcolm X puts it quite bluntly: "Then, early in the 1920s, music and entertainment sprang up as an industry in Harlem, supported by downtown whites who poured uptown every night." A more serious side of the Harlem Renaissance saw the emergence of black intellectuals and literary artists such as Langston Hughes and Hurston, who also wrote mainly for white audiences; the black audience for poetry and novels was still too small to sustain a professional writer.

White audiences were interested in black theater and literature because they perceived blacks as an exotic *other* in the terms defined in Edward Said's *Orientalism*. Western culture has an ideal image of itself and projects any of its own disfavored features onto a figurative *other* that becomes associated with any group that is

perceived as foreign or alien, particularly one that is deemed inferior. In the 1920s, black culture was used for this purpose. The strong emotions associated with sex and violence are always a key ingredient in popular art. If one could imagine, however, that they belong to the *other* and that they can be viewed safely, without having to admit their effect in one's own inner life, then one can maintain one's idealized self-identity at the expense of the *other*.

The popular entertainer Josephine Baker exemplified this idea. The open sexuality of her appeal was termed exotic, even animalistic, and she was put in shows with stereotypical African themes including caged lions on stage, although she had been born in east St. Louis. She was compelled to act out onstage an Orientalist fantasy. Black music and drama in general was praised as authentic and unspoiled because it was supposedly isolated from the mainstream of Western culture, but the very fact that it was primarily viewed by white audiences proves the opposite. Instead these terms—*wild, exotic, African, unspoiled*—are part of a constellation of imposed qualities that included simple and emotional instead of complex and intellectual. The

Hurston's set includes a portiere upstage. (© Sergey Chirkov | Shutterstock.com)

very factors that supposedly made the black performer or writer excellent also testified to a fantasy of black inferiority. Black entertainment became a mirror for the face of American culture that it did not want to look at.

Hurston's work, with its source in folklore studies, was ready-made for this sort of treatment, although many of its themes come directly from white culture. Her use of black dialect made her work seem safe, meaning it could not possibly be related to white culture. One of the most intellectually dangerous ideas in *Poker!* for mainstream American culture is the suspicion that ideas about God and divine justice are just childish fables that do not fit with the moral complexities of the real world. Hurston, who was an atheist, certainly intended it partly as a burlesque of religion. At the same time, the white audience could safely laugh at what seemed to them the superstitious simplicity of black religion without consciously examining their own beliefs.

CRITICAL OVERVIEW

Poker! was one of four one-act plays that Hurston wrote in 1931 for the revue *Fast and Furious*, which was one of the last expressions of Harlem Renaissance theater written to attract the lucrative white audience. The other plays were *Woofing* (a term referring to the ritualized trading of insults to demonstrate mastery of language as a claim to social status), *Lawing and Jawing*, and *Forty Yards*. Given the economic conditions of the Great Depression, the show was a flop and ran for only a week of performances.

The text of the plays would have been completely lost except for the fact that Hurston preserved her original manuscript copies, which were among her papers that were eventually collected by the Library of Congress. They were given a public reading in 2005 but were not printed until the edition made by Jean Lee Cole and Charles Mitchell in their 2008 *Collected Plays*, which included all of Hurston's drama.

Given the fact that *Poker!* was completely unknown to the critical and scholarly communities, it has naturally received very little attention as yet. In their introduction, Cole and Mitchell note that Hurston mentioned the play a few times in her surviving correspondence to criticize the artistic choices made by the producer Forbes Robinson. She nevertheless thought the experience would stand in her good stead in any future dramatic projects. Indeed, she did have several more successful productions, such as *The Great Day* (1932) on Broadway and in touring companies, such as *All De Livelong Day* (1933), which gained Hurston a reputation sufficient to secure her a visiting professorship in drama at Bethune-Cookman College in 1933–34.

The only published (anonymously) review of *Fast and Furious* denounced the show in racist terms directed as much against the Jewish musical composers who collaborated on the show as the black cast and writers. The review suggests that *Poker!* and *Woofing*—almost the only spoken parts of the revue—had more merit than the other predominantly musical sections, recognizing the greater authenticity achieved by Hurston's play. In their introduction to Hurston's collected plays, Cole and Mitchell observe that,

> *Poker!* finally, shows the darker side of "woofing" as a form of aggression that explodes into violence among the poor denizens of a "shotgun house." However, the stage business of all

the players cheating at the same time and a humorous tag line suggests that Hurston is winking at her audience.

Lucy Anne Hurston (the playwright's niece and a sociology professor) and John Lowe, in their articles in *"The Inside Light,"* both note the foundation of Hurston's *Fast and Furious* plays in the author's anthropological work. Lowe additionally observes that Hurston's patron Charlotte Mason opposed Hurston's work in the theater because she did not consider it entirely respectable.

CRITICISM

Rita M. Brown

Brown is an English professor. In the following essay, she examines Poker! *as an allegory of Hurston's political views.*

Hurston, like many sophisticated writers, sometimes represented her ideas through metaphor. She found it easier, or perhaps more pointed, to explain the intricacies of a situation through an analogy with everyday life, the Bible, or anything else that would already be familiar to her audience. The technique goes back to Aesop. His animal fables, generally treated as charming children's literature today, were really intended as a set of stock metaphors that an advocate in court could use to explain his theory of a case to the jurors.

A well-known example of Hurston's use of metaphor concerns her own trial. In 1948, she was accused of sexual assault against the ten-year-old son of her landlady in Harlem and two of his friends, both eleven years old. The circumstances of the case are anything but clear, but Hurston claimed in a series of letters to her patrons that she was falsely accused by one Richard D. Rochester, who may have been a Democratic political operative opposed to her support of the Republican Party. The boy's mother was ready to testify against her because Hurston told her that her son was developmentally delayed and offered to put her in touch with social services that could help him. The mother had taken offense over what she perceived as an insult. The case went to trial but was dismissed after Hurston established in court that she had been in Honduras at the time of the supposed molestation.

> TO HURSTON, ANY PATERNALISTIC ATTEMPT TO HELP BLACKS WAS JUST AS DISCRIMINATORY AS THE SEGREGATION AND RACISM THAT SO LONG OPPRESSED THEM."

Rochester went out of his way to make his accusations personally to Hurston's patrons and publishers. Whether simply because of the suspicion against her or whether the shock to her inner equilibrium affected her talent as a writer, Hurston never published a significant work afterward but piled up rejection notices for years. She never stopped writing but eventually gave up attempting to publish.

Hurston's artistic reaction to the trial was her novel, *Herod the Great*, which has never been published but exists in manuscript among her papers in the Library of Congress. She presents Herod as a virtuous hero whose evil reputation in the New Testament derives from slanders circulated by those jealous of him. In particular, she denies the episode of the slaughter of innocents from the Gospel of Matthew ever occurred. According to this story, Herod became jealous when the magi from the east told him of the birth of a Jewish savior other than himself and ordered that all of the children under two years of age in Bethlehem be murdered by his soldiers in order to make sure of killing the infant Jesus. Using biblical scholarship in a very insightful way, Hurston argued that Herod died four years before Jesus was born. In letters and other documents, she makes it quite clear that she intended Herod to be taken as a symbol for herself, and the accusation of the slaughter of the innocents represented her own trial.

This kind of extended metaphor is known as an allegory, in which a story is told that seems on the surface to be about one thing, but in which everything in the story is a symbol that corresponds point by point to another story that is told on a different level of meaning. In the case of *Herod the Great*, the surface meaning of the story concerns the biblical and historical figure of Herod, but the reader is invited to interpret

WHAT DO I READ NEXT?

- Lucy Hurston's biography of her aunt, *Speak, So You Can Speak Again: The Life of Zora Neale Hurston* (2004), appropriate for young-adult readers, includes a CD of black folk songs recorded by Hurston as part of her anthropological field work and dozens of facsimiles of documents relating to her personal life, including letters to other black intellectuals like Langston Hughes, family Christmas cards, and the manuscripts of her unpublished works rescued from being burned by the janitor at the Saint Lucie County Welfare Home.

- The *Encyclopedia of the Harlem Renaissance*, edited in 2004 by Cary D. Wintz and Paul Finkelman, covers the entire cultural spectrum of Harlem in the 1920s, with a good concentration on the graphic and performing arts.

- Hurston's friend and colleague Langston Hughes, perhaps the most important writer of the Harlem Renaissance, wrote for children and young adults and was often active in primary and secondary education. *The Dream Keeper and Other Poems* (1922) was the first of his many books for a juvenile audience.

- The Zora Neale Hurston website (http://zoranealehurston.com/), maintained by Hurston's niece, sociology professor Lucy Anne Hurston, collects an array of web-based resources on Hurston aimed at students and teachers.

- Hurston's *Tell My Horse*, originally published in 1938 and reissued several times in recent years, reports the results of her anthropological research into voodoo and similar religions in Haiti and Jamaica.

- Joseph Holloway and Winifred K. Vass's *The African Heritage of American English* (1997) is a scientific study of the influences and survival of West African languages in Gullah and black dialect, many of which have also made their way into standard English.

- Many of the folktales that Hurston collected as part of her anthropological work have been adapted in a series of illustrated children's books published by the Zora Neale Hurston Trust, such as *What's the Hurry, Fox?* illustrated by Bryan Collier and published in 2004.

everything in the story as a symbol for events in Hurston's own life. This suggests an interesting way to read *Poker!*, as an allegory in which the surface story of a group of gangsters killing each other in a fight over cheating at cards conceals another, more significant meaning. Hurston left plenty of clues that the reader can use to understand the allegory in *Herod the Great*, but not so for the obscure *Poker!* In reading the play, the reader must conjecture what the allegorical meaning might be.

An allegory can have more levels of meaning than the surface story and one extended metaphor, and that seems to be the case with *Poker!*

The play can read as a moral fable by scarcely dipping below the surface. Gambling, according to the conventional morality, is a sin, and the punishment for that sin is death, which is duly paid out to the sinners. A moral allegory like this is liable to find easy acceptance with any audience because its wisdom is entirely conventional. For this reason, there will be little doubt that the audience will understand it.

The punch-line ending of the play operates almost entirely on this level, because it plays on the Christian belief that hell is a fitting place for wicked sinners. There, the poker players' sins will make them outstanding among the damned, which is not, perhaps, what the gangsters who die at the end of the play had in mind in cultivating their "tough" macho images. Hurston worked in this moral fable to please her audience, but it probably had little personal meaning for her because she was an atheist (although she was quick to include her own traditional church-lady personae in her correspondence with the devout Christian patron Charlotte Osgood Mason when it was to her advantage to do so). Also, in practice, gambling was not very much looked down upon by the citizens of Harlem or by her sophisticated white audience.

Any further interpretation of *Poker!* must be more speculative, but Hurston's other writings provide some guidance in the matter. Allegories are often political. Particularly when one wishes to present political views that are either unpopular or subject to censorship. A well-known example of this phenomenon that is roughly contemporary with Hurston is the *Antigone* of the French playwright Jean Anouilh that premiered in early 1944 in Paris under Nazi occupation. Anouilh's play is closely based on the ancient Greek dramatist Sophocles's *Antigone*, which balances the human needs to obey and to reject authority. Anouilh subtly changed the original material, however, into a criticism of Nazi oppression, but not so blatantly as to attract the attention of Nazi censors. In the same way, perhaps Hurston used *Poker!* to express her own political views.

One can hardly speak of a unified political belief system in the black community of the 1920s and 1930s. Because most American blacks were denied the right to vote, many were apolitical. Some factions in the black community, like the Nation of Islam, were frankly separatist, while Marcus Garvey's back-to-Africa movement still had a political following, even if it did not inspire much actual emigration. Like white intellectuals of the time, some leading black figures like Langston Hughes and Kenneth Robeson flirted with soviet communism, which promised the equality of all men. Others, like Josephine Baker and the novelist Richard Wright, emigrated to France to escape the racism that prevailed in America.

As a practical matter, the artists and intellectuals of the Harlem Renaissance realized that segregation was not going to end any time soon and worked to build up black culture as a separate institution, which Langston Hughes called *negritude*, a term borrowed from the same kind of movement among blacks from the French colonial empire living in France. Most blacks had an abiding hope of eventually winning social and political equality and were happy to accept any help along those lines offered by the federal government, which was increasingly more favorable to the black community than state governments, and the white population at large, especially in the South where most blacks still lived. This led in due course to the civil rights movement. In response to pressure from black civil rights leaders like Martin Luther King and Malcolm X, the federal government began to enforce existing laws that would ensure equality for blacks (as well as all other Americans) and to pass new laws that would level the uneven playing field that had been created by a century of segregation and discrimination, a process that is still ongoing.

Although most blacks supported the civil rights movement, ideas like affirmative action, the notion that the government would interfere with education, employment, and many other areas of life to ensure that blacks received equal treatment, deeply offended Hurston's libertarian sensibilities. To Hurston, any paternalistic attempt to help blacks was just as discriminatory as the segregation and racism that so long oppressed them. If people were going to be equal, she thought, they should be just that and not receive quotas at schools or jobs that effectively advanced blacks at the expense of whites. She had confidence that blacks could make their own way without receiving special privileges. She addresses her beliefs about racial equality in her 1942 memoir, *Dust Trackson a Road*, and explains her position using the game of poker as an explanatory metaphor:

> If I say a whole system must be upset for me to win, I am saying that I cannot sit in the game, and that safer rules must be made to give me a chance. I repudiate that. If others are in there, deal me a hand and let me see what I can make of it, even though I know some in there are dealing from the bottom and cheating like hell in other ways.

In Hurston's view, affirmative action is a kind of cheating, and she would rather play fairly even if she is forced to play against cheaters (white racists). It is easy to see how the brief dramatic sketch *Poker!* expresses the same idea. A group of black men cheat at poker (life), are corrupted by the process, and are ultimately

Tush Hawg begins the dialogue by admonishing Nunkie to stop holding up the game. *(© Africa Studio /*
Shutterstock.com)

destroyed by the very means they had hoped to use to win.

Source: Rita M. Brown, Critical Essay on *Poker!*, in *Drama for Students*, Gale, Cengage Learning, 2013.

Barbara Speisman

In the following excerpt, Speisman reviews Hurston's career up to 1930, which included the time during which Poker! *was written.*

On 12 April 1926, in a letter to Langston Hughes, Zora Neale Hurston asked Hughes a question: "Did I tell you before I left about the new, the REAL Negro art theater I Plan? Well I shall, or rather we shall act out the folk tales, however short with the abrupt angularity and naivete of the primitive 'bama Nigger.... What do you think?" (Hemenway 115). From 1927 to 1930 Hurston had the opportunity to interpret what "had gone unseen for three hundred years" (113), and she shared many of her discoveries with Hughes, her colleague and friend. Traveling to isolated, rural African American communities, such as Magazine Point, Alabama, as well

as her home village of Eatonville, Florida, Hurston came to realize that the folktales and songs she heard during her travels were not creations of the past, but of the everchanging present.

Pretending to be a gangster's girlfriend on the run in a Loughman, Florida, turpentine camp, she had become friends with Big Sweet, a "jook" woman who could out-talk, out-fight, and out-love her male counterparts in the camp. Big Sweet had been instrumental in teaching Hurston the importance of the jook in the development of the "real Negro theater," the theater of "the people farthest down." Hurston came to believe that the real Negro theater was in the "jooks" of the South "where women, like Big Sweet, could hoist a jook song from her belly and lam it against the front door of the theater" ("Characteristics" 254). Hurston was persuaded that only theater could truly convey the mercurial nature, as well as cultural richness, of the folklife, tales, and songs she learned. She wanted to share not only her subject matter with Langston Hughes, but also her vision of a script that would not follow the standard two- or three-act

> " HURSTON CAME TO HER DEFINITION OF A
> REAL NEGRO ART THEATER AFTER THE THREE YEARS
> SHE SPENT RESEARCHING IN THE SOUTH, BUT HER
> ODYSSEY AS A PLAYWRIGHT BEGAN SEVERAL YEARS
> EARLIER."

format. Hurston also advanced the concept that the real Negro play should be angular in structure, which was similar to African dance ("Characteristics" 247). Thus, at the beginning of her professional career as a folklorist, Hurston was forming a totally different concept of the type of play that she hoped to write; one that would be radically different, not only in theme and subject matter, but in structure as well.

Hughes shared Hurston's enthusiasm for an authentic folk theater in which African Americans would write, direct, and perform their own material. Like Hurston, Hughes believed that "The Negro outstanding characteristic is drama" ("Characteristics" 247), and he proposed to coauthor a folk play with Hurston that would be a real departure in the drama. Hurston's dream of a "real Negro art theater" (Hemenway 115) was one that she would hold onto for much of her creative life. It was, however, one that brought her great frustration and disappointment and even caused her to be alienated from Hughes, a sharer of her dream.

Although Hurston's published work has received much critical attention, her role as a playwright still needs more investigation. Perhaps one of the chief reasons her plays have not received the attention they deserve is that so few of her manuscripts are in published form. Lynda Marion Hill points out in her ground-breaking study *Social Rituals and the Verbal Art of Zora Neale Hurston*:

> Hurston's theatrical career is virtually a lost segment of Hurston's work, and that having available documentation of her staged productions is essential not only to be able to write a thorough historical account but to reproduce the play, in writing or on stage. (201)

During the spring and summer of 1997, however, several of Hurston's play manuscripts have surfaced. Wyatt Hourston Day, an African American manuscript collector, discovered "Spears" which was first published in Hurston's sorority yearbook, the Zeta Phi Beta *X RAY* for 1925. Alice L. Birney, historian of American literature at the Library of Congress, has discovered three full-length plays and several dramatic skits copyrighted by Hurston from 1925 to 1944. The plays include "Meet the Mamma," a musical play, copyrighted 12 July 1925, less than three months after the *Opportunity* Award Banquet at which Hurston won second prize for her play *Color Struck* and an honorable mention for "Spears." "Cold Keener," a musical revue, and "De Turkey and de Law," a comedy in three acts, were both copyrighted 29 October 1930, shortly before an argument between Hurston and Langston Hughes over authorship of *Mule Bone*. On 21 July 1931, Hurston copyrighted four comical sketches: "Poker," "Lawing and Jawing," "Woolfing," and "Forty Yards." Hurston did not copyright another play until 15 June 1935, when she copyrighted "Spunk." With Hurston's permission, Josephine Van Dolzen Pease copyrighted, on 7 April 1936, "Three Authentic Folk Dances from the Deep South," which are dances to be performed by children. These dances consist of "Rabbit Dance," "Chick-Ma Chick, Ma, Cranney Crow," and "Sissie in the Barn." The final play, and one familiar to Hurston scholars, was "Polk County" which Hurston coauthored with Dorothy Waring; its copyright date was 9 December 1944.

Collectively these manuscripts are over three hundred pages in length, and provide the reader a rich selection with which to analyze Hurston's conviction that the folklife material she had collected in the South would best reach a greater audience "as the product of folk performance" (Abrahams and Kalcik 229). Hurston came to her definition of a real Negro art theater after the three years she spent researching in the South, but her odyssey as a playwright began several years earlier.

Hurston's first association with drama probably came in 1915 to 1916 while she was employed as a maid in the Gilbert and Sullivan troupe which introduced her to professional actors and musicians. Although she did not actively participate in any of the performances, she certainly had the opportunity to explore the structure of plays, acting, and directing techniques. Later, from 1916 to 1919, Hurston moved to Baltimore where her sister

Sarah had a rooming house near Pennsylvania Avenue which was renowned for its theaters. Here well-known African American performers, like Ethel Waters, often performed. Hurston, therefore, had ample opportunity to observe the then current African American stage drama and musical entertainment. In 1919 Hurston graduated from Morgan Academy and was encouraged by Mae Miller, a young Washington playwright and poet, to enter Howard University's drama department (Perkins 77). This fact suggests Hurston's early interest in the theater.

Her formal study of drama and, in particular, African American drama was at Howard University. Hurston's initial concept of theater was formed under the tutelage of Thomas Montgomery Gregory who had organized the Howard Players to perform plays about Negro life. Gregory had been a member of Professor Baker's famous English 47 Workshop at Harvard University that had served as the dramatic training ground for Thomas Woolf and Eugene O'Neill. Gregory was friends with O'Neill, and O'Neill visited Howard's drama department in 1923 while Hurston was a student. O'Neill and his Provincetown Players took an active interest in the Howard Players and Gregory's hope of developing a national Negro theater. Gregory was also unique in that he believed that African American women were capable of writing plays, and encouraged his women students to become playwrights (Perkins 78). Although Hurston wrote *Color Struck*, "Spears," and "Meet the Mamma" while studying with Gregory, no record has been located that would indicate whether or not Hurston had any of her plays produced while a member of the Howard Players. Gregory kept excellent files, but Hurston's only mention is as a violinist for the Howard orchestra.

However, Gregory was one of the judges for the *Opportunity* Award Banquet, held on 1 May 1925, which formally ushered in the Harlem Renaissance. There Hurston won second prize for her play *Color Struck* and honorable mention for "Spears." These plays, African American in content, followed the traditional one- and two-act structure. No mention was made of "Meet the Mamma," her blues musical. Not long after the *Opportunity* presentation, the Negro Art Theater of Harlem opened with her play, *Color Struck*. With this formal production, Hurston began to make a name for herself as a playwright.

Color Struck, a play about miscegenation, has received much critical attention, but "Spears" has yet to be examined. It appears that in writing "Spears" Hurston was influenced by the Tarzan craze that was sweeping the country at the time—her characters are dressed in lion skins and loin cloths, with bone jewelry and rings in their noses and ears. Hurston was gambling that she could capitalize on the myth of Africa popular in white America's imagination. Although the characters in the play are unbelievable, the plot contrived, and the ending expected, Hurston's sense of humor and satirical style are evident. "Spears" was not part of Hurston's efforts to establish an authentic American Negro theater, but was rather an attempt to satirize the white concept of what they thought African primitivism to be, and perhaps to produce a commercial success.

The play centers on the Luallaba tribe who have been unable to find food and are starving, making them vulnerable to their enemies, the Wahehes. Monanga, King of the Luallabas, meets with Bombay, his old counselor, to debate their predicament. Bombay, like Polonius in Shakespeare's *Hamlet*, provides bombastic, silly advice. Bombay tells his chief that their problem may be solved by "selling our young women to the Wahehes for good." Zaida, the King's beautiful daughter, appears on the scene to announce that she and the other women are hungry, and to ask what her father means to do about it. Uledi, a warrior in love with her, has hidden food and provides Zaida with something to eat. As Zaida eats, the rest of the tribe follows each morsel of meat from the girl's hand to her mouth with their eyes and mimic swallowing when she does. Act 1 ends when the King demands that his medicine man "make medicine for rain" which will solve their problem. The Medicine Man and his accomplices, the Witch Woman and a chicken, participate in a rain dance and, as the drums beat furiously, the dancing grows wilder and Hurston's stage directions are "that this will continue for nine minutes."

In act 2, a Wahehe warrior accuses Uledi of stealing food and, as a result, Uledi must die or the tribe will fight the Luallabas. When presented with this decision, Monanga quickly agrees that Ulede must perish in order that the tribe may be preserved. However, in Pocahontas style, Zaida begs her father to save Ulede's life. Monanga's answer is "that women were not made to counsel men but to serve them." Zaida's reply is that "we women have no minds at all. We know nothing . . . what we saw yesterday is today forgotten." She then cleverly reminds her father of Uledi's many heroic adventures, how he saved her life, and "How he is first to hear your voice always. If Uledi has done wrong let me be killed in his place. Your slave has spoken." The play ends with the Luallaba tribe overcoming their enemies and Uledi and Zaida in each other's arms. Although "Spears" was published, we do not know if Hurston ever managed to have it performed.

From 1926 to 1930, Hurston may not have written plays, but she was developing ideas about what should constitute the real Negro art theater, and shared with Hughes much of the folk material she had collected. For financial reasons, both Hurston and Hughes had entered into an agreement with Charlotte Osgood Mason, a wealthy patron of the arts, which allowed her to have a great measure of control over their lives and writings. In particular, Hurston had signed a contract with Mason on 8 December 1927 which gave Mason complete ownership of Hurston's collected material and the methods by which it would be presented and published (Hemenway 109). Although Mason informed Hurston that she should not consider using her folk material for theatrical purposes, Hurston persevered in her desire for the "glorious . . . departure in the drama" (Hemenway 115). . . .

Source: Barbara Speisman, "From 'Spears' to *The Great Day*: Zora Neale Hurston's Vision of a Real Negro Theater," in *Southern Quarterly*, Vol. 36, No. 3, Spring 1998, pp. 34–46.

John Lowe

In the following excerpt, Lowe examines Hurston's works, including the play Mule Bone, *and the influence of Hurston's life situation on her dramatic writings.*

Zora Neale Hurston has recently been rescued from literary oblivion and installed as a major figure in the American literary canon. Her stature thus far, however, has stemmed from her success as a novelist, especially in her masterwork, *Their Eyes Were Watching God* (1937). Some Hurston aficionados were therefore surprised when the play she coauthored with Langston Hughes, *Mule Bone*, had its Broadway debut in 1991. Did Hurston write plays as well? Indeed she did. In fact, one of her

> THE MOST IMPORTANT HURSTON PLAY IS A COLLABORATION WITH LANGSTON HUGHES, *MULE BONE*, WHICH THEY WROTE IN 1930 BUT NEVER PRODUCED, AS THE AUTHORS HAD A 'FALLING OUT' RIGHT AFTER IT WAS WRITTEN AND NEVER RECONCILED."

first publications was a play, and she never gave up trying to mount a successful production.

As a preacher's daughter, Hurston came by her dramatic gifts naturally. John Hurston, born a slave, overcame his humble origins by marrying Lucy Potts, the daughter of a well-to-do farmer and by heeding a call from God. A strapping man, he was a commanding figure in the pulpit and made the most of his booming voice and musical gifts. Zora Neale was born on either 7 January or 15 January 1891 in Notasulga, Alabama, not far from Booker T. Washington's Tuskegee Institute. She was the sixth of John and Lucy's children. One son, Isaac, died in childhood, and three more sons were born after the family relocated in Eatonville, an all-black town in central Florida, in the early 1890s. In her autobiography, Hurston vividly recalls learning the dynamics of African American performance style from the men swapping lies on the porch of Joe Clarke's general store.

Hurston's apparently happy life fell apart in 1904 when her mother died. She did not get along with her stepmother and eventually left Florida as a lady's maid for a traveling Gilbert and Sullivan company, thus inaugurating her theatrical experiences. After a series of jobs and a sequence of college courses at Morgan State and Howard University, Hurston won a scholarship to Barnard College, where she studied with Ruth Benedict and Franz Boas, the founders of American anthropology. While in New York she also met the leading figures of the New Negro literary movement and soon became one of the leading "niggerati," as she called them, herself. One of her several contributions to the Harlem Renaissance, as it has become known, was a play, *Color Struck*, which she published in a short-lived magazine, *Fire!!* She also submitted a play, "Spears" (since lost), to *Opportunity*'s writing contest in 1925; the piece was awarded an honorable mention.

Aside from the material surrounding *Mule Bone*'s publication and premiere, some brief commentary by her biographer, Robert E. Hemenway, and articles by Adele Newsome on "The Fiery Chariot" and Lynda Hill on plays that dramatize Hurston's life and work, virtually nothing has been written on Hurston as dramatist. One finds some insight into her dramatic program, however, by examining the nature of her few published and several unpublished plays, a sequence initiated with *Color Struck.*

This four-scene play initially depicts a group of laughing, animated friends boarding the Jim Crow railway car in Jacksonville enroute to a cakewalk contest in St. Augustine in 1900. The crowd predicts that John and Emma will win: "They's the bestest cakewalkers in dis state." When these two appear, however, they argue because the dark Emma thinks brown-skinned John has been flirting with the mulatto Effie. Throughout the play, Emma's jealousy and morbid self-hatred keep her from accepting John's love. Her tragedy, however, is played out in the early scenes against the boisterous comedy enacted by her friends, and the lovingly detailed cakewalk contest in scenes 2 and 3. Joe Clarke, mayor of Eatonville, who plays a prominent role in much of Hurston's fiction, appears for the first time here. Emma, jealous again, refuses to perform with John, who goes on anyway, partnering Effie. As Emma watches, they win the contest.

The fourth and final scene takes place twenty years later. Emma is revealed nursing her light-skinned, invalid daughter when John enters. Although he has not seen her since the cakewalk and has since been married and widowed, he still loves Emma. She supposes he married a light-skinned woman, but John says he chose a dark wife because he longed for Emma. He teases her when he discovers her invalid teenage daughter is nearly white. He tells her he will stay with the girl while Emma goes for the white doctor she insists on. Instead of going for the doctor, however, Emma doubles back and accuses John of lust for her daughter. Disgusted, John leaves. The doctor arrives, but he is too late to save Emma's daughter and tells her that she might have lived had she sent for him sooner. The play's melodrama makes it top heavy, but it succeeds in suggesting the creativity and exuberance of African American culture and in sketching in the parameters of color prejudice within the African American community.

Hurston was asked to contribute a piece to Charles S. Johnson's *Ebony and Topaz: A Collectanea*, an anthology of black writing that appeared in 1927, and she chose a play. *The First One: A Play in One Act* is set in the Valley of Ararat three years after the flood and features Noah, his wife, their three sons Shem, Japeth and Ham, Eve, Ham's wife and the sons' wives and children. This was the first of several pieces that Hurston would set in biblical times, frequently in black dialect. Here, however, Hurston uses standard speech. As the play opens, Noah and everyone else stand fuming because Ham, the wayward son, is once again late for the annual commemoration of the delivery from the flood. Ham comes in playing a harp, dressed in a goat-skin and a green wreath, obviously linking him with both Orpheus and Bacchus. Shem's wife criticizes Ham because he doesn't bring an offering and because, unlike his brothers who toil in the fields, he merely tends flocks and sings. After a brief ceremony, the characters recall the flood and the deliverance in dramatic language. Noah calls upon Ham to play and sing to help them forget. Noah gets drunk to forget the images of the dead faces that floated by the ark. When Ham, also inebriated, laughingly reports on his father's nakedness in the tent—"The old Ram . . . he has had no spring for years." Shem's jealous wife seizes the opportunity and wakes Noah, reporting the deed but not the identity of the perpetrator. Noah, enraged, roars that "His skin shall be black . . . He and his seed forever. He shall serve his brothers and they shall rule over him." Later, all involved are appalled and try to reverse the curse, but Ham comes in laughing, unaware that he has been turned black. His son has changed color as well. Noah banishes them, fearing that blackness is contagious. Ham, rather than show dismay, laughs cynically, saying "Oh, remain with your flocks and fields and vineyards, to covet, to sweat, to die and to know no peace, I go to the sun."

Two things are worth noting about this play. First is that the origin of a race is in its founding father's joke. Second, the ending suggests that "The First [Black] One," a being who knows the true value of life, is superior to whites. Thus Hurston's playlet both embraces and inverts the traditional interpretation of the biblical passage upon which it is based.

In the meantime, Hurston continued her education at Columbia. Encouraged by Boas, she began a series of trips to Florida to gather folklore materials. This work was facilitated for years by the sponsorship of a wealthy white woman, Mrs. Osgood Mason, who also supported the careers of Hurston's gifted friends, the writers Langston Hughes and Alain Locke, as well as the musician Hall Johnson, who was active in the Broadway theater. All of them called Mrs. Mason "Godmother."

Even during the years of this patron's largesse, Hurston had to scramble to make ends meet. In 1931 she was hired to write some sketches for *Fast and Furious*, a black musical review produced by Forbes Randolph. She also appeared as a pom-pom girl in a football sketch and helped direct the show, which folded after a week. Her next theatrical adventure was writing sketches for the revue *Jungle Scandals*, which also closed quickly. Hurston had nothing but scorn for both of these shows and saw an opportunity to correct their errors with a musical of her own. Accordingly, she sought out Hall Johnson, who had directed the chorus of the wildly successful *Green Pastures* in 1931. Hurston thought that the play, written by a white man, Marc Connelly, was a dreadful hash of black culture, but she knew Johnson was master of his craft. She decided to set a single day in a railroad work camp to music. At first she thought of calling it *Spunk* but settled on *The Great Day*. Johnson worked on the project desultorily, but finally withdrew, only to filch some of Hurston's material for his production *Run Little Chillun*, which opened to favorable reviews in 1931.

In spite of these early disappointments, Hurston perservered. By pawning some of her possessions to raise funds and wheedling the final backing from Godmother, *The Great Day* was presented at New York's John Golden Theater on 10 January 1932. It used a concert format, and Alain Locke wrote the program notes. In the first part of the program, the audience saw workers arising and going to the job, singing songs as they laid track, returning to their homes where their children played folk games, and listening to a preacher's sermons accompanied by spirituals. Part 2 presented an evening's entertainment at the local "jook" (nightclub), consisting mainly of blues songs, ending with half the cast doing a blues song, half singing "Deep River." No

theatrical producer came forward to offer an extended run and the show lost money, even though it attracted a good crowd and favorable reviews. Godmother refused to let Hurston ever again put on the play as written and also forbade the theatrical use of other portions of *Mules and Men*. Hurston did succeed in mounting an edited version of *The Great Day* at Manhattan's New School on 29 March 1932. A program of this production survives, and *Theatre Arts* published a photo of the cast.

The next year, back home in Florida, Hurston and her friend Robert Wunsch of the Rollins College English department produced a January performance of the revised *The Great Day* to great acclaim, using a new title, *From Sun to Sun*. A second performance was given in February. In this form, the musical was mounted in a number of other cities in Florida, including Eatonville. Two years later, Hurston repeated the show in abbreviated concert form at Fisk University in Nashville and followed with a performance in Chicago, using still another title, *Singing Steel*, casting it with aspiring singers from the YWCA. Once again the show received good reviews, but, more importantly, officials from the Rosenwald Foundation, impressed by Hurston's research, offered to sponsor her return to Columbia to work on a PhD in anthropology.

We have no script for these musicals, but the Library of Congress owns tapes of many of the musical numbers. A version was pieced together for a performance at the 1993 Zora Neale Hurston Festival of the Arts in Eatonville.

Hurston did write down a one-act play that was part of the Rollins *From Sun to Sun* performance in 1933. The unpublished version, now in the Hurston Collection of the University of Florida, "The Fiery Chariot," creates a seven-page drama out of an old folktale. The play takes place in Dinah and Ike's slave cabin. Initially Ike comically wars with his little son over a baked sweet potato but soon switches to a comic duel with Dinah, who criticizes Ike in lively vernacular for praying every night to God to come get him in his fiery chariot. "Ah betcher God gits so tired uh yo' noise dat when He sees you gittin' down, he gwan in his privy house and slam de door." Ole Massa hears Ike praying and appears before the door wearing a sheet, claiming to be the Lord come in his chariot. Ike hides under the bed and tells Dinah to tell him he isn't there. Ole Massa says Dinah will do, and Ike urges her to go. When Dinah reveals Ike, he comes out and quivers at the sight of the Lord in his white sheet and stalls by saying he needs to put his Sunday shirt on. Then it's his Sunday pants. Finally, he persuades Ole Massa to step back some and bolts out the door and away. When Ike's son asks if God will catch him, Dinah answers, "You know God aint got no time wid yo' pappy and him barefooted too." Although the play builds on an old comic tradition, it has serious undertones. Ike prays for death because Ole Massa works him so hard; Ole Massa's decision to take Dinah instead verges toward the habit actual owners had of appropriating the bodies of their female slaves. Finally, Ike's clever method of escaping Ole Massa/God links him with the heroics of the legendary trickster slave, High John de Conquer.

The most important Hurston play is a collaboration with Langston Hughes, *Mule Bone*, which they wrote in 1930 but never produced, as the authors had a "falling out" right after it was written and never reconciled. In 1985 Henry Louis Gates, Jr. read the play at Yale and began a campaign to have it produced, but the revival almost did not come about. A staged reading before one hundred prominent black writers and theater people in 1988 led over half of them to urge the project be shelved, partly because its humor seemed stereotypical—it made extensive use of vernacular and racial humor, including the word "nigger." Changes were duly made, and *Mule Bone* was finally brought to the New York stage in March 1991, edited and revised by George Houston Bass, Ann Cattaneo, Henry Louis Gates, Jr., Arnold Rampersad and the director, Michael Schultz. Taj Mahal provided the musical numbers, which included lyrics drawn from some poems by Hughes. Bass wrote a "frame" story involving Hurston herself, who pronounced to the audience that the evening's event was a result of her scientific folklore expeditions.

In both the original and revised versions, the plot is based on Hurston's short story "The Bone of Contention," which detailed the falling out of two friends who quarrel over a turkey one of them has shot. In the three-act version, the two men, Jim Weston, a musician, and Dave Carter, a dancer, form a musical team. They quarrel over a flirtatious local domestic worker, Daisy Taylor, who skillfully plays them off against each other. The real voice in the play, however,

belongs to the community. The men on Joe Clarke's porch and the women who stroll by offer a continual stream of commentary on the triangle, tell jokes and stories, and play local card games and checkers. A political parallel emerges in the Reverend Simms's public campaign to unseat Joe Clarke as mayor. Even children contribute, playing out classic African American folk games for the audience. The community takes sides according to religious denominations after Jim (a Methodist) knocks Dave (a Baptist) out with a mule bone. Act 2 largely consists of the "trial," held at the Macedonia Baptist Church, presided over by Mayor Clarke. But his leadership is challenged by Reverend Simms, who later spars with Reverend Childers. Their rivalry is matched by the wickedly comic duel between the Methodist Sister Lewis and the Baptist Sister Taylor, who signify to each other to beat the band, seemingly setting off various other quarrels. A continuing joke is the general ineffectiveness of the town marshall, Lum Boger, to coerce anyone, of any denomination. The latter proves that the mule bone is indeed a dangerous weapon by quoting Samson's story from the Bible. Clarke rules that Dave be banished for two years.

The brief third act focuses on the romantic triangle. After toying with the rivals, Daisy chooses Jim and demands that he take a good job as the white folks' yardman. When Jim refuses, she sidles up to Dave, but he too rejects her. The play ends with the two men back together, determined to make the town accept them both.

Mule Bone enjoyed limited success at the box office. It closed on 14 April 1991 after twenty-seven previews and sixty-seven performances. Although a few critics found it funny and historic (Kissel), an "exuberant" theatrical event (Beaufort) and a "wonderful piece of black theater" (Barnes), it was deemed "an amiable curiosity" (Winer), "one of the American theater's more tantalizing might-have-beens" (Rich), "pleasant but uneventful" (Wilson) and a "theatrical curio" (Watt) by other critics, who found it charming but dramatically deficient.

During the thirties, Hurston spent most of her time in Florida writing her novels, two books of folklore and working for the Federal Writers' Project. In October 1934 she wrote from Chicago to her friend James Weldon Johnson about a visit she had just made to Fisk University. There,

President Jones asked Hurston to consider attending Yale Drama School for a year to study directing and the allied dramatic arts as preparation for establishing an experimental theater at Fisk. The idea, Hurston wrote, was "to create the Negro drama out of the Negro himself" (Yale, James Weldon Johnson Collection). Despite this and other ambitious but ultimately unrealized plans to create a new and authentic "negro drama," Hurston wrote mostly nonfiction afterward, but did publish an autobiography in 1942 and a final novel in 1948....

Source: John Lowe, "From *Mule Bones* to Funny Bones: The Plays of Zora Neale Hurston," in *Southern Quarterly*, Vol. 33, Nos. 2–3, Winter/Spring 1995, pp. 65–78.

Joyce Irene Middleton

In the following essay, Middleton relates the importance of Hurston's own life to her works.

The name of Zora Neale Hurston is so familiar that many new readers might easily assume she has always enjoyed a considerable degree of literary status. Yet a sustained reading of the chronology of her life, admirably written by editor Cheryl Wall in this beautiful, two-volume Library of America collection, reanimates the complex cultural and political forces that shaped the world in which we see Zora Hurston laughing and lying, fighting and loving, speaking and writing.

I am, of course, reminded of Alice Walker's research and writing in the 1970s, which led to the powerful movement to "remember" Zora. This movement would uncover new evidence to help us more fully understand why Hurston was forgotten, and why her work, clearly the most substantial literary production of any black woman writer of the period, was abandoned—completely out of print within her own lifetime. (Wall notes that in 1956, Hurston "[e]ngages a 'book hunting agency' to find copies of *Dust Tracks* and *Their Eyes Were Watching God* to send to Dutch translator Margrit Sabloniere.") For those of us who found an ancestral voice in Hurston's writings, the answers to these questions became our own as well as historical or academic. In her essay "Looking for Zora," Walker gathered together Hurston's memories, interweaving both oral and written testimonies, and tried to convey the magic that she herself felt about this woman's life.

> IN AN ASSIMILATIONIST ERA, HURSTON WAS ESPECIALLY CONCERNED WITH THE DANGER OF LOSING THE BLACK ORAL MEMORY—WITH THE WAY MEMORY IS CONSTRUCTED AND ESTEEMED IN BLACK CULTURE."

Given Hurston's contradictions and complexities, if there is one dominant image that fascinates readers it is certainly her self-possession—her life was her own. Yet as a black woman writer, publishing in the late 1920s and 1930s—the age of the "New Negro" or "Harlem Renaissance"—her desire for self-definition wasn't simply personal. Her writings reflect a significant moment in the African American evolutionary shift from oral to written memory. Early on, she recognized the poetic, bardic value of the oral idiom, not simply the dialect of black language use—and the literary world responded favorably to this aspect of her unique contribution to African American literature. In "Art and Such," from the first volume of the collection, she writes:

> The Negro's poetical flow of language, his thinking in images and figures was called to the attention of the outside world. It gave verisimilitude to the narrative by stewing the subject in its own juice. (p. 910)

Wall's new edited collection—the first volume of essays and autobiographical writing, the second of fiction—allows her readers to celebrate Hurston's many achievements. Indeed, Hurston's reanimated voice speaks strongly to the current literary scene, in which African American literature and its relation to theory are enjoying rich debates—a new "renaissance"—on issues such as the social construction of race and class; black writers and the African diaspora; the literary history of African American women; black feminist theory; gender and language use; and the politics of literacy—that is, writing in a racialized society.

Hurston was certainly one of the first to articulate theories of a social construction of race through language. Her "Characteristics of Negro Expression," published in Negro in 1934 (the anthology edited by Nancy Cunard) represents the earliest American example of its kind. As an anthropologist, Hurston formed a foundation for thinking about cultural language use in this essay. She categorized contrasting features calling Western abstract expression "cheque words." "Language is like money," she writes. "The people with highly developed language have words for detached ideas. That is legal tender.... [W]e might say that *Paradise Lost* ... [is] written in cheque words."

In contrast, Hurston points out that the early language use rooted in black cultural expression is "all close fitting":

> ... the Negro, even with detached words in his vocabulary—not evolved in him but transplanted on his tongue by contact—must add action to it to make it do. So we have "chop-axe," "sitting-chair," "cook-pot" and the like because the speaker has in his mind the picture of the object in use. Action. Everything illustrated. So we can say the white man thinks in written language and the Negro thinks in hieroglyphics. (pp. 830–831)

Writing in the 1920s, Hurston had very specific reasons for resisting the view of black language use as inferior. This foundation not only informs her collections of black folklore in, for example, *Mules and Men*—the first collection published by an African American—and *Tell My Horse*, but it also evolves through her experiments with prose fiction. Although the contrast between the oral and written word is implicit in Hurston's theory of language, her work reveals a deep-rooted, historical and anthropological concern: how can a writer use written language without losing the "oral consciousness" that informs it? How does one create the "speakerly text," a sense of a speaker's "presence," or intimacy in the writing itself?

In an assimilationist era, Hurston was especially concerned with the danger of losing the black oral memory—with the way memory is constructed and esteemed in black culture. Other black intellectuals of the time—what she called the "black literati"—were often more concerned with assimilating Western values for written language use and representing the race.

Many contemporary writers and scholars, black women and women of color, have revisited these issues, experimenting with oral and written values—for example, prose fiction writers Paula Gunn Allen, Gloria Anzualdua, Toni Cade Bambara, Gayl Jones, Maxine Hong Kingston, Toni Morrison, Ntozake Shange, Leslie Marmon Silko; critical writers Elsa Barkley Brown, Barbara Christian, June Jordan, Trinh Min-Ha, Trudier Harris, Deborah McDowell, Nellie McKay, Marilyn Mobley, Harryette Mullen, Valerie Smith, Mary Helen Washington. Historically, these aesthetic and political language issues also link Zora Neale Hurston with William Faulkner (although we rarely think about them as contemporaries), who also assumed a bardic ethos as an American writer, reconceiving the values of writing, cultural oral memory and the Southern folk idiom in his novels.

Hurston's accomplishments as a writer speak strongly to the current feminist and gender studies scene as well. Her big, bodacious voice insists—at every turn—on an interrogation of gender in addition to race. Hurston was one of the earliest women writers to create a powerful realism in her novels, illustrating a woman's feelings and spaces with striking metaphors, drama and ethnographic detail.

In one of her lesser-known novels, *Moses, Man of the Mountain*, she sets her retelling of the Moses story in biblical Egypt. The story unfolds quickly to the scene of Moses' birth. Hurston, who remained childless throughout her life, graphically depicts the physical, emotional and psychological violence of birthing a child in silence. The mother fears bearing a male child, because Pharaoh has proclaimed that all boys will be killed. The breaking of her water, the ebb-and-flow pain of childbirth, are combined with the violent gestures of the father who attempts to muffle, smother and silence his wife's cries. Fear dominates the scene. Hurston also includes a slave midwife practicing her herbal healing arts. Effectively, this opening signifies Eve, dramatizing the curse on Eve and all women to bear children in pain.

This intense focus on giving birth and a woman's sacred space moves Hurston's readers to feel the direct impact of these metaphorical violations on women's rights and freedoms within the long history of patriarchal repression, alienation, infantilizing and silencing of the female voice. The feminist themes in her fiction mirror the irony of Hurston's own life; she was a black woman writer in a new literary movement dominated by men and patriarchal values.

Yet despite such cultural and gender conflicts, Hurston articulates her desire for a good life in her controversial autobiography, *Dust Tracks on a Road*, fully restored in the first volume of this collection. Reflectively, she writes, "What all my work shall be, I don't know that either, every hour being a stranger to you until you live it. I want a busy life, a just mind and a timely death."

Hurston wrote this in 1942, at a time when she viewed herself as only midway through her career as a writer. One can only contemplate the irony of her desire and the significance of her "untimely" death in 1960. But her outstanding literary production remains a monument to her life, which was always subconsciously directed by her mother's voice and inspiration to "jump at de sun"—surely the call to become an African griotte—and to reflect that light on earth for all to see, and love, and "pass it on."

Source: Joyce Irene Middleton, "Where to Look for Zora," in *Women's Review of Books*, Vol. 13, No. 2, November 1995, pp. 28–29.

SOURCES

Cole, Jean Lee, and Charles Mitchell, Introduction to *Collected Plays*, edited by Jean Lee Cole and Charles Mitchell, Rutgers University Press, 2008, pp. xv–xxxi.

Cunard, Nancy, "Harlem Reviewed," in *Negro: An Anthology*, edited by Nancy Cunard, abridged by Hugh Ford, Continuum International, 1996, pp. 47–55.

Gannett, Lewis, Review of *Mules and Men*, in *Zora Neale Hurston: Critical Perspectives Past and Present*, edited by Henry Louis Gates and K. A. Appiah, Amistad, 1993, pp. 11–13; originally published in *New York Herald Tribune Weekly Book Review*, October 11, 1935.

Hughes, Langston, "The Twenties: Harlem and Its Negritude," in *The Collected Works of Langston Hughes*, Vol. 9, *Essays on Art, Race, Politics, and World Affairs*, edited by Christopher C. De Santis, University of Missouri Press, 2002, 465–74; originally published in *African Forum*, Vol. 1, 1966, pp. 11–20.

Hurston, Lucy Anne, "Zora Neale Hurston: Pioneering Social Scientist," in *"The Inside Light": New Critical Essays on Zora Neale Hurston*, edited by Deborah G. Plant, Praeger, 2010, pp. 15–21.

Hurston, Zora Neale, "Characteristics of Negro Expression," in *Negro: An Anthology*, edited by Nancy Cunard, abridged by Hugh Ford, Continuum International, 1996, pp. 24–46.

———, *Dust Tracks on a Road*, Harper Perennial, 2006, p. 263.

———, *Poker!*, in *Collected Plays*, edited by Jean Lee Cole and Charles Mitchell, Rutgers University Press, 2008, pp. 201, 217–19.

Hutchinson, George, *The Harlem Renaissance in Black and White*, Belknap, 1997 pp. 62–69, 170–208.

Lowe, John, "Hurston, Toomer, and the Dream of a Negro Theater," in *"The Inside Light": New Critical Essays on Zora Neale Hurston*, edited by Deborah G. Plant, Praeger, 2010, pp. 79–92.

McCrum, Robert, William Cran, and Robert MacNeil, *The Story of English*, Viking, 1986, pp. 195–233.

Said, Edward, *Orientalism*, Vintage Books, 1979, pp. 1–28.

Wall, Cheryl A., "Zora Neale Hurston: Changing Her Own Words," in *Zora Neale Hurston: Critical Perspectives Past and Present*, edited by Henry Louis Gates and K. A. Appiah, Amistad, 1993, pp. 76–97.

Wright, Richard, "Between Laughter and Tears," in *New Masses*, Vol. 5, October 5, 1937, pp. 22–23.

X, Malcolm, *The Autobiography of Malcolm X as Told to Alex Haley*, Ballantine, 1999, pp. 73–153.

FURTHER READING

Hill, Lynda Marion, *Social Rituals and the Verbal Art of Zora Neale Hurston*, Howard University Press, 1996.
    Hill explores the anthropological component of Hurston's work from many different viewpoints including the social complexity of the black community and the role of superstition and magic in black folk tradition.

Jones, Sharon L., *Critical Companion to Zora Neale Hurston: A Literary Reference to Her Life and Work*, Facts on File, 2009.
    This introductory reference work contains a biography of Hurston together with two encyclopedic sections: one devoted to Hurston's works and one to her literary and social environment, with entries on topics such as the Harlem Renaissance and Langston Hughes.

Minnick, Lisa Cohen, *Dialect and Dichotomy: Literary Representations of African American Speech*, University of Alabama Press, 2004.
    Cohen studies the ways in which black dialect has been incorporated into American literary works, focusing on four main works: Mark Twain's *Huckleberry Finn*, Charles W. Chestnutt's *The Conjure Woman*, William Faulkner's *The Sound and the Fury*, and Hurston's *Their Eyes Were Watching God*.

Smith, Katherine Capshaw, ed., *Children's Literature of the Harlem Renaissance*, Indiana University Press, 2004.
    The essays in this volume consider the children's literature produced by black authors in light of the black experience in America. There is particular attention paid to the aesthetic qualities of the children's literature written by Hurston's colleague Langston Hughes in collaboration with Arna Bontemps during the Harlem Renaissance.

SUGGESTED SEARCH TERMS

Zora Neale Hurston

Poker! AND Hurston

Harlem Renaissance

minstrel show

libertarianism

patter

negritude

voodoo

black folklore

Radio Golf

AUGUST WILSON

2005

August Wilson, playwright and two-time Pulitzer Prize winner, set out early in his career to win a place on America's stages for African American work. Not only did he succeed beyond all doubt—with the majority of his plays completing successful runs on Broadway—but he also brought full casts and crews of black artists along with him, granting them recognition on the best stages in the country. His ten-play cycle chronicling black life over a century in Pittsburgh, Pennsylvania, broke down barriers in its multicultural appeal, bringing many African Americans into theaters for the first time while inspiring as well as educating white audiences who were already regular theatergoers.

Radio Golf (2005) is the last of these ten plays, set in the economic boom of the late 1990s. Harmond Wilks, a candidate for mayor of Pittsburgh as well as a hopeful redeveloper of the rundown Hill District, must choose between succeeding at the cost of his morality or embracing the community he loves at the cost of his career. Through the play, Wilson urges the increasingly successful black middle and upper classes not to forget those suffering below them, while discouraging assimilation with white society at the expense of black cultural traditions. *Radio Golf* is a story of ambitions, contradictions, and, ultimately, love—a sweeping morality play complete with musical numbers, monologues, and every emotion in the spectrum—all contained within a single-room real-estate office. Wilson died shortly after this

August Wilson (© AP Images / Ted S. Warren)

AUTHOR BIOGRAPHY

Wilson, born April 27, 1945, in Pittsburgh, Pennsylvania, as Frederick August Kittel, was the son of a black mother descended from slaves and a white German immigrant father, who had no part in his upbringing. At the age of fifteen, Wilson dropped out of high school after he was wrongly accused of plagiarizing a paper on Napoleon that he had passionately researched and written. To avoid telling his mother, who was sure to be heartbroken, Wilson spent his days at the Carnegie Library, reading whatever he pleased. A naturally gifted writer, Wilson at first wanted to become a poet, but was lured into the world of drama by Rob Penny, with whom he formed the Black Horizons Theater Company in 1968.

In 1978, Wilson moved from Pittsburgh to St. Paul, Minnesota, where the sudden absence of African American voices around him brought their language into sharp focus. In his introduction to *The Cambridge Companion to August Wilson*, Christopher Bigsby quotes the playwright:

> I was removed from the black community and, perhaps as a result, for the first time I began to hear the voices that I had grown up with all my life. And I began to discover, to recognize, the value of those voices.

Ma Rainey's Black Bottom (1984) was his first major success and proved Wilson a capable writer of authentic dialogue, sympathetic characters, and

cross-culturally compelling drama. Partnering with acclaimed director Lloyd Richards, Wilson began his cycle of ten plays chronicling ten decades of African American life known as the "Twentieth-Century Cycle" or the "Pittsburgh Cycle," for their common setting in Wilson's hometown. Wilson's plays would generally begin at the O'Neil Playwrights Conference, move on to the Yale Repertory Theatre, and finally appear on Broadway—an unprecedented continuous success story for a black playwright. Harry J. Elam Jr. states in *The Past as Present in the Drama of August Wilson*,

> He has changed the face of American theater, and his emergence has enabled other black writers to follow. As director Marion McClinton states, "A lot of black writers had doors opened to them basically because August Wilson knocked them out."

Wilson was awarded the Pulitzer Prize for Drama twice—in 1987 for *Fences*, which also won the Tony Award that year, and again in 1990 for *The Piano Lesson*—along with countless other accolades in recognition of his groundbreaking work on the stage. His plays have provided up-and-coming black actors the chance to play powerful and memorable lead roles, along with providing black audiences the experience of seeing their own lives represented onstage.

Radio Golf, the final entry in Wilson's ten-play cycle, premiered in 2005 and progressed to Broadway. A tale of moral responsibility in the upwardly mobile black middle class in the increasingly diverse American landscape of the cusp of the new millennium, *Radio Golf* opened to excellent reviews. Wilson passed away shortly after completing his "Pittsburgh Cycle," on October 2, 2005, of liver cancer, leaving behind his third wife, Constanza Wilson, and two daughters.

PLOT SUMMARY

Act 1

SCENE 1

As *Radio Golf* opens, the scene is Bedford Hills Redevelopment, Inc., an office cluttered with unopened packing boxes. Harmond Wilks enters with more boxes in his hands, accompanied by his wife, Mame. She is not impressed and insists his campaign office should look better. He tells her that his mayoral campaign office will be elsewhere in the Hill District of Pittsburgh, as

play, the last in the cycle, premiered; his work was, indisputably, complete.

this is the construction office for the redevelopment of the neighborhood. Mame suggests the upscale Shadyside neighborhood for the site of his campaign office, but Harmond disagrees succinctly: "I'm from the Hill District."

Harmond's business partner, Roosevelt Hicks, enters with a rendering of their multimillion-dollar redevelopment plan, with corporate storefronts including a Starbucks, Barnes & Noble, and Whole Foods. Roosevelt hangs a poster of Tiger Woods on the wall, while Mame leaves to handle the press side of Harmond's campaign for mayor. Harmond is confident that his announcement of his mayoral candidacy will ensure the blight will be declared on time for the groundbreaking ceremony. *Blight* means that the area is too badly decayed to be useful, and the government may step in to rebuild. They discuss golf, a favorite pastime of both men.

Mame calls to tell Harmond that a man is painting an old house in the district, despite the presence of signs announcing it will be torn down in a week. Roosevelt leaves to confront the man. Harmond, left alone, hangs a portrait of Martin Luther King Jr. on the wall. Sterling Johnson, an ex-con from the neighborhood looking for a job, enters; he admits to serving jail time for bank robbery. When Harmond says he plans on changing the name of the Hill District to Bedford Hills, Sterling says there is no use, because the neighborhood is dead. Roosevelt enters. Sterling leaves his phone number and exits.

Roosevelt confronted the man painting the house, who claims it is his property. Roosevelt threatened to call the police, but the man did not seem to care. Roosevelt leaves to pick up his new business cards to pass out on the golf course, where he socializes with white businessmen: "Without them cards they'll think I'm the caddie."

SCENE 2

With the local radio station, WBTZ, playing in the background, Harmond hangs a new rendering of the redevelopment plan. Elder Joseph Barlow (Old Joe) enters, looking for a lawyer. He acknowledges that Harmond is "a big man" but says the powers that be will not let a black man become mayor. Old Joe realizes he knew Harmond's twin brother and his father.

Roosevelt enters, recognizing Old Joe as the man who was painting the abandoned house.

Asked for an explanation, Old Joe replies that the house is his: he owns the deed. But he stopped painting the house after the police confronted him, giving him a court summons. Harmond calls in to have the summons dismissed. Old Joe recalls seeing Harmond as a child riding by in his father's car eating ice cream, passing everyone on foot. Roosevelt shows him the demolition order for 1839 Wylie Street that they have on file and tells him to prove he has the deed by retrieving it from the courthouse. Old Joe leaves, offended by Roosevelt's rudeness. Roosevelt brags to Harmond that he was asked to play golf with an influential businessman.

SCENE 3

Mame and Harmond have an argument in the office about his upcoming speech announcing his run for mayor. Old Joe enters, to tell Harmond his car has been broken into. Harmond leaves in a rush and returns upset at the loss of his golf clubs, stolen out of his trunk. Mame exits disappointedly after Harmond calls the newspaper to demand that they print his speech in whole, without the cuts Mame approved. Alone, the two men talk about the house on Wylie Street. Old Joe was told by the clerk at the courts that his deed was sold off because of unpaid taxes. Harmond promises to look into the matter as a favor to Old Joe. Roosevelt enters, fresh off the golf course. Old Joe excuses himself from the office.

Roosevelt had a great day on the course, and was asked by the influential millionaire Bernie Smith to partner in his radio station. Bernie Smith is seeking to buy the radio station at a reduced price, because there is a tax incentive for the seller if he sells to a minority buyer. Bernie Smith would secretly partner in the company with Roosevelt acting as a front. Harmond thinks the plan sounds awful, but Roosevelt says he will take what he can get to advance his career. Roosevelt wants to go out for another round of golf with Harmond, but Harmond admits his clubs have been stolen. Roosevelt says he warned Harmond about parking his car in the Hill District. He does not trust the locals.

SCENE 4

Harmond realizes after some research that, in buying 1839 Wylie Street, he has made an illegal purchase. The complex history of 1839 Wylie Street began when the government took over the property as a result of unpaid property taxes. Legally, the government must post an announcement in the newspaper stating they have taken the house as a result of unpaid taxes. When Harmond bought the property from the government, he assumed the purchase was legal. However, the home is technically still owned by Old Joe because no announcement was ever published in the newspaper, meaning the city took it without notifying Old Joe first. Mame arrives, ecstatic to have landed a government job. But when Harmond suggests that she start as soon as possible, she refuses because of her duties to his campaign. They discuss possible slogans for the mayoral race. Sterling Johnson arrives, at first congratulating, then warning Harmond about his decision to run for mayor. Mame leaves while Sterling begins to read the announcement in the paper. He asks about a job, but Harmond denies him. Old Joe enters, mourning to Sterling that the city is going to tear his house down. Harmond promises he will find a legal solution to the problem. Harmond receives a paper from Old Joe stating that Harmond's own father paid the taxes on 1839 Wylie. But neither Harmond nor Old Joe can imagine why.

SCENE 5

Roosevelt tells Harmond that they can bring Bernie Smith into the redevelopment deal in case the city does not declare blight in time, but Harmond will not hear of it. Harmond confides in Roosevelt about the legal problems surrounding 1839 Wylie. Because Harmond bought the house before auction, before notice was given to Old Joe, the sale is illegal. Harmond insists that Old Joe must be paid the value of his house if the city is going to demolish it. Roosevelt reluctantly agrees.

The two men receive a phone call that the city has declared blight, and they burst into celebration. Sterling interrupts, grimly demanding to be refunded the money he spent painting the door of 1839 Wylie for Old Joe. The city went over the fresh paint job with an X. Roosevelt mocks him, but Harmond goes to get the twenty-six dollars he demands. Still, he says, "Rightly or wrongly we're going to tear down the house." Sterling, incensed, argues that you cannot just destroy someone's home. He threatens revenge on anyone who harms the house on Wylie Street: "You the cowboys. I'm the Indians. See who win this war."

Act 2

SCENE 1

The radio plays WBTZ, and it is Roosevelt's voice on his new radio show, giving golf advice. Harmond's campaign poster hangs on the wall with his slogan: "Hold Me to It." Sterling enters, handing Harmond a flyer for a paint party he has organized at 1839 Wylie on the day of the demolition. In addition to the flyer, Sterling brings Harmond's golf clubs, demanding twenty dollars for their return. Harmond pays him.

Old Joe enters, greeting Sterling. Harmond gives Old Joe a check for ten thousand dollars but Old Joe will not take it. He does not want to sell his house. Harmond tries to argue with him, using the fact of the house's inevitable demolition, but Old Joe leaves without the check. Harmond tries to explain to Sterling why Old Joe needs to take the money, but Sterling puts him in his place: "You stole Mr. Barlow's house. As it is Bedford Hills is in the possession of stolen property and you and him are the only ones who know you stole it." He says that while no one will listen to Old Joe tell the truth, if Harmond even whispers, everyone takes notice. He gives Harmond's twenty dollars back and leaves.

SCENE 2

Roosevelt, his desk cluttered with WBTZ paraphernalia, practices his golf swing. He brags to Harmond that his new office at the radio station is being painted "light money green." Harmond congratulates him with a touch of sarcasm, and then asks if he has ever been to 1839 Wylie. Roosevelt has not, but Harmond has just come from there. The house is beautiful. Harmond, touched by its history, reveals a new redevelopment plan that preserves the house in the middle of the new construction. Roosevelt is beside himself at his partner's decision. He leaves, telling Harmond not to make any rash moves without consulting him. As soon as he is alone, Harmond calls off the demolition.

Old Joe enters with one hundred dollars, for the taxes he owes. Harmond tells him the good news about the house. Old Joe takes his money back. Harmond asks Old Joe why Harmond's father as well as his grandfather were paying taxes on 1839 Wylie. They begin to trace their ancestors back together and realize that they each have a woman named Black Mary in their family: she is Harmond's aunt and Old Joe's mother. They each write the name of their grandfather on pieces of paper, to be sure. They both write the name Henry Samuel. The two men are cousins. Amazed, they share a hug.

SCENE 3

Roosevelt and Mame wait for Harmond to arrive at the office, worried about his obsession with Old Joe's house. Mame says Harmond wants to move back to the Hill District from their affluent suburb; she remarks, "I can't move back here, Roosevelt. I don't want to go backward." Harmond comes in thrilled about preserving the house, but Roosevelt informs him that the redevelopment project has collapsed overnight due to his decision—the investors are angry. Additionally, Roosevelt hands Harmond a long rap sheet detailing Old Joe's criminal history. Harmond dismisses it. Roosevelt says he called to reschedule the house's demolition. Harmond says the demolition is illegal, and he will reveal it to the authorities at the expense of his own career. Roosevelt warns him not to throw their hard work away.

SCENE 4

With the phones in the office ringing off the hook, Harmond, alone, sits at his desk. He cannot reach Roosevelt or any of his associates. He starts to yank the phone cords out of the wall when Mame walks in. She saw two bulldozers parked near 1839 Wylie, but the paint party is raging: "Got music blasting. Got the barbecue cooking. Kids running around. Looks like the Fourth of July." She makes Harmond admit that he ruined his chances for mayor, and also that he ruined her chances, too. They won't have her in for another interview for her government job. Harmond apologizes. She does not know if she can stay with him, but decides they will work through it together, as they always have. She leaves to wait for him at home.

Sterling enters, hailing Harmond as a desperado. He reads aloud from the newspaper how Harmond blew the cover on the illegal sale of houses at auction by the government. Harmond filed a temporary injunction against the demolition of 1839 Wylie, but Sterling is skeptical. Roosevelt enters, quickly getting into an argument with Sterling and finally threatening to call the cops if he does not leave the office. Sterling dips his finger into the bucket of paint he's carrying and marks his face as if before a battle. He exits. Roosevelt tells Harmond that the judge dismissed his injunction and the demolition is

imminent. Harmond says the decision is not fair. Roosevelt tells him he is buying Harmond out of their company. Harmond realizes Roosevelt is getting the money for the buyout from Bernie Smith—that he will once again act as a minority front to a white-owned operation. The two friends exchange harsh words, and Harmond kicks Roosevelt out of the office. As the lights go down, Harmond dips his finger into the paint can Sterling left behind and begins to mark his face for battle.

CHARACTERS

Elder Joseph "Old Joe" Barlow

Old Joe is a resident of the Hill District whose house was sold illegally to Bedford Hills Redevelopment, Inc. He has no wish to vacate the house, insisting on painting it to fix it up for his daughter. He will not accept money for the house, either. He simply has no desire to leave. Old Joe remembers Harmond as a little boy, as well as Harmond's father, whom Old Joe disliked for his air of superiority. When Old Joe and Harmond discover they are cousins, Harmond turns completely to Old Joe's cause.

Roosevelt Hicks

Roosevelt Hicks is Harmond's money-hungry partner in Bedford Hills Redevelopment, Inc. He dislikes the Hill District, never parking his car out of sight. Old Joe and Sterling Johnson are fools as far as Roosevelt is concerned: he never respects their concerns or worries. He is ambitious, prone to bragging about his connections in the white business world. He sees Bernie Smith as the answer to his prayers—a man capable of making him rich through a questionable deal in which Roosevelt will be the front to a silent partnership. Roosevelt loves golf, hanging a poster of Tiger Woods in his office and frequenting the golf course where he rubs shoulders with the white business elite. After Harmond reveals the illegality of the government auctions, Roosevelt betrays him by partnering with Bernie Smith to buy out Harmond's share in the company. The two longtime friends part painfully in the final scene.

Sterling Johnson

Sterling Johnson is an ex-con living in the Hill District. He meets Roosevelt and Harmond when he enters their office to ask for a job. They cannot hire him for construction because he is nonunion. However, Sterling continues to visit the office, offering his advice and admonishments as the drama progresses. Sterling likes Harmond, who generally respects and listens to his opinions. Roosevelt and Sterling do not get along at all, with Roosevelt insulting him and threatening to call the police if he does not stop loitering around their office. Sterling is hired by Old Joe to help paint the house on 1839 Wylie Street. He later organizes the paint party to support his friend against the city's demolition of his house.

Bernie Smith

Bernie Smith is a wealthy, white businessman who is offstage for the entirety of *Radio Golf*. However, his influence over Roosevelt, who sees him as a promising investor, is felt throughout the play. After inviting Roosevelt out for a round of golf, Bernie Smith brings him in on a deal that would allow Smith to be a silent partner in the WBTZ radio station while Roosevelt acts as the minority front—ensuring that Smith gets a better price on the sale because the seller will benefit from a minority tax incentive. Bernie is using Roosevelt's color for his own profit, but Roosevelt is too taken with the idea of accumulating wealth to notice or care. Harmond, however, sees through Smith's shady business plan. He refuses to even entertain the idea of Bernie Smith joining his and Roosevelt's partnership in Bedford Hills Redevelopment. After Harmond goes down in flames, Roosevelt buys Harmond out of their partnership with money from Bernie Smith, who will once again profit off of the color of Roosevelt's skin.

Harmond Wilks

Harmond Wilks, the protagonist of *Radio Golf*, is, simply put, a good man. Hoping to revitalize the downtrodden and mostly abandoned Hill District with a slew of new corporate businesses and high-rise apartments, he and Roosevelt are partners in Bedford Hills Redevelopment, Inc. He comes from money: his father, too, was in real estate. Additionally, Harmond is running a campaign for mayor under the slogan "Hold Me to It." When he discovers that he has bought 1839 Wylie illegally, Harmond is wracked with guilt and seeks a legal way to compensate Old Joe for his loss. Instead, upon discovering that he is related to Old Joe, he joins the growing

community of disapproving residents of the Hill District and suggests to his wife that they move back to the troubled neighborhood. Unable to run a dishonest business, Harmond gives up his dream of becoming mayor of Pittsburgh by exposing the illegal purchase. Roosevelt abandons him, taking the redevelopment plan with him. Mame stays true to him. Left alone in his office at the end of the play, he paints himself like a warrior and leaves the office to join Sterling's paint party at 1839 Wylie.

Mame Wilks

Mame Wilks, Harmond Wilks's wife, is in charge of the details of his mayoral campaign. She is strong, decisive, and intelligent, with no time for the antics of Sterling and Old Joe. In addition to these duties, she is also courting a high-status job in the government as the governor's press representative—an opportunity she loses as a result of Harmond's decision to go public with the news of the illegal sale of houses by the government. Like Roosevelt, Mame is extremely ambitious. However, she decides to forgive Harmond for his campaign failure and stay by his side: "I can't live my life for you. And you can't live yours for me. But I'm still standing here."

THEMES

Community

Roosevelt, Harmond, and Mame do not presently belong to the community they hope to redevelop as well as rename (from the Hill District to Bedford Hills). In fact, they are attempting to enforce their own values of commoditization and corporations onto a neighborhood once sprinkled with little shops and restaurants. The global culture of attainment that they would like to bring to the Hill District includes Whole Foods, Starbucks, and Barnes & Noble. Clearly the uneducated Old Joe and ex-con Sterling Johnson have no place in this fantasy. As Wilson's representative voices for the community of the Hill District, their rejection from this corporate dreamscape means the rejection of all the local residents. Roosevelt, who is always about to call the cops on one local or another, displays the elite's discomfort loudly. Mame, Roosevelt, and Harmond simply do not get it.

TOPICS FOR FURTHER STUDY

- After finishing *Radio Golf*, read another installment in the Pittsburgh Cycle. Write a comparative essay about the two plays in which you identify common themes and major differences in the works. The plays of the cycle you can choose from are as follows (listed chronologically by the decade in which they are set, beginning with the 1900s): *Gem of the Ocean* (2003), *Joe Turner's Come and Gone* (1988), *Ma Rainey's Black Bottom* (1984), *The Piano Lesson* (1990), *Seven Guitars* (1997), *Fences* (1987), *Two Trains Running* (1991), *Jitney* (1982), and *King Hedley II* (1999).

- Using Kristen Dabrowski's *Twenty 10-Minute Plays for Teens* (2004), break into groups to plan a performance. Dabrowski's plays cover a variety of issues important to young adults, making the classroom the perfect theater. Or, if you prefer, choose a scene from *Radio Golf* to perform.

- Go see a play at your local theater. How did they do? Write a comprehensive review, highlighting the performances you found best, while commenting on the scenery, the directing, and making suggestions for the company's next production. Touch briefly on the themes of the play in your review.

Did the play share any major themes with *Radio Golf*? Touch on the similarities or differences between the two plays. Be sure to hold on to your playbill for the names of the actors and crew. Attach the playbill to your review when you turn it in.

- Have you ever tried your hand at playwriting? Now is your chance. Compose your own play of any length, on any subject. Use your imagination, write from the heart, and do not forget stage directions! Use *Radio Golf* as a guide and inspiration by limiting the action of your play to a single room.

- Many of the technical terms in *Radio Golf* may be unfamiliar to you. Using your online search skills, research a few of these terms (such as *back taxes*, *blight*, *injunction*, and *deeds*), making a list of definitions in your own words along with any examples you can find—for instance, a newspaper article about a case of a government declaring blight on a neighborhood. Then write an essay in which you explain the technical aspects of *Radio Golf* by providing your definitions and elaborating on real-life examples to illustrate different ways such situations concerning property may turn out.

Harmond, though, has pride in coming from the Hill District and awakens to the error of his plans to improve the culture of the neighborhood by literally destroying it. The paint party becomes the active site of the Hill District's culture. Mame describes it as a "Fourth of July." One would assume the neighborhood is derelict, crime-ridden, and mostly abandoned from the speeches heard inside the redevelopment office, but outside blossoms a celebration of the spirit that truly defines the Hill District, which is not abandoned but bursting with life. The "desperado," as Sterling describes the newly awakened

Harmond, finds his place within the community. Roosevelt leaves him for the pursuit of money, but Harmond paints his face and dives into the celebration of a unique, endangered culture hidden to the wealthy redevelopers.

Morality

In essence, *Radio Golf* is a morality play. At stake is the community of the Hill District. Harmond, who at first believes he is saving the neighborhood, must come to the conclusion that he is in fact about to flatten it in favor of culturally and morally bankrupt corporate interests. The

Radio Golf *is set in the Hill District of Pittsburgh, Pennsylvania. (© Svetlana Larina / Shutterstock.com)*

theme of right and wrong is prevalent throughout the play, as Harmond navigates the difference between them. His first indication that he is on the wrong side is the illegal purchase of 1839 Wylie Street. Once Harmond discovers this fact, Roosevelt's nonchalance over the matter disturbs him. The further he strays from his partner's money-driven ideology, the closer Harmond comes to his moral and spiritual awakening as a warrior for the Hill District. Old Joe and Sterling are his moral guides, questioning his past, present, and future with each move he makes. When Harmond claims that they will demolish Old Joe's house "rightly or wrongly," Sterling's strong objection begins to change Harmond's mind. Old Joe and Sterling are there to point out that Harmond grew up with a porch, a house, and his father's car to ride in while others sat on stoops and watched him roll past. Roosevelt is his moral opposite, a bad influence who does not respect anything but cash. After the revelation that Old Joe and Harmond are cousins, there is no turning back. At first Harmond tries to work within the system he knows so well to save his people, but when that fails, he goes guerrilla, donning the painted face of a warrior and following Sterling to the community's last hurrah for Old Joe's home.

Money

The division of wealth is stark in *Radio Golf*, with those in the upper echelons (Mame, Harmond, and Roosevelt) meddling in the lives of those in poverty (Old Joe and Sterling Johnson). The multimillion-dollar redevelopment plan, the high-end corporate investors, and the campaign for mayor are just a few of many examples of wealth in action. Meanwhile, Sterling's search for a job, the low-tech rebellion of the paint party, and the setting in the dilapidated Hill District of Pittsburgh mark the presence of lower-class interests in jeopardy. Money, when not discussed outright by the characters, is symbolized in the game of golf. A leisure sport of the wealthy, golf in the play represents the carefree and questionable business dealings of the upper class. Roosevelt, who loves his "light money green" painted office, is most hypnotized by golf, just as he is the most obsessed with money among the characters. Significantly, Roosevelt was not born into money and thus may appreciate it more than the born-wealthy Harmond. But Harmond is ultimately a humane member of the upper class: when he hands the ten-thousand-dollar check over to Old Joe, he cannot understand why his generosity is rejected. But for Old Joe, money will not solve his problem, as he simply states, "I like my house. Don't you like your house?" This moment shows the disconnection between Old Joe's and Harmond's values. Old Joe values community, togetherness, the future of his daughter, for whom he wants to fix the house up. But Harmond cannot comprehend what would be more valuable than his check. Money also equals power, and when Sterling points this out to Harmond, he also hands Harmond's money back to him. Sterling and Old Joe's dual rejection of what Harmond believes everyone and anyone would want plants the seed in his mind that he is doing something inherently wrong by calling for blight in a neighborhood where residents still live and love, still have a community of support despite their downtrodden surroundings and economic position. While Roosevelt continues to chase money, Harmond decides to pursue community, and the result is an all-out war over 1839 Wylie Street.

STYLE

Dialogue

Wilson, who struggled with realistic dialogue as a young writer, had become a master of writing believable and compelling conversation between his characters by the end of his career. Dialogue, the spoken words of the characters, may be the most important aspect in drama, and when reading a play as opposed to watching a play in performance, the dialogue between the characters—interrupted only by stage directions—is all a reader has to go on. Looking closely at Wilson's dialogue, one sees that his characters each speak in a distinct way. For example, confusing the dialogue of Harmond with that of Sterling would be unlikely. How characters speak (their syntax) and the vocabularies they choose to express themselves (diction) are determined by many factors, but in *Radio Golf* the main division determining speech is wealth. Margaret Booker's essay "*Radio Golf*: The Courage of His Convictions—Survival, Success and Spirituality" breaks the difference down: "Harmond

and Mame speak with near-perfect grammar about marketing and business deals and their relationship." Harmond, born into wealth as a result of his father's real-estate business, "like a true politician, can adjust his speech pattern to his constituency." Roosevelt, who is a self-made man desperately scrambling toward the top of the ladder, "retains the poor grammar and colourful swearing of his youth in addition to the vocabularies he learnt in college." But Harmond, Mame, and Roosevelt travel to the Hill District from their affluent suburbs. The Hill District residents, Old Joe and Sterling, speak imperfect, slang-filled idiosyncratic English with heart and soul. Booker notes, quoting Ben Brantley from the *New York Times*, "Old Joe and Sterling possess the 'Shakespearean richness that Mr. Wilson has devised for residents of the hill...the wayward anecdotal vigor that is Mr. Wilson's blissful specialty.'" The differences in speech between the residents of the Hill District and the three outsiders not only result in distinct voices but moreover encapsulate the issues of race and class that *Radio Golf* raises for the audience's consideration.

Conflict

Tension-creating conflict drives narratives, and *Radio Golf* is no exception. Many conflicts are present in the play, but the conflict between Harmond and Roosevelt is central to the story's moral conundrum, with 1839 Wylie serving as the symbolic battleground. Wilson customarily leaves white characters offstage, leaving the black characters alone to act. Nonetheless, Bernie Smith's creeping influence on the morally weak Roosevelt causes tension between Roosevelt and Harmond. Although they are friends, money and sympathy divide them. Roosevelt does not trust the neighborhood, preens over his new position at the radio station, and (though he, unlike Harmond, was not born wealthy) shows no sympathy for the residents of the Hill District. As Harmond pulls further away from Roosevelt, Roosevelt's anger grows, until he takes the redevelopment company out from under Harmond. Roosevelt chooses money, Harmond chooses community. Thus the morality play ends in a sort of draw, with one partner against the other. Booker writes of the grander implications of their battle, which she believes "embodies and crystallizes in time...the moment of danger in which the unique African American history and cultural values could disappear, if those in leadership positions do not assume responsibility for their continuance." Significantly, the tension is not resolved—the fate of 1839 Wylie still hangs in the air—but the battle lines are crisply drawn and the moral implications made obvious. Money and power lead to corrupt assimilation into the dominant culture, while sympathy and community lead to Harmond's spiritual awakening as a warrior for his people.

HISTORICAL CONTEXT

1990s Liminality

Wilson situates the final play of his cycle, as with eight of the others, in his hometown of Pittsburgh, Pennsylvania—specifically the Hill District, where Wilson grew up. The 1990s brought the decay and partial abandonment of the neighborhood, as upwardly mobile blacks (like Mame and Harmond, who is originally from the Hill District) fled to safer, more exclusive neighborhoods. Significantly, Wilson did not extensively research the historical periods in which he set his plays; rather, his details come from more organic observations and assumptions about each period. In this way, Wilson avoided feeling trapped by historical facts. Of the historical background he creates, Booker remarks, "*Radio Golf* depicts Pittsburgh's Hill District in 1997, a year which marks the critical moment of its possible extinction in the name of progress. As the city proceeds to rid itself from blight, it also creates a 'moment of danger.'" That danger, Booker argues, is that with the extinction of the historical site of an African American community in favor of supersized, faceless corporations, the people themselves will lose their spiritual connection to their shared culture.

The result of this, Elam argues, is that "Wilson depicts black people in liminal space, displaced and disconnected from their history, separated from their individual identity and in search of spiritual resurrection and socio-political reconnection." A liminal space, or liminality, refers to being in between two states of rest. It is a state of transition which is often not defined; for example, a train moving between Pittsburgh and Washington, DC, can be said to occupy a liminal space, because it is neither here nor there but moving in between. Likewise, a student who has finished high school and is about to enter college occupies a liminal space during the summer after graduation, as the student waits for classes to begin. Most importantly in the context of *Radio Golf*, 1839 Wylie Street is a liminal property as a result of its illegal sale: at once held by Bedford Redevelopment, Inc., as well as owned by Old Joe, the house becomes symbolic of the people of the Hill District who are similarly caught in between definitions. In a decade of growing opportunity for African Americans, the 1990s were also a liminal time in terms of black progress forward toward inclusion and acceptance. Elam states, "Throughout Wilson's cycle as a whole, the liminality of the times provides a metaphor for the characters' own dilemma and developments." As barriers broke down in the 1990s—exemplified by the poster of Tiger Woods that Roosevelt hangs lovingly on his office wall, heralding the first black man to succeed in the white-dominated arena of professional golf—a greater number of black Americans rose to their rightful place as equal participants in society at large. But barriers do not come down all at once, and remnants of discrimination in business are on prominent display in *Radio Golf* in the offstage person of Bernie Smith.

For Wilson, responsibility for the extinction or failure of African American cultural traditions is placed firmly on the shoulders of these vanguard African Americans who rise up to match the success of the dominant white culture. Will they join the culture—assimilating as Roosevelt yearns to do? Or will they reach back and help others up, establishing a firmly African American version of success that stays true to their historical roots? Harmond (as with Wilson as he rose to prominence himself) chooses the latter. For Harmond it means the end of his campaign for mayor. For Wilson it meant a moral obligation to honestly represent the complexity and beauty in the lives of black Americans through art. He believed that, for blacks to be cured of their liminal status in the nation, as Bigsby states, "the need was for communal strength, an acknowledgement of a shared past and hence a sense of shared identity in the present." As Harmond paints his face in the final scene of *Radio Golf*, Wilson is demonstrating his belief in community as the savior during uncertain and unpredictable times.

Harmond Wilkes is Ivy-league educated. *(© Thomas Barrat | Shutterstock.com)*

CRITICAL OVERVIEW

Wilson will go down in history as one of the most decorated and important playwrights of the twentieth century. *Radio Golf* premiered to positive reviews coupled with a long run on Broadway, with similar productions around the country. The election of America's first African American president shortly after the debut of Wilson's political drama only helped bolster the popularity and relevance of the play. Elam states of Wilson's broad commercial appeal, "Like music that finds listeners across racial and ethnic borders, Wilson's works contain meanings and messages that are accessible to a wider audience."

Booker remarks in admiration of Wilson's final work, "Never one to mince words, even in the last few months of his life, he sounds his challenge to the black middle class to engage in the battle for the black man's soul." That battle, the battle of 1839 Wylie Street, the battle of right versus wrong, leads to the baptism in paint of Harmond Wilks as a cultural warrior. Sandra G.

Shannon comments in *The Dramatic Vision of August Wilson*, "Wilson leads his audiences to recurring cultural epiphanies about their collective pasts and sweeps them toward the cathartic awareness that therein lie their greatest strengths." Harmond and Old Joe's realization of their shared past is one such instance. From that point in the drama forward, Harmond works for the community rather than for his own success. Similarly, Joan Herrington states in *"I Ain't Sorry for Nothin' I Done": August Wilson's Process of Playwriting*, "It is only when the characters tap into the wellspring of their history and their culture that they are empowered. Wilson believes that individual strength and transcendence is achieved through connections to a larger universe." Money and power are fine, but at the cost of social connection to those with whom one shares a past—a cost Roosevelt is willing to pay—they are not enough to make a person whole.

In his obituary of Wilson in the *New York Times*, Charles Isherwood praises the skill of the playwright: "In his work, Mr. Wilson depicted the struggles of black Americans with uncommon lyrical richness, theatrical density and emotional heft, in plays that gave vivid voices to people on the frayed margins of life." John Lahr, in his early review of *Radio Golf* for the *New Yorker*, puts the tenth and final play in perspective: "Although the play cycle has reached the nineteen-nineties, Wilson's characters are still under assault, still marginalized.... His heroes here, however, have learned how to play the dominant culture's game." Lahr goes on, "Whether it's a success or not hardly matters to the reputation of the cycle; Wilson is a heavyweight, and his oeuvre is a glorious and enduring victory."

CRITICISM

Amy Lynn Miller

Miller is a graduate of the University of Cincinnati and now resides in New Orleans, Louisiana. In the following essay, she discusses the roles of Old Joe and Sterling Johnson in Radio Golf *as representatives of their community, working to preserve their culture against an overwhelming outside force of destructive change.*

Although Harmond is the focal center of the battle between right and wrong in August Wilson's *Radio Golf*, Old Joe and Sterling Johnson actively work throughout the play to save their community as well as Harmond's soul. If the redevelopment office is the site of reason, 1839 Wylie Street is the site of the spiritual world transcending hegemonic logic. Old Joe and Sterling belong to this site, gain energy from it, and speak for it tirelessly. The house at 1839 Wylie Street represents a defiant black cultural tradition with its own rules and roots. Prominent, unruly, and historically significant, the house stands as a symbol for all of the Hill District, for all once-thriving but underfunded black neighborhoods, for all of society's cast-offs. Old Joe and Sterling are two such cast-offs, yet through their wisdom and dedication they bring about change in Harmond's heart.

The Hill District appears in all but one play of Wilson's cycle, and 1839 Wylie Street, Old Joe, and Sterling Johnson have each had roles in earlier plays. The newcomers—Roosevelt, Mame, and Harmond—do not belong to the larger narrative. Their place in the play is to

> WHEN HARMOND CHOOSES COMMUNITY OVER HIS CAREER, HIS AMERICAN DREAM ENDS, AND A NEW ONE BEGINS AS HE IS REBORN AS A CULTURAL WARRIOR."

threaten the future of the cycle's setting itself. Old Joe and Sterling, then, act on behalf of all the characters who have come before them in their efforts to save their rightful inheritance: the historical site of black American lives for the last century in the cycle's time line. Important, too, is Wilson's own origins in the Hill District. After dropping out of high school, the playwright spent his days at a local library and his nights haunting popular Hill District hangouts. The adults called him Youngblood and told him all about their world. Wilson could be found sitting off to the side of the main action, scribbling away on napkins. Absorbing everything, he honed his powers of observation. After moving away, Isherwood writes, "His spiritual home remained the rough streets of the Hill District, where as a young man he sat in thrall to the voices of African-American working men and women." In representing the Hill District, Old Joe and Sterling also represent Wilson's own history as well as his grave concern for his hometown's future.

First hearing of Harmond's fantasy of redeveloping, renaming, and reclaiming the Hill District, Sterling—as he always does—hits Harmond hard with a dose of realism: "How you gonna bring it back? It's dead.... What you mean is you gonna put something else in its place. Say that. But don't talk about bringing the Hill back." A local who walked in off the street looking for work, Sterling will not stand by silently and listen to this stranger's ultimately destructive vision. He recognizes immediately that there is no place for himself or the community to which he belongs in the future mayor Harmond's Bedford Hills. After hearing Harmond's plan, Sterling visits the office regularly under various pretenses to pick moral fights, doubt grand schemes, teach lessons, and generally be a thorn in the side of so-called progress. With each

WHAT DO I READ NEXT?

- The poet, playwright, author, and essayist Amiri Baraka's influence on Wilson cannot be overstated, though Baraka can be characterized as the more extreme of the two writers. Baraka's *Four Black Revolutionary Plays* (1969) served as an instruction manual for Wilson when he first became involved with the Black Horizons Theater Company. A controversial author, Baraka's focus, like Wilson's, rests squarely on the black experience in America—the trials of living, the joyous victories, and the bitter defeats.

- Perhaps Wilson's most surprising major influence was the Argentinian author Jorge Luis Borges. Borges's *Selected Poems* (2000), edited by Alexander Coleman, collects many of Borges's most popular poems as well as some unpublished works. All are typical of Borges's metaphysical, transcendental, and rule-defying style of writing. Newcomers to Borges will love his playful ability to turn an assumption on its head, trick his reader, rewrite the rules of time, and create fantastically imaginative characters and scenarios. In particular, it was Borges's treatment of time that Wilson identified with and learned for himself, as seen in his blending of past and present within the ten-play cycle.

- August Wilson's *Ma Rainey's Black Bottom* (1984) is a story of blues musicians waiting for their singer to arrive at the recording studio. Ma Rainey, a powerful woman, must dodge the tricks of her white producers as they scheme to steal the rights to her songs. The waiting musicians, meanwhile, debate the situation heatedly, leading to a disastrous black-on-black crime. *Ma Rainey's Black Bottom* takes place in the 1920s but has many thematic similarities to Wilson's last play, *Radio Golf*, despite being the only play of his cycle not set in Pittsburgh.

- *August Wilson and Black Aesthetics* (2004), edited by Sandra Shannon and Dana Williams, is a collection of essays published not long before Wilson's death. The political and cultural implications of his cycle of plays are examined alongside speeches and interviews with Wilson concerning the role of black theater in America. In particular, a controversial and polarizing speech that Wilson gave in 1996, titled "The Ground on Which I Stand," is addressed as a key to understanding the playwright and his work.

- *Fierce & True: Plays for Teen Audiences* (2010), by the Children's Theatre Company and edited by Peter Brosius and Elissa Adams, includes young-adult works by Naomi Iizuka, Will Power, Lonnie Carter, and Whit MacLaughlin. Intended to address the important and often complicated issues in young-adult lives in America, *Fierce and True* reaches out to young audiences in an effort to engage them in the traditions of drama and theater.

- Lorraine Hansberry's *A Raisin in the Sun* (1959) was the first play by a black woman to make it on Broadway, paving the way for Wilson's later success. A Chicago family is divided when insurance money pays out after the patriarch's death. Each with their own dreams of success, the siblings and loved ones fall to infighting that reaches a breaking point. Taking its name from a line in the famous Langston Hughes poem "Harlem," Hansberry translated Hughes's brilliant poetry into a fascinating dramatic reality. The original director of *A Raisin in the Sun* was Lloyd Richards—the first black director on Broadway—who later worked closely with Wilson, directing much of his ten-play cycle.

visit, Sterling chips away at Harmond's ideologies, leading him through the moral maze of right and wrong. It is Sterling who coins Harmond's campaign slogan, "Hold Me to It." But by embracing Sterling's suggestion, sensitive Harmond creates for himself a strong moral obligation to remember his own promises to his people. Sterling knows this. He and Old Joe are wise men posing as fools, so that their frequent lessons go down easier in the mind of the college-educated man. Playing up their weaknesses, they chip away at Harmond's ignorance. That an ex-con and a crazy old man are deeply involved in educating a candidate for mayor who speaks with perfect grammar is an irony Wilson savors in his gradual development of Harmond's spiritual journey home to 1839 Wylie.

But Harmond, for all his education, is ultimately naive. For instance, he believes he can judge people based on superficial qualities like their mode of speech. "Where was they going?" Sterling asks. "Where were they going?" Harmond repeats. But his correction of Sterling's grammar has no effect on Sterling, who has no reasonable use for this intangible lesson on proper diction. To the contrary, Sterling's corrections of Harmond are based in reality, in emotion, in real human lives, and have a lasting effect on the mayoral candidate. Sterling teaches. Harmond follows. When he paints his face in the last moments of the play, Harmond is miming Sterling's earlier act. He follows his teacher's example. Yet for Harmond, the painting is his final triumphant act on stage, a powerful moment when a genuine "big man," as Old Joe calls him, prepares to battle the hegemony.

Hegemony refers to the dominant power of a culture and its suggestive power over other cultures. In *Radio Golf*, the established hegemonic power is that of white America. We could also notice that power is represented by males, with the only woman—Mame—cast in a supporting role alongside her husband. In this way, we understand hegemony to express whatever values the dominant members hold: white values, upper-class values, and male values. This means that those outside these definitions are marked as inherently other or as outsiders subject to the dominant group's rule. Elam speaks of "the fault in black capitalist strategies that depend upon a system of white hegemony to assess their worth. Inevitably, such dependencies result in exploitation." In Roosevelt, this exploitation is expressed

in his misguided belief that he is striking a fair deal with the millionaire Bernie Smith. Roosevelt leans so heavily on white hegemony as to describe other members of his race in white racist terms, frequently criticizing Hill residents as lazy or criminals or both. His triumphant presentation of Old Joe's criminal record to Harmond—as if it would surprise Harmond, who has listened to Old Joe's speeches, that Old Joe has a history with the police—shows just how lost Roosevelt becomes in the world of white business, white reputations, and white ideals of pristine records. Hegemony, represented by the golf course and Bernie Smith, stays offstage. Likewise the counterculture, represented by 1839 Wylie Street, is never shown. Instead, all paths intersect, mingle, and repel in the liminal space of the office of Bedford Hills Redevelopment, Inc.: a crossroads of cultural beliefs and symbol of the conflict within Harmond's own mind. Herrington states, "The characters in Wilson's plays are struggling to define themselves as individuals and to understand their place in the world. It is only through internal change that they can successfully face external affliction." This internal change in Harmond is acted out by the characters around him: fights between Sterling and Roosevelt might as well be voices arguing in his head.

Another teacher arrives for Harmond in the person of Old Joe. He appears, on first impression, out of his mind. His opening lines—asking around the office for a Christian, then suddenly a lawyer, then just as suddenly recognizing Harmond from the old days in the Hill—suggest a disorganized, illogical, and unpredictable man. But Old Joe is the historical and cultural link that Harmond most desires when he proudly claims, "I'm from the Hill District." In fact, Old Joe is not at all a crazy man, but a profound spiritual connection to the old Hill District as it lives on through his residence at 1839 Wylie Street. His behaviors, which seem to defy logic, such as painting a house about to be demolished, are actually methods of resistance, healing, and renewal. Elam states, "Madness enables these characters both figuratively and literally to transfigure discord into harmony and to agitate for communal and cultural change." Painting his house sends a message of hope to other Hill residents, a beacon of defiance against an overwhelming foe. Indeed, no one knows better the destructive power of mandated progress than Old Joe, who is losing his past, present, and future in the forced destruction of a house that was stolen from him by the same powers and laws that produced Old Joe's long rap sheet which Roosevelt so happily throws in Harmond's face. Where is the government's rap sheet? Of course, there is none, or else the powers that be would have to answer for their own crimes. For blowing the lid off the illegal acts of the government, Harmond loses his hopes of joining and influencing that same government. Yet, would Wilson's Pittsburgh not be better off with more people like Harmond in power, wielding it honestly with moral integrity? His loss is an irony worthy of 1839 Wylie Street, and so that is exactly where Harmond goes after watching his dream dissolve. Herrington writes that Wilson "promotes self-definition, self-determination, and cultural nationalism even at the possible cost of exclusion from the American dream." When Harmond chooses community over his career, his American dream ends, and a new one begins as he is reborn as a cultural warrior.

Elam declares, "Through his madmen, Wilson establishes a bridge between past and present, a way of connection to tradition even in the face of progress." Old Joe and Sterling Johnson, defiant heroes of the Hill District, use the force of their cultural convictions to, if not save the Hill District, then recapture the soul of one of their own. Awakening Harmond to his rightful place beside Old Joe and Sterling at 1839 Wylie, the warriors prepare for the final battle. Wilson leaves the fate of his people, his neighborhood, and black America hanging in the balance in this, his final play. His magnificent contribution to American drama will forever guide lost souls back into the strength of their community. Lahr summarizes the effect of his work: "Taken as a whole, the cycle, with its humor and its poetic scope, both claims and interprets, for black and white audiences, the experience and the idiom of the African-American world." Wilson's work immortalizes the African American past, promotes the talents of black casts and crews in their productions, and points the way to a future of self-defined success.

Source: Amy Lynn Miller, Critical Essay on *Radio Golf*, in *Drama for Students*, Gale, Cengage Learning, 2013.

Sandra G. Shannon

In the following excerpt, Shannon examines the first and last plays in the Pittsburgh Cycle to

> AS THE OCTOBER ANNIVERSARY OF AUGUST WILSON'S DEATH APPROACHES, HIS WORK FEELS EVER MORE VITAL, NOT JUST FOR CULTURAL HEALING AMONG AFRICANS IN AMERICA, BUT FOR SIMILAR HEALING AMONG ALL PEOPLES OF THE WORLD."

verify Wilson's claim that the two plays are very closely connected thematically, and that the other eight plays have an inter-textual relationship with these two.

On April 28, 2005, one day after August Wilson's sixtieth birthday, the last play in his 10-play cycle—*Radio Golf*—opened at the Yale Repertory Theatre in New Haven, Connecticut. In late August of that same year, August Wilson divulged to the press that he was suffering from advanced liver cancer. On October 2, 2005, August Wilson died at age 60. The all-too-sudden passing of this two-time Pulitzer Prize winning and internationally acclaimed playwright suggests a troubling and ironic twist of fate that occurred only months after he had completed a 26-year-long magnum opus—a staggering body of dramatic work that virtually frames African American cultural identity in a series of plays set in fictive time frames that span from 1904 to 1997. While Wilson's death continues to be mourned extensively, we may take comfort in the completed cycle that he leaves behind as one of the greatest artistic achievements of the twentieth century.

Some time during the early 1980s, August Wilson began touting his idea of writing ten plays chronicling decisive moments in the history of African Americans in the twentieth century. After succeeding at crafting individual plays set in two separate decades, Wilson decided to extend the reach of his proven talents and set his sights on an entire cycle of plays. He recalled in a 1984 interview,

> As it turns out, I've written plays that take place in 1911, 1927, 1941, 1957, and 1971. Somewhere along the way it dawned on me that I was writing one play for each decade. Once I became conscious of that, I realized I was trying to focus on what I felt were the most

important issues confronting black Americans for that decade, so ultimately they could stand as a record of black experience over the past hundred years presented in the form of dramatic literature. (Powers 2005, 4–5)

Understandably, then, August Wilson may be regarded as the consummate cultural architect. But instead of designing a blueprint for a new cultural construct, he directed his efforts toward resurrecting a culture already within a culture. In other words, he dedicated his energies as an artist toward retrieving and reconnecting the disparate parts of an African American cultural identity that already exists, albeit subsumed into the dominant western white culture. Wilson's notion of this reconstituted African American cultural identity urged a figurative and spiritual return to the starting place, which he saw as Africa. The blueprint for this job, of course, took the form of ten dramatic installments written at an unprecedented pace: *Jitney* (1979), *Ma Rainey's Black Bottom* (1982), *Fences* (1983), *Joe Turner's Come and Gone* (1984), *The Piano Lesson* (1987), *Two Trains Running* (1990), *Seven Guitars* (1995), *King Hedley II* (1999), *Gem of the Ocean* (2002), and *Radio Golf* (2005).

From this point of departure, Wilson wanted to write on a grand scale. He wanted to magnify the African American experience—to write around, through, and against recorded history in order to give voice to the nameless masses of Africans in America and to tap the never-ending supply of untold stories about African American life and culture in the United States. Inspired by the limitless possibilities of his aesthetic of excavation, August Wilson envisioned an ambitious plan and acquired a dogged determination to

write about the unique particulars of black American culture…to place this culture onstage in all its richness and fullness and to demonstrate its ability to sustain us in all areas of human life and endeavor and through profound moments of our history in which the larger society has thought less of us than we have thought of ourselves. (Wilson 2005, viii–ix)

In addition to earning the title of cultural architect, August Wilson donned the title of cultural critic for his efforts to shape the cultural experiences of those who encountered his dramatic works. In numerous recorded conversations, he revealed a conscious plan to communicate in each of his plays certain types of African American cultural awareness: "I try to actually keep all of

the elements of the culture alive in the work," he told me in a 1991 interview,

and myth is certainly a part of it. Mythology, history, social organizations—all of these kinds of things—economics—are all part of the culture. I make sure—I purposefully go through and make sure each element of that is in some way represented—some more so than other in the plays, which I think gives them a fullness and a completeness—that is an entire world. (Shannon 1995, 202–03)

As cultural critic and cultural architect, Wilson advanced critic Henry Louis Gates's affirmation that,

the black Africans who survived the dreaded "Middle Passage" from the west coast of Africa to the New World did not sail alone. Violently and radically abstracted from their civilizations, these Africans nevertheless carried within them to the Western hemisphere aspects of their cultures that were meaningful, that could not be obliterated, and that they chose, by acts of will, not to forget: their music… their myths, their expressive institutional structures, their metaphysical systems of order, and their forms of performance. (Gates 1988, 3–4)

Toward this end, I want to examine the intertextual relationships within and among five of August Wilson's cycle plays but pay particularly close attention to two of Wilson's plays that are strategically positioned within his ninety-six-year time line as bookends: *Gem of the Ocean* (1904) and *Radio Golf* (1997). In various interviews, Wilson divulged the "special relationship" of these two plays and further explained that his ultimate aim in writing the cycle was to ". . . build an umbrella under which the rest of the plays can sit…a bridge. The subject matter of these two plays is going to be very similar and connected thematically, meaning that the other eight will be part and parcel of these two. You should be able to see how they all fit inside these last two plays" (Jones 1999, 16).

Dramatically unfolding between Wilson's so-called "bookend plays"—*Gem of the Ocean* and *Radio Golf*—is a narrative depicting over ninety years' worth of African American history, all of which is filtered and recast through August Wilson's cultural memory. This type of memory he labeled "blood's memory" or recollections of a shared past that emerges unexplained from irrepressible ancestral ties with Africa. By varying degrees, each of the ten plays that make up

Wilson's cycle reaffirms some aspect of this recast identity. However, I want to focus on five of his ten plays that best exemplify his strategies of identity construction. In addition to the two bookend or frame plays, I want to examine certain cultural building blocks in *Joe Turner's Come and Gone*, *The Piano Lesson*, and *Two Trains Running* to reveal strategies August Wilson uses to convey the passionate and persistent assertion that "we are African people, and we have a culture that's separate and distinct from the mainstream white American culture. We have different philosophical ideas, different ways of responding to the world, different ideas and attitudes, different values, different ideas about style and linguistics, different aesthetics" (Moyers 2006, 68–9).

Let me begin by describing what I consider to be essential building blocks in Wilson's identity-building strategy. Primarily, I want to inject August Wilson's own personal stakes in setting forth a distinct African American cultural identity. This agenda, it would appear, was not just for African American people in general but for the playwright as well. The son of an emotionally and physically distant German baker and an adoring African American mother, August Wilson made his own decisions about his cultural identity based upon parental allegiance and his belief in the aesthetic and political principles of the Black Arts movement, the prevailing artistic cultural nationalist movement of the 1960s. Taunted and called "nigger" during his abbreviated enrollment at Pittsburgh, Pennsylvania's predominantly white Central Catholic High School, growing up with neither the presence or oversight of his German father, he immersed himself in all aspects of his African American mother's culture. In 1989, he shared candid recollections of this period in his life with journalist Bill Moyers: "The cultural environment of my life, the forces that have shaped me, the nurturing, the learning, have all been black ideas about the world that I learned from my mother" (2006, 72).

While eclipsing the playwright's quest to negotiate a definition for his own cultural identity, Africa serves as the largest block and central frame of reference in defining, containing and shaping African American cultural identity in the five plays referenced above. It is an identity culled out of the concept of re-memory whereby one questions the past and chooses what to do

with it. Does one allow past selves to take over and overrule the present self in importance? Does one attempt to meld the past and the present? Or does one utilize the lessons of selves past and forge a new present and future with added insight gained from these personal ancestors? Wilson's approach privileges the latter. Without the characteristic schizophrenia of Du Boisian double consciousness, Wilson depicts an African American cultural identity that can and must naturally and unapologetically exist both separate from and as a part of American society. As Amritjit Singh, Joseph Skerrett, and Robert Hogan observe in Memory and Cultural Politics, ". . . since the 1960s, this search for African roots (ending, for some, no farther back than the American South) has altered the nature of African American remembering by focusing on positive ways of constructing a new identity, even out of the painful experiences of the past" (1996, 7). Filling out Wilson's portrait of African American cultural identity are instances of recovered myths, belief systems, and identifiable cultural rituals. And, though by no means the end of his list of cultural building blocks, I include the pervasive influence of the blues in defining the world in which Wilson's African American characters live.

Africa—easily considered by Wilson to be the very salt of African American cultural identity—is but a ritual, a dance or a nuance away in each of his five plays under investigation here. Its various manifestations underscore the playwright's refrain "I am African!" and support his constant pronouncement that "There's an inner strength that comes with recognizing that . . . there's nothing wrong with being African" (Moyers 2006, 71). In *Gem of the Ocean* (1904), for example, Africa is summoned onto stage by the 285 year-old African American woman named Aunt Ester Tyler—considered by Harry Elam Jr. to be ". . . a critical figure mediating between the African past and the African American present, between the practice of Christianity and an Africanist-based spirituality . . ." (2006, 184).

The storyline of Wilson's 1904 play, *Gem of the Ocean*, establishes a clear framework for his dramatic rendering of African American cultural identity. Loyalty, honor, truth, redemption, and ancestral reverence are but a few of the ideal personality traits that emerge in this play. Citizen Barlow stole a bucket of nails, but he frames another man for the crime. Garret Brown, the man he falsely accused, stages a private protest by jumping into a nearby river and—despite the pleas of many—refuses to leave his watery confinement until, exhausted from treading water, he sinks to his death. All of this is witnessed by the sheriff and the townspeople who stood by and watched him pay with his life to prove his innocence.

In the wake of this innocent man's death, Citizen Barlow, the actual perpetrator of the crime, is tormented by guilt and seeks out the ageless and wise Aunt Ester for help and sanctuary. Aunt Ester agrees to help Citizen "wash his soul," as she tells him, "You're on an adventure, Mr. Citizen. You signed up for it and didn't even know it" (Wilson 2006, 24). In a fantastical ritual of redemption, Aunt Ester transfixes Citizen and leads him on a metaphysical journey to the bottom of the ocean. This site of memory, which stupefies Barlow, captures in stark images the ravages of the Middle Passage in the North American slave trade: "There it is! It's made of bones! All the buildings and everything. Head bones and leg bones and rib bones. The streets look like silver. The trees are made of bones. The trees and everything made of bone" (Wilson 2006, 68). Dazed and humbled, Barlow metaphysically enters the gated City of Bones constructed by the skeletons of slaves who perished on their way from Africa to America. Once inside the City of Bones, he encounters the spirit of the accused man and confesses his crime. At that, his journey ends, and he returns to consciousness a changed man.

What is the nature of African American cultural identity in *Gem of the Ocean*? What framework does this play, which occupies the distinct position as being the first in August Wilson's cycle, establish in the shaping of that identity? How does this play, set in the early years of the twentieth century, reach across the temporal divide to connect with another set on the brink of the 21st century? What, ultimately, does this inter-textual conversation mean? If we look beyond the fantastical elements of the play for a moment, we find a simple tale involving very basic codes of ethical behavior. A man's lie has caused harm to another. Burdened by the weight of a guilty conscience, he seeks atonement from the community of elders. That atonement, however, cannot occur unless the sinner embarks on a journey back to a sacred place bearing the spirits of his ancestors. While it is cast in terms of individual conflict limited to a specific time and specific place, this narrative of crime, punishment, and redemption may also serve to suggest Wilson's larger pronouncement on cultural identity. As critic Harry Elam, Jr., notes, ". . . history both shackles his African American characters and empowers them. They must discover how both to embrace the past [according to Du Bois's theory] and to let it go . . . there is not simply a matter of unfinished business with the past but a hunger for redress and regeneration in the present . . ." (2006, xiv).

In *Gem of the Ocean* Wilson also demonstrates the function of myth and belief systems to affirm African American cultural identity. In both are registered "the substance of things hoped for; the evidence of things not seen." Whether one is asked to throw $20 of their hard-earned money into the Monongahela River or to go out into the streets to find two pennies lying side by side, one should not question the sanity of the act. Suspending disbelief and accepting unlikely scenarios as truthful stems from an African cosmology, which becomes the source of hope for many in the face of destitution. Aunt Ester devises such a belief system as part of her plan to rehabilitate Citizen Barlow. She implores him to locate and bring to her two pennies positioned side by side on the ground. Her exact—seemingly irrational— demands are just enough to valorize the search and to appreciate its value. Critic Paul Carter Harrison describes the importance of such lore in the construction of African American cultural identity, noting:

> The stories and gestures that codify collective experience are framed ideologically by myths which serve to preserve the essential metaphors of the cultural worldview. . . . Thus, embedded in the mythological store of black experience are the many symbolic gestures that correspond to the changing ideals that lead to moral and ethical perfection. (Harrison 1984, 293–94)

. . . Aunt Ester, who either figures as a character or as an offstage presence, makes her presence known one way or another in *Gem of the Ocean*, *King Hedley II*, *Two Trains Running*, and Wilson's final play, *Radio Golf*. With the 2005 completion of *Radio Golf*, set in 1997, August Wilson ended the tenth and final chapter in a narrative that was twenty years in the making. But in 2003—just two years prior to this resounding finale—Wilson made a sharp U-turn to complete his 1904 play, *Gem of the Ocean*—a pivotal play that answers a number of questions that emerge when one looks at the plays as separate installments in a single master narrative.

The conflict of the 1990s play, *Radio Golf*, revolves around real estate developers who want to tear down the home of Aunt Ester, the play's central character, now a familiar name within the cycle. Harmond Wilks and Roosevelt Hicks are members of the black middle class, blinded by desires to make it big in the real estate industry while faced with the same questions raised throughout Wilson's cycle: what should you do with our culture? How can you best put it to use? Though Aunt Ester has died by 1997, she still influences Wilks's ultimate decision to quell his ambitions and pay homage to symbols of black cultural identity rather than sell it to the highest bidder. And so the house where Aunt Ester resided at 1839 Wylie Street is left standing leaving a powerful symbol of cultural memory and allowing for healing to occur within the community.

Up until Wilson completed *Radio Golf*, one of the most pressing questions that lingered throughout the entire cycle hinged upon the recurring presence of the powerful cultural figure Aunt Ester. Who is she really? What meaning lies in her on and onstage presence? How does she hold the cycle together? How can any human live to be as old as the black presence in America—over 322 years! It is Aunt Ester who initiates and sustains the inter-textual conversations that take place within the cycle and who holds the ten plays together. Though she is not physically present throughout, she is still a constant force that defines and shapes the finer aspects of African American cultural identity. She is Wilson's living metaphor of black experience and the model for present and future black cultural identity. She also embodies decades of cultural memory. Existing on the fringes of the play's reality, she demonstrates mystical powers by "laying on the hands" and has a near god-like following.

Less than forty years in the wake of slavery's end, the images that *Gem of the Ocean* summons to the stage and to the forefront of African American consciousness draw a direct line to Africa. In sometimes jolting, sometimes mesmerizing images and details, Wilson fashions a blueprint for cultural identity directly linked to this site of memory. Some ninety-three years later, Wilson's message on cultural identity remains the same, but the role of Africa as the ultimate liminal zone a source of cultural healing and

definition is threatened by the noise, greed, and corruption that come with modernity. But Wilson finds a way to remind his characters and his audiences that Africa is within them and that it is this blood's memory they should return to for moral direction.

Radio Golf and *Gem of the Ocean*, the so-called bookend plays, the beginning and the end, hold special positions in the entire cycle, for not only do they mark the growth of a visionary artist—the likes of whom we rarely see among us—but they also represent the playwright's own "four-hundred-year autobiography," as he once told me, as it is a revision of the cultural history of African Americans in the twentieth century.

As the October anniversary of August Wilson's death approaches, his work feels ever more vital, not just for cultural healing among Africans in America, but for similar healing among all peoples of the world.

Source: Sandra G. Shannon, "Framing African-American Cultural Identity: The Bookend Plays in August Wilsons's 10-Play Cycle," in *College Literature*, Vol. 36, No. 2, Spring 2009, pp. 26–40.

Patricia M. Gantt

In the following excerpt, Gantt pulls Radio Golf *from the Pittsburgh Cycle to examine its characters and recurring concerns, including the use of black culture.*

... *Radio Golf* (2004), the conclusive play of the Pittsburgh Cycle, takes place in 1997. The protagonist is Harmond Wilks, an affluent graduate of Cornell, who now lives in an upscale suburb of the Hill and is well on his way to becoming Pittsburgh's first black mayor. Set in the real-estate development office he shares with his partner Roosevelt Hicks, the play chronicles what happens when Wilks tries to stop the demolition of 1839 Wylie, the former neighborhood sanctuary inhabited by Aunt Ester. Wilks becomes aware of the historical and aesthetic significance of 1839 Wylie, and he feels guilty for acquiring the property through a legal loophole that takes advantage of his cousin, Elder Barlow, with whom he has recently become reacquainted. Despite the fact that the house is slated for demolition, Barlow insists on painting it and fixing it up. In response to Harmond's claim that America is the land of opportunity, he says,

> But you got to have the right quarter. America
> is a giant slot machine. You walk up and put in

WITHOUT A DOUBT, HIS WORK WILL LIVE ON, BOTH FOR ITS DRAMATIC QUALITY AND FOR ITS MES- SAGE OF ENCOURAGEMENT TO DRAMATISTS WHO FOLLOW—TO PUT THEIR CULTURES ON STAGE, AS HE HAS SO EXPRESSIVELY DONE."

your coin and it spits it back out. You look at your coin. You think maybe it's a Canadian quarter. It's the only coin you got. If this coin ain't no good then you out of luck. You look at it and sure enough it's an American quarter. But it don't spend for you. It spend for every- body else but it don't spend for you. (Wilson 2007, 21)

This speech, a poignant reminder of King Hedley II's declaration that "I know which way the Wind blow too. It don't blow my way," enforces Wilson's frequent visitation of the unfairness of economic life for the black man in America (2005, 55). Barlow's life, too, has been a series of disappointments, but he is determined to win out this time.

Old Joe Barlow may have inherited the house, but one of Wilks' former schoolmates, Sterling Johnson, seems to have inherited Aunt Ester's moral and ethical voice. Throughout the play he reminds Harmond of his responsibility to do not only what goes by the letter of the law, but by a larger code of humanity and justice. He sets his feet on high moral ground from his first appear- ance in the play, when he stops by to ask Wilks for a job: "I'd take something you couldn't spend over money any day" (Wilson 2007, 15). A man with a dubious background, Sterling has served time in prison; nevertheless, his priorities are firmly in order. Realizing at last that Roosevelt Hicks is willing to sell his soul for advancement, Sterling accuses him, with his repeated compromises to ingratiate himself to whites, of being complicitous in the black man's destruction:

You know what you are? It took me a while to figure it out. You a Negro. White people will get confused and call you a nigger but they don't know like I know. I know the truth of it. I'm a nigger. Negroes are the worst thing in God's creation. Niggers got style. Negroes got blindyitis. A dog knows it's a dog. A cat knows

it's a cat. But a Negro don't know he's a Negro. He thinks he's a white man. It's Negroes like you who hold us back. (Wilson 2007, 76)

Sterling's cautions fall on fallow ground for Hicks, but not for Harmond Wilks, who is pre- disposed to honor his forebears, their history, and their achievements. Even in the first scene of the play, he draws his wife Mame's attention to the tin-embossed ceiling in his office, telling her, "See those marks. It's all hand tooled. That's the only way you get pattern detail like that" (Wilson 2007, 7). Although he realizes that the ceiling is "worth some money," he has no intention of tearing it down and selling it, as Mame suggests. Wilks is one man who appreci- ates his heritage, a sensitivity Wilson encourages in all of his plays. Even more importantly, Wilks has a conscience, and is genuinely trying to become mayor so he can build a better city. Unlike several of those around him—most nota- bly Hicks—Harmond is neither willing to com- promise his integrity or become a toady for white politicos.

Ultimately Hicks betrays Wilks and their heritage by serving as a "black face" for white investors, by enforcing the demolition, and by forcing Wilks' removal from the project. Unwill- ing to compromise his values, Wilks is caught between his worlds. He can save neither Aunt Ester's house nor his role as the project's devel- oper, suggesting that black assimilation and material success require unethical practices and a lack of reverence for one's heritage. As the play concludes, however, he chooses the side of right over might that Sterling has so consistently advocated. Ordering Hicks from his office, he takes up a paintbrush and rushes out, heading for Wylie Street to confront the bulldozers poised at Aunt Ester's threshold.

Remembering the impulse that began his career as a dramatist, Wilson spoke many times of his deeply-felt desire to emulate the blues, which he saw as "a flag bearer of self-definition, and within the scope of the larger world which lay beyond its doorstep, it carved out a life, set down rules, and urged a manner of being that corre- sponded to the temperament and sensibilities of its creators" (1991b, x). Early on, he recalled,

I turned my ear, my heart, and whatever ana- lytical tools I possessed to embrace this world. I elevated it, rightly or wrongly, to biblical sta- tus. I rooted out the ideas and attitudes expressed in the music, charted them and bent and twisted and stretched them. I gave my whole being, muscle and bone and sinew and flesh and spirit, over to the emotional reference provided by the music. . . . This was life being lived in all its timbre and horrifies, with the zest and purpose and the affirmation of the self of worthy of the highest possibilities and the highest celebration. What more fertile ground could any artist want? (Wilson 1991b, x)

Throughout the decades of his dramatic creation, Wilson continued to write "with the blues and what [he] call[ed] the blood's memory as [his] only guide and companion" (xii). The world-class plays he created as a result of this strong commitment assure Wilson's place in the artistic life of the United States.

Shortly after Wilson learned in June of 2005 that he had liver cancer and would have a mere three to five months to live, he told Christopher Rawson, drama editor of the *Pittsburgh Post-Gazette,* "It's not like poker, you can't throw your hand in. I've lived a blessed life. I'm ready. I'm glad I finished the cycle [of plays]" (2005, C1). At the time of Wilson's death, *Time* critic Richard Zoglin offered this assessment of the dramatist's contribution:

> His work stood apart from, and above, nearly everything else in contemporary American theater. While others wrote spare, personal, ironic plays, Wilson's were big, verbose and passionate, brimming with social protest and epic poetry. Offstage, too, he was a maverick, opposing color-blind casting and advocating what some felt was a separatist black theater. Yet his work will endure, for everyone. (Zoglin 2005, 27)

In addition to the many awards Wilson won for individual plays, he also won the Whiting Writers Award, the William Inge Award for Distinguished Achievement in the American Theatre, several honorary doctorates; the Rockefeller, Guggenheim, and McKnight fellowships; a National Humanities Medal; and the 2003 Heinz Award in Arts and Humanities. He was a member of both the American Academy of Arts and Sciences and the American Academy of Arts and Letters. In 1995 Wilson was nominated for an Emmy for his screenplay for *The Piano Lesson.* The New Dramatists, America's oldest nonprofit workshop, gave him a Lifetime Achievement award in 2003, and, shortly after his death, Broadways Virginia Theatre was rechristened the August Wilson. The 2006 season of New York's Signature Theatre was dedicated to Wilson's dramatic achievements, and in 2008 the Kennedy Center ran an August Wilson

> **THE PRESS OF HISTORY AND ITS CHALLENGES IS ALWAYS PRESENT IN A WILSON PLAY, BUT HE USES HISTORY TO SITUATE US IN A MOMENT WHERE WE MIGHT ASK WHAT WE ARE TO DO NEXT."**

festival of plays, mounting all ten in the cycle. Without a doubt, his work will live on, both for its dramatic quality and for its message of encouragement to dramatists who follow—to put their cultures on stage, as he has so expressively done.

Source: Patricia M. Gantt, "Putting Black Culture on Stage: August Wilson's Pittsburgh Cycle," in *College Literature,* Vol. 36, No. 2, Spring 2009, pp. 1–26.

Elizabeth Alexander

In the following essay, Alexander provides a brief recap of Wilson's career and expresses profound admiration for his writing skills, intellect, and compassion.

Something was happening in New Haven, Connecticut, in the blossoming spring of 1984. Creative black people seemed to be everywhere: in earnest conversation over endless cups of coffee, talking big and doing big, believing in culture and its power and possibility. The Afro-American Cultural Center at Yale—then and now known affectionately as the House—opened its doors to this burgeoning creativity. As a college senior at the time, I was editing a magazine based at the House called *Ritual and Dissent,* and today I am amazed when I look in its pages: original interviews, conducted that year in New Haven, with Wole Soyinka, Audre Lorde, and Melvin Dixon, as well as stories and poems and reviews by writers and scholars who went on to great acclaim, all of us products of that remarkable time and place.

That spring came a play by a new playwright named August Wilson. We'd see him around New Haven, wearing some variety of old-school hat, drinking coffee, and writing in notebooks, or sitting quietly in the back of rehearsals, many of which were held right at the House. Angela Bassett and Charles "Roc" Dutton had performed scenes from Shakespeare at the House; its imposing, Gothic "enormous room" was beautifully suited to theater. Now in that same space, as well as at the University School of Drama, with those same actors and others, Lloyd Richards was rehearsing the Wilson play.

Of course we all knew who Lloyd Richards was. The legendary director was not only dean of the Yale School of Drama at the time but also the director of the 1959 Broadway production of Lorraine Hansberry's *A Raisin in the Sun*, starring Sidney Poitier, Diana Sands, Ruby Dee, and others in the black theater firmament. He was American theater royalty and a black theater deity. But this playwright, this new guy, this August Wilson, was something else, working right here in our hothouse. Even as a college senior, I knew when the curtain fell on those first performances of *Ma Rainey's Black Bottom* that something not just important but shifting had happened. We'd spent two hours (or probably three, because Wilson plays ran famously long in their early incarnations) in a Chicago recording studio in the 1920s, at the dawn of recorded jazz and blues and thus a new era for African-American popular culture, and we had listened to characters with historical integrity talk, really talk, about profound issues of black progress. No matter the decade, no matter the characters, all of August Wilson's plays ask black people: Where do we go from here? What is progress? Can we do it together? What is our inheritance? Lest you imagine that talk as dissertational, however, August Wilson makes characters named Slow Drag and Levee and Toledo and Cutler lie, woof, and signify, in the great oral tradition of Negro talk in the spaces we've made our own.

I went to the premiere of *Radio Golf* this past spring at the Yale Repertory Theater. It would be Wilson's last opening in New Haven before his death at age 60 on October 2, and the play was the 10th and final of his 20th-century cycle. The curtain came up on the same stage where I'd seen *Ma Rainey*. This time the milieu (for in Wilson's plays, workplaces were spaces where human beings speak their minds and hearts) was an office in which people came in and out singing their arias (metaphorically speaking), and the same questions were raised, approached from different angles: What does black progress mean if it does not attempt to bring along a community and respect a community? What do

we need to know and bring forward from our history? And why is none of this a straightforward enterprise? In *Radio Golf*, the discursive tug of war (or the rational distance) between Harmond Wilks and Elder Joseph Barlow does not yield easy or immediate answers to these questions. This is apt, for we have not yet overcome, nor reached the promised land. The play ends on a hopeful note, with family ties revealed between the "progress-seeking" bourgeoisie and the materially dispossessed "folk." Wilson sees black people of different classes as necessarily connected. The folk character in this play gets all the good lines, but he does not have the answers. Difficult interactions across class lines move the community closer together—connections made tenuously, perhaps, with the string and Scotch tape of conversation.

In Elder Joseph Barlow we have a familiar Wilson type: the street poet, corner philosopher, mother wit, or half-wit character he writes like no one else. Wilson understood the street-corner poets with rural Southern roots who abound in urban America, and he imbues them with a Southern sense of the aphoristic and the mysterious, that kind of hyperbole and non-sequitur that tends toward wisdom. "I want my ham!" is a *cri de coeur* from his play *Two Trains Running*, and it is not just idle exclamation, but an existential howl, time signature, grace note, cipher. Levee's obsession with his footwear in *Ma Rainey's Black Bottom* shows us that a pair of shoes is not always only a pair of shoes. Wilson understood the symbolic dimensions in which everyday life presents itself to us if we pay attention. The metaphorical is ever present, which is to say that life and its lessons are not always best apprehended straight on but rather after the groundwork of associative thinking or attuned listening. When, in the play *Fences*, Troy Maxon makes his speech about fences, we understand how the most quotidian and familiar objects give us a way to think about historical wrongs and the complex pride of character. In all Wilson's plays, the men, especially, strive for dignity, despite the soul-crushing challenges they face and have faced for generations.

In *The Piano Lesson*, Wilson asks what we, as black people, do with our cultural and familial legacies, symbolized in the play by an elaborately carved piano whose decoration tells a story reaching back to slavery. He asks the question about black people in a specific historical context, and that is part of what is extraordinary about his work. While white people—indeed anybody—can, of course, hear the question and appreciate the plays, he is speaking to black people, without winks or smiles, dilution or translation. What to do with our cultural legacy is, ultimately, our question. How families remember is our question. The press of history and its challenges is always present in a Wilson play, but he uses history to situate us in a moment where we might ask what we are to do next. *So high, you can't get over it / so low you can't get under it / so wide, you can't go around it. You gotta come in at the door.* That is the truth of history.

When writing is called poetic, it usually means something conventionally beautiful and mellifluous in style. I would call Wilson a poetic writer in the way he understands the poetics of speech and how he recognizes the potent allusiveness of conversation. The stage directions that open *Ma Rainey's Black Bottom* point to the kind of rich talk to come and also to the grand historical sweep in which Wilson worked: "Chicago in 1927 is a rough city, a bruising city, a city of millionaires and derelicts, gangsters and roughhouse dandies, whores and Irish grandmothers who move through its streets fingering long black rosaries. Somewhere a man is wrestling with the taste of a woman in his cheek. Somewhere a dog is barking. Somewhere the moon has fallen through the window and broken into thirty pieces of silver." Spoken language is rich and nuanced and oratorical in the traditions of black talk Wilson feeds on, and thus is his prose poetic.

One aspect of African-American history is a melancholia that comes from the interruption— the violent fissure of the Middle Passage and its subsequent soul-annihilating indignities. The never-to-be-resolved fissure, the never-to-be-known homeland, coexist with the great possibilities of reinvention that gave the world jazz and blues, music heavily influenced by African music but utterly, yes, purely, completely, African-American, which is to say American. Our death came at the bottom of the ocean and then at the hands of the brutal slave system and then from the privations of Jim Crow, and then at the hands of the police and of each other. That's a lot of unending blues. Wilson is always attuned to the "sea of bones": that it is there, that it is unresolved, that it is a crossroads, that it presses on the present, that it forms a

hieroglyphics that the griot needs to unlock in order to prophesy.

I think of poet Gwendolyn Brooks's wonderful words—"I am a black. I am one of the Blacks. We occur everywhere. Don't call me out of my name"—and her wish that to be called black links her to other African people, diasporized and not. Does that linkage hold? Is our wish for it to hold sentimental? What is the motherland that each of us may wish for, and what does it mean to try to heal that need with words, deeds, and culture, our bottle trees and shell-studded graves? Wilson's genius as a writer was his ability to keep the listening ear open, both for the literal sounds of the oral tradition he clearly loved as well as for a proverbial logic and structure that must be called African. In grappling with the literary possibilities of a realist theater, trying consistently to bring the spoken word into the written form, Wilson consistently brought the genius of African-American language into his plays.

In some ways, August Wilson doesn't feel like a writer of the 1980s, a decade not known for its attention to history. But it was in the '80s—when so much was new, when theory and multiculturalism were changing the arts dramatically, when the shape of art went in a million different directions—that Wilson began his un-trendy but radical project of looking to the past. It took vision to recognize, as he did, that until we examine our history we will not be able to look or move forward. And looking at that history is also how we come to recognize our seers. In a ravishing speech about "the secret of life" in *Joe Turner's Come and Gone*, the rootworker Bynum Walker says:

> "[M]y daddy taught me the meaning of this thing that I had seen and showed me how to find my song. He told me he was the One Who Goes Before and Shows the Way. Said there was lots of shiny men and if I ever saw one again before I died then I would know that my song had been accepted and worked its full power in the world and I could lay down and die a happy man. A man who done left his mark on life . . . So I takes the power of my song and binds [people] together."

Some part of the artist knew that the moment had come when the century could be surveyed, intimately and in the terms and language of black urban folks whose wisdom was sometimes practical and sometimes potently mystical.

Wilson audaciously redefined the American theater canon in just 25 years. He finished the cycle he began, one play for each decade of the

20th century, and while it does not make up for his absence from our midst, let alone for the absent promise of more words, he chiseled something in granite that will stand like Shakespeare. I wonder what he might have said about evanescence and black culture, the way so much of our genius is neglected or misnamed, misplaced, destroyed. Wilson's genius is at hand; he built his own boat to last.

I am satisfied to have watched him from a short distance 25 years ago and to be able to say today that I was right: something very important was happening. This was a shiny man, humbly telling the village's tales. He revered the word, and the brilliance with which black people have shaped it. He knew a good story when he saw one. His narrative sense was unerring. He loved black people enough to celebrate us and challenge us. Loving black people to my mind means loving humanity. My favorite-ever quote of his—and he made many rich and profound statements—is one that makes me catch my breath before writing, humble before the task at hand and also wild-eyed with the excitement and ambition his words inspire. He said, "You have responsibilities as a global citizen. Your history dictates your duty. And by writing about black people, you are not limiting yourself. The experiences of African-Americans are as wide open as God's closet."

In his work and in his deeds, August Wilson was what the old folks call a righteous man.

Source: Elizabeth Alexander, "The One Who Went Before: Remembering the Playwright August Wilson, 1945–2005," in *American Scholar*, Vol. 75, No. 1, Winter 2006, pp. 122–25.

SOURCES

Bigsby, Christoper, ed., "August Wilson: The Ground on Which He Stood," in *The Cambridge Companion to August Wilson*, Cambridge University Press, 2007, pp. 3, 13.

Booker, Margaret, "*Radio Golf*: The Courage of His Convictions—Survival, Success, and Spirituality," in *The Cambridge Companion to August Wilson*, edited by Christopher Bigsby, Cambridge University Press, 2007, pp. 183, 186, 192.

Elam, Harry J., Jr., *The Past as Present in the Drama of August Wilson*, University of Michigan Press, 2006, pp. xiii, 13, 29–30, 58, 64–65.

Herrington, Joan, *"I Ain't Sorry for Nothin' I Done": August Wilson's Process of Playwriting*, Limelight Editions, 1998, pp. 33, 39.

Isherwood, Charles, "August Wilson, Theater's Poet of Black America, Is Dead at 60," in *New York Times*, October 3, 2005, http://theater.nytimes.com/2005/10/03/theater/newsandfeatures/03wilson.html?_r=1&adxnnl=1&pagewanted=all&adxnnlx=1347586087-o+dX3bLVqKy+jIWMYsbEKQ (accessed September 10, 2012).

Lahr, John, Review of *Radio Golf*, in *New Yorker*, May 16, 2005, http://www.newyorker.com/archive/2005/05/16/050516crth_theatre (accessed September 10, 2012).

Shannon, Sandra G., *The Dramatic Vision of August Wilson*, Howard University Press, 1995, p. 4.

Wilson, August, *Radio Golf*, Theatre Communications Group, 2007.

FURTHER READING

Bryer, Jackson R., and Mary C. Hartig, eds., *Conversations with August Wilson*, University Press of Mississippi, 2006.

This volume is a collection of interviews with the playwright ranging from 1984 to 2004 on the subjects of his life, influences, and writing methods and the ten-play cycle that defined his career.

Cohen, Cathy J., *Democracy Remixed: Black Youth and the Future of American Politics*, Oxford University Press, 2012.

Cohen sets out to discover the state of black youth in this well-researched and personal discussion of race and politics in America. Including the voices of the youth themselves in her presentation, Cohen makes a compelling argument toward what can be done in American politics today to build a better, more inclusive future for all.

Harrison, Paul Carter, Victor Leo Walker II, and Gus Edwards, eds., *Black Theatre: Ritual Performance in the African Diaspora*, Temple University Press, 2002.

The birth and life of black theater from its origins in Africa to its performance on stages today is examined in Harrison, Walker, and Edwards's extensive work on the cultural art's transformative power. Beginning in the tribal settings of ancient villages and proceeding to the lights of Broadway, black performance art's long history is detailed and celebrated.

Nadel, Alan, ed., *August Wilson: Completing the Twentieth-Century Cycle*, University of Iowa Press, 2010.

Nadel's study of Wilson's cycle of ten plays focuses on the final five installments in the series and their place in the narrative arc of the work as a whole. The final five plays—*Jitney*, *Seven Guitars*, *King Hedley II*, *Gem of the Ocean*, and *Radio Golf*—fill in the remaining decades of Wilson's century of black life and make connections between the works through repeating characters, themes, settings, and even dialogue. Nadel examines and explicates these connections one by one, revealing the blueprint for Wilson's great cycle.

SUGGESTED SEARCH TERMS

Radio Golf

August Wilson

Contemporary Drama

black theater

Broadway AND black theater

Pittsburgh AND August Wilson

Pittsburgh AND Contemporary Drama

Pittsburgh Cycle

Twentieth-Century Cycle

Tape

JOSÉ RIVERA
1992

José Rivera's short play *Tape* was published in a group of plays called *Giants Have Us in Their Books: Six Children's Plays for Adults* in 1992 and first performed in 1993. The play explores the relationship between a sinner being punished in the afterlife for lies he told while alive and the supernatural being tasked with guiding him through the process of listening to reel-to-reel tapes of every single one of those lies . . . all ten thousand boxes' worth of them. *Tape*, like most of Rivera's work, is written in a magical-realist style, as first popularized by fiction writers such as Gabriel García Márquez and Jorge Luis Borges. Magical realism incorporates supernatural or fantastic elements within straightforward depictions of reality to create a world in which magic is not only possible but accepted.

Despite the occasional use of profanity, *Tape* is an appropriate introduction to the genre of magical-realist drama for middle- and high-school students. Although Rivera's *Giants Have Us in Their Books* is no longer in print, *Tape* can also be found in *30 Ten-Minute Plays for 2 Actors*, a volume of plays from the Actors Theatre of Louisville's ten-minute play contest, edited by Michael Bigelow Dixon, Amy Wegener, and Karen Petruska.

AUTHOR BIOGRAPHY

Rivera was born on March 24, 1955, in San Juan, Puerto Rico, but moved to Long Island

José Rivera (© *Everett Collection Inc / Alamy*)

with his family when he was five years old, where his father was a taxi driver. Childhood exposure to the oral storytelling tradition of his Puerto Rican grandparents, combined with seeing a production of *Rumpelstiltskin* at the age of twelve, convinced him that he wanted to be a writer, and soon after he wrote his first play. "I was lucky," he told the *New York Times* in 2006, "because my grandparents, who lived with us, were illiterate but they were great storytellers, so I got a kind of storytelling bug from them." After he received his BA in theater from Denison University, in Ohio, in 1977, Rivera considered a career in acting. As an apprentice actor at the Great Lakes Shakespeare Festival in Cleveland, he met and worked with a young Tom Hanks. Witnessing Hanks's passion and talent for acting made Rivera realize that he felt the same way about playwriting.

In 1989, Rivera was awarded a Fulbright scholarship to study in England, where he completed his play *Marisol*, which went on to receive an Obie Award for Best Play in 1993. He attended the Sundance Institute's writing workshop to study under Gabriel García Márquez, the Nobel Prize–winning Colombian author known for his prolific and masterful use of the style of magical realism. Rivera went on to become a pioneer in the genre of magical-realist drama, as evidenced by plays such as *Tape*, published in 1992.

Rivera's plays have been translated into some seven languages. He has received grants from the National Endowment for the Arts, the Rockefeller Foundation, and the New York Foundation for the Arts. In addition to his Obie Award for *Marisol* and another for *References to Salvador Dalí Make Me Hot* in 2001, he was nominated for an Academy Award in 2005 for his adapted screenplay for *The Motorcycle Diaries*. He lives in Los Angeles, California.

PLOT SUMMARY

The lights come up on a small room with no windows and one door. In the room are a table with a reel-to-reel tape recorder, a chair, and two people, the Person and the Attendant. The Person complains about the lack of lighting, and the Attendant says that if it is too dark, he will have one of the other attendants replace the bulb because they do not want to cause the Person any "undue suffering." The Person says that it does not matter anyway, and asks the Attendant if this is the room in which the action will take place, though the audience does not know yet what he is talking about. The Attendant says that the Person will be in the room and the Attendant will be outside "the entire time," and that he can send out for snacks, sodas, and maybe a beer on the Person's birthday, to make him more comfortable.

The Attendant says that the Person should feel free to ask him however many questions he needs to in order to understand exactly what is going to happen, and not to worry about taking too much time because they have "a lot of time." He is disappointed when the Person says he does not have any questions but just wants to sit down. The Person is bitter that he has to be there and snaps at the Attendant, but then apologizes because he knows it is not the Attendant's fault. He asks the Attendant's name, and the Attendant tells him that names are not allowed;

it is one of many rules established during the "long and extensive training course" for attendants. The Attendant is proud of having been chosen for his position, despite the long hours and other rules like not being allowed to dream.

The Attendant tells the Person that he knows everything that has ever happened in the Person's life because of that training, and he then asks if the Person knows how to operate the reel-to-reel. He shows the Person the buttons for Play, Pause, and Rewind, but says that there is no Fast Forward function. The Person asks if there is only the one tape, and the Attendant informs him that there are in fact ten thousand boxes full of tapes. He says that although everyone goes through this process in the same kind of room, not everyone has to spend the same amount of time in the room.

The Attendant finally explains what will happen in the room. The Person will have to sit and listen to his voice repeat every lie he has ever told. Every time in his life the Person lied, the attendants were listening and recording, even if the Person was just lying to himself. Now, the Person has to listen to them all. He tries to apologize, but the Attendant tells him that it is "too late." The Person says he does not want to listen, and the Attendant replies, "Neither did we." He presses Play, and a woman's voice comes on, asking a small child to tell her where he has been all day. The lights fade before the audience hears the answer.

CHARACTERS

The Attendant

The Attendant is in charge of working the reel-to-reel tape recorder that will play back every lie that the Person has ever told. Though the details of exactly who he is and where he works never get explained, through contextual clues one can surmise that he is tasked with forcing the Person to face the lies he told when he was alive as part of the Person's punishment after his death. The Attendant, then, is presumably neither alive nor dead, but a part of a purgatorial other world or afterlife. He may not even be human, though he was not always an attendant. He describes the honor he felt at being chosen for his position and the "long" and "rigorous" training course he was required to complete before becoming an attendant. As he puts it, to be an attendant he has "to

be a little bit of everything. Confidant, confessor, friend, stern taskmaster. Guide." He is proud of his job and is eager to do it well, but also shows regret and sadness at the sacrifices he makes. He must stand outside of the room with the tape recorder and see to the comfort of the Person the entire time the Person is listening. He is not allowed to have a name. He is not even allowed to dream.

The Attendant knows everything there is to know about the Person. He knows everything that ever happened to him and everything he has ever thought or felt. It is "part of the training" to know these things before the Person's arrival so that he can be prepared to guide him through what will be a long and painful process of self-confrontation for the Person. He is genuinely sorry for the pain that the Person will experience and offers no judgment on the volume of lies the Person told, but he does not shy away from his duty. It has been his job to listen to and record all the lies the Person told when he was alive and store them until the time came to force the Person to listen to them all. Though he is empathetic, he tells the person that the attendants do not want to hear the lies any more than do the people who tell them. Each of them, nonetheless, has a task to fulfill.

The Person

The Person has died and is now in a purgatory-like place where he must sit and listen to ten thousand boxes of reel-to-reel tape recordings of every lie he ever told while he was alive. The Person is being instructed and guided by the Attendant to sit on a chair in a small room and listen to the tapes until he has heard every lie. At first, he is not quite sure of exactly what the process will entail. All he knows is that he is dead, and he is despondent, saying that nothing really matters now. It does not matter if the room is too dark or if he is uncomfortable; he knows there is no way out of this place except to do as the Attendant tells him. Although he is unhappy with his situation, he is aware that it is not the Attendant's fault that he is there. As the Attendant empathizes with the Person, the Person also feels bad for the thankless nature of the Attendant's job. He tries to be friendly, apologizing when his fear of what awaits him on the tapes makes him snap at the Attendant. Though he is intrigued by the Attendant and asks him questions about his existence, he is distracted by his own worry and despair. Even when he tries to engage the Attendant in conversation, it proves impossible because the Attendant already knows everything about him.

The Person is dumbfounded when the Attendant informs him that there are ten thousand boxes of tapes for him to listen to. It seems impossible that he lied that much, but the Attendant explains that it is not only the lies he told others that he must relive, but "every betrayal, every lying thought, every time you lied to yourself." As the Attendant explains, the Person grows more and more frightened and despondent. He tries to apologize, but it is "too late" for apologies. Once each lie was told, it was recorded and saved for the Person to hear again after death. There are no exceptions. Everyone who dies goes through this process, but the length of time it takes varies with each person depending on how many lies are recorded. In the end, despite his dread, he is forced to sit and listen as the tapes play back every lie of his, starting with the very first one from when he was a child.

THEMES

Religion

Religion, in particular the Roman Catholicism that is practiced so widely in Latin America, is a theme that suits itself well to the magical realism style. Writers and artists within this genre often twist the commonplace traditions and myths of established religion in order to question socially accepted norms and inspire similar questions within their audiences. In *Tape*, Rivera explores the notion of an afterlife and karmic retribution. Ultimately, the play serves as a spark to ignite a spiritual examination by the viewer, who, in asking where the meaning of the play lies, engages in a process of searching for personal answers to the questions Rivera raises. The mythical references to the Christian afterlife in the play suggest Rivera's own Latino heritage and roots in the Roman Catholicism practiced largely throughout the Puerto Rican community both on the island and in the United States, and the allusion to purgatory is spiritually evocative for audience members. Many modern writers, scholars, and critics attribute a great deal of the development of magical realism to Latino religious traditions and the various cultural influences of the Catholic Church.

Some Latino writers, in their struggle to assimilate their cultural traditions within the fairly secular culture of America, use their craft to express their own questions or opinions. Mysticism may begin at an institutional level, but it can only truly be experienced through a personal spiritual journey. In works of literature like *Tape*, the writer and the audience or reader embark on that journey together, ideally leading to further spiritual insight.

Afterlife

As ancient Greco-Roman concepts of the afterlife merged with that of early Christianity in the medieval period, certain beliefs from these different mythologies faded from use, while others grew entrenched. By the early fourteenth century, the notion of an afterlife where both the nature and the severity of sin result in corresponding and appropriate punishment was established, laying the perfect social framework for the inferno in Dante's *Divine Comedy*. Published between 1308 and the author's death in 1321, the *Divine Comedy* synthesized the classical underworld with Christian hell in two ways, according to Jean-Charles Seigneuret. First, Dante brought together characters from classical mythology with actual historical figures, so that fiction and history existed side by side. Second, he shifted Aristotle's three classes of "evil dispositions," which were more like vices than sins, to accommodate a Christian context. This made sins of "incontinence (uncontrolled appetite)" such as lust, gluttony, avarice, and wrath, much less serious than those of "fraud or malice (abuse of reason)" such as seduction, betrayal, hypocrisy, and deceit. In the middle were the sins of violence, either against oneself, another person, or God in the form of blasphemy. The sins of fraud and malice were punishable in the lowest levels of hell. According to hell as illustrated by Dante, then, the Person in *Tape* has committed one of the most grievous sins repeatedly throughout his life. Just as in *Tape*, the punishments in Dante's hell follow a law of karmic retribution called *contrapasso*, where the divinely mandated punishment is symbolically reflective of the earthly sin. However, whereas the punishments described by Dante were quite physically violent, the pain of the punishment for liars in *Tape* is emotional.

TOPICS FOR FURTHER STUDY

- In *Tape*, the Person's afterlife (or at least a significant portion of it) consists of listening to tapes of all the lies he has ever told, presumably as some metaphysical punishment for his acts of deceit during his life. Assuming that most people have led a varied life featuring greater virtues than honesty and worse sins than lies, what other experiences might the afterlife as depicted in *Tape* hold, besides hearing one's lies? How might a thief be punished, or a faithful person be rewarded? With a group, write and perform a one-scene play exploring further the notion of *contrapasso* introduced in *Tape*, wherein your "Person" has led a particularly virtuous or sinful life. How does the punishment fit the crime in your story?

- The Attendant in *Tape* has been tasked with watching all of the Person's life, noting and recording the lies told, and overseeing the Person's listening to the tapes. From this, it can be inferred that the Attendant must have experienced exactly what the Person has experienced, even in his own mind, from birth to death to afterlife; just as the Person says "I don't want to listen!," the Attendant replies "Neither did we." Aside from identity and language, what differentiates the Attendant and the Person, if both must suffer through the lies when neither wanted to? Of what value is punishment when the innocent must suffer it to ensure justice is brought against the guilty? Examine a current penal issue in the United States such as military detainees, the use of the death penalty, or the effort and cost of prisoner rehabilitation. Using the Internet, research newspaper and magazine articles, news reports, and personal accounts to gather data that illustrate the debate. Create a website and post your findings, then write and post an essay on your opinions as to

what you feel best demonstrates the relationship between the responsibilities of the innocent and the punishment of the guilty.

- Read *City of the Beasts* (2002), a young-adult novel by Isabel Allende that contains elements of magical realism. Vivid imagery, myth, realistic action, and mystical elements combine to tell the story of fifteen-year-old Alex, whose grandmother has taken him to the Amazon on a quest for a legendary beast. Find three examples of magical realism in the novel and identify the ways in which the style enhances the major themes. Write an essay on your conclusions, making sure to identify the major themes and how their portrayal was made more or less successful because of the magical realism.

- Though magical realism is a style that began in fiction, it quickly found a home in the theater and in film. Movies such as *Pleasantville*, *Run Lola Run*, *Scott Pilgrim vs. The World*, and *Pan's Labyrinth* portray fantastical elements, mythical allusions, and mystical overtones as being part of an enhanced reality. These movies mix those and other characteristics with realistic settings and characters to create magical-realist cinema. Choose a film that you feel can be classified as magical realism, and identify the stylistic traits of the film that support your choice. How does the style enhance the thematic overtones of the film? Pay close attention to things like music and sound effects, cinematic lighting, camera angles, and special effects, things that are unique to the medium of film. How do these techniques attempt to reflect magical realism? Do you think they are successful? Pick three to five clips that exemplify your findings and present them, along with your opinions on their effectiveness, to the class.

Tape *takes place in a darkened interrogation room.* *(© Wilm Ihlenfeld / Shutterstock.com)*

STYLE

Magical Realism

Originally coined to describe the work of certain Latin American novelists such as Gabriel García Márquez and Jorge Luis Borges, *magical realism* is a style that combines miraculous or magical elements with differing degrees of realistic depictions, with the expectation that the reader or viewer will accept those elements as a natural part of the world in the story. The style is a vital part of the Latin American literary tradition, widely attributed as being a result of the clash between mystical, traditional cultures in Latin America and the modern, fast-paced world of Western culture and other industrial societies. Daniel Wood, in his article "'Magical Realism' and the Latino Theatre Lab," quotes Rivera as saying that magical realism is "Latin America's reaction against poverty, political repression, emotional starvation, cultural assimilation."

As Luis Leal writes in his essay "Magical Realism in Spanish American Culture," included in *Magical Realism*, "In magical realism the writer confronts reality and tries to untangle it, to discover what is mysterious in things, in life, in human acts." It seeks to elevate the mundane by injecting it with a degree of supernatural nuance, but it also aims to demystify the abstract by examining it from the perspective of the average world. As Rivera told Janice Arkatov in a 1988 *Los Angeles Times* interview, "The magic serves the lives of these people, their psychological truths." It contrasts everyday situations and characters with fantastical imagery and poetic language. Metaphor and allegory are sometimes deliberately woven into the story by the writer, and other times become apparent to the reader or viewer only when the work is considered in relation to the rest of culture. In either case, the magic is drawn from what is already mysterious and not easily understood in average life. Since mystery is all around people, the magical aspects of life do not require elaborate description; the writer only needs to draw attention to what is already there. "People still have lives the way we know them," Rivera told Arkatov, "and magic is the color; it flavors their world. Nothing stops so it can have an effect." The style often thematically brings together two or more discordant worlds, many times with one being more abstract than the other. In *Tape*, the world of the living and the dead as well as the world of myth and the contemporary world are brought together in a fusion of realities. By contrasting different planes of reality and introducing sometimes jarring and paradoxical belief systems, magical realism suits itself well to social and cultural commentary.

Though often the language of magical realism is more poetic or lyrical than other styles, it is still approachable and understandable. The dreamlike and the real are presented equally, so that together they present a new reality, both mysterious and familiar. As Rivera told Tad Simons of *American Theatre* in 1993, "We all think magically when we sleep. In our dreams there are monsters and angels. . . . In my work, the internal psychology of the characters is just reflected onstage." The style combines history, including mythical elements and dreams of the future, and then contrasts them with the present, which is so often felt as much more harshly realistic. For this reason, magical realism elevates the reality of the play to the level of myth and imbues it with a timeless sense of mysticism. There is a sense that the larger themes of the work, such as the spiritual atonement theme in *Tape*, are not specific to contemporaneous times, but instead are cyclical; it has all happened before, and it will all happen again. All of the various components of magical realism serve to reveal deeper meanings to readers or viewers about the world in which they live and force them to face mysterious and supernatural unknowns that threaten the security of unchallenged social norms.

Postmodernism

In the early part of the twentieth century, the modernist movement sought to find meaning in a world in which most forms of tradition had been thrown into chaos. Industrialization, the collapse of established class systems, the dwindling influence of authority structures such as religion and traditional families, and the psychological wreckage from World War I led to a widespread identity crisis, and writers and artists explored the changing meaning of the individual's relationship to the society in which one lived. After World War II, postmodernism developed as a reaction to modernism's strict rejection of traditional form and style. Postmodernist philosophers, artists, and writers focused more on the creation of the work of art itself, studying each piece as a whole instead of in relation to society or the world, as a way of finding meaning separate from outside influence. Postmodern literature and drama invert expectations, such as with magical realism, twisting situations to show the absurdity in things that one might typically view as normal and vice versa. It is a style that forces the reader or viewer to question what is thought of as "true." Irony and satire, as seen in *Tape*, combine with a reverence for myth and universality intrinsic to all people. Postmodernist works often play with tradition rather than completely repudiating it, as modernists tended to do. For example, the afterlife depicted in *Tape* is one in which the Person and the Attendant are mutually dependent upon one another, as opposed to the supernatural having pure authority over the human. This particular afterlife is also unique unto the play; it can be studied in relation to other stylistic or thematic elements in the work itself, but it would be difficult to compare it to other plays about the afterlife since it is a situation that exists only in the world of *Tape*.

Postmodernist works often contain multiple layers of meaning which become apparent only after they have been read or viewed multiple times in an effort to study them. They spark conversation about what certain elements symbolize or what the writer "meant" by certain things. In *Tape*, the very intriguing suggestion that the Person led an incredibly deceptive life contrasts with his mostly pleasant demeanor in the play, but the audience is left to wonder about it with no real elucidation from Rivera. Similarly, though the audience is given a brief description of what lies in store for both the Attendant and the Person during the listening process, Rivera cuts off the action before it can be clarified, leaving viewers to wonder what happens next and how it affects each character. Postmodernism seeks to show a "truth" of the writer's world in unconventional ways. Rivera does not moralize in the play, but he makes clear that he thinks lying is a grave offense that should be punished in a way that is emotionally painful to the liar.

In the twenty-first century, some critics have made references to "post-postmodernism," but it remains unclear whether the postmodern era is at an end and, if so, just when it ended.

Language

Rivera time and time again has stressed the importance of language to a playwright and the successful execution of a concept onstage. He uses a more poetic and lyrical tone in his magical-realist plays to create a mood of mystery and carry the audience into the world of his characters. "Theatre is closer to poetry and music than it is to the novel," Rivera wrote in his article "36 Assumptions about Writing Plays," in *American Theatre*, adding, "Language is a form of entertainment. Beautiful language can be like beautiful music. It can amuse, inspire, mystify, enlighten." Language, for Rivera, is far more than just the meaning of the words. "Rhythm is key," he states in his *American Theatre* article, instructing playwrights to envision "dialogue as a form of percussive music." The many beats, or pauses, that he writes into his scripts, including *Tape*, demonstrate what he means.

Each of these *beats* indicates a pause in the flow of dialogue. But there are many tools available to the playwright to control cadence, as Rivera notes in his article: "You can vary the speed of language, the beats per line, volume, density. You can use silences, fragments, elongated sentences, interruptions, overlapping conversation, physical activity, monologues, nonsense, non-sequiturs, foreign languages." In *Tape*, almost all of these elements are written into the script, revealing how it is ultimately the playwright's job to use language to evoke a desired response from those hearing it. As Rivera wrote in *Cinema Journal* in 2006, "Theater is powered by spoken language." In theater, language, any spoken expression, is the primary vehicle to character-audience identification and connection.

Antihero

Although the audience may find the Attendant a more sympathetic character than the Person, the Person is the protagonist of *Tape* for two reasons: first, because it is his immediate conflict—having to listen to the tapes of his lies—that drives the action of the narrative, and second, because while one may admire the Attendant more, it is the Person with whom one can best identify. In many cases, the protagonist of a story is called the hero, and the antagonist is the villain, but *Tape* is an interesting case study

for the concepts of hero and villain because though it is the Attendant who is guiding the Person through his conflict, he is neither the source of the conflict nor is he preventing it from being resolved. It is the Person's own fault that he is there, and the Attendant has no control over whether he stays or goes. Therefore, unless the Person is classified as the villain in his own story (which is indeed a literary trope), there is no real villain in this piece. Neither is there a true hero. Even though the Person can be classified as the protagonist, he is not heroic in any way. His past actions are what resulted in the conflict and drive the plot; within the context of *Tape*, he can do nothing but endure. If one takes on faith that he is there by divine mandate or supernatural law, then he cannot hope to escape and can take no action to better his situation.

A protagonist who can be classified as neither a hero nor a villain is often referred to as an antihero. An antihero is a main character of a narrative who exists outside of normal society, rejected in some way by the world. Characters that fall into this category often display both good qualities and flaws. Often, an antihero is not evil, but simply lacks moral conviction, insight, or courage. Antiheroes are not villainous, but they are not completely admirable, either. They do not hold the same status in the eyes of the reader or viewer that a traditional hero does.

Allusion

Allusion is the term for when a piece of literature references a specific event or figure from history or literature. Allusions draw upon the reader's or viewer's prior knowledge in order to capitalize on preexisting feelings or opinions which will help increase the emotional impact of the action. In *Tape*, the overarching allusion is vague but obvious, since the setting of the play is clearly some version of hell or purgatory. It is a place where people must pay for the sins they committed when they were alive. Any emotions or thoughts held by a viewer in relation to atonement in the afterlife are therefore automatically engaged by the story. Although Rivera never specifically references a religious doctrine or text, the spiritual themes evoke the audience member's own feelings toward and knowledge of the religious afterlife, especially in Western traditions where the concept of hell or purgatory is common.

COMPARE
&
CONTRAST

- **1990s:** The postmodern fascination with the role of the individual within a larger cultural context is the focus of much literary output, and experimental modes of this identity examination lead to innovative approaches to the ways in which writers play with structural elements in their efforts to symbolically represent their views.

  Today: Although the twenty-first century has not yet been classified by an all-encompassing definition such as "postmodern," literature and the performing arts have in many ways returned to more lyrical and traditional forms of narrative in the study of society and the human condition.

- **1990s:** Religious affiliation shows a marked decline from previous decades, as scandal, corruption, and instances of social intolerance instill mistrust in many Americans who come of age in this decade.

Today: As the children of those members of generation X who disaffiliated themselves from organized religion are raised outside of church, membership in religious institutions has not increased significantly in the twenty-first century.

- **1990s:** Latinos in America are heavily marginalized in much of the performing arts, film, and television. Many American actors of Hispanic or Latino descent are relegated to roles playing domestic or unskilled workers, gang members, or other negative ethnic stereotypes.

Today: As the Latino population in America grows rapidly, far outpacing the growth of other ethnic demographics, mainstream theater, cinema, and television are beginning to showcase Hispanic characters in roles that signify their permanent status as valued members of American society.

HISTORICAL CONTEXT

Puerto Rican Theater in the Twentieth and Twenty-First Centuries

Edna Acosta-Belén, in her article "Haciendo patria desde la metrópoli: The Cultural Expressions of the Puerto Rican Diaspora," says that the history of Puerto Rican performing arts in the United States, as with most aspects of Puerto Rican cultural expression, is "linked to a long professional and working-class tradition" that began to emerge in the late nineteenth century, flourished in the interwar period, and underwent a massive renaissance in the 1970s. The development of Puerto Rican theater took place mainly in New York City, where due to their large presence, Puerto Ricans were able to establish a foothold for themselves in the world of the stage. A great deal of dramatic literature produced by Puerto Ricans offers reactions to US policies in their homeland. Starting with the *teatro obrero*

(worker's theater) in the 1920s, working-class struggles and ideologies became the backbone of Puerto Rican theater both in the United States and on the island. In the 1960s, writer-activists such as Miriam Colon and Miguel Algarín created companies and workshops designed to promote the development of Puerto Rican and Nuyorican playwrights and performers.

Rivera is one of the few Puerto Rican playwrights to achieve definitive commercial and critical success in off-Broadway caliber productions, as well as in film. His emergence in the 1990s coincided with a renewed interest in Puerto Rican and minority studies in American universities that placed emphasis on the Puerto Rican diaspora and explored identity confusion in Latino immigrants, whose traditional cultural practices often collide with mainstream American society. Though Puerto Ricans, like many Latinos, still struggle to find success in theater and film while avoiding ethnic typecasting, inroads are slowly being made. In the late twentieth century, as the Hispanic demographic in the United States grew too large to ignore, Latino writers in general began to see more widespread exposure and opportunity, though Rivera still remains the only Puerto Rican to be nominated for an Academy Award for screenwriting, for his screen adaptation of *The Motorcycle Diaries* in 2002.

Where much of Puerto Rican and Latino theater of the 1960s and 1970s focused on political activism, magical realism became the predominant theatrical style in the last decades of the twentieth century as the influence of writers like Gabriel García Márquez began to show in the theater. In fact, Rivera went so far in 1993 as to tell Tad Simons of *American Theatre* that while it was gratifying to see a shift away from ethnic stereotypes imposed on Latinos by mainstream theater, he was wary of how much Latino theater, specifically from Puerto Rican artists, was in the style of magical realism. As he told Simons, "In the 1970s, Puerto Rican theater clichés ran more along the lines of drug dealers, pimps, murderers and child molesters. That's changed now, but I'd hate to see it get to the point where people are disappointed if they don't see any flying angels or chicken sacrifices."

Jade Powers, in her article "Two Stages/ Spaces in Puerto Rican Theater: A Report from the Field," in the *Latin American Theatre Review*, says that *el otro teatro*, or "'alternative' theater," still thrives in Puerto Rico in the twenty-first century: "I am glad to report that this movement of experimental performance continues, both within and outside of the confines of designated theatrical spaces." The message of resistance to authority, from Puerto Rican police to the "looming presence of the US federal government," is central particularly among youths. This is unsurprising given the often-undesired vast amount of influence exerted over Puerto Rico by what is happening in the states. In a country that is in essence split in half by a sea—there are approximately the same number of people who are Puerto Rican or of Puerto Rican descent living stateside as there are on the island itself—theater, so often an expression of political or social dissent, continues "to grapple with questions of belonging, authenticity, and the Caribbean history of colonial oppression," according to Powers.

Simultaneously, Puerto Rican theater continues to produce more traditional plays that, while not innovative or experimental in nature, celebrate Puerto Rico's long struggle for an identity of its own. Ideological themes such as independence continue to rouse standing ovations. These two very different types of theater nonetheless share a dissatisfaction with Puerto Rico's current political situation that resonates extremely well with contemporary audiences. This discontent with the economy and social situation of Puerto Rico, states Powers, is "rooted in a frustration with its continued colonial status." One approach to expressing dissidence is to celebrate Puerto Rico's history and glorify past attempts at independence; another is to represent the manifestations of that heritage in contemporary life.

Religion in the 1990s

According to a 2002 report by Gill Donovan in the *National Catholic Reporter*, the percentage of Americans who identified with no specific religious doctrine doubled in the 1990s, though sociologists such as Michael Hout and Claude Fischer believe the phenomenon actually began in the mid- to late 1980s. However, while church affiliation was drastically reduced, the percentage of Americans who professed belief in a higher power remained the same. Though participation in traditional religious practices and identification with specific ideologies declined, Americans continued to pray, choosing to classify themselves as spiritual rather than religious. According to the report referenced by Donovan, a lack of faith in intolerant religious leaders and institutions led to general disillusionment with organized religion as a whole. In a 2009 issue of *Religion Watch*, further findings of Hout and Fischer were cited to corroborate this conclusion, indicating that "church political involvement...was a factor in alienating" churchgoers. This trend has continued to increase, according to the findings of Hout and Fischer reported in *Religion Watch*, as more Americans are raised outside of any religious organization.

As represented in *Tape*, beliefs in God or gods, an afterlife, and a divinely sanctioned moral code became more general notions in the 1990s as Americans turned away from dogmatic teachings and explored their personal belief systems. Susannah Schmidt states in her 2004 article "Virtually Abandoned: Reflections on 'Gen X'

The characters are called "person" and "attendant," signifying anonymity. (© Diez Artwork / Shutterstock.com)

Faith and the Church" that generation X, which came of age in the 1980s and 1990s, "showed signs of displacement, fragmented work and economies, a disconnection from a cultural and natural history of the land, and a deep attachment to shared pop culture as the site of deliverance." Schmidt cites scholars like Douglas Coupland and Tom Beaudoin and notes that the communal experience of pop culture replaced that of religious congregations for this generation. In the 1990s, even as young Americans questioned religion, they explored their own notions of spirituality. This helps explain why spiritual themes such as those explored in *Tape* resonated so strongly in that decade.

CRITICAL OVERVIEW

Writing for the *Dallas Morning News* in 1999, critic Lawson Taitte called Rivera "one of the three or four most important Latino playwrights in the country." Indeed, Rivera's magical realism plays have been drawing critical attention since the early 1990s. Tad Simons, writing in *American Theatre* in 1993 of Rivera's play *Marisol*, says that in a single "bold stroke of imagination, José Rivera connects heaven and Earth, spirituality and survival, the fantastic and mundane, drapes it in mystery and delivers it to the stage as

one grand multi-layered metaphor for the human condition." This is the ultimate goal of magical realism, and Rivera has consistently aimed to convey the defining characteristics of the style onstage. In his plays, the supernatural and the everyday almost always attempt to inhabit the same reality. "José Rivera writes with half his mind on credible reality and the other half in fantasyland," critic Bruce Weber states in a 2001 *New York Times* review of Rivera's Obie Award–winning play *References to Salvador Dalí Make Me Hot*, adding, "His characters tend to live in a world where magical and concrete forces coexist." Rivera's reverence for the process of modernizing mythological traditions is not lost on critics like David Román, who, writing for *Theatre Journal* in 1997, discusses the reason behind Rivera's use of myth, saying that it "call[s] the myth into question even as it is conjured."

Still, not all critics have found Rivera's attempts worthy of praise. In a 1992 piece for the *Christian Science Monitor*, for example, Marilynne S. Mason comments on the symbolism inherent in Rivera's magical-realist work, noting that "Mr. Rivera says his mythopoetic imagery offers a metaphor" for social commentary. However, she is not convinced of its success. She admits that Rivera "is a considerably talented man of poetic sensibility" but says that "his oil and water mix of myth and politically correct proselytizing seems overwrought, simplistic, and finally moralistic." And Jorge Morales writes in a 2006 review of the same play, "strip away Rivera's poetic flair and you're left with the thin plot contrivances of a lost *Twilight Zone* episode."

Other criticisms seem directed not at Rivera's execution, per se, but on his very attempt to portray magical realism on the stage. Paul Hodgins, writing for the *Orange County Register* in 1995, is critical of Rivera's ability to translate magical realism from fiction to drama in his play *Cloud Tectonics*. Rivera, the reviewer remarks, "gambles everything on the viewer's willingness to be carried away by its spell, to the point that weaknesses of plot and character can be dismissed as part of the chiaroscuro." In the view of Hodgins and other critics of magical-realist theater, "There's a good reason why the novels of Gabriel Garcia Marquez have never made it to the big screen: Their magic-realist qualities were meant to be imagined, not seen."

However, these detractors remain in the minority, and even critics like Mason who complain about the sometimes unattainable lofty goals of Rivera's plays are capable of pointing out when they work. In her 1993 review of a number of Actors Theatre of Louisville festival performances, including *Tape*, for the *Christian Science Monitor*, Mason calls the play "terrific," saying that it "assails the viewer's conscience in a single short play." A review in the *Spartanburg Herald-Journal* describes the play as "a brief fable about retribution and the possibility of redemption," calling attention to the way it examines "a life of deceit."

"If you're looking for a clear-cut plot and resolution," writes Irene Backalenick in a 2006 review in *Back Stage East*, "Rivera doesn't provide them." But he is not trying to. His goal is to raise social consciousness and inspire questions, not answer them. His lyrical language is always his primary focus, and he relies on his dialogue more than on convoluted characters. Rivera's work contains "fine writing and powerful moments," according to *Globe and Mail* critic Kate Taylor, who adds, "Rivera's characters are little more than briefly observed types . . . but his ability to make them exist simultaneously as small people and big themes can be wonderful to watch."

CRITICISM

Kristy Blackmon

Blackmon is a writer, editor, and critic from Dallas, Texas. In the following essay, she examines the magical-realist evolution of myth in José Rivera's short play Tape.

Myths are cultural constructs. They are metaphors for the human experience because they are created to account for what we find inexplicable in the world. Since recorded history, there have been myths to explain death, love, time, weather, the nature of good and evil, God, and so on. Myths have their roots in people's using what is available to them to understand what is mysterious to them. We pull from the world around us to form the foundation of myths, constructing them of archetypes that make them familiar to us. Thus, culture is both the making of and the result of myth. Myth reflects cultural beliefs while simultaneously evolving to fit the needs of the cultural present.

> IN HIS PLAY *TAPE*, JOSÉ RIVERA SUBVERTS THE TRADITIONAL CHRISTIAN AFTERLIFE MYTHOLOGY IN ORDER TO HIGHLIGHT ITS ANACHRONISMS, CREATING A NEW MYTHOLOGY THAT HAS ITS ROOTS IN OUR CULTURAL PAST BUT THAT REACHES INTO OUR PRESENT TO EXPOSE AND COMMENT UPON CONTEMPORARY SOCIAL THOUGHT."

When a mythology is no longer satisfactory, society adapts it to fit new cultural norms and societal structures. Myth forces us to continually face our own past in order to shape our future. Magical realism deals heavily in myth, both to recount shared cultural histories and modify existing social mythologies by forcing the readers or viewers to admit their inherent inadequacies. In his play *Tape*, José Rivera subverts the traditional Christian afterlife mythology in order to highlight its anachronisms, creating a new mythology that has its roots in our cultural past but that reaches into our present to expose and comment upon contemporary social thought.

Naomi Iizuka, in her 1999 article "What Myths May Come," in *American Theatre*, discusses the role of myth in American theater and literature, quoting several well-respected writers to supplement her elucidation of myth as a means to understanding ourselves and our worlds. Among the writers she references is Rivera, whom she quotes as explaining that myth is intrinsic to his experience as a Latino artist. For Rivera, myth lies in

> the stories recorded on the fragile tape of my child's recollections, those told by abuelas and god fathers and second cousins from Newark, New Jersey, those stored in the clothing my father wore, the Virgin Mary statues guarding the sacred, private spaces on my mother's bureau.

For Rivera, myth is everywhere, in every human interaction and experience: "Once I started to really listen, the noises and cries and howls were impossible to silence. Myth became actual. Myth became Living Material." This idea of living myth is important to a full understanding of both how

WHAT DO I READ NEXT?

- "The Lie," a short story by T. C. Boyle published in the *New Yorker* in 2008, tells the story of a bored man who tells a lie that eventually grows to infect every part of his life.

- Franz Kafka's novella *Metamorphosis*, first published in 1915, is a point of debate for literary scholars attempting to determine if it fits the requirements of magical realism. The protagonist, Gregor Samsa, awakes one morning to discover that he has been transformed into a cockroach. Kafka's depiction of Gregor's reality is nightmarish and otherworldly, yet grounded in ordinary reality.

- *Bless Me, Ultima* (1972), by Rudolfo Anaya, tells the story of six-year-old Antonio Marez and his aunt Ultima, who is a *curandera*, or healer. Ultima introduces Antonio to the mystical traditions of his ancestral roots and helps him navigate the conflicting worlds of his father, a traditional Mexican *vaquero* rancher, and his mother, a devout Catholic. Winner of the Premio Quinto Sol award, *Bless Me, Ultima* is a coming-of-age story told with magical-realist overtones.

- Louise Erdrich is of mixed German American and Chippewa Indian descent, and her 1984 novel *Love Medicine* draws upon her Native American ancestral roots to tell the story of multiple families living on a North Dakota Ojibwe reservation. The narrative comprises stories told from the points of view of multiple characters and takes

advantage of a nonlinear timeline and mystical Native American tradition to impart what some scholars consider a sense of magical realism. It won the National Book Critics Circle Award.

- *Secret Weavers: Stories of the Fantastic by Latin American Women*, edited by Marjorie Agosín, is a 1991 anthology of over forty short stories from Latin American magical-realist writers, including Isabel Allende, Alicia Steimberg, and Silvina Ocampo. The stories collected here prove that magical realism is the result of a shared history and geography and not the sole province of celebrated Latin American male writers like Jorge Luis Borges and Gabriel García Márquez.

- Rivera's *Marisol and Other Plays*, published in 1997, contains his Obie Award–winning play *Marisol* as well as *Each Day Dies with Sleep* and *Cloud Tectonics*, which has been performed and received with mixed reviews.

- *Magic(al) Realism*, by Maggie Bowers, published in 2004, is a valuable resource for students wishing to learn about the genre in relation to both literature and visual art. Bowers provides definitions and historical overviews, examines magical realism's relation to other literary movements, and draws from writers and artists such as Salman Rushdie and Frida Kahlo to provide examples.

---

myth operates and the magical-realist fascination with it. Myth lies at the center of social revolution and change, because the "truths" it presents—the explanations it provides—are constantly evolving.

There are traditional mythologies and there are modern mythologies. Traditional mythologies are basic illustrations of shared cultural histories. Every culture has its myths, but in

magical realism, the mythological traditions that are reflected in the literature, steeped as it is in Latin American and Western culture, are those most prevalent in the Americas. Donald Shaw says in his essay "The Presence of Myth in Borges, Carpentier, Asturias, Rulfo and García Márquez" (included in the 2005 essay collection *A Companion to Magical Realism*) that "there are really three kinds of myth which come into play: Classical, Christian and indigenous Latin American." Classical mythology is characterized by references to the stories of the gods and goddesses of Greco-Roman antiquity. Christian—more specifically Roman Catholic—mythology spread from the church into the collective consciousness of most of the Caribbean and Central and South America beginning with the Spanish imperial conquests of the fifteenth and sixteenth centuries. But the natives never forgot nor completely abandoned their traditional beliefs, and indigenous mythology still permeates much of Latin America.

Modern myths are those that are particular to a specific societal structure rather than a whole cultural tradition. We are surrounded by myth. As Iizuka writes, "We live in a culture saturated by myth—myths about what's normal and what's freakish, what's appropriate and what's obscene." These modern myths represent the way we conceive of ourselves and of others, and of the world around us. Everything we do and are is in the process of being amalgamated into a continuously evolving, living mythology. Modern myths are reflected in customs and traditions such as the modern commercialization of Christmas or wishing on a shooting star. Others can be seen most clearly in stereotypes: the dumb blonde, the greedy lawyer, the starving writer. Stereotypes based on race, ethnicity, and class are often the modern myths that magical realists choose to showcase in an effort to subvert them. We can take the reality of the Latino members of the American theater and film communities as an example. Through the twentieth century and into the twenty-first, roles written for Latino or Hispanic Americans were in large part relegated to stereotypes of the ignorant immigrant, violent gang member, or domestic/unskilled worker. Latino writers began to create characters that played on these modern myths in order to expose their falsity. The *actos* of Luis Valdez and other activist-playwrights exemplify this practice, which involves addressing the modern myth of stereotype and then showing where it is lacking in order to create new modern myths.

The frank confrontation of myth as a means to exposing its inadequacies is common in magical realism, where the line between reality and non-reality is blurred, and the supernatural is treated as commonly accepted truth. Magical realism links the "modern, rational, 'disenchanted' subject of the West with forgotten but recoverable spiritual realities" that exist in mythology, as Christopher Warnes says in his 2005 article "Naturalizing the Supernatural: Faith, Irreverence and Magical Realism." In this way, traditional mythologies and modern mythologies are addressed as equivalents; the truth lies in the knowledge gap between the two. The past and the present combine to form mythologies that "are living, electric patterns: the ferocious menagerie of voices," as Rivera, quoted by Iizuka, puts it.

According to Shaw, magical realism does not include mythic elements in order to simply point out any inherent truth of a mythology. "On the contrary," he says, "they are devices employed by the writers in question to function as a relatively new and effective way of expressing their own attitudes and ideas." In other words, myth is referenced by magical realists as a social critique of traditional points of view and value systems toward the goal of social change. This is one of the three main purposes as defined by Shaw that myth serves in magic realism, especially that of the Latin world: it conveys the writer's view of "Latin American reality, including myths of nationality and mythic representations of socio-political or historical forces for purposes of interpretation, criticism or protest." Second, it functions to show a new reality in the clash between different belief systems, particularly between the mystical culture of Latin America and the industrialized culture of the United States. Cultural truth lies in the mythologies of the culture in question, so that an examination of the myths is in essence an examination of what a people take as truth. Shaw concludes that the third purpose of myth in magical realism is "to express the author's wider view of the Human Condition generally." The mysteries that myths seek to explain have remained fairly constant throughout history, and it is these mysteries that magical realists are most interested in. Rivera, in his 2003 *American Theatre* article "36 Assumptions about Writing Plays," defines them as "the great themes: death, war, sexuality, identity, fate, God, existence, politics, love."

Shaw points out that one additional purpose that myth serves in the literature of magical realism is to function as a way to structure the narrative. Myths provide a structural framework upon which the writer can build. Archetypal characters, conflict and resolution, and plot structure are provided in varying degrees by myths since they are preexisting stories. Writers can use these elements as a foundation from which to explore new meaning and insights, knowing that the narrative frame of the myth is always there to bring them back to a central idea. In addition, as P. Gabrielle Foreman explains in her essay "Past on Stories: History and the Magically Real, Morrison and Allende on Call," "Magical realism, unlike the fantastic or the surreal, presumes that the individual requires a bond with the traditions and the faith of the community, that s/he is historically constructed and connected." The referencing of myths in magical-realist texts serves to point out that bond, strengthen it and, finally, to throw it into question by subverting the mythological expectations of the audience and introducing new, evolved cultural beliefs in the form of new modern myths.

Rivera, speaking to Karen Fricker for the *New York Times* in 1993, explained the need for a new take on the traditional Christian mythologies: "We need to find new heroes and new myths for our society—the old ones just aren't working. The God we know now is a right-wing, white male, corporate God, in whose world racism, sexism and political injustice are rampant." Rivera feels that the traditional Christian myths no longer suffice in modern society. Moreover, they are noninclusive of many groups within contemporary American culture. This view of religion is one that many Americans adopted in the 1990s and 2000s, when religious intolerance was widely viewed as a source of cultural conflict and dissonance. Organized religion, rather than bringing people together in peace, was seen by some as a source of divisiveness in modern America, as Gill Donovan reported for the *National Catholic Reporter* in 2002. This resulted in a marked decrease in the number of Americans who affiliated themselves with a religious tradition or congregation, depriving them of a sufficient mythology to reference in the face of the unknown mysteries religion once served to explain. In the void created by the rejection of religious tradition, where Christian mythologies remained well known but were no longer adequate, Americans substituted the warped ideologies that were most relevant to them, leading to an ultimately unfulfilling deification of concepts such as consumerism and materialism. Celebrities take the place of saints, professional success becomes a substitute for spiritual attainment, and a new moral code as portrayed in mass

media and pop culture steps into the space that traditional religious teachings once occupied.

The conflict between the traditional Christian myths and the new modern myths is the phenomenon that Rivera explores in *Tape*, where the details of Christian afterlife mythology no longer seem plausible but modern myths that focus on the immediate present offer no alternative. The idea of a mandated atonement performed after death for sins committed in life is a universal concept that transcends Christian tradition. However, the gruesome Dantean vision of eternal physical torment no longer resonates as it once did. Rivera modernized and individualized the myth of biblical hell, altering its purpose and effectiveness, making it more powerful by rendering the punishment psychological rather than physical. This aligns the idea of hell with our modern pathological fear of emotional pain and also comments on the pervasiveness of certain societal behaviors that illustrate a flexible moral code with an apparent central tenet that sin is excusable as long as the sinner is not caught.

The incorporation of biblical elements in *Tape* prompts a cultural memory of spiritual karma and allows no escape from the intrinsic fear of punishment in an afterlife. Rivera attempts to temper the discomfort that being forced to confront this fear engenders in many American audiences by making the setting more conducive to modern sensibilities. The Attendant is no righteous, wrathful hand of the Christian God who mercilessly doles out the Person's punishment. Instead, Rivera twists the archetypal characters so that the Attendant and the Person both take part in the pain given by this *contrapasso*-like punishment. The Attendant expresses a wish that he did not have to listen to the Person lying during life and says that the process of listening to the tapes is one that "we have to get through together." This notion of a compassionate deity who suffers for the sins of humanity is reminiscent of the Christ tradition, but the Attendant is accessible and available to every person. "There's no differentiation," the Attendant says; "everyone's equal." This is a pointed line designed to illustrate the alienation felt by many modern Americans, ostracized by mainstream religion for their nontraditional beliefs. In *Tape*, therefore, Rivera evolves the myth of the Christian afterlife by infusing it with elements that are relevant to modern

The entire conversation in the play is being recorded. *(© Viktor Gmyria / Shutterstock.com)*

society, providing us with a new afterlife mythology that addresses the concerns of contemporary America.

Source: Kristy Blackmon, Critical Essay on *Tape*, in *Drama for Students*, Gale, Cengage Learning, 2013.

Norma Jenckes and Jose Rivera

In the following excerpt, Jenckes and Rivera discuss how he became a playwright, the influence of Caryl Churchill on him, and his view of the term "ethnic" in literature.

Two days after Thanksgiving 2000, I talked with playwright Jose Rivera in his home in the Los Feliz section of Los Angeles. We had met a few weeks earlier when he accepted my invitation to appear at the University of Cincinnati as part of the 10th anniversary celebration of the Helen Weinberger Center for the Study of Drama and Playwriting. He held a master class in Playwriting and also participated in a spirited discussion of writing and American theater with a large audience. He attended the UC Drama Department's production of his play *Marisol*. He made a strong positive impact on the students, especially those involved in the *Marisol* production with whom he had been holding an extended consultation by e-mail while they were in the rehearsal process.

Rivera's enthusiasm, charisma, generosity, and thoughful engagement with writing and contemporary drama made me ask him for an interview. Happily, he agreed.

Norma Jenckes: How did you decide to become a playwright, or how did you discover yourself as a playwright?

Jose Rivera: I think the first decision, actually, was for theater, I decided on theater very early having seen a production of *Rumpelstiltskin* that was touring my elementary school when I was twelve years old in sixth grade. I had never forgotten it. I just loved the whimsy of it and the kind of communal interaction between the audience and the performers. And how everybody would laugh at the same time, and I just thought that had some real power to it, something very powerful about that experience. So I knew that the theater in some way was something that I felt naturally drawn to. It became a process of becoming more familiar

> **I'M NOT A BIG FAN OF LABELS FOR ARTISTS. I DON'T PARTICULARLY THINK THEY'RE NECESSARY, BECAUSE I THINK IN SOME WAYS WE'RE MORE BONDED BY THE ART THAN WE ARE SEPARATED BY RACE IN A LOT OF WAYS."**

with the theater and then realizing at one point that plays are written, as opposed to just made up on the spot or improvised. That came a little bit later around the time I was a senior in high school I had decided that writing plays was the thing I wanted to do more than anything else.

NJ: What was your major in college?

Rivera: I majored in theater and English in college at Denison University in Ohio, and it wasn't a great Theater Department, then. It had been really good apparently in the sixties, but by the time I got there it wasn't all that terrific. But I did have the freedom to write and direct and produce my work. So in the four years I was there I wrote and directed and produced four plays.

NJ: Those were your first?

Rivera: Yeah. Well, I had written some things in high school, but these were the first things I had actually seen performed.

NJ: Were you acting as well or doing anything like that?

Rivera: Yeah, I was doing a lot of acting. I was sort of the token ethnic actor at Denison. I played the Chinese water carrier, the Puerto Rican delivery boy in a Neil Simon play, and that kind of thing. But yeah, I did a lot of work and felt that I actually learned a lot about the craft of playwriting through acting, had to interpret the words and understand the beats in a scene and understand the arc of a character, and understand where a particular theme is going, from having to embody that work. I really learned a great deal of many playwriting lessons from that.

NJ: Do you recall your first work?

Rivera: Very first work? Was a play in high school called *Just Dirt*. About a girl, a homeless

girl named Dirt, who is caught picking through the garbage in a middle class Long Island neighborhood. And the reactions of all the neighbors to this girl, this homeless girl who's just looking through it.

NJ: Can you tell us a little bit about the movement in your own writing towards becoming a playwright full time and how that happened?

Rivera: The four years at college, were really pivotal in at least my trying to learn some craft and then directing it. Right after college, I went to New York and worked, because I didn't know how to support myself, I worked in some bookstores, I worked in a warehouse, and eventually worked nine to five in a publishing company. And for about four years worked nine to five while I was still writing plays at night. And the play *Marisol* really covers a lot of that time period in my life when I was living in the Bronx and commuting to Manhattan and working nine to five. I didn't go to graduate school. I had never taken a writing class. I didn't know any other way to do it except to write every day and spend time with writers. I joined a small theater company in New York called Theater Matrix and constantly brought in new work, constantly talking to other writers. It was probably a slower form of education, but the lessons were very deep and they did leave some strong impressions.

NJ: A really concentrated form of education.

Rivera: Yeah. . . .

NJ: Tell me a little bit about Caryl Churchill's appeal to you.

Rivera: I respect what she's doing on so many levels, I mean, on the political level I think that she is obviously in plays like *Fen* and *Top Girls* she's really examining the class situation in England, capitalism run amuck, Thatcherism run amuck. I think she deals with many ways people are cruel to each other, sometimes how that cruelty is related to class and wealth. I think *Mad Forest* is an incredible play about political manipulation and powerlessness. So I love her themes, politically, I think she's trying to tackle some of the most important issues. And one of the things I learned in my year in England was that at least, on a rhetorical level, they really view theater as being part of the social debate. That was a lesson I took home with me when I finished that year there. And Caryl Churchill really embodies that. But on a whole other level, I just think she's wildly original. I've never read a play quite like *The Skriker*, which is mind-boggling. Just on the level of language and the mythology that she explores, and *Blue Hearts*. Who else in the world has that kind of range? She has an old play which I encountered out there. It's something like *Not Not Not Not Enough Oxygen*. It's set in the future. She's great.

NJ: I hear the Churchill influence, but I also recall that in your mention of your very first play, you showed social concern. Would you talk about that, what you think the sources might be for that, early concerns of yours with a girl like Dirt?

Rivera: Well I think maybe part of it's growing up—

NJ: Your experience, in other words?

Rivera: Yeah, there's nothing like growing up poor in America. I mean, it's not everyone's experience, and certainly artists seem to be drawn more from the middle and upper classes than from the lower class I guess. So we don't hear about poverty as much. We don't have the Ivy League schools turn out a lot of kids who were once poor. But it's a big part of a lot of Americans' experience, and it shapes you forever. To this day, there are certain things I can't do because of growing up poor. I'm stingy with money, and I can't walk past a homeless person. There's many things that really psychologically were shaped by those years. And I think being we came to the States in '59 from Puerto Rico, and we were the only Puerto Rican family in an Italian neighborhood for many many years. And we were always outsiders. That experience of being outside, to me, is essentially an artist's experience. That has shaped the political nature of my writing. Always feeling that you're sort of the bottom of the totem pole, and wondering what it is that, why are you there and they're up there, and that kind of thing. Especially in the States, class is determined so much by race and ethnic origin, and country of origin, and when you arrived, and all that kind of thing. It's one of those subjects in America, like coming from a family of an alcoholic father, that nobody wants to talk about. It's a 400 pound elephant. It's the thing nobody really wants to talk about—class in America. It's a big part of my make-up.

NJ: I was struck by that when reading your work, or seeing your sense of class being instrumental at the most intimate levels. It forms and influences what people can be or what they can

aspire to. *Yet, I'm baffled by your writing myself, because of the risks you take. I find them really quite breathtaking. So I wonder whether you accept this "magic realism" designation or description, whether that was something that helped you to see a way of framing those kinds of social concerns in a way that so dazzles, the form is very dazzling, I think.*

Rivera: Yeah, I remember coming across the phrase "magic realism," and in an article about Gabriel Garcia-Marquez. I had never heard the phrase.

NJ: But somewhere you had absorbed it—

Rivera: Yeah. I read about it. It seemed to me really quite a perfect phrase, even though I can't quite define what it means. Nobody I know really seems to have a definition. But put those two words together, I understand them, magic and realism. I understand what that is about. That's always been in my nature, that kind of sort of theatrical whimsy on some level, and a willingness to look at really dark issues in a really dark way. That's always been part of my nature.

NJ: But yet it's like the world suddenly cracks open and all sorts of things are shown to us. The surface breaks; you break the surface in your work.

Rivera: Yeah. Once when I was at Intar, watching a play, and afterwards Max, the artistic director, was talking to the audience and he said that the mission of Intar is to take the audience on a journey. And that essentially your buying a ticket's like getting a passport. And so, it's the responsibility of the writer to create the world in which that journey will take place. And I've always found that to be very useful guide in my work. And I've always been puzzled by playwrights who stick to the real world.

NJ: Stay home?

Rivera: Yeah. I think it's like if you're given the chance, if you're given the talent to write, why stay here? Even though there's a lot to talk about here, absolutely. But you can also talk about here by inventing there. And to me, part of the fun is, in some ways, just seeing how much you can get away with. Just trying to push audience's tolerance and perception and patience, and that kind of thing. So, to me, that's part of the joy of it. Because in the profession sometimes joy is hard to come by (laughter).

NJ: I know our students really responded to the whimsical and playful, even, as you said, sometimes very dark playfulness, if that's a kind of a strange question, too, but that idea of "Let's try it. Let's go there. Let's see what we can do." And I wonder where that comes from. You say it's in your nature. Did you always feel that as a child? Were you mischievous? Were you testing things?

Rivera: (Laughter)

NJ: Did you enjoy that?

Rivera: Well, first of all, my grandparents lived with us, and they were very superstitious, religious people. They were—

NJ: They broke boundaries for you.

Rivera: Yeah, And they brought in another world for me. I grew up fairly standard American childhood with television, but my grandparents brought in this whole other pre-television world, where there was an oral tradition that was more predominant than the television tradition. And they told outrageous stories that they said were true, and they couldn't have been true, and that kind of thing. But I grew up the oldest of six, and when we moved out to the Island, it was Old World. And I spent hundreds of hours alone in the woods in Long Island, where I grew up. I mean, hundreds of hours just playing pretend in the woods. Cowboys and Indians, or whatever those games were. And I know everyone does that, but there was something about the isolation that was really important for me. And even to this day I have a hard time not living in my mind, and living in the real world. That's one thing about being a father, it has forced me to really confront the actual world. But sometimes it's more comfortable in there. It's safer, and it's easier, and you make the rules. . . .

NJ: Tell me a little bit about your sense of this term "ethnic." Is there such a thing? Is that a useful category?

Rivera: I'm not a big fan of labels for artists. I don't particularly think they're necessary, because I think in some ways we're more bonded by the art than we are separated by race in a lot of ways. And, I've worked with artists who are completely different from me racially and religiously, in sexual orientation, and in every other way, but we're so bonded on the work. That's to me the art, the type of artist is an ethnic term, and that should be the ethnic term. But the sort of social and racial categories, I mean, I think they're important in so far as historically the theater has been a white, middle class place, just historically. It hasn't been really until the

60s that that began to change. It's changing more and more, as years go by. And I think that can only be good. I think that the American stage needs to reflect the American reality, which is that we all, we share this big space with a lot of different kinds of people.

NJ: So you see ethnicity as sort of a democratization.

Rivera: Yeah. I think it's essential. And I think we have so much to learn from each other. When I saw this play, *Under the Western Sky*, I think it's called, about African American women homesteaders who came to the West after the Civil War. And the freed slaves, recently emancipated slaves who had gone West. And I just was so appreciative of that play. I learned so much about that population in that time in history. We have so much to learn from each other, and the greater diversity in our voices, the better off we're all going to be. Even though not every ethnic play is going to be a great play, as not every white play is a great play, and we're going to have to suffer through a lot of mediocrity. But I think the ultimate goal is really laudable.

NJ: Mining that experience.

Rivera: Absolutely. If people go to the theater, I think they want to see their reality reflected back to them. . . .

Source: Norma Jenckes and Jose Rivera, "An Interview with Jose Rivera," in *American Drama*, Vol. 10, No. 2, Summer 2001, pp. 21–47.

SOURCES

Acosta-Belén, Edna, "Haciendo patria desde la metropoli: The Cultural Expressions of the Puerto Rican Diaspora," in *CENTRO Journal*, Vol. 21, No. 2, Fall 2009, pp. 63–65.

"Allusion," in *Merriam Webster's Encyclopedia of Literature*, Merriam-Webster, 1995, p. 37.

"Although More Americans Are Joining the Ranks of the Unchurched . . . ," in *Religion Watch*, Vol. 24, No. 6, September–October 2009, p. 4.

"Antihero," in *Merriam Webster's Encyclopedia of Literature*, Merriam-Webster, 1995, p. 57.

Arkatov, Janice, "A Magical 'Promise' from Playwright Jose Rivera," in *Los Angeles Times*, February 13, 1988, p. E9.

Backalenick, Irene, Review of *Cloud Tectonics*, in *Back Stage East*, July 27, 2006, Vol. 47, No. 30, p. 43.

Donovan, Gill, "Proportion of Those Preferring No Religion Doubled in 1990s," in *National Catholic Reporter*, Vol. 38, No. 31, June 7, 2002, p. 11.

Foreman , P. Gabrielle, "Past-On Stories: History and the Magically Real, Morrison and Allende on Call," in *Magical Realism: Theory, History, Community*, edited by Lois Parkinson Zamora and Wendy Faris, Duke University Press, 1995, p. 286.

Fricker, Karen, "Another Playwright Confronts an Angel and the Apocalypse," in *New York Times*, May 16, 1993, p. 1.

Geyh, Paula E., "Postmodernism," in *New Dictionary of the History of Ideas*, edited by Maryanne Cline Horowitz, Vol. 5, Charles Scribner's Sons, 2005, pp. 1867–70.

Hodgins, Paul, "Getting Lost in the Clouds," in *Orange County Register*, July 6, 1995, p. F3.

Iizuka, Naomi, "What Myths May Come," in *American Theatre*, Vol. 16, No. 7, September 1999, pp. 18–19, 78.

Leal, Luis, "Magical Realism in Spanish American Literature," in *Magical Realism: Theory, History, Community*, edited by Lois Parkinson Zamora and Wendy Faris, Duke University Press, 1995, p. 121.

Mason, Marilynne S., "Louisville's Window on New Plays," in *Christian Science Monitor*, April 2, 1992, p. 12.

———, "New Plays to Rouse the Social Conscience," in *Christian Science Monitor*, March 30, 1993, p. 10.

McElroy, Steven, "Nine to Watch, Onstage and Off," in *New York Times*, February 26, 2006, p. 12.

Morales, Jorge, "Unstuck in Time," in *Village Voice*, July 18, 2006, http://www.villagevoice.com/content/printVersion/204312/ (accessed September 7, 2012).

Newcomb, Paul R., "Mysticism," in *International Encyclopedia of the Social Sciences*, 2nd ed., edited by William A. Darity, Jr., Vol. 5, Macmillan Reference USA, 2008, pp. 352–53.

Powers, Jade, "Two Stages/Spaces in Puerto Rican Theater: A Report from the Field," in *Latin American Theatre Review*, Vol. 43, No. 1, Fall 2009, pp. 189, 191, 193.

Rivera, José, "Split Personality: Random Thoughts on Writing for Theater and Film," in *Cinema Journal*, Vol. 45, No. 2, Winter 2006, pp. 89–92.

———, *Tape*, in *30 Ten-Minute Plays for 2 Actors, from the National Ten-Minute Play Contest*, edited by Michael Bigelow Dixon, Amy Wegener, and Karen C. Petruska, Smith & Kraus, 2001, pp. 241–46.

———, "36 Assumptions about Writing Plays," in *American Theatre*, Vol. 20, No. 2, February 2003, pp. 22–23.

Román, David, Review of *The Street of the Sun*, in *Theatre Journal*, Vol. 50, No. 1, March 1998, p. 96.

Schmidt, Susannah, "Virtually Abandoned: Reflections on 'Gen X' Faith and the Church," in *Catholic New Times*, Vol. 28, No. 4, February 29, 2004, p. 14.

Seigneuret, Jean-Charles, "Afterlife," in *Dictionary of Literary Themes and Motifs*, edited by Jean-Charles

Seigneuret, A. Owen Aldridge, Armin Arnold, and Peter H. Lee, Greenwood Press, 1988, p. 13.

Shaw, Donald, "The Presence of Myth in Borges, Carpentier, Asturias, Rulfo and García Márquez," in *A Companion to Magical Realism*, edited by Stephen M. Hart and Wen-Chin Ouyang, Tamesis, 2005, pp. 46–47, 49, 54.

Simons, Tad, "Jose Rivera: We All Think Magically in Our Sleep," in *American Theatre*, Vol. 10, Nos. 7–8, July–August 1993, p. 46.

Taitte, Lawson, "A Dream Job—Latino Playwright Jose Rivera Brings His Work to SMU," in *Dallas Morning News*, February 6, 1999, p. 1C.

Taylor, Kate, Review of *Marisol*, in *Globe and Mail*, January 17, 1997, p. C6.

Warnes, Christopher, "Naturalizing the Supernatural: Faith, Irreverence and Magical Realism," in *Literature Compass*, Vol. 2, No. 1, January 2005, p. 1.

Weber, Bruce, "She's Venus, He's Mars, in a Regimented Match," in *New York Times*, April 12, 2001, p. E5.

"Wofford Theatre Plans Series of Short Plays," in *Spartanburg Herald-Journal*, November 6, 2011.

Wood, Daniel B., "'Magical Realism' and the Latino Theatre Lab," in *Christian Science Monitor*, January 3, 1989, p. 10.

FURTHER READING

García Márquez, Gabriel, *One Hundred Years of Solitude*, translated by Gregory Rabassa, Demco Media, 2004.

> This widely acclaimed novel by Nobel Prize–winner García Márquez is considered by many to be the seminal work in the genre of magical-realist fiction. It tells the story of the mythical town of Macondo by chronicling the history of the Buendía family over many generations, incorporating symbolically fantastical imagery and a nonlinear timeline. Originally published in Spanish in 1967, it is now available in thirty-seven languages.

Hollaman, Keith, and David Young, eds., *Magical Realist Fiction: An Anthology*, Longman, 1984.

> This anthology includes examples of magical realism in works published before the term was well known and gives attention to a diverse array of nationalities and ethnicities. The introduction by Young and Hollaman outlines the general characteristics of the genre while making an argument that the definition of magical realism is fluid.

Otfinoski, Steve, *1990s to 2010*, "Hispanic America" series, Benchmark Books, 2009.

> In 2003, Hispanics became the largest minority group in America, and some experts predict that by 2020, Hispanics will constitute 20

percent of the US population. Otfinoski's book chronicles the explosive growth of this demographic in the late twentieth and early twenty-first centuries, focusing on the results of assimilation, the question of immigration, and what the future holds for Hispanic Americans.

Reyes, Luis, and Peter Rubie, *Hispanics in Hollywood: A Celebration of 100 Years in Film and Television*, Lone Eagle, 2000.

Reyes and Rubie provide an exhaustive reference guide on prominent Hispanics in American film and television, supplemented by biographical information, essays, photographs, and plot summaries.

SUGGESTED SEARCH TERMS

Jose Rivera

Jose Rivera AND Tape

Jose Rivera AND ten minute play

magical realism

Jose Rivera AND magical realism

Latino theater AND Jose Rivera

Gabriel Garcia Marquez AND Jose Rivera

mythology AND magical realism

Well

LISA KRON
2006

Lisa Kron's play *Well* premiered in 2004 and was first published in 2006. In this autobiographical work, Kron features a character meant to represent herself, as well as a character based on her mother. It is overtly structured as a "theatrical exploration" of themes of individual and community wellness. As the character Lisa explains during the course of the play, she intends as a playwright to use vignettes and montages as a means of exploring the past. She recalls her mother's role as a community organizer who helped integrate her Lansing, Michigan, neighborhood, and remembers scenes from her own time spent in the hospital overcoming symptoms believed by her fatigue-plagued family—her mother in particular—to be the result of allergies. But as the play progresses, the structures Lisa intended to incorporate begin to disintegrate as Lisa's mother inserts herself into the "intended" play, commenting about the play and about Lisa's mistakes and bonding with the actors, who encourage Lisa to confront the issues Lisa clearly has with her mother. Only after the actor playing Lisa's mother breaks character and speaks to Lisa directly is Lisa finally able to speak truthfully about the past.

First staged in 2004 in New York, *Well* premiered on the West Coast in 2005 and on Broadway in 2006. It was published in 2006 by Theatre Communications Group.

Lisa Kron (© *Alamy Celebrity | Alamy*)

AUTHOR BIOGRAPHY

Kron was born in Ann Arbor, Michigan, on May 20, 1961, to parents Walter and Ann Kron. Her mother is a community activist known for founding the Westside Neighborhood Organization in Lansing, Michigan, a group that fought the tide of racial segregation in neighborhoods during the 1960s. Kron's father is a Holocaust survivor and a retired lawyer. In 1965, just after Kron's brother David was born, the family moved to Lansing. Kron graduated as valedictorian from Everett High School in 1979. Afterward, she majored in theater at Kalamazoo College. Kron continued her theatrical studies after college at the Chautauqua Professional Actors Studio and at the British European Studies Group in London. In 1984, Kron moved to New York and worked at various odd jobs while pursuing a career in theater. She found work as an actor at the WOW Café in Manhattan's East Village. Kron, along with four other women—Maureen Angelos, Dominique Dibbell, Peg Healey and Babs Davy—founded the

theatrical company The Five Lesbian Brothers in 1989. The group writes and performs satirical works inspired by a feminist and lesbian perspective. Their work has been performed by such groups as the New York Theatre Workshop and the WOW Café Theatre. Kron's 1996 play *2.5 Minute Ride*, which focuses on the murder of her Jewish grandparents by the Nazis, received an OBIE Award, while Kron's performance as herself received Drama Desk and Outer Critics Circle nominations for best solo performance. In 2004, Kron's play *Well* premiered at the Public Theater; it received favorable reviews and premiered on the West Coast in 2005. *Well* made its Broadway debut in 2006 at the Longacre Theater and received two Tony nominations. Kron continues to live and work in New York. She has received a number of prestigious fellowships and grants, including a Guggenheim Fellowship. Kron's latest work is a musical, *Fun Home*, with music by Jeanine Tesori, and the playbook and lyrics by Kron. The musical premiered in the fall of 2012.

PLOT SUMMARY

While characters in the play refer to specific scenes, the play is not structured in terms of acts and scenes, but proceeds as a one-act play. The format is self-reflexive, in that the characters in the play refer to the play itself and their role in it. The play as a whole is an incorporation of the play the character Lisa intends to produce as well as the disintegration of this "intended" play into what is depicted as "real" interaction between the actors in the "intended" play and Lisa's mother. The stage is set "as if Lisa has plucked her mother out of her house, shaken off all she could, and then plopped her down onto the stage along with everything that stuck." The play opens with Lisa Kron addressing the audience and explaining the play's format. In this explanation, Lisa describes the play she intends to perform with the actors on set; she does not anticipate the derailing that is about to occur. This derailment begins almost immediately, when Ann Kron, asleep in a chair on the portion of the stage meant to represent Ann's house, begins to groan and talk in her sleep. As Ann wakes up, she addresses the audience briefly. When she disappears upstairs, Lisa explains Ann's lifelong battle with the debilitating allergies that have sapped all of her strength. Lisa seems suspicious of her mother's attribution of her fatigue and general sense of illness to allergies. Growing increasingly annoyed at her mother's insistence on offering drinks to the audience members, Lisa marvels at the energy Ann puts into annoying her daughter by throwing packets of potato chips at audience members, an act Ann performs to amuse the audience.

Lisa continues to try to explain the focus of the play—on individual and community wellness—to her mother, seeking to skirt the fact that the play will necessarily be *about* Lisa and her mother. Ann suspects that Lisa's play is really about her, and she fears that Lisa will portray her as a hypochondriac. Lisa steps into a spotlight identified in the stage directions as "her 'special light.'" It is a space from which Lisa confidentially addresses the audience after stepping outside the action of the play.

The "intended" play, as it is repeatedly referred to, thus commences, beginning with a scene that takes place in the Allergy Unit at Henrotin Hospital in Chicago. Lisa is greeted by the character identified as "Head Nurse." As they discuss the procedures at the hospital, a woman named Kay enters. Kay is introduced to Lisa and talks to the head nurse briefly. The head nurse and Lisa then enter what will be Lisa's room, which she will share with a woman named Joy. As the Head Nurse tells Lisa about the water and food testing she will undergo, Joy becomes agitated and annoyed with Lisa and excuses herself. The Head Nurse explains that Lisa might have some auto exhaust residue in her hair, which triggered Joy's allergies.

Lisa turns from this scene and explains to the audience that she "believed in allergies" when she entered the hospital and that her family believed in two things—allergies and racial integration. The scene then shifts to a neighborhood meeting, as Lisa states that her mother was the president of the West Side Neighborhood Association from the time Lisa was seven until she was fourteen. At the meeting now being enacted, Jim greets Lisa and informs her that two of her friends, Cynthia and Bridget, are outside playing. Another neighbor, Howard, compliments Lisa on the way she helps with the coffee and cookies. Other neighbors introduced at this time include Mrs. Price, who comments on how fat

Lisa is getting, and Dottie. The neighbors discuss the fact that the "City of Lansing and the real-estate industry believe this neighborhood is sick and is going to die because there's no such thing as an integrated neighborhood." Ann's role in creating a neighborhood association to foster a sense of unity within the community is discussed; her focus is on social activities that bring people together. Lisa explains that some neighbors are skeptical about Ann's approach.

Ann interrupts the scene and criticizes Lisa for compressing too much important information about the neighborhood. They are interrupted by a girl named Lori Jones, a tormenter from Lisa's youth. Lisa is surprised to see Lori, as she has not written her into the play. The scene transfers back to the Allergy Unit, where Nurse 2 is administering the "water test" to see which types of water Lisa may safely drink without an allergic reaction. Joy and Kay discuss Lisa's symptoms with her.

Lisa once again addresses the audience, describing her childhood friends Oscar and Cynthia and the fact that Lisa and her brother are the only white children in an all-black school as well as being the only Jews in the school. A new scene begins, with Oscar and Cynthia and Lisa portraying a scene from Lisa's childhood in which the three are playing outside together. To an audience member, Ann explains that Lisa and her friends used to play a game in which they discussed which girl—Lisa or Carol, the girl Lisa has named Cynthia in the play—was going to marry Otis, the boy Lisa has named Oscar in the play. Lisa remembers her mother chastising her for calling Oscar "black boy," a term that was part of a game they played. Ann interrupts the scene by questioning Lisa's portrayal of this memory. Ann goes on to introduce herself to the actors playing Cynthia and Oscar. The other two actors, identified in the script as "A" and "D" are also called out to be introduced to Ann. The four actors and Ann discuss the "confusing" nature of the structure of Lisa's play. Lisa defends the play and attempts to get the play back on track. She invites her mother to discuss her vision for the neighborhood association, and she and Lisa remember the various parties that were attended by the whole neighborhood.

As Lisa tries to get her actors to begin the next scene, in the Allergy Unit, "B" asks Lisa how those scenes should be played. She is not sure if Lisa intends the patients at the hospital to be depicted as "a little whacked" or if people actually improved their health there. Ann interrupts, assuring "B" that people did get better there, while Lisa hesitates. "A" and "B" carry on a conversation with Ann about allergies. All four actors rush to Ann's aid as she returns to her "living room" to search for pamphlets on allergies to give to them.

Meanwhile, Lisa sets up the next scene by herself. When she calls out to the actors, they finally get in place for the next scene, which opens with the Head Nurse discussing Lisa's progress with her. Joy comments about how big Lisa's arms are when the topic of skin testing comes up. After Joy and the head nurse exit, Lori enters the scene, teasing Lisa about the way she dances. Lori exits, and Nurse 2 enters; Joy has returned as well. As they both undergo a food test, eating and monitoring their responses, Lisa to corn, Joy to pineapple, Joy becomes intensely aggressive toward Lisa. Ann interrupts the scene by gasping in pain. The woman playing Joy, "A," breaks character and runs to Ann's side to help her. Ann gives "A" a pamphlet to give to "B" about environmental allergies. As they discuss such allergies, "A" begins to suspect that some of her health problems have been caused by these allergies. Lisa calls "A" back to the scene, but not before Ann hands "A" a piece of paper to give to Lisa. As Joy, the actress known as "A" infuses the scene about a chemical allergy test with her emotional response to her discussion with Ann about the reality of such allergies.

The next scene takes place in Lisa's old neighborhood. Big Oscar, or Mr. Harris, is a friend and neighbor to the Krons. The scene depicts Big Oscar's drunken attempts to flirt with Ann. When Little Oscar is heard screaming, Lisa says that her mother ran out the door, just as other neighbors, including Dottie, played by "A" and Howard, played by "D," come to see what is going on as well. Lisa narrates the unfolding of the scene, saying that Ann went into the house and retrieved Little Oscar and took him away from the house for the evening. The scene is interrupted by Lori, who teases Lisa about her hair. Hearing the commotion, Ann inserts herself into the action to see what is happening. Cornered by Lori, Lisa attempts to explain the point of the scene and to insist that the racial integration of the neighborhood was marked by the supportive and cooperative

atmosphere among the adults, while there was tension among the children. Ann disagrees, insisting that tension existed among the adults as well. Lori exits.

Ann and Lisa continue to discuss the neighborhood, while "C" and "D" break character and join in the conversation. Ann explains more of the history of the association and criticizes the fact that Lisa has summarized too much and has glossed over important details in the process. Ann then goes on to talk about Lisa's lack of friends during this period, while the actors listen eagerly. Lisa interrupts and pushes the actors offstage to get ready for the next scene. Meanwhile, Lisa tells the audience about her Halloween costumes and how she always tried to be creative, but in doing so, isolated herself from her peers. Yet she insists that she did have friends and begins another anecdote that is soon interrupted by Lori, who teases Lisa mercilessly, all while Lisa tries to insist that Lori's presence does not accurately represent her childhood experience. Lori exits after being scolded by Ann. Before Lisa begins the next Allergy Unit scene, Ann attempts to correct Lisa's interpretation of the Little Oscar scene. Kay, played by "B," enters and discusses her impending departure from the hospital. Lisa appears moved and steps into her "special light" to talk about an incident in which her mother almost died. The event had been downplayed by Lisa and her family at the time because it seemed tied to the fact that Ann was *always* sick.

Lisa attempts to return to the scene but is interrupted by Ann, who asks why Lisa has not included a scene about Lisa's allergic reaction to wheat. Lisa gets angry and stomps up the stairs. Ann begins a lengthy speech about how and why neighborhood integration was so important to her and how her illness impaired her. She then falls into a chair, exhausted. The actors enter and discuss their confusion about the play's structure. "D" apologizes to the audience, and the four actors discuss leaving the play. Lisa returns and attempts to mobilize them to do the next scene. They protest and express their sympathy with Ann. The actors go on to insist that Lisa has a lot of issues to work out with her mother. They decide to leave and bid Ann farewell.

Lisa apologizes to the audience. Ann encourages her to simply say what she wants to say to her; Ann accuses her daughter of being afraid to be candid with her. Lisa steps into her "special light" and begins a long speech about how she overcame her illness or allergies. She seems to disregard her symptoms as medical in nature and expresses her resentments about the "sick people" in her life. She differentiates herself from them. Ann calls out to Lisa to step out of her "special light" and deal with her directly. Lisa is surprised that Ann can hear her.

Ann questions Lisa, forcing her to confront the issues she has avoided throughout the play. Lisa defends herself and the play. As Ann questions, Lisa admits that she has left out how people at the Allergy Unit actually got better, but she admits to not knowing why she left things out. Ann continues to insist that Lisa say what she needs to say, and Lisa finally blurts, "Why can't you make yourself well?!" Ann becomes upset, thinking the question is unfair. Lisa underscores how very much alike they were and confesses that she got well by leaving home, by getting away from her mother's sickness. The actress playing Ann, identified in the script as Jayne, breaks character and addresses Lisa. She says that she cannot continue with the ending as it is currently written. Jayne asks Lisa about the paper that she, as Ann, gave to "A" to give to Lisa, telling her it is something her mother wrote. They discuss the way the story has progressed, and Jayne contends that Lisa has made it into a "comfortable" story. Jayne further addresses Lisa's fear that she will become her mother, and she reflects on the separation process she went through with her own mother.

The play closes with Lisa reading the speech her mother wrote about the neighborhood association and the people in the neighborhood. In it, she discusses integration in terms of wholeness.

CHARACTERS

A

Throughout the play, the character designated as "A," played by a white woman, plays herself, as well as Joy and Dottie. Like the other ensemble actors, "A" frequently breaks character to interact with Lisa and Ann during the play. In performance, the actors referred to in the script by the letters "A," "B," "C," and "D" are referred to by the actual names of the actors playing these roles.

B

Throughout the play, the character designated as "B," played by an African American woman, plays herself, as well as Lori Jones, Kay, Mrs. Price, and Cynthia. Like the other ensemble actors, "B" frequently breaks character to interact with Lisa and Ann during the play. In performance, the actors referred to in the script by the letters "A," "B," "C," and "D" are referred to by the actual names of the actors playing these roles.

Big Oscar

Big Oscar, or Mr. Harris, is one of the African American neighbors of the Krons. He is the father of Little Oscar, one of Lisa's friends, and he appears in scenes involving the neighborhood association. He is played by the actor identified as "C."

Bridget

Bridget does not appear in the play, but she is referred to in one of the neighborhood scenes as a friend of Lisa's.

C

Throughout the play, the character designated as "C," played by an African American man, plays himself, along with Jim Richardson, Nurse 2, Little Oscar, and Big Oscar. Like the other ensemble actors, "C" frequently breaks character to interact with Lisa and Ann during the play. In performance, the actors referred to in the script by the letters "A," "B," "C," and "D" are referred to by the actual names of the actors playing these roles.

Cynthia

Cynthia is one of Lisa's childhood African American friends. She is played by the actress designated as "B." Ann notes that Lisa has changed this character's name for the play, commenting that Cynthia's real name was Carol.

D

Throughout the play, the character designated as "D," played by a white man, plays himself, as well as Howard Norris and Head Nurse. Like the other ensemble actors, "D" frequently breaks character to interact with Lisa and Ann during the play. In performance, the actors referred to in the script by the letters "A," "B," "C," and "D" are referred to by the actual names of the actors playing these roles.

Dottie

Dottie, played by "A," is a white member of the neighborhood association. She appears in some of the neighborhood scenes helping Ann.

Mr. Harris

See *Big Oscar*

Head Nurse

The character of the head nurse is played by the actor designated as "C." He appears in the Allergy Unit scenes, administering to Lisa.

Jayne

Jayne is the actor who plays Ann Kron. She breaks character at the end of the play to confront Lisa about her relationship with her mother and to urge her to change the play's ending. Unlike the other actors in the play, Jayne does not break character until late in the play.

Joy

Joy is Lisa's roommate in the Allergy Unit. She repeatedly expresses her annoyance with Lisa. Joy is played by the actress designated as "A."

Lori Jones

Lori Jones is a character played by "B." She is a figure from Lisa's childhood, a young girl who teased Lisa relentlessly. She appears throughout the play at key points, calling attention to places within the play where Lisa appears to be leaving out important pieces of her personal history and her presentation of the neighborhood.

Kay

Kay appears in the Allergy Unit scenes as Lisa's fellow patient. Along with Joy, Kay discusses with Lisa allergy symptoms and their treatment. Her release from the hospital prompts Lisa to reflect upon a near-fatal event in her mother's life.

Ann Kron

Ann is Lisa's mother. She is portrayed by the actress identified in the script as "Jayne." Ann repeatedly interrupts Lisa's play, questions the format, and worries over how she will be portrayed. Because of the way Ann engages with the actors in the play, she garners their sympathy. They begin to question Lisa's format and express the fact that they prefer talking to Ann to performing Lisa's scenes. For Lisa, Ann is defined by two things: her illness and her role in integrating the Lansing neighborhood where Lisa grew up. Ann criticizes the way Lisa has left out the complexities and tensions of the relationships among the neighbors, and she possesses a growing sense that Lisa harbors some resentment against her that she is afraid to voice. Eventually, Ann compels her daughter to tell the truth about her feelings for her.

Lisa Kron

The character of Lisa Kron in *Well* is a theatrical version of the playwright and actor based on herself. In some theatrical productions of the play, Kron played the role, blurring the boundaries between drama and reality. As a character in the play, Lisa struggles to maintain control of the production. She grows frustrated with the interruptions by her mother, Ann, and with the way her actors break character and converse with Ann. Lisa attempts to portray a version of her own past and that of her mother in an effort to contrast the notions of sickness and wellness in herself, in her mother, and in the community her mother rehabilitated. As the play progresses, however, a defiant and often confused Lisa is forced to confront facts she omitted in her retelling of the past. She eventually must come to terms with her mother and with her own mixed feelings about her relationship with her.

Little Oscar

Little Oscar is one of Lisa's African American friends. The son of Big Oscar, or Mr. Harris, he creates a game in which he shouts "Hey, white girl!" at Lisa and she responds by shouting "Hey, black boy," at him. Lisa is reprimanded for this by her mother. Ann notes that in real life, Oscar's name was "Otis."

Howard Norris

Howard Norris, played by the actor designated as "D," appears in the first scene involving the neighborhood association. Like other neighbors, specifically Jim Richardson, Howard is skeptical about Ann's plan for the neighborhood association.

Nurse 2

Nurse 2, played by the actor designated as "C," appears in the Allergy Unit scenes. He assists Lisa with some of her tests.

Mrs. Price

Mrs. Price appears in the first of the neighborhood scenes. After telling Lisa that she is getting fat, Mrs. Price expresses concerns about the future of the neighborhood.

Jim Richardson

Jim Richardson, played by the actor designated as "C," appears in the first scene involving the neighborhood association. He is depicted as critical of Ann's plans for the association, which are rooted in social events designed to build a sense of community.

THEMES

Mother-Child Relationships

Despite Lisa's assertion at the beginning of *Well* that "this play is *not* about my mother and me," *Well* is, in fact, intently focused on that relationship. Lisa exhibits admiration for and idolization of her mother and at the same time treats her in a condescending manner and grows irritated with her frequently. Amazed by what Ann accomplished by creating a healthy, vibrant, integrated neighborhood in the 1960s, Lisa seeks to gloss over elements of her mother's work that do not reflect positively on the neighborhood. While Lisa seeks to present a polished, idealized view of the neighborhood, her mother attests to the struggles and tensions that existed. Ann's energetic efforts to improve her community stand in stark contrast—at least in Lisa's eyes—to her mother's pervasive sense of sickness. Lisa cannot comprehend the way a woman who was as unwell as her mother claimed to be could have accomplished so much. For this reason, Lisa seems to believe her mother can *will* herself to get better, as Lisa feels she herself did. It is during the moments when Ann seems most fatigued that Lisa grows the most irritated with her. Despite these conflicts, Ann and Lisa both speak of their closeness, of the way their lives seemed connected. Ann says of Lisa, "She is like an amazing star to me—my daughter. . . . It's like we were one thing. Or we were rooted in the same place and she kept growing which was the most wonderful thing." Later, when Lisa compares her sickness to her mother's, Ann insists upon their differences, stating, "But we are not the same person," to enforce the idea that just because Lisa got better does not mean that she

could. Lisa replies, "But, we were, Mom. We were—entwined. And that was good in a lot of ways." Lisa continues to express a daughter's adoration of her mother, stating, "there is no place better, safer, warmer, than right up against you. . . . I wanted to be just like you. . . . Mom, I thought I was going to become you." At the same time, Lisa recognizes that she needed to get away from her mother to become better, to become herself. She maintains, "I got better when I left," and goes on to explain, "I think I was sick because you were sick, Mom." Enveloped as she was in her mother's existence, Lisa realizes that this experience was simultaneously wonderful and damaging. Stepping out of her role as Ann, the actress Jayne discusses her own similar experience with her own mother, claiming, "I wanted to crawl right into her skin and I couldn't push her far enough away." But Jayne gives Lisa permission to stop pushing Ann away and insists that Lisa does not have to fear losing her own identity any longer, because she has successfully separated her self from her mother. "Stop fighting her. Just let her in," Jayne urges. By voicing her mother's words at the end of the play, Lisa seems finally able to begin to embrace her mother and let her in.

Sickness

In *Well*, Kron explores the notion of sickness and, through contrast, the idea of wellness. As the play opens, Lisa states that the play is concerned with such questions as "Why are some people sick and other people are well? Why are some people sick for years and years and other people are sick for a while but then they get better?" Although the play evolves into an exploration of Lisa's relationship with her mother, the notions of sickness and health continue to pervade the work. Lisa uses the Allergy Unit scenes to discuss her own battle with sickness. She believes, due to her mother's experience, that the vague array of symptoms she experiences may be attributed to allergies. The Allergy Unit scenes seem to indicate Lisa's skepticism about allergies and their treatment. The ensemble characters notice this and ask Lisa if they should be playing the characters as slightly crazy or as people who actually received treatment that improved their health. Lisa's answer conveys her doubts, while Ann voices her opinion that people actually got better at the hospital. Ann presses Lisa to portray the positive outcomes; Lisa resists, even though Ann eventually

TOPICS FOR FURTHER STUDY

- Robert Sharenow's highly acclaimed 2007 young-adult novel, *My Mother the Cheerleader*, concerns race relations in the 1960s. It takes place in the South, in a white neighborhood that is protesting the court-ordered integration of their school. With a small group, read Sharenow's novel. Consider the ways in which Sharenow depicts the attitudes of the white community toward the black students entering the school system. Compare Lisa's childhood experience as one of the few white children in an all-black school, as depicted in *Well*, with the portrayal of the school integration in Sharenow's novel. How do the children's views in Sharenow's book reflect those of their parents? Are they positively or negatively impacted by their parents' activities? How does this compare with Lisa's experience in *Well*? Create an online blog in which you discuss these and other issues related to the two novels. Alternatively, engage in a "live" book group discussion and present a summary of your comparison of the two works to your teacher and your class.

- Discrimination based on ethnic, religious, and racial difference remains a pervasive part of twenty-first-century culture. In Azadeh Moaveni's memoir, *Lipstick Jihad: A Memoir of Growing Up Iranian in America and American in Iran*, the author recounts her experiences as an Iranian-born American who returns to Iran but is perceived now as more American than Iranian—she is discriminated against in both the worlds she inhabits. Read Moaveni's work and explore the sources of such discrimination. What spurred the reaction she generated among her American and Iranian peers? Were the fears and prejudices rooted in political, religious, ethnic, or racial stereotypes? How does Moaveni's relationship with her mother factor into her experiences with struggle in both countries? Write a report in which you discuss Moaveni's journey and the themes she explores along the way.

- *Well* explores the importance of integrated neighborhoods and the way Ann Kron was able to help establish and maintain an integrated Michigan neighborhood in the 1960s. Research the history of race relations during this decade and explore the factors that contributed to the segregation of neighborhoods by race. Write a detailed research paper in which you describe race relations during this time period. Cite all your sources. Share your work with your class either in print form, through a visual presentation such as a timeline or a PowerPoint, or as a web page.

- In *Well*, Kron utilizes an unconventional format, incorporating a self-reflexive style and a disjointed, montage-based structure. Using one or both of these techniques, compose a one-act play by yourself or with a group. Focus on incorporating elements of the past with the present time, and ground the play in themes related to family relationships. If you are working alone, present your play to your class as a script. If you are working with a group, perform the play for your class.

---

compels Lisa to reveal that her own allergy to wheat was undeniable, and that she did in fact see people cured at the hospital. Ann's own experience confuses Lisa. Throughout her entire childhood, Lisa has witnessed her mother's fatigue and the way Ann attributes every symptom of sickness to a food-related or environmental allergen. At the same time, Lisa marvels at the remarkable energy Ann exhibited in healing their Lansing neighborhood. Ann's approach

A scene from Well *with the characters of Kron and her mother.* (© *Alamy Celebrity | Alamy*)

toward a healthy neighborhood involves bringing people together in celebration of one another and their community—she urges her neighbors to embrace social activity and togetherness. Similarly, Lisa realizes that, at least in part, she healed herself through activity and connection with other people. She considers the way her girlfriend, her move to New York, getting therapy, eating healthy food, and her study of theater all contributed to her wellness. Throughout the play, Lisa seems insistent on contrasting sickness and wellness, dividing people into those two categories—the sick and the well—and being angry with her mother for not being able to transition to the group of the well as she herself has. Yet at the play's end, as Lisa reads Ann's words about the neighborhood, Lisa begins to realize that just as the neighborhood strove to be a healthy, integrated one, it also continued to battle tensions. The neighborhood here serves as a metaphor for the self. Each

person embraces wellness but continues to battle symptoms of their own physical or mental sickness. Kron emphasizes that people should regard themselves in terms of wholeness, a state in which sickness and wellness and one's experiences with both states of being contribute to an integrated sense of self.

STYLE

Meta-theater

Well is a work of meta-theater, a theatrical production in which the characters refer to the play as a play and understand the work they are performing as a theatrical production. The actors step out of their roles and interact with Lisa as the playwright and with Ann as Lisa's mother, even though the character of Ann herself is played by an actor. Lisa addresses the audience directly, as does Ann. The actors discuss various scenes with Ann, who is perpetually interrupting scenes in progress. Ann's interruptions and the actors' breaking character are presented as if they are interfering with what the stage directions refer to as the "intended" play, or the play the character of Lisa is attempting to present. Yet all of these features are in fact part of the true play as presented by Lisa Kron, the playwright. Given that Kron played herself in the performances of *Well*, the lines between theater and reality become muddied. The interruptions are designed to seem genuine, and the criticisms of the play by the actors and Ann are depicted as spontaneous. At one point in the play, the ensemble actors—that is, the four actors who play the various roles in the montages—become frustrated with the way Lisa is portraying her mother and her past and with the way the play they have rehearsed is disintegrating. Near the end of the play, they "abandon" Lisa and the production. After the actors depart, Lisa attempts to regain control of the play. Underscoring the self-reflexive and self-aware nature of the play as a play, Lisa states, "Wow! This avant-garde meta-theatrical thing will just bite you in your ass!"

Experimental Structure

In addition to the meta-theatrical style employed by Kron in *Well*, the playwright also incorporates a structure that can be described as experimental in its nonlinear format. The play Kron presents does not convey a traditional narrative; that is, she is not telling a story in a chronological manner. Rather, Kron incorporates a series of brief scenes presented as flashbacks from the current time in which Lisa and Ann appear on stage. Ann's presence on stage is explained as though she has been plucked out of her current existence in her living room and deposited on stage, and Lisa is there to mediate between her mother and the play she intends to present. At the outset of the play, Lisa indicates that while experimental, the play—as the character of Lisa intends to present it—exhibits its own sense of structure. Reading from a notecard, Lisa describes the work as "a multicharacter theatrical exploration of issues of health and illness both in the individual and the community." Throughout the work, Lisa attempts to explain the format to her mother, describing her depiction of the neighborhood as a montage, or a series of images or scenes that work together to

create a composite whole. The scenes from the neighborhood, along with the Allergy Unit scenes, are presented in a disconnected manner, seemingly performed as they occur to Lisa, and with frequent interruptions from Ann. Although the scenes from the past are presented in a disjointed fashion, they are nevertheless intended to convey a meaning that is designed to gradually coalesce. As Lisa explains to the audience, "I had a plan, and if we had followed it, a pattern would have emerged. Didn't you assume a pattern was going to emerge? Yes. Because that's the way it works." In fact, patterns do emerge, particularly in the way Lisa repeatedly avoids telling the whole truth about her past. While these are not the patterns the character of Lisa intended to emerge, they reveal the intent of Kron, the playwright.

HISTORICAL CONTEXT

Neighborhood Racial Segregation and Integration

In *Well*, Kron shines a spotlight on her mother Ann's role as a community activist dedicated to maintaining a racially integrated neighborhood during the 1960s. This element of the play is rooted in Ann's real-life experience as a community organizer. In the play, the neighbors discuss the way pressures from both the local government and the real-estate industry contribute to segregated neighborhoods by either keeping blacks out of white neighborhoods or by scaring whites out of neighborhoods in which blacks have settled. As the neighbors discuss the closing of neighborhood schools, Lisa informs them, "That is how a slum is made. It's not that the people who live in the neighborhood aren't taking care of themselves. The city withdraws all the resources." As Michael T. Maly maintains in *Beyond Segregation: Multiracial and Multiethnic Neighborhoods in the United States*, Realtors colluded in racial segregation by selling to blacks in a predominantly white neighborhood, then instigated fear among the white residents that "the neighborhood was about to change." They then bought property "from the panicked whites at bargain basement prices" and proceeded to sell the properties "to middle-class blacks looking for a nice neighborhood at higher prices." Maly cites additional documentation and explains that "until the

In the play, Lisa's mother "heals" a diverse neighborhood. (© June Marie Sobrito | Shutterstock.com)

1970s Realtors were obligated to steer potential home seekers to neighborhoods whose residents shared their race or nationality." Furthermore, Maly asserts, "Federal policies institutionalized many of these discriminatory acts and exacerbated racial tensions and color lines in cities." Several pieces of legislation were passed in the 1960s and 1970s that were designed to prevent discrimination and segregation, including the Federal Fair Housing Act of 1968 and the Equal Credit Opportunity Act of 1974. While some neighborhoods remain racially segregated despite such legislation, other communities, Maly points out, "have organized and struggled to maintain a stable integrated racial composition." In fact, recent studies indicate that racial segregation in cities is declining. Sam Roberts reports in an article for the *New York Times* that a study based on census data finds that "the nation's cites are more racially integrated than at any time since 1910." The Manhattan

Institution study by Edward Glaeser and Jacob Vigdor states that "gentrification and immigration have made a dent in segregation. While these phenomena are clearly important in some areas, the rise of black suburbanization explains much more of the decline in segregation."

Chronic Fatigue Syndrome and Multiple Chemical Sensitivity

Kron attributes the symptoms she suffers in *Well* to allergies. Lisa notes that today, her mother's symptoms might be classified as chronic fatigue syndrome or fibromyalgia, which causes symptoms such as pain and fatigue. Ann additionally describes an array of chemical sensitivities suffered by many, which she also attributes to allergies, but which might now be classified as multiple chemical sensitivity. These syndromes and diagnoses are labels assigned to specific symptoms that cannot be attributed to any other causes. For this reason, they are sometimes not regarded as legitimate health concerns. Brant Wenegrat, in *Theater of Disorder: Patients, Doctors, and the Construction of Illness*, describes the diagnoses of chronic fatigue syndrome that arose during the 1980s. The mysterious disorder is characterized by fatigue "sufficiently severe to produce at least a 50 percent impairment in daily activities for at least six months." Viruses and immune system abnormalities have been cited as possible causes of the disorder. The symptoms of chronic fatigue syndrome in many ways mirror those of people who claim to suffer from multiple chemical sensitivity. Wenegrat explains, "Patients with multiple chemical sensitivity complain of diffuse symptoms that they attribute to exposure to common chemicals at levels far below those believed to have toxic effects." Among the most common symptoms is disabling fatigue. Wenegrat cites a study in which all of the chemical sensitivity patients studied had adverse reactions to such things as gas, smoke, and paint fumes, and more than half of the chronic fatigue patients also reported experiencing adverse effects. Wenegrat also discusses the way various symptoms in the 1950s were attributed to food and chemical allergies and says that, as these case reports increased, the label of multiple chemical sensitivity evolved. Allergies continue to be linked to chronic fatigue syndrome, depression, and headaches, as Rick Ansorge and Eric Metcalf point out in *Prevention*. The authors quote Dr. Leo Galland, director of the Foundation for Integrated Medicine, who points out for example, "Mold allergy is an important cause of fatigue and muscle aches. A significant proportion of people with chronic fatigue syndrome and fibromyalgia have mold sensitivity." Ansorge and Metcalf also cite studies that link allergens to irritability and mild depression and note that research has suggested that "pollen, food, and other allergens" may trigger headaches.

CRITICAL OVERVIEW

Well received positive reviews following its 2006 Broadway premiere. Ben Brantley of the *New York Times* characterizes the work as a "sparkling autobiographical play" and describes the production as "a deliberately self-conscious, calculatedly awkward exercise in recapturing the past." Brantley praises the way in which Kron

WHAT DO I READ NEXT?

- Two of Kron's plays, *2.5 Minute Ride* and *101 Most Humiliating Stories*, were published in the same volume in 2000. Both are autobiographical in nature and explore various aspects of Kron's family history.

- Joyce A. Baugh's *The Detroit School Busing Case: Milliken v. Bradley and the Controversy over Desegregation*, published in 2001, explores the issue of school desegregation in Kron's home state of Michigan.

- *Brave Smiles . . . Another Lesbian Tragedy* is a play written by the Five Lesbian Brothers, a theatrical group that includes Kron, along with Maureen Angelos, Babs Davy, Dominique Dibbell, and Peg Healey. The satirical farce examines clichés about gender identity. The play premiered in 1992 and was published in 2000.

- Elizabeth Wong, a Chinese American playwright, wrote *Kimchee and Chitlins* in 1990; it was produced in various locations and published in 1996. Like Kron, Wong presents themes rooted in tensions between races. Wong explores contemporary tensions among Korean Americans and African Americans in Brooklyn.

- Indian-born author Anjali Banerjee's young-adult novel *Maya Running*, published in 2005, centers around the Indian protagonist's attempts to fit into a new, predominantly white school after her family moves to Canada. Banerjee examines racial and cultural differences and the feelings of isolation they produce.

- Anne Lipscomb's memoir, *Poisoned by Pollution: An Unexpected Spiritual Journey*, published in 2009, traces the author's journey toward understanding the relationship between illness, chemical sensitivity, and fatigue.

"uses autobiography to point out the limitations of the artificial forms we naturally impose on memory." In *Contemporary American Drama*,

Annette J. Saddick states that Kron's play "brilliantly fuses autobiographical solo performance, memory play and traditional theatre to create a complex net of identifications and disrupt the boundaries between representation and reality." In a review for *New York Magazine*, Jeremy McCarter discusses the play's themes, maintaining that Kron "finds graceful ways to make wellness echo other issues, such as race." McCarter goes on to comment about the way the play's structure works with its themes, stating, "All the complicated apparatus seems, in the end, like a grand effort by Lisa to put off dealing with her mother." Like McCarter, Misha Berson of the *Seattle Times*, observes the complications in the play's structure, describing the work as "tricky," but "insightful." Yet the work's appeal diminished throughout the course of its run. Robert Simonson of *Playbill* maintains that the work "struggled to find an audience" and that attendance dropped notably toward the end of the play's Broadway run.

CRITICISM

Catherine Dominic

Dominic is a novelist and a freelance writer and editor. In the following essay, she examines the key role the character of Lori Jones plays in Well, *demonstrating the way Lori is used to signal the areas and instances in which Lisa purposefully avoids truthfulness.*

In *Well*, Kron uses a disjointed, avant-garde structure to examine her relationship with her mother, along with a variety of other themes, including sickness, wellness, wholeness, race relations, and community. Throughout the play, a minor character, one Lisa did not include in the "intended" play, repeatedly interrupts the action. This character, Lori, is a young girl from Lisa's past. She breaks into various scenes and teases Lisa mercilessly, much in the same way she did throughout Lisa's childhood. Lori receives almost no attention from the other characters, although Ann does scold her once. She is similarly glossed over in most critical assessments of the play, yet she plays an important role in the drama. Lori appears at instances in the play when Lisa is deliberately obfuscating. The more Lisa avoids revealing significant truths, the more persistent Lori becomes with her teasing. She is a key figure in determining

> LORI RECEIVES ALMOST NO ATTENTION FROM THE OTHER CHARACTERS, ALTHOUGH ANN DOES SCOLD HER ONCE. SHE IS SIMILARLY GLOSSED OVER IN MOST CRITICAL ASSESSMENTS OF THE PLAY, YET SHE PLAYS AN IMPORTANT ROLE IN THE DRAMA."

the facts that Ann repeatedly accuses Lisa of omitting from the play.

Lori makes her first appearance after the first neighborhood scene, in which the adult neighbors are discussing the establishment of neighborhood organization and questioning the changes such a group could possibly make in their community. As the scene ends, Ann criticizes Lisa's depiction of the nascent neighborhood association, telling Lisa that the scene "seemed awfully compressed." Lisa defends the scene despite Ann's insistence that the time period in question was filled with "an awful lot of complications." As Ann asks Lisa what else she remembers, Lori bursts onto the scene; the stage directions indicate that she is ten years old. She states accusingly to Lisa, "Ooh! You think you're so big," and then "stomps off." Ann remembers Lori as the girl who was mean to Lisa in school. Based on Ann's questions and concerns that she voices to Lisa about the neighborhood, it is clear that Lisa has glossed over some critical details in her exploration of the past. The audience is as yet unaware of what these details might be, or why Lisa has left them out. Still, Ann's reaction and Lori's unexpected presence both serve to indicate that Lisa's picture of the way the neighbors dealt with one another is too rosy.

Appearing again in one of the Allergy Unit scenes, Lori interrupts Lisa, who has just been subtly insulted by Joy. Joy has commented on the size of Lisa's arms. Lori suddenly appears, demanding that Lisa demonstrate the way she dances. Lisa insists that Lori is not a part of the play. Lori is unconcerned and states that she and her friends want to see Lisa dance. Lisa begins to narrate a memory in which she is nine years old, and the teacher has left the classroom. Someone has put on a record, and everyone knows the song except Lisa. This reminds Lisa of going to conventions for young Jewish people in which all the other girls come wearing the same trendy clothing. She remembers wondering, "How are these people communicating with each other??" Lisa's sense of disconnection from her peers is underscored in this memory and is intensified by Lori's repeated taunting. When Lisa refuses to dance, Lori departs, calling out to the audience, "See? What'd I tell you." Lori's appearance in the Allergy Unit scene highlights Lisa's sense of exclusion from other people in her adult life. In addition to being reminded of her painful youth when Joy comments about her weight, Lisa feels isolated in another the way: she distances herself from the other patients in the Allergy Unit. As is gradually revealed in the course of the play, Lisa does not *want* to identify with people she perceives to be *sick*. She wants to be *well*.

In a scene focused on the neighborhood, Lori appears again, just as Lisa is narrating the way her mother helped rescue Little Oscar from his home while Big Oscar was drunk. Lori teases Lisa about her hair and eventually corners her. Lisa insists to the audience that "the Association stabilized the neighborhood and by the way, it is still a stable racially integrated neighborhood today in 2006.... Okay, there might have been a little bit of tension between some of the kids. But the big picture is that the Neighborhood Association was working. The adults were getting along." When Ann disputes Lisa's claim about the adults, Lori departs. The stage directions indicate that Lori "*having proven her point*" proclaims, "HA!" before her departure. Both Ann's comment and Lori's presence make clear that Lisa again has attempted to depict the adults in the neighborhood as working together harmoniously and to diminish the conflicts between the children. As the play continues and as Lori's later presence will demonstrate, the "little bit of tension" among the children is actually quite intense.

Later in the play, Lisa's propensity to isolate herself from her peers is brought up again. Ann reminds Lisa, "It's true you had some tension with some of the black kids, but, honey, you didn't fit in particularly well with the white kids either. You were your own person." The conversation that ensues between Lisa and her mother, with the other actors chiming in, leads Lisa to relate the story of her Halloween costumes. She fervently believed in being "original and

creative," which led her to choose costumes very different from the princess costumes her friends were wearing. Lisa recalls how the incidents compelled her to ask herself, "What is wrong with me?!" Nevertheless, she insists that she did in fact have two friends. Like Lisa, the girls were "daughters of progressive whites," and they shared a love of Laura Ingalls Wilder. The girls decide to wear prairie dresses, inspired by their reading of Wilder's books, to school. Lisa remembers realizing as she got to school that she had made a horrible mistake. She does not have time to finish the story, or to let the audience know whether or not the other girls dressed up too, because she is interrupted again by Lori, who enters the scene laughing loudly at Lisa. Gathering herself to withstand the assault, Lisa proclaims to the audience, "I would like you to know that Lori Jones is not representative of my experience growing up in this neighborhood." Lori proceeds to emphasize Lisa's difference from the otherwise all-black student population at school as she makes fun of Lisa's Jewish last name. She then launches a series of insults, all while Lisa continues to insist that her childhood experiences were largely positive. Lisa expresses her fear that Lori is feeding into stereotypes and is not helping Lisa to make her point. Provoked by Lori's taunting, Lisa tries to fight back. The stage directions indicate, "*A lame girl-fight ensues in which Lisa falls and Lori tries to drag her offstage.*" Ann appears and scolds Lori, dragging her away from Lisa. Lori appears to be subdued, but before she leaves, she turns to the audience, and describes Lisa as a "stupid white girl" who "acts like she's scared of me so I give her something to be scared of."

Lisa has been attempting, throughout the play, to characterize her childhood as positive, to depict the neighborhood as a nurturing community. She has attempted to minimize the tensions that existed among the adults, much to her mother's disapproval, and has similarly downplayed the tensions between the children. Lori, however, refuses to let this version of the truth stand. She appears to remind Lisa, and the audience, that Lisa's childhood was painful and lonely. Although Ann has insisted that Lisa had trouble making friends with both white and black girls, Lori's comments suggest that despite the role Lisa's mother played in the community as an advocate for integration, Lisa had deep fears about not fitting in at her nearly all-black school. Lisa seems reluctant to address these fears because she is leery about depicting either her own discomfort or the attitudes of the black children as stemming from racial prejudice or fear. And yet, this fear, whether it was rooted in social or racial insecurity, or simply in the insecurity of youth, did exist, as Lori's comment—"stupid white girl acts like she's scared of me"—indicates.

Ann is frustrated with Lisa's reasoning for wanting Lori out of the play. Ann tells Lisa, "Kick Lori out of the play for acting like a crumb if you want, but not because she's not an appropriate 'representation.'" Ann goes on to emphasize that Lori "was just one little girl," not a representation of racial aggression or a symbol of racial disharmony. While Ann insists that Lori "didn't have that kind of power," it is clear that Lisa fears she might. Lori might have the power, by virtue of inclusion in Lisa's play, to convey a set of perceptions that Lisa does not wish to convey. The point remains unresolved as Lisa attempts to push forward, brushing off her mother's observations about Lori by saying, "That's not what my issue—that's not my issue."

Lori does not make another appearance in the play. She has served her purpose of pointing out that Lisa does in fact have some "issue" with her and with the way Lori's presence informs her depiction of her experience of growing up in the neighborhood. Ann explains, after Lori's departure, "Part of the point of growing up in an integrated neighborhood was that you didn't have to extrapolate from abstract impressions of black people, because you knew actual people." Ann stated earlier in the play, when discussing the elections for the neighborhood association, that "though there was divisiveness, it never fell along racial lines." Ann seems to believe firmly that the neighborhood, though not free from tensions and disagreements, was successfully integrated in that its inhabitants regarded each other as neighbors and worked together as such for a common good. She understands that, through the experience of living in an integrated community, people gain enough insight about each other as individuals to avoid having opinions that devolve into stereotypes. Lisa, however, seems to regard this as a slightly naïve perspective. She fears that to depict a black girl—Lori—taunting a white girl—herself—in her play may lead her audience to believe that the neighborhood integration Ann fought for

Lisa refers to her time in an environmental ecology clinic. *(© Paul Matthew Photography / Shutterstock.com)*

was fruitless because the white children and the black children were not getting along. They fought each other, and they feared each other.

Yet Ann's speech, originally given during a neighborhood association meeting and read by Lisa at the end of the play, gives evidence to the contrary. As Ann has written and Lisa reads, "This is what integration means. It means weaving into the whole even the parts that are uncomfortable or don't seem to fit. Even the parts that are complicated and painful. What is more worthy of our time and our love than this?" Ann's words and Lisa's repeating those words emphasize the shared understanding the Kron women have gained that integration and wholeness are not diminished by the presence of fighting, fear, and tension. Through the course of the play, Ann is shown to be not as naïve as Lisa has believed, and the neighborhood is revealed to be less idyllic than Lisa wanted to remember it and portray it. Lisa's own childhood is something she can at last come to terms with. Lori helps Lisa face her individual struggles and view them within the context of her own past as an integration of positive and negative experiences.

These experiences, as Lisa comes to appreciate, were separate from the neighborhood and her mother's work, even as they exist as part of a whole, a composite of the experiences of all the individuals within the community.

Source: Catherine Dominic, Critical Essay on *Well*, in *Drama for Students*, Gale, Cengage Learning, 2013.

Vanessa Lawrence

In the following review, Lawrence explains the uniqueness of Kron's approach to Mother-daughter issues in her play Well.

Mother-daughter issues have been fodder for a veritable library of self-help books. But few people have tried the approach of playwright-actress Lisa Kron and put those conflicts on stage—along with mom herself.

In her critically acclaimed play *Well*, opening this week at the Longacre Theatre after a sold-out run at the Public Theatre two years ago, Kron takes audiences on a dramatic and hilarious journey exploring ideas on race, mental and physical illness and, of course, Mommie Dearest. Posing as a fictitious version of herself, Kron, along with a supporting chorus of actors, narrates the autobiographical tale of trying to put on a play about her memories of growing up in a black neighborhood in Michigan, time spent in the allergy unit of a hospital and her mother Ann's chronic illness. Throughout, actress Jayne Houdyshell sits on stage in an armchair as Kron's mother, interrupting her storytelling attempts. Actors fall out of character, interacting with Houdyshell; scenes fall apart, and Kron loses her cool as general chaos ensues, much to the audience's amusement.

Like any fruitful—or frustrating—relationship, *Well* has been a work in progress since Kron began writing the piece six years ago. And so has, naturally, the actress's career. Raised in Lansing, Mich., Kron studied theater at Kalamazoo College and toured with the National Repertory Theatre for a season before moving to New York in 1984.

"I was pretty hapless for a long time," she says. "I sort of found my way by accident to the East Village into the performance art scene." There, she clocked many hours telling and improvising anecdotal stories on stage, working at the theater collective at the Wild Caf and going on with a group to found the company the Five Lesbian Brothers. Kron began writing

plays, and her solo theater career was born (though she still performs with the Five Lesbian Brothers).

After writing and performing in *2.5 Minute Ride*, about her Holocaust survivor father and her brother's marriage, Kron started work on *Well*, not without some anxiety on her mother's part.

"In the creation of the play, she was very nervous, in the way that the character of her is on stage, and that what I was saying was I got better and so she should be able to get better," explains Kron, referring to her stint in the allergy ward. Now, many years and multiple viewings later, mom is a big fan, though she offers her occasional criticism. For example, an earlier version of the play had her collecting thimbles.

"My mother was, like, 'I have never had a thimble collection—I never would collect thimbles. I think that's a stupid collection,'" laughs Kron, who obligingly changed it to candle snuffers, the one thing her mother admits to collecting. "The director and dramaturge were kind of horrified, because it seemed wordy, but I said, 'Listen—I'm gonna give that one to my mom.'"

Navigating the factual details was one of the many challenges Kron incurred in structuring the story. But one shouldn't mistake the play disintegrating on stage for Kron's actual, much lengthier struggles in crafting it.

"I think the problem with writing a play about how hard it is to do a play is that I certainly have seen plays like that and thought, 'Well, why don't you figure out how to make your play work, and then I'll sit here and pay some money and spend my time watching it!'" she says. "So I don't think that the play is about the real difficulty we had writing it. It uses an imagined difficulty to make a form that is reflective of the content."

If the end result has landed her on a Broadway stage for an open-ended run, no one is more surprised than Kron herself. "It's certainly not what anybody pictured, ever!" she laughs. "You know, it's like, how will I get to Broadway? I'm going to become a lesbian performance artist and write these really weird plays. That'll work!"

Source: Vanessa Lawrence, "*Well* Deserved," in *WWD*, March 28, 2006, p. 4.

Leonard Jacobs

In the following review, Jacobs praises the play, but worries that Broadway audiences won't understand the themes of Well.

One of the most wonderful moments in *Well*, Lisa Kron's emotionally fulfilling meta-theatrical triple play—about how to be physically healthy within yourself, how to be emotionally healthy with your mother, and how these intertwine comes when you wonder if Broadway audiences, used to far blander fare, will get what the playwright and her gifted 31-year-old director, Leigh Silverman, are doing. I hope so. The play, which ran to acclaim at the Public Theater in spring 2004, has only grown more enamoring and affecting over time. Well should be prescribed to everyone.

Dressed in costume designer Miranda Hoffman's chic black pantsuit, Kron announces that the play is a "theatrical exploration of issues of health and illness both in an individual and a community." The brilliant Jayne Houdyshell plays Ann Kron, her mother, who is on stage with her; the audience is acknowledged, too. Ann is chronically ill—in a pitch-perfect flat Midwestern accent, she blames it on "the allergies"—and she's always been sickly, it seems, even during an amazing moment in Lisa's youth when her mother led the fight to racially integrate their Lansing, Mich., neighborhood. Lisa similarly suffered in college, but after a long-term visit to an allergy clinic, she got better. Yet how could that have happened when her mother stayed the same?

Ann Kron's plight isn't far-fetched. For years, the mother of a dear friend of mine was housebound due to allergies; I remember seeing the same clippings boxes pulled from drawers and shelves that Ann accesses on Tony Walton's well-designed (pardon the pun) set. The point here, however, isn't neuroscience. It's how Lisa Kron, working off personal memory and with gut-busting honesty, theatrically reimagines that hard-boiled crucible: the mother-daughter dynamic.

In the play that Kron has "written," she aids herself by presenting childhood flashbacks (in which she plays herself), scenes from her mother's grass-roots efforts, and still other scenes from the allergy clinic. Actors John Hoffman, Saidah Arrika Ekulona, Daniel Breaker, and Christina Kirk play all the other roles, including the actors in the "play." Kirk is a hoot as Joy, an

expressionless sad sack who was Lisa's woebegone roommate at the clinic. Ekulona epitomizes everyone's worst nightmare as a 9-year-old bully who tormented Lisa as a girl.

Except the bully isn't, as a frightened Lisa immediately notes, in her play. Indeed, there have been quite a few cracks in what the actor-playwright has tried to pass off as a fine-as-clockwork dramaturgical construct. Her mother's endless interruptions to fix inaccuracies in Lisa's flashbacks or to offer the audience drinks, for example, are already impeding the flow of the "exploration." The other actors' mounting fascination with Ann, in addition to telling Lisa they don't understand what she's doing, only adds insult to injury. All hell breaks loose: An upstage flat collapses, onstage lights are fooled with, and a set piece seems to be missing. Lisa, in a desperate moment, tries to haul it on stage and restore order.

But there is order—just not the order the actor-playwright has tried to impose on what she cannot understand. It is the order that comes from accepting how things are, not how they ought to be. What's so great about *Well*—aside from how the story of Lansing's racial integration is married with personal memoir—is its dramaturgical corollary: a clear belief that walls shouldn't exist between action and audience. And that is why I wonder whether Broadway theatregoers will understand what a gift *Well* is. There are a few moments when the play seems lost, unformed, even nebulous. But just because Lisa Kron is playing herself as a woman who may not know where her exploration will lead doesn't mean that Lisa Kron, the actor-playwright, doesn't know what she's doing. This is postmodern Pirandello, polished with sure-handed craftsmanship. Broadway should welcome such talent within its fold....

Source: Leonard Jacobs, "*Well* at the Longacre Theatre," in *Back Stage East*, Vol. 47, No. 14, April 6, 2006, p. 10.

Gerard Raymond

In the following review, Raymond analyzes the performance of Jayne Houdyshell in her Broadway debut as Lisa Kron's mother in Well.

"It's really nice to think that one can be a new kid on the block at the age of 52," says Jayne Houdyshell. Currently appearing as the dynamic but chronically ill mother in Lisa Kron's autobiographical play *Well*, she chuckles over the

> **THEN THERE IS THE COMPLICATED, CONTRA-DICTORY PERSONALITY OF ANN, THE CHRONICALLY AILING WOMAN WHO ATTEMPTED TO HEAL AN ENTIRE COMMUNITY."**

circumstances of her breakout role—a triumphant Broadway debut.

In the critically acclaimed metatheatrical comedy, Houdyshell plays the playwright's mother, Ann Kron, who spends most of the play lying inert in a La-Z-Boy recliner, felled by what she calls "allergies." In the 1960s and '70s, however, Ann Kron was the real-life driving force behind the racial integration of her Lansing, Mich., neighborhood. Her daughter, Lisa Kron, who also stars in the play, has put the character of her mother onstage to advance her own self-serving theories about wellness in individuals and society. But by the end of the evening—barely moving from her chair—Ann has effectively overturned her daughter's carefully planned agenda, winning the hearts of the audience in the process. "It's the most generous thing imaginable, what Lisa has written: She allows her own mother to hijack her own play," Houdyshell marvels. "What an astounding way to come to Broadway."

Houdyshell has been hooked on theatre since she was 10 years old, growing up in Topeka, Kan. "My principal exposure to the theatre was listening to cast albums of Broadway musicals," she recalls. "I'd listen to them over and over and drove my folks nuts. I'd gaze at the pictures on the album covers and create the whole scenario in my head, fleshing out the scenes, guessing from the lyrics." In her early teens, she joined a group of precocious older adolescents and college students who produced, directed, and acted in plays for other teens. "There were a lot of bright people there, and I can remember being introduced to Brecht and seeing Peter Brook's [production of] *Marat/Sade* at the age of 14. I can't tell you I necessarily understood a lot of it, but I knew it was great theatre," she says. Her next big influence was a high school teacher, an Anglophile who

introduced her to the great British acting tradition through films and touring shows. Seeing the formidable Dame Judith Anderson, at age 73, play the title role in *Hamlet* on tour in 1971 made an impression on Houdyshell.

"I developed this deep respect for what the British were doing in terms of training," Houdyshell says. "The acting school curriculum was very appealing because of the particular emphasis on technique, text, period work, and the classics." Spurred on by the same Anglophile teacher, she enrolled in an intensive conservatory program at Oakland University in Rochester, Mich.: the now-defunct Academy of Dramatic Art, whose faculty came from London's Royal Academy of Dramatic Art. "I got some really spectacular training there," she recalls. "It instilled an awesome work ethic that has kept me in good stead for a long time in the theatre, and it also instilled in me a hunger to play a broad range of roles. I wanted to work nonstop and to do big parts, and it seemed to me that the best place to do that was in regional theatre."

In theatres mostly in the Midwest and Northeast, Houdyshell proceeded to build an impressive resume, pursuing major regional-theatre roles even after moving to New York in 1980. "I traveled between nine and 11 months out of the year, going from job to job for about 20 years until I finally burned out on it," she says. The payoff came in the roles she played (Martha in *Who's Afraid of Virginia Woolf?*, Serafina in *The Rose Tattoo*, Lady Bracknell in *The Importance of Being Earnest*, Linda Loman in *Death of a Salesman*, Big Mama in *Cat on a Hot Tin Roof*) and where she played them (Peterborough Players, Missouri Rep, the Wilma Theatre, Delaware Theatre Company, Asolo Theatre Festival, the Alabama Shakespeare Festival, Yale Repertory Theatre).

"When you chew on beautiful roles—" Houdyshell starts to say. "I don't want to go on about that or I'll sound pompous and I don't mean to be." What she doesn't spell out is that this rich experience is what prepared her for her remarkable breakout role. By this stage of her career, she was also craving something different: "I really hadn't had the opportunity when I hit my mid-40s to know what it was like to originate a role or to be around a playwright who was developing work." That ambition was realized in 2002 with *Well.*

GETTING *WELL*

Playwright-performer Lisa Kron, at the time best known for her solo performance pieces (*2.5 Minute Ride, 101 Humiliating Stories*) and her collective work with the Five Lesbian Brothers, was looking for someone to play her mother in a weeklong workshop of a new play at Baltimore's Center Stage. On a recommendation, Kron caught a performance of Charles L. Mee's *True Love* at the Zipper Theatre in New York, in which Houdyshell was playing a woman addicted to sex. The role was the polar opposite of Ann Kron, but Houdyshell still got the job. *Well* had yet to evolve into the playfully Pirandellian, emotionally complex theatrical experience it is today, but "even at that very early stage, [Ann Kron] just leapt off the page and I was able to intuit who she was," she recalls. From then on, the role was hers.

"Everything about the way I approached this role and worked on it is totally out of the norm—and that made perfect sense to me because this whole play is so out of the box," she says. "Because of the extraordinary circumstance of playing a woman's mother onstage, opposite the woman herself, who also happens to be the playwright, it was clear to me that I didn't want to try to imitate Ann Kron.

"Once I felt really deep under the skin of the role and very comfortable, then I felt it was perfectly natural to meet Ann," she continues. "I could get to know her on her own terms, just two women meeting." The actor and the playwright's mother exchanged emails and talked on the phone but didn't meet in person until 2004, when Ann attended a performance of *Well* during its premiere Off-Broadway run at the Public Theater. After the show, Houdyshell says, Ann Kron exclaimed, "Oh, my goodness, Jayne. I watched you there up onstage and thought 'Even I want to be Ann Kron!'" The two have since become great friends, and the actor has visited Ann at her home in Lansing. Moreover, Houdyshell says she is thrilled when after a performance of *Well*, she is accosted by audience members who seem to believe she's really Lisa Kron's mother: "That's such a compliment to me as an actor, but also the greatest compliment because Ann is a very cool person. I have so much admiration for her ethics, her politics, her integrity, and her humanity."

The role, Houdyshell says, is also one of the hardest she's ever tackled. "Many people say,

'Wow, you've got it easy,' meaning I spend a great deal of time onstage in the La-Z-Boy. But it's a very odd challenge to try to project when you're in a jackknife position. By the end of the show, I'm really worn out." For half an hour before the play even begins, Houdyshell pretends to be asleep in her chair—in full view of the incoming audience. "That was my bright idea way back when we were doing readings and workshops," she says, laughing ruefully. "I never dreamed for a moment we would do a long run of the play." It serves to establish that Ann has spent a significant part of her life unwell and chairbound, but, Houdyshell reveals, there are nights when "I feel like I'm going to jump out of my skin!" The best nights are when she listens to the rise and fall of the audience chatter and can "go into some Zen-like zone and feel totally refreshed and alert when the play starts." Her fear is that one night she may indeed drift off to sleep and wake up to find Lisa standing there and talking to her. "Actors do so many strange things; this is just one of those odd jobs that I do."

Then there is the complicated, contradictory personality of Ann, the chronically ailing woman who attempted to heal an entire community. "There is this deep power in her that feels archetypal and universal, as big as Medea," Houdyshell says. "When you have to play someone who has to be so real, but at the same time you have to project to a 1,200-seat house, every muscle in my body is being worked. I feel myself using my training in the classics and all that vocal and text work that I had as a student in acting school."

In the two years between the Off-Broadway production of *Well* and its current Broadway run, Houdyshell continued to pursue roles in new works. In 2005 she won two prestigious regional theatre prizes: a Barrymore Award for her supporting role as a neurotic woman obsessed with tidiness in Sarah Ruhl's *The Clean House* at Philadelphia's Wilma Theatre, and a Joseph Jefferson Award for playing a Midwestern mother very different from Ann Kron in Bruce Norris' *The Pain and the Itch* at Chicago's Steppenwolf Theatre Company.

"I've never thought in terms of the smart career move. I have always gone from job to job," Houdyshell says. "It's a gift and I don't know where that comes from, because this is a business that is all about insecurity. I've been very fortunate to trust that the next job will always be there." So what comes next for an actor who is now the toast of Broadway? Houdyshell laughs. "Another great role in a great play."

Source: Gerard Raymond, "Striking the Mother Lode: Jayne Houdyshell," in *Back Stage West*, Vol. 13, No. 16, April 20, 2006, p. 9.

SOURCES

Ansorge, Rick, Eric Metcalf, et al., "Tired? Depressed? It May be Hidden Allergies," MSNBC website, http://www.msnbc.msn.com/id/35932711/ns/health-allergies_and_asthma/t/tired-depressed-it-may-be-hidden-allergies/#.UFNig-3leDk (accessed September 14, 2012).

Berson, Misha, "Lisa Kron's *Well* a Story of Mothers and Daughters, Opens at Repertory Actors Theatre," in *Seattle Times*, http://seattletimes.com/html/thearts/2004393546_zart05well.html (accessed September 14, 2012).

"Biography," Lisa Kron website, http://www.lisakron.com/bio.html (accessed September 14, 2012).

Brantley, Ben, "Lisa Kron's *Well* Opens on Broadway, with Mom Keeping Watch," in *New York Times*, March 31, 2006, http://theater2.nytimes.com/2006/03/31/theater/reviews/31well.html?pagewanted=all (accessed September 14, 2012).

Glaeser, Edward, and Jacob Vigdor, "The End of the Segregated Century: Racial Separation in America's Neighborhoods, 1890–2010," in *Civic Report*, Manhattan Institute for Policy Research website, No. 66, January 2012, http://www.manhattan-institute.org/html/cr_66.htm (accessed September 14, 2012).

"Jeanine Tesori and Lisa Kron's *Fun Home* to Have Public Theatre Lab, 10/17–11/4," Broadway World website, http://broadwayworld.com/article/Jeanine-Tesori-and-Lisa-Krons-FUN-HOME-to-Have-Public-Theater-Lab-1017-114-20120911 (accessed September 14, 2012).

Kron, Lisa, *Well*, Theatre Communications Group, 2006.

Maly, Michael T., "Racial and Ethnic Segregation and Integration in Urban America," in *Beyond Segregation: Multiracial and Multiethnic Neighborhoods in the United States*, Temple University Press, 2005, pp. 8–28.

McCarter, Jeremy, "Heal Thyself," in *New York Magazine*, April 9, 2006, http://nymag.com/arts/theater/reviews/16638/ (accessed September 14, 2012).

"The Playwright, Lisa Kron," in *Inside Out*, The Denver Center for the Performing Arts website, November–December 2009, pp. 3–4, http://www.denvercenter.org/Libraries/Study_Guides/Well.sflb.ashx (accessed September 14, 2012).

Roberts, Sam, "Segregation Curtailed in U. S. Cities, Study Finds," in *New York Times*, January 30, 2012, http://www.nytimes.com/2012/01/31/us/Segregation-Curtailed-in-US-Cities-Study-Finds.html?pagewanted=all (accessed September 14, 2012).

Saddik, Annette J., Conclusion to *Contemporary American Drama*, Edinburgh University Press, 2007, pp. 207–12.

Simonson, Robert, "*Well* Runs Dry: Lisa Kron Play to Close on Broadway May 14," in *Playbill*, http://www.playbill.com/news/article/99566-Well-Runs-Dry-Lisa-Kron-Play-to-Close-on-Broadway-May-14 (accessed September 14, 2012).

Wenegrat, Brant, "Hysteria and Hysteria-like Disorders," in *Theater of Disorder: Patients, Doctors, and the Construction of Illness*, Oxford University Press, 2001, pp. 81–136.

FURTHER READING

Frazier, John W., and Florence M. Margai, eds., *Multicultural Geographies: The Changing Racial/Ethnic Patterns of the United States*, Global Academic Publishing, 2010.

Frazier and Margai collect a series of essays on the history of racial and ethnic trends in the United States. The essays focus on African American, Asian American, and Latino populations and geographical trends.

Lane, Eric, and Nina Shengold, eds., *Talk to Me: Monologue Plays*, Vintage, 2004.

The editors collect plays composed as monologues and written by a number of different authors, including Kron. The works include full-length monologue plays along with shorter pieces and one-act plays.

Pall, Martin L., *Explaining 'Unexplained Illnesses': Disease Paradigm for Chronic Fatigue Syndrome, Multiple Chemical Sensitivity, Fibromyalgia, Post-Traumatic Stress Disorder, and Gulf War Syndrome*, Harrington Park Press, 2007.

Pall examines the symptoms and triggers of these mysterious disorders, suggests relationships among them, and asserts that an understanding of biochemical cycles can aid in understanding and treating the disorders.

Sugrue, Thomas J., *The Origins of the Urban Crisis: Race and Inequality in Postwar Detroit*, Princeton University Press, 1996.

Sugrue analyzes the transformation that Detroit underwent in the 1950s and 1960s, tracing the racial tensions and the city's path toward creating an increasingly segregated community.

Weisman, Wendy, and Lisa Kron, "The Importance of Being Lisa Kron: In *Well*, She Plays Herself Writing a

Play about Herself. Will Broadway Get It?," in *American Theatre*, March 2006, Vol. 23, No. 3, p. 34.

Weisman interviews Kron, discussing the structure, themes, and production of *Well*.

SUGGESTED SEARCH TERMS

Lisa Kron AND Well

Lisa Kron AND Ann Kron

Lisa Kron AND autobiography

Lisa Kron AND Michigan

Lisa Kron AND experimental theatre

Lisa Kron AND meta-theatre

Lisa Kron AND race relations

Lisa Kron AND segregation

Lisa Kron AND activism

Lisa Kron AND feminism

Glossary of Literary Terms

A

Abstract: Used as a noun, the term refers to a short summary or outline of a longer work. As an adjective applied to writing or literary works, abstract refers to words or phrases that name things not knowable through the five senses. Examples of abstracts include the *Cliffs Notes* summaries of major literary works. Examples of abstract terms or concepts include "idea," "guilt" "honesty," and "loyalty."

Absurd, Theater of the: See *Theater of the Absurd*

Absurdism: See *Theater of the Absurd*

Act: A major section of a play. Acts are divided into varying numbers of shorter scenes. From ancient times to the nineteenth century plays were generally constructed of five acts, but modern works typically consist of one, two, or three acts. Examples of five-act plays include the works of Sophocles and Shakespeare, while the plays of Arthur Miller commonly have a three-act structure.

Acto: A one-act Chicano theater piece developed out of collective improvisation. *Actos* were performed by members of Luis Valdez's Teatro Campesino in California during the mid-1960s.

Aestheticism: A literary and artistic movement of the nineteenth century. Followers of the movement believed that art should not be mixed with social, political, or moral teaching. The statement "art for art's sake" is a good summary of aestheticism. The movement had its roots in France, but it gained widespread importance in England in the last half of the nineteenth century, where it helped change the Victorian practice of including moral lessons in literature. Oscar Wilde is one of the best-known "aesthetes" of the late nineteenth century.

Age of Johnson: The period in English literature between 1750 and 1798, named after the most prominent literary figure of the age, Samuel Johnson. Works written during this time are noted for their emphasis on "sensibility," or emotional quality. These works formed a transition between the rational works of the Age of Reason, or Neoclassical period, and the emphasis on individual feelings and responses of the Romantic period. Significant writers during the Age of Johnson included the novelists Ann Radcliffe and Henry Mackenzie, dramatists Richard Sheridan and Oliver Goldsmith, and poets William Collins and Thomas Gray. Also known as Age of Sensibility

Age of Reason: See *Neoclassicism*

Age of Sensibility: See *Age of Johnson*

Alexandrine Meter: See *Meter*

Allegory: A narrative technique in which characters representing things or abstract ideas are used to convey a message or teach a lesson. Allegory is typically used to teach moral, ethical, or religious lessons but is sometimes used for satiric or political purposes. Examples of allegorical works include Edmund Spenser's *The Faerie Queene* and John Bunyan's *The Pilgrim's Progress.*

Allusion: A reference to a familiar literary or historical person or event, used to make an idea more easily understood. For example, describing someone as a "Romeo" makes an allusion to William Shakespeare's famous young lover in *Romeo and Juliet.*

Amerind Literature: The writing and oral traditions of Native Americans. Native American literature was originally passed on by word of mouth, so it consisted largely of stories and events that were easily memorized. Amerind prose is often rhythmic like poetry because it was recited to the beat of a ceremonial drum. Examples of Amerind literature include the autobiographical *Black Elk Speaks,* the works of N. Scott Momaday, James Welch, and Craig Lee Strete, and the poetry of Luci Tapahonso.

Analogy: A comparison of two things made to explain something unfamiliar through its similarities to something familiar, or to prove one point based on the acceptedness of another. Similes and metaphors are types of analogies. Analogies often take the form of an extended simile, as in William Blake's aphorism: "As the caterpillar chooses the fairest leaves to lay her eggs on, so the priest lays his curse on the fairest joys."

Angry Young Men: A group of British writers of the 1950s whose work expressed bitterness and disillusionment with society. Common to their work is an anti-hero who rebels against a corrupt social order and strives for personal integrity. The term has been used to describe Kingsley Amis, John Osborne, Colin Wilson, John Wain, and others.

Antagonist: The major character in a narrative or drama who works against the hero or protagonist. An example of an evil antagonist is Richard Lovelace in Samuel Richardson's *Clarissa,* while a virtuous antagonist is Macduff in William Shakespeare's *Macbeth.*

Anthropomorphism: The presentation of animals or objects in human shape or with human characteristics. The term is derived from the Greek word for "human form." The fables of Aesop, the animated films of Walt Disney,

and Richard Adams's *Watership Down* feature anthropomorphic characters.

Anti-hero: A central character in a work of literature who lacks traditional heroic qualities such as courage, physical prowess, and fortitude. Anti-heros typically distrust conventional values and are unable to commit themselves to any ideals. They generally feel helpless in a world over which they have no control. Anti-heroes usually accept, and often celebrate, their positions as social outcasts. A well-known anti-hero is Yossarian in Joseph Heller's novel *Catch-22.*

Antimasque: See *Masque*

Antithesis: The antithesis of something is its direct opposite. In literature, the use of antithesis as a figure of speech results in two statements that show a contrast through the balancing of two opposite ideas. Technically, it is the second portion of the statement that is defined as the "antithesis"; the first portion is the "thesis." An example of antithesis is found in the following portion of Abraham Lincoln's "Gettysburg Address"; notice the opposition between the verbs "remember" and "forget" and the phrases "what we say" and "what they did": "The world will little note nor long remember what we say here, but it can never forget what they did here."

Apocrypha: Writings tentatively attributed to an author but not proven or universally accepted to be their works. The term was originally applied to certain books of the Bible that were not considered inspired and so were not included in the "sacred canon." Geoffrey Chaucer, William Shakespeare, Thomas Kyd, Thomas Middleton, and John Marston all have apocrypha. Apocryphal books of the Bible include the Old Testament's Book of Enoch and New Testament's Gospel of Peter.

Apollonian and Dionysian: The two impulses believed to guide authors of dramatic tragedy. The Apollonian impulse is named after Apollo, the Greek god of light and beauty and the symbol of intellectual order. The Dionysian impulse is named after Dionysus, the Greek god of wine and the symbol of the unrestrained forces of nature. The Apollonian impulse is to create a rational, harmonious world, while the Dionysian is to express the irrational forces of personality. Friedrich Nietzche uses these terms in *The Birth of Tragedy* to designate contrasting elements in Greek tragedy.

Apostrophe: A statement, question, or request addressed to an inanimate object or concept or to a nonexistent or absent person. Requests for inspiration from the muses in poetry are examples of apostrophe, as is Marc Antony's address to Caesar's corpse in William Shakespeare's *Julius Caesar*: "O, pardon me, thou bleeding piece of earth, That I am meek and gentle with these butchers!... Woe to the hand that shed this costly blood!..."

Archetype: The word archetype is commonly used to describe an original pattern or model from which all other things of the same kind are made. This term was introduced to literary criticism from the psychology of Carl Jung. It expresses Jung's theory that behind every person's "unconscious," or repressed memories of the past, lies the "collective unconscious" of the human race: memories of the countless typical experiences of our ancestors. These memories are said to prompt illogical associations that trigger powerful emotions in the reader. Often, the emotional process is primitive, even primordial. Archetypes are the literary images that grow out of the "collective unconscious." They appear in literature as incidents and plots that repeat basic patterns of life. They may also appear as stereotyped characters. Examples of literary archetypes include themes such as birth and death and characters such as the Earth Mother.

Argument: The argument of a work is the author's subject matter or principal idea. Examples of defined "argument" portions of works include John Milton's *Arguments* to each of the books of *Paradise Lost* and the "Argument" to Robert Herrick's *Hesperides*.

Aristotelian Criticism: Specifically, the method of evaluating and analyzing tragedy formulated by the Greek philosopher Aristotle in his *Poetics*. More generally, the term indicates any form of criticism that follows Aristotle's views. Aristotelian criticism focuses on the form and logical structure of a work, apart from its historical or social context, in contrast to "Platonic Criticism," which stresses the usefulness of art. Adherents of New Criticism including John Crowe Ransom and Cleanth Brooks utilize and value the basic ideas of Aristotelian criticism for textual analysis.

Art for Art's Sake: See *Aestheticism*

Aside: A comment made by a stage performer that is intended to be heard by the audience but supposedly not by other characters. Eugene O'Neill's *Strange Interlude* is an extended use of the aside in modern theater.

Audience: The people for whom a piece of literature is written. Authors usually write with a certain audience in mind, for example, children, members of a religious or ethnic group, or colleagues in a professional field. The term "audience" also applies to the people who gather to see or hear any performance, including plays, poetry readings, speeches, and concerts. Jane Austen's parody of the gothic novel, *Northanger Abbey,* was originally intended for (and also pokes fun at) an audience of young and avid female gothic novel readers.

Avant-garde: A French term meaning "vanguard." It is used in literary criticism to describe new writing that rejects traditional approaches to literature in favor of innovations in style or content. Twentieth-century examples of the literary *avant-garde* include the Black Mountain School of poets, the Bloomsbury Group, and the Beat Movement.

B

Ballad: A short poem that tells a simple story and has a repeated refrain. Ballads were originally intended to be sung. Early ballads, known as folk ballads, were passed down through generations, so their authors are often unknown. Later ballads composed by known authors are called literary ballads. An example of an anonymous folk ballad is "Edward," which dates from the Middle Ages. Samuel Taylor Coleridge's "The Rime of the Ancient Mariner" and John Keats's "La Belle Dame sans Merci" are examples of literary ballads.

Baroque: A term used in literary criticism to describe literature that is complex or ornate in style or diction. Baroque works typically express tension, anxiety, and violent emotion. The term "Baroque Age" designates a period in Western European literature beginning in the late sixteenth century and ending about one hundred years later. Works of this period often mirror the qualities of works more generally associated with the label "baroque" and sometimes feature elaborate conceits. Examples of Baroque works include

John Lyly's *Euphues: The Anatomy of Wit,* Luis de Gongora's *Soledads,* and William Shakespeare's *As You Like It.*

Baroque Age: See *Baroque*

Baroque Period: See *Baroque*

Beat Generation: See *Beat Movement*

Beat Movement: A period featuring a group of American poets and novelists of the 1950s and 1960s—including Jack Kerouac, Allen Ginsberg, Gregory Corso, William S. Burroughs, and Lawrence Ferlinghetti—who rejected established social and literary values. Using such techniques as stream of consciousness writing and jazz-influenced free verse and focusing on unusual or abnormal states of mind—generated by religious ecstasy or the use of drugs—the Beat writers aimed to create works that were unconventional in both form and subject matter. Kerouac's *On the Road* is perhaps the best-known example of a Beat Generation novel, and Ginsberg's *Howl* is a famous collection of Beat poetry.

Black Aesthetic Movement: A period of artistic and literary development among African Americans in the 1960s and early 1970s. This was the first major African-American artistic movement since the Harlem Renaissance and was closely paralleled by the civil rights and black power movements. The black aesthetic writers attempted to produce works of art that would be meaningful to the black masses. Key figures in black aesthetics included one of its founders, poet and playwright Amiri Baraka, formerly known as LeRoi Jones; poet and essayist Haki R. Madhubuti, formerly Don L. Lee; poet and playwright Sonia Sanchez; and dramatist Ed Bullins. Works representative of the Black Aesthetic Movement include Amiri Baraka's play *Dutchman,* a 1964 Obie award-winner; *Black Fire: An Anthology of Afro-American Writing,* edited by Baraka and playwright Larry Neal and published in 1968; and Sonia Sanchez's poetry collection *We a BaddDDD People,* published in 1970. Also known as Black Arts Movement.

Black Arts Movement: See *Black Aesthetic Movement*

Black Comedy: See *Black Humor*

Black Humor: Writing that places grotesque elements side by side with humorous ones in an attempt to shock the reader, forcing him or her

to laugh at the horrifying reality of a disordered world. Joseph Heller's novel *Catch-22* is considered a superb example of the use of black humor. Other well-known authors who use black humor include Kurt Vonnegut, Edward Albee, Eugene Ionesco, and Harold Pinter. Also known as Black Comedy.

Blank Verse: Loosely, any unrhymed poetry, but more generally, unrhymed iambic pentameter verse (composed of lines of five two-syllable feet with the first syllable accented, the second unaccented). Blank verse has been used by poets since the Renaissance for its flexibility and its graceful, dignified tone. John Milton's *Paradise Lost* is in blank verse, as are most of William Shakespeare's plays.

Bloomsbury Group: A group of English writers, artists, and intellectuals who held informal artistic and philosophical discussions in Bloomsbury, a district of London, from around 1907 to the early 1930s. The Bloomsbury Group held no uniform philosophical beliefs but did commonly express an aversion to moral prudery and a desire for greater social tolerance. At various times the circle included Virginia Woolf, E. M. Forster, Clive Bell, Lytton Strachey, and John Maynard Keynes.

Bon Mot: A French term meaning "good word." A *bon mot* is a witty remark or clever observation. Charles Lamb and Oscar Wilde are celebrated for their witty *bon mots.* Two examples by Oscar Wilde stand out: (1) "All women become their mothers. That is their tragedy. No man does. That's his." (2) "A man cannot be too careful in the choice of his enemies."

Breath Verse: See *Projective Verse*

Burlesque: Any literary work that uses exaggeration to make its subject appear ridiculous, either by treating a trivial subject with profound seriousness or by treating a dignified subject frivolously. The word "burlesque" may also be used as an adjective, as in "burlesque show," to mean "striptease act." Examples of literary burlesque include the comedies of Aristophanes, Miguel de Cervantes's *Don Quixote,* Samuel Butler's poem "Hudibras," and John Gay's play *The Beggar's Opera.*

C

Cadence: The natural rhythm of language caused by the alternation of accented and unaccented syllables. Much modern poetry—notably free verse—deliberately manipulates cadence to create complex rhythmic effects. James Macpherson's "Ossian poems" are richly cadenced, as is the poetry of the Symbolists, Walt Whitman, and Amy Lowell.

Caesura: A pause in a line of poetry, usually occurring near the middle. It typically corresponds to a break in the natural rhythm or sense of the line but is sometimes shifted to create special meanings or rhythmic effects. The opening line of Edgar Allan Poe's "The Raven" contains a caesura following "dreary": "Once upon a midnight dreary, while I pondered weak and weary...."

Canzone: A short Italian or Provencal lyric poem, commonly about love and often set to music. The *canzone* has no set form but typically contains five or six stanzas made up of seven to twenty lines of eleven syllables each. A shorter, five- to ten-line "envoy," or concluding stanza, completes the poem. Masters of the *canzone* form include Petrarch, Dante Alighieri, Torquato Tasso, and Guido Cavalcanti.

Carpe Diem: A Latin term meaning "seize the day." This is a traditional theme of poetry, especially lyrics. A *carpe diem* poem advises the reader or the person it addresses to live for today and enjoy the pleasures of the moment. Two celebrated *carpe diem* poems are Andrew Marvell's "To His Coy Mistress" and Robert Herrick's poem beginning "Gather ye rosebuds while ye may...."

Catharsis: The release or purging of unwanted emotions—specifically fear and pity—brought about by exposure to art. The term was first used by the Greek philosopher Aristotle in his *Poetics* to refer to the desired effect of tragedy on spectators. A famous example of catharsis is realized in Sophocles's *Oedipus Rex,* when Oedipus discovers that his wife, Jacosta, is his own mother and that the stranger he killed on the road was his own father.

Celtic Renaissance: A period of Irish literary and cultural history at the end of the nineteenth century. Followers of the movement aimed to create a romantic vision of Celtic myth and legend. The most significant works of the Celtic Renaissance typically present a dreamy, unreal world, usually in reaction against the reality of contemporary problems. William Butler Yeats's *The Wanderings of Oisin* is among the most significant works of the Celtic Renaissance. Also known as Celtic Twilight.

Celtic Twilight: See *Celtic Renaissance*

Character: Broadly speaking, a person in a literary work. The actions of characters are what constitute the plot of a story, novel, or poem. There are numerous types of characters, ranging from simple, stereotypical figures to intricate, multifaceted ones. In the techniques of anthropomorphism and personification, animals—and even places or things—can assume aspects of character. "Characterization" is the process by which an author creates vivid, believable characters in a work of art. This may be done in a variety of ways, including (1) direct description of the character by the narrator; (2) the direct presentation of the speech, thoughts, or actions of the character; and (3) the responses of other characters to the character. The term "character" also refers to a form originated by the ancient Greek writer Theophrastus that later became popular in the seventeenth and eighteenth centuries. It is a short essay or sketch of a person who prominently displays a specific attribute or quality, such as miserliness or ambition. Notable characters in literature include Oedipus Rex, Don Quixote de la Mancha, Macbeth, Candide, Hester Prynne, Ebenezer Scrooge, Huckleberry Finn, Jay Gatsby, Scarlett O'Hara, James Bond, and Kunta Kinte.

Characterization: See *Character*

Chorus: In ancient Greek drama, a group of actors who commented on and interpreted the unfolding action on the stage. Initially the chorus was a major component of the presentation, but over time it became less significant, with its numbers reduced and its role eventually limited to commentary between acts. By the sixteenth century the chorus—if employed at all—was typically a single person who provided a prologue and an epilogue and occasionally appeared between acts to introduce or underscore an important event. The chorus in William Shakespeare's *Henry V* functions in this way. Modern dramas rarely feature a chorus, but T. S. Eliot's *Murder in the Cathedral* and Arthur Miller's *A View from the Bridge* are notable exceptions. The Stage Manager in Thornton Wilder's *Our Town* performs a role similar to that of the chorus.

Chronicle: A record of events presented in chronological order. Although the scope and level of detail provided varies greatly among the chronicles surviving from ancient times, some, such as the *Anglo-Saxon Chronicle,* feature vivid descriptions and a lively recounting of events. During the Elizabethan Age, many dramas—appropriately called "chronicle plays"—were based on material from chronicles. Many of William Shakespeare's dramas of English history as well as Christopher Marlowe's *Edward II* are based in part on Raphael Holinshead's *Chronicles of England, Scotland, and Ireland.*

Classical: In its strictest definition in literary criticism, classicism refers to works of ancient Greek or Roman literature. The term may also be used to describe a literary work of recognized importance (a "classic") from any time period or literature that exhibits the traits of classicism. Classical authors from ancient Greek and Roman times include Juvenal and Homer. Examples of later works and authors now described as classical include French literature of the seventeenth century, Western novels of the nineteenth century, and American fiction of the mid-nineteenth century such as that written by James Fenimore Cooper and Mark Twain.

Classicism: A term used in literary criticism to describe critical doctrines that have their roots in ancient Greek and Roman literature, philosophy, and art. Works associated with classicism typically exhibit restraint on the part of the author, unity of design and purpose, clarity, simplicity, logical organization, and respect for tradition. Examples of literary classicism include Cicero's prose, the dramas of Pierre Corneille and Jean Racine, the poetry of John Dryden and Alexander Pope, and the writings of J. W. von Goethe, G. E. Lessing, and T. S. Eliot.

Climax: The turning point in a narrative, the moment when the conflict is at its most intense. Typically, the structure of stories, novels, and plays is one of rising action, in which tension builds to the climax, followed by falling action, in which tension lessens as the story moves to its conclusion. The climax in James Fenimore Cooper's *The Last of the Mohicans* occurs when Magua and his captive Cora are pursued to the edge of a cliff by Uncas. Magua kills Uncas but is subsequently killed by Hawkeye.

Colloquialism: A word, phrase, or form of pronunciation that is acceptable in casual conversation but not in formal, written communication. It is considered more acceptable than slang. An example of colloquialism can be found in Rudyard Kipling's *Barrack-room Ballads:* When' Omer smote' is bloomin' lyre He' d' eard men sing by land and sea; An' what he thought' e might require' E went an' took—the same as me!

Comedy: One of two major types of drama, the other being tragedy. Its aim is to amuse, and it typically ends happily. Comedy assumes many forms, such as farce and burlesque, and uses a variety of techniques, from parody to satire. In a restricted sense the term comedy refers only to dramatic presentations, but in general usage it is commonly applied to nondramatic works as well. Examples of comedies range from the plays of Aristophanes, Terrence, and Plautus, Dante Alighieri's *The Divine Comedy,* Francois Rabelais's *Pantagruel* and *Gargantua,* and some of Geoffrey Chaucer's tales and William Shakespeare's plays to Noel Coward's play *Private Lives* and James Thurber's short story "The Secret Life of Walter Mitty."

Comedy of Manners: A play about the manners and conventions of an aristocratic, highly sophisticated society. The characters are usually types rather than individualized personalities, and plot is less important than atmosphere. Such plays were an important aspect of late seventeenth-century English comedy. The comedy of manners was revived in the eighteenth century by Oliver Goldsmith and Richard Brinsley Sheridan, enjoyed a second revival in the late nineteenth century, and has endured into the twentieth century. Examples of comedies of manners include William Congreve's *The Way of the World* in the late seventeenth century, Oliver Goldsmith's *She Stoops to Conquer* and Richard Brinsley Sheridan's *The School for Scandal* in the eighteenth century, Oscar Wilde's *The Importance of Being Earnest* in the nineteenth century, and W. Somerset Maugham's *The Circle* in the twentieth century.

Comic Relief: The use of humor to lighten the mood of a serious or tragic story, especially in plays. The technique is very common in Elizabethan works, and can be an integral part of the plot or simply a brief event designed to break the tension of the scene. The Gravediggers' scene in William Shakespeare's *Hamlet* is a frequently cited example of comic relief.

Commedia dell'arte: An Italian term meaning "the comedy of guilds" or "the comedy of professional actors." This form of dramatic comedy was popular in Italy during the sixteenth century. Actors were assigned stock roles (such as Pulcinella, the stupid servant, or Pantalone, the old merchant) and given a basic plot to follow, but all dialogue was improvised. The roles were rigidly typed and the plots were formulaic, usually revolving around young lovers who thwarted their elders and attained wealth and happiness. A rigid convention of the *commedia dell'arte* is the periodic intrusion of Harlequin, who interrupts the play with low buffoonery. Peppino de Filippo's *Metamorphoses of a Wandering Minstrel* gave modern audiences an idea of what *commedia dell'arte* may have been like. Various scenarios for *commedia dell'arte* were compiled in Petraccone's *La commedia dell'arte, storia, technica, scenari,* published in 1927.

Complaint: A lyric poem, popular in the Renaissance, in which the speaker expresses sorrow about his or her condition. Typically, the speaker's sadness is caused by an unresponsive lover, but some complaints cite other sources of unhappiness, such as poverty or fate. A commonly cited example is "A Complaint by Night of the Lover Not Beloved" by Henry Howard, Earl of Surrey. Thomas Sackville's "Complaint of Henry, Duke of Buckingham" traces the duke's unhappiness to his ruthless ambition.

Conceit: A clever and fanciful metaphor, usually expressed through elaborate and extended comparison, that presents a striking parallel between two seemingly dissimilar things—for example, elaborately comparing a beautiful woman to an object like a garden or the sun. The conceit was a popular device throughout the Elizabethan Age and Baroque Age and was the principal technique of the seventeenth-century English metaphysical poets. This usage of the word conceit is unrelated to the best-known definition of conceit as an

arrogant attitude or behavior. The conceit figures prominently in the works of John Donne, Emily Dickinson, and T. S. Eliot.

Concrete: Concrete is the opposite of abstract, and refers to a thing that actually exists or a description that allows the reader to experience an object or concept with the senses. Henry David Thoreau's *Walden* contains much concrete description of nature and wildlife.

Concrete Poetry: Poetry in which visual elements play a large part in the poetic effect. Punctuation marks, letters, or words are arranged on a page to form a visual design: a cross, for example, or a bumblebee. Max Bill and Eugene Gomringer were among the early practitioners of concrete poetry; Haroldo de Campos and Augusto de Campos are among contemporary authors of concrete poetry.

Confessional Poetry: A form of poetry in which the poet reveals very personal, intimate, sometimes shocking information about himself or herself. Anne Sexton, Sylvia Plath, Robert Lowell, and John Berryman wrote poetry in the confessional vein.

Conflict: The conflict in a work of fiction is the issue to be resolved in the story. It usually occurs between two characters, the protagonist and the antagonist, or between the protagonist and society or the protagonist and himself or herself. Conflict in Theodore Dreiser's novel *Sister Carrie* comes as a result of urban society, while Jack London's short story "To Build a Fire" concerns the protagonist's battle against the cold and himself.

Connotation: The impression that a word gives beyond its defined meaning. Connotations may be universally understood or may be significant only to a certain group. Both "horse" and "steed" denote the same animal, but "steed" has a different connotation, deriving from the chivalrous or romantic narratives in which the word was once often used.

Consonance: Consonance occurs in poetry when words appearing at the ends of two or more verses have similar final consonant sounds but have final vowel sounds that differ, as with "stuff" and "off." Consonance is found in "The curfew tolls the knells of parting day" from Thomas Grey's "An Elegy Written in a Country Church Yard." Also known as Half Rhyme or Slant Rhyme.

Convention: Any widely accepted literary device, style, or form. A soliloquy, in which a character reveals to the audience his or her private thoughts, is an example of a dramatic convention.

Corrido: A Mexican ballad. Examples of *corridos* include "Muerte del afamado Bilito," "La voz de mi conciencia," "Lucio Perez," "La juida," and "Los presos."

Couplet: Two lines of poetry with the same rhyme and meter, often expressing a complete and self-contained thought. The following couplet is from Alexander Pope's "Elegy to the Memory of an Unfortunate Lady": 'Tis Use alone that sanctifies Expense, And Splendour borrows all her rays from Sense.

Criticism: The systematic study and evaluation of literary works, usually based on a specific method or set of principles. An important part of literary studies since ancient times, the practice of criticism has given rise to numerous theories, methods, and "schools," sometimes producing conflicting, even contradictory, interpretations of literature in general as well as of individual works. Even such basic issues as what constitutes a poem or a novel have been the subject of much criticism over the centuries. Seminal texts of literary criticism include Plato's *Republic*, Aristotle's *Poetics*, Sir Philip Sidney's *The Defence of Poesie*, John Dryden's *Of Dramatic Poesie*, and William Wordsworth's "Preface" to the second edition of his *Lyrical Ballads*. Contemporary schools of criticism include deconstruction, feminist, psychoanalytic, poststructuralist, new historicist, postcolonialist, and reader-response.

D

Dactyl: See *Foot*

Dadaism: A protest movement in art and literature founded by Tristan Tzara in 1916. Followers of the movement expressed their outrage at the destruction brought about by World War I by revolting against numerous forms of social convention. The Dadaists presented works marked by calculated madness and flamboyant nonsense. They stressed total freedom of expression, commonly through primitive displays of emotion and illogical, often senseless, poetry. The movement ended shortly after the war, when it was replaced by surrealism. Proponents of Dadaism include Andre

Breton, Louis Aragon, Philippe Soupault, and Paul Eluard.

Decadent: See *Decadents*

Decadents: The followers of a nineteenth-century literary movement that had its beginnings in French aestheticism. Decadent literature displays a fascination with perverse and morbid states; a search for novelty and sensation—the "new thrill"; a preoccupation with mysticism; and a belief in the senselessness of human existence. The movement is closely associated with the doctrine Art for Art's Sake. The term "decadence" is sometimes used to denote a decline in the quality of art or literature following a period of greatness. Major French decadents are Charles Baudelaire and Arthur Rimbaud. English decadents include Oscar Wilde, Ernest Dowson, and Frank Harris.

Deconstruction: A method of literary criticism developed by Jacques Derrida and characterized by multiple conflicting interpretations of a given work. Deconstructionists consider the impact of the language of a work and suggest that the true meaning of the work is not necessarily the meaning that the author intended. Jacques Derrida's *De la grammatologie* is the seminal text on deconstructive strategies; among American practitioners of this method of criticism are Paul de Man and J. Hillis Miller.

Deduction: The process of reaching a conclusion through reasoning from general premises to a specific premise. An example of deduction is present in the following syllogism: Premise: All mammals are animals. Premise: All whales are mammals. Conclusion: Therefore, all whales are animals.

Denotation: The definition of a word, apart from the impressions or feelings it creates in the reader. The word "apartheid" denotes a political and economic policy of segregation by race, but its connotations—oppression, slavery, inequality—are numerous.

Denouement: A French word meaning "the unknotting." In literary criticism, it denotes the resolution of conflict in fiction or drama. The *denouement* follows the climax and provides an outcome to the primary plot situation as well as an explanation of secondary plot complications. The *denouement* often involves a character's recognition of his or her state of mind or moral condition. A well-known example of *denouement* is the last scene of the play *As You Like It* by William Shakespeare, in which couples are married, an evildoer repents, the identities of two disguised characters are revealed, and a ruler is restored to power. Also known as Falling Action.

Description: Descriptive writing is intended to allow a reader to picture the scene or setting in which the action of a story takes place. The form this description takes often evokes an intended emotional response—a dark, spooky graveyard will evoke fear, and a peaceful, sunny meadow will evoke calmness. An example of a descriptive story is Edgar Allan Poe's *Landor's Cottage,* which offers a detailed depiction of a New York country estate.

Detective Story: A narrative about the solution of a mystery or the identification of a criminal. The conventions of the detective story include the detective's scrupulous use of logic in solving the mystery; incompetent or ineffectual police; a suspect who appears guilty at first but is later proved innocent; and the detective's friend or confidant—often the narrator—whose slowness in interpreting clues emphasizes by contrast the detective's brilliance. Edgar Allan Poe's "Murders in the Rue Morgue" is commonly regarded as the earliest example of this type of story. With this work, Poe established many of the conventions of the detective story genre, which are still in practice. Other practitioners of this vast and extremely popular genre include Arthur Conan Doyle, Dashiell Hammett, and Agatha Christie.

Deus ex machina: A Latin term meaning "god out of a machine." In Greek drama, a god was often lowered onto the stage by a mechanism of some kind to rescue the hero or untangle the plot. By extension, the term refers to any artificial device or coincidence used to bring about a convenient and simple solution to a plot. This is a common device in melodramas and includes such fortunate circumstances as the sudden receipt of a legacy to save the family farm or a last-minute stay of execution. The *deus ex machina* invariably rewards the virtuous and punishes evildoers. Examples of *deus ex machina*

include King Louis XIV in Jean-Baptiste Moliere's *Tartuffe* and Queen Victoria in *The Pirates of Penzance* by William Gilbert and Arthur Sullivan. Bertolt Brecht parodies the abuse of such devices in the conclusion of his *Threepenny Opera.*

Dialogue: In its widest sense, dialogue is simply conversation between people in a literary work; in its most restricted sense, it refers specifically to the speech of characters in a drama. As a specific literary genre, a "dialogue" is a composition in which characters debate an issue or idea. The Greek philosopher Plato frequently expounded his theories in the form of dialogues.

Diction: The selection and arrangement of words in a literary work. Either or both may vary depending on the desired effect. There are four general types of diction: "formal," used in scholarly or lofty writing; "informal," used in relaxed but educated conversation; "colloquial," used in everyday speech; and "slang," containing newly coined words and other terms not accepted in formal usage.

Didactic: A term used to describe works of literature that aim to teach some moral, religious, political, or practical lesson. Although didactic elements are often found in artistically pleasing works, the term "didactic" usually refers to literature in which the message is more important than the form. The term may also be used to criticize a work that the critic finds "overly didactic," that is, heavy-handed in its delivery of a lesson. Examples of didactic literature include John Bunyan's *Pilgrim's Progress,* Alexander Pope's *Essay on Criticism,* Jean-Jacques Rousseau's *Emile,* and Elizabeth Inchbald's *Simple Story.*

Dimeter: See *Meter*

Dionysian: See *Apollonian and Dionysian*

Discordia concours: A Latin phrase meaning "discord in harmony." The term was coined by the eighteenth-century English writer Samuel Johnson to describe "a combination of dissimilar images or discovery of occult resemblances in things apparently unlike." Johnson created the expression by reversing a phrase by the Latin poet Horace. The metaphysical poetry of John Donne, Richard Crashaw, Abraham Cowley, George Herbert, and Edward Taylor among others, contains many examples of *discordia concours.* In

Donne's "A Valediction: Forbidding Mourning," the poet compares the union of himself with his lover to a draftsman's compass: If they be two, they are two so, As stiff twin compasses are two: Thy soul, the fixed foot, makes no show To move, but doth, if the other do; And though it in the center sit, Yet when the other far doth roam, It leans, and hearkens after it, And grows erect, as that comes home.

Dissonance: A combination of harsh or jarring sounds, especially in poetry. Although such combinations may be accidental, poets sometimes intentionally make them to achieve particular effects. Dissonance is also sometimes used to refer to close but not identical rhymes. When this is the case, the word functions as a synonym for consonance. Robert Browning, Gerard Manley Hopkins, and many other poets have made deliberate use of dissonance.

Doppelganger: A literary technique by which a character is duplicated (usually in the form of an alter ego, though sometimes as a ghostly counterpart) or divided into two distinct, usually opposite personalities. The use of this character device is widespread in nineteenth- and twentieth- century literature, and indicates a growing awareness among authors that the "self" is really a composite of many "selves." A well-known story containing a *doppelganger* character is Robert Louis Stevenson's *Dr. Jekyll and Mr. Hyde,* which dramatizes an internal struggle between good and evil. Also known as The Double.

Double Entendre: A corruption of a French phrase meaning "double meaning." The term is used to indicate a word or phrase that is deliberately ambiguous, especially when one of the meanings is risque or improper. An example of a *double entendre* is the Elizabethan usage of the verb "die," which refers both to death and to orgasm.

Double, The: See *Doppelganger*

Draft: Any preliminary version of a written work. An author may write dozens of drafts which are revised to form the final work, or he or she may write only one, with few or no revisions. Dorothy Parker's observation that "I can't write five words but that I change seven" humorously indicates the purpose of the draft.

Drama: In its widest sense, a drama is any work designed to be presented by actors on a stage. Similarly, "drama" denotes a broad literary genre that includes a variety of forms, from pageant and spectacle to tragedy and comedy, as well as countless types and subtypes. More commonly in modern usage, however, a drama is a work that treats serious subjects and themes but does not aim at the grandeur of tragedy. This use of the term originated with the eighteenth-century French writer Denis Diderot, who used the word *drame* to designate his plays about middle- class life; thus "drama" typically features characters of a less exalted stature than those of tragedy. Examples of classical dramas include Menander's comedy *Dyscolus* and Sophocles' tragedy *Oedipus Rex.* Contemporary dramas include Eugene O'Neill's *The Iceman Cometh,* Lillian Hellman's *Little Foxes,* and August Wilson's *Ma Rainey's Black Bottom.*

Dramatic Irony: Occurs when the audience of a play or the reader of a work of literature knows something that a character in the work itself does not know. The irony is in the contrast between the intended meaning of the statements or actions of a character and the additional information understood by the audience. A celebrated example of dramatic irony is in Act V of William Shakespeare's *Romeo and Juliet,* where two young lovers meet their end as a result of a tragic misunderstanding. Here, the audience has full knowledge that Juliet's apparent "death" is merely temporary; she will regain her senses when the mysterious "sleeping potion" she has taken wears off. But Romeo, mistaking Juliet's drug-induced trance for true death, kills himself in grief. Upon awakening, Juliet discovers Romeo's corpse and, in despair, slays herself.

Dramatic Monologue: See *Monologue*

Dramatic Poetry: Any lyric work that employs elements of drama such as dialogue, conflict, or characterization, but excluding works that are intended for stage presentation. A monologue is a form of dramatic poetry.

Dramatis Personae: The characters in a work of literature, particularly a drama. The list of characters printed before the main text of a play or in the program is the *dramatis personae.*

Dream Allegory: See *Dream Vision*

Dream Vision: A literary convention, chiefly of the Middle Ages. In a dream vision a story is presented as a literal dream of the narrator. This device was commonly used to teach moral and religious lessons. Important works of this type are *The Divine Comedy* by Dante Alighieri, *Piers Plowman* by William Langland, and *The Pilgrim's Progress* by John Bunyan. Also known as Dream Allegory.

Dystopia: An imaginary place in a work of fiction where the characters lead dehumanized, fearful lives. Jack London's *The Iron Heel,* Yevgeny Zamyatin's *My,* Aldous Huxley's *Brave New World,* George Orwell's *Nineteen Eighty-four,* and Margaret Atwood's *Handmaid's Tale* portray versions of dystopia.

E

Eclogue: In classical literature, a poem featuring rural themes and structured as a dialogue among shepherds. Eclogues often took specific poetic forms, such as elegies or love poems. Some were written as the soliloquy of a shepherd. In later centuries, "eclogue" came to refer to any poem that was in the pastoral tradition or that had a dialogue or monologue structure. A classical example of an eclogue is Virgil's *Eclogues,* also known as *Bucolics.* Giovanni Boccaccio, Edmund Spenser, Andrew Marvell, Jonathan Swift, and Louis MacNeice also wrote eclogues.

Edwardian: Describes cultural conventions identified with the period of the reign of Edward VII of England (1901-1910). Writers of the Edwardian Age typically displayed a strong reaction against the propriety and conservatism of the Victorian Age. Their work often exhibits distrust of authority in religion, politics, and art and expresses strong doubts about the soundness of conventional values. Writers of this era include George Bernard Shaw, H. G. Wells, and Joseph Conrad.

Edwardian Age: See *Edwardian*

Electra Complex: A daughter's amorous obsession with her father. The term Electra complex comes from the plays of Euripides and Sophocles entitled *Electra,* in which the character Electra drives her brother Orestes to kill their mother and her lover in revenge for the murder of their father.

Elegy: A lyric poem that laments the death of a person or the eventual death of all people. In a conventional elegy, set in a classical world, the poet and subject are spoken of as shepherds. In modern criticism, the word elegy is often used to refer to a poem that is melancholy or mournfully contemplative. John Milton's "Lycidas" and Percy Bysshe Shelley's "Adonais" are two examples of this form.

Elizabethan Age: A period of great economic growth, religious controversy, and nationalism closely associated with the reign of Elizabeth I of England (1558-1603). The Elizabethan Age is considered a part of the general renaissance—that is, the flowering of arts and literature—that took place in Europe during the fourteenth through sixteenth centuries. The era is considered the golden age of English literature. The most important dramas in English and a great deal of lyric poetry were produced during this period, and modern English criticism began around this time. The notable authors of the period—Philip Sidney, Edmund Spenser, Christopher Marlowe, William Shakespeare, Ben Jonson, Francis Bacon, and John Donne—are among the best in all of English literature.

Elizabethan Drama: English comic and tragic plays produced during the Renaissance, or more narrowly, those plays written during the last years of and few years after Queen Elizabeth's reign. William Shakespeare is considered an Elizabethan dramatist in the broader sense, although most of his work was produced during the reign of James I. Examples of Elizabethan comedies include John Lyly's *The Woman in the Moone,* Thomas Dekker's *The Roaring Girl, or, Moll Cut Purse,* and William Shakespeare's *Twelfth Night.* Examples of Elizabethan tragedies include William Shakespeare's *Antony and Cleopatra,* Thomas Kyd's *The Spanish Tragedy,* and John Webster's *The Tragedy of the Duchess of Malfi.*

Empathy: A sense of shared experience, including emotional and physical feelings, with someone or something other than oneself. Empathy is often used to describe the response of a reader to a literary character. An example of an empathic passage is William Shakespeare's description in his narrative poem *Venus and Adonis* of: the snail, whose tender horns being hit, Shrinks backward in his shelly cave with pain. Readers of Gerard Manley Hopkins's *The Windhover* may experience some of the physical sensations evoked in the description of the movement of the falcon.

English Sonnet: See *Sonnet*

Enjambment: The running over of the sense and structure of a line of verse or a couplet into the following verse or couplet. Andrew Marvell's "To His Coy Mistress" is structured as a series of enjambments, as in lines 11-12: "My vegetable love should grow/Vaster than empires and more slow."

Enlightenment, The: An eighteenth-century philosophical movement. It began in France but had a wide impact throughout Europe and America. Thinkers of the Enlightenment valued reason and believed that both the individual and society could achieve a state of perfection. Corresponding to this essentially humanist vision was a resistance to religious authority. Important figures of the Enlightenment were Denis Diderot and Voltaire in France, Edward Gibbon and David Hume in England, and Thomas Paine and Thomas Jefferson in the United States.

Epic: A long narrative poem about the adventures of a hero of great historic or legendary importance. The setting is vast and the action is often given cosmic significance through the intervention of supernatural forces such as gods, angels, or demons. Epics are typically written in a classical style of grand simplicity with elaborate metaphors and allusions that enhance the symbolic importance of a hero's adventures. Some well-known epics are Homer's *Iliad* and *Odyssey,* Virgil's *Aeneid,* and John Milton's *Paradise Lost.*

Epic Simile: See *Homeric Simile*

Epic Theater: A theory of theatrical presentation developed by twentieth-century German playwright Bertolt Brecht. Brecht created a type of drama that the audience could view with complete detachment. He used what he termed "alienation effects" to create an emotional distance between the audience and the action on stage. Among these effects are: short, self-contained scenes that keep the play from building to a cathartic climax; songs that comment on the action; and techniques of

acting that prevent the actor from developing an emotional identity with his role. Besides the plays of Bertolt Brecht, other plays that utilize epic theater conventions include those of Georg Buchner, Frank Wedekind, Erwin Piscator, and Leopold Jessner.

Epigram: A saying that makes the speaker's point quickly and concisely. Samuel Taylor Coleridge wrote an epigram that neatly sums up the form: What is an Epigram? A Dwarfish whole, Its body brevity, and wit its soul.

Epilogue: A concluding statement or section of a literary work. In dramas, particularly those of the seventeenth and eighteenth centuries, the epilogue is a closing speech, often in verse, delivered by an actor at the end of a play and spoken directly to the audience. A famous epilogue is Puck's speech at the end of William Shakespeare's *A Midsummer Night's Dream.*

Epiphany: A sudden revelation of truth inspired by a seemingly trivial incident. The term was widely used by James Joyce in his critical writings, and the stories in Joyce's *Dubliners* are commonly called "epiphanies."

Episode: An incident that forms part of a story and is significantly related to it. Episodes may be either self-contained narratives or events that depend on a larger context for their sense and importance. Examples of episodes include the founding of Wilmington, Delaware in Charles Reade's *The Disinherited Heir* and the individual events comprising the picaresque novels and medieval romances.

Episodic Plot: See *Plot*

Epitaph: An inscription on a tomb or tombstone, or a verse written on the occasion of a person's death. Epitaphs may be serious or humorous. Dorothy Parker's epitaph reads, "I told you I was sick."

Epithalamion: A song or poem written to honor and commemorate a marriage ceremony. Famous examples include Edmund Spenser's "Epithalamion" and e. e. cummings's "Epithalamion." Also spelled Epithalamium.

Epithalamium: See *Epithalamion*

Epithet: A word or phrase, often disparaging or abusive, that expresses a character trait of someone or something. "The Napoleon of crime" is an epithet applied to Professor

Moriarty, arch-rival of Sherlock Holmes in Arthur Conan Doyle's series of detective stories.

Exempla: See *Exemplum*

Exemplum: A tale with a moral message. This form of literary sermonizing flourished during the Middle Ages, when *exempla* appeared in collections known as "example-books." The works of Geoffrey Chaucer are full of *exempla*.

Existentialism: A predominantly twentieth-century philosophy concerned with the nature and perception of human existence. There are two major strains of existentialist thought: atheistic and Christian. Followers of atheistic existentialism believe that the individual is alone in a godless universe and that the basic human condition is one of suffering and loneliness. Nevertheless, because there are no fixed values, individuals can create their own characters—indeed, they can shape themselves—through the exercise of free will. The atheistic strain culminates in and is popularly associated with the works of Jean-Paul Sartre. The Christian existentialists, on the other hand, believe that only in God may people find freedom from life's anguish. The two strains hold certain beliefs in common: that existence cannot be fully understood or described through empirical effort; that anguish is a universal element of life; that individuals must bear responsibility for their actions; and that there is no common standard of behavior or perception for religious and ethical matters. Existentialist thought figures prominently in the works of such authors as Eugene Ionesco, Franz Kafka, Fyodor Dostoyevsky, Simone de Beauvoir, Samuel Beckett, and Albert Camus.

Expatriates: See *Expatriatism*

Expatriatism: The practice of leaving one's country to live for an extended period in another country. Literary expatriates include English poets Percy Bysshe Shelley and John Keats in Italy, Polish novelist Joseph Conrad in England, American writers Richard Wright, James Baldwin, Gertrude Stein, and Ernest Hemingway in France, and Trinidadian author Neil Bissondath in Canada.

Exposition: Writing intended to explain the nature of an idea, thing, or theme. Expository writing is often combined with description, narration, or argument. In dramatic writing, the exposition is the introductory material which presents the characters, setting, and tone of the play. An example of dramatic exposition occurs in many nineteenth-century drawing-room comedies in which the butler and the maid open the play with relevant talk about their master and mistress; in composition, exposition relays factual information, as in encyclopedia entries.

Expressionism: An indistinct literary term, originally used to describe an early twentieth-century school of German painting. The term applies to almost any mode of unconventional, highly subjective writing that distorts reality in some way. Advocates of Expressionism include dramatists George Kaiser, Ernst Toller, Luigi Pirandello, Federico Garcia Lorca, Eugene O'Neill, and Elmer Rice; poets George Heym, Ernst Stadler, August Stramm, Gottfried Benn, and Georg Trakl; and novelists Franz Kafka and James Joyce.

Extended Monologue: See *Monologue*

F

Fable: A prose or verse narrative intended to convey a moral. Animals or inanimate objects with human characteristics often serve as characters in fables. A famous fable is Aesop's "The Tortoise and the Hare."

Fairy Tales: Short narratives featuring mythical beings such as fairies, elves, and sprites. These tales originally belonged to the folklore of a particular nation or region, such as those collected in Germany by Jacob and Wilhelm Grimm. Two other celebrated writers of fairy tales are Hans Christian Andersen and Rudyard Kipling.

Falling Action: See *Denouement*

Fantasy: A literary form related to mythology and folklore. Fantasy literature is typically set in non-existent realms and features supernatural beings. Notable examples of fantasy literature are *The Lord of the Rings* by J. R. R. Tolkien and the Gormenghast trilogy by Mervyn Peake.

Farce: A type of comedy characterized by broad humor, outlandish incidents, and often vulgar subject matter. Much of the "comedy" in film and television could more accurately be described as farce.

Feet: See *Foot*

Feminine Rhyme: See *Rhyme*

Femme fatale: A French phrase with the literal translation "fatal woman." A *femme fatale* is a sensuous, alluring woman who often leads men into danger or trouble. A classic example of the *femme fatale* is the nameless character in Billy Wilder's *The Seven Year Itch,* portrayed by Marilyn Monroe in the film adaptation.

Fiction: Any story that is the product of imagination rather than a documentation of fact. characters and events in such narratives may be based in real life but their ultimate form and configuration is a creation of the author. Geoffrey Chaucer's *The Canterbury Tales,* Laurence Sterne's *Tristram Shandy,* and Margaret Mitchell's *Gone with the Wind* are examples of fiction.

Figurative Language: A technique in writing in which the author temporarily interrupts the order, construction, or meaning of the writing for a particular effect. This interruption takes the form of one or more figures of speech such as hyperbole, irony, or simile. Figurative language is the opposite of literal language, in which every word is truthful, accurate, and free of exaggeration or embellishment. Examples of figurative language are tropes such as metaphor and rhetorical figures such as apostrophe.

Figures of Speech: Writing that differs from customary conventions for construction, meaning, order, or significance for the purpose of a special meaning or effect. There are two major types of figures of speech: rhetorical figures, which do not make changes in the meaning of the words, and tropes, which do. Types of figures of speech include simile, hyperbole, alliteration, and pun, among many others.

Fin de siecle: A French term meaning "end of the century." The term is used to denote the last decade of the nineteenth century, a transition period when writers and other artists abandoned old conventions and looked for new techniques and objectives. Two writers commonly associated with the *fin de siecle* mindset are Oscar Wilde and George Bernard Shaw.

First Person: See *Point of View*

Flashback: A device used in literature to present action that occurred before the beginning of the story. Flashbacks are often introduced as the dreams or recollections of one or more characters. Flashback techniques are often used in films, where they are typically set off by a gradual changing of one picture to another.

Foil: A character in a work of literature whose physical or psychological qualities contrast strongly with, and therefore highlight, the corresponding qualities of another character. In his Sherlock Holmes stories, Arthur Conan Doyle portrayed Dr. Watson as a man of normal habits and intelligence, making him a foil for the eccentric and wonderfully perceptive Sherlock Holmes.

Folk Ballad: See *Ballad*

Folklore: Traditions and myths preserved in a culture or group of people. Typically, these are passed on by word of mouth in various forms—such as legends, songs, and proverbs—or preserved in customs and ceremonies. This term was first used by W. J. Thoms in 1846. Sir James Frazer's *The Golden Bough* is the record of English folklore; myths about the frontier and the Old South exemplify American folklore.

Folktale: A story originating in oral tradition. Folktales fall into a variety of categories, including legends, ghost stories, fairy tales, fables, and anecdotes based on historical figures and events. Examples of folktales include Giambattista Basile's *The Pentamerone,* which contains the tales of Puss in Boots, Rapunzel, Cinderella, and Beauty and the Beast, and Joel Chandler Harris's Uncle Remus stories, which represent transplanted African folktales and American tales about the characters Mike Fink, Johnny Appleseed, Paul Bunyan, and Pecos Bill.

Foot: The smallest unit of rhythm in a line of poetry. In English-language poetry, a foot is typically one accented syllable combined with one or two unaccented syllables. There are many different types of feet. When the accent is on the second syllable of a two syllable word (con-*tort*), the foot is an "iamb"; the reverse accentual pattern (*tor* -ture) is a "trochee." Other feet that commonly occur in poetry in English are "anapest," two unaccented syllables followed by an accented syllable as in in-ter-*cept*, and "dactyl," an accented syllable followed by two unaccented syllables as in *su*-i-cide.

Foreshadowing: A device used in literature to create expectation or to set up an explanation of later developments. In Charles Dickens's *Great Expectations,* the graveyard encounter at the beginning of the novel between Pip and the escaped convict Magwitch foreshadows the baleful atmosphere and events that comprise much of the narrative.

Form: The pattern or construction of a work which identifies its genre and distinguishes it from other genres. Examples of forms include the different genres, such as the lyric form or the short story form, and various patterns for poetry, such as the verse form or the stanza form.

Formalism: In literary criticism, the belief that literature should follow prescribed rules of construction, such as those that govern the sonnet form. Examples of formalism are found in the work of the New Critics and structuralists.

Fourteener Meter: See *Meter*

Free Verse: Poetry that lacks regular metrical and rhyme patterns but that tries to capture the cadences of everyday speech. The form allows a poet to exploit a variety of rhythmical effects within a single poem. Free-verse techniques have been widely used in the twentieth century by such writers as Ezra Pound, T. S. Eliot, Carl Sandburg, and William Carlos Williams. Also known as *Vers libre.*

Futurism: A flamboyant literary and artistic movement that developed in France, Italy, and Russia from 1908 through the 1920s. Futurist theater and poetry abandoned traditional literary forms. In their place, followers of the movement attempted to achieve total freedom of expression through bizarre imagery and deformed or newly invented words. The Futurists were self-consciously modern artists who attempted to incorporate the appearances and sounds of modern life into their work. Futurist writers include Filippo Tommaso Marinetti, Wyndham Lewis, Guillaume Apollinaire, Velimir Khlebnikov, and Vladimir Mayakovsky.

G

Genre: A category of literary work. In critical theory, genre may refer to both the content of a given work—tragedy, comedy, pastoral—and to its form, such as poetry, novel, or drama. This term also refers to types of popular literature, as in the genres of science fiction or the detective story.

Genteel Tradition: A term coined by critic George Santayana to describe the literary practice of certain late nineteenth-century American writers, especially New Englanders. Followers of the Genteel Tradition emphasized conventionality in social, religious, moral, and literary standards. Some of the best-known writers of the Genteel Tradition are R. H. Stoddard and Bayard Taylor.

Gilded Age: A period in American history during the 1870s characterized by political corruption and materialism. A number of important novels of social and political criticism were written during this time. Examples of Gilded Age literature include Henry Adams's *Democracy* and F. Marion Crawford's *An American Politician.*

Gothic: See *Gothicism*

Gothicism: In literary criticism, works characterized by a taste for the medieval or morbidly attractive. A gothic novel prominently features elements of horror, the supernatural, gloom, and violence: clanking chains, terror, charnel houses, ghosts, medieval castles, and mysteriously slamming doors. The term "gothic novel" is also applied to novels that lack elements of the traditional Gothic setting but that create a similar atmosphere of terror or dread. Mary Shelley's *Frankenstein* is perhaps the best-known English work of this kind.

Gothic Novel: See *Gothicism*

Great Chain of Being: The belief that all things and creatures in nature are organized in a hierarchy from inanimate objects at the bottom to God at the top. This system of belief was popular in the seventeenth and eighteenth centuries. A summary of the concept of the great chain of being can be found in the first epistle of Alexander Pope's *An Essay on Man,* and more recently in Arthur O. Lovejoy's *The Great Chain of Being: A Study of the History of an Idea.*

Grotesque: In literary criticism, the subject matter of a work or a style of expression characterized by exaggeration, deformity, freakishness, and disorder. The grotesque often includes an element of comic absurdity. Early examples of literary grotesque include Francois Rabelais's *Pantagruel* and *Gargantua* and Thomas Nashe's *The Unfortunate Traveller,* while more recent examples can be found in the works of Edgar Allan Poe, Evelyn Waugh, Eudora Welty, Flannery O'Connor, Eugene Ionesco, Gunter Grass, Thomas Mann, Mervyn Peake, and Joseph Heller, among many others.

H

Haiku: The shortest form of Japanese poetry, constructed in three lines of five, seven, and five syllables respectively. The message of a *haiku* poem usually centers on some aspect of spirituality and provokes an emotional response in the reader. Early masters of *haiku* include Basho, Buson, Kobayashi Issa, and Masaoka Shiki. English writers of *haiku* include the Imagists, notably Ezra Pound, H. D., Amy Lowell, Carl Sandburg, and William Carlos Williams. Also known as *Hokku.*

Half Rhyme: See *Consonance*

Hamartia: In tragedy, the event or act that leads to the hero's or heroine's downfall. This term is often incorrectly used as a synonym for tragic flaw. In Richard Wright's *Native Son,* the act that seals Bigger Thomas's fate is his first impulsive murder.

Harlem Renaissance: The Harlem Renaissance of the 1920s is generally considered the first significant movement of black writers and artists in the United States. During this period, new and established black writers published more fiction and poetry than ever before, the first influential black literary journals were established, and black authors and artists received their first widespread recognition and serious critical appraisal. Among the major writers associated with this period are Claude McKay, Jean Toomer, Countee Cullen, Langston Hughes, Arna Bontemps, Nella Larsen, and Zora Neale Hurston. Works representative of the Harlem Renaissance include Arna Bontemps's poems "The Return" and "Golgotha Is a Mountain," Claude McKay's novel *Home to Harlem,* Nella Larsen's novel *Passing,* Langston Hughes's poem "The Negro Speaks of Rivers," and the journals *Crisis* and *Opportunity,* both founded during this period. Also known as Negro Renaissance and New Negro Movement.

Harlequin: A stock character of the *commedia dell'arte* who occasionally interrupted the action with silly antics. Harlequin first appeared on the English stage in John Day's *The Travailes of the Three English Brothers.* The San Francisco Mime Troupe is one of the few modern groups to adapt Harlequin to the needs of contemporary satire.

Hellenism: Imitation of ancient Greek thought or styles. Also, an approach to life that focuses on the growth and development of the intellect. "Hellenism" is sometimes used to refer to the belief that reason can be applied to examine all human experience. A cogent discussion of Hellenism can be found in Matthew Arnold's *Culture and Anarchy.*

Heptameter: See *Meter*

Hero/Heroine: The principal sympathetic character (male or female) in a literary work. Heroes and heroines typically exhibit admirable traits: idealism, courage, and integrity, for example. Famous heroes and heroines include Pip in Charles Dickens's *Great Expectations,* the anonymous narrator in Ralph Ellison's *Invisible Man,* and Sethe in Toni Morrison's *Beloved.*

Heroic Couplet: A rhyming couplet written in iambic pentameter (a verse with five iambic feet). The following lines by Alexander Pope are an example: "Truth guards the Poet, sanctifies the line,/ And makes Immortal, Verse as mean as mine."

Heroic Line: The meter and length of a line of verse in epic or heroic poetry. This varies by language and time period. For example, in English poetry, the heroic line is iambic pentameter (a verse with five iambic feet); in French, the alexandrine (a verse with six iambic feet); in classical literature, dactylic hexameter (a verse with six dactylic feet).

Heroine: See *Hero/Heroine*

Hexameter: See *Meter*

Historical Criticism: The study of a work based on its impact on the world of the time period in which it was written. Examples of postmodern historical criticism can be found in the work of Michel Foucault, Hayden White, Stephen Greenblatt, and Jonathan Goldberg.

Hokku: See *Haiku*

Holocaust: See *Holocaust Literature*

Holocaust Literature: Literature influenced by or written about the Holocaust of World War II. Such literature includes true stories of survival in concentration camps, escape, and life after the war, as well as fictional works and poetry. Representative works of Holocaust literature include Saul Bellow's *Mr. Sammler's Planet,* Anne Frank's *The Diary of a Young Girl,* Jerzy Kosinski's *The Painted Bird,* Arthur Miller's *Incident at Vichy,* Czeslaw Milosz's *Collected Poems,* William Styron's *Sophie's Choice,* and Art Spiegelman's *Maus.*

Homeric Simile: An elaborate, detailed comparison written as a simile many lines in length. An example of an epic simile from John Milton's *Paradise Lost* follows: Angel Forms, who lay entranced Thick as autumnal leaves that strow the brooks In Vallombrosa, where the Etrurian shades High over-arched embower; or scattered sedge Afloat, when with fierce winds Orion armed Hath vexed the Red-Sea coast, whose waves o'erthrew Busiris and his Memphian chivalry, While with perfidious hatred they pursued The sojourners of Goshen, who beheld From the safe shore their floating carcasses And broken chariot-wheels. Also known as Epic Simile.

Horatian Satire: See *Satire*

Humanism: A philosophy that places faith in the dignity of humankind and rejects the medieval perception of the individual as a weak, fallen creature. "Humanists" typically believe in the perfectibility of human nature and view reason and education as the means to that end. Humanist thought is represented in the works of Marsilio Ficino, Ludovico Castelvetro, Edmund Spenser, John Milton, Dean John Colet, Desiderius Erasmus, John Dryden, Alexander Pope, Matthew Arnold, and Irving Babbitt.

Humors: Mentions of the humors refer to the ancient Greek theory that a person's health and personality were determined by the balance of four basic fluids in the body: blood, phlegm, yellow bile, and black bile. A dominance of any fluid would cause extremes in behavior. An excess of blood created a sanguine person who was joyful, aggressive, and passionate; a phlegmatic person was shy, fearful, and sluggish; too much yellow bile led to a choleric temperament characterized by impatience, anger, bitterness, and stubbornness; and excessive black bile created melancholy, a state of laziness, gluttony, and lack of motivation. Literary treatment of the humors is exemplified by several characters in Ben Jonson's plays *Every Man in His Humour* and *Every Man out of His Humour.* Also spelled Humours.

Humours: See *Humors*

Hyperbole: In literary criticism, deliberate exaggeration used to achieve an effect. In William Shakespeare's *Macbeth,* Lady Macbeth hyperbolizes when she says, "All the perfumes of Arabia could not sweeten this little hand."

I

Iamb: See *Foot*

Idiom: A word construction or verbal expression closely associated with a given language. For example, in colloquial English the construction "how come" can be used instead of "why" to introduce a question. Similarly, "a piece of cake" is sometimes used to describe a task that is easily done.

Image: A concrete representation of an object or sensory experience. Typically, such a representation helps evoke the feelings associated with the object or experience itself. Images are either "literal" or "figurative." Literal images are especially concrete and involve little or no extension of the obvious meaning of the words used to express them. Figurative images do not follow the literal meaning of the words exactly. Images in literature are usually visual, but the term "image" can also refer to the representation of any sensory experience. In his poem "The Shepherd's Hour," Paul Verlaine presents the following image: "The Moon is red through horizon's fog;/ In a dancing mist the hazy meadow sleeps." The first line is broadly literal, while the second line involves turns of meaning associated with dancing and sleeping.

Imagery: The array of images in a literary work. Also, figurative language. William Butler

Yeats's "The Second Coming" offers a powerful image of encroaching anarchy: Turning and turning in the widening gyre The falcon cannot hear the falconer; Things fall apart....

Imagism: An English and American poetry movement that flourished between 1908 and 1917. The Imagists used precise, clearly presented images in their works. They also used common, everyday speech and aimed for conciseness, concrete imagery, and the creation of new rhythms. Participants in the Imagist movement included Ezra Pound, H. D. (Hilda Doolittle), and Amy Lowell, among others.

In medias res: A Latin term meaning "in the middle of things." It refers to the technique of beginning a story at its midpoint and then using various flashback devices to reveal previous action. This technique originated in such epics as Virgil's *Aeneid*.

Induction: The process of reaching a conclusion by reasoning from specific premises to form a general premise. Also, an introductory portion of a work of literature, especially a play. Geoffrey Chaucer's "Prologue" to the *Canterbury Tales*, Thomas Sackville's "Induction" to *The Mirror of Magistrates*, and the opening scene in William Shakespeare's *The Taming of the Shrew* are examples of inductions to literary works.

Intentional Fallacy: The belief that judgments of a literary work based solely on an author's stated or implied intentions are false and misleading. Critics who believe in the concept of the intentional fallacy typically argue that the work itself is sufficient matter for interpretation, even though they may concede that an author's statement of purpose can be useful. Analysis of William Wordsworth's *Lyrical Ballads* based on the observations about poetry he makes in his "Preface" to the second edition of that work is an example of the intentional fallacy.

Interior Monologue: A narrative technique in which characters' thoughts are revealed in a way that appears to be uncontrolled by the author. The interior monologue typically aims to reveal the inner self of a character. It portrays emotional experiences as they occur at both a conscious and unconscious level. images are often used to represent sensations or emotions. One of the best-known interior monologues in English is the Molly Bloom section at the close of James Joyce's *Ulysses*. The interior monologue is also common in the works of Virginia Woolf.

Internal Rhyme: Rhyme that occurs within a single line of verse. An example is in the opening line of Edgar Allan Poe's "The Raven": "Once upon a midnight dreary, while I pondered weak and weary." Here, "dreary" and "weary" make an internal rhyme.

Irish Literary Renaissance: A late nineteenth- and early twentieth-century movement in Irish literature. Members of the movement aimed to reduce the influence of British culture in Ireland and create an Irish national literature. William Butler Yeats, George Moore, and Sean O'Casey are three of the best-known figures of the movement.

Irony: In literary criticism, the effect of language in which the intended meaning is the opposite of what is stated. The title of Jonathan Swift's "A Modest Proposal" is ironic because what Swift proposes in this essay is cannibalism—hardly "modest."

Italian Sonnet: See *Sonnet*

J

Jacobean Age: The period of the reign of James I of England (1603-1625). The early literature of this period reflected the worldview of the Elizabethan Age, but a darker, more cynical attitude steadily grew in the art and literature of the Jacobean Age. This was an important time for English drama and poetry. Milestones include William Shakespeare's tragedies, tragi-comedies, and sonnets; Ben Jonson's various dramas; and John Donne's metaphysical poetry.

Jargon: Language that is used or understood only by a select group of people. Jargon may refer to terminology used in a certain profession, such as computer jargon, or it may refer to any nonsensical language that is not understood by most people. Literary examples of jargon are Francois Villon's *Ballades en jargon*, which is composed in the secret language of the *coquillards*, and Anthony Burgess's *A Clockwork Orange*, narrated in the fictional characters' language of "Nadsat."

Juvenalian Satire: See *Satire*

K

Knickerbocker Group: A somewhat indistinct group of New York writers of the first half of the nineteenth century. Members of the group were linked only by location and a common theme: New York life. Two famous members of the Knickerbocker Group were Washington Irving and William Cullen Bryant. The group's name derives from Irving's *Knickerbocker's History of New York*.

L

Lais: See *Lay*

Lay: A song or simple narrative poem. The form originated in medieval France. Early French *lais* were often based on the Celtic legends and other tales sung by Breton minstrels—thus the name of the "Breton lay." In fourteenth-century England, the term "lay" was used to describe short narratives written in imitation of the Breton lays. The most notable of these is Geoffrey Chaucer's "The Minstrel's Tale."

Leitmotiv: See *Motif*

Literal Language: An author uses literal language when he or she writes without exaggerating or embellishing the subject matter and without any tools of figurative language. To say "He ran very quickly down the street" is to use literal language, whereas to say "He ran like a hare down the street" would be using figurative language.

Literary Ballad: See *Ballad*

Literature: Literature is broadly defined as any written or spoken material, but the term most often refers to creative works. Literature includes poetry, drama, fiction, and many kinds of nonfiction writing, as well as oral, dramatic, and broadcast compositions not necessarily preserved in a written format, such as films and television programs.

Lost Generation: A term first used by Gertrude Stein to describe the post-World War I generation of American writers: men and women haunted by a sense of betrayal and emptiness brought about by the destructiveness of the war. The term is commonly applied to Hart Crane, Ernest Hemingway, F. Scott Fitzgerald, and others.

Lyric Poetry: A poem expressing the subjective feelings and personal emotions of the poet. Such poetry is melodic, since it was originally accompanied by a lyre in recitals. Most Western poetry in the twentieth century may be classified as lyrical. Examples of lyric poetry include A. E. Housman's elegy "To an Athlete Dying Young," the odes of Pindar and Horace, Thomas Gray and William Collins, the sonnets of Sir Thomas Wyatt and Sir Philip Sidney, Elizabeth Barrett Browning and Rainer Maria Rilke, and a host of other forms in the poetry of William Blake and Christina Rossetti, among many others.

M

Mannerism: Exaggerated, artificial adherence to a literary manner or style. Also, a popular style of the visual arts of late sixteenth-century Europe that was marked by elongation of the human form and by intentional spatial distortion. Literary works that are self-consciously high-toned and artistic are often said to be "mannered." Authors of such works include Henry James and Gertrude Stein.

Masculine Rhyme: See *Rhyme*

Masque: A lavish and elaborate form of entertainment, often performed in royal courts, that emphasizes song, dance, and costumery. The Renaissance form of the masque grew out of the spectacles of masked figures common in medieval England and Europe. The masque reached its peak of popularity and development in seventeenth-century England, during the reigns of James I and, especially, of Charles I. Ben Jonson, the most significant masque writer, also created the "antimasque," which incorporates elements of humor and the grotesque into the traditional masque and achieved greater dramatic quality. Masque-like interludes appear in Edmund Spenser's *The Faerie Queene* and in William Shakespeare's *The Tempest*. One of the best-known English masques is John Milton's *Comus*.

Measure: The foot, verse, or time sequence used in a literary work, especially a poem. Measure is often used somewhat incorrectly as a synonym for meter.

Melodrama: A play in which the typical plot is a conflict between characters who personify extreme good and evil. Melodramas usually end happily and emphasize sensationalism. Other literary forms that use the same techniques are often labeled "melodramatic." The term was formerly used to describe a combination of drama and music; as such, it was synonymous with "opera." Augustin Daly's *Under the Gaslight* and Dion Boucicault's *The Octoroon, The Colleen Bawn,* and *The Poor of New York* are examples of melodramas. The most popular media for twentieth-century melodramas are motion pictures and television.

Metaphor: A figure of speech that expresses an idea through the image of another object. Metaphors suggest the essence of the first object by identifying it with certain qualities of the second object. An example is "But soft, what light through yonder window breaks?/ It is the east, and Juliet is the sun" in William Shakespeare's *Romeo and Juliet.* Here, Juliet, the first object, is identified with qualities of the second object, the sun.

Metaphysical Conceit: See *Conceit*

Metaphysical Poetry: The body of poetry produced by a group of seventeenth-century English writers called the "Metaphysical Poets." The group includes John Donne and Andrew Marvell. The Metaphysical Poets made use of everyday speech, intellectual analysis, and unique imagery. They aimed to portray the ordinary conflicts and contradictions of life. Their poems often took the form of an argument, and many of them emphasize physical and religious love as well as the fleeting nature of life. Elaborate conceits are typical in metaphysical poetry. Marvell's "To His Coy Mistress" is a well-known example of a metaphysical poem.

Metaphysical Poets: See *Metaphysical Poetry*

Meter: In literary criticism, the repetition of sound patterns that creates a rhythm in poetry. The patterns are based on the number of syllables and the presence and absence of accents. The unit of rhythm in a line is called a foot. Types of meter are classified according to the number of feet in a line. These are the standard English lines: Monometer, one foot; Dimeter, two feet; Trimeter, three feet; Tetrameter, four feet; Pentameter, five feet; Hexameter, six feet (also called the Alexandrine); Heptameter, seven feet (also called the "Fourteener" when the feet are iambic). The most common English meter is the iambic pentameter, in which each line contains ten syllables, or five iambic feet, which individually are composed of an unstressed syllable followed by an accented syllable. Both of the following lines from Alfred, Lord Tennyson's "Ulysses" are written in iambic pentameter: Made weak by time and fate, but strong in will To strive, to seek, to find, and not to yield.

Mise en scene: The costumes, scenery, and other properties of a drama. Herbert Beerbohm Tree was renowned for the elaborate *mises en scene* of his lavish Shakespearean productions at His Majesty's Theatre between 1897 and 1915.

Modernism: Modern literary practices. Also, the principles of a literary school that lasted from roughly the beginning of the twentieth century until the end of World War II. Modernism is defined by its rejection of the literary conventions of the nineteenth century and by its opposition to conventional morality, taste, traditions, and economic values. Many writers are associated with the concepts of Modernism, including Albert Camus, Marcel Proust, D. H. Lawrence, W. H. Auden, Ernest Hemingway, William Faulkner, William Butler Yeats, Thomas Mann, Tennessee Williams, Eugene O'Neill, and James Joyce.

Monologue: A composition, written or oral, by a single individual. More specifically, a speech given by a single individual in a drama or other public entertainment. It has no set length, although it is usually several or more lines long. An example of an "extended monologue"—that is, a monologue of great length and seriousness—occurs in the one-act, one-character play *The Stronger* by August Strindberg.

Monometer: See *Meter*

Mood: The prevailing emotions of a work or of the author in his or her creation of the work. The mood of a work is not always what might be expected based on its subject matter. The poem "Dover Beach" by Matthew Arnold offers examples of two different moods originating from the same experience: watching the ocean at night. The mood of the first three lines—The sea is calm tonight The tide is full, the moon lies fair Upon the straights.... is in sharp contrast to the mood of the last three lines—And we are here as on a darkling plain Swept with confused alarms of struggle and flight, Where ignorant armies clash by night.

Motif: A theme, character type, image, metaphor, or other verbal element that recurs throughout a single work of literature or occurs in a number of different works over a period of time. For example, the various manifestations of the color white in Herman Melville's *Moby Dick* is a "specific" *motif,* while the trials of star-crossed lovers is a "conventional" *motif* from the literature of all periods. Also known as *Motiv* or *Leitmotiv.*

Motiv: See *Motif*

Muckrakers: An early twentieth-century group of American writers. Typically, their works exposed the wrongdoings of big business and government in the United States. Upton Sinclair's *The Jungle* exemplifies the muckraking novel.

Muses: Nine Greek mythological goddesses, the daughters of Zeus and Mnemosyne (Memory). Each muse patronized a specific area of the liberal arts and sciences. Calliope presided over epic poetry, Clio over history, Erato over love poetry, Euterpe over music or lyric poetry, Melpomene over tragedy, Polyhymnia over hymns to the gods, Terpsichore over dance, Thalia over comedy, and Urania over astronomy. Poets and writers traditionally made appeals to the Muses for inspiration in their work. John Milton invokes the aid of a muse at the beginning of the first book of his *Paradise Lost:* Of Man's First disobedience, and the Fruit of the Forbidden Tree, whose mortal taste Brought Death into the World, and all our woe, With loss of Eden, till one greater Man Restore us, and regain the blissful Seat, Sing Heav'nly Muse, that on the secret top of Oreb, or of Sinai, didst inspire That Shepherd, who first taught the chosen Seed, In the Beginning how the Heav'ns and Earth Rose out of Chaos....

Mystery: See *Suspense*

Myth: An anonymous tale emerging from the traditional beliefs of a culture or social unit. Myths use supernatural explanations for natural phenomena. They may also explain cosmic issues like creation and death. Collections of myths, known as mythologies, are common to all cultures and nations, but the best-known myths belong to the Norse, Roman, and Greek mythologies. A famous myth is the story of Arachne, an arrogant young girl who challenged a goddess, Athena, to a weaving contest; when the girl won, Athena was enraged and turned Arachne into a spider, thus explaining the existence of spiders.

N

Narration: The telling of a series of events, real or invented. A narration may be either a simple narrative, in which the events are recounted chronologically, or a narrative with a plot, in which the account is given in a style reflecting the author's artistic concept of the story. Narration is sometimes used as a synonym for "storyline." The recounting of scary stories around a campfire is a form of narration.

Narrative: A verse or prose accounting of an event or sequence of events, real or invented. The term is also used as an adjective in the sense "method of narration." For example, in literary criticism, the expression "narrative technique" usually refers to the way the author structures and presents his or her story. Narratives range from the shortest accounts of events, as in Julius Caesar's remark, "I came, I saw, I conquered," to the longest historical or biographical works, as in Edward Gibbon's *The Decline and Fall of the Roman Empire,* as well as diaries, travelogues, novels, ballads, epics, short stories, and other fictional forms.

Narrative Poetry: A nondramatic poem in which the author tells a story. Such poems may be of any length or level of complexity. Epics such as *Beowulf* and ballads are forms of narrative poetry.

Narrator: The teller of a story. The narrator may be the author or a character in the story through whom the author speaks. Huckleberry Finn is the narrator of Mark Twain's *The Adventures of Huckleberry Finn.*

Naturalism: A literary movement of the late nineteenth and early twentieth centuries. The movement's major theorist, French novelist Emile Zola, envisioned a type of fiction that would examine human life with the objectivity of scientific inquiry. The Naturalists typically viewed human beings as either the products of "biological determinism," ruled by hereditary instincts and engaged in an endless struggle for survival, or as the products of "socioeconomic determinism," ruled by social and economic forces beyond their control. In their works, the Naturalists generally ignored the highest levels of society and focused on degradation: poverty, alcoholism, prostitution, insanity, and disease. Naturalism influenced authors throughout the world, including Henrik Ibsen and Thomas Hardy. In the United States, in particular, Naturalism had a profound impact. Among the authors who embraced its principles are Theodore Dreiser, Eugene O'Neill, Stephen Crane, Jack London, and Frank Norris.

Negritude: A literary movement based on the concept of a shared cultural bond on the part of black Africans, wherever they may be in the world. It traces its origins to the former French colonies of Africa and the Caribbean. Negritude poets, novelists, and essayists generally stress four points in their writings: One, black alienation from traditional African culture can lead to feelings of inferiority. Two, European colonialism and Western education should be resisted. Three, black Africans should seek to affirm and define their own identity. Four, African culture can and should be reclaimed. Many Negritude writers also claim that blacks can make unique contributions to the world, based on a heightened appreciation of nature, rhythm, and human emotions— aspects of life they say are not so highly valued in the materialistic and rationalistic West. Examples of Negritude literature include the poetry of both Senegalese Leopold Senghor in *Hosties noires* and Martiniquais Aime-Fernand Cesaire in *Return to My Native Land.*

Negro Renaissance: See *Harlem Renaissance*

Neoclassical Period: See *Neoclassicism*

Neoclassicism: In literary criticism, this term refers to the revival of the attitudes and styles of expression of classical literature. It is generally used to describe a period in European history beginning in the late seventeenth century and lasting until about 1800. In its purest form, Neoclassicism marked a return to order, proportion, restraint, logic, accuracy, and decorum. In England, where Neoclassicism perhaps was most popular, it reflected the influence of seventeenth- century French writers, especially dramatists. Neoclassical writers typically reacted against the intensity and enthusiasm of the Renaissance period. They wrote works that appealed to the intellect, using elevated language and classical literary forms such as satire and the ode. Neoclassical works were often governed by the classical goal of instruction. English neoclassicists included Alexander Pope, Jonathan Swift, Joseph Addison, Sir Richard Steele, John Gay, and Matthew Prior; French neoclassicists included Pierre Corneille and Jean-Baptiste Moliere. Also known as Age of Reason.

Neoclassicists: See *Neoclassicism*

New Criticism: A movement in literary criticism, dating from the late 1920s, that stressed close textual analysis in the interpretation of works of literature. The New Critics saw little merit in historical and biographical analysis. Rather, they aimed to examine the text alone, free from the question of how external events— biographical or otherwise—may have helped shape it. This predominantly American school was named "New Criticism" by one of its practitioners, John Crowe Ransom. Other important New Critics included Allen Tate, R. P. Blackmur, Robert Penn Warren, and Cleanth Brooks.

New Negro Movement: See *Harlem Renaissance*

Noble Savage: The idea that primitive man is noble and good but becomes evil and corrupted as he becomes civilized. The concept of the noble savage originated in the Renaissance period but is more closely identified with such later writers as Jean-Jacques Rousseau and Aphra Behn. First described in John Dryden's play *The Conquest of Granada,* the noble savage is portrayed by the various Native Americans in James Fenimore Cooper's "Leatherstocking Tales," by Queequeg, Daggoo, and Tashtego in Herman Melville's *Moby Dick,* and by John the Savage in Aldous Huxley's *Brave New World.*

O

Objective Correlative: An outward set of objects, a situation, or a chain of events corresponding to an inward experience and evoking this experience in the reader. The term frequently appears in modern criticism in discussions of authors' intended effects on the emotional responses of readers. This term was originally used by T. S. Eliot in his 1919 essay "Hamlet."

Objectivity: A quality in writing characterized by the absence of the author's opinion or feeling about the subject matter. Objectivity is an important factor in criticism. The novels of Henry James and, to a certain extent, the poems of John Larkin demonstrate objectivity, and it is central to John Keats's concept of "negative capability." Critical and journalistic writing usually are or attempt to be objective.

Occasional Verse: poetry written on the occasion of a significant historical or personal event. *Vers de societe* is sometimes called occasional verse although it is of a less serious nature. Famous examples of occasional verse include Andrew Marvell's "Horatian Ode upon Cromwell's Return from England," Walt Whitman's "When Lilacs Last in the Dooryard Bloom'd"—written upon the death of Abraham Lincoln—and Edmund Spenser's commemoration of his wedding, "Epithalamion."

Octave: A poem or stanza composed of eight lines. The term octave most often represents the first eight lines of a Petrarchan sonnet. An example of an octave is taken from a translation of a Petrarchan sonnet by Sir Thomas Wyatt: The pillar perisht is whereto I leant, The strongest stay of mine unquiet mind; The like of it no man again can find, From East to West Still seeking though he went. To mind unhap! for hap away hath rent Of all my joy the very bark and rind; And I, alas, by chance am thus assigned Daily to mourn till death do it relent.

Ode: Name given to an extended lyric poem characterized by exalted emotion and dignified style. An ode usually concerns a single, serious theme. Most odes, but not all, are addressed to an object or individual. Odes are distinguished from other lyric poetic forms by their complex rhythmic and stanzaic patterns. An example of this form is John Keats's "Ode to a Nightingale."

Oedipus Complex: A son's amorous obsession with his mother. The phrase is derived from the story of the ancient Theban hero Oedipus, who unknowingly killed his father and married his mother. Literary occurrences of the Oedipus complex include Andre Gide's *Oedipe* and Jean Cocteau's *La Machine infernale,* as well as the most famous, Sophocles' *Oedipus Rex.*

Omniscience: See *Point of View*

Onomatopoeia: The use of words whose sounds express or suggest their meaning. In its simplest sense, onomatopoeia may be represented by words that mimic the sounds they denote such as "hiss" or "meow." At a more subtle level, the pattern and rhythm of sounds and rhymes of a line or poem may be onomatopoeic. A celebrated example of onomatopoeia is the repetition of the word "bells" in Edgar Allan Poe's poem "The Bells."

Opera: A type of stage performance, usually a drama, in which the dialogue is sung. Classic examples of opera include Giuseppi Verdi's *La traviata,* Giacomo Puccini's *La Boheme,* and Richard Wagner's *Tristan und Isolde.* Major twentieth-century contributors to the form include Richard Strauss and Alban Berg.

Operetta: A usually romantic comic opera. John Gay's *The Beggar's Opera,* Richard Sheridan's *The Duenna,* and numerous works by William Gilbert and Arthur Sullivan are examples of operettas.

Oral Tradition: See *Oral Transmission*

Oral Transmission: A process by which songs, ballads, folklore, and other material are transmitted by word of mouth. The tradition of oral transmission predates the written record systems of literate society. Oral transmission preserves material sometimes over generations, although often with variations. Memory plays a large part in the recitation and preservation of orally transmitted material. Breton lays, French *fabliaux,* national epics (including the Anglo-Saxon *Beowulf,* the Spanish *El Cid,* and the Finnish *Kalevala*), Native American myths and legends, and African folktales told by plantation slaves are examples of orally transmitted literature.

Oration: Formal speaking intended to motivate the listeners to some action or feeling. Such public speaking was much more common before the development of timely printed communication such as newspapers. Famous examples of oration include Abraham Lincoln's "Gettysburg Address" and Dr. Martin Luther King Jr.'s "I Have a Dream" speech.

Ottava Rima: An eight-line stanza of poetry composed in iambic pentameter (a five-foot line in which each foot consists of an unaccented syllable followed by an accented syllable), following the abababcc rhyme scheme. This form has been prominently used by such important English writers as Lord Byron, Henry Wadsworth Longfellow, and W. B. Yeats.

Oxymoron: A phrase combining two contradictory terms. Oxymorons may be intentional or unintentional. The following speech from William Shakespeare's *Romeo and Juliet* uses several oxymorons: Why, then, O brawling love! O loving hate! O anything, of nothing first create! O heavy lightness! serious vanity! Mis-shapen chaos of well-seeming forms! Feather of lead, bright smoke, cold fire, sick health! This love feel I, that feel no love in this.

P

Pantheism: The idea that all things are both a manifestation or revelation of God and a part of God at the same time. Pantheism was a common attitude in the early societies of Egypt, India, and Greece—the term derives from the Greek *pan* meaning "all" and *theos* meaning "deity." It later became a significant part of the Christian faith. William Wordsworth and Ralph Waldo Emerson are among the many writers who have expressed the pantheistic attitude in their works.

Parable: A story intended to teach a moral lesson or answer an ethical question. In the West, the best examples of parables are those of Jesus Christ in the New Testament, notably "The Prodigal Son," but parables also are used in Sufism, rabbinic literature, Hasidism, and Zen Buddhism.

Paradox: A statement that appears illogical or contradictory at first, but may actually point to an underlying truth. "Less is more" is an example of a paradox. Literary examples include Francis Bacon's statement, "The most corrected copies are commonly the least correct," and "All animals are equal, but some animals are more equal than others" from George Orwell's *Animal Farm*.

Parallelism: A method of comparison of two ideas in which each is developed in the same grammatical structure. Ralph Waldo Emerson's "Civilization" contains this example of parallelism: Raphael paints wisdom; Handel sings it, Phidias carves it, Shakespeare writes it, Wren builds it, Columbus sails it, Luther preaches it, Washington arms it, Watt mechanizes it.

Parnassianism: A mid nineteenth-century movement in French literature. Followers of the movement stressed adherence to well-defined artistic forms as a reaction against the often chaotic expression of the artist's ego that dominated the work of the Romantics. The Parnassians also rejected the moral, ethical, and social themes exhibited in the works of French Romantics such as Victor Hugo. The aesthetic doctrines of the Parnassians strongly influenced the later symbolist and decadent movements. Members of the Parnassian school include Leconte de Lisle, Sully Prudhomme, Albert Glatigny, Francois Coppee, and Theodore de Banville.

Parody: In literary criticism, this term refers to an imitation of a serious literary work or the signature style of a particular author in a ridiculous manner. A typical parody adopts the style of the original and applies it to an inappropriate subject for humorous effect. Parody is a form of satire and could be considered the literary equivalent of a caricature or cartoon. Henry Fielding's *Shamela* is a parody of Samuel Richardson's *Pamela*.

Pastoral: A term derived from the Latin word "pastor," meaning shepherd. A pastoral is a literary composition on a rural theme. The conventions of the pastoral were originated by the third-century Greek poet Theocritus, who wrote about the experiences, love affairs, and pastimes of Sicilian shepherds. In a pastoral, characters and language of a courtly nature are often placed in a simple setting. The term pastoral is also used to classify dramas, elegies, and lyrics that exhibit the use of country settings and shepherd characters. Percy Bysshe Shelley's "Adonais" and John Milton's "Lycidas" are two famous examples of pastorals.

Pastorela: The Spanish name for the shepherds play, a folk drama reenacted during the Christmas season. Examples of *pastorelas* include Gomez Manrique's *Representacion del nacimiento* and the dramas of Lucas Fernandez and Juan del Encina.

Pathetic Fallacy: A term coined by English critic John Ruskin to identify writing that falsely endows nonhuman things with human intentions and feelings, such as "angry clouds" and "sad trees." The pathetic fallacy is a required convention in the classical poetic form of the pastoral elegy, and it is used in the modern poetry of T. S. Eliot, Ezra Pound, and the Imagists. Also known as Poetic Fallacy.

Pelado: Literally the "skinned one" or shirtless one, he was the stock underdog, sharp-witted picaresque character of Mexican vaudeville and tent shows. The *pelado* is found in such works as Don Catarino's *Los effectos de la crisis* and *Regreso a mi tierra*.

Pen Name: See *Pseudonym*

Pentameter: See *Meter*

Persona: A Latin term meaning "mask." *Personae* are the characters in a fictional work of literature. The *persona* generally functions as a mask through which the author tells a story in a voice other than his or her own. A *persona* is usually either a character in a story who acts as a narrator or an "implied author," a voice created by the author to act as the narrator for himself or herself. *Personae* include the narrator of Geoffrey Chaucer's *Canterbury Tales* and Marlow in Joseph Conrad's *Heart of Darkness*.

Personae: See *Persona*

Personal Point of View: See *Point of View*

Personification: A figure of speech that gives human qualities to abstract ideas, animals, and inanimate objects. William Shakespeare used personification in *Romeo and Juliet* in the lines "Arise, fair sun, and kill the envious moon,/ Who is already sick and pale with grief." Here, the moon is portrayed as being envious, sick, and pale with grief—all markedly human qualities. Also known as *Prosopopoeia*.

Petrarchan Sonnet: See *Sonnet*

Phenomenology: A method of literary criticism based on the belief that things have no existence outside of human consciousness or awareness. Proponents of this theory believe that art is a process that takes place in the mind of the observer as he or she contemplates an object rather than a quality of the object itself. Among phenomenological critics are Edmund Husserl, George Poulet, Marcel Raymond, and Roman Ingarden.

Picaresque Novel: Episodic fiction depicting the adventures of a roguish central character ("picaro" is Spanish for "rogue"). The picaresque hero is commonly a low-born but clever individual who wanders into and out of various affairs of love, danger, and farcical intrigue. These involvements may take place at all social levels and typically present a humorous and wide-ranging satire of a given society. Prominent examples of the picaresque novel are *Don Quixote* by Miguel de Cervantes, *Tom Jones* by Henry Fielding, and *Moll Flanders* by Daniel Defoe.

Plagiarism: Claiming another person's written material as one's own. Plagiarism can take the form of direct, word-for-word copying or the theft of the substance or idea of the work. A student who copies an encyclopedia entry and turns it in as a report for school is guilty of plagiarism.

Platonic Criticism: A form of criticism that stresses an artistic work's usefulness as an agent of social engineering rather than any quality or value of the work itself. Platonic criticism takes as its starting point the ancient Greek philosopher Plato's comments on art in his *Republic*.

Platonism: The embracing of the doctrines of the philosopher Plato, popular among the poets of the Renaissance and the Romantic period. Platonism is more flexible than Aristotelian Criticism and places more emphasis on the supernatural and unknown aspects of life. Platonism is expressed in the love poetry of the Renaissance, the fourth book of Baldassare Castiglione's *The Book of the Courtier,* and the poetry of William Blake, William Wordsworth, Percy Bysshe Shelley, Friedrich Holderlin, William Butler Yeats, and Wallace Stevens.

Play: See *Drama*

Plot: In literary criticism, this term refers to the pattern of events in a narrative or drama. In its simplest sense, the plot guides the author in composing the work and helps the reader follow the work. Typically, plots exhibit causality and unity and have a beginning, a middle, and an end. Sometimes, however, a plot may consist of a series of disconnected events, in which case it is known as an "episodic plot." In his *Aspects of the Novel,* E. M. Forster distinguishes between a story, defined as a "narrative of events arranged in their time-sequence," and plot, which organizes the events to a "sense of causality." This definition closely mirrors Aristotle's discussion of plot in his *Poetics.*

Poem: In its broadest sense, a composition utilizing rhyme, meter, concrete detail, and expressive language to create a literary experience with emotional and aesthetic appeal. Typical poems include sonnets, odes, elegies, *haiku,* ballads, and free verse.

Poet: An author who writes poetry or verse. The term is also used to refer to an artist or writer who has an exceptional gift for expression, imagination, and energy in the making of art in any form. Well-known poets include Horace, Basho, Sir Philip Sidney, Sir Edmund Spenser, John Donne, Andrew Marvell, Alexander Pope, Jonathan Swift, George Gordon, Lord Byron, John Keats, Christina Rossetti, W. H. Auden, Stevie Smith, and Sylvia Plath.

Poetic Fallacy: See *Pathetic Fallacy*

Poetic Justice: An outcome in a literary work, not necessarily a poem, in which the good are rewarded and the evil are punished, especially in ways that particularly fit their virtues or crimes. For example, a murderer may himself be murdered, or a thief will find himself penniless.

Poetic License: Distortions of fact and literary convention made by a writer—not always a poet—for the sake of the effect gained. Poetic license is closely related to the concept of "artistic freedom." An author exercises poetic license by saying that a pile of money "reaches as high as a mountain" when the pile is actually only a foot or two high.

Poetics: This term has two closely related meanings. It denotes (1) an aesthetic theory in literary criticism about the essence of poetry or (2) rules prescribing the proper methods, content, style, or diction of poetry. The term poetics may also refer to theories about literature in general, not just poetry.

Poetry: In its broadest sense, writing that aims to present ideas and evoke an emotional experience in the reader through the use of meter, imagery, connotative and concrete words, and a carefully constructed structure based on rhythmic patterns. Poetry typically relies on words and expressions that have several layers of meaning. It also makes use of the effects of regular rhythm on the ear and may make a strong appeal to the senses through the use of imagery. Edgar Allan Poe's "Annabel Lee" and Walt Whitman's *Leaves of Grass* are famous examples of poetry.

Point of View: The narrative perspective from which a literary work is presented to the reader. There are four traditional points of view. The "third person omniscient" gives the reader a "godlike" perspective, unrestricted by time or place, from which to see actions and look into the minds of characters. This allows the author to comment openly on characters and events in the work. The "third person" point of view presents the events of the story from outside of any single character's perception, much like the omniscient point of view, but the reader must understand the action as it takes place and without any special insight into characters' minds or motivations. The "first person" or "personal" point of view relates events as they are perceived by a single character. The main character "tells" the story and may offer opinions about the action and characters which differ from those of the author. Much less common than omniscient, third person, and first person is the "second person" point of view, wherein the author tells the story as if it is happening to the reader. James Thurber employs the omniscient point of view in his short story "The Secret Life of Walter Mitty." Ernest Hemingway's "A Clean, Well-Lighted Place" is a short story told from the third person point of view. Mark Twain's novel *Huck Finn* is presented from the first person viewpoint. Jay McInerney's *Bright Lights, Big City* is an example of a novel which uses the second person point of view.

Polemic: A work in which the author takes a stand on a controversial subject, such as abortion or religion. Such works are often extremely argumentative or provocative. Classic examples of polemics include John Milton's *Aeropagitica* and Thomas Paine's *The American Crisis.*

Pornography: Writing intended to provoke feelings of lust in the reader. Such works are often condemned by critics and teachers, but those which can be shown to have literary value are viewed less harshly. Literary works that have been described as pornographic include Ovid's *The Art of Love,* Margaret of Angouleme's *Heptameron,* John Cleland's *Memoirs of a Woman of Pleasure; or, the Life of Fanny Hill,* the anonymous *My Secret Life,* D. H. Lawrence's *Lady Chatterley's Lover,* and Vladimir Nabokov's *Lolita.*

Post-Aesthetic Movement: An artistic response made by African Americans to the black aesthetic movement of the 1960s and early '70s. Writers since that time have adopted a somewhat different tone in their work, with less emphasis placed on the disparity between black and white in the United States. In the words of post-aesthetic authors such as Toni Morrison, John Edgar Wideman, and Kristin Hunter, African Americans are portrayed as looking inward for answers to their own questions, rather than always looking to the outside world. Two well-known examples of works produced as part of the post-aesthetic movement are the Pulitzer Prize-winning novels *The Color Purple* by Alice Walker and *Beloved* by Toni Morrison.

Postmodernism: Writing from the 1960s forward characterized by experimentation and continuing to apply some of the fundamentals of modernism, which included existentialism and alienation. Postmodernists have gone a step further in the rejection of tradition begun with the modernists by also rejecting traditional forms, preferring the anti-novel over the novel and the anti-hero over the hero. Postmodern writers include Alain Robbe-Grillet, Thomas Pynchon, Margaret Drabble, John Fowles, Adolfo Bioy-Casares, and Gabriel Garcia Marquez.

Pre-Raphaelites: A circle of writers and artists in mid nineteenth-century England. Valuing the pre-Renaissance artistic qualities of religious symbolism, lavish pictorialism, and natural sensuousness, the Pre-Raphaelites cultivated a sense of mystery and melancholy that influenced later writers associated with the Symbolist and Decadent movements. The major members of the group include Dante Gabriel Rossetti, Christina Rossetti, Algernon Swinburne, and Walter Pater.

Primitivism: The belief that primitive peoples were nobler and less flawed than civilized peoples because they had not been subjected to the tainting influence of society. Examples of literature espousing primitivism include Aphra Behn's *Oroonoko: Or, The History of the Royal Slave,* Jean-Jacques Rousseau's *Julie ou la Nouvelle Heloise,* Oliver Goldsmith's *The Deserted Village,* the poems of Robert Burns, Herman Melville's stories *Typee, Omoo,* and *Mardi,* many poems of William Butler Yeats and Robert Frost, and William Golding's novel *Lord of the Flies.*

Projective Verse: A form of free verse in which the poet's breathing pattern determines the lines of the poem. Poets who advocate projective verse are against all formal structures in writing, including meter and form. Besides its creators, Robert Creeley, Robert Duncan, and Charles Olson, two other well-known projective verse poets are Denise Levertov and LeRoi Jones (Amiri Baraka). Also known as Breath Verse.

Prologue: An introductory section of a literary work. It often contains information establishing the situation of the characters or presents information about the setting, time period, or action. In drama, the prologue is spoken by a chorus or by one of the principal characters. In the "General Prologue" of *The Canterbury Tales,* Geoffrey Chaucer describes the main characters and establishes the setting and purpose of the work.

Prose: A literary medium that attempts to mirror the language of everyday speech. It is distinguished from poetry by its use of unmetered, unrhymed language consisting of logically related sentences. Prose is usually grouped into paragraphs that form a cohesive whole such as an essay or a novel. Recognized masters of English prose writing include Sir Thomas Malory, William Caxton, Raphael Holinshed, Joseph Addison, Mark Twain, and Ernest Hemingway.

Prosopopoeia: See *Personification*

Protagonist: The central character of a story who serves as a focus for its themes and incidents and as the principal rationale for its development. The protagonist is sometimes referred to in discussions of modern literature as the hero or anti-hero. Well-known protagonists are Hamlet in William Shakespeare's *Hamlet* and Jay Gatsby in F. Scott Fitzgerald's *The Great Gatsby*.

Protest Fiction: Protest fiction has as its primary purpose the protesting of some social injustice, such as racism or discrimination. One example of protest fiction is a series of five novels by Chester Himes, beginning in 1945 with *If He Hollers Let Him Go* and ending in 1955 with *The Primitive*. These works depict the destructive effects of race and gender stereotyping in the context of interracial relationships. Another African American author whose works often revolve around themes of social protest is John Oliver Killens. James Baldwin's essay "Everybody's Protest Novel" generated controversy by attacking the authors of protest fiction.

Proverb: A brief, sage saying that expresses a truth about life in a striking manner. "They are not all cooks who carry long knives" is an example of a proverb.

Pseudonym: A name assumed by a writer, most often intended to prevent his or her identification as the author of a work. Two or more authors may work together under one pseudonym, or an author may use a different name for each genre he or she publishes in. Some publishing companies maintain "house pseudonyms," under which any number of authors may write installations in a series. Some authors also choose a pseudonym over their real names the way an actor may use a stage name. Examples of pseudonyms (with the author's real name in parentheses) include Voltaire (Francois-Marie Arouet), Novalis (Friedrich von Hardenberg), Currer Bell (Charlotte Bronte), Ellis Bell (Emily Bronte), George Eliot (Maryann Evans), Honorio Bustos Donmecq (Adolfo Bioy-Casares and Jorge Luis Borges), and Richard Bachman (Stephen King).

Pun: A play on words that have similar sounds but different meanings. A serious example of the pun is from John Donne's "A Hymne to God the Father": Sweare by thyself, that at my death thy sonne Shall shine as he shines now, and hereto fore; And, having done that, Thou haste done; I fear no more.

Pure Poetry: poetry written without instructional intent or moral purpose that aims only to please a reader by its imagery or musical flow. The term pure poetry is used as the antonym of the term "didacticism." The poetry of Edgar Allan Poe, Stephane Mallarme, Paul Verlaine, Paul Valery, Juan Ramoz Jimenez, and Jorge Guillen offer examples of pure poetry.

Q

Quatrain: A four-line stanza of a poem or an entire poem consisting of four lines. The following quatrain is from Robert Herrick's "To Live Merrily, and to Trust to Good Verses": Round, round, the root do's run; And being ravisht thus, Come, I will drink a Tun To my *Propertius*.

R

Raisonneur: A character in a drama who functions as a spokesperson for the dramatist's views. The *raisonneur* typically observes the play without becoming central to its action. *Raisonneurs* were very common in plays of the nineteenth century.

Realism: A nineteenth-century European literary movement that sought to portray familiar characters, situations, and settings in a realistic manner. This was done primarily by using an objective narrative point of view and through the buildup of accurate detail. The standard for success of any realistic work depends on how faithfully it transfers common experience into fictional forms. The realistic method may be altered or extended, as in stream of consciousness writing, to record highly subjective experience. Seminal authors in the tradition of Realism include Honore de Balzac, Gustave Flaubert, and Henry James.

Refrain: A phrase repeated at intervals throughout a poem. A refrain may appear at the end of each stanza or at less regular intervals. It may be altered slightly at each appearance. Some refrains are nonsense expressions—as with "Nevermore" in Edgar Allan Poe's "The Raven"—that seem to take on a different significance with each use.

Renaissance: The period in European history that marked the end of the Middle Ages. It began in Italy in the late fourteenth century. In broad terms, it is usually seen as spanning the fourteenth, fifteenth, and sixteenth centuries, although it did not reach Great Britain, for example, until the 1480s or so. The Renaissance saw an awakening in almost every sphere of human activity, especially science, philosophy, and the arts. The period is best defined by the emergence of a general philosophy that emphasized the importance of the intellect, the individual, and world affairs. It contrasts strongly with the medieval worldview, characterized by the dominant concerns of faith, the social collective, and spiritual salvation. Prominent writers during the Renaissance include Niccolo Machiavelli and Baldassare Castiglione in Italy, Miguel de Cervantes and Lope de Vega in Spain, Jean Froissart and Francois Rabelais in France, Sir Thomas More and Sir Philip Sidney in England, and Desiderius Erasmus in Holland.

Repartee: Conversation featuring snappy retorts and witticisms. Masters of *repartee* include Sydney Smith, Charles Lamb, and Oscar Wilde. An example is recorded in the meeting of "Beau" Nash and John Wesley: Nash said, "I never make way for a fool," to which Wesley responded, "Don't you? I always do," and stepped aside.

Resolution: The portion of a story following the climax, in which the conflict is resolved. The resolution of Jane Austen's *Northanger Abbey* is neatly summed up in the following sentence: "Henry and Catherine were married, the bells rang and every body smiled."

Restoration: See *Restoration Age*

Restoration Age: A period in English literature beginning with the crowning of Charles II in 1660 and running to about 1700. The era, which was characterized by a reaction against Puritanism, was the first great age of the comedy of manners. The finest literature of the era is typically witty and urbane, and often lewd. Prominent Restoration Age writers include William Congreve, Samuel Pepys, John Dryden, and John Milton.

Revenge Tragedy: A dramatic form popular during the Elizabethan Age, in which the protagonist, directed by the ghost of his murdered father or son, inflicts retaliation upon a powerful villain. Notable features of the revenge tragedy include violence, bizarre criminal acts, intrigue, insanity, a hesitant protagonist, and the use of soliloquy. Thomas Kyd's *Spanish Tragedy* is the first example of revenge tragedy in English, and William Shakespeare's *Hamlet* is perhaps the best. Extreme examples of revenge tragedy, such as John Webster's *The Duchess of Malfi,* are labeled "tragedies of blood." Also known as Tragedy of Blood.

Revista: The Spanish term for a vaudeville musical revue. Examples of *revistas* include Antonio Guzman Aguilera's *Mexico para los mexicanos,* Daniel Vanegas's *Maldito jazz,* and Don Catarino's *Whiskey, morfina y marihuana* and *El desterrado.*

Rhetoric: In literary criticism, this term denotes the art of ethical persuasion. In its strictest sense, rhetoric adheres to various principles developed since classical times for arranging facts and ideas in a clear, persuasive, appealing manner. The term is also used to refer to effective prose in general and theories of or methods for composing effective prose. Classical examples of rhetorics include *The Rhetoric of Aristotle,* Quintillian's *Institutio Oratoria,* and Cicero's *Ad Herennium.*

Rhetorical Question: A question intended to provoke thought, but not an expressed answer, in the reader. It is most commonly used in oratory and other persuasive genres. The following lines from Thomas Gray's "Elegy Written in a Country Churchyard" ask rhetorical questions: Can storied urn or animated bust Back to its mansion call the fleeting breath? Can Honour's voice provoke the silent dust, Or Flattery soothe the dull cold ear of Death?

Rhyme: When used as a noun in literary criticism, this term generally refers to a poem in which words sound identical or very similar and appear in parallel positions in two or more lines. Rhymes are classified into different types according to where they fall in a line or stanza or according to the degree of similarity they exhibit in their spellings and sounds. Some major types of rhyme are "masculine" rhyme, "feminine" rhyme, and "triple" rhyme. In a masculine rhyme, the rhyming sound falls in a single accented syllable, as with "heat" and "eat." Feminine rhyme is a rhyme of two syllables, one stressed and one unstressed, as with "merry" and "tarry." Triple rhyme matches the sound of the accented syllable and the two unaccented syllables that follow: "narrative" and "declarative." Robert Browning alternates feminine and masculine rhymes in his "Soliloquy of the Spanish Cloister": Gr-r-r—there go, my heart's abhorrence! Water your damned flower-pots, do! If hate killed men, Brother Lawrence, God's blood, would not mine kill you! What? Your myrtle-bush wants trimming? Oh, that rose has prior claims— Needs its leaden vase filled brimming? Hell dry you up with flames! Triple rhymes can be found in Thomas Hood's "Bridge of Sighs," George Gordon Byron's satirical verse, and Ogden Nash's comic poems.

Rhyme Royal: A stanza of seven lines composed in iambic pentameter and rhymed *ababbcc*. The name is said to be a tribute to King James I of Scotland, who made much use of the form in his poetry. Examples of rhyme royal include Geoffrey Chaucer's *The Parlement of Foules,* William Shakespeare's *The Rape of Lucrece,* William Morris's *The Early Paradise,* and John Masefield's *The Widow in the Bye Street.*

Rhyme Scheme: See *Rhyme*

Rhythm: A regular pattern of sound, time intervals, or events occurring in writing, most often and most discernably in poetry. Regular, reliable rhythm is known to be soothing to humans, while interrupted, unpredictable, or rapidly changing rhythm is disturbing. These effects are known to authors, who use them to produce a desired reaction in the reader. An example of a form of irregular rhythm is sprung rhythm poetry; quantitative verse, on the other hand, is very regular in its rhythm.

Rising Action: The part of a drama where the plot becomes increasingly complicated. Rising action leads up to the climax, or turning point, of a drama. The final "chase scene" of an action film is generally the rising action which culminates in the film's climax.

Rococo: A style of European architecture that flourished in the eighteenth century, especially in France. The most notable features of *rococo* are its extensive use of ornamentation and its themes of lightness, gaiety, and intimacy. In literary criticism, the term is often used disparagingly to refer to a deca-dent or over-ornamental style. Alexander Pope's "The Rape of the Lock" is an example of literary *rococo.*

Roman à clef: A French phrase meaning "novel with a key." It refers to a narrative in which real persons are portrayed under fictitious names. Jack Kerouac, for example, portrayed various real-life beat generation figures under fictitious names in his *On the Road.*

Romance: A broad term, usually denoting a narrative with exotic, exaggerated, often idealized characters, scenes, and themes. Nathaniel Hawthorne called his *The House of the Seven Gables* and *The Marble Faun* romances in order to distinguish them from clearly realistic works.

Romantic Age: See *Romanticism*

Romanticism: This term has two widely accepted meanings. In historical criticism, it refers to a European intellectual and artistic movement of the late eighteenth and early nineteenth centuries that sought greater freedom of personal expression than that allowed by the strict rules of literary form and logic of the eighteenth-century neoclassicists. The Romantics preferred emotional and imaginative expression to rational analysis. They considered the individual to be at the center of all experience and so placed him or her at the center of their art. The Romantics believed that the creative imagination reveals nobler truths—unique feelings and attitudes—than those that could be discovered by logic or by scientific examination. Both the natural world and the state of childhood were important sources for revelations of "eternal truths." "Romanticism" is also used as a general term to refer to a type of sensibility found in all periods of literary history and usually considered to be in opposition to the principles of classicism. In this sense, Romanticism signifies any work or philosophy in which the exotic or dreamlike figure strongly, or that is devoted to individualistic expression, self-analysis, or a pursuit of a higher realm of knowledge than can be discovered by human reason. Prominent Romantics include Jean-Jacques Rousseau, William Wordsworth, John Keats, Lord Byron, and Johann Wolfgang von Goethe.

Romantics: See *Romanticism*

Russian Symbolism: A Russian poetic movement, derived from French symbolism, that flourished between 1894 and 1910. While some Russian Symbolists continued in the French tradition, stressing aestheticism and the importance of suggestion above didactic intent, others saw their craft as a form of mystical worship, and themselves as mediators between the supernatural and the mundane. Russian symbolists include Aleksandr Blok, Vyacheslav Ivanovich Ivanov, Fyodor Sologub, Andrey Bely, Nikolay Gumilyov, and Vladimir Sergeyevich Solovyov.

S

Satire: A work that uses ridicule, humor, and wit to criticize and provoke change in human nature and institutions. There are two major types of satire: "formal" or "direct" satire speaks directly to the reader or to a character in the work; "indirect" satire relies upon the ridiculous behavior of its characters to make its point. Formal satire is further divided into two manners: the "Horatian," which ridicules gently, and the "Juvenalian," which derides its subjects harshly and bitterly. Voltaire's novella *Candide* is an indirect satire. Jonathan Swift's essay "A Modest Proposal" is a Juvenalian satire.

Scansion: The analysis or "scanning" of a poem to determine its meter and often its rhyme scheme. The most common system of scansion uses accents (slanted lines drawn above syllables) to show stressed syllables, breves (curved lines drawn above syllables) to show unstressed syllables, and vertical lines to separate each foot. In the first line of John Keats's *Endymion,* "A thing of beauty is a joy forever:" the word "thing," the first syllable of "beauty," the word "joy," and the second syllable of "forever" are stressed, while the words "A" and "of," the second syllable of "beauty," the word "a," and the first and third syllables of "forever" are unstressed. In the second line: "Its loveliness increases; it will never" a pair of vertical lines separate the foot ending with "increases" and the one beginning with "it."

Scene: A subdivision of an act of a drama, consisting of continuous action taking place at a single time and in a single location. The beginnings and endings of scenes may be indicated by clearing the stage of actors and props or by the entrances and exits of important characters. The first act of William Shakespeare's *Winter's Tale* is comprised of two scenes.

Science Fiction: A type of narrative about or based upon real or imagined scientific theories and technology. Science fiction is often peopled with alien creatures and set on other planets or in different dimensions. Karel Capek's *R.U.R.* is a major work of science fiction.

Second Person: See *Point of View*

Semiotics: The study of how literary forms and conventions affect the meaning of language. Semioticians include Ferdinand de Saussure, Charles Sanders Pierce, Claude Levi-Strauss, Jacques Lacan, Michel Foucault, Jacques Derrida, Roland Barthes, and Julia Kristeva.

Sestet: Any six-line poem or stanza. Examples of the sestet include the last six lines of the Petrarchan sonnet form, the stanza form of Robert Burns's "A Poet's Welcome to his love-begotten Daughter," and the sestina form in W. H. Auden's "Paysage Moralise."

Setting: The time, place, and culture in which the action of a narrative takes place. The elements of setting may include geographic location, characters' physical and mental environments, prevailing cultural attitudes, or the historical time in which the action takes place. Examples of settings include the romanticized Scotland in Sir Walter Scott's "Waverley" novels, the French provincial setting in Gustave Flaubert's *Madame Bovary,* the fictional Wessex country of Thomas Hardy's novels, and the small towns of southern Ontario in Alice Munro's short stories.

Shakespearean Sonnet: See *Sonnet*

Signifying Monkey: A popular trickster figure in black folklore, with hundreds of tales about this character documented since the 19th century. Henry Louis Gates Jr. examines the history of the signifying monkey in *The Signifying Monkey: Towards a Theory of Afro-American Literary Criticism,* published in 1988.

Simile: A comparison, usually using "like" or "as," of two essentially dissimilar things, as in "coffee as cold as ice" or "He sounded like a broken record." The title of Ernest Hemingway's "Hills Like White Elephants" contains a simile.

Slang: A type of informal verbal communication that is generally unacceptable for formal writing. Slang words and phrases are often colorful exaggerations used to emphasize the speaker's point; they may also be shortened versions of an often-used word or phrase. Examples of American slang from the 1990s include "yuppie" (an acronym for Young Urban Professional), "awesome" (for "excellent"), wired (for "nervous" or "excited"), and "chill out" (for relax).

Slant Rhyme: See *Consonance*

Slave Narrative: Autobiographical accounts of American slave life as told by escaped slaves. These works first appeared during the abolition movement of the 1830s through the 1850s. Olaudah Equiano's *The Interesting Narrative of Olaudah Equiano, or Gustavus Vassa, The African* and Harriet Ann Jacobs's *Incidents in the Life of a Slave Girl* are examples of the slave narrative.

Social Realism: See *Socialist Realism*

Socialist Realism: The Socialist Realism school of literary theory was proposed by Maxim Gorky and established as a dogma by the first Soviet Congress of Writers. It demanded adherence to a communist worldview in works of literature. Its doctrines required an objective viewpoint comprehensible to the working classes and themes of social struggle featuring strong proletarian heroes. A successful work of socialist realism is Nikolay Ostrovsky's *Kak zakalyalas stal* (*How the Steel Was Tempered*). Also known as Social Realism.

Soliloquy: A monologue in a drama used to give the audience information and to develop the speaker's character. It is typically a projection of the speaker's innermost thoughts. Usually delivered while the speaker is alone on stage, a soliloquy is intended to present an illusion of unspoken reflection. A celebrated soliloquy is Hamlet's "To be or not to be" speech in William Shakespeare's *Hamlet*.

Sonnet: A fourteen-line poem, usually composed in iambic pentameter, employing one of several rhyme schemes. There are three major types of sonnets, upon which all other variations of the form are based: the "Petrarchan" or "Italian" sonnet, the "Shakespearean" or "English" sonnet, and the "Spenserian" sonnet. A Petrarchan sonnet consists of an octave rhymed *abbaabba* and a "sestet" rhymed either *cdecde, cdccdc,* or *cdedce.* The octave poses a question or problem, relates a narrative, or puts forth a proposition; the sestet presents a solution to the problem, comments upon the narrative, or applies the proposition put forth in the octave. The Shakespearean sonnet is divided into three quatrains and a couplet rhymed *abab cdcd efef gg.* The couplet provides an epigrammatic comment on the narrative or problem put forth in the quatrains. The Spenserian sonnet uses three quatrains and a couplet like the Shakespearean, but links their three rhyme schemes in this way: *abab bcbc cdcd ee.* The Spenserian sonnet develops its theme in two parts like the Petrarchan, its final six lines resolving a problem, analyzing a narrative, or applying a proposition put forth in its first eight lines. Examples of sonnets can be found in Petrarch's *Canzoniere,* Edmund Spenser's *Amoretti,* Elizabeth Barrett Browning's *Sonnets from the Portuguese,* Rainer Maria Rilke's *Sonnets to Orpheus,* and Adrienne Rich's poem "The Insusceptibles."

Spenserian Sonnet: See *Sonnet*

Spenserian Stanza: A nine-line stanza having eight verses in iambic pentameter, its ninth verse in iambic hexameter, and the rhyme scheme ababbcbcc. This stanza form was first used by Edmund Spenser in his allegorical poem *The Faerie Queene.*

Spondee: In poetry meter, a foot consisting of two long or stressed syllables occurring together. This form is quite rare in English verse, and is usually composed of two monosyllabic words. The first foot in the following line from Robert Burns's "Green Grow the Rashes" is an example of a spondee: Green grow the rashes, O.

Sprung Rhythm: Versification using a specific number of accented syllables per line but disregarding the number of unaccented syllables that fall in each line, producing an irregular rhythm in the poem. Gerard Manley Hopkins, who coined the term "sprung rhythm," is the most notable practitioner of this technique.

Stanza: A subdivision of a poem consisting of lines grouped together, often in recurring patterns of rhyme, line length, and meter. Stanzas may also serve as units of thought in a poem much like paragraphs in prose. Examples of stanza forms include the quatrain, *terza rima, ottava rima,* Spenserian, and the so-called *In Memoriam* stanza from Alfred, Lord Tennyson's poem by that title. The following is an example of the latter form: Love is and was my lord and king, And in his presence I attend To hear the tidings of my friend, Which every hour his couriers bring.

Stereotype: A stereotype was originally the name for a duplication made during the printing process; this led to its modern definition as a person or thing that is (or is assumed to be) the same as all others of its type. Common stereotypical characters include the absent-minded professor, the nagging wife, the troublemaking teenager, and the kind-hearted grandmother.

Stream of Consciousness: A narrative technique for rendering the inward experience of a character. This technique is designed to give the impression of an ever-changing series of thoughts, emotions, images, and memories in the spontaneous and seemingly illogical order that they occur in life. The textbook example of stream of consciousness is the last section of James Joyce's *Ulysses.*

Structuralism: A twentieth-century movement in literary criticism that examines how literary texts arrive at their meanings, rather than the meanings themselves. There are two major types of structuralist analysis: one examines the way patterns of linguistic structures unify a specific text and emphasize certain elements of that text, and the other interprets the way literary forms and conventions affect the meaning of language itself. Prominent structuralists include Michel Foucault, Roman Jakobson, and Roland Barthes.

Structure: The form taken by a piece of literature. The structure may be made obvious for ease of understanding, as in nonfiction works, or may obscured for artistic purposes, as in some poetry or seemingly "unstructured" prose. Examples of common literary structures include the plot of a narrative, the acts and scenes of a drama, and such poetic forms as the Shakespearean sonnet and the Pindaric ode.

Sturm und Drang: A German term meaning "storm and stress." It refers to a German literary movement of the 1770s and 1780s that reacted against the order and rationalism of the enlightenment, focusing instead on the intense experience of extraordinary individuals. Highly romantic, works of this movement, such as Johann Wolfgang von Goethe's *Gotz von Berlichingen,* are typified by realism, rebelliousness, and intense emotionalism.

Style: A writer's distinctive manner of arranging words to suit his or her ideas and purpose in writing. The unique imprint of the author's personality upon his or her writing, style is the product of an author's way of arranging ideas and his or her use of diction, different sentence structures, rhythm, figures of speech, rhetorical principles, and other elements of composition. Styles may be classified according to period (Metaphysical, Augustan, Georgian), individual authors (Chaucerian, Miltonic, Jamesian), level (grand, middle, low, plain), or language (scientific, expository, poetic, journalistic).

Subject: The person, event, or theme at the center of a work of literature. A work may have one or more subjects of each type, with shorter works tending to have fewer and longer works tending to have more. The subjects of James Baldwin's novel *Go Tell It on the Mountain* include the themes of father-son relationships, religious conversion, black life, and sexuality. The subjects of Anne Frank's *Diary of a Young Girl* include Anne and her family members as well as World War II, the Holocaust, and the themes of war, isolation, injustice, and racism.

Subjectivity: Writing that expresses the author's personal feelings about his subject, and which may or may not include factual information about the subject. Subjectivity is demonstrated in James Joyce's *Portrait of the Artist as a Young Man,* Samuel Butler's *The Way of All Flesh,* and Thomas Wolfe's *Look Homeward, Angel.*

Subplot: A secondary story in a narrative. A subplot may serve as a motivating or complicating force for the main plot of the work, or it may provide emphasis for, or relief from, the main plot. The conflict between the Capulets and the Montagues in William Shakespeare's *Romeo and Juliet* is an example of a subplot.

Surrealism: A term introduced to criticism by Guillaume Apollinaire and later adopted by Andre Breton. It refers to a French literary and artistic movement founded in the 1920s. The Surrealists sought to express unconscious thoughts and feelings in their works. The best-known technique used for achieving this aim was automatic writing—transcriptions of spontaneous outpourings from the unconscious. The Surrealists proposed to unify the contrary levels of conscious and unconscious, dream and reality, objectivity and subjectivity into a new level of "super-realism." Surrealism can be found in the poetry of Paul Eluard, Pierre Reverdy, and Louis Aragon, among others.

Suspense: A literary device in which the author maintains the audience's attention through the buildup of events, the outcome of which will soon be revealed. Suspense in William Shakespeare's *Hamlet* is sustained throughout by the question of whether or not the Prince will achieve what he has been instructed to do and of what he intends to do.

Syllogism: A method of presenting a logical argument. In its most basic form, the syllogism consists of a major premise, a minor premise, and a conclusion. An example of a syllogism is: Major premise: When it snows, the streets get wet. Minor premise: It is snowing. Conclusion: The streets are wet.

Symbol: Something that suggests or stands for something else without losing its original identity. In literature, symbols combine their literal meaning with the suggestion of an abstract concept. Literary symbols are of two types: those that carry complex associations of meaning no matter what their contexts, and those that derive their suggestive meaning from their functions in specific literary works. Examples of symbols are sunshine suggesting happiness, rain suggesting sorrow, and storm clouds suggesting despair.

Symbolism: This term has two widely accepted meanings. In historical criticism, it denotes an early modernist literary movement initiated in France during the nineteenth century that reacted against the prevailing standards of realism. Writers in this movement aimed to evoke, indirectly and symbolically, an order of being beyond the material world of the five senses. Poetic expression of personal emotion figured strongly in the movement, typically by means of a private set of symbols uniquely identifiable with the individual poet. The principal aim of the Symbolists was to express in words the highly complex feelings that grew out of everyday contact with the world. In a broader sense, the term "symbolism" refers to the use of one object to represent another. Early members of the Symbolist movement included the French authors Charles Baudelaire and Arthur Rimbaud; William Butler Yeats, James Joyce, and T. S. Eliot were influenced as the movement moved to Ireland, England, and the United States. Examples of the concept of symbolism include a flag that stands for a nation or movement, or an empty cupboard used to suggest hopelessness, poverty, and despair.

Symbolist: See *Symbolism*

Symbolist Movement: See *Symbolism*

Sympathetic Fallacy: See *Affective Fallacy*

T

Tale: A story told by a narrator with a simple plot and little character development. Tales are usually relatively short and often carry a simple message. Examples of tales can be found in the work of Rudyard Kipling, Somerset Maugham, Saki, Anton Chekhov, Guy de Maupassant, and Armistead Maupin.

Tall Tale: A humorous tale told in a straightforward, credible tone but relating absolutely impossible events or feats of the characters. Such tales were commonly told of frontier adventures during the settlement of the west in the United States. Tall tales have been spun around such legendary heroes as Mike Fink, Paul Bunyan, Davy Crockett, Johnny Appleseed, and Captain Stormalong as well as the real-life William F. Cody and Annie Oakley. Literary use of tall tales can be found in Washington Irving's *History of New York,* Mark Twain's *Life on the Mississippi,* and in the German R. F. Raspe's *Baron Munchausen's Narratives of His Marvellous Travels and Campaigns in Russia.*

Tanka: A form of Japanese poetry similar to *haiku*. A *tanka* is five lines long, with the lines containing five, seven, five, seven, and seven syllables respectively. Skilled *tanka* authors include Ishikawa Takuboku, Masaoka Shiki, Amy Lowell, and Adelaide Crapsey.

Teatro Grottesco: See *Theater of the Grotesque*

Terza Rima: A three-line stanza form in poetry in which the rhymes are made on the last word of each line in the following manner: the first and third lines of the first stanza, then the second line of the first stanza and the first and third lines of the second stanza, and so on with the middle line of any stanza rhyming with the first and third lines of the following stanza. An example of *terza rima* is Percy Bysshe Shelley's "The Triumph of Love": As in that trance of wondrous thought I lay This was the tenour of my waking dream. Methought I sate beside a public way Thick strewn with summer dust, and a great stream Of people there was hurrying to and fro Numerous as gnats upon the evening gleam,...

Tetrameter: See *Meter*

Textual Criticism: A branch of literary criticism that seeks to establish the authoritative text of a literary work. Textual critics typically compare all known manuscripts or printings of a single work in order to assess the meanings of differences and revisions. This procedure allows them to arrive at a definitive version that (supposedly) corresponds to the author's original intention. Textual criticism was applied during the Renaissance to salvage the classical texts of Greece and Rome, and modern works have been studied, for instance, to undo deliberate correction or censorship, as in the case of novels by Stephen Crane and Theodore Dreiser.

Theater of Cruelty: Term used to denote a group of theatrical techniques designed to eliminate the psychological and emotional distance between actors and audience. This concept, introduced in the 1930s in France, was intended to inspire a more intense theatrical experience than conventional theater allowed. The "cruelty" of this dramatic theory signified not sadism but heightened actor/audience involvement in the dramatic event. The theater of cruelty was theorized by Antonin Artaud in his *Le Theatre et son double* (*The Theatre and Its Double*), and also appears in the work of Jerzy Grotowski, Jean Genet, Jean Vilar, and Arthur Adamov, among others.

Theater of the Absurd: A post-World War II dramatic trend characterized by radical theatrical innovations. In works influenced by the Theater of the Absurd, nontraditional, sometimes grotesque characterizations, plots, and stage sets reveal a meaningless universe in which human values are irrelevant. Existentialist themes of estrangement, absurdity, and futility link many of the works of this movement. The principal writers of the Theater of the Absurd are Samuel Beckett, Eugene Ionesco, Jean Genet, and Harold Pinter.

Theater of the Grotesque: An Italian theatrical movement characterized by plays written around the ironic and macabre aspects of daily life in the World War I era. Theater of the Grotesque was named after the play *The Mask and the Face* by Luigi Chiarelli, which was described as "a grotesque in three acts." The movement influenced the work of Italian dramatist Luigi Pirandello, author of *Right You Are, If You Think You Are*. Also known as *Teatro Grottesco*.

Theme: The main point of a work of literature. The term is used interchangeably with thesis. The theme of William Shakespeare's *Othello*—jealousy—is a common one.

Thesis: A thesis is both an essay and the point argued in the essay. Thesis novels and thesis plays share the quality of containing a thesis which is supported through the action of the story. A master's thesis and a doctoral dissertation are two theses required of graduate students.

Thesis Play: See *Thesis*

Three Unities: See *Unities*

Tone: The author's attitude toward his or her audience may be deduced from the tone of the work. A formal tone may create distance or convey politeness, while an informal tone may encourage a friendly, intimate, or intrusive feeling in the reader. The author's attitude toward his or her subject matter may also be deduced from the tone of the words he or she uses in discussing it. The tone of John F. Kennedy's speech which included the appeal to "ask not what your country can do for you" was intended to instill feelings of camaraderie and national pride in listeners.

Tragedy: A drama in prose or poetry about a noble, courageous hero of excellent character who, because of some tragic character flaw or *hamartia*, brings ruin upon him- or herself. Tragedy treats its subjects in a dignified and serious manner, using poetic language to help evoke pity and fear and bring about catharsis, a purging of these emotions. The tragic form was practiced extensively by the ancient Greeks. In the Middle Ages, when classical works were virtually unknown, tragedy came to denote any works about the fall of persons from exalted to low conditions due to any reason: fate, vice, weakness, etc. According to the classical definition of tragedy, such works present the "pathetic"—that which evokes pity—rather than the tragic. The classical form of tragedy was revived in the sixteenth century; it flourished especially on the Elizabethan stage. In modern times, dramatists have attempted to adapt the form to the needs of modern society by drawing their heroes from the ranks of ordinary men and women and defining the nobility of these heroes in terms of spirit rather than exalted social standing. The greatest classical example of tragedy is Sophocles' *Oedipus Rex*. The "pathetic" derivation is exemplified in "The Monk's Tale" in Geoffrey Chaucer's *Canterbury Tales*. Notable works produced during the sixteenth century revival include William Shakespeare's *Hamlet, Othello,* and *King Lear*. Modern dramatists working in the tragic tradition include Henrik Ibsen, Arthur Miller, and Eugene O'Neill.

Tragedy of Blood: See *Revenge Tragedy*

Tragic Flaw: In a tragedy, the quality within the hero or heroine which leads to his or her downfall. Examples of the tragic flaw include Othello's jealousy and Hamlet's indecisiveness, although most great tragedies defy such simple interpretation.

Transcendentalism: An American philosophical and religious movement, based in New England from around 1835 until the Civil War. Transcendentalism was a form of American romanticism that had its roots abroad in the works of Thomas Carlyle, Samuel Coleridge, and Johann Wolfgang von Goethe. The Transcendentalists stressed the importance of intuition and subjective experience in communication with God. They rejected religious dogma and texts in favor of mysticism and scientific naturalism. They pursued truths that lie beyond the "colorless" realms perceived by reason and the senses and were active social reformers in public education, women's rights, and the abolition of slavery. Prominent members of the group include Ralph Waldo Emerson and Henry David Thoreau.

Trickster: A character or figure common in Native American and African literature who uses his ingenuity to defeat enemies and escape difficult situations. Tricksters are most often animals, such as the spider, hare, or coyote, although they may take the form of humans as well. Examples of trickster tales include Thomas King's *A Coyote Columbus Story,* Ashley F. Bryan's *The Dancing Granny* and Ishmael Reed's *The Last Days of Louisiana Red.*

Trimeter: See *Meter*

Triple Rhyme: See *Rhyme*

Trochee: See *Foot*

U

Understatement: See *Irony*

Unities: Strict rules of dramatic structure, formulated by Italian and French critics of the Renaissance and based loosely on the principles of drama discussed by Aristotle in his *Poetics*. Foremost among these rules were the three unities of action, time, and place that compelled a dramatist to: (1) construct a single plot with a beginning, middle, and end that details the causal relationships of action and character; (2) restrict the action to the events of a single day; and (3) limit the scene to a single place or city. The unities were observed faithfully by continental European writers until the Romantic Age, but they were never regularly observed in English drama. Modern dramatists are typically more concerned with a unity of impression or emotional effect than with any of the classical unities. The unities are observed in Pierre Corneille's tragedy *Polyeuctes* and Jean-Baptiste Racine's *Phedre*. Also known as Three Unities.

Urban Realism: A branch of realist writing that attempts to accurately reflect the often harsh facts of modern urban existence. Some works by Stephen Crane, Theodore Dreiser, Charles Dickens, Fyodor Dostoyevsky, Emile Zola, Abraham Cahan, and Henry Fuller feature urban realism. Modern examples include Claude Brown's *Manchild in the Promised Land* and Ron Milner's *What the Wine Sellers Buy.*

Utopia: A fictional perfect place, such as "paradise" or "heaven." Early literary utopias were included in Plato's *Republic* and Sir Thomas More's *Utopia,* while more modern utopias can be found in Samuel Butler's *Erewhon,* Theodor Herzka's *A Visit to Freeland,* and H. G. Wells' *A Modern Utopia.*

Utopian: See *Utopia*

Utopianism: See *Utopia*

V

Verisimilitude: Literally, the appearance of truth. In literary criticism, the term refers to aspects of a work of literature that seem true to the reader. Verisimilitude is achieved in the work of Honore de Balzac, Gustave Flaubert, and Henry James, among other late nineteenth-century realist writers.

Vers de societe: See *Occasional Verse*

Vers libre: See *Free Verse*

Verse: A line of metered language, a line of a poem, or any work written in verse. The following line of verse is from the epic poem *Don Juan* by Lord Byron: "My way is to begin with the beginning."

Versification: The writing of verse. Versification may also refer to the meter, rhyme, and other mechanical components of a poem. Composition of a "Roses are red, violets are blue" poem to suit an occasion is a common form of versification practiced by students.

Victorian: Refers broadly to the reign of Queen Victoria of England (1837-1901) and to anything with qualities typical of that era. For example, the qualities of smug narrowmindedness, bourgeois materialism, faith in social progress, and priggish morality are often considered Victorian. This stereotype is contradicted by such dramatic intellectual developments as the theories of Charles Darwin, Karl Marx, and Sigmund Freud (which stirred strong debates in England) and the critical attitudes of serious Victorian writers like Charles Dickens and George Eliot. In literature, the Victorian Period was the great age of the English novel, and the latter part of the era saw the rise of movements such as decadence and symbolism. Works of Victorian literature include the poetry of Robert Browning and Alfred, Lord Tennyson, the criticism of Matthew Arnold and John Ruskin, and the novels of Emily Bronte, William Makepeace Thackeray, and Thomas Hardy. Also known as Victorian Age and Victorian Period.

Victorian Age: See *Victorian*

Victorian Period: See *Victorian*

W

Weltanschauung: A German term referring to a person's worldview or philosophy. Examples of *weltanschauung* include Thomas Hardy's view of the human being as the victim of fate, destiny, or impersonal forces and circumstances, and the disillusioned and laconic cynicism expressed by such poets of the 1930s as W. H. Auden, Sir Stephen Spender, and Sir William Empson.

Weltschmerz: A German term meaning "world pain." It describes a sense of anguish about the nature of existence, usually associated with a melancholy, pessimistic attitude. *Weltschmerz* was expressed in England by George Gordon, Lord Byron in his *Manfred* and *Childe Harold's Pilgrimage,* in France by Viscount de Chateaubriand, Alfred de Vigny, and Alfred de Musset, in Russia by Aleksandr Pushkin and Mikhail Lermontov, in Poland by Juliusz Slowacki, and in America by Nathaniel Hawthorne.

Z

Zarzuela: A type of Spanish operetta. Writers of *zarzuelas* include Lope de Vega and Pedro Calderon.

Zeitgeist: A German term meaning "spirit of the time." It refers to the moral and intellectual trends of a given era. Examples of *zeitgeist* include the preoccupation with the more morbid aspects of dying and death in some Jacobean literature, especially in the works of dramatists Cyril Tourneur and John Webster, and the decadence of the French Symbolists.

Cumulative Author/Title Index

Gregg, Stephen
This Is a Test: V28
Guare, John
The House of Blue Leaves: V8
Six Degrees of Separation: V13
Guys and Dolls (Burrows, Loesser, Swerling): V29

H

Habitat (Thompson): V22
Hackett, Albert
The Diary of Anne Frank: V15
The Hairy Ape (O'Neill): V4
Hammerstein, Oscar II
The King and I: V1
Hanff, Helene
84, Charing Cross Road: V17
Hansberry, Lorraine
A Raisin in the Sun: V2
A Raisin in the Sun (Motion picture): V29
Hare, David
Blue Room: V7
Plenty: V4
The Secret Rapture: V16
Harris, Bill
Robert Johnson: Trick the Devil: V27
Hart, Moss
Once in a Lifetime: V10
You Can't Take It with You: V1
Harvey (Chase): V11
Havel, Vaclav
The Memorandum: V10
Having Our Say: The Delany Sisters' First 100 Years (Mann): V28
Hay Fever (Coward): V6
Hayes, Joseph
The Desperate Hours: V20
Heather Raffo's 9 Parts of Desire (Raffo): V27
Hecht, Ben
The Front Page: V9
Hedda Gabler (Ibsen): V6
Heggen, Thomas
Mister Roberts: V20
The Heidi Chronicles (Wasserstein): V5
Hellman, Lillian
The Children's Hour: V3
The Little Foxes: V1
Watch on the Rhine: V14
Henley, Beth
Crimes of the Heart: V2
Impossible Marriage: V26
The Miss Firecracker Contest: V21
Henrietta (Jones Meadows): V27
Highway, Tomson
The Rez Sisters: V2
Hippolytus (Euripides): V25
Hollmann, Mark
Urinetown: V27

Holmes, Rupert
The Mystery of Edwin Drood: V28
The Homecoming (Pinter): V3
The Hostage (Behan): V7
Hot L Baltimore (Wilson): V9
The House of Bernarda Alba (GarcíaLorca, Federico): V4
The House of Blue Leaves (Guare): V8
How I Learned to Drive (Vogel): V14
Howard, Sidney
They Knew What They Wanted: V29
Hughes, Langston
Mulatto: V18
Mule Bone: V6
Hurston, Zora Neale
Mule Bone: V6
Poker!: V30
Hwang, David Henry
M. Butterfly: V11
The Sound of a Voice: V18
Trying to Find Chinatown: V29

I

I Am My Own Wife (Wright): V23
I Hate Hamlet (Rudnick): V22
I Never Saw Another Butterfly (Raspanti): V27
I Remember Mama (Van Druten): V30
I, Too, Speak of the Rose (Carballido): V4
Ibsen, Henrik
Brand: V16
A Doll's House: V1
An Enemy of the People: V25
Ghosts: V11
Hedda Gabler: V6
The Master Builder: V15
Peer Gynt: V8
The Wild Duck: V10
The Iceman Cometh (O'Neill): V5
An Ideal Husband (Wilde): V21
Idiot's Delight (Sherwood): V15
Iizuka, Naomi
36 Views: V21
Ile (O'Neill): V26
I'm Not Rappaport (Gardner): V18
Imaginary Friends (Ephron): V22
The Imaginary Invalid (Molière): V20
The Importance of Being Earnest (Wilde): V4
Impossible Marriage (Henley): V26
Inadmissible Evidence (Osborne): V24
India Song (Duras): V21
Indian Ink (Stoppard): V11
Indians (Kopit): V24
Indiscretions (Cocteau): V24
Inge, William
Bus Stop: V8
Come Back, Little Sheba: V3
Picnic: V5

Inherit the Wind (Lawrence and Lee): V2
The Insect Play (Capek): V11
Into the Woods (Sondheim and Lapine): V25
Ionesco, Eugène
The Bald Soprano: V4
The Chairs: V9
Rhinoceros: V25
Iphigenia in Taurus (Euripides): V4
Ives, David
Time Flies: V29

J

J. B. (MacLeish): V15
Jarry, Alfred
Ubu Roi: V8
Jensen, Erik
The Exonerated: V24
Jesus Christ Superstar (Webber and Rice): V7
The Jew of Malta (Marlowe): V13
Joe Turner's Come and Gone (Wilson): V17
Jones, LeRoi
see Baraka, Amiri
Jones Meadows, Karen
Henrietta: V27
Jonson, Ben(jamin)
The Alchemist: V4
Volpone: V10

K

Kaufman, George S.
Once in a Lifetime: V10
You Can't Take It with You: V1
Kaufman, Moisés
The Laramie Project: V22
Kennedy, Adam P.
Sleep Deprivation Chamber: V28
Kennedy, Adrienne
Funnyhouse of a Negro: V9
Sleep Deprivation Chamber: V28
The Kentucky Cycle (Schenkkan): V10
Kesselring, Joseph
Arsenic and Old Lace: V20
The King and I (Hammerstein and Rodgers): V1
Kingsley, Sidney
Detective Story: V19
Men in White: V14
Kopit, Arthur
Indians: V24
Oh Dad, Poor Dad, Mamma's Hung You in the Closet and I'm Feelin' So Sad: V7
Y2K: V14
Kotis, Greg
Urinetown: V27
Kramm, Joseph
The Shrike: V15

Cumulative Nationality/Ethnicity Index

Middleton, Thomas
  The Changeling: V22
  A Chaste Maid in Cheapside:
    V18
Nicholson, William
  Shadowlands: V11
Orton, Joe
  Entertaining Mr. Sloane: V3
  What the Butler Saw: V6
Osborne, John
  Inadmissible Evidence: V24
  Look Back in Anger: V4
  Luther: V19
Pinter, Harold
  The Birthday Party: V5
  The Caretaker: V7
  The Dumb Waiter: V25
  The Homecoming: V3
  Mountain Language: V14
Rattigan, Terence
  The Browning Version: V8
Rice, Tim
  Jesus Christ Superstar: V7
Shaffer, Anthony
  Sleuth: V13
Shaffer, Peter
  Amadeus: V13
  Equus: V5
Shakespeare, William
  Much Ado About Nothing (Motion
    picture): V30
  Othello: V20
  Romeo and Juliet: V21
Stoppard, Tom
  Arcadia: V5
  *Dogg's Hamlet, Cahoot's Mac
    beth:* V16
  Indian Ink: V11
  The Real Thing: V8
  *Rosencrantz and Guildenstern Are
    Dead:* V2
  Travesties: V13
Van Druten, John
  I Remember Mama: V30
Webber, Andrew Lloyd
  Jesus Christ Superstar: V7
Webster, John
  The Duchess of Malfi: V17
  The White Devil: V19
Wheeler, Hugh
  *Sweeney Todd: The Demon Barber
    of Fleet Street:* V19

French

Anouilh, Jean
  Antigone: V9
  Becket, or the Honor of God:
    V19
  Ring Around the Moon: V10
Artaud, Antonin
  The Cenci: V22

Beckett, Samuel
  Endgame: V18
  Krapp's Last Tape: V7
  Waiting for Godot: V2
Cocteau, Jean
  Indiscretions: V24
Corneille, Pierre
  Le Cid: V21
de Beaumarchais, Pierre-Augustin
  The Barber of Seville: V16
  The Marriage of Figaro: V14
Duras, Marguerite
  India Song: V21
Genet, Jean
  The Balcony: V10
Giraudoux, Jean
  The Madwoman of Chaillot: V28
Ionesco, Eugène
  The Bald Soprano: V4
  The Chairs: V9
  Rhinoceros: V25
Jarry, Alfred
  Ubu Roi: V8
Molière
  The Imaginary Invalid: V20
  The Misanthrope: V13
  Tartuffe: V18
Racine, Jean
  Andromache: V28
Reza, Yasmina
  Art: V19
Rostand, Edmond
  Cyrano de Bergerac: V1
Sartre, Jean-Paul
  The Flies: V26
  No Exit: V5

German

Brecht, Bertolt
  The Good Person of Szechwan: V9
  *Mother Courage and Her
    Children:* V5
  The Threepenny Opera: V4
Weiss, Peter
  Marat/Sade: V3

Greek

Aeschylus
  Agamemnon: V26
  Prometheus Bound: V5
  Seven Against Thebes: V10
Aristophanes
  Lysistrata: V10
Euripides
  The Bacchae: V6
  Hippolytus: V25
  Iphigenia in Taurus: V4
  Medea: V1
  The Trojan Women: V27
Sophocles
  Ajax: V8
  Antigone: V1

  Electra: V4
  Oedipus Rex: V1
  Women of Trachis: Trachiniae:
    V24

Guatemalan

Solórzano, Carlos
  Crossroads: V26

Hispanic

Cruz, Nilo
  Anna in the Tropics: V21
Fornes, Maria Irene
  Fefu and Her Friends: V25
Sanchez-Scott, Milcha
  The Cuban Swimmer: V29
Valdez, Luis
  Los Vendidos: V29
  Zoot Suit: V5

Indian

Tagore, Rabindranath
  The Post Office: V26

Indochinese

Duras, Marguerite
  India Song: V21

Irish

Beckett, Samuel
  Endgame: V18
  Krapp's Last Tape: V7
  Waiting for Godot: V2
Behan, Brendan
  The Hostage: V7
Friel, Brian
  Dancing at Lughnasa: V11
Leonard, Hugh
  The Au Pair Man: V24
  Da: V13
O'Casey, Sean
  Red Roses for Me: V19
Shaw, George Bernard
  Arms and the Man: V22
  Candida: V30
  Major Barbara: V3
  Man and Superman: V6
  Mrs. Warren's Profession: V19
  Pygmalion: V1
  Saint Joan: V11
Sheridan, Richard Brinsley
  The Critic: V14
  The Rivals: V15
  School for Scandal: V4
Synge, J. M.
  Playboy of the Western World: V18
Wilde, Oscar
  An Ideal Husband: V21
  The Importance of Being Earnest:
    V4

Subject/Theme Index